ACCOUNTING in the headlines

Accounting in the Headlines.

One of the biggest challenges for accounting instructors is that students often feel disengaged from the course material, which can seem abstract and unrelated to their personal experiences. But by incorporating real-life examples, instructors can spark student interest and engagement, especially when teaching accounting at the introductory level.

Accounting in the Headlines, an award-winning blog by renowned author Wendy Tietz, does just that with stories about real companies and events that can be used in the accounting classroom to illustrate introductory financial and managerial accounting concepts.

Concise, tailorable, and updated on a weekly basis, these articles easily fit into the typical introductory accounting curriculum, whether the course is delivered in-person or online. **Accounting in the Headlines articles, along with multiple-choice and polling questions, can be assigned through** MyAccountingLab **and Learning Catalytics™. Instructors are also provided with discussion questions, PowerPoint slides, and handout files, to support learning initiatives.**

http://accountingintheheadlines.com

Karen Wilken Braun • Wendy M. Tietz

Managerial Accounting

ACC 202

Second Custom Edition for Michigan State University

Taken from:
Managerial Accounting, Fifth Edition
by Karen Wilken Braun and Wendy M. Tietz

Cover Art: Courtesy of Brian A. Jackson.Shutterstock and Maksym Dykha.Shutterstock.

Taken from:

Managerial Accounting, Fifth Edition
by Karen Wilken Braun and Wendy M. Tietz
Copyright © 2018, 2015, 2013 by Pearson Education, Inc.
New York, NY 10013

Pearson Education, Inc., 330 Hudson Street, New York, New York 10013
A Pearson Education Company
www.pearsoned.com

Printed in the United States of America

2   17

000200010272094757

EJ

ISBN 10: 1-323-65704-5
ISBN 13: 978-1-323-65704-1

BRIEF CONTENTS

CONTENTS

4 Activity-Based Costing, Lean Operations, and the Costs of Quality   175

6 Cost Behavior   307

7 Cost-Volume-Profit Analysis 381

8 Relevant Costs for Short-Term Decisions 443

9 The Master Budget 507

15 Sustainability   894

Visual Walk-Through

Technology Makes it Simple
Expanded to include several new topics, these features give students step-by-step directions on how to use Microsoft Excel 2016 to perform the accounting task with more efficiency. Examples include: scatterplots, regression analysis, capital budgeting, CVP graphs, budgeting, and sensitivity analysis.

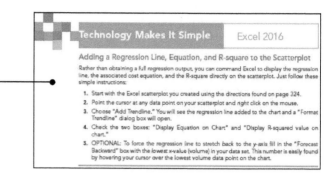

Try It! Interactive Questions
Found throughout the chapter, Try It! interactive questions give students the opportunity to apply the concept they just learned. Linking in the eText will allow students to practice in MyAccountingLab® without interrupting their interaction with the eText. Students' performance on the questions creates a precise adaptive study plan for additional practice.

Video Solutions
Found in the eText and MyAccountingLab, the video solutions feature the author walking through the Try It! problems on a white board. Designed to give students detailed help when they need it.

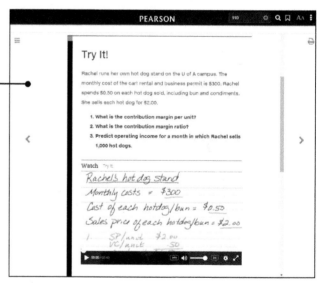

Excel Exhibits
To give students a glimpse into the real world presentation of managerial accounting topics, all financial statements and schedules are presented in Excel. In the eText, a video link on selected exhibits will teach students how to create the same schedule using Excel.

Sustainability

Within every chapter is a section on how sustainability relates to the main chapter topic.

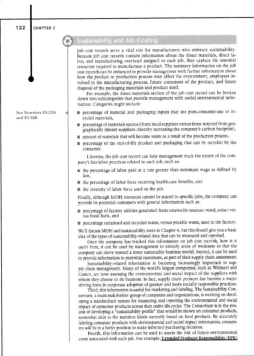

Also included is a quick reference on which end-of-chapter problems correspond to the sustainability concept.

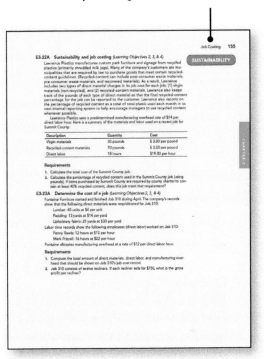

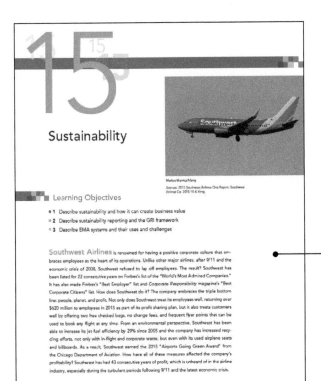

Sustainability Chapter

This chapter provides a deeper dive into how sustainability can generate business value. It also includes sections on sustainability reporting, the Sustainability Accounting Standards Board, and environmental management accounting systems.

Why is this important?
Found throughout the chapter, this feature connects accounting with the business environment so that students can better understand the business significance of managerial accounting.

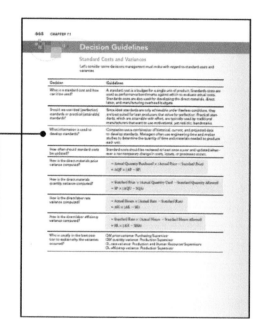

Decision Guidelines
Found at the midpoint and end of each chapter, this feature uses a business decision context to summarize key terms, concepts, and formulas from the chapter in question and answer format.

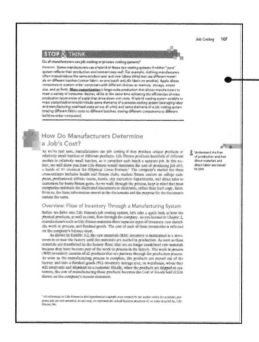

Stop & Think
Found at various points within each chapter, this feature includes a question-and-answer snapshot asking students to critically examine a concept they just learned.

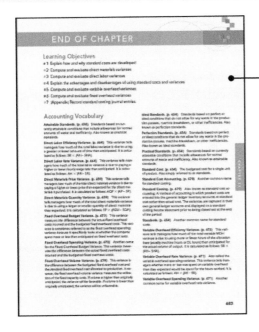

End-of-Chapter Problems

The end-of-chapter content for short exercises, exercises, and problems has been refreshed for this edition. End-of-chapter items are structured to allow students to progress from simple to more rigorous as they move from item to item.

New short exercises based on real world situations have been added to every chapter to help students make the connection between the real world and the concepts being studied.

Serial Case

A serial (continuing) case that focuses on one real world company has been added to the end-of-chapter material. The serial case consists of several small cases, one per chapter. These cases are meant to inspire critical thinking and to connect the content with real life by following one company through all of the chapters in managerial accounting.

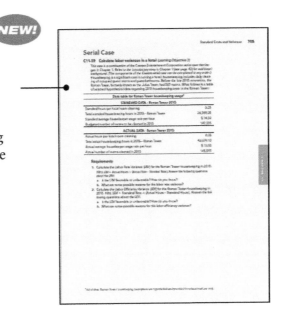

Critical Thinking

Problems are included to provide students with the opportunity for applied critical thinking. These problems include ethical topics, mini cases, and decision-making cases in real companies.

- Ethics Mini Cases based on the IMA Statement of Professional Practice are highlighted with an icon.

  ETHICS

- Real Life Mini Cases focusing on a real company and the decisions presented in business are highlighted with an icon.

  REAL LIFE

Excel in MyAccountingLab

- Students will download and complete problem in Microsoft Excel.

- Students receive personalized, detailed feedback upon uploading their completed spreadsheets.

- Questions will be autograded and reported to the grade book.

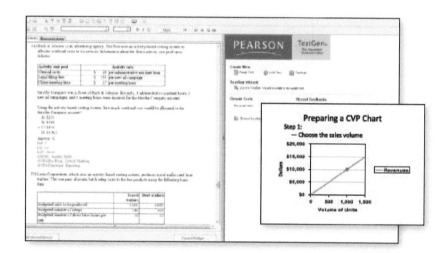

Test Bank and PowerPoints

Test bank includes algorithmic questions and 30% new material. PowerPoints have been updated and refreshed for the new edition. Worked-out problems contain the entire problem statement.

Directed Reading Guides

Directed reading guides, which have been prepared by the authors, help students take thorough notes while reading the text and glean the most important information from each chapter. Each chapter's reading guide follows the text, paragraph-by-paragraph, asking students to answer questions and fill in the blanks, thereby keeping students actively engaged while preparing for class.

Accounting in the Headlines Blog

Accounting in the Headlines, www.accountingintheheadlines.com is a blog written by Wendy Tietz. New stories are added to the blog each week. The blog contains short stories about real-life companies and current events that can be used in the accounting classroom to illustrate introductory accounting concepts. The blog posts contain discussion questions, PowerPoint slides, and handout files, making it a turnkey solution for instructors wanting to use real-life examples in their classes. All content is intended to be brief and fit easily into the typical introductory accounting class. In addition to the content found on the blog site, multiple-choice questions related to each blog post can be found in MyAccountingLab and in Learning Catalytics.

Concept Videos for Students

Short videos focusing on key concepts are available in MyAccountingLab to further emphasize major concepts. These videos can be assigned in homework or used as part of a flipped classroom strategy.

CONTENT CHANGES TO THE FIFTH EDITION

Both students and instructors will benefit from a variety of new content in the fifth edition.

New and updated content within the text:

- Refreshed chapter opening stories attract student attention and lay the groundwork for the chapter using recognizable, real-world companies.

- Updated sustainability features in each chapter show how sustainability relates to the chapter content.

- Select modifications and enhancements were made to each chapter to make it easier for students to grasp difficult concepts. Some of these modifications include the following:

Chapter 1   Redesigned to focus on the professional nature of management accounting, including the American Accounting Association's Vision Model, IMA's definition of management accounting, technical and soft skills required by professionals, summary of CMA exam requirements, and a step-by-step model for critical thinking that can be referenced and used throughout the course. The chapter also includes a section on why management accounting is important to students majoring in other fields of study.

Chapter 2   Simplified language used for product costs (rather than inventoriable product costs) now used throughout the book; revised discussion of direct and indirect costs.

Chapter 3   Introduction and illustration of manufacturing overhead as a cost pool; Decision Guidelines now include job costing journal entries.

Chapter 7   Learning objective 3 expanded to illustrate the impact of changing business conditions on operating income as well as on the breakeven point.

Chapter 8   Streamlined introduction on relevant data; new company example for pricing, special order, and product discontinuation decisions; new "pitfalls to avoid" section with each decision; additional summary problem with worked out solution.

Chapter 10   To provide continuity between budgeting and performance evaluation, the flexible budgeting example now includes the entire income statement using the company featured in Chapter 9; updated PepsiCo data illustrates responsibility accounting.

Chapter 11   Company example tied to Chapters 9 and 10 to provide continuity between chapter topics; variance exhibits are more specifically labeled to better serve as references for students.

Chapter 15   Updated for recent company examples and new data on sustainability reporting; new sections on the Sustainability Accounting Standards Board and inclusion of the landmark 2015 Paris Agreement.

New and updated content within the end-of-chapter material:

Quick Checks   Updated quick checks in each chapter. These questions are conceptual in nature.

ABOUT THE AUTHORS

Karen Wilken Braun is a professor for the Department of Accountancy in the Weatherhead School of Management at Case Western Reserve University. Dr Braun is also the Beta Alpha Psi adviser and the director of the undergraduate accounting program. Professor Braun was on the faculty of the J.M. Tull School of Accounting at the University of Georgia before her appointment at Case Western Reserve University. She has received several student-nominated Outstanding Teacher of the Year awards at both business schools, and is regularly asked to speak to student clubs and organizations about personal financial planning.

Professor Braun is a Certified Public Accountant and holds membership in the American Accounting Association (AAA), the Institute of Management Accountants, and the American Institute of Certified Public Accountants. She also holds the Chartered Global Management Accountant designation, and is a member of the AAA's Management Accounting Section as well as the Teaching, Learning and Curriculum Section. Dr. Braun has has regularly held leadership positions with the AAA's Conference on Teaching and Learning in Accounting (CTLA) including co-chairing the 2015 and 2016 conferences. She was awarded the 2016 Bea Sanders/AICPA Teaching Innovation Award for her development of Excel-based active-learning resources for introductory managerial accounting courses. Dr. Braun's research and teaching interests revolve around lean operations, sustainability, corporate responsibility, and accounting education. Dr. Braun's work has been published in *Contemporary Accounting Research, Issues in Accounting Education*, and *Journal of Accounting Education*.

Dr. Braun received her Ph.D. from the University of Connecticut and her B.A., summa cum laude, from Luther College, where she was a member of Phi Beta Kappa. Dr. Braun gained public accounting experience while working at Arthur Andersen & Co. and accumulated additional business and management accounting experience as a corporate controller.

Professor Braun has two daughters who are both in college. In her free time, she enjoys biking, gardening, hiking, skiing, and spending time with family and friends.

To my children, Rachel and Hannah, who are the joy of my life,
and to my students, who inspire me daily.

Karen W. Braun

Wendy M. Tietz is a professor for the Department of Accounting in the College of Business Administration at Kent State University. She teaches introductory financial and managerial accounting in a variety of formats, including large sections, small sections, and web-based sections. She has received numerous college and university teaching awards while at Kent State University.

Dr. Tietz is a Certified Public Accountant, a Certified Management Accountant, and a Chartered Global Management Accountant. She is a member of the American Accounting Association (AAA), the Institute of Management Accountants and the American Institute of Certified Public Accountants. She is a member of the AAA's Management Accounting Section as well as the Teaching, Learning and Curriculum Section. She has published in *Strategic Finance, IMA Educational Case Journal, Issues in Accounting Education, Accounting Education: An International Journal*, and *Journal of Accounting & Public Policy*. She regularly presents at AAA regional and national meetings.

Dr. Tietz authors a blog, Accounting in the Headlines, which has real-world news stories and resources for use in the introductory accounting classroom. Dr. Tietz was awarded the Bea Sanders/AICPA Teaching Innovation Award for her blog in 2014 and the Jim Bulloch/IMA Award for Innovations in Management Accounting Education in 2016. She was also awarded the Best Educational/Case Award for the Teaching, Learning and Curriculum Section (AAA, Ohio Region) in 2016. Dr. Tietz earned her Ph.D. from Kent State University. She received both her M.B.A. and B.S.A. from the University of Akron. She worked in industry for several years, both as a controller for a financial institution and as the operations manager and controller for a recycled plastics manufacturer.

Dr. Tietz and her husband, Russ, have two grown sons. In her spare time, she enjoys walking, reading, and spending time with family and friends. She is also intensely interested in using technology and social media in education.

To my husband, Russ, who steadfastly and enthusiastically supports every new project.

Wendy M. Tietz

ACKNOWLEDGMENTS

We'd like to extend a special thank you to our reviewers who took the time to help us develop teaching and learning tools for Managerial Accounting courses to come. We value and appreciate their commitment, dedication, and passion for their students and the classroom:

Managerial Accounting, 5e and prior editions

Arinola Adebayo, University of South Carolina Aiken, *Nasrollah Ahadiat*, California State Polytechnic University, *Markus Ahrens*, St. Louis Community College, *Dave Alldredge*, Salt Lake Community College; *Natalie Allen*, Texas A&M University; *Vern Allen*, Central Florida Community College; *Lynn Almond*, Virginia Tech; *Felix E. Amenkhienan*, Radford University; *Arnold I. Barkman*, Texas Christian University; *Gary Barnett*, Salt Lake Community College; *Scott Berube*, University of New Hampshire; *Michael T. Blackwell*, West Liberty State College; *Phillip A. Blanchard*, The University of Arizona; *Charles Blumer*, St. Charles Community College; *Kevin Bosner*, SUNY Genesco; *Anna Boulware*, St. Charles Community College; *Ann K. Brooks*, University of New Mexico; *Molly Brown*, James Madison University; *Nina E. Brown*, Tarrant County College; *Helen Brubeck*, San Jose State University; *Janet B. Butler*, Texas State University–San Marcos; *Jennifer Cainas*, University of South Florida; *David Centers*, Grand Valley State University; *Sandra Cereola*, James Madison University; *Mike Chatham*, Radford University; *Julie Chenier*, Louisiana State University; *Robert Clarke*, Brigham Young University–Idaho; *Thomas Clevenger*, Washburn University; *Jay Cohen*, Oakton Community College; *Cheryl Copeland*, California State University Fresno; *Robert Cornell*, Oklahoma State University; *Deb Cosgrove*, University of Nebraska at Lincoln; *Patrick Cunningham*, Dawson Community College; *Alan B. Czyzewski*, Indiana State University; *Kreag Danvers*, Clarion University; *David L. Davis*, Tallahassee Community College; *Mike Deschamps*, MiraCosta College; *Patricia A. Doherty*, Boston University School of Management; *Jimmy Dong*, Sacramento City College; *Kevin Dooley*, Kapiolani Community College; *Jan Duffy*, Iowa State University; *Barbara Durham*, University of Central Florida; *Lisa Dutchik*, Kirkwood Community College; *Darlene K. Edwards*, Bellingham Technical College; *Robert S. Ellison*, Texas State University–San Marcos; *Anita Ellzey*, Harford Community College; *Gene B. Elrod*, The University of North Texas; *Jame M. Emig*, Villanova University; *Martin Epstei*, Central New Mexico Community College; *Diane Eure*, Texas State University; *Robert Everett*, Lewis & Clark Community College; *Dr. Kurt Fanning*, Grand Valley State University; *Amanda Farmer*, University of Georgia; *Janice Fergusson*, University of South Carolina; *Richard Filler*, Franklin University; *Jean Fornasieri*, Bergen Community College; *Ben Foster*, University of Louisville; *Faith Fugate*, University of Nevada, Reno; *Mary Anne Gaffney*, Temple University; *Karen Geiger*, Arizona State University; *Lisa Gillespie*, Loyola University–Chicago; *Shirley Glass*, Macomb Community College; *Marina Grau*, Houston Community College; *Timothy Griffin*, Hillsborough Community College; *Michael R. Hammond*, Missouri State University; Michael R. Hammond, Missouri State University; *Fei Han*, Robert Morris University; *Sheila Handy*, East Stroudsburg University; *Christopher Harper*, Grand Valley State University; *Sueann Hely*, West Kentucky Community & Technical College; *Pamela Hopcroft*, Florida State College at Jacksonville; *Audrey S. Hunter*, Broward College; *Frank Ilett*, Boise State University; *Ron Jastrzebski*, Penn State University–Berks; *Catherine Jeppson*, California State University, Northridge; *Nancy Jones*, California State University-Chico; *Mark T. Judd*, University of San Diego; *David Juriga*, St. Louis Community College; *Thomas Kam*, Hawaii Pacific University; *Ken Koerber*, Bucks County Community College; *Emil Koren*, Saint Leo University; *Ron Lazer*, University of Houston–Bauer College; *Pamela Legner*, College of DuPage; *Elliott Levy*, Bentley University; *Harold T. Little*, Western Kentucky University; *William Lloyd*, Lock Haven University D. Jordan Lowe, Arizona State University, West Campus; *Lois S. Mahoney*, Eastern Michigan University; *Diane Marker*, University of Toledo; *Linda Marquis*, Northern Kentucky University; *Lizbeth Matz*, University of Pittsburgh at Bradford; *David Mautz*, University of North Carolina–Wilmington; *Florence McGovern*, Bergen Community College; *Noel McKeon*, Florida State College at Jacksonville; *Mallory McWilliams*, San Jose State University; *Robert Meyer*, Parkland College; *Michael Newman*, University of Houston; *Kitty O'Donnell*, Onondaga Community College; *Mehmet Ozbilgin*, Baruch College, City University of New York; *Abbie Gail Parham*, Georgia Southern University; *Glenn Pate*, Palm Beach Community College; *Paige Paulsen*, Salt Lake Community College; *Deborah Pavelka*, Roosevelt University; *Sheldon Peng*, Washburn University; *Tamara Phelan*, Northern Illinois University; *Letitia Pleis*, Metropolitan State College of Denver; *Cindy Powell*, Southern Nazarene University; *Will Quilliam*, Florida Southern College; *Paulette A. Ratliff-Miller*, Grand Valley State University; *Donald Reynolds*, Calvin College; *Christina M. Ritsema*, University of Northern Colorado; *Doug Roberts*, Appalachian State University; *Amal Said*, University of Toledo; *Anwar Salimi*, California State Polytechnic University; *Kathryn Savage*, Northern Arizona University; *Christine Schalow*, California State University–San Bernadino; *Tony Scott*, Norwalk Community College; *Lloyd Seaton*, University of Northern Colorado; *David Skougstad*, Metropolitan State College of Denver; *John Stancil*, Florida Southern College; *Jenny Staskey*, Northern Arizona University; *Dennis Stovall*, Grand Valley State University; *Olin Scott Stovall*, Abilene Christian University; *Gloria Stuart*, Georgia Southern University; *Iris Stuart*, California State University, Fullerton; *Gracelyn V. Stuart-Tuggle*, Palm Beach State College, Boca Raton; *Jan Sweeney*, Baruch College, City University of New York; *Pavani Tallapally*, Slippery Rock University; *Lloyd Tanlu*, University of Washington; *Diane Tanner*, University of North Florida; *Linda Hayden Tarrago*, Hillsborough Community College; *Steven Thoede*, Texas State University; *Geoffrey Tickell*, Indiana University of Pennsylvania; *Don Trippeer*, SUNY Oneonta; *Igor Vaysman*, Baruch College; *John Virchick*, Chapman University; *Terri Walsh*, Seminole State; *Andy Williams*, Edmonds Community College; *Jeff Wong*, University of Nevada Reno; *Michael Yampuler*, University of Houston (Main Campus); *Jeff Jiewei Yu*, Southern Methodist University; *Judith Zander*, Grossmont College; *James Zeigler*, Bowling Green State University

Introduction to Managerial Accounting

Pickture/Alamy

Sources: Starbucks 2015 10-K filing www
.starbucks.com/about-us/company-information/
starbucks-company-timeline; starbucks.com/
responsibility

Learning Objectives

- **1** Identify managers' three primary responsibilities

- **2** Distinguish financial accounting from managerial accounting

- **3** Describe the roles and skills required of management accountants within the organization

- **4** Describe the role of the Institute of Management Accountants (IMA) and apply its ethical standards

- **5** Discuss the business trends and regulations affecting management accounting

Starbucks Corporation, which began operations in 1971 as a sole coffee bean shop in Seattle's well-known Pike Street Market, now has over 23,000 company-owned and licensed stores in 68 countries around the world. The company's success can be attributed to innovative thinking, carefully disciplined expansion, and a focus on corporate responsibility. The company believes that its commitment to ethically sourced coffee, contributions to local communities, and superior employee benefits to part-time as well as full-time employees contribute to the company's objective of being one of the most recognized and respected brands in the world. Management accounting plays a role in implementing the company's strategy. Without information on the costs and benefits of different beverages, programs, distribution channels, and geographic areas, Starbucks would not be able to make responsible, yet profitable, decisions. Starbucks uses management accounting to make operating decisions that focus on corporate responsibility, while also keeping the company financially strong. Case in point: $100 invested in Starbucks's stock in 2010 would have been worth $480 at the end of fiscal 2015, a return well above the S&P 500.

As the Starbucks story shows, managers use accounting information for much more than preparing annual financial statements. They use managerial accounting information to guide their actions and decisions. For Starbucks, these decisions might include opening new stores, adding new products, or even providing new employee benefits, such as Starbucks's new tuition reimbursement plan. Management accounting information helps management decide whether any or all of these actions will help accomplish the company's ultimate goals. In this chapter, we'll introduce managerial accounting, describe how it differs from financial accounting, and discuss the skills and ethics management accountants need. We will also discuss the regulatory and business environment in which today's managers and management accountants operate.

What Is Managerial Accounting?

Managerial accounting, also referred to as management accounting, focuses on the financial insight needed for an organization to achieve success. In the words of the Institute of Management Accountants,

> **Management accounting** *is a profession that involves partnering in management decision making, devising planning and performance management systems, and providing expertise in financial reporting and control to assist management in the formulation and implementation of an organization's strategy.*[1]

As you will see throughout the book, managerial accounting is very different from financial accounting. Financial accounting focuses on providing stockholders and creditors with the information they need to make investment and lending decisions. This information takes the form of financial statements: the balance sheet, income statement, statement of shareholders' equity, and statement of cash flows. On the other hand, managerial accounting focuses on identifying, interpreting, analyzing, and implementing the financial information internal management needs to run the company efficiently, effectively, and profitably. This information takes many forms depending on management's needs.

To understand the kind of information managers need, let's first look at their primary responsibilities.

Managers' Three Primary Responsibilities

Managerial accounting helps managers fulfill their three primary responsibilities, as shown in Exhibit 1-1: planning, directing, and controlling. Integrated throughout these responsibilities is **decision making** (identifying alternative courses of action and choosing among them).

1 Identify managers' three primary responsibilities

EXHIBIT 1-1 Managers' Three Primary Responsibilities

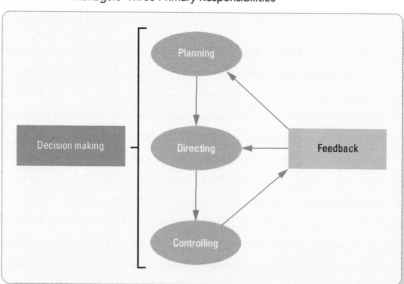

[1]Statement on Management Accounting, "Definition of Management Accounting," Institute of Management Accountants, 2008.

■ <u>Planning</u> involves setting goals and objectives for the company and determining how to achieve them. For example, one of Starbucks's goals is to generate more sales. One strategy to achieve this goal is to open more retail locations. For example, the company opened 731 new company-operated stores in fiscal 2015, roughly half in the United States and half in China and the Asia-Pacific.[2] Another strategy is to develop new products and new distribution channels (such as selling coffee through grocery stores and warehouse clubs). Managerial accounting translates these plans into <u>**budgets**</u>—the quantitative expression of a plan. Management analyzes the budgets before proceeding to determine whether its expansion plans make financial sense.

■ <u>Directing</u> means overseeing the company's day-to-day operations. Management uses sales and costs information by store, region, and distribution channel, to run daily business operations. For example, Starbucks managers use sales data to determine which beverages on the menu and products in the stores are generating the most sales. They use that information to adjust product offerings, marketing strategies, and retail expansion decisions.

■ <u>Controlling</u> means evaluating the results of business operations against the plan and making adjustments to keep the company pressing toward its goals. Starbucks uses performance reports to compare each store's actual performance against the budget and then based on that *feedback* take corrective actions if needed. If actual costs are higher than planned, or actual sales are lower than planned, then management may revise its plans or adjust operations.

Management is continually making decisions while it plans, directs, and controls operations. Starbucks management must decide where to open new stores, which stores to refurnish, what prices to set for beverages and other products in the store, and so forth. Managerial accounting provides the financial insight needed to help make these decisions.

A Road Map: How Managerial Accounting Fits In

This book will show you how managerial accounting helps managers fulfill their responsibilities. The rest of the text is organized around the following themes:

1. **Managerial Accounting Building Blocks**   Chapter 1 helps you understand more about the management accounting profession and today's business environment. Chapter 2 teaches you some of the language that is commonly used in managerial accounting. Just as musicians must know the notes to the musical scale, management accountants *and* managers must have a common understanding of these terms to communicate effectively with one another.

2. **Determining Unit Cost (Product Costing)**   To run a business profitably, managers must be able to identify the costs associated with manufacturing its products or delivering its services. For example, Starbucks's managers need to know the cost of producing each beverage on the menu as well as the cost of operating each retail location. Managers must have this information so that they can set prices high enough to cover costs and generate an adequate profit. Chapters 3, 4, and 5 show you how businesses determine these costs. Chapter 4 also shows how managers can effectively control costs by eliminating wasteful activities and focusing on quality.

3. **Making Decisions**   Before Harold Schultz opened the first Starbucks coffee house, he must have thought about the volume of sales needed just to break even—that is, just to cover costs. In order to do so, he had to first identify and estimate the types of costs the coffee house would incur, as well as the profit that would be generated on each beverage served. These topics are covered in Chapters 6 and 7. Chapter 6 shows how managers identify different types of cost behavior, while Chapter 7 shows how managers determine the profitability of each unit sold as well as the

[2]Starbucks 2015 10-K filing.

company's breakeven point. Chapter 8 continues to use cost behavior information to walk through common business decisions, such as outsourcing and pricing decisions. Finally, Chapter 12 shows how managers decide whether to invest in new equipment, new projects, or new locations.

4. **Planning** Budgets are management's primary tool for expressing its plans. Chapter 9 discusses all of the components of the master budget and the way companies like Starbucks use the budgeting process to implement their business goals and strategies.

5. **Controlling and Evaluating** Management uses many different performance evaluation tools to determine whether individual segments of the business are reaching company goals. Chapters 10 and 11 describe these tools in detail. Chapters 13 and 14 describe how the statement of cash flows and financial statement analysis can be used to evaluate the performance of the company as a whole. Finally, Chapter 15 discusses how companies are beginning to address the sustainability of their operations, by measuring, reporting, and minimizing the negative impact of their operations on people and the environment. As you saw in the opening story, some of Starbucks's primary business concerns are to use ethically sourced coffee, contribute to local communities, and provide superior employee benefits to part-time as well as full-time employees.

Differences Between Managerial Accounting and Financial Accounting

2 Distinguish financial accounting from managerial accounting

Managerial accounting information differs from financial accounting information in many respects. Exhibit 1-2 summarizes these differences. Take a few minutes to study the exhibit (on page 5), and then we'll apply it to Starbucks.

Starbucks's *financial accounting* system is geared toward producing annual and quarterly consolidated financial statements that will be used by investors and creditors to make investment and lending decisions. Since Starbucks is a publicly traded company, its financial statements can be easily found on the Internet by searching for its 10-K (annual) and 10-Q (quarterly) SEC filings. The financial statements, which must be prepared in accordance with Generally Accepted Accounting Principles (GAAP), objectively summarize the transactions that occurred between Starbucks and external parties during the previous period. The Securities and Exchange Commission (SEC) requires that the annual financial statements of publicly traded companies, such as Starbucks, be audited by independent certified public accountants (CPAs). Starbucks's financial statements are useful to its investors and creditors, but they do not provide management with enough information to run the company effectively.

Starbucks's *managerial accounting* system is designed to provide internal managers with the accounting information needed to plan, direct, and control operations. Since managerial accounting information is specifically designed to help *internal* management, it is confidential information that is generally *not* available to the public. There are no GAAP-type standards or audits required for managerial accounting. To provide Starbucks's management with the information needed to make good business decisions, managerial accounting reports focus on smaller segments of the company (such as individual retail locations, geographic areas, and specific beverages and products) rather than the company as a whole. Rather than preparing reports just once a year, Starbucks prepares managerial accounting reports as often as needed, which could be as frequently as daily or even hourly. Many companies even use "real-time performance dashboards" that constantly update so that managers have the financial information they need to control operations and make timely decisions. Since managerial accounting revolves around planning and decision making, much of it focuses on the *future* rather than on the past. Any information that is *relevant* to management will be included. Finally, since every company is different, managerial accounting systems will vary from company to company. In designing

EXHIBIT 1-2 Managerial Accounting Versus Financial Accounting

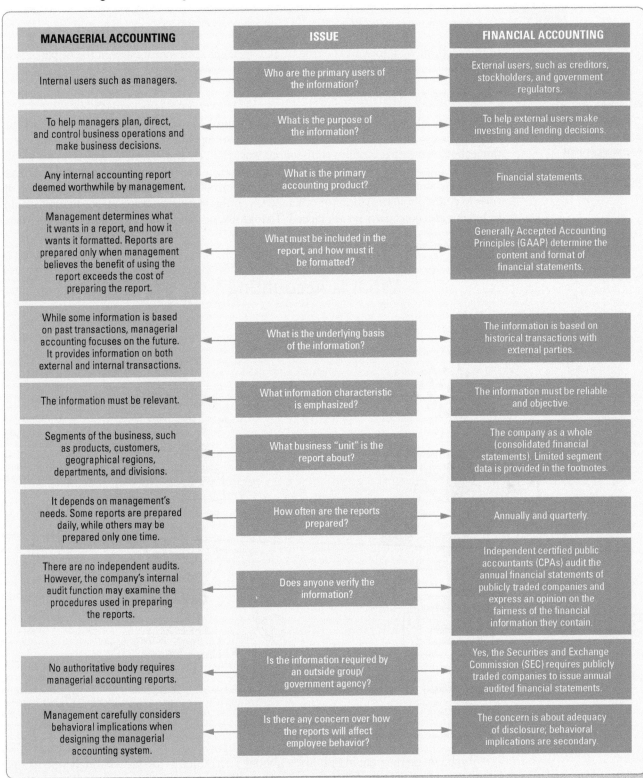

MANAGERIAL ACCOUNTING	ISSUE	FINANCIAL ACCOUNTING
Internal users such as managers.	Who are the primary users of the information?	External users, such as creditors, stockholders, and government regulators.
To help managers plan, direct, and control business operations and make business decisions.	What is the purpose of the information?	To help external users make investing and lending decisions.
Any internal accounting report deemed worthwhile by management.	What is the primary accounting product?	Financial statements.
Management determines what it wants in a report, and how it wants it formatted. Reports are prepared only when management believes the benefit of using the report exceeds the cost of preparing the report.	What must be included in the report, and how must it be formatted?	Generally Accepted Accounting Principles (GAAP) determine the content and format of financial statements.
While some information is based on past transactions, managerial accounting focuses on the future. It provides information on both external and internal transactions.	What is the underlying basis of the information?	The information is based on historical transactions with external parties.
The information must be relevant.	What information characteristic is emphasized?	The information must be reliable and objective.
Segments of the business, such as products, customers, geographical regions, departments, and divisions.	What business "unit" is the report about?	The company as a whole (consolidated financial statements). Limited segment data is provided in the footnotes.
It depends on management's needs. Some reports are prepared daily, while others may be prepared only one time.	How often are the reports prepared?	Annually and quarterly.
There are no independent audits. However, the company's internal audit function may examine the procedures used in preparing the reports.	Does anyone verify the information?	Independent certified public accountants (CPAs) audit the annual financial statements of publicly traded companies and express an opinion on the fairness of the financial information they contain.
No authoritative body requires managerial accounting reports.	Is the information required by an outside group/ government agency?	Yes, the Securities and Exchange Commission (SEC) requires publicly traded companies to issue annual audited financial statements.
Management carefully considers behavioral implications when designing the managerial accounting system.	Is there any concern over how the reports will affect employee behavior?	The concern is about adequacy of disclosure; behavioral implications are secondary.

the system, management will weigh the costs of collecting and analyzing information with the benefits they expect to receive. Management will also consider how the system will affect employees' behavior. Employees try to perform well on the parts of their jobs that the accounting system measures and rewards.

What Role Do Management Accountants Play?

In this section, we'll look at the role of management accountants within the organization and the skills they need to help their organizations succeed.

The Role of Management Accountants

3 Describe the roles and skills required of management accountants within the organization

When you think of accountants, what do you picture? Many people picture accountants the way they were 50 to 100 years ago, before the widespread use of computers when everything about measuring business transactions was relatively simplistic. As shown on the left in Exhibit 1-3, many people have the erroneous conception that accountants are nothing more than "bean counters," plugging numbers into set formulas and using a black and white set of rules to churn out information for others to use. If this were true, being an accountant would be tedious and noncreative work indeed. Thankfully, nothing could be farther from the truth.

EXHIBIT 1-3 The Perception and the Reality

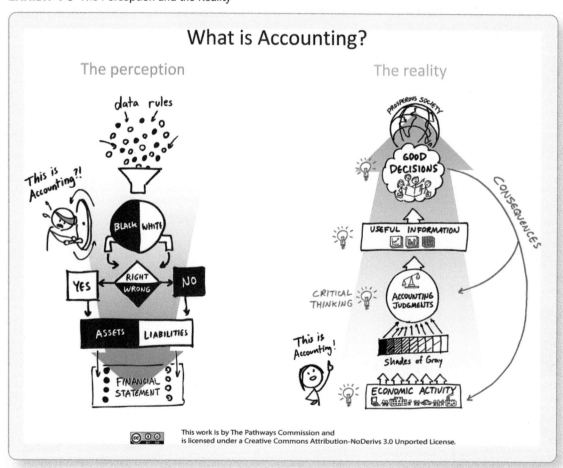

Source: © American Accounting Association. Used with permission.

As shown on the right in Exhibit 1-3, today's accountants are professionals who use an immense amount of critical thinking, insight, and judgment to capture the reality of today's complex economic events. As valued financial advisors, managerial accountants partner with management to make critical business decisions that have widespread and significant consequences for the business and for society. Let's face it: the business world is much more complex than it was in your grandparents' day. With rapidly changing technology and continual business innovation, the role of accountants has drastically changed from what it used to be. In fact, management accountants are rarely referred to by that name any more; instead, they are usually referred to as business advisors, analysts, or finance professionals.

As you go through each topic in this book, keep the blue picture in Exhibit 1-3 in mind, and ask yourself the following questions:

1. **What is the business issue, event, or problem, and how can accounting help to solve it?** Management accounting always begins with some relevant business issue that management is facing or some economic event that occurred in the past or might occur in the future. Management accounting is used to shed light on the issue and direct management's path.

2. **What are the "gray areas"?** In other words, what differences in methods, assumptions, estimates, measurement choices, and judgment calls might impact the information that is used for decision making? Because of the gray areas and judgment involved, accounting numbers are rarely as precise as they may seem.

3. **What are the implications for the business if the accounting information used in the decision is "wrong"?** Because of the gray areas, it's difficult to say that accounting information is ever "wrong." However, judgment in these gray areas could lead to financial estimates that are on the high side or on the low side. What are the consequences of numbers that are too high or too low? Would estimates that are "off" in one direction be worse than the other direction?

Since you are studying management accounting for the first time, the topics in the book may at first appear very straightforward and immutable. However, if you consider the three questions listed above, you'll begin to see the significance of the judgment calls that go into management accounting and the ramifications to the business decisions that are consequently made.

The Skills Required of Management Accountants

To understand the skills required of management accountants, let's go back to the definition of management accounting with which we started the chapter:

> *Management accounting is a profession that involves partnering in management decision making, devising planning and performance management systems, and providing expertise in financial reporting and control to assist management in the formulation and implementation of an organization's strategy.*[3]

First and foremost, management accounting is a profession (in a later section, we'll describe the professional organizations that represent management accountants). Since management accountants work in a professional advisory role, they need a vast array of

EXHIBIT 1-4 Technical and Nontechnical Competencies Needed by Management Accountants

Technical Competencies	Nontechnical Competencies
• Planning, budgeting, and forecasting	• Ethics
• Internal financial reporting	• Communication
• Performance management	• Customer service
• Cost management	• Adaptability
• Internal controls	• Strategic thinking
• Technology	• Process improvement
• Decision analysis	• Leadership
• Financial statement analysis	• Collaboration
• Investment decision making	• Business acumen
• Enterprise risk management	• Change management

[3]Statement on Management Accounting, "Definition of Management Accounting," Institute of Management Accountants, 2008.

skills. Some of these skills are technical, whereas others are nontechnical competencies, which are often referred to as "soft-skills." A recent survey of management accounting professionals revealed some of the top skills they need to help their organizations achieve success. Exhibit 1-4 summarizes some of these competencies.[4]

This book will introduce you to most of the technical competencies listed in Exhibit 1-4, as well as give you the opportunity to advance many of your nontechnical skills. As you can see in the exhibit, the ability to use technology and common software, such as Microsoft Excel, is a critical skill management accountants need to possess. Because Excel is used so pervasively in business, you will see many of the exhibits in this book featured in Excel. You will also see features in several chapters that teach you how to use Excel to perform various tasks. Regardless of your future career path, becoming as proficient as you can with Excel during this course will help you become more marketable and more valuable to your future employer.

Managerial Accounting Is Important to All Careers

As you can see, management accountants don't fit the stereotypical accountant portrayed in movies and shows. Because of their expanding role, management accountants have truly become trusted and valued internal business advisors. But what if you don't plan to major in accounting? How can this course be of use to you? Here are just a few specific ways this course can help you prepare for your future business career:

- **Entrepreneurs** If you are planning to be an entrepreneur, you'll first want to know if your business idea makes financial sense. How high will volume have to be for your business to at least break even? How high will it have to be for your business to earn the level of profit that you want to achieve? As you begin to implement your business plan, should you negotiate sales contracts that are more fixed (flat fee) or variable (fee per activity)? What about costs? Would having more fixed costs or variable costs be better? How sensitive will your profits be to changes in volume if the economy booms or if it takes a turn for the worse? How will you decide whether to invest in new equipment and technology? As your business grows in size, how will you divide it into manageable segments and relinquish oversight of day-to-day operations to others, while at the same time retain control? How can you design systems to ensure your managers will make decisions that are consistent with your goals? And if you decide to raise capital or sell your business, what will potential investors want to see when they analyze your financial statements and study your statement of cash flows? All of these topics are addressed in this book.

- **Business Management** If you are planning to be a general business manager, not a day will go by in which you don't consider the financial ramifications of your decisions. You'll need to have a firm grasp on the costs of obtaining or manufacturing every product you sell and/or every service you deliver. You'll also want to understand how costly every activity within the company is to perform and have specific strategies in hand for controlling and reducing those costs. You'll need to understand which costs will increase as your volume increases and which costs will be unaffected by changes in volume. Cost information will drive many, if not all, of your decisions about where to locate, what to produce, which suppliers to use, whether to outsource, which products to emphasize, whether to implement quality improvement initiatives, whether to automate some of your processes, how to price your products or bid for jobs, whether to discontinue certain products or operations, and so forth. Every business decision you make will be rooted in revenue and cost information, so it will be important for you to understand how those costs were obtained and what they include. Different costs will be used for different purposes. All of these topics are addressed in this book.

- **Marketing and Sales** If you are planning to be in marketing and sales, your marketing strategy, assumptions, and predictions will be the driving force behind the company's entire budget. As a result, you will be intimately involved with developing the budget. Product-line profitability reports will show you which products are most profitable and will guide your decisions about which products to emphasize. Cost information

[4]"The Skills Gap in Entry-level Management Accounting and Finance," Institute of Management Accountants and American Quality and Productivity Center, 2014.

will drive many of your pricing decisions, as well as decisions about whether to accept special orders at reduced sales prices or give volume discounts. The company's stance on sustainability may impact your ability to attract various customers and target different markets. All of these topics are addressed in this book.

■ **Nonbusiness Majors** Even if you are planning to be a nurse, engineer, musician, or fashion designer, the information you learn in this course will be of consequence to you. All organizations, including nonprofits and governmental agencies, use cost and revenue information to guide their plans, actions, and decisions. No matter what your career path, every activity you engage in will impact the costs and revenues of your organization. That holds true, whether you are tending to sick patients, designing bridges, managing a symphony orchestra, or designing clothes. Management will expect you to operate under limited resources and will often look to you for revenue and expense estimates for specific projects or for specific periods of time. Management may also hand you budgets, cost data, and performance reports and expect you to understand it and use it for making decisions. The more you understand the underlying financial information, the better prepared you will be.

We've chosen to highlight just a few specific business career tracks here, but many of the same issues will pertain to all business careers, including those in logistics, supply chain management, production, and finance. There is such a huge overlap in business between managerial accounting and finance that both are often referred to as the "finance function," and the people who work in this function, regardless of whether they were accounting or finance majors, are often referred to as analysts. No matter what your eventual career, you will be using managerial accounting information. As is often said, accounting is the language of business, so the more you know about it, the more valuable you will be to your organization.

Accounting within the Organizational Structure

Most corporations are too large to be governed directly by their stockholders. Therefore, stockholders elect a **board of directors** to oversee the company. Exhibit 1-5 shows a typical organizational structure, with the green boxes representing employees of the firm and the orange and blue boxes representing nonemployees.

The board members meet only periodically, so they hire a **chief executive officer (CEO)** to manage the company on a daily basis. The CEO hires other executives to run various aspects

EXHIBIT 1-5 Typical Organizational Structure

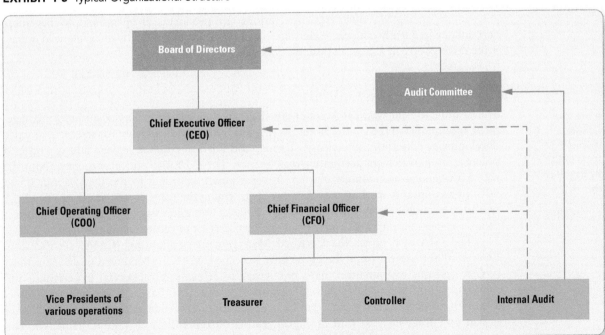

of the organization, including the <u>chief operating officer (COO)</u> and the <u>chief financial officer (CFO)</u>. The COO is responsible for the company's operations, such as research and development (R&D), production, and distribution. The CFO is responsible for all of the company's financial concerns. The <u>treasurer</u> and the <u>controller</u> report directly to the CFO. The treasurer is primarily responsible for raising capital (through issuing stocks and bonds) and investing funds. The controller is usually responsible for general financial accounting, managerial accounting, and tax reporting. Many organizations have other C-Suite personnel not pictured in Exhibit 1-5, such as Chief Information Officer (in charge of the company's technology infrastructure) and the Chief Sustainability Officer (in charge of devising, implementing, and reporting on the company's sustainability initiatives). The CFO, controller, and others within the accounting function work closely with these individuals since technology plays a significant role in collecting managerial accounting information, and, as you'll see later in the chapter and book, managerial accounting both impacts, and is impacted by, sustainability initiatives.

Let's now turn our attention to the right side of Exhibit 1-5. The New York Stock Exchange requires that listed companies have an <u>internal audit function</u>. The role of the internal audit function is to ensure that the company's internal controls and risk management policies are functioning properly. The Internal Audit Department reports directly to a subcommittee of the board of directors called the <u>audit committee</u>. The audit committee oversees the internal audit function as well as the annual audit of the financial statements by independent CPAs. Both the Internal Audit Department and the independent CPAs report directly to the audit committee for one very important reason: to ensure that management will not intimidate them or bias their work. However, since the audit committee meets only periodically, it is not practical for the audit committee to manage the internal audit function on a day-to-day basis. Therefore, the internal audit function also reports to a senior executive, such as the CFO or CEO, for administrative matters.

When you look at the organizational chart pictured in Exhibit 1-5, where do you think management accountants work? It depends on the company. Management accountants used to work in accounting departments and reported directly to the controller. Now, over half of management accountants are located throughout companies and work on cross-functional teams. <u>Cross-functional teams</u> consist of employees representing various functions of the company, such as R&D, design, production, marketing, distribution, and customer service. Cross-functional teams are effective because each member can address business decisions from a different viewpoint. These teams often report to various vice presidents of operations. Management accountants frequently take the leadership role in cross-functional teams since financial impact is the driving force in almost all business decisions.

> ■ **Why is this important?**
>
> "Management **accountants** act as internal business advisors. They provide the **financial** information and in-depth **analysis** needed to make good business **decisions**."

Professional Associations

4 Describe the role of the Institute of Management Accountants (IMA) and apply its ethical standards

The <u>Institute of Management Accountants (IMA)</u> is the professional association for management accountants in the United States. Its mission is to provide a forum for research, practice development, education, knowledge sharing, and advocacy of the highest ethical and best practices in management accounting *and* finance. The IMA also educates society about the role management accountants play in organizations. According to the IMA, about 85 to 90% of accountants work in organizations, performing the roles discussed earlier. The IMA publishes a monthly journal called *Strategic Finance* that addresses current topics of interest to management accountants and helps them keep abreast of recent techniques and trends.

The IMA also issues the <u>Certified Management Accountant (CMA)</u> certification. Over 50,000 people around the globe have become CMAs. To become a CMA, you must pass a rigorous examination, gain two years of relevant professional experience, and maintain continuing professional education. You must also have a baccalaureate degree, although the degree does *not* need to be in accounting. One nice feature of the CMA exam is that you don't have to wait until you graduate from college to take it. Thus, you can start working on valuable credentials that will earn you a higher salary even before you graduate from college. A recent global survey conducted by the IMA revealed that, globally, CMAs earn 61% higher salaries than their non-CMA peers.

The CMA exam consists of two parts. Each part of the exam is 4 hours long and consists of 100 multiple-choice questions as well as two essay questions. As shown in the following, most of the topics on the exam are introduced in this textbook:

Part 1-Financial Reporting, Planning, Performance and Control—Financial Reporting (the financial statements, including the Statement of Cash Flows, Chapter 13); Planning, Budgeting and Forecasting (Chapters 9 and 6), Performance Management (Chapters 10 and 11); Cost Management (Chapters 2, 3, 4, 5, and 6); and Internal Controls.

Part 2-Financial Decision Making—Financial Statement Analysis (Chapter 14); Corporate Finance; Risk Management; Decision Analysis (Chapters 7 and 8); Investment Decisions (Chapter 12); and Professional Ethics (Chapter 1).

The CMA exam topics reinforce the technical skills, shown in Exhibit 1-4, that management accountants are expected to have. If you like the material in this course as well as in your finance course, you should strongly consider taking the CMA exam. You can also become a student member of the IMA for a significantly reduced annual fee, which will give you access to its job posting website as well as all of its publications. Finally, the IMA hosts an annual three-day student leadership conference at a different location in the United States each year. You can find out more about the IMA at its website: www.imanet.org.

In 2012, the <u>**American Institute of Certified Public Accountants (AICPA)**</u>, the world's largest association representing the accounting profession, joined forces with England's Chartered Institute of Management Accountants (CIMA) to launch a separate specialized credential geared toward members who work, or have worked, in accounting roles in business, industry, or government. The <u>**Chartered Global Management Accountant (CGMA)**</u> designation, which is available to qualifying AICPA and CIMA members, is meant to recognize the unique business and accounting skill set possessed by those certified public accountants (CPAs) who fill, or have filled, accounting roles within an organization, as opposed to strictly public accounting roles. The CGMA has issued a "Competency Framework" that covers many of the same technical and nontechnical skills shown in Exhibit 1-4. Currently, 36% of AICPA members work in management accounting rather than public accounting.[5] Qualification for the CGMA designation is based on examination and professional experience. You can find out more about the CGMA designation, qualifications, and benefits at www.CGMA.org.

▶ Try It!

Throughout each chapter you will see several "Try It!" features. These features will allow you to see if you understand something you just learned about in the reading. Click the Try It! Icon to practice and get immediate feedback in the etext.

Determine whether each of the following statements is true or false:

1. Managers' three primary responsibilities are planning, directing, and controlling.
2. Management accounting is geared toward external stakeholders, such as investors and creditors.
3. Management accountants often work in cross-functional teams throughout the organization.
4. The internal audit function reports to the audit committee of the board of directors.
5. Management accountants are now more often looked upon as internal business advisors rather than "bean counters" recording historical transactions.
6. Management accountants should be technically proficient, but they don't need strong oral and written communication skills.
7. Management accountants should be proficient in Excel.
8. The AICPA (American Institute of Certified Public Accountants) issues the CMA (Certified Management Accountant) certification.

Please see page 47 for solutions.

[5]www.aicpa.org/About/Pages/About.aspx

Average Salaries of Management Accountants

The average salaries of management accountants reflect their large skill set. Naturally, salaries will vary with the accountant's level of experience, his or her specific job responsibilities, and the size and geographical location of the company. However, to give you a general idea, in 2015, the average base salary (before benefits, profit sharing, or bonuses) of *all* IMA members in the United States was $115,022, while the median base salary of IMA members in the United States with only one to five years of experience was $64,900. Those professionals in the United States with the CMA or CPA certification earned 31% more in total compensation than members with no certification, while those who held *both* the CMA and CPA certifications earned 45% more than noncertified members. You can obtain more specific salary information in the IMA's 2015 Salary Survey.[6]

Robert Half International, Inc., is another good source for salary information. Robert Half publishes a free yearly guide to average salaries for all types of finance professionals. The guide also provides information on current hiring trends. In addition, Robert Half offers a free online interactive salary calculator, which allows you to drill down to salary information by zip code, years of experience, job title, and company size. To explore salaries in the fields of accounting and finance, do a web search on the phrase, "Robert Half Salary Guide and Calculator."

ETHICS

Professional Ethics

Management accountants continually face ethical challenges. The IMA has developed principles and standards to help management accountants deal with these challenges. The principles and standards remind us that society expects professional accountants to exhibit the highest level of ethical behavior. The IMA's *Statement of Ethical Professional Practice* requires management accountants to do the following:

- Maintain their professional competence.
- Preserve the confidentiality of the information they handle.
- Uphold their integrity.
- Perform their duties with credibility.

These ethical standards are summarized in Exhibit 1-6, while the full *Statement of Ethical Professional Practice* appears in Exhibit 1-7.

EXHIBIT 1-6 Summary of Ethical Standards

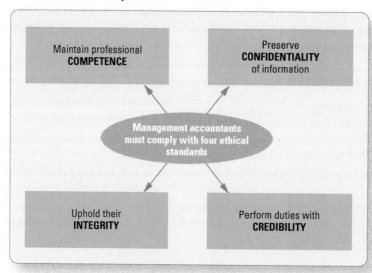

[6]IMA 2015 U.S. Salary Survey, May 2016. http://www.imanet.org/resources-publications/thought-leadership-new/salary-survey

EXHIBIT 1-7 IMA Statement of Ethical Professional Practice

Members of IMA shall behave ethically. A commitment to ethical professional practice includes: overarching principles that express our values, and standards that guide our conduct.

Principles

IMA's overarching ethical principles include: Honesty, Fairness, Objectivity, and Responsibility. Members shall act in accordance with these principles and shall encourage others within their organizations to adhere to them.

Standards

A member's failure to comply with the following standards may result in disciplinary action.

I. Competence

Each member has a responsibility to:
1. Maintain an appropriate level of professional expertise by continually developing knowledge and skills.
2. Perform professional duties in accordance with relevant laws, regulations, and technical standards.
3. Provide decision support information and recommendations that are accurate, clear, concise, and timely.
4. Recognize and communicate professional limitations or other constraints that would preclude responsible judgment or successful performance of an activity.

II. Confidentiality

Each member has a responsibility to:
1. Keep information confidential except when disclosure is authorized or legally required.
2. Inform all relevant parties regarding appropriate use of confidential information. Monitor subordinates' activities to ensure compliance.
3. Refrain from using confidential information for unethical or illegal advantage.

III. Integrity

Each member has a responsibility to:
1. Mitigate actual conflicts of interest. Regularly communicate with business associates to avoid apparent conflicts of interest. Advise all parties of any potential conflicts.
2. Refrain from engaging in any conduct that would prejudice carrying out duties ethically.
3. Abstain from engaging in or supporting any activity that might discredit the profession.

IV. Credibility

Each member has a responsibility to:
1. Communicate information fairly and objectively.
2. Disclose all relevant information that could reasonably be expected to influence an intended user's understanding of the reports, analyses, or recommendations.
3. Disclose delays or deficiencies in information, timeliness, processing, or internal controls in conformance with organization policy and/or applicable law.

Institute of Management Accountants. Adapted with permission (2006).

Source: Courtesy of IMA (Institute of Management Accountants, www.imanet.org). Adapted with permission.

To resolve ethical dilemmas, the IMA suggests that management accountants first follow their company's established policies for reporting unethical behavior. If the conflict is not resolved through the company's procedures, the management accountant should:

- Discuss the unethical situation with the immediate supervisor unless the supervisor is involved in the unethical situation. If so, notify the supervisor at the next higher managerial level. If the immediate supervisor involved is the CEO, notify the audit committee or board of directors.
- Discuss the unethical situation with an objective advisor. The IMA offers a confidential "Ethics Hotline" to its members. Members may call the hotline and discuss their ethical dilemma. The ethics counselor will not provide a specific resolution but will clarify how the dilemma relates to the IMA's *Statement of Ethical Professional Practice* shown in Exhibit 1-7.
- Consult an attorney regarding legal obligations and rights.

Examples of Ethical Dilemmas

Because professional ethical behavior is so critical, we have included short exercises and cases related to ethical behavior in each chapter of the book. An ethics icon will mark each of these exercises so that they are readily identifiable to you and your instructor.

Unfortunately, the ethical path is not always clear. You may want to act ethically and do the right thing, but the consequences can make it difficult to decide what to do. Let's consider several ethical dilemmas in light of the IMA *Statement of Ethical Professional Practice.*

Dilemma #1

Sarah Baker is examining the expense reports of her staff, who counted inventory at Top-Flight's warehouses in Arizona. She discovers that Mike Flinders has claimed but not included hotel receipts for over $1,000 of accommodation expenses. Other staff, who also claimed $1,000, did attach hotel receipts. When asked about the receipts, Mike admits that he stayed with an old friend, not in the hotel, but he believes that he deserves the money he saved. After all, the company would have paid his hotel bill.

By asking to be reimbursed for hotel expenses he did not incur, Flinders violated the IMA's integrity standards (conflict of interest in which he tried to enrich himself at the company's expense). Because Baker discovered the inflated expense report, she would not be fulfilling her ethical responsibilities of integrity and credibility if she allowed the reimbursement.

Dilemma #2

As the accountant of Entreé Computer, you are aware of your company's weak financial condition. Entreé is close to signing a lucrative contract that should ensure its future success. To do so, the controller states that the company must report a profit this year (ending December 31). He suggests, "Two customers have placed orders that are really not supposed to be shipped until early January. Ask production to fill and ship those orders on December 31 so we can record them in this year's sales."

The resolution of this dilemma is less clear-cut. Many people believe that following the controller's suggestion to manipulate the company's income would violate the standards of competence, integrity, and credibility. Others would argue that because Entreé Computer already has the customer orders, shipping the goods and recording the sale in December is still ethical behavior. In this situation, you might discuss the available alternatives with the next managerial level or the IMA ethics hotline counselor.

Dilemma #3

As a new accounting staff member at Central City Hospital, your supervisor has asked you to prepare the yearly Medicare Cost Report, which the government uses to determine its reimbursement to the hospital for serving Medicare patients. The report requires specialized knowledge that you don't believe you possess. Your supervisor is busy planning for the coming year and cannot offer much guidance while you prepare the report.

This situation is not as rare as you might think. You may be asked to perform tasks that you don't feel qualified to perform. The competence standard requires you to perform professional duties in accordance with laws, regulations, and technical standards; but laws and regulations are always changing. For this reason, the competence standard also requires you to continually develop knowledge and skills. CPAs and CMAs are required to complete annual continuing professional education (about 40 hours per year) to fulfill this responsibility. However, even continuing professional education courses will not cover every situation you may encounter.

In the Medicare cost report situation, advise your supervisor that you currently lack the knowledge required to complete the Medicare report. By doing so, you are complying with the competence standard that requires you to recognize and communicate any limitations that would preclude you from fulfilling an activity. You should ask for training on the report preparation and supervision by someone experienced in preparing the report. If the supervisor denies your requests, you should ask him or her to reassign the Medicare report to a qualified staff member.

Dilemma #4

Your company is negotiating a large multiyear sales contract that, if won, would substantially increase the company's future earnings. At a dinner party over the weekend, your friends ask you how you like your job and the company you work for. In your enthusiasm, you tell them not only about your responsibilities at work, but also about the contract negotiations. As soon as the words pop out of your mouth, you worry that you've said too much.

This situation is difficult to avoid. You may be so excited about your job and the company you work for that information unintentionally "slips out" during casual conversation with friends and family. The confidentiality standard requires you to refrain from disclosing information or using confidential information for unethical or illegal advantage. Was the contract negotiation confidential? If so, would your friends invest in company stock in hopes that the negotiations increase stock prices? Or were the negotiations public knowledge in the financial community? If so, your friends would gain no illegal advantage from the information. Recent cases in the news remind us that insider trading (use of inside knowledge for illegal gain) has serious consequences. Even seemingly mundane information about company operations could give competitors an advantage. Therefore, it's best to disclose only information that is meant for public consumption.

Unethical Versus Illegal Behavior

Finally, is there a difference between unethical and illegal behavior? Not all unethical behavior is illegal, but all illegal behavior is unethical. For example, consider the competence standard. The competence standard states that management accountants have a responsibility to provide decision support information that is accurate, clear, concise, and timely. Failure to follow this standard is unethical but in most cases not illegal. Now, consider the integrity standard. It states that management accountants must abstain from any activity that might discredit the profession. A management accountant who commits an illegal act is violating this ethical standard. In other words, ethical behavior encompasses more than simply following the law. The IMA's ethical principles include honesty, fairness, objectivity, and responsibility—principles that are much broader than what is codified in the law.

> **Why is this important?**
>
> "At the **root** of all business relationships is **trust**. Would you put your **money** in a bank that you didn't trust, invest in a company you knew was '**cooking the books**,' or lend money to someone you thought would never pay you back? As a **manager**, your trust in the other party's **ethical** behavior, and vice versa, will be a vital component of the business **decisions** you make."

Decision Guidelines

Managerial Accounting and Management Accountants

Starbucks had to consider the following in designing its managerial accounting system.

Decision	Guidelines
What is the primary purpose and focus of managerial accounting?	Managerial accounting provides information that helps managers plan, direct, and control operations. By focusing on *relevant* information, managerial accounting assists managers in formulating and implementing the organization's strategy and making good business decisions.
What should managers take into consideration when designing managerial accounting systems?	Managers need to weigh the costs of the system (for example, collecting and analyzing data) with the benefits that are expected from using the information to make better decisions. Managers must carefully consider the behavioral effects of the system since employees tend to focus on those aspects of performance that are measured.
Where should management accountants be placed within the organizational structure?	In the past, most management accountants worked in accounting departments. Now, over 50% of management accountants work on cross-functional teams across the organization, where they serve in an advisory role.
What skills should management accountants possess?	Because of their expanding role within the organization, management accountants need both technical skills (such as managerial and financial accounting knowledge and technology skills) and nontechnical skills (such as ethics, communication, critical thinking, and leadership).
What professional associations advocate for management accountants in the United States?	The Institute of Management Accountants (IMA) is the premier organization advocating strictly for the advancement of the management accounting profession. The IMA also issues the CMA certification. In addition, the American Institute of Certified Public Accountants (AICPA) has launched a specialized credential (the CGMA) for CPAs who have experience in industry, business, and government.
By what ethical principles and standards should management accountants abide?	The IMA's overarching ethical *principles* include the following: • Honesty • Objectivity • Fairness • Responsibility The IMA's ethical *standards* include the following: • Competence • Integrity • Confidentiality • Credibility

SUMMARY PROBLEM 1

Requirements

1. Each of the following statements describes a responsibility of management. Match each statement to the management responsibility being fulfilled.

Statement	Management Responsibility
1. Identifying alternative courses of action and choosing among them	a. Planning
2. Running the company on a day-to-day basis	b. Decision making
3. Determining whether the company's units are operating according to plan	c. Directing
4. Setting goals and objectives for the company and determining strategies to achieve them	d. Controlling

2. Are the following statements more descriptive of managerial accounting or financial accounting information?

   a. Describes historical transactions with external parties
   b. Is not required by any authoritative body, such as the SEC
   c. Reports on the company's subunits, such as products, geographical areas, and departments
   d. Is intended to be used by creditors and investors
   e. Is formatted in accordance with GAAP

3. Each of the following statements paraphrases an ethical responsibility. Match each statement to the standard of ethical professional practice being fulfilled. Each standard may be used more than once or not at all.

Responsibility	Standard of Ethical Professional Practice
1. Do not disclose company information unless authorized to do so.	a. Competence
2. Continue to develop skills and knowledge.	b. Confidentiality
3. Don't bias the information and reports presented to management.	c. Integrity
4. If you do not have the skills to complete a task correctly, do not pretend that you do.	d. Credibility
5. Avoid actual *and* apparent conflicts of interest.	

▪ SOLUTIONS

Requirement 1
1. (b) Decision making
2. (c) Directing
3. (d) Controlling
4. (a) Planning

Requirement 2
a. Financial accounting
b. Managerial accounting
c. Managerial accounting
d. Financial accounting
e. Financial accounting

Requirement 3
1. (b) Confidentiality
2. (a) Competence
3. (d) Credibility
4. (a) Competence
5. (c) Integrity

What Business Trends and Regulations Affect Management Accounting?

Business trends and regulations are continually changing. To remain competitive, companies need to be nimble and adaptable. In this section, we'll describe some of the business trends and regulations that are significantly affecting management accounting.

Big Data, Data Analytics, and Critical Thinking

5 Discuss the business trends and regulations affecting management accounting

The collection of data from sensors, social media, GPS signals, texts, pictures, customer reward cards, and so forth is increasing at an unprecedented rate. In fact, over 90% of the world's data has been created in the last two years.[7] Big, unstructured data, coupled with traditional business transaction data, are changing the ways in which companies operate. Although the power of much of this data still remains untapped, companies are using data visualization software, such as Tableau, and predictive modeling to become more cost-efficient, to better target their sales markets, to uncover fraud, and to innovate.

For business transaction data, many small businesses use ready-to-use accounting software packages, such as QuickBooks or Sage 50, to track their costs and to develop the information that owners and managers need to run the business. But large companies use **enterprise resource planning (ERP)** systems that can integrate all of a company's worldwide functions, departments, and data. ERP systems such as SAP and Oracle gather company data into a centralized data warehouse. The system feeds the data into software for all of the company's business activities, from budgeting and purchasing to production and customer service.

Advantages of ERP systems include the following:

- Companies streamline their operations before mapping them into ERP software. Streamlining operations saves money.

- ERP helps companies respond quickly to changes. A change in sales instantly ripples through the ERP's purchases, production, shipping, and accounting systems.

- An ERP system can replace hundreds of separate software systems, such as different software in different regions, or different payroll, shipping, and production software.

Gone are the days when decisions are made based on gut feelings. Data-driven decision making is here to stay. What can you do to prepare yourself for a data-driven business career? Data are only data, unless they are turned into useful information. The way to turn big data into information is to use critical thinking skills in conjunction with technological skills, such as competency in Excel, SAP, and Tableau. As mentioned earlier in the chapter, management accountants are expected to possess both technical *and* critical thinking skills. In other words, data cannot stand on their own; they require analysis and interpretation if they are to be of use to management.

Critical Thinking

You will need to use critical thinking throughout this course and throughout your career. But what does critical thinking really entail? **Critical thinking** can be described as improving the quality of thought by skillfully analyzing, assessing, and reconstructing it.[8] Critical thinking can be improved by asking yourself the following series of questions about any issue or problem you encounter:[9]

1. What is the purpose, goal, or objective? In other words, what am I trying to accomplish?

2. What is the specific question I'm trying to address? The question will guide your thought process.

3. What data will I need to answer the question? With the sheer magnitude of data available, you'll need to hone in solely on the data that will help you answer the question at hand.

[7]www-01.ibm.com/software/data/bigdata/what-is-big-data.html
[8]Criticalthinking.org
[9]www.criticalthinking.org/ctmodel/logic-model1.htm

4. What concepts am I using, and what assumptions might I be taking for granted? Make sure you clearly identify the concepts and assumptions you are using, since a change in assumption might impact your conclusions.

5. What conclusions am I coming to, and are my inferences logical? *Always* check for logic.

6. What are the implications and consequences of these conclusions? All decisions have repercussions. Think ahead to what the outcome might be.

7. What is my point of view or reference point through which I have viewed the problem? Could I look at the problem from another equally valid point of view? Recognize that your point of view, which is the lens through which you view an issue, might be only one of several equally valid viewpoints.

Often in business, school, and life, you may be faced with problems you don't feel you know how to attack. By asking yourself the series of questions listed above, you can put a thoughtful, intellectual framework around the problem that will help guide your journey toward a solution.

STOP & THINK

Companies are constantly faced with decisions about investing in technological innovations that could potentially save money. While Chapter 12 discusses investment decisions in more detail, we'll consider a simple one-year cost-benefit analysis here. Faced with rising pressure for a $15 per hour minimum wage rate, the fast-food industry is currently exploring the possible use of robotics for order-taking and food preparation tasks. Assume the following facts:

1. By investing in one robotic arm, a fast-food restaurant could potentially save $15 per hour plus 7.65% payroll tax. While the tasks performed by a human associate are more flexible and adaptable than those performed by a robot, assume the robot would replace 10 hours of human labor, 365 days per year.

2. The robotic arm is estimated to cost $35,000 plus $5,000 for installation. While the equipment itself may be in workable condition for up to five years, the company is viewing its implementation as a one-year experiment.

3. The annual cost of running the robotic arm, including utilities and servicing, is expected to be $1,500.

Perform a cost-benefit analysis for the first year of implementation to determine whether the robotic arm would be a financially viable investment if the minimum wage were to be raised to $15 per hour.

Answer:

	A	B	C
1	**Cost-Benefit Analysis**		**Total**
2	**Expected benefits (cost savings):**		
3	Wages: $15 per hour × 10 hours per day × 365 days per year	$ 54,750	
4	Payroll taxes: 7.65% of gross wages	4,188	
5	Total expected benefits		$ 58,938
6	**Expected costs:**		
7	Robotic arm and installation	$ 40,000	
8	Cost of operating and servicing	1,500	
9	Total expected costs		41,500
10	**Net expected benefit in first year**		$ 17,438
11			

Based on this one-year cost-benefit analysis, the fast-food restaurant would expect to benefit from investing in the robotic technology. This analysis is based on several key assumptions (hours of labor replaced, hourly wage rate, and equipment fully expensed in one year). As with most decisions, the projected financial impact would vary under different assumptions.

Shifting Economy

The U.S. economy is becoming a "knowledge economy" in which more and more people are being employed for their intellectual capital than for their ability to provide manual labor in agricultural and manufacturing roles. Outside of government, more people are now employed in the service sector of the U.S. economy (77 million) than in retail and whole-sale merchandising (21 million); manufacturing, construction, and mining (19 million); and agriculture (2 million) combined.[10] Service companies provide health care, communication, transportation, banking, professional consulting, education, hospitality and leisure activities, and other important benefits to society. The critical thinking framework outlined earlier highlights the importance of these skills to knowledge workers in the new economy.

Many managerial accounting practices were first developed to meet the needs of manufacturers during the industrial age of the early twentieth century. However, since the U.S. economy has shifted away from manufacturing, managerial accounting has *expanded* to meet the needs of merchandising companies and service firms as well as manufacturers. For example, consider the following:

1. Manufacturers still need to know how much each unit of their product costs to produce. In addition to using this information for inventory valuation and pricing decisions, manufacturers also use cost information to determine whether they should outsource production to another company or to an overseas location, or even whether they should reshore (relocate) it back in the United States.

2. Because such a large percentage of goods are now produced overseas rather than domestically, retailers must now consider foreign currency translation, shipping costs, and import tariffs when determining the cost of imported products. Managers of merchandising companies also need cost and revenue information about operating their brick and mortar locations as well as their online sales platforms. All of this information helps managers make more strategic and profitable decisions.

3. Service companies also need cost information to make decisions. For example, health care providers need to know the cost of performing procedures and running lab tests; hotel managers need to know the cost of providing rooms and amenities to guests; cell phone carriers and Internet service providers need to know the cost of providing texts, data, and cloud computing services; and entrepreneurs that develop apps, such as Uber and Airbnb, need to have a good understanding of their cost structure and how they will monetize the site. No matter what the service, cost information helps managers make vital business decisions, such as pricing decisions, marketing decisions, decisions to invest in new technology, and market expansion decisions.

Globalization

The barriers to international trade have fallen over the past decades, allowing foreign companies to compete with domestic companies. Firms that are not highly efficient, innovative, and responsive to business trends will vanish from the global market. However, global markets also provide highly competitive domestic companies with great opportunities for growth.

Globalization has several implications for managerial accounting:

■ Stiffer competition means managers need more accurate and timely information to make wise business decisions. Companies can no longer afford to make decisions by the "seat of their pants." Detailed, accurate, and real-time cost information has become a necessity for survival.

■ Companies must decide whether to expand sales and/or production into foreign countries. To do so, managers need comprehensive estimates of the costs of running international operations and the benefits that can be reaped. They also need to be aware of regulations and laws in other countries that could impact their operations. For example, England

[10]www.bls.gov/emp/ep_table_201.htm

and Europe tend to have much stricter environmental protection laws than the United States.

- Companies can learn new management techniques by observing their international competitors. For example, lean thinking, which is discussed next, was developed in Japan by Toyota. Lean practice has now been adopted, expanded upon, and refined by U.S. companies.

Lean Thinking and Focus on Quality

To be competitive in the global market, companies need to be acutely aware of their costs, customer response time, and quality. Market share goes to any company that can do the same thing cheaper, faster, or better. To address these issues, many companies espouse **lean thinking**, which is both a philosophy and a business strategy of operating without waste. The more *wasteful activities* that can be eliminated, the lower the company's costs. The more *wasted time* that can be removed between receiving an order and delivering the product or service, the faster the customer response time. And the more *defects* that can be prevented or removed from the process, the less costly the production process and the higher the customer satisfaction. **Six Sigma**—the goal of producing near perfection (with less than 3.4 defects per million opportunities)—often goes hand in hand with lean thinking. In the second half of Chapter 4, we'll look at some of the unique characteristics of lean operations which companies in every sector of the economy are using with great success. We'll also show how companies analyze the costs associated with their current level of quality as well as make decisions about quality improvement initiatives.

Sustainability, Social Responsibility, and the Triple Bottom Line

Recent years have witnessed an increasing awareness and growing interest in sustainability and social responsibility by both consumers and corporations. The dictionary definition of **sustainability** refers to the ability of a system to maintain its own viability, endure without giving way, or use resources so that they are not depleted or permanently damaged.[11] In other words, it's the ability of a system to operate in such a manner that it is able to continue indefinitely. The United Nations has defined sustainability as "the ability to meet the needs of the present without compromising the ability of future generations to meet their own needs."[12] Others have defined sustainability as an expansion of the golden rule: "Do unto others, including future generations, as you would have done unto you."[13]

As pictured in Exhibit 1-8, sustainability has three pillars: environmental, social, and economic. A company will be viable in the long run only if all three of these factors are

EXHIBIT 1-8 The Three Pillars of Sustainability

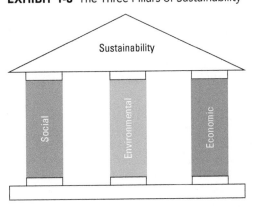

---

[11]www.merriam-webster.com; http://dictionary.reference.com

[12]1987 World Commission on Environment and Development, www.un.org/documents/ga/res/42/ares42-187.htm

[13]Gary Langenwalter, "Business Sustainability: Keeping Lean but with More Green for the Company's Long Haul," 2010, AICPA, Lewisville, Texas.

considered when making business decisions. For example, a company will not be able to survive in the long run if the natural resources (e.g., air, water, soil, minerals, plants, fuel supplies, etc.) or people (e.g., suppliers, customers, employees, communities) it relies on are put in jeopardy. Thus, sustainability is also viewed as the intersection of all three factors, as pictured in Exhibit 1-9. As a result, many companies are beginning to adhere to the notion of a triple bottom line. The <u>triple bottom line</u> recognizes that a company's performance should be viewed not only in terms of its ability to generate economic profits for its owners, as has traditionally been the case, but also in terms of its impact on people and the planet.

EXHIBIT 1-9 Sustainability as the Intersection of Three Factors

Social

Environmental

Economic

Sustainable

To move toward sustainability, companies are introducing "green initiatives"—ways of doing business that have fewer negative consequences for the earth's resources. They are innovating new products and manufacturing processes that use recycled materials to reduce the amount of waste going to landfills. The drive is toward a circular economy, where nothing goes to waste. Companies have also recognized the need to be socially responsible—carefully considering how their business affects employees, consumers, citizens, and entire communities. Many companies have introduced means of giving back to their local communities by supporting local schools, employee volunteerism, and charities. Most of the leading companies in the world are now issuing Corporate Social Responsibility (CSR) reports through which they communicate their social and environmental impacts. Businesses are now viewing sustainability and social responsibility as opportunities for innovation and business development. These initiatives not only allow a company to "do the right thing," but they also can lead to economic profits by increasing demand for a company's products and services and reducing costs.

 In every chapter of this text, you will see a special section illustrating how management accounting can help companies pursue sustainable, socially responsible business practices. These sections will be marked with a green recycle symbol and will also point you to corresponding homework problems. In addition, Chapter 15 is devoted to sustainability, examining the reasons sustainability makes good business sense and the framework and methods companies use to measure and report on their social and environmental impact.

Integrated Reporting

The corporate reporting landscape is constantly changing. One of the most notable recent global movements is toward integrated reporting. According to the International Integrated Reporting Committee (IIRC), <u>integrated reporting</u> (symbolized as < IR >) "is a process that results in communication, most visibly a periodic 'integrated report,' about value creation over time. An integrated report is a concise communication about how an organization's strategy, governance, performance and prospects lead to the creation of value over the short, medium and long term."[14] As such, it is a

[14]www.theiirc.org

broader, more holistic, balanced, and future-looking report than traditional financial statements, which tend to focus on short-term financial measures of past performance. An integrated report essentially describes and measures all material elements of value creation, not just those relating to financial capital. In addition to financial capital, the report considers manufactured, intellectual, human, social, and natural (environmental) capital, which are often more difficult for investors to access through traditional financial reporting.

Integrated reporting, which is still in its infancy, is being driven by businesses and institutional investors who want more information for better decision making than that offered by traditional financial statements. Several well-known companies, including Microsoft, Prudential, and Coca-Cola, as well as the Big Four accounting firms, the Chartered Financial Analyst (CFA) Institute, and Goldman Sachs, are working closely with the IIRC to help further develop and refine the $<$ IR $>$ reporting framework. You may keep abreast of current developments in $<$ IR $>$ by visiting www.theiirc.org.

The Sarbanes-Oxley Act of 2002

As a result of corporate accounting scandals, such as those at Enron and WorldCom, the U.S. Congress enacted the **Sarbanes-Oxley Act of 2002 (SOX)**. The purpose of SOX is to restore trust in publicly traded corporations, their management, their financial statements, and their auditors. SOX enhances internal control and financial reporting requirements and establishes new regulatory requirements for publicly traded companies and their independent auditors. Publicly traded companies have spent millions of dollars upgrading their internal controls and accounting systems to comply with SOX regulations.

As shown in Exhibit 1-10, SOX requires the company's CEO and CFO to assume responsibility for their company's financial statements and disclosures. The CEO and CFO must certify that the financial statements and disclosures fairly present, in all material respects, the operations and financial condition of the company. Additionally, they must accept responsibility for establishing and maintaining an adequate internal control structure and procedures for financial reporting. The company must have its internal controls and financial reporting procedures assessed annually.

EXHIBIT 1-10 Some Important Features of SOX

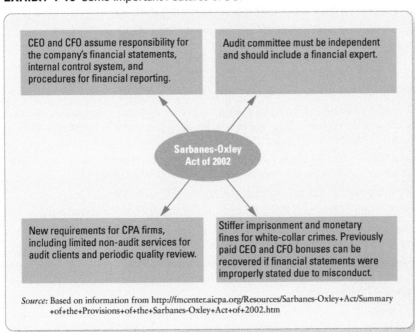

Source: Based on information from http://fmcenter.aicpa.org/Resources/Sarbanes-Oxley+Act/Summary +of+the+Provisions+of+the+Sarbanes-Oxley+Act+of+2002.htm

SOX also requires audit committee members to be independent; that is, they may not receive any consulting or advisory fees from the company other than for their service on the board of directors. In addition, at least one of the members should be a financial expert. The audit committee oversees not only the internal audit function but also the company's audit by independent CPAs.

To ensure that CPA firms maintain independence from their client company, SOX does not allow CPA firms to provide certain nonaudit services (such as bookkeeping and financial information systems design) to companies during the same period of time in which they are providing audit services. If a company wants to obtain such services from a CPA firm, it must hire a different firm to do the nonaudit work. Tax services may be provided by the same CPA firm if pre-approved by the audit committee. The audit partner must rotate off the audit engagement every five years, and the audit firm must undergo quality reviews every one to three years.

SOX also increases the penalties for white-collar crimes such as corporate fraud. These penalties include both monetary fines and substantial imprisonment. For example, knowingly destroying or creating documents to "impede, obstruct, or influence" any federal investigation can result in up to 20 years of imprisonment.[15]

SOX also contains a "clawback" provision in which previously paid CEO's and CFO's incentive-based compensation can be recovered if the financial statements were misstated due to misconduct. The Dodd-Frank Wall Street Reform and Consumer Protection Act of 2010 further strengthens the clawback rules, such that firms *must* recover all incentive compensation paid to *any* current or former executive, in the three years preceding the restatement, if that compensation would not have been paid under the restated financial statements. In other words, executives will not be allowed to profit from misstated financial statements, even if the misstatement was not due to misconduct.[16]

Since its enactment in 2002, SOX has significantly affected the internal operations of publicly traded corporations and their auditors. SOX will continue to play a major role in corporate management and the auditing profession.

▶ Try It!

Determine whether each of the following statements is true or false:

1. The Sarbanes-Oxley Act of 2002 (SOX) imposes stricter requirements for financial reporting and internal controls and stricter consequences for those who engage in financial statement misconduct and other white-collar crimes.

2. Most business decisions are now based on gut feelings and hunches, rather than being data-driven.

3. Critical thinking can be improved by asking yourself a series of questions about any issue or problem you encounter. These questions, for example, include: What is the objective? What data will I need? What assumptions am I making? Is my conclusion logical?

4. The triple bottom line assesses company performance on three factors: people (social impact), planet (environmental impact), and profit (economic impact).

5. Manufacturing makes up the largest sector of the U.S. economy.

6. The globalization of business has little bearing on management accounting.

7. Computer systems that integrate all of a company's worldwide functions into one database are known as Integrated Worldwide Systems (IWSs).

8. Lean thinking focuses on eliminating waste from operations.

Please see page 47 for solutions.

---

[15]Go to www.AICPA.org to learn more about SOX.

[16]http://www.pwc.com/us/en/cfodirect/publications/in-brief/sec-dodd-frank-clawback-rule-954.html

Decision Guidelines

The Changing Business and Regulatory Environment

Successful companies have to respond to changes in the business and regulatory environment. Managers have many decisions to make as they adapt to current business trends.

Decision	Guidelines
What impact will big data and data analytics have on our organization?	The abundance of data allows managers to make data-driven decisions, rather than decisions that are made on a hunch. However, critical thinking is needed to turn data into useful information.
How can we use critical thinking to help solve business issues?	The following steps provide a framework for critically examining any issue or problem: 1. What is the purpose, goal, or objective? In other words, what am I trying to accomplish? 2. What is the specific question I'm trying to address? The question will guide your thought process. 3. What data will I need to answer the question? With the sheer magnitude of data available, you'll need to hone in solely on the data that will help you answer the question at hand. 4. What concepts am I using, and what assumptions might I be taking for granted? Make sure you clearly identify the concepts and assumptions you are using, since a change in assumption might impact your conclusions. 5. What conclusions am I coming to, and are my inferences logical? *Always* check for logic. 6. What are the implications and consequences of these conclusions? All decisions have repercussions. Think ahead to what the outcome might be. 7. What is my point of view or reference point through which I have viewed the problem? Could I look at the problem from another equally valid point of view? Recognize that your point of view, which is the lens through which you view an issue, might be only one of several equally valid viewpoints.
Is management accounting useful in the growing knowledge economy, or is it only applicable to manufacturers?	Managerial accounting has expanded to meet the needs of companies in all sectors of the economy. Managers in service industries need detailed cost and revenue data to plan, control, and direct operations just as much as manufacturers do.
How do companies compete in a global economy?	The globalization of business means more competition but more opportunity as well. To remain competitive, companies must constantly focus on costs, customer response times, and quality. Companies use lean thinking and Six Sigma to reduce wasted resources, reduce wasted time, and improve quality.
How does the concept of sustainability affect business?	Businesses will be viable in the long run only if they take a sustainable approach to operations, carefully considering the impact of the company's operations on people and the planet as well as on profit. Thus, company performance is often evaluated using a triple-bottom-line approach. Businesses are viewing sustainability as an opportunity to "do the right thing" while simultaneously increasing the company's value through innovation, risk minimization, and cost reduction.
Which companies need to comply with SOX?	Publicly traded companies must comply with SOX. To better ensure the legitimacy of companies' financial information, many of the law's specific requirements focus on implementing adequate internal controls, employing better financial reporting procedures, and maintaining independence from the company's auditors.

SUMMARY PROBLEM 2

EZ-Rider Motorcycles is considering whether to expand into Germany. If gas prices increase, the company expects more interest in fuel-efficient transportation such as motorcycles. As a result, the company is considering setting up a motorcycle assembly plant on the outskirts of Berlin.

EZ-Rider Motorcycles estimates that it will cost $850,000 to convert an existing building to motorcycle production. Workers will need training, at a total cost of $65,000. The additional cost to organize the business and to establish relationships is estimated to be $150,000.

The CEO believes the company can earn profits from this expansion (before considering the costs in the preceding paragraph) of $1,624,000.

Requirement

Use cost-benefit analysis to determine whether EZ-Rider should expand into Germany.

▪ SOLUTION

The following cost-benefit analysis indicates that the company should expand into Germany because expected benefits exceed expected costs:

	A	B	C	D
1	**Cost-Benefit Analysis**		**Total**	
2	***Expected Benefits:***			
3	Expected profits from increase in sales		$ 1,624,000	
4	***Expected Costs:***			
5	Conversion of building	$ 850,000		
6	Workforce training	65,000		
7	Organizing and establishing relationships	150,000		
8	Total expected costs		1,065,000	
9	**Net expected benefit**		$ 559,000	
10				

END OF CHAPTER

Learning Objectives

- 1 Identify managers' three primary responsibilities
- 2 Distinguish financial accounting from managerial accounting
- 3 Describe the roles and skills required of management accountants within the organization
- 4 Describe the role of the Institute of Management Accountants (IMA) and apply its ethical standards
- 5 Discuss the business trends and regulations affecting management accounting

Accounting Vocabulary

American Institute of Certified Public Accountants (AICPA). **(p. 11)** The world's largest association representing the accounting profession; together with the Chartered Institute of Management Accountants (CIMA), offers the Chartered Global Management Accountant (CGMA) designation.

Audit Committee. (p. 10) A subcommittee of the board of directors that is responsible for overseeing both the internal audit function and the annual financial statement audit by independent CPAs.

Board of Directors. (p. 9) The body elected by shareholders to oversee the company.

Budget. (p. 3) Quantitative expression of a plan that helps managers coordinate and implement the plan.

Certified Management Accountant (CMA). (p. 10) A professional certification issued by the IMA to designate expertise in the areas of managerial accounting, economics, and business finance.

Chartered Global Management Accountant (CGMA). **(p. 11)** A designation available to qualifying American Institute of Certified Public Accountants (AICPA) members that is meant to recognize the unique business and accounting skill set possessed by those CPAs who work, or have worked, in business, industry, or government.

Chief Executive Officer (CEO). (p. 9) The position hired by the board of directors to oversee the company on a daily basis.

Chief Financial Officer (CFO). (p. 10) The position responsible for all of the company's financial concerns.

Chief Operating Officer (COO). (p. 10) The position responsible for overseeing the company's operations.

Controller. (p. 10) The position responsible for general financial accounting, managerial accounting, and tax reporting.

Controlling. (p. 3) One of management's primary responsibilities; evaluating the results of business operations against the plan and making adjustments to keep the company pressing toward its goals.

Cost-Benefit Analysis. (p. 19) Weighing costs against benefits to help make decisions.

Critical Thinking. (p. 18) Improving the quality of thought by skillfully analyzing, assessing, and reconstructing it.

Cross-Functional Teams. (p. 10) Corporate teams whose members represent various functions of the organization, such as R&D, design, production, marketing, distribution, and customer service.

Decision Making. (p. 2) Identifying possible courses of action and choosing among them.

Directing. (p. 3) One of management's primary responsibilities; running the company on a day-to-day basis.

Enterprise Resource Planning (ERP). (p. 18) Software systems that can integrate all of a company's worldwide functions, departments, and data into a single system.

Institute of Management Accountants (IMA). (p. 10) The professional organization that promotes the advancement of the management accounting profession.

Integrated Reporting. (p. 22) A process resulting in a report that describes how a company is creating value over time using financial, manufactured, intellectual, human, social, and natural capital.

Internal Audit Function. (p. 10) The corporate function charged with assessing the effectiveness of the company's internal controls and risk management policies.

Lean Thinking. (p. 21) A philosophy and business strategy of operating without waste.

Management Accounting (p. 2) A profession that involves partnering in management decision making, devising planning and performance management systems, and providing expertise in financial reporting and control to assist management in the formulation and implementation of an organization's strategy.

Planning. (p. 3) One of management's primary responsibilities: setting goals and objectives for the company and deciding how to achieve them.

Sarbanes-Oxley Act of 2002 (SOX). (p. 23) A congressional act that enhances internal control and financial reporting requirements and establishes new regulatory requirements for publicly traded companies and their independent auditors.

Six Sigma. (p. 21) The goal of producing near perfection with less than 3.4 defects per million opportunities.

Sustainability. (p. 21) The ability to meet the needs of the present without compromising the ability of future generations to meet their own needs.

Treasurer. (p. 10) The position responsible for raising the firm's capital and investing funds.

Triple Bottom Line. (p. 22) Evaluating a company's performance not only by its ability to generate economic profits, but also by its impact on people and on the planet.

MyAccountingLab

Go to http://myaccountinglab.com/ **for the following Quick Check, Short Exercises, Exercises, and Problems. They are available with immediate grading, explanations of correct and incorrect answers, and interactive media that acts as your own online tutor.**

Quick Check

1. *(Learning Objective 1)* Which of the following management responsibilities often involves evaluating the results of operations against the budget?
   a. Planning
   b. Directing
   c. Controlling
   d. None of the above

2. *(Learning Objective 2)* Managerial accounting differs from financial accounting in that managerial accounting
   a. tends to report on the company as a whole rather than segments of the company.
   b. emphasizes data relevance over data objectivity.
   c. is used primarily by external decision makers.
   d. is required by Generally Accepted Accounting Principles (GAAP).

3. *(Learning Objective 3)* Which of the following corporate positions is responsible for general financial accounting, managerial accounting, and tax reporting?
   a. Controller
   b. Treasurer
   c. Internal audit
   d. Chief operating officer (COO)

4. *(Learning Objective 3)* Of the following skills, which are needed by today's management accountants?
   a. Strategic thinking
   b. Cost management
   c. Decision analysis
   d. All of the above

5. *(Learning Objective 4)* Which of the following organizations is the professional association specifically for management accountants?
   a. FASB
   b. AICPA
   c. IMA
   d. IFRS

6. *(Learning Objective 4)* Which of the following professional standards requires management accountants to continually develop their knowledge and skills?
   a. Competence
   b. Confidentiality
   c. Integrity
   d. Credibility

7. *(Learning Objective 4)* Which of the following professional standards requires management accountants to not disclose private information about their organizations?
   a. Competence
   b. Confidentiality
   c. Integrity
   d. Credibility

8. *(Learning Objective 5)* Which of the following requires the company's CEO and CFO to assume responsibility for the company's financial statements and disclosures?
   a. Sarbanes-Oxley Act of 2002 (SOX)
   b. Institute of Management Accountants (IMA)
   c. Enterprise Resource Planning (ERP)
   d. Lean operations

9. *(Learning Objective 5)* Which of the following is *false*?
   a. Globalization has increased the necessity for more detailed and accurate cost information.
   b. The triple bottom line focuses on three items: net income, net assets, and return on investment.
   c. ERP systems integrate information from all company functions into a centralized data warehouse.
   d. Lean operations is a philosophy and business strategy of operating without waste.

10. *(Learning Objective 5)* All of the following are business trends affecting management accounting **except:**
    a. shifting economy.
    b. sustainability.
    c. big data.
    d. all of the above.

Quick Check Answers

1.c 2.b 3.a 4.d 5.c 6.a 7.b 8.a 9.b 10.d

2

Building Blocks
of Managerial
Accounting

lev radin/Alamy

Source: http://www.toyota-global.com/company/vision_philosophy/
toyota_global_vision_2020.html; http://www.statista.com/
statistics/275520/ranking-of-car-manufacturers-based-on-global-sales/

Learning Objectives

- **1** Distinguish among service, merchandising, and manufacturing companies
- **2** Describe the value chain and its elements
- **3** Distinguish between direct and indirect costs
- **4** Identify product costs and period costs
- **5** Prepare the financial statements for service, merchandising, and manufacturing companies
- **6** Describe costs that are relevant and irrelevant for decision making
- **7** Classify costs as fixed or variable and calculate total and average costs at different volumes

As the world's largest automotive manufacturer, Toyota has been guided by a global vision designed "to lead the way to the future of mobility, enriching lives around the world with the safest and most responsible ways of moving people." In order to achieve this vision, company managers must focus on researching and developing new, safe, and environmentally friendly technologies, and on designing, marketing, and distributing new models that will appeal to a diverse array of global markets. Toyota must also produce vehicles in the most efficient manner possible and provide customers with exceptional post-sales service. All of these business activities, which cost money to perform, impact Toyota's bottom line by driving market share and sales revenue. Toyota's keys to financial success include its focus on performing these business activities as cost efficiently as possible and using cost and revenue information to make profitable business decisions. In this chapter, we discuss the costs incurred by these different business activities: costs that both managers and accountants must understand in order to make profitable business decisions.

So far, we have seen how managerial accounting provides information that managers use to run their businesses more efficiently. Managers must understand basic managerial accounting terms and concepts before they can use the information to make good decisions. This terminology provides the common ground through which managers and accountants communicate. Without a common understanding of these concepts, managers may ask for (and accountants may provide) the wrong information for making decisions. As you will see, different types of costs are useful for different purposes. Both managers and accountants must have a clear understanding of the types of costs that are relevant to the decision at hand.

What Are the Most Common Business Sectors and Their Activities?

Before we talk about specific types of costs, let's consider the three most common types of companies and the business activities they perform.

Service, Merchandising, and Manufacturing Companies

Recall from Chapter 1 that many companies are beginning to adhere to the notion of a **triple bottom line**, in which the company's performance is evaluated not only in terms of profitability, but also in terms of its impact on people and the planet. Even so, for a business to flourish and grow in the long run, it will need to generate economic profits that are sufficiently large to attract and retain investors, as well as fuel future business expansion. Companies typically generate profit through one of three basic business models: they provide a service, they sell merchandise, or they manufacture products.

1 Distinguish among service, merchandising, and manufacturing companies

Service Companies

Service companies are in business to sell intangible services—such as health care, insurance, banking, and consulting. Recall from Chapter 1 that service firms now make up the largest sector of the U.S. economy. Because these types of companies sell services, they generally don't carry inventory. Some service providers carry a minimal amount of supplies inventory; however, this inventory is typically used for internal operations—not sold for profit. Service companies incur costs to provide services, advertise, and develop new services. For many service providers, salaries and benefits make up the majority of their costs.

Merchandising Companies

Merchandising companies such as Walmart and Best Buy resell tangible products they buy from manufacturers and suppliers. For example, Walmart buys clothing, toys, and electronics and resells them to customers at higher prices than what it pays for these goods. Merchandising companies include retailers (such as Walmart) and wholesalers. **Retailers** sell to consumers like you and me. **Wholesalers**, often referred to as "middlemen," buy products in bulk from manufacturers, mark up the prices, and then sell those products to retailers.

Because merchandising companies are in business to sell tangible goods, they carry a substantial amount of inventory. The cost of inventory includes the cost merchandisers pay for the goods *plus* all costs necessary to get the merchandise in place and ready to sell, such as freight-in costs and any import duties or tariffs paid on merchandise purchased from overseas suppliers. A merchandiser's balance sheet has just one inventory account called "Inventory" or "Merchandise Inventory." Besides incurring inventory-related costs, merchandisers also incur costs to operate their retail stores and websites, advertise, research new products and new store locations, and provide customer service.

Manufacturing Companies

<u>Manufacturing companies</u> use labor, plant, and equipment to convert raw materials into new finished products. For example, Toyota converts steel, tires, and fabric into high-performance vehicles using production labor and advanced manufacturing equipment. The vehicles are then sold to car dealerships at a price that is high enough to cover costs and generate a profit. As shown in Exhibit 2-1, manufacturers carry three types of inventory:

1. **Raw materials inventory**: *All raw materials that will be used in manufacturing.* Toyota's raw materials include steel, glass, tires, upholstery fabric, engines, and other automobile components. They also include other physical materials used in the plant, such as machine lubricants and janitorial supplies.

2. **Work in process inventory**: *Goods that are partway through the manufacturing process but not yet complete.* At Toyota, the work in process inventory consists of partially completed vehicles.

3. **Finished goods inventory**: *Completed goods that have not yet been sold.* Toyota is in business to sell completed cars, not work in process. Once the vehicles are completed, they are no longer considered work in process, but rather they become part of finished goods inventory.

EXHIBIT 2-1 Manufacturers' Three Types of Inventory

Exhibit 2-2 summarizes the differences among service, merchandising, and manufacturing companies.

EXHIBIT 2-2 Service, Merchandising, and Manufacturing Companies

	Service Companies	Merchandising Companies	Manufacturing Companies
Examples	Southwest Airlines	Amazon.com	Procter & Gamble
	Bank of America	Best Buy	General Mills
	Progressive Insurance	Walmart	Apple
	Goldman Sachs	The Home Depot	Toyota
Primary Output	Intangible services	Tangible products purchased from manufacturers and suppliers	New tangible products made using raw materials, labor, and production equipment
Type(s) of Inventory	None	Inventory (or Merchandise Inventory)	Raw materials inventory Work in process inventory Finished goods inventory

STOP & THINK

What type of company is Chipotle?

Answer: Some companies don't seem to fit nicely into one of the three categories previously discussed. For example, Chipotle has some elements of a service company (it serves hungry patrons), some elements of a manufacturing company (employees convert raw ingredients into finished meals), and some elements of a merchandising company (it sells ready-to-serve bottled drinks). Despite all of these different operating activities, restaurants are considered to be in the service sector.

As the "Stop & Think" feature shows, not all companies are strictly service, merchandising, or manufacturing firms. Recall from Chapter 1 that the U.S. economy is shifting more toward service-based companies. Many traditional manufacturers, such as General Electric (GE) and Ford, have developed profitable service segments that add additional profit to the company's bottom line. Even merchandising firms are getting into the "service game." For example, retailers often sell extended warranties on products ranging from furniture and major appliances to sporting equipment and consumer electronics. While the merchandiser recognizes a liability for these warranties, the price charged to customers for the warranties greatly exceeds the company's cost of fulfilling its warranty obligations, thus providing additional profit to the merchandiser.

Why is this important?

"All employees should have an **understanding** of their company's basic business model. The **Enron scandal** was finally brought to light as a **result** of someone seriously asking, "How does this company actually **make money?**" If the business model does not make **logical sense**, something fishy may be going on."

Which Business Activities Make Up the Value Chain?

Many people describe Toyota, General Mills, and Apple as manufacturing companies. But it would be more accurate to say that these are companies that *do* manufacturing. Why? Because companies that do manufacturing also do many other things. For example, even though Apple is a manufacturing company, it may be best known for its technological design innovations. Likewise, although Toyota is a manufacturer, it also conducts research to determine what type of new technology to integrate into next year's models. Toyota designs the new models based on its research and then produces, markets, distributes, and services the cars. These activities form Toyota's <u>value chain</u>—the activities that add value to the company's products and services. The value chain is pictured in Exhibit 2-3.

2 Describe the value chain and its elements

EXHIBIT 2-3 The Value Chain

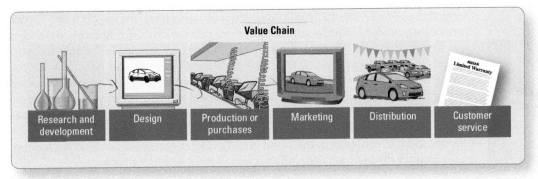

The value chain activities also cost money. To set competitive, yet profitable selling prices, Toyota must consider all of the costs incurred along the value chain, not just the costs incurred in manufacturing vehicles. Let's briefly consider some of the costs incurred in each element of the value chain.[1]

[1] Toyota Motor Corp 2014 Annual report and Toyota.com.

Research and Development (R&D): *Researching and developing new or improved products or services and the processes for producing them.* Toyota continually engages in researching and developing new technologies to incorporate in its vehicles (such as fuel cells, artificial intelligence, and pre-crash safety systems). Much of the R&D is aimed at safety and accessibility; improving how machines and humans work together. Toyota also researches and develops new technologies to use in its manufacturing plants (such as advanced manufacturing robotics). In 2014, Toyota spent 910.5 billion yen (approximately $7.7 billion) on R&D.

Design: *Detailed engineering of products and services and the processes for producing them.* Toyota's goal is to design vehicles that create total customer satisfaction, including satisfaction with vehicle style, features, safety, and quality. As a result, Toyota updates the design of older models (such as the Corolla) and designs new prototypes on a regular basis (such as the i-Road, a three-wheel electric commuter vehicle, and the Mirai, the first fuel cell vehicle for the mass market). Part of the design process also includes determining how to mass-produce the vehicles. Because Toyota produces over 8 million vehicles per year, engineers must design production plants that are efficient, yet flexible enough to allow for new features and models.

Production or Purchases: *Resources used by manufacturers to produce a product or by merchandising companies to purchase finished merchandise intended for resale.* For Toyota, the production activity includes all costs incurred to *make* the vehicles. These costs include raw materials (such as steel), plant labor (such as machine operators' wages), and manufacturing overhead (such as factory utilities and depreciation). As you can imagine, factories are very expensive to build and operate.

For a merchandiser such as Best Buy, this value chain activity includes the cost of purchasing the inventory that the company plans to sell to customers. It also includes all costs associated with getting the inventory to the store, including freight-in costs and any import duties and tariffs that might be incurred if the merchandise was purchased from overseas.

Marketing: *Promotion and advertising of products or services.* The goal of marketing is to create consumer demand for products and services. Toyota uses print advertisements in magazines and newspapers, billboards, television commercials, and the Internet to market its vehicles in both existing and emerging global markets. Some companies use star athletes and sporting events to market their products. Each method of advertising costs money but adds value by reaching different target customers.

Distribution: *Delivery of products or services to customers.* On the one hand, Toyota sells most of its vehicles through traditional brick-and-mortar dealerships. On the other hand, Amazon sells and distributes its products almost entirely using a web-based sales platform and then ships the products directly to customers. Other industries use different distribution mechanisms, such as catalog sales and home-based parties.

Customer Service: *Support provided for customers after the sale.* Toyota incurs substantial customer service costs, especially in connection with warranties on new car sales. Toyota generally warranties its vehicles for the first three years and/or 36,000 miles, whichever comes first. Historically, Toyota has had one of the best reputations in the auto industry for excellent quality. However, 2009–2010 proved to be costly and difficult years for the company, as recalls were made on over 14 million vehicles. In addition to the cost of repairing the vehicles, the company incurred millions of dollars in costs related to government fines, lawsuits, and public relations campaigns. However, as a result of the company's commitment to building safe and reliable vehicles, Toyota once again regained the title of the number-one carmaker in the world in 2012 and has continued to hold the number one position for the last four years, selling over 10 million vehicles per year.

Coordinating Activities Across the Value Chain

Many of the value chain activities occur in the order discussed here. However, managers cannot simply work on R&D and not think about customer service until after selling the car. Rather, cross-functional teams work on R&D, design, production, marketing, distribution, and customer service simultaneously. As the teams develop new model features, they also plan how to produce, market, and distribute the redesigned vehicles. They also consider how the new design will affect warranty costs. Recall from the last chapter that management accountants typically participate in these cross-functional teams. Even at the highest level of global operations, Toyota uses cross-functional teams to implement its business goals and strategy.

The value chain pictured in Exhibit 2-3 also reminds managers to control costs over the value chain as a whole. For example, Toyota spends more in R&D and product design to increase the quality of its vehicles, which in turn reduces customer service costs. Even though R&D and design costs are higher, the total cost of the vehicle—as measured throughout the entire value chain—is potentially lower as a result of this trade-off. Enhancing its reputation for safe, high-quality, innovative products has also enabled Toyota to increase its market share.

Sustainability and the Value Chain

Progressive companies will incorporate sustainability throughout every function of the value chain. However, experts estimate that 90% of sustainability occurs at the design stage. At the design stage, companies determine how the product will be used by customers, how easily the product can be repaired or eventually recycled, and the types of raw materials and manufacturing processes necessary to produce the product. Thus, good design is essential to the creation of environmentally friendly, safe products that enhance people's lives. For example, companies can integrate sustainability throughout the value chain by:

- **Researching and developing environmentally safe packaging.** Many companies are actively researching ways to reduce the amount of packaging used with their products as well as developing new types of packaging that are less harmful to the environment. In 2015, McDonald's achieved the goal of sourcing 100% of its packaging for its European operations from recycled sources or from forests certified by the Forest Stewardship Council. That same year, the company also pledged to end deforestation across the company's entire global supply chain.[2]

- **Designing products using life-cycle assessment and biomimicry.** Life-cycle assessment means the company analyzes the environmental impact of a product, from "cradle-to-grave," in an attempt to minimize negative environmental consequences throughout the entire lifespan of the product. For example, after studying the life cycles of its products, Procter & Gamble (P&G) discovered that about three-quarters of the energy used by consumers in washing their clothes comes from heating the water. As a result, the company developed Coldwater Tide, which is effective for laundering in cold water, thereby conserving energy. This product is a win–win for the environment and the company: the product is saving energy while also generating millions in annual sales revenue.[3]

  Biomimicry means that a company tries to mimic, or copy, natural biological features and processes. For example, Ford Motor Company and P&G are studying the gecko, nature's perfect example of a creature able to stick to surfaces without any liquids or adhesive substances, and then release from the surface, without any leaving sticky residue. The companies envision innovative adhesive applications from this research that will generate revenue, save money, and be more environmentally friendly.[4] Another aspect of biomimicry

[2]http://www.environmentalleader.com/2015/11/10/mcdonalds-achieves-100-sustainable-packaging-goal/

[3]http://www.nytimes.com/2011/09/17/business/cold-water-detergents-get-a-chilly-reception.html?pagewanted=1&_r=0

[4]http://www.environmentalleader.com/2015/10/21/ford-looks-to-lizards-to-increase-recyclability-improve-adhesives/

revolves around eliminating the concept of waste by creating "cradle-to-cradle" product life cycles. For example, Ricoh's copiers were designed so that at the end of a copier's useful life, Ricoh would collect and dismantle the product for usable parts, shred the metal casing, and use the parts and shredded material to build new copiers. The entire copier was designed so that nothing is wasted, or thrown out, except the dust from the shredding process. PT Tirta Marta has developed a "plastic" bag made from tapioca that can biodegrade in as little as two weeks,[5] whereas traditional plastic bags, according to the Environmental Protection Agency (EPA), can take as long as 1,000 years.[6]

■ **Adopting sustainable purchasing practices.** Many of the world's largest companies, such as Walmart, Costco, and The Home Depot, are now actively assessing the sustainability level of potential suppliers as a factor in selecting suppliers. As leading retailers in the world, these companies' purchasing policies are forcing other companies to adopt more sustainable business practices.

■ **Marketing with integrity.** Consumers are driving much of the sustainability movement by demanding that companies produce environmentally friendly products and limit or eliminate operational practices that have a detrimental impact on the environment and society. The LOHAS (Lifestyles of Health and Sustainability) market segment is estimated at $355 billion per year.[7] Thus, many companies are successfully spotlighting their sustainability initiatives in order to increase market share as well as attract potential investors and employees. However, <u>greenwashing</u>, the unfortunate practice of *overstating* a company's commitment to sustainability, can ultimately backfire as investors and consumers learn the truth about company operations. Hence, honesty and integrity in marketing are imperative.

■ **Distributing using fossil-fuel alternatives and carbon offsets.** While the biofuel industry is still in its infancy, the production and use of biofuels, especially those generated from nonfood waste, are expected to grow exponentially in the near future. Companies whose business is heavily reliant upon fossil fuels, such as oil companies (Valero), airlines (United), and distribution companies (UPS), are especially interested in the development of sustainable fuel sources. In fact, many companies, such as UPS and Walmart, are investing in hybrid fleets in order to reduce energy consumption, which thereby reduces their costs. In addition, many companies are investing in carbon offsets through such measures as reforestation projects. For example, in 2013 UPS planted 1.3 million trees, and in 2014 it pledged to plant 2 million trees as part of its efforts to offset greenhouse gas emissions.[8] United Airlines offers a carbon-offset program that allows customers, as soon as they purchase their ticket, to offset the carbon emissions resulting from their air travel by donating to reforestation and renewable energy projects. The website automatically calculates the donation amount needed to offset the greenhouse gas emissions.

■ **Providing customer service past the warranty date.** Environmentally conscious companies don't want customers discarding products that are in need of repair, or no longer serve the customer's needs or wants, thus, they provide the customer with other options. REI Co-op and Patagonia provide customers with free repair tips and offer repair services at a nominal charge. Best Buy recycles any electronic equipment regardless of where the customer bought it, and Apple buys back iPhones, iPads, and iPods by issuing credit toward the purchase of a new device.

If you are interested in learning more about what companies are doing to become more sustainable, visit the Environmentalleader.com website and sign up for its daily e-mail.

See Exercises
E2-20A and E2-32B

---

[5]http://www.tirtamarta.com/green-plastic-solutions/about-us/
[6]http://www.nytimes.com/2007/04/01/weekinreview/01basics.html
[7]http://www.lohas.com/whos-changing
[8]http://compass.ups.com/how-ups-helps-turn-world-greener

How Do Companies Define Cost?

Now that you understand the most common types of companies and the primary business activities they perform, let's consider some of the specialized language that accountants use when referring to costs.

Cost Objects, Direct Costs, and Indirect Costs

A **cost object** is anything for which managers want to know the cost. Toyota's cost objects may include the following:

■ Individual units (a specific, custom-ordered Prius)

■ Different models (the Prius, Rav4, and Corolla)

■ Alternative marketing strategies (television advertising, sponsorship of athletic events)

■ Geographic segments of the business (United States, Europe, Japan)

■ Departments (human resources, R&D, legal)

■ Sustainability initiatives ("Toyota TogetherGreen" conservation programs)

Costs are classified as either direct or indirect with respect to the cost object.

■ A **direct cost** is a cost that can be traced to the cost object, meaning the company can readily identify or associate the cost with the cost object. For example, say the cost object is one Prius. Toyota can easily trace, or associate, the cost of four tires with one specific Prius. Therefore, the tires are a direct cost of the vehicle.

■ An **indirect cost**, in contrast, is a cost that relates to the cost object but cannot be traced specifically to it. Think of an indirect cost as a cost that is jointly used or shared by several cost objects. For example, Toyota incurs substantial cost to run a manufacturing plant, including utilities, property taxes, and depreciation. Toyota cannot build a Prius without incurring these costs, so the costs are related to the Prius. However, it's impossible to trace a specific amount of these costs to one Prius. These costs are shared by all of the vehicles produced in the plant during the period. Therefore, these costs are considered indirect costs of a single Prius.

Another example might help. Think about your university's football team. Direct costs of the football team would include their uniforms, footballs, coach's salary, and travel to away games. These costs are easily identifiable with and traceable to the football team, so they are considered direct costs of the football team. Indirect costs would include costs shared by the football team and other university athletic teams, such as the athletic director's salary, shared training facilities, and shared locker rooms. Since these resources are jointly used or shared by several athletic teams, not just the football team, they are considered indirect costs of the football team.

As shown in Exhibit 2-4, the same costs can be indirect with respect to one cost object, yet direct with respect to another cost object. For example, plant depreciation, plant property taxes, and plant utilities are indirect costs of a single Prius. However, if management wants to know how much it costs to operate the Prius manufacturing plant, the plant becomes the cost object; so the same depreciation, tax, and utility costs are direct costs of the manufacturing facility. Whether a cost is direct or indirect depends on the specified cost object. In this chapter, we'll be talking about a unit of product (such as one Prius) as the cost object.

If a company wants to know the *total* cost attributable to a cost object, it must **assign** all direct *and* indirect costs to the cost object. Assigning a cost simply means that you are "attaching" a cost to the cost object. For example, if Toyota wants to know the entire cost of manufacturing a Prius, it will need to assign both direct costs (such as the tires on the car) and indirect costs (such as

3 Distinguish between direct and indirect costs

Why is this important?

"As a manager **making decisions**, you'll need different types of **cost information** for different types of decisions. To get the **information** you really want, you'll have to **communicate** with the accountants using precise **definitions** of cost."

EXHIBIT 2-4 The Same Cost Can Be Direct or Indirect, Depending on the Cost Object

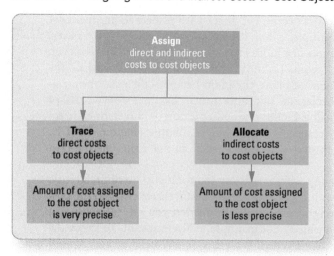

Cost object: One Prius

Cost object: Prius manufacturing plant

Indirect cost

Direct cost

Cost of plant and equipment depreciation, plant property taxes, and plant utilities

factory utilities) to the vehicle. Similarly, if the university wants to know the total cost of having a football team, it will have to consider both the direct and indirect costs related to the team.

The manner in which Toyota assigns costs depends on whether the costs are direct or indirect costs of the cost object. In our example, a specific vehicle is the cost object. Toyota can easily identify direct costs, such as tires, with specific vehicles. Therefore Toyota is able to **trace** direct costs to each vehicle manufactured in the plant. This results in a very precise cost figure, giving managers great confidence in the the amount of direct cost assigned to each vehicle. However, Toyota cannot trace indirect costs, such as utilities, to specific vehicles. Therefore, Toyota must **allocate** these indirect costs among all of the vehicles produced at the plant. The allocation process results in a less precise cost figure being assigned to each vehicle. We will discuss the allocation process in more detail in the following two chapters; but for now, think of allocation as dividing up the total indirect costs over all of the units produced, just as you might divide a pizza among friends. Exhibit 2-5 illustrates these concepts.

EXHIBIT 2-5 Assigning Direct and Indirect Costs to Cost Objects

Assign
direct and indirect
costs to cost objects

Trace
direct costs
to cost objects

Allocate
indirect costs
to cost objects

Amount of cost assigned
to the cost object
is very precise

Amount of cost assigned
to the cost object
is less precise

Try It!

Please see page 103 for solutions.

Assume a grocery store manager wants to know the cost of running the Produce Department. Thus, the Produce Department is the cost object. Which of the following would be considered direct costs of the Produce Department?

1. Wages of checkout clerks
2. Wages for workers in the Produce Department
3. Depreciation on refrigerated produce display cases
4. Cost of weekly advertisements in local newspaper
5. Cost of bananas, lettuce, and other produce
6. Baggies and twist ties available for shoppers in the Produce Department
7. Monthly lease payment for grocery store retail location
8. Cost of scales hanging in the Produce Department

Costs for Internal Decision Making and External Reporting

4 Identify product costs and period costs

Let's now consider how managers define the cost of one of their most important cost objects: their products. Managers need this information to determine the profitability of each product as well as to make other important business decisions. Managers define costs based on how the information will be used. Will the information be used for 1) internal decision making, or for 2) external reporting?

Costs for Internal Decision Making

When making internal decisions, managers must consider all costs incurred across the value chain. For example, when determining a suitable selling price for a Prius, Toyota must consider the cost to research, design, manufacture, market, distribute, and service that model. A Prius's **total cost** includes the costs of *all resources used throughout the value chain*. For Toyota, the total cost of a particular model, such as the Prius, is the total cost to research, design, manufacture, market, distribute, and service that model. Before launching a new model, managers predict the total cost of the model to set a selling price that will cover *all costs* plus return a profit. By comparing each model's sales revenue with its total cost across the value chain, Toyota can determine which models are most profitable. Perhaps Rav4s are more profitable than Corollas. Marketing can then focus on advertising and promoting the most profitable models. We'll talk more about total costs in Chapter 8, where we discuss many common business decisions.

Costs for External Reporting

For external reporting purposes, management must follow Generally Accepted Accounting Principles (GAAP). For external reporting purposes, GAAP requires that certain costs of the company be attached, or assigned, to units of product in inventory, while other costs are treated as operating expenses of the period. Let's define each of these types of costs.

- **Product costs** are the costs incurred by *manufacturers to produce* their products or incurred by *merchandisers to purchase* their products. Notice how these costs relate to *obtaining inventory*, either through manufacturing the products or purchasing them. Thus, these costs are incurred in the production or purchases function of the value chain. For external financial reporting, GAAP requires that these costs be assigned to inventory until the related products are sold. When the products are sold, these costs are removed from the company's inventory and expensed as Cost of Goods Sold.

- **Period costs** are the costs incurred by the company that do *not* get treated as inventory, but rather, are expensed immediately in the period in which they are incurred. These costs do *not* relate to manufacturing or purchasing product. Rather, they include costs incurred in every other function of the value chain, including R&D, design, marketing, distribution, and customer service. In essence, any cost that is not treated as inventory, is treated as a period cost. While accountants refer to these costs as "period costs," most other people refer to them as "operating expenses" or "selling, general, and administrative expenses" (SG&A). These terms are essentially synonymous and arise from the fact that these are costs of operating the business over a specific period of time.

Keep the following two important rules of thumb in mind:

> Product costs are costs assigned to the company's inventory on the balance sheet. In essence, they are the costs of manufacturing or purchasing the company's products.
>
> Period costs are often called "operating expenses" or "selling, general, and administrative expenses" (SG&A) on the company's income statement. Period costs are always expensed in the period in which they are incurred and never become part of an inventory account.

Exhibit 2-6 shows that a company's total costs can be divided into two categories: product costs (those costs treated as part of inventory until the product is sold) and period costs (those costs expensed in the current period regardless of when inventory is sold). GAAP requires this distinction for external financial reporting. Study the exhibit carefully to make sure you understand how the two types of costs affect the income statement and balance sheet.

EXHIBIT 2-6 Total Costs, Product Costs, and Period Costs

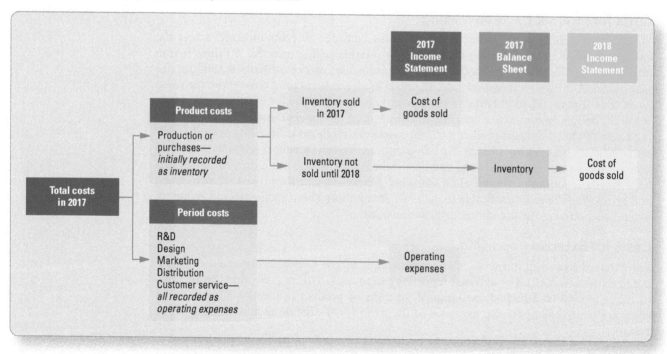

Now that you understand the difference between product costs and period costs, let's take a closer look at the specific costs that are treated as product costs in merchandising and manufacturing companies.

Merchandising Companies' Product Costs

Merchandising companies' product costs include *only* the cost of purchasing the inventory from suppliers plus any costs incurred to get the merchandise to the merchandiser's place of business and ready for sale. Typically, these additional costs include freight-in costs and import duties or tariffs, if the products were purchased from overseas. Why does the cost of the inventory include freight-in charges? Think of the last time you made a purchase from an online website, such as Amazon.com. The website may have shown the product's price as $15, but by the time you paid the shipping and handling charges, the product really cost you around $20. Likewise, merchandising companies pay freight-in charges to get the goods to their place of business. If they purchased the goods from overseas, there is a good chance they also had to pay import duties to bring the goods into the United States. As shown in Exhibit 2-7, these charges become part of the cost of their inventory.

EXHIBIT 2-7 Summary of a Merchandising Company's Total Costs

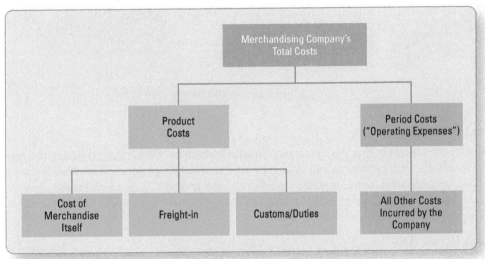

For example, The Home Depot's product costs include what the company paid for its store merchandise plus freight-in and import duties. The Home Depot records these costs in an asset account—Inventory—until it *sells* the merchandise. Once the merchandise is sold, it belongs to the customer, not The Home Depot. Therefore, The Home Depot takes the cost out of its inventory account and records it as an expense—the *cost of goods sold*. The Home Depot expenses all other costs incurred during the period, such as salaries, utilities, advertising, and property lease payments, as "operating expenses."

▶ **Try It!**

Which of the following costs are treated as product costs by a *merchandising company,* such as Walmart? Which costs are treated as period costs?

1. Cost of leasing the retail locations
2. Cost of managers' and sales associates' salaries
3. Cost of merchandise purchased for resale
4. Cost of designing and operating the company's website
5. Cost of shipping merchandise to the store
6. Cost of providing free shipping to customers who buy product online
7. Cost of utilities used in running the retail locations
8. Cost of import duties paid on merchandise purchased from overseas suppliers
9. Depreciation on store shelving and shopping carts

Please see page 103 for solutions.

Manufacturing Companies' Product Costs

Manufacturing companies' product costs include *only* those costs related to producing, or manufacturing, their products. As shown in Exhibit 2-8, manufacturers such as Toyota incur three types of manufacturing costs when making a vehicle: direct materials, direct labor, and manufacturing overhead.

EXHIBIT 2-8 Summary of the Three Types of Manufacturing Costs

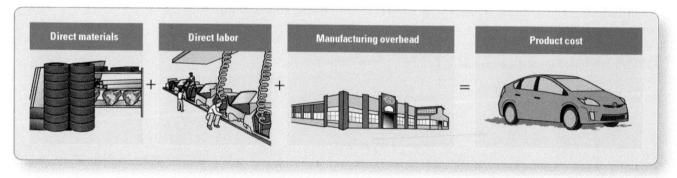

Direct Materials (DM)

Manufacturers convert raw materials into finished products. **Direct materials** are the *primary* materials that become a physical part of the finished product. The Prius's direct materials include steel, tires, engines, upholstery, and so forth. Toyota can trace the cost of these materials (including freight-in and any import duties) to specific units or batches of vehicles; thus, they are considered direct costs of the vehicles.

Direct Labor (DL)

Although many manufacturing facilities are highly automated, most still require some direct labor to convert raw materials into a finished product. **Direct labor** is the cost of compensating employees who physically convert raw materials into the company's products. At Toyota, direct labor includes the wages and benefits of machine operators and technicians who build and assemble the vehicles. Toyota can trace the time each of these employees spends working on specific units or batches of vehicles; thus, the cost of this labor is considered a direct cost of the vehicles.

Manufacturing Overhead (MOH)

The third production cost, **manufacturing overhead,** *includes all manufacturing costs other than direct materials and direct labor.* In other words, manufacturing overhead includes *all indirect manufacturing costs.* Manufacturing overhead is also referred to as factory overhead because all of these costs relate to the factory. Manufacturing overhead has three components: indirect materials, indirect labor, and other indirect manufacturing costs.

■ **Indirect materials** include materials used in the plant that are not easily traced to individual units. For example, indirect materials often include janitorial supplies, oil and lubricants for the machines, and any physical components of the finished product that are very inexpensive. For example, Toyota might treat the invoice sticker placed on each vehicle's window as an indirect material rather than a direct material. Even though the cost of the sticker (roughly 10 cents) *could* be traced to the vehicle, it wouldn't make much sense to do so. Why? Because the cost of tracing the sticker to the vehicle outweighs the benefit management receives from the increased accuracy of the information.

■ **Indirect labor** includes the cost of all employees working *in the plant* other than those employees directly converting the raw materials into the finished product. For example, at Toyota, indirect labor includes the salaries, wages, and benefits of plant forklift operators, plant security officers, plant janitors, and plant supervisors.

■ **Other indirect manufacturing costs** include such *plant-related* costs as depreciation on the plant and plant equipment, plant property taxes and insurance, plant repairs and maintenance, and plant utilities. Indirect manufacturing costs have grown tremendously in recent years as manufacturers automate their plants with the latest advanced manufacturing technology.

Exhibit 2-9 summarizes how manufacturers classify their costs.

EXHIBIT 2-9 Summary of a Manufacturing Company's Total Costs

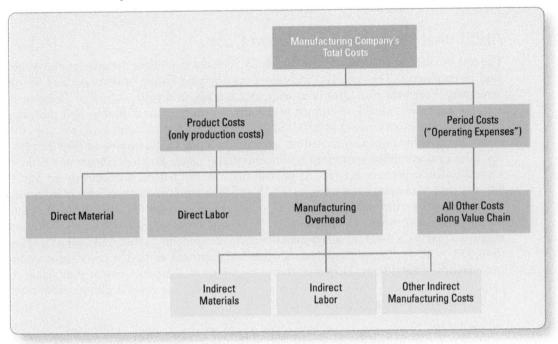

Prime and Conversion Costs

Managers and accountants sometimes talk about certain combinations of manufacturing costs. As shown in Exhibit 2-10, **prime costs** refer to the combination of direct materials and direct labor. Prime costs used to be the primary costs of production. However, as companies have automated production with expensive machinery, manufacturing overhead has become a greater cost of production. **Conversion costs** refer to the combination of direct labor and manufacturing overhead. These are the costs of *converting* raw materials into finished goods.

EXHIBIT 2-10 Prime and Conversion Costs

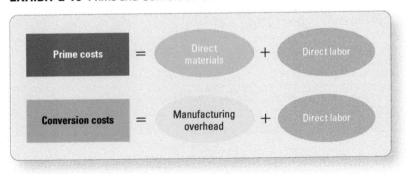

STOP & THINK

What is the difference between raw materials, direct materials, and indirect materials?

Raw materials are materials that have not yet been used. Once used, materials can be classified as direct or indirect. Direct materials are the primary physical components of a product. Indirect materials are materials used in the production plant that don't become part of the product (such as machine lubricants) or materials that do become part of the product but are insignificant in cost (such as the price sticker on a car).

Additional Labor Compensation Costs

The cost of labor, in all areas of the value chain, includes more than the salaries and wages paid to employees. The cost also includes company-paid fringe benefits such as health insurance, retirement plan contributions, payroll taxes, and paid vacations. These costs are very expensive. Health insurance premiums, which have seen double-digit increases for many years, often amount to $500–$1,500 per month for each employee electing coverage. Many companies also contribute an amount equal to 3% to 6% of their employees' salaries to company-sponsored retirement 401(k) plans. Employers must pay Federal Insurance Contributions Act (FICA) payroll taxes to the federal government for Social Security and Medicare, amounting to 7.65% of each employee's gross pay. In addition, most companies offer paid vacation and other benefits. Together, these fringe benefits usually cost the company an *additional* 35% beyond gross salaries and wages. Thus, an employee making a $40,000 salary actually costs the company about $54,000 to employ ($40,000 × 1.35). These fringe-benefit costs are expensed as period costs for all non-manufacturing employees. However, they are treated as a product cost if they relate to employees working in the manufacturing plant. In Chapter 3 we'll discuss how these additional labor costs get assigned to products.

Recap: Product Costs Versus Period Costs

In this half of the chapter, you have learned about the activities and costs incurred by three different types of companies. You have also learned the difference between direct and indirect costs. Finally, you have learned the difference between product costs and period costs. Exhibit 2-11 summarizes some of these concepts for you.

EXHIBIT 2-11 Summary of Product Costs Versus Period Costs

	-----Total Costs Across the Value Chain-----	
	Product Costs	**Period costs**
Service Companies	None	All costs across value chain
Merchandising Companies	Cost of merchandise itself Freight-in Import duties and customs, if any	All costs across value chain except product costs
Manufacturing Companies	Direct materials Direct labor Manufacturing overhead	All costs across value chain except product costs
Accounting Treatment	Treat as inventory until product is sold. When sold, expense as "Cost of Goods Sold."	Expense in period incurred as "Operating Expenses" or "Selling, General, and Administrative Expenses."

Decision Guidelines

Building Blocks of Managerial Accounting

Dell engages in *manufacturing* when it assembles its computers, *merchandising* when it sells them on its website, and support *services* such as start-up and implementation services. Dell had to make the following types of decisions as it developed its accounting systems.

Decision	Guidelines
How do you distinguish among service, merchandising, and manufacturing companies? How do their balance sheets differ?	*Service companies:* • Provide customers with intangible services • Have no inventories on the balance sheet *Merchandising companies:* • Resell tangible products purchased ready-made from suppliers • Have only one category of inventory *Manufacturing companies:* • Use labor, plant, and equipment to transform raw materials into new finished products • Have three categories of inventory: 　1. Raw materials inventory 　2. Work in process inventory 　3. Finished goods inventory
What business activities add value to companies?	All of the elements of the value chain, including the following: • R&D • Design • Production or purchases • Marketing • Distribution • Customer service
What costs should be assigned to cost objects such as products, departments, and geographic segments?	Both direct and indirect costs are assigned to cost objects. Direct costs are traced to cost objects, whereas indirect costs are allocated to cost objects.
Which costs are useful for internal decision making, and how are costs classified for external reporting?	Managers use *total costs* for internal decision making. However, GAAP requires companies to distinguish between product costs and period costs for external reporting purposes.
What costs are treated as product costs under GAAP?	• *Service companies:* Usually no product costs since they don't carry inventory • *Merchandising companies:* The cost of merchandise purchased for resale plus all of the costs of getting the merchandise to the company's place of business (for example, freight-in and import duties) • *Manufacturing companies:* Direct materials, direct labor, and manufacturing overhead
How are product costs treated on the financial statements?	Product costs are initially treated as an asset (inventory) on the balance sheet. These costs are expensed (as cost of goods sold) on the income statements when the products are sold.

SUMMARY PROBLEM 1

Requirements

1. Classify each of the following business costs into one of the six value chain elements:
   a. Costs associated with warranties and recalls
   b. Cost of shipping finished goods to overseas customers
   c. Costs a pharmaceutical company incurs to develop new drugs
   d. Cost of a 30-second commercial during the SuperBowl™
   e. Cost of making a new product prototype
   f. Cost of assembly labor used in the plant

2. For a manufacturing company, identify the following as either a product cost or a period cost. If it is a product cost, classify it as direct materials, direct labor, or manufacturing overhead.
   a. Depreciation on plant equipment
   b. Depreciation on salespeoples' automobiles
   c. Insurance on plant building
   d. Marketing manager's salary
   e. Cost of major components of the finished product
   f. Assembly-line workers' wages
   g. Costs of shipping finished products to customers
   h. Plant forklift operator's salary

▪ SOLUTIONS

Requirement 1
a. Customer service
b. Distribution
c. Research and development
d. Marketing
e. Design
f. Production

Requirement 2
a. Product cost; manufacturing overhead
b. Period cost
c. Product cost; manufacturing overhead
d. Period cost
e. Product cost; direct materials
f. Product cost; direct labor
g. Period cost
h. Product cost; manufacturing overhead

How Are Product Costs and Period Costs Shown in the Financial Statements?

5 Prepare the financial statements for service, merchandising, and manufacturing companies

The difference between product costs and period costs is important because these costs are treated differently in the financial statements. All product costs remain in inventory accounts until the merchandise is sold; then, these costs become the cost of goods sold. In contrast, all period costs are expensed as "operating expenses" in the period in which they are incurred. Keep these differences in mind as we review the income statements of service firms (which have no inventory), merchandising companies (which purchase their inventory), and manufacturers (which make their inventory). We'll finish the section by comparing the balance sheets of these three different types of companies.

Service Companies

Service companies have the simplest income statement. Exhibit 2-12 shows the income statement of WSC Consulting, an e-commerce consulting firm. The firm has no inventory and thus, no product costs. Therefore, WSC Consulting's income statement has no Cost of Goods Sold. Rather, all of the company's costs are period costs, so they are expensed in the current period as "operating expenses."

EXHIBIT 2-12 Service Company Income Statement

	A	B	C	D
1	WSC Consulting			
2	Income Statement			
3	Year Ended December 31			
4				
5	Revenues		$ 160,000	
6	Less operating expenses:			
7	Salary expense	$ 106,000		
8	Office rent expense	18,000		
9	Depreciation expense	3,500		
10	Marketing expense	2,500		
11	Total operating expenses		130,000	
12	Operating income		$ 30,000	
13				

In this textbook, we will always be evaluating the company's "operating income" rather than its "net income." Why? Because internal managers are particularly concerned with the income generated through the company's ongoing, primary operations. To arrive at net income, we would need to add or subtract non-operating income and expenses, such as interest, and subtract income taxes. In general, **operating income** is simply the company's earnings before interest and income taxes.

Merchandising Companies

In contrast with service companies, a merchandiser's income statement features Cost of Goods Sold as the major expense. Exhibit 2-13 illustrates the income statement for Wholesome Foods, a regional grocery store chain. Notice how Cost of Goods Sold is deducted from Sales Revenue to yield the company's gross profit. Next, all operating expenses (*all period costs*) are deducted to arrive at the company's operating income.

EXHIBIT 2-13 Merchandiser's Income Statement

	A	B	C	D
1	**Wholesome Foods**			
2	**Income Statement**			
3	**For the Year Ended December 31**			
4	*(all figures shown in thousands of dollars)*			
5				
6	Sales revenues		$ 150,000	
7	Less: Cost of goods sold		106,500	
8	Gross profit		$ 43,500	
9	Less operating expenses:			
10	Salaries and wages	$ 5,000		
11	Rent and utilities	3,000		
12	Marketing	1,000		
13	Total operating expenses		9,000	
14	Operating income		$ 34,500	
15				

But how does a merchandising company calculate the Cost of Goods Sold?

■ Most likely, the company uses bar coding to implement a **perpetual inventory** system during the year. If so, all inventory is labeled with a unique bar code that reflects (1) the sales price that will be charged to the customer, and (2) the "product cost" of the merchandise to the store. Every time a bar-coded product is scanned at the checkout counter, the company's accounting records are automatically updated to reflect (1) the sales revenue earned, (2) the cost of goods sold, and (3) the removal of the product from merchandise inventory.

■ However, at the end of the period, merchandisers must also calculate Cost of Goods Sold using the **periodic inventory** method. Why? Because the company's accounting records only reflect those products that were scanned during checkout. Thus, the records would not reflect any breakage, theft, input errors, or obsolescence that occurred during the year. Exhibit 2-14 shows how to calculate Cost of Goods Sold using the periodic method.

EXHIBIT 2-14 Calculation of Cost of Goods Sold for a Merchandising Firm

	A	B	C	D
1	**Calculation of Cost of Goods Sold**			
2	Beginning inventory	$ 9,500		
3	Plus: Purchases, freight-in, and any import duties	110,000		
4	Cost of goods available for sale	$ 119,500		
5	Less: Ending inventory	13,000		
6	Cost of goods sold	$ 106,500		
7				

In this calculation, we start with the beginning inventory and add to it all of the company's *product costs* for the period: the cost of the merchandise purchased from suppliers, freight-in, and any import duties. The resulting total reflects the cost of all goods that were available for sale during the period. Then we subtract the cost of the products still in ending inventory to arrive at the Cost of Goods Sold.

Try It!

Compute Cost of Goods Sold for Ralph's Sporting Goods, a merchandising company, given the following information:

Advertising expense...	$ 25,000
Purchases of merchandise..............................	400,000
Salaries expense..	80,000
Freight-in and import duties	20,000
Lease of store...	75,000
Beginning inventory	35,000
Ending inventory	38,000

Please see page 103 for solutions.

Manufacturing Companies

Exhibit 2-15 shows the income statement for Proquest, a manufacturer of tennis balls. As you can see, the income statement for a manufacturer is essentially identical to that of a merchandising company. The only *real* difference is that the company is selling product that it has *made*, rather than merchandise that it has *purchased*. As a result, the calculation of Cost of Goods Sold is different from that shown in Exhibit 2-14.

EXHIBIT 2-15 Manufacturer's Income Statement

	A	B	C	D
1	Proquest			
2	Income Statement			
3	For the Year Ended December 31			
4	(all figures shown in thousands of dollars)			
5				
6	Sales revenues		$ 65,000	
7	Less: Cost of goods sold		40,000	
8	Gross profit		$ 25,000	
9	Less operating expenses:			
10	Selling and marketing expenses	$ 8,000		
11	General and administrative expenses	2,000		
12	Total operating expenses		10,000	
13	Operating income		$ 15,000	
14				

Calculating Cost of Goods Manufactured and Cost of Goods Sold

Exhibit 2-16 illustrates how the manufacturer's *product costs* (direct material used, direct labor, and manufacturing overhead) flow through the three inventory accounts before they become part of Cost of Goods Sold. In order to calculate Cost of Goods Sold, a manufacturer must first figure out the amount of direct materials *used* and the Cost of Goods Manufactured.

As you see in Exhibit 2-16, the **Cost of Goods Manufactured** represents the cost of those goods that were completed and moved to Finished Goods Inventory during the period.

EXHIBIT 2-16 Flow of Costs Through a Manufacturer's Financial Statements

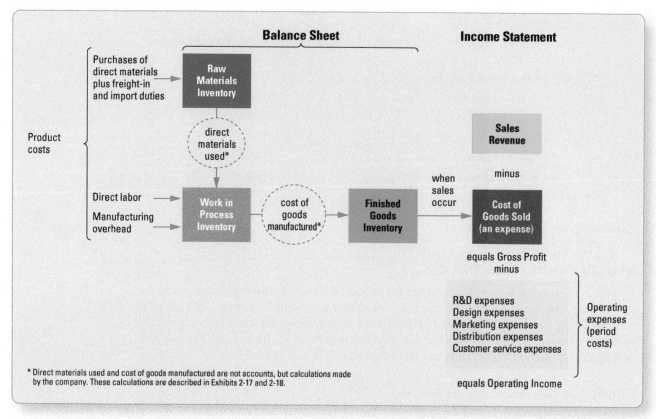

Using Exhibit 2-16 as a guide, let's walk through the calculation of Cost of Goods Sold. We'll use three steps. Each step focuses on a different inventory account: Raw Materials, Work in Process, and Finished Goods.

STEP 1:   Calculate the cost of the direct materials used during the year

Step 1 simply analyzes what happened in the *Raw Materials Inventory* account during the year. As shown in Exhibit 2-17, we start with the beginning balance in the Raw Materials Inventory account and add to it all of the direct materials purchased during the year, including any freight-in and import duties. This tells us the cost of materials that were available for use during the year. Finally, by subtracting out the ending balance of Raw Materials Inventory, we are able to back into the cost of the direct materials that were used.[9]

EXHIBIT 2-17 Calculation of Direct Materials Used

	A	B	C
1	**Calculation of Direct Materials Used**		
2	**(Analyze Raw Materials Inventory account)**		
3			
4	Beginning Raw Materials Inventory	$ 9,000	
5	Plus: Purchases of direct materials, freight-in, and import duties	27,000	
6	Materials available for use	$ 36,000	
7	Less: Ending Raw Materials Inventory	22,000	
8	Direct materials used	$ 14,000	
9			

[9]In this chapter, we'll assume that the Raw Materials account only contains direct materials because the company uses indirect materials as soon as they are purchased. In Chapter 3, we expand the discussion to include manufacturers who store both direct and indirect materials in the Raw Materials Inventory account.

STEP 2: Calculate the cost of goods manufactured

Step 2 simply analyzes what happened in the *Work in Process* account during the year. As shown in Exhibit 2-18, we start with the beginning balance in Work in Process and then add to it all three manufacturing costs that were incurred during the year (direct materials used, direct labor, and materials overhead). Finally, by subtracting out the goods still being worked on at year-end (ending Work in Process Inventory), we are able to back into the Cost of Goods Manufactured (CGM). This figure represents the cost of manufacturing the units that were *completed* and sent to Finished Goods Inventory during the year.

EXHIBIT 2-18 Calculation of Cost of Goods Manufactured

	A	B	C
1	**Calculation of Cost of Goods Manufactured**		
2	**(Analyze Work in Process Inventory account)**		
3			
4	Beginning Work in Process Inventory	$ 2,000	
5	Plus manufacturing costs incurred:		
6	Direct materials used	14,000	
7	Direct labor	19,000	
8	Manufacturing overhead	12,000	
9	Total manufacturing costs to account for	$ 47,000	
10	Less: Ending Work in Process Inventory	5,000	
11	Cost of goods manufactured (CGM)	$ 42,000	
12			

STEP 3: Calculate the cost of goods sold

Step 3 simply analyzes what happened in the *Finished Goods Inventory* account during the year. As shown in Exhibit 2-19, we start with the beginning balance of Finished Goods Inventory and add to it the product that was manufactured during the year (CGM) to arrive at the cost of the total goods available for sale. Finally, just like with a merchandiser, we subtract what was left in Finished Goods Inventory to back into the Cost of Goods Sold.

EXHIBIT 2-19 Calculation of Cost of Goods Sold

	A	B	C
1	**Calculation of Cost of Goods Sold**		
2	**(Analyze Finished Goods Inventory account)**		
3			
4	Beginning Finished Goods Inventory	$ 6,000	
5	Plus: Cost of goods manufactured (CGM)	42,000	
6	Cost of goods available for sale	$ 48,000	
7	Less: Ending Finished Goods Inventory	8,000	
8	Cost of goods sold	$ 40,000	
9			

By analyzing, step by step, what occurred in each of the three inventory accounts, we were able to calculate the Cost of Goods Sold shown on the company's Income Statement (see Exhibit 2-15). Some companies combine Steps 1 and 2 into one schedule called the Schedule of Cost of Goods Manufactured. Others combine all three steps into a Schedule of Cost of Goods Sold.

You may be wondering where all of the data come from. The beginning inventory balances were simply last year's ending balances. The purchases of direct materials and the incurrence of direct labor and manufacturing overhead would have been captured in the company's accounting records when those costs were incurred. Finally, the ending inventory balances come from doing a physical inventory count at the end of the year. In the coming chapters, we'll show you different systems manufacturers use to keep track of the product cost associated with the units still in the three inventory accounts.

Comparing Balance Sheets

Now that we've looked at the income statement for each type of company, let's consider their balance sheets. The only difference relates to how inventory is shown in the current asset section:

- Service companies show no Inventory.
- Merchandising companies show Inventory or Merchandise Inventory.
- Manufacturing companies show Raw Materials, Work in Process, and Finished Goods Inventory.

Sometimes manufacturers just show "Inventories" on the face of the balance sheet but disclose the breakdown of the inventory accounts (Raw Materials, Work in Process, and Finished Goods) in the footnotes to the financial statements.

 Sustainability and Corporate Reporting

In addition to generating a full set of financial statements for external users, many companies are now preparing and issuing Corporate Social Responsibility, or CSR, reports. These reports provide sustainability-related information to a variety of stakeholders, including investors and creditors, customers, government regulators, nongovernmental organizations (NGOs), and the general public. Although these reports are still voluntary in the United States, the move toward providing stakeholders with more sustainability-related data is growing. For example, the following issued CSR reports:

- 92% of the world's 250 largest companies (2015)[10]
- 75% of the S&P 500 companies (2014)[11]

Although sustainability reporting is still in its infancy, the Global Reporting Initiative, or GRI, has become the dominant framework for sustainability reporting. The GRI report follows the triple-bottom-line approach (people, planet, profit) by specifying metrics that companies should report on related to each of the three pillars of sustainability:

- Social performance metrics—for example, fair labor and human rights practices
- Environmental performance metrics—for example, greenhouse gas emissions and total water use
- Economic performance metrics—for example, revenues, operating costs, and so forth.

Sustainability reporting is not just for external reporting; companies also use it as a tool for internal change management. The GRI reporting process helps an organization illuminate areas of social and environmental impact that need improvement. It also helps management track the company's social and environmental progress by comparing baseline performance metrics with those achieved over time. The old adage proves just as true for nonfinancial data as it does for financial data: "You can't manage what you don't measure."

Finally, in a 2014 survey, Verdantix found that the Big Four accounting firms dominated both the sustainability consulting and sustainability assurance services markets.[12] Thus, students who wish to enter the accounting profession should be aware of these reporting developments.

---

[10]KPMG, 2015 Survey of Corporate Responsibility Reporting.

[11]Governance and Accountability Institute, http://www.ga-institute.com/nc/issue-master-system/news-details/article/flash-report-seventy-five-percent-75-of-the-sp-index-published-corporate-sustainability-rep.html.

[12]http://research.verdantix.com/index.cfm/papers/Press.Details/press_id/105/verdantix-global-survey-finds-the-big-four-accounting-firms-continue-to-dominate-the-sustainability-brands-landscape/

What Other Cost Terms Are Used by Managers?

So far in this chapter, we have discussed direct versus indirect costs and product costs versus period costs. Now let's turn our attention to other cost terms that managers and accountants use when planning and making decisions.

6 Describe costs that are relevant and irrelevant for decision making

Controllable Versus Uncontrollable Costs

When deciding to make business changes, management needs to distinguish controllable costs from uncontrollable costs. In the long run, most costs are **controllable**, meaning management is able to influence or change them. However, in the short run, companies are often locked in to certain costs arising from previous decisions. These are called **uncontrollable costs**. For example, Toyota has little or no control over the property tax and insurance costs of its existing plants. These costs were locked in when Toyota built its plants. Toyota could replace existing production facilities with different-sized plants in different areas of the world that might cost less to operate, but that would take time. To see *immediate* benefits, management must change those costs that are controllable at the present time. For example, management can control costs of research and development, design, and advertising. Sometimes Toyota's management chose to *increase* rather than decrease these costs in order to successfully gain market share. However, Toyota was also able to *decrease* other controllable costs, such as the price paid for raw materials, by working with its suppliers.

Relevant and Irrelevant Costs

Decision making involves identifying various courses of action and then choosing among them. When managers make decisions, they focus on only those costs and revenues that are relevant to the decision.

Say you want to buy a new car and you have narrowed your decision to two choices: the Nissan Sentra or the Toyota Corolla. As shown in Exhibit 2-20, say the Sentra you like costs $18,480, whereas the Corolla costs $19,385. Because sales tax is based on the sales price, the Corolla's sales tax is higher. However, your insurance agent quotes you a higher price to insure the Sentra ($195 per month versus $149 per month for the Corolla). All of these costs are relevant to your decision because they differ between the two cars. The **differential cost**, is the difference in cost between two alternative courses of action.

EXHIBIT 2-20 Comparison of Relevant Information

	A	B	C	D
1	**Relevant Costs**	**Sentra**	**Corolla**	**Differential Cost**
2	Car's price	$ 18,480	$ 19,385	$ (905)
3	Sales tax (8%) (rounded)	1,478	1,551	(73)
4	Insurance*	11,700	8,940	2,760
5	Total relevant costs	31,658	$ 29,876	$ 1,782
6				

*Over the five years (60 months) you plan to keep the car.

Other costs are not relevant to your decision. For example, both cars run on regular unleaded gasoline and have about the same fuel economy ratings, so the cost of operating the vehicles is about the same. Likewise, you don't expect cost differences in servicing the vehicles because they both carry the same warranty and have received excellent quality ratings. Because you project operating and maintenance costs to be the same for both cars, these costs are irrelevant to your decision. In other words, they won't influence your decision either way. Based on your analysis, the differential cost is $1,782 in favor of the Corolla. Does this mean that you will choose the Corolla? Not necessarily.

The Sentra may have some characteristics you like better, such as a particular paint color, more comfortable seating, or more trunk space. When making decisions, management must also consider qualitative factors, such as effect on employee morale, in addition to differential costs.

Another cost that is irrelevant to your decision is the price you paid for the vehicle you currently own. Say you just bought a Ford F-150 pickup truck two months ago, but you've decided you need a small sedan rather than a pickup truck. The cost of the truck is a <u>sunk cost</u>. Sunk costs are costs that have already been incurred. Nothing you do now can change the fact that you already bought the truck. Thus, the cost of the truck is not relevant to your decision of whether to choose between the Sentra and the Corolla. The only thing you can do now is (1) keep your truck or (2) sell it for the best price you can get.

Managers often have trouble ignoring sunk costs when making decisions, even though they should. Perhaps they invested in a factory or a computer system that no longer serves the company's needs. Many times, new technology makes managers' past investments in older technology look like bad decisions, even though they weren't at the time. Managers should ignore sunk costs because their decisions about the future cannot alter decisions made in the past.

Fixed and Variable Costs

7 Classify costs as fixed or variable and calculate total and average costs at different volumes

Managers cannot make good plans and decisions without first knowing how their costs behave. Costs generally behave as fixed costs or variable costs. We will spend all of Chapter 6 discussing cost behavior. For now, let's look just at the basics. <u>Fixed costs</u> stay constant in total over a wide range of activity levels. For example, let's say you decide to buy the Corolla, so your insurance cost for the year is $1,788 ($149 per month × 12 months). As shown in Exhibit 2-21, your total insurance cost stays fixed whether you drive your car 0 miles, 1,000 miles, or 10,000 miles during the year.

EXHIBIT 2-21 Fixed Cost Behavior

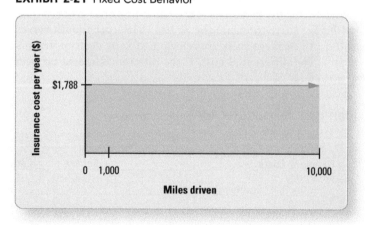

Why is this important?

"Most **business decisions** depend on how costs are **expected** to change at different volumes of **activity**. Managers can't make good decisions without first **understanding** how their costs **behave**."

However, the total cost of gasoline to operate your car varies depending on whether you drive 0 miles, 1,000 miles, or 10,000 miles. The more miles you drive, the higher your total gasoline cost for the year. If you don't drive your car at all, you won't incur any costs for gasoline. As shown in Exhibit 2-22, <u>variable costs</u>, such as your gasoline cost, change in total in direct proportion to changes in volume. To accurately forecast the total cost of operating your car during the year, you need to know which costs are fixed and which are variable.

EXHIBIT 2-22 Variable Cost Behavior

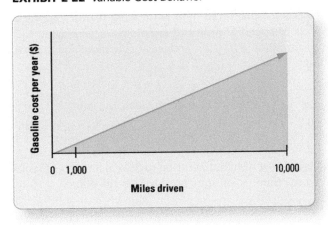

How Manufacturing Costs Behave

Most companies have both fixed and variable costs. At a manufacturer, materials are considered to be variable costs. The more cars Toyota makes, the higher its total cost for tires, steel, and parts. The behavior of direct labor is harder to characterize. Salaried employees are paid a fixed amount per year. Hourly wage earners are paid only when they work. The more hours they work, the more they are paid. Nonetheless, direct labor is generally treated as a variable cost because the more cars Toyota produces, the more assembly-line workers and machine operators it must employ. Manufacturing overhead includes both variable and fixed costs. For example, the cost of indirect materials is variable, while the cost of property tax, insurance, and straight-line depreciation on the plant and equipment is fixed. The cost of utilities is partially fixed and partially variable. Factories incur a certain level of utility costs just to keep the lights on. However, when more cars are produced, more electricity is used to run the production equipment. Exhibit 2-23 summarizes the behavior of manufacturing costs.

EXHIBIT 2-23 The Behavior of Manufacturing Costs

Direct materials	→	A variable cost
+		
Direct labor	→	Generally treated as a variable cost
+		
Manufacturing overhead	→	A mixture of fixed and variable costs
=		
Product cost	→	A mixture of fixed and variable costs

Calculating Total and Average Costs

Why is cost behavior important? Managers need to understand how costs behave to predict total costs and calculate average costs. In our example, we'll look at Toyota's total and average *production* costs, but the same principles apply to period costs.

Let's say Toyota wants to estimate the total cost of manufacturing 10,000 vehicles at one of its plants next year. To do so, Toyota must estimate (1) the total fixed manufacturing costs at the plant, and (2) the variable cost of manufacturing each vehicle. Let's say Toyota expects to spend $20 million on fixed manufacturing costs at the plant. In addition, it expects to spend $5,000 of variable costs producing each vehicle.[13] How much total product cost should Toyota budget at this plant for the year? Toyota would calculate it as follows:

Total fixed cost + (Variable cost per unit × Number of units) = Total product cost
$20,000,000   + ($5,000 per vehicle   ×   10,000 vehicles) = $70,000,000

What is the **average cost** of manufacturing each vehicle at this plant next year? It's the total cost divided by the number of units produced at the plant:

$$\frac{\text{Total cost}}{\text{Number of units}} = \frac{\text{Average product}}{\text{cost per unit}}$$

$$\frac{\$70,000,000}{10,000 \text{ vehicles}} = \$7,000 \text{ per vehicle}$$

If Toyota's managers decide they need to produce 12,000 vehicles at this plant instead, can they simply predict total product cost as follows?

Average cost per unit × Number of units = Total product cost???
$7,000   ×   12,000   = $84,000,000???

No! They cannot! Why? *Because the average product cost per unit is NOT appropriate for predicting total costs at different levels of output.* Toyota's managers should forecast total product costs based on cost behavior:

Total fixed cost + (Variable cost per unit × Number of units) = Total product cost
$20,000,000   + ($5,000 per vehicle   ×   12,000 vehicles) = $80,000,000

Why is the *correct* forecasted cost of $80 million less than the *faulty* prediction of $84 million? The difference stems from fixed costs. Remember, Toyota incurs $20 million of fixed manufacturing costs whether it makes 10,000 vehicles or 12,000 vehicles. As Toyota makes more vehicles, the fixed manufacturing costs are spread over more vehicles, so the average product cost per vehicle declines. If Toyota ends up making 12,000 vehicles, the new average product cost per vehicle decreases as follows:

$$\frac{\text{Total cost}}{\text{Number of units}} = \text{Average product cost per unit}$$

$$\frac{\$80,000,000}{12,000 \text{ vehicles}} = \$6,667 \text{ per vehicle (rounded)}$$

The average product cost per unit is lower when Toyota produces more vehicles because the company is using the fixed manufacturing costs more efficiently—taking the same $20 million of resources and making more vehicles with it.

---

[13]All references to Toyota in this hypothetical example were created by the author solely for academic purposes and are not intended in any way to represent the actual business practices of, or costs incurred by, Toyota-Motor Corporation.

Keep the following two important rules of thumb in mind:

- Managers like to operate near 100% capacity in order to spread fixed costs over more units. By doing so, they are able to reduce the average cost per unit.
- The average cost per unit is valid only at ONE level of output—the level used to compute the average cost per unit. NEVER use average costs to forecast costs at different output levels; if you do, you will miss the mark.

Finally, a **marginal cost** is the cost of making *one more unit*. Fixed costs will not change when Toyota makes one more vehicle unless the plant is operating at 100% capacity and simply cannot make one more unit. If that's the case, Toyota will need to incur additional costs to expand the plant. So, unless the plant is operating at 100% capacity, the marginal cost of a unit is simply its variable cost.

As you have seen, management accountants and managers use specialized terms for discussing costs. They use different costs for different purposes. To be able to communicate effectively with other people in the organization and get the correct cost information for different business decisions, managers and accountants need a solid understanding of these terms.

Decision Guidelines

Building Blocks of Managerial Accounting

Toyota also needs to know many characteristics about its costs in order to plan and make decisions. It also needs to know how to differentiate between product costs and period costs for external reporting. The following guidelines help managers with these types of decisions.

Decision	Guidelines
How do you compute cost of goods sold?	*Service companies:* No cost of goods sold because they don't sell tangible goods • *Merchandising companies:* Beginning inventory + Purchases plus freight-in and import duties, if any = Cost of goods available for sale − Ending inventory = Cost of goods sold • *Manufacturing companies:* Beginning finished goods inventory + Cost of goods manufactured = Cost of goods available for sale − Ending finished goods inventory = Cost of goods sold
How do you compute the cost of goods manufactured?	Beginning work in process inventory + Total manufacturing costs incurred during year (direct materials used + direct labor + manufacturing overhead) = Total manufacturing costs to account for − Ending work in process inventory = Cost of goods manufactured
How do managers decide which costs are relevant to their decisions?	Costs are relevant to a decision when they differ between alternatives and affect the future. Thus, *differential* costs are relevant, whereas *sunk costs* and costs that don't differ are not relevant.
How should managers forecast total costs for different production volumes?	Total cost = Total fixed costs + (Variable cost per unit × Number of units) Managers should *not* use a product's *average cost* to forecast total costs because it will change as production volume changes. As production increases, the average cost per unit declines (because fixed costs are spread over more units).

SUMMARY PROBLEM 2

Requirements

1. Show how to compute cost of goods manufactured. Use the following amounts: direct materials used ($24,000), direct labor ($9,000), manufacturing overhead ($17,000), beginning work in process inventory ($5,000), and ending work in process inventory ($4,000).

2. Auto-USA spent $300 million in total to produce 50,000 cars this year. The $300 million breaks down as follows: The company spent $50 million on fixed costs to run its manufacturing plants and $5,000 of variable costs to produce each car. Next year, it plans to produce 60,000 cars using the existing production facilities.

   a. What is the current *average product cost* per car this year?

   b. Assuming there is no change in fixed costs or variable costs per unit, what is the *total forecasted cost* to produce 60,000 cars next year?

   c. What is the *forecasted average product cost* per car next year?

   d. Why does the average product cost per car vary between years?

▪ SOLUTIONS

Requirement 1

Cost of goods manufactured:

	A	B	C	D
1	**Calculation of Cost of Good Manufactured**			
2	Beginning Work in Process Inventory	$ 5,000		
3	Plus manufacturing costs incurred:			
4	Direct materials used	24,000		
5	Direct labor	9,000		
6	Manufacturing overhead	17,000		
7	Total manufacturing costs to account for	$ 55,000		
8	Less: Ending Work in Process Inventory	4,000		
9	Cost of goods manufactured (CGM)	$ 51,000		
10				

Requirement 2

a.

Total cost ÷ Number of units = Current average product cost

$300 million ÷ 50,000 cars = $6,000 per car

b.

Total fixed costs + Total variable costs = Total projected product cost

$50 million + (60,000 cars × $5,000 per car) = $350 million

c.

Total cost ÷ Number of units = Projected average product cost

$350 million ÷ 60,000 cars = $5,833 per car

d. The average product cost per car decreases because Auto-USA will use the same fixed costs ($50 million) to produce more cars next year. Auto-USA will be using its resources more efficiently, so the average cost per unit will decrease.

END OF CHAPTER

Learning Objectives

- 1 Distinguish among service, merchandising, and manufacturing companies
- 2 Describe the value chain and its elements
- 3 Distinguish between direct and indirect costs
- 4 Identify product costs and period costs
- 5 Prepare the financial statements for service, merchandising, and manufacturing companies
- 6 Describe costs that are relevant and irrelevant for decision making
- 7 Classify costs as fixed or variable and calculate total and average costs at different volumes

Accounting Vocabulary

Allocate. (p. 56) To assign an *indirect* cost to a cost object.

Assign. (p. 55) To attach a cost to a cost object.

Average Cost. (p. 74) The total cost divided by the number of units.

Biomimicry. (p. 53) A means of product design in which a company tries to mimic, or copy, the natural biological process in which dead organisms (plants and animals) become the input for another organism or process.

Controllable Costs. (p. 71) Costs that can be influenced or changed by management.

Conversion Costs. (p. 61) The combination of direct labor and manufacturing overhead costs.

Cost Object. (p. 55) Anything for which managers want to know the cost.

Cost of Goods Manufactured. (p. 67) The cost of manufacturing the goods that were *finished* during the period.

Customer Service. (p. 52) Support provided for customers after the sale.

Design. (p. 52) Detailed engineering of products and services and the processes for producing them.

Differential Cost. (p. 71) The difference in cost between two alternative courses of action.

Direct Cost. (p. 55) A cost that can be traced to a cost object; a cost that is readily identifiable or associated with the cost object.

Direct Labor. (p. 60) The cost of compensating employees who physically convert raw materials into the company's products; labor costs that are directly traceable to the finished product.

Direct Materials. (p. 60) Primary raw materials that become a physical part of a finished product and whose costs are traceable to the finished product.

Distribution. (p. 52) Delivery of products or services to customers.

Finished Goods Inventory. (p. 50) Completed goods that have not yet been sold.

Fixed Costs. (p. 72) Costs that stay constant in total despite wide changes in volume.

Greenwashing. (p. 54) The unfortunate practice of *overstating* a company's commitment to sustainability.

Indirect Cost. (p. 55) A cost that relates to the cost object but cannot be traced specifically to it; a cost that is jointly used or shared by more than one cost object.

Indirect Labor. (p. 60) Labor costs that are difficult to trace to specific products.

Indirect Materials. (p. 60) Materials whose costs are difficult to trace to specific products.

Life-Cycle Assessment. (p. 53) A method of product design in which the company analyzes the environmental impact of a product, from cradle to grave, in an attempt to minimize negative environmental consequences throughout the entire lifespan of the product.

Manufacturing Company. (p. 50) A company that uses labor, plant, and equipment to convert raw materials into new finished products.

Manufacturing Overhead. (p. 60) All manufacturing costs other than direct materials and direct labor; also called factory overhead and indirect manufacturing cost.

Marginal Cost. (p. 75) The cost of producing one more unit.

Marketing. (p. 52) Promotion and advertising of products or services.

Merchandising Company. (p. 49) A company that resells tangible products previously bought from suppliers.

Operating Income. (p. 65) Earnings generated from the company's primary ongoing operations; the company's earnings before interest and taxes.

Other Indirect Manufacturing Costs. (p. 61) All manufacturing overhead costs aside from indirect materials and indirect labor.

Period Costs. (p. 57) The costs incurred by the company to operate the business that do *not* get treated as inventory, but rather are expensed immediately in the period in which they are incurred. These costs do *not* relate to manufacturing or purchasing product. Period costs are often called operating expenses or selling, general, and administrative expenses.

Periodic Inventory. (p. 66) An inventory system in which Cost of Goods Sold is calculated at the end of the period rather than every time a sale is made.

Perpetual Inventory. (p. 66) An inventory system in which both Cost of Goods Sold and Inventory are updated every time a sale is made.

Prime Costs. (p. 61) The combination of direct material and direct labor costs.

Product Costs. (p. 57) The costs incurred by *manufacturers to produce* their products or incurred by *merchandisers to purchase* their products. For external financial reporting, GAAP requires that these costs be assigned to inventory until the products are sold, at which point they are expensed as Cost of Goods Sold.

Production or Purchases. (p. 52) Resources used to produce a product or service or to purchase finished merchandise intended for resale.

Raw Materials Inventory. (p. 50) All raw materials (direct materials and indirect materials) not yet used in manufacturing.

Research and Development (R&D). (p. 52) Researching and developing new or improved products or services or the processes for producing them.

Retailer. (p. 49) Merchandising company that sells to consumers.

Service Company. (p. 49) A company that sells intangible services rather than tangible products.

Sunk Cost. (p. 72) A cost that has already been incurred.

Total Cost. (p. 57) The cost of all resources used throughout the value chain.

Trace. (p. 56) To assign a *direct* cost to a cost object.

Triple Bottom Line. (p. 49) Evaluating a company's performance not only by its ability to generate economic profits, but also by its impact on people and the planet.

Uncontrollable Costs. (p. 71) Costs that cannot be changed or influenced in the short run by management.

Value Chain. (p. 51) The activities that add value to a firm's products and services; includes R&D, design, production or purchases, marketing, distribution, and customer service.

Variable Costs. (p. 72) Costs that change in total in direct proportion to changes in volume.

Wholesaler. (p. 49) Merchandising companies that buy in bulk from manufacturers, mark up the prices, and then sell those products to retailers.

Work in Process Inventory. (p. 50) Goods that are partway through the manufacturing process but not yet complete.

MyAccountingLab Go to http://myaccountinglab.com/ **for the following Quick Check, Short Exercises, Exercises, and Problems. They are available with immediate grading, explanations of correct and incorrect answers, and interactive media that acts as your own online tutor.**

Quick Check

1. (*Learning Objective 1*) Which of the following types of companies would have work in process inventory?
   a. Service
   b. Merchandising
   c. Manufacturing
   d. All of the above

2. (*Learning Objective 2*) Which of the following is *not* an activity in the value chain?
   a. Marketing
   b. Customer Service
   c. Design
   d. Administration

3. (*Learning Objective 3*) A cost that can be traced to a cost object is known as a
   a. period cost.
   b. product cost.
   c. direct cost.
   d. indirect cost.

4. (*Learning Objective 4*) Period costs are often referred to as
   a. manufacturing expenses.
   b. operating expenses.
   c. direct costs.
   d. product costs.

5. (*Learning Objective 4*) Conversion costs consist of
   a. direct materials and manufacturing overhead.
   b. direct labor and manufacturing overhead.
   c. direct materials and direct labor.
   d. direct materials, direct labor, and manufacturing overhead.

6. (*Learning Objective 4*) Which of the following is *not* part of manufacturing overhead?
   a. Period costs, such as depreciation on office computers
   b. Indirect materials, such as machine lubricants
   c. Indirect labor, such as plant forklift operators' wages
   d. Other indirect manufacturing costs, such as plant utilities

7. (*Learning Objective 5*) Which of the following is a calculated amount, rather than a general ledger account?
   a. Finished goods inventory
   b. Cost of goods manufactured
   c. Sales revenue
   d. Cost of goods sold

8. (*Learning Objective 5*) Which of the following types of companies will always have the Cost of Goods Sold account on their income statements?
   a. Service and merchandising companies
   b. Merchandising and manufacturing companies
   c. Service and manufacturing companies
   d. Service, merchandising, and manufacturing companies

9. (*Learning Objective 6*) Which of the following is *false*?
   a. Uncontrollable costs are costs over which the company has little or no control in the short run.
   b. Sunk costs are costs that have already been incurred.
   c. Sunk costs are generally relevant to decisions.
   d. The difference in cost between two alternatives is known as a differential cost.

10. (*Learning Objective 7*) Which of the following is *true*?
   a. The average cost per unit can be used for predicting total costs at many different output levels.
   b. Manufacturing overhead is composed of only variable costs.
   c. Fixed costs stay constant in total over a wide range of activity levels.
   d. Direct materials are considered to be fixed costs.

Quick Check Answers

1. c 2. d 3. c 4. b 5. b 6. a 7. b 8. b 9. c 10. c

3

Job Costing

Learning Objectives

- **1** Distinguish between job costing and process costing
- **2** Understand the flow of production and how direct materials and direct labor are traced to jobs
- **3** Compute a predetermined manufacturing overhead rate and use it to allocate MOH to jobs
- **4** Determine the cost of a job and use it to make business decisions
- **5** Compute and dispose of overallocated or underallocated manufacturing overhead
- **6** Prepare journal entries for a manufacturer's job costing system
- **7** (Appendix) Use job costing at a service firm as a basis for billing clients

Nithid Memanee/Shutterstock

Sources: Brunswick Corp. 2015 10(k) filing; http://lifefitness.com

With annual sales of over $794 million, Life Fitness, a division of the Brunswick Corporation, is the world's largest manufacturer of commercial fitness equipment and a global leader in consumer fitness equipment. The company began in the 1970s by introducing the world's first-ever computerized stationary exercise bicycle. Since then, the company has grown to design and manufacture hundreds of different products, including treadmills, elliptical cross-trainers, stair climbers, strength equipment, and, of course, exercise bikes. While the company's growth has been propelled in part by consumers' ever-increasing zeal for personal fitness, the company has also grown through carefully analyzing the profit margins on each of its products and adjusting its operations accordingly.

How do managers determine the profit margins on each of the company's different models of fitness equipment? Managers first determine how much it costs to manufacture a batch of each model. Each batch of units produced is called a "job." The company's job costing system traces the cost of direct materials and direct labor used to each job. It also allocates some manufacturing overhead to each job. By adding up the direct materials, direct labor, and manufacturing overhead assigned to each job, the company can determine the cost of the job, as well as the average cost of each unit in the job. The company then uses this information to prepare the company's financial reports and make vital business decisions.

Whether you plan a career in marketing, engineering, production, general management, or accounting, you'll need to understand how much each of the company's products cost to produce. This chapter will show you the way companies determine their product costs when they make unique products or products made in relatively small batches.

What Methods Are Used to Determine the Cost of Manufacturing a Product?

1 Distinguish between job costing and process costing

Most manufacturers use one of two product costing systems in order to find the cost of producing their products:

- Process costing
- Job costing

The end goal of both product costing systems is the same: to find the cost of manufacturing one unit of the product. However, the manner in which this goal is achieved differs. Management chooses the product costing system that works best for its particular manufacturing environment. Let's go over the basics of each system and identify the types of companies that would be most likely to use them.

Process Costing

Process costing is used by companies that produce extremely large numbers of identical units through a series of uniform production steps or processes. Because each unit is identical, in theory, each unit should cost the same to make. In essence, process costing averages manufacturing costs across all units produced so that each identical unit bears the same cost.

For example, let's assume Pace Foods uses two processes to make picante sauce: (1) cleaning and chopping vegetables and (2) mixing and bottling the sauce. First, Pace accumulates all manufacturing costs incurred in the cleaning and chopping process over a period of time, such as a month. The costs incurred in this process include the cost of the vegetables themselves, as well as the cost of cleaning and chopping the vegetables. Next, the company averages the total costs of this process over all units passing through the process during the same period of time.

For example, let's say Pace spends $500,000 on purchasing, cleaning, and chopping the vegetables to make 1 million jars of picante sauce during the month. The average cost per jar of the cleaning and chopping process is as follows:

$$\text{Average cost per jar of the cleaning and chopping process} = \frac{\$500,000}{1,000,000 \text{ jars}} = \$0.50 \text{ per jar}$$

Now the cleaned and chopped vegetables go through the second production process, mixing and bottling, where a similar calculation is performed to find the average cost of that process. The cost of the second process would include any direct materials used, such as the cost of the glass jars, as well as the cost of mixing the sauce and filling the jars with the sauce. Let's say the average cost to mix and bottle each jar of sauce is $0.25.

Now Pace can determine the total cost to manufacture each jar of picante sauce:

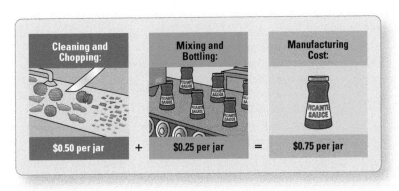

Each jar of picante sauce is identical to every other jar, so each bears the same average cost: $0.75. Once managers know the cost of manufacturing each jar of sauce, they can use that information to help set sales prices and make other business decisions. To generate a profit, the sales price will have to be high enough to cover the $0.75 per jar product cost as well as the company's operating costs incurred in other areas of the value chain, including research and development (R&D), design, marketing, distribution, and customer service. We'll delve more deeply into process costing in Chapter 5. For now, just remember that any company that mass-produces identical units of product will most likely use process costing to determine the cost of making each unit.

> ## ■ Why is this important?
>
> "Managers need the most accurate **cost information** they can get in order to make good **business decisions**. They will choose a costing system (usually **job costing** or **process costing**) based on which system best fits their operations."

Job Costing

Whereas process costing is used by companies that mass-manufacture identical units, <u>job costing</u> (also called job order costing) is used by companies that produce unique, custom-ordered products, or relatively small batches of different products. Each unique product or batch of units is considered a separate "job." Different jobs can vary considerably in direct materials, direct labor, and manufacturing overhead costs, so job costing tracks these costs separately for each individual job. For example, Life Fitness produces hundreds of different models of fitness equipment, including cross-trainers, bikes, stairclimbers, and strength equipment. Each model is produced in relatively small, separate batches. Each batch is considered a separate job. Job costing would also be used by Boeing (airplanes), custom-home builders (unique houses), high-end jewelers (unique jewelry), furniture manufacturers (sofas and chairs with different fabrics), and any other manufacturers that build relatively unique products in small batches.

Job costing is not limited to manufacturers. Professional service providers such as law firms, accounting firms, consulting firms, and marketing firms use job costing to determine the cost of serving each client. People working in trades, such as mechanics, plumbers, and electricians, also use job costing to determine the cost of performing separate jobs for clients. In both cases, the job cost is used as a basis for billing the client. The appendix to this chapter illustrates a complete example of how a law firm would use job costing to bill its clients.

In summary, companies use job costing when their products or services vary in terms of materials needed, time required to complete the job, and/or the complexity of the production process. Because the jobs are so different, it would not be reasonable to assign them equal costs. Therefore, the cost of each job is compiled separately. We'll spend the rest of this chapter looking at how companies compile, record, and use job costs to make important business decisions. Before moving on, take a look at Exhibit 3-1, which summarizes the key differences between job and process costing.

EXHIBIT 3-1 Differences Between Job and Process Costing

	Job Costing	Process Costing
Cost object:	Job	Process
Outputs:	Single units or small batches with large differences between jobs	Large quantities of identical units
Extent of averaging:	Less averaging—costs are averaged over the small number of units in a job (often one unit in a job)	More averaging—costs are averaged over the thousands or millions of identical units that pass through each process

STOP & THINK

Do all manufacturers use job costing or process costing systems?

Answer: Some manufacturers use a hybrid of these two costing systems if neither "pure" system reflects their production environment very well. For example, clothing manufacturers often mass-produce the same product over and over (dress shirts) but use different materials on different batches (cotton fabric on one batch and silk fabric on another). Apple allows consumers to custom order computers with different choices on memory, storage, screen size, and so forth. **Mass customization** is large-scale production that allows manufacturers to meet a variety of consumer desires, while at the same time achieving the efficiencies of mass production (economies of scale) that drive down unit costs. A hybrid costing system suitable to mass customization would include some elements of a process costing system (averaging labor and manufacturing overhead costs across all units) and some elements of a job costing system (tracing different fabric costs to different batches; tracing different components to different build-to-order computers).

How Do Manufacturers Determine a Job's Cost?

As we've just seen, manufacturers use job costing if they produce unique products or relatively small batches of different products. Life Fitness produces hundreds of different models in relatively small batches, so it considers each batch a separate job. In this section, we will show you how Life Fitness would determine the cost of producing Job 603, a batch of 50 identical X4 Elliptical Cross-Trainers.[1] The company's market for these cross-trainers includes health and fitness clubs, student fitness centers on college campuses, professional athletic teams, hotels, city recreation departments, and direct sales to customers for home fitness gyms. As we walk through the process, keep in mind that most companies maintain the illustrated documents in electronic, rather than hard copy, form. Even so, the basic information stored in the documents and the purpose for the documents remain the same.

2 Understand the flow of production and how direct materials and direct labor are traced to jobs

Overview: Flow of Inventory Through a Manufacturing System

Before we delve into Life Fitness's job costing system, let's take a quick look at how the physical products, as well as costs, flow through the company. As you learned in Chapter 2, manufacturers such as Life Fitness maintain three separate types of inventory: raw materials, work in process, and finished goods. The cost of each of these inventories is reflected on the company's balance sheet.

As shown in Exhibit 3-2, the raw materials (RM) inventory is maintained in a storeroom in or near the factory until the materials are needed in production. As soon as these materials are transferred to the factory floor, they are no longer considered raw materials because they have become part of the work in process in the factory. The work in process (WIP) inventory consists of all products that are partway through the production process. As soon as the manufacturing process is complete, the products are moved out of the factory and into a finished goods (FG) inventory storage area, or warehouse, where they will await sale and shipment to a customer. Finally, when the products are shipped to customers, the cost of manufacturing those products becomes the Cost of Goods Sold (CGS) shown on the company's income statement.

[1] All references to Life Fitness in this hypothetical example were created by the author solely for academic purposes and are not intended, in any way, to represent the actual business practices of, or costs incurred by, Life Fitness, Inc.

EXHIBIT 3-2 Flow of Inventory Through a Manufacturing System

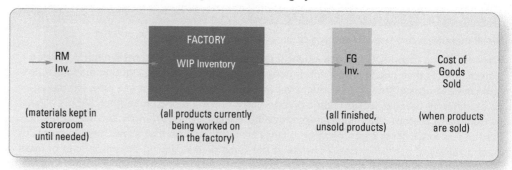

Keep the basic flow of inventory shown in Exhibit 3-2 in mind as we delve into Life Fitness's job costing system.

Scheduling Production

Job costing begins with management's decision to produce a batch of units. Sometimes companies produce a batch of units just to meet a particular customer order. For example, the Chicago Bears may custom order treadmills that have characteristics not found on other models. This batch of unique treadmills would become its own job. On the other hand, most companies also produce **stock inventory** for products they sell on a regular basis. They want to have stock available to quickly fill customer orders. By forecasting demand for the product, the manufacturer is able to estimate the number of units that should be produced during a given time period. As shown in Exhibit 3-3, the **production schedule** indicates the quantity and types of inventory that are scheduled to be manufactured during the period. Depending on the company, the types of products it offers, and the production time required, production schedules may cover periods of time as short as one day (Dell, producing customized laptops), several months (Boeing, manufacturing 737 airplanes), or several years (bridges, roads, large commercial buildings and stadiums).

EXHIBIT 3-3 Monthly Production Schedule

Production Schedule
For the Month of December

Job	Model Number	Stock or Customer	Quantity	Scheduled Start Date	Scheduled End Date
603	X4 Cross-Trainer	For stock	50	12/2	12/6
604	T5 Treadmill	For stock	60	12/7	12/17
605	Custom T6-C Treadmill	Chicago Bears	15	12/18	12/21
606	Custom S3-C Stair-Climber	Chicago Bears	12	12/22	12/24
	FACTORY CLOSED FOR HOLIDAYS and ANNUAL MAINTENANCE			12/25	12/31

The production schedule is very important in helping management determine the direct labor and direct materials needed during the period. To complete production on time, managers must ensure they have the right amounts and types of raw materials and skilled labor available to meet production requirements. The next section shows how this is accomplished.

Purchasing Raw Materials

Production engineers prepare a **bill of materials** for each job. The bill of materials is like a recipe card: It simply lists all of the raw materials needed to manufacture the job. Exhibit 3-4 illustrates a partial bill of materials for Job 603:

EXHIBIT 3-4 Bill of Materials (Partial Listing)

Bill of Materials

Job: 603

Model: X4 Elliptical Cross-Trainer   Quantity: 50 units

Part Number	Description	Quantity Needed
HRM50812	Heart rate monitor	50
LCD620	LCD entertainment screen	50
B4906	Front and rear roller base	100
HG2567	Hand grips	100
FP689	Foot platform	100
	Etc.	

After the bill of materials has been prepared, the purchasing department checks the raw materials inventory to determine which raw materials needed for the job are currently in stock and which raw materials must be purchased. As shown in Exhibit 3-5, a **raw materials record** shows detailed information about each item in stock, including the number of units received, the number of units used, and the running balance of units currently in stock. Additionally, the raw materials record shows the cost of each unit purchased, the cost of each unit used, and the cost of the units currently in the raw materials inventory.

EXHIBIT 3-5 Raw Materials Record

Raw Materials Record

Item No.: HRM50812   Description: Heart rate monitor

	Received			Used				Balance		
Date	Units	Cost	Total	Requisition Number	Units	Cost	Total	Units	Cost	Total
11-25	100	$60	$6,000					100	$60	$6,000
11-30				#7235	70	$60	$4,200	30	$60	$1,800

According to the raw materials record pictured in Exhibit 3-5, only 30 heart rate monitors are currently in stock. However, the bill of materials shown in Exhibit 3-4 indicates that 50 heart rate monitors are needed for Job 603. Therefore, the purchasing department will need to buy 20 more monitors. The purchasing department must also consider other jobs that will be using heart rate monitors in the near future, as well as the time it takes to obtain the monitors from the company's suppliers. According to the production schedule, Job 603 is scheduled to begin production on December 2; therefore, the purchasing department must make sure all necessary raw materials are on hand by that date.

Life Fitness's purchasing department will issue a **purchase order** to its suppliers for any needed parts. Incoming shipments of raw materials are counted and then recorded on a **receiving report**, as well as on the individual raw materials records. The receiving report is typically a duplicate of the purchase order, except it does not pre-list the quantity of parts ordered. The quantity ordered is intentionally left blank to ensure the receiving dock personnel will actually count and record the quantity of materials received. Progressive companies use bar-coding systems to electronically update the raw materials records as soon as incoming shipments are received.

Life Fitness's accounting department will not pay the **invoice** (bill from the supplier) unless the amount billed agrees with the quantity of parts both ordered *and* received. By matching the purchase order, receiving report, and invoice, Life Fitness ensures that it pays for only those parts that were ordered and received, *and nothing more*. This is an important control that helps companies avoid scams in which businesses are sent and billed for inventory that was not ordered.

In addition to tracking the current level of individual inventory items, the raw materials records also form the basis for valuing the Raw Materials Inventory account found on the balance sheet. On a given date, by adding together the balances in the individual raw materials records, the company is able to substantiate the total Raw Materials Inventory shown on the balance sheet. For example, as shown in Exhibit 3-6, on November 30, Life Fitness had $1,800 of heart rate monitors in stock, $24,000 of LCD entertainment screens, $1,200 of roller bases, and so forth. When added together, these individual balances sum to the Raw Materials Inventory balance shown on Life Fitness's November 30 balance sheet.

EXHIBIT 3-6 Individual Raw Materials Records Sum to the Raw Materials Inventory Balance

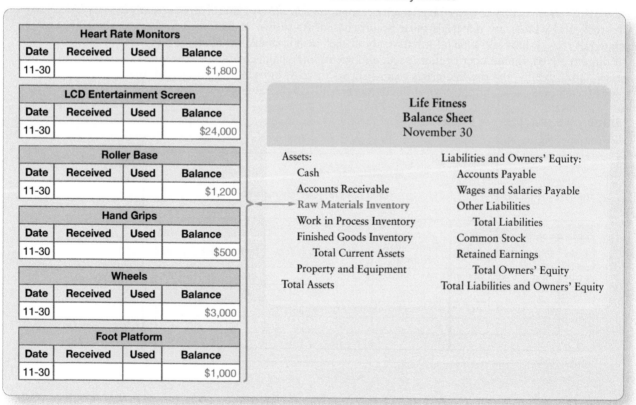

Using a Job Cost Record to Keep Track of Job Costs

Job 603 will be started when the scheduled production date arrives. A **job cost record**, as pictured in Exhibit 3-7, will be used to keep track of all the direct materials and direct labor used on the job, as well as the manufacturing overhead allocated to the job.

▶ Try It!

Match the following concepts to their descriptions:

1. Document specifying when jobs will be manufactured
2. Product costing system used by mass manufacturers
3. Bill from supplier
4. Document specifying parts needed to produce a job
5. Product costing system used by manufacturers of unique products
6. Document containing the details and balance of each part in stock
7. Document for recording incoming shipments
8. Products normally kept on hand in order to fill orders quickly

a. Process costing
b. Stock inventory
c. Raw materials records
d. Production schedule
e. Receiving report
f. Invoice
g. Bill of materials
h. Job costing

Please see page 174 for solutions.

EXHIBIT 3-7 Job Cost Record

Job Cost Record

Job Number: 603

Customer: For stock

Job Description: 50 units of X4 Elliptical Cross-Trainers

Date Started: Dec. 2   **Date Completed:** _____

Manufacturing Cost Information:	Cost Summary
Direct Materials	$
Direct Labor	$
Manufacturing Overhead	$
Total Job Cost	$
Number of Units	÷ 50 units
Cost per Unit	$

Shipping Information:			
Date	Quantity Shipped	Units Remaining	Cost Balance

> **Why is this important?**
> "**Job cost records** keep track of **all manufacturing costs** assigned to **individual jobs** so that **managers** know the **cost** of making each product."

Each job will have its own job cost record. Note that the job cost record is merely a form (electronic or hard copy) for keeping track of the three manufacturing costs associated with each job:

- direct materials,
- direct labor, and
- manufacturing overhead.

The job cost records also show the number of units produced on the job, as well as the cost per unit.

As we saw in the last section, the individual raw materials records add up to the total Raw Materials Inventory account shown on the balance sheet. Likewise, as shown in Exhibit 3-8, the job cost records on *incomplete* jobs provide the supporting detail for the total Work in Process Inventory account shown on the balance sheet.

EXHIBIT 3-8 Job Cost Records on Incomplete Jobs Sum to the WIP Inventory Balance

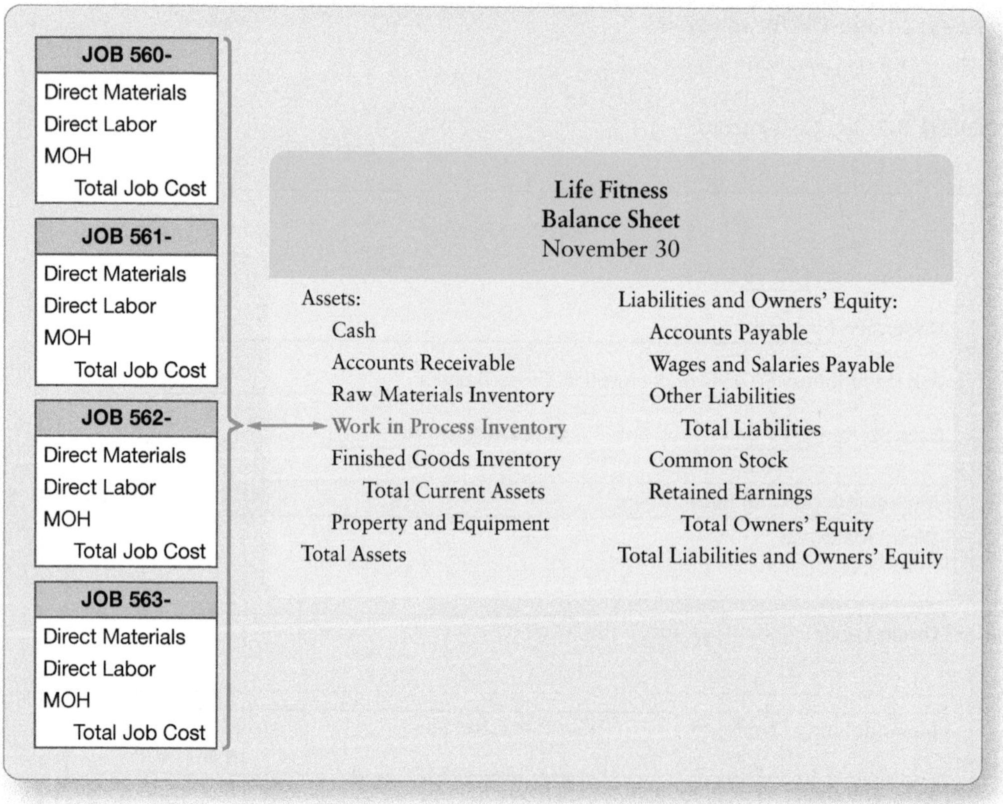

Once jobs are completed, the job cost records serve as a basis for valuing the Finished Goods Inventory account. As shown near the bottom of Exhibit 3-7, job cost records typically list the date and quantity of units shipped to customers, the number of units remaining in finished goods inventory, and the cost of those units. The balance of *unsold* units from *completed* job cost records add up to the total Finished Goods Inventory account shown on the balance sheet.

As you can see, the job cost records serve a vital role in a job costing system. Now let's take a look at how Life Fitness accumulates manufacturing costs on the job cost record. We'll begin by looking at how direct materials costs are traced to individual jobs.

Tracing Direct Materials Cost to a Job

Production will eventually need all of the parts shown on the bill of materials for Job 603 (Exhibit 3-4). However, according to the production schedule (Exhibit 3-3), this job is scheduled to take five days to complete, so the production crew may not want all of the raw materials at once. Each time materials are needed, production personnel will fill out a **materials requisition**. As shown in Exhibit 3-9, the materials requisition is a document itemizing the materials currently needed from the storeroom. Notice that the root word of *requisition* is *request*. In essence, production personnel use this document to *request* that certain materials be sent from the storeroom into the factory. Most progressive companies use electronic forms, but we show a hard copy here.

EXHIBIT 3-9 Materials Requisition

Materials Requisition

Date: 12/2   Number: #7568

Job: 603

Part Number	Description	Quantity	Unit Cost	Amount
HRM50812	Heart rate monitor	50	$60	$3,000
LCD620	LCD entertainment screen	50	$100	5,000
B4906	Front and rear roller base	100	$5	500
	Total			$8,500

As soon as the materials requisition is received by the raw materials storeroom, workers **pick** the appropriate materials and send them to the factory floor. Picking is just what it sounds like: storeroom workers pick the needed materials off of the storeroom shelves. The unit cost and total cost of all materials picked are posted to the materials requisition based on the cost information found in the individual raw materials records. The individual raw materials records are also updated as soon as the materials are picked, often using bar-coding systems to simplify the process and provide real-time information. For example, in Exhibit 3-10, we show how the raw material record for heart rate monitors is updated after requisition #7568 (Exhibit 3-9) has been picked.

EXHIBIT 3-10 Raw Materials Record Updated for Materials Received and Used

Raw Materials Record

Item No.: HRM50812   Description: Heart rate monitor

	Received			Used				Balance		
Date	Units	Cost	Total	Requisition Number	Units	Cost	Total	Units	Cost	Total
11-25	100	$60	$6,000					100	$60	$6,000
11-30				#7235	70	$60	$4,200	30	$60	$1,800
12-1	75	$60	$4,500					105	$60	$6,300
12-2				#7568	50	$60	$3,000	55	$60	$3,300

Finally, the raw materials requisitioned for the job are posted to the job cost record. As shown in Exhibit 3-11, each time raw materials are requisitioned for Job 603, they are posted to the direct materials section of the job cost record. Again, bar-coding systems allow this process to be completed with more efficiency. These materials are considered direct materials (rather than indirect materials), because they can be traced specifically to Job 603. By using this system to trace direct materials to specific jobs, managers know *exactly* how much direct materials cost is incurred by each job.

EXHIBIT 3-11 Posting Direct Materials Used to the Job Cost Record

Job Cost Record

Job Number: 603

Customer: For stock

Job Description: 50 units of X4 Elliptical Cross-Trainers

Date Started: Dec. 2   Date Completed: _____

Manufacturing Cost Information:	Cost Summary
Direct Materials	
Req. #7568: $ 8,500 (shown in Exhibit 3-9)	
Req. #7580: $14,000	
Req. #7595: $13,500	
Req. #7601: $ 4,000	$ 40,000
Direct Labor	
	$
Manufacturing Overhead	
	$
Total Job Cost	$
Number of Units	÷ 50 units
Cost per Unit	$

Tracing Direct Labor Cost to a Job

Now let's look at how direct labor costs are traced to individual jobs. All direct laborers in the factory fill out **labor time records**. As shown in Exhibit 3-12, a labor time record simply records the time spent by each employee on each job he or she worked on throughout the day. Often, these records are kept electronically. Rather than using old-fashioned time tickets and punch clocks, factory workers now "swipe" their bar-coded employee identification cards on a computer terminal and enter the appropriate job number. Based on each employee's unique hourly wage rate, the computer calculates the direct labor cost to be charged to the job. Companies that are even more progressive use biometric scanning devices to quickly capture information about how long individual employees work on each job.

For example, in Exhibit 3-12, we see that Hannah Smith, who is paid a wage rate of $20 per hour, worked on both Jobs 602 and 603 during the week. Hannah spent five hours working on Job 603 on December 2. Therefore, $100 of direct labor cost ($20 × 5) will be charged to Job 603 for Hannah's work on that date. On December 3, Hannah's eight hours of work on Job 603 resulted in another $160 ($20 × 8) of direct labor being charged to the job. The cost of each direct laborer's time will be computed using each employee's unique wage rate, just as was done with Hannah Smith's time. Then, as shown in Exhibit 3-13, the information from the individual labor time records is posted to the direct labor section of the job cost record. Again, this posting is normally done automatically, and often in real time, by the company's computer system.

As you can see, by tracing direct labor cost in this fashion, individual jobs are charged only for the exact amount of direct labor actually used in their production.

EXHIBIT 3-12 Labor Time Record

Labor Time Record					

Employee: Hannah Smith   **Week:** 12/2 – 12/9

Hourly Wage Rate: $20   **Record #:** 324

Date	Job Number	Start Time	End Time	Hours	Cost
12/2	602	8:00	11:00	3	$60
12/2	603	12:00	5:00	5	$100
12/3	603	8:00	4:00	8	$160
12/4 etc.					

EXHIBIT 3-13 Posting Direct Labor Used to the Job Cost Record

Job Cost Record

Job Number: 603

Customer: For stock

Job Description: 50 units of X4 Elliptical Cross-Trainers

Date Started: Dec. 2   **Date Completed:** _____

Manufacturing Cost Information:	Cost Summary	
Direct Materials		
Req. #7568: $ 8,500		
Req. #7580: $14,000		
Req. #7595: $13,500		
Req. #7601: $ 4,000	$	40,000
Direct Labor		
No. #324 (30 DL hours): $100, $160, etc. (shown in Exhibit 3-12)		
No. #327 (40 DL hours): $240, $210, etc.		
No. #333 (36 DL hours): $80, $120, etc.		
Etc.		
(a total of 500 DL hours)	$	10,000
Manufacturing Overhead		
	$	
Total Job Cost	$	
Number of Units	÷	50 units
Cost per Unit	$	

What about employee benefits, such as employee-sponsored retirement plans, health insurance, payroll taxes, and other benefits? As discussed in Chapter 2, these payroll-related benefits often add another 30% or more to the cost of gross wages and salaries. Some companies factor, or load, these costs into the hourly wage rate charged to the jobs. For example, if a factory worker earns a wage rate of $10 per hour, the job cost records would show a loaded hourly rate of about $13 per hour, which would include all benefits associated with employing the worker. However, because coming up with an *accurate* loaded hourly rate such as this is difficult, many companies treat these extra payroll-related costs as part of manufacturing overhead, rather than loading these costs into the direct labor wage rates. Either method is acceptable. We'll next discuss how manufacturing overhead costs are handled.

Allocating Manufacturing Overhead to a Job

3 Compute a predetermined manufacturing overhead rate and use it to allocate MOH to jobs

So far we have traced the direct materials and direct labor costs to Job 603. Recall, however, that Life Fitness incurs many other manufacturing costs that cannot be directly traced to specific jobs. These indirect manufacturing costs, otherwise known as manufacturing overhead (MOH), include depreciation on the factory plant and equipment, utilities to run the plant, property taxes and insurance on plant, equipment maintenance, the salaries of plant janitors and supervisors, machine lubricants, and so forth. Because of the nature of these costs, we cannot tell exactly how much of these costs are attributable to producing a specific job. Therefore, we cannot trace these costs to specific jobs, as we did with direct materials and direct labor. Rather, we will have to allocate some reasonable amount of these costs to each job. Why bother? Generally Accepted Accounting Principles (GAAP) requires that manufacturing overhead *must* be treated as a product cost for external financial reporting purposes. The rationale is that these costs are a *necessary* part of the production process: Jobs could not be produced without incurring these costs, so they must become part of each job's stated product cost. Let's now look at how companies allocate manufacturing overhead costs to jobs.

What Does Allocating Mean?

Allocating manufacturing overhead[2] to jobs simply means that we will be "splitting up" or "dividing" the total manufacturing overhead costs among the jobs we produced during the year. There are many different ways we could split up the total manufacturing overhead costs among jobs. For example, there are a number of different ways you could split up a pizza pie among friends: You could give equal portions to each friend, you could give larger portions to the largest friends, or you could give larger portions to the hungriest friends. All in all, you have a set amount of pizza, but you could come up with several different reasonable bases for splitting it among your friends (based on number of friends, size of friends, or hunger level of friends).

Likewise, a manufacturer has a total amount of manufacturing overhead that must be split among all of the jobs produced during the year. Because each job is unique in size and resource requirements, it wouldn't be fair to allocate an equal amount of manufacturing overhead to each job. Rather, management needs some other reasonable basis for splitting up the total manufacturing overhead costs among jobs. In this chapter, we'll discuss the most basic method of allocating manufacturing overhead to jobs. This method has traditionally been used by most manufacturers, but more progressive companies are learning to use better, more accurate allocation systems, which we will discuss in Chapter 4. However, for now, we'll start with a basic allocation system.

Steps to Allocating Manufacturing Overhead

Manufacturers follow four steps to implement this basic allocation system. The first three steps are taken *before the year begins:*

STEP 1: The company estimates its total manufacturing overhead costs for the coming year.

This is the total "pie" to be allocated. For Life Fitness, let's assume management estimates total manufacturing overhead costs for the year to be $1 million.

---

[2] The term *applying* manufacturing overhead is often used synonymously with "allocating" manufacturing overhead.

STEP 2: **The company selects an allocation base and estimates the total amount that will be used during the year.**

> This is the *basis* management has chosen for "dividing up the pie." For Life Fitness, let's assume management has selected direct labor hours as the allocation base. Furthermore, management estimates that 62,500 of direct labor hours will be used during the year.

Ideally, the allocation base should be the **cost driver** of the manufacturing overhead costs. As the term implies, a cost driver is the primary factor that causes, or drives, a cost. For example, in many companies, manufacturing overhead costs rise and fall with the amount of work performed in the factory. Because of this, most companies traditionally use either direct labor hours or direct labor cost as their allocation base. This information is also easy to gather from the labor time records or job cost records. However, for manufacturers that have automated much of their production process, machine hours is a more appropriate allocation base because the amount of time spent running the machines drives the utility, maintenance, and equipment depreciation costs in the factory. As you'll learn in Chapter 4, some companies use multiple allocation bases to more accurately allocate manufacturing overhead costs to individual jobs. The important point is that the allocation base selected should bear a strong, positive relationship to the manufacturing overhead costs.

STEP 3: **The company calculates its *predetermined* manufacturing overhead (MOH) rate using the information estimated in Steps 1 and 2:**

$$\text{Predetermined MOH rate} = \frac{\text{Total estimated manufacturing overhead costs}}{\text{Total estimated amount of the allocation base}}$$

For example, Life Fitness calculates its predetermined MOH rate as follows:

$$\text{Predetermined MOH rate} = \frac{\$1,000,000}{62,500 \text{ DL hours}} = \$16 \text{ per direct labor hour}$$

This rate will be used throughout the coming year. It is not revised unless the company finds that either the manufacturing overhead costs or the total amount of the allocation base being used in the factory (direct labor hours in our example) has substantially shifted away from the estimated amounts. If this is the case, management might find it necessary to revise the rate part way through the year.

Why does the company use a **predetermined MOH rate**, based on *estimated or budgeted data*, rather than an actual MOH rate based on actual data for the year? In order to get actual data, the company would have to wait until the *end of the year* to set its MOH rate. By then, the information is too late to be useful for making pricing and other decisions related to individual jobs. Managers are willing to sacrifice some accuracy in order to get timely information on how much each job costs to produce.

Once the company has established its predetermined MOH rate, it uses that rate throughout the year to calculate the amount of manufacturing overhead to allocate to each job produced, as shown in Step 4.

STEP 4: **The company allocates some manufacturing overhead to each individual job as follows:**

MOH allocated to a job = Predetermined MOH rate × Actual amount of allocation base used by the job

Let's see how this works for Life Fitness's Job 603. Because the predetermined MOH rate is based on direct labor (DL) hours ($16 per DL hour), we'll need to know how many direct labor hours were used on Job 603. From Exhibit 3-13, we see that Job 603 required a total of 500 DL hours. This information was collected from the individual labor time records and summarized on the job cost record. Therefore, we calculate the amount of manufacturing overhead to be allocated to Job 603 as follows:

$$\text{MOH to be allocated to Job 603} = \$16 \text{ per direct labor hour} \times 500 \text{ direct labor hours}$$
$$= \$8,000$$

The $8,000 of manufacturing overhead allocated to Job 603 is now posted to the job cost record, as shown in Exhibit 3-14.

EXHIBIT 3-14 Posting Manufacturing Overhead and Completing the Job Cost Record

Job Cost Record

Job Number: 603

Customer: For stock

Job Description: 50 units of X4 Elliptical Cross-Trainers

Date Started: Dec. 2   **Date Completed:** Dec. 6

Manufacturing Cost Information:	Cost Summary
Direct Materials	
Req. #7568: $ 8,500	
Req. #7580: $14,000	
Req. #7595: $13,500	
Req. #7601: $ 4,000	$ 40,000
Direct Labor	
No. #324 (30 DL hours): $100, $160, etc.	
No. #327 (40 DL hours): $240, $210, etc.	
No. #333 (36 DL hours): $80, $120, etc.	
Etc.	
(a total of 500 DL hours)	$ 10,000
Manufacturing Overhead	
$16/DL hour × 500 DL hours = $8,000	$ 8,000
Total Job Cost	$ 58,000
Number of Units	÷ 50 units
Cost per Unit	$ 1,160

When Is Manufacturing Overhead Allocated to Jobs?

The point in time at which manufacturing overhead is allocated to a job depends on the sophistication of the company's computer system. In most sophisticated systems, some manufacturing overhead is allocated to a job each time some of the allocation base is posted to the job cost record. In our Life Fitness example, every time an hour of direct labor is posted to a job, $16 of manufacturing overhead would also be posted to the same job. In less sophisticated systems, manufacturing overhead is allocated only once: as soon as the job is complete and the total amount of allocation base used by the job is known (as shown in Exhibit 3-14). However, if the balance sheet date (for example, December 31) arrives before the job is complete, Life Fitness would need to allocate some manufacturing overhead to the job based on the number of direct labor hours used on the job thus far. Only by updating the job cost records will the company have the most accurate Work in Process Inventory on its balance sheet.

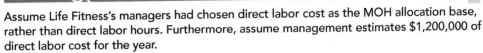

STOP & THINK

Assume Life Fitness's managers had chosen direct labor cost as the MOH allocation base, rather than direct labor hours. Furthermore, assume management estimates $1,200,000 of direct labor cost for the year.

1. Calculate the company's predetermined MOH rate based on direct labor cost.

2. How much MOH would have been allocated to Job 603?

Answer:

1. Predetermined MOH rate $= \dfrac{\$1,000,000}{\$1,200,000 \text{ of DL cost}} = .8333$ or 83.33% of direct labor cost

2. MOH allocated to Job 603 $= 83.33\% \times \$10,000$ direct labor cost
(from Exhibit 3-14)
$= \$8,333$

Note that this allocation differs from that shown in Exhibit 3-14 ($8,000). That's because the amount of MOH allocated to an individual job is highly dependent on the allocation base chosen by management as well as the amount of the allocation base used by the job. Although there is no one "correct" allocation, the most accurate allocation occurs when the company uses the MOH cost driver as its allocation base.

Completing the Job Cost Record and Using It to Make Business Decisions

As shown in Exhibit 3-14, now that all three manufacturing costs have been posted to the job cost record, Life Fitness can determine the total cost of manufacturing Job 603 ($58,000) as well as the cost of producing each of the 50 identical units in the job ($1,160 each). Let's look at a few ways management uses this information.

4 Determine the cost of a job and use it to make business decisions

REDUCING FUTURE JOB COSTS   Management will use the job cost information to control costs. By examining the exact costs traced to the job, management might be able to determine ways of reducing the cost of similar jobs produced in the future. For example, are the heart rate monitors costing more than they did on previous jobs? Perhaps management can renegotiate the contracts with its primary suppliers, or identify different suppliers that are willing to sell the parts more cheaply, without sacrificing quality.

What about direct labor costs? By examining the time spent by various workers on the job, management may be able to improve the efficiency of the process so that less production time is required. Management will also examine the hourly wage rates paid to the individuals who worked on the job to determine if less skilled and therefore less costly workers could accomplish the same production tasks, freeing up the more highly skilled employees for more challenging work.

ASSESSING AND COMPARING THE PROFITABILITY OF EACH MODEL   Management will also use job cost information to determine the profitability of the various models. Assume the X4 Elliptical Cross-Trainer is listed on the company's website at a sales price of $1,900. That means the company can expect the following gross profit on each unit sold:

Sales price per unit	$1,900
Cost of goods sold per unit (computed on job cost record in Exhibit 3-14)	1,160
Gross profit per unit	$ 740

This profit analysis shows that the company would generate a gross profit of $740 on each unit sold from this job. Although this may seem fairly high, keep in mind that companies incur many operating costs, outside of manufacturing costs, that must be covered by the gross profit earned by product sales. For example, in 2014, Life Fitness spent over $23 million on research and development in the fitness segment.[3] Managers will compare the gross profit on this model to the gross profit of other models to determine which products should be emphasized in sales effort. Obviously, management will want to concentrate on marketing those models that yield the higher profit margins.

DEALING WITH PRICING PRESSURE FROM COMPETITORS Management can also use job cost information to determine how it will deal with pricing pressure. Say a competitor drops the price of its similar elliptical cross-trainer to $1,500. The profit analysis shows that Life Fitness could drop its sales price to $1,500 and still generate $340 of gross profit on the sale ($1,500 − $1,160). In fact, Life Fitness could use a sales promotion to *undercut* competitors' prices. As long as Life Fitness charges at least $1,161 for each unit in this job, the company will be earning a positive gross profit on the sale.

ALLOWING DISCOUNTS ON HIGH-VOLUME SALES Customers will often expect discounts for high-volume sales. For example, say the City of Westlake wants to order 40 of these cross-trainers for the city's recreation center and has asked for a 25% volume discount off of the regular sales price. If Life Fitness won't agree to the discount, the city will take its business to the competitor. Can Life Fitness agree to this discount and still earn a profit on the sale? Let's see:

Discounted sales price per unit	$ 1,425
Cost of goods sold per unit	1,160
Gross profit per unit	$ 265
Multiplied by: Number of units	× 40
Total gross profit on sale	$ 10,600

Why is this important?

"Once managers know how much it **costs** to complete a **job**, they use that **information** to do the following:

- Find **cheaper** ways of completing similar jobs in the future,
- Determine which products are **most profitable**, and
- Establish prices for **custom-ordered** jobs."

These calculations show that the discounted sales price will still provide a gross profit. We'll talk more about special orders like this in Chapter 8.

BIDDING FOR CUSTOM ORDERS Management also uses product cost information to bid for custom orders. Let's say that the Atlanta Falcons training facility would like to order 15 custom treadmills and is accepting bids from various fitness equipment manufacturers. Management can use the job cost records from past treadmill jobs to get a good idea of how much it will cost to complete the custom order. For example, the custom treadmills may require additional components not found on the standard models. Life Fitness will factor in these additional costs to get an estimate of the total job cost before it is produced. Life Fitness will most likely use <u>cost-plus pricing</u> to determine a bid price for the custom job. When companies use cost-plus pricing, they take the cost of the job (from the estimated or actual job cost record) and add a markup to help cover operating expenses and generate a profit:

Cost plus price = Cost + Markup on cost

Usually, the markup percentage or final bid price is agreed upon in a written contract before the company goes ahead with production. For example, let's say that Life Fitness typically adds a 40% markup on cost to help cover operating costs and generate a reasonable profit. If the estimated total job cost for the 15 treadmills is $25,000, then the bid price would be calculated as follows:

[3] Brunswick Corp., 2014 10-K filing. Life Fitness is a division of Brunswick Corporation.

$$\text{Cost-plus price} = \$25,000 + (40\% \times \$25,000)$$
$$= \$35,000$$

Once the management team of the Atlanta Falcons has received Life Fitness's bid as well as bids from other companies, the team will decide which bid to accept based on price, quality, reputation for service, and so forth.

PREPARING THE FINANCIAL STATEMENTS   Finally, the job cost information is critical to preparing the company's financial statements. Why? Because the information is used to determine the total Cost of Goods Sold shown on the income statement, as well as the Work in Process and Finished Goods Inventory accounts shown on the balance sheet. Every time a cross-trainer from Job 603 is sold, its cost ($1,160) becomes part of the Cost of Goods Sold during the period. Likewise, every time a cross-trainer from the job is sold, the balance in Finished Goods Inventory is reduced by $1,160. As shown earlier (Exhibit 3-8), the cost-to-date of unfinished jobs remains in the company's Work in Process Inventory.

How Can Job Costing Information Be Enhanced for Decision Making?

We have just finished developing a traditional job cost record and have seen how managers use the information to make vital business decisions. With the help of today's advanced information systems, the job cost information can be further enhanced to help managers make even more informed decisions. This section describes just a few of these enhancements.

Non-Manufacturing Costs

Job costing has traditionally focused on assigning only manufacturing-related costs to jobs. The focus on manufacturing costs arises because GAAP requires that *only* direct materials, direct labor, and manufacturing overhead be assigned to units of inventory for external financial reporting purposes. Costs incurred by other activities in the value chain are not assigned to products for external financial reporting but instead are treated as operating expenses (period costs).

However, for setting long-term average sales prices and making other critical decisions, manufacturers must take into account the total costs of researching and developing, designing, producing, marketing, distributing, and providing customer service for new or existing products. In other words, *they want to know the total cost of the product across the entire value chain.* But how do managers figure this out?

The same principles of tracing direct costs and allocating indirect costs apply to all costs incurred in other activities of the value chain. Managers add these non-manufacturing costs to the production-related job costs to build the *total cost of the product across the entire value chain.* For example, say Life Fitness spent $2 million designing and marketing the X4 Elliptical Cross-Trainer. These costs are direct costs of the X4 Elliptical product line. On the other hand, the company may have spent $3 million researching basic technology for the video screen that is used on all of its products, making it an indirect cost of the X4 Elliptical, shared with other products that use the same video screen. Life Fitness may choose to add an additional cost section to the job cost record, indicating specific operating expenses associated with each job. By adding this information to the job cost record, managers have a more complete understanding of the total job costs, not just the job's manufacturing costs.

Keep in mind that these non-manufacturing costs are assigned to products *only* for internal decision making, never for external financial reporting, because GAAP does not allow it. For financial reporting, non-manufacturing costs must *always* be expensed on the income statement as operating expenses in the period in which they are incurred.

Why is this important?
"**Job cost records** can provide managers with the detailed **environmental** and social **impact** information needed to develop more sustainable **products** and manufacturing processes."

Sustainability and Job Costing

Job cost records serve a vital role for manufacturers who embrace sustainability. Because job cost records contain information about the direct materials, direct labor, and manufacturing overhead assigned to each job, they capture the essential resources required to manufacture a product. The summary information on the job cost records can be enhanced to provide management with further information about how the product or production process may affect the environment, employees involved in the manufacturing process, future consumers of the product, and future disposal of the packaging materials and product itself.

For example, the direct materials section of the job cost record can be broken down into subcategories that provide management with useful environmental information. Categories might include:

See Exercises E3-22A and E3-36B

■ percentage of material and packaging inputs that are post-consumer-use or recycled materials,

■ percentage of materials sourced from local suppliers versus those sourced from geographically distant suppliers (thereby increasing the company's carbon footprint),

■ amount of materials that will become waste as a result of the production process,

■ percentage of the end-of-life product and packaging that can be recycled by the consumer.

Likewise, the job cost record can help management track the extent of the company's fair-labor practices related to each job, such as:

■ the percentage of labor paid at a rate greater than minimum wage as defined by law,

■ the percentage of labor force receiving health-care benefits, and

■ the diversity of labor force used on the job.

Finally, although MOH resources cannot be traced to specific jobs, the company can provide its potential customers with general information such as:

■ percentage of factory utilities generated from renewable sources (wind, solar) versus fossil fuels, and

■ percentage reclaimed and recycled water, versus potable water, used in the factory.

We'll discuss MOH and sustainability more in Chapter 4, but this should give you a basic idea of the types of sustainability-related data that can be measured and reported.

Once the company has tracked this information on job cost records, how is it used? First, it can be used by management to identify areas of weakness so that the company can move toward a more sustainable business model. Second, it can be used to provide information to potential customers, as part of their supply chain assessment.

Sustainability-related information is becoming increasingly important in supply chain management. Many of the world's largest companies, such as Walmart and Costco, are now assessing the environmental and social impact of the suppliers with whom they choose to do business. In fact, supply chain pressure has become a major driving force in corporate adoption of greener and more socially responsible practices.

Third, this information is useful for marketing and labeling. The Sustainability Consortium, a multi-stakeholder group of companies and organizations, is working on developing a standardized system for measuring and reporting the environmental and social impact of consumer products across their entire life cycles. The Consortium is in the process of developing a "sustainability profile" that would be shown on consumer products, somewhat akin to the nutrition labels currently found on food products. By accurately labeling consumer products with environmental and social impact information, consumers will be in a better position to make informed purchasing decisions.

Fourth, this information can be used to assess the risk of future environmental costs associated with each job. For example, **Extended Producer Responsibility (EPR)**

laws, more commonly known as "take-back" laws, create future costs associated with the production of electronic devices and other problem waste, such as mattresses, paint, and batteries. EPR laws, which have been passed in over 25 states as well as several European countries, require manufacturers of electronic devices and other problem waste to take back a large percentage of their products at the end of the products' useful lives. For example, the Wisconsin E-waste Law requires electronics manufacturers to take back 80% of the products they have produced (by weight) in the previous three years; manufacturers that violate this law are subject to a fine.

The goal of EPR laws is to reduce the amount of potentially dangerous waste in landfills by shifting the end-of-life disposal cost back to the manufacturer. By bearing the disposal cost, manufacturers should be motivated to design products and components that are more easily repairable, reusable, and recyclable, and have a longer life cycle.

How do e-waste EPR laws work? Major electronics retailers, such as Best Buy and Staples, collect unused electronics from consumers free of charge, and then partner with responsible recyclers to ensure that the e-waste is dismantled and recycled rather than dumped in landfills or exported to developing nations. Electronics manufacturers partner with these retailers and recyclers by subsidizing their costs.

To put the size of e-waste into perspective, consider the following. In the first quarter of 2016, Apple sold over 74 million iPhones, 16 million iPads, and 5 million Macs.[4] And that's just for three months of sales! When you consider all of the other computer, TV, and smartphone producers, you begin to understand the size of the potential e-waste issue. In fact, a study funded by the EPA and carried out by MIT and others indicated that in 2010, approximately 258 million units of used electronics such as cell phones, TVs, and computers (equating to 1.6 million tons) were generated in the United States, but only 66% were collected.[5] As a result, many electronics producers, such as Apple, HP, and Dell, are supporting take-back policies and providing recycling options for their old products.

In addition to state EPR laws, the federal government is also considering a bill (the Responsible Electronics Recycling Act) that will restrict the export of toxic e-waste, which historically has been shipped to developing countries. This bill, if passed, will not only help with environmental and public health issues caused by e-waste but will also create even more incentive for manufacturers and recyclers to find alternative uses for outdated electronic equipment.

Direct or Variable Costing

Even though the job cost records contain information about all three manufacturing costs, managers base certain decisions on just the direct costs (direct materials and labor) or variable costs found on a job cost record. Why? For two reasons: (1) The simple allocation of MOH that we have described in this chapter results in a fairly arbitrary amount of MOH being allocated to jobs, and (2) because many MOH costs are fixed and will not be affected as a result of producing a job. Later in the book, we'll see how management accountants have addressed these issues. In Chapter 4, we'll show how managers can improve the allocation system so that the amount of manufacturing overhead assigned to the job is much more accurate. In Chapters 6 and 8, we'll discuss how direct costing or variable costing can be used to improve the decision-making process.

---

[4] www.apple.com; http://electronicstakeback.com/promote-good-laws/state-legislation

[5] December 2013, "Quantitative Characterization of Domestic and Transboundary Flows of Used Electronics: Analysis of Generation, Collection, Export in the United States." www.epa.gov/international-cooperation/cleaning-electronic-waste-e-waste

Decision Guidelines

Job Costing

Life Fitness uses a job costing system that assigns manufacturing costs to each batch of exercise machines that it makes. These guidelines explain some of the decisions Life Fitness made in designing its costing system.

Decision	Guidelines
Should we use job costing or process costing?	Managers use the costing system that best fits their production environment. Job costing is best suited to manufacturers that produce unique, custom-built products or relatively small batches of different products. Process costing is best suited to manufacturers that mass-produce identical units in a series of uniform production processes.
How do we determine the cost of manufacturing each job?	The exact amount of direct materials and direct labor can be traced to individual jobs using materials requisitions and labor time records. However, the exact amount of manufacturing overhead attributable to each job is unknown and therefore *cannot* be traced to individual jobs. To deal with this issue, companies *allocate* some manufacturing overhead to each job.
Should we use a predetermined manufacturing overhead rate or the actual manufacturing overhead rate?	Although it would be more accurate to use the actual manufacturing overhead rate, companies would have to wait until the end of the year to have that information. Most companies are willing to sacrifice some accuracy for the sake of having timely information that will help them make decisions throughout the year. Therefore, most companies use a predetermined overhead rate to allocate manufacturing overhead to jobs as they are produced throughout the year.
How do we calculate the predetermined MOH rate?	$$\text{Predetermined MOH rate} = \frac{\text{Total estimated manufacturing overhead cost}}{\text{Total estimated amount of the allocation base}}$$
What allocation base should we use for allocating manufacturing overhead?	If possible, companies should use the cost driver of manufacturing overhead as the allocation base. The most common allocation bases are direct labor hours, direct labor cost, and machine hours. Some companies use multiple bases in order to more accurately allocate MOH. This topic will be covered in Chapter 4.
How should we allocate manufacturing overhead to individual jobs?	The MOH allocated to a job is calculated as follows: = Predetermined MOH rate $\times$ Actual amount of allocation base used by the job
Can job cost records help companies in their journey toward sustainability?	Job cost records can be enhanced to provide more detail about the environmental and social impact of the resources used on the job. In addition to satisfying supply chain assessment, managers can use this information to determine how a product, or production process, can become more sustainable.
Can manufacturers also assign operating expenses to jobs?	Operating expenses can also be assigned to jobs, but *only* for *internal decision-making* purposes. Operating expenses are *never* assigned to jobs for external financial reporting purposes. Direct operating costs would be traced to jobs (such as the sales commission on a particular job or the design costs related to a particular job) whereas indirect operating costs (such as the R&D costs associated with several product lines) would be allocated to jobs.

SUMMARY PROBLEM 1

E-Z-Boy Furniture makes sofas, loveseats, and recliners. The company allocates manufacturing overhead based on direct labor hours. E-Z-Boy estimated a total of $2 million of manufacturing overhead and 40,000 direct labor hours for the year.

Job 310 consists of a batch of 10 recliners. The company's records show that the following direct materials were requisitioned for Job 310:

Lumber: 10 units at $30 per unit

Padding: 20 yards at $20 per yard

Upholstery fabric: 60 yards at $25 per yard, sourced from a local manufacturer

Labor time records show the following employees (direct labor) worked on Job 310:

Jesse Slothower: 10 hours at $12 per hour

Becky Wilken: 15 hours at $18 per hour

Chip Lathrop: 12 hours at $15 per hour

Requirements

1. Compute the company's predetermined manufacturing overhead rate.

2. Compute the total amount of direct materials, direct labor, and manufacturing overhead that should be shown on Job 310's job cost record.

3. Compute the total cost of Job 310, as well as the cost of each recliner produced in Job 310.

4. The company's customers are concerned about environmental responsibility and social justice and require additional sustainability-related information prior to making their purchasing decisions. To meet customer concerns, determine (a) which materials used for the product are sourced locally, and (b) the percentage of labor paid at a rate greater than minimum wage. Currently, the federal minimum wage is $7.25 per hour.

■ SOLUTIONS

1. The predetermined MOH rate is calculated as follows:

$$\text{Predetermined MOH rate} = \frac{\text{Total estimated manufacturing overhead cost}}{\text{Total estimated amount of the allocation base}}$$

For E-Z-Boy:

$$\text{Predetermined MOH rate} = \frac{\$2,000,000}{40,000 \text{ direct labor hours}} = \$50 \text{ per direct labor hour}$$

2. The total amount of direct materials ($2,200) and direct labor ($570) incurred on Job 310 is determined from the materials requisitions and labor time records, as shown on the following job cost record. Because the job required 37 direct labor hours, we determine the amount of manufacturing overhead to allocate to the job is as follows:

$$= \text{Predetermined MOH rate} \times \text{Actual amount of allocation base used by the job}$$
$$= \$50 \text{ per direct labor hour} \times 37 \text{ direct labor hours used on Job 310}$$
$$= \$1,850$$

These costs are summarized on the following job cost record:

Job Cost Record

Job Number: 310

Job Description: 10 recliners

Manufacturing Cost Information:	Cost Summary	
Direct Materials		
Lumber: 10 units × $30 = $300		
Padding: 20 yards × $20 = $400		
Fabric: 60 yards × $25 = $1,500	$	2,200
Direct Labor		
Slothower: 10 hours × $12 = $120		
Wilken: 15 hours × $18 = $270		
Lathrop: 12 hours × $15 = $180		
Total hours: 37 hours	$	570
Manufacturing Overhead		
37 direct labor hours × $50 = $1,850	$	1,850
Total Job Cost	$	4,620
Number of Units	÷	10 units
Cost per Unit	$	462

3. The direct materials ($2,200), direct labor ($570), and manufacturing overhead ($1,850) sum to a total job cost of $4,620. When the total job cost is averaged over the 10 recliners in the job, the cost per recliner is $462.

4. Supplemental sustainability information for Job 310:

   a. All fabric contained in the product was sourced locally.

   b. All labor used in the manufacturing was paid at a rate higher than minimum wage.

How Do Managers Deal with Underallocated or Overallocated Manufacturing Overhead?

In the first half of the chapter, we showed how managers find the cost of completing a job. Direct materials and direct labor are traced to each job using materials requisitions and labor time records, and manufacturing overhead is allocated to each job using a predetermined overhead rate. At the end of the period, all manufacturers will have a problem to deal with: Invariably, they will have either <u>underallocated manufacturing overhead</u> or <u>overallocated manufacturing overhead</u> to the jobs worked on during the period.

Recall that manufacturing overhead is allocated to jobs using a *predetermined rate* that is calculated using *estimates* of the company's total annual manufacturing overhead costs and *estimates* of the total annual allocation base (such as direct labor hours). By the end of the period, the *actual* manufacturing overhead costs incurred by the company will be known, and they will likely differ from the total amount allocated to jobs during the period.

For example, suppose Life Fitness incurred the following *actual* manufacturing overhead costs during the month of December:

"Why is this important?"

Because managers **allocate** MOH to jobs using a **predetermined** rate that is based on **estimates**, the amount of **MOH allocated** to jobs during the year will not be quite right. At the **end of the period**, managers find out whether the jobs have been allocated **too much** or **too little** MOH and then **fix** the error in the **financial** records.

Manufacturing Overhead Incurred	Actual MOH Costs
Indirect materials used (janitorial supplies, machine lubricants, etc.).........	$ 2,000
Indirect labor (janitors' and supervisors' wages, etc.)	13,000
Other indirect manufacturing costs	
(Plant utilities, depreciation, property taxes, insurance, etc.)...........	10,000
Total actual manufacturing overhead costs incurred	$25,000

5 Compute and dispose of overallocated or underallocated manufacturing overhead

Now let's look at the total amount of manufacturing overhead that was *allocated* to individual jobs during the month using the predetermined manufacturing overhead rate of $16 per direct labor hour. For simplicity, we'll assume only two jobs were worked on during December.

Jobs	Amount of MOH Allocated to Job
603 (from Exhibit 3-14) ($16 per DL hour × 500 DL hours)	$ 8,000
604 (not shown) ($16 per DL hour × 1,000 DL hours)	16,000
Total MOH allocated to jobs ($16 per DL hour × 1,500 DL hours).........	$24,000

Notice that we don't need to have the individual job cost records available to figure out the total amount of MOH allocated to jobs during the period. Rather, we can calculate the total amount of MOH allocated to jobs as follows:

Total MOH allocated = Predetermined MOH rate × Actual *total* amount of allocation base used on all jobs

= $16 per DL hour × 1,500 direct labor hours

= $24,000 total MOH allocated to jobs during the period

To determine whether manufacturing overhead had been overallocated or underallocated, we simply compare the amount of MOH actually incurred during the period with the amount of MOH that was allocated to jobs during the same period. The difference between the *actual manufacturing overhead costs incurred* by the company and the amount of manufacturing overhead *allocated to jobs* shows that Life Fitness *underallocated* manufacturing overhead by $1,000 during December:

Actual manufacturing overhead costs **incurred**.......................................	$25,000
Manufacturing overhead **allocated** to jobs	24,000
Underallocated manufacturing overhead..	$ 1,000

By underallocating manufacturing overhead, Life Fitness *did not allocate enough* manufacturing overhead cost to the jobs worked on during the period. In other words, the jobs worked on during the period should have had a total of $1,000 more manufacturing overhead cost allocated to them than the job cost records indicated. These jobs have been undercosted, as shown in Exhibit 3-15. If, on the other hand, a manufacturer finds that the amount of manufacturing overhead allocated to jobs is *greater* than the actual amount of manufacturing overhead incurred by the company, we would say that manufacturing overhead had been overallocated, resulting in overcosting these jobs.

EXHIBIT 3-15 Underallocated Versus Overallocated Manufacturing Overhead

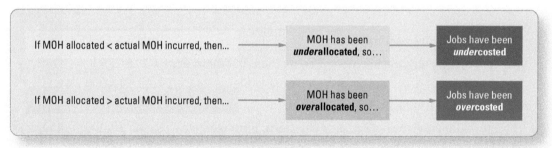

What do manufacturers do about this problem? *Assuming that the amount of underallocation or overallocation is immaterial, or that most of the inventory produced during the period has been sold,* manufacturers typically adjust Cost of Goods Sold for the total amount of the under- or overallocation. Why? Because (1) as a result of using a *predetermined* MOH rate, too much or too little MOH was originally recorded on the job cost records and (2) when the jobs were sold, the job cost records were used as a basis for recording Cost of Goods Sold. Hence, the Cost of Goods Sold account will be wrong unless it is corrected. As shown in Exhibit 3-16, by increasing Cost of Goods Sold when manufacturing overhead has been underallocated, or by decreasing Cost of Goods Sold when manufacturing overhead has been overallocated, the company actually corrects the error that exists in Cost of Goods Sold.

EXHIBIT 3-16 Correcting Cost of Goods Sold for Underallocated or Overallocated MOH

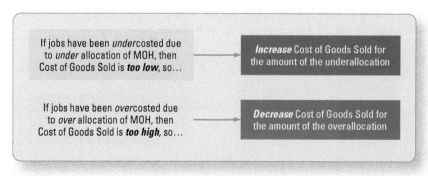

What if the amount of under- or overallocation is large, and the company has *not* sold almost all of the units produced during the period? Then the company will prorate the total amount of under- or overallocation among Work in Process Inventory, Finished Goods Inventory, and Cost of Goods Sold based on the current status of the jobs worked on during the period. For example, if 30% of the jobs are still in Work in Process, 20% are still in Finished Goods, and 50% were sold, then the total amount of underallocation ($1,000 in the case of Life Fitness) would be roughly allocated as follows: 30% ($300) to Work in Process Inventory, 20% ($200) to Finished Goods Inventory, and 50% ($500) to Cost of Goods Sold. The exact procedure for prorating is covered in more advanced accounting textbooks.

▶ Try It!

Recall that Life Fitness had estimated $1,000,000 of MOH for the year and 62,500 DL hours, resulting in a predetermined MOH rate of $16/DL hour. By the end of the year, the company had actually incurred $975,000 of MOH costs and used a total of 60,000 DL hours on jobs. By how much had Life Fitness overallocated or underallocated MOH for the year?

Please see page 174 for solutions.

What Journal Entries Are Needed in a Manufacturer's Job Costing System?

Now that you know how manufacturers determine job costs and how those costs are used to make business decisions, let's look at how these costs are entered into the company's general ledger accounting system. We'll consider the journal entries needed to record the flow of costs through Life Fitness's accounts during the month of December. We'll use the same examples used earlier in the chapter. For the sake of simplicity, we'll continue to assume that Life Fitness only worked on two jobs during the month:

6 Prepare journal entries for a manufacturer's job costing system

- Job 603: 50 units of the X4 Elliptical Cross-Trainers
- Job 604: 60 units of the T5 Treadmill

You may wish to review the basic mechanics of journal entries, shown in Exhibit 3-17, before we begin our discussion.

EXHIBIT 3-17 Review of Journal Entry and T-account Mechanics

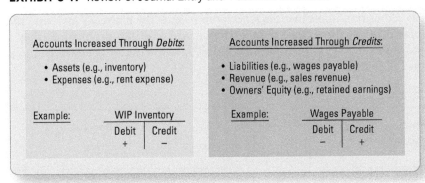

Additionally, keep in mind the flow of inventory that was first described in Exhibit 3-2. You may find this visual reminder helpful as we describe how the journal entries reflect the flow of inventory through the manufacturing system. In Exhibit 3-18, each arrow represents a journal entry that must be made to reflect activities that occur along the process: purchasing raw materials, using direct materials, using direct labor, recording actual MOH costs, allocating MOH to jobs, moving the jobs out of the factory after completion, and, finally, selling the units from a job. We'll now walk through journal entries associated with each of these activities.

EXHIBIT 3-18   Flow of Costs through a Manufacturing Plant

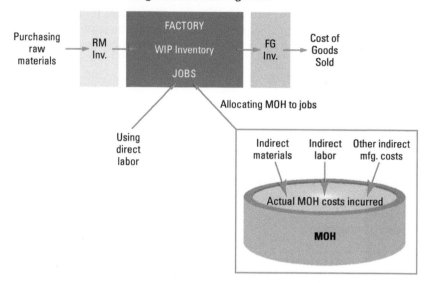

Purchase of Raw Materials

Assume that Life Fitness ordered and received $90,000 of raw materials during December. Once the materials are received and verified against the purchase order and the invoice received from the supplier, the purchase is recorded as follows:

(1)	Raw Materials Inventory	90,000	
	Accounts Payable		90,000
	(to record purchases of raw materials on account)		

These materials will remain in the raw materials storeroom until they are needed for production. The liability in Accounts Payable will be removed when the supplier is paid.

Use of Direct Materials

Recall that direct materials are the primary physical components of the product. Each time production managers need particular direct materials for Jobs 603 and 604, they fill out a materials requisition informing the storeroom to pick the materials and send them into the manufacturing facility. Once these materials are sent into production, they become part of the work in process on Jobs 603 and 604, so their cost is added to the job cost records, as follows:

Job Cost Record

Job Number: 603 (50 Cross-trainers)

Manufacturing Cost Information:	Cost Summary
Direct Materials	$40,000
Direct Labor	
Manufacturing Overhead	
Total Job Cost	

Job Cost Record

Job Number: 604 (60 Treadmills)

Manufacturing Cost Information:	Cost Summary
Direct Materials	$72,000
Direct Labor	
Manufacturing Overhead	
Total Job Cost	

From an accounting perspective, the cost of these materials must also be moved into Work in Process Inventory (through a debit) and out of Raw Materials Inventory (through a credit). The following journal entry is made:

(2)	Work in Process Inventory ($40,000 + $72,000)	112,000	
	Raw Materials Inventory		112,000
	(to record the use of direct materials on jobs)		

Recall from the first half of the chapter that the individual job cost records form the underlying support for Work in Process Inventory shown on the balance sheet.[6] Therefore, the amount posted to the general ledger account ($112,000) must be identical to the sum of the amounts posted to the individual job cost records ($40,000 + $72,000 = $112,000). Keep this important rule of thumb in mind:

> Whenever a cost is added to a job cost record, a corresponding journal entry is made to increase WIP Inventory.

Use of Indirect Materials

Indirect materials are materials used in the manufacturing plant that *cannot* be traced to individual jobs and therefore are *not* recorded on any job cost record. Examples include janitorial supplies used in the factory and machine lubricants for the factory machines. Once again, materials requisitions inform the raw materials storeroom to release these materials. However, instead of becoming part of the Work in Process account for a particular job, the indirect materials used in the factory (let's say $2,000) become part of the Manufacturing Overhead account. Therefore, the Manufacturing Overhead account is debited (to increase the account) and Raw Materials Inventory is credited (to decrease the account) as follows:

(3)	Manufacturing Overhead	2,000	
	Raw Materials Inventory		2,000
	(to record the use of indirect materials in the factory)		

All indirect manufacturing costs, including indirect materials, indirect labor, and other indirect manufacturing costs (such as plant insurance and depreciation), are accumulated, or gathered together, in the Manufacturing Overhead account. The Manufacturing Overhead account is a *temporary* account used to "pool" (gather together) indirect manufacturing costs until those costs can be allocated to individual jobs. In fact, the MOH account is sometimes referred to as the "MOH cost pool."

---

[6] The job cost records of unfinished jobs form the subsidiary ledger for the Work in Process Inventory account. Recall that a **subsidiary ledger** is simply the supporting detail for a general ledger account. Many other general ledger accounts (such as Accounts Receivable, Accounts Payable, and Plant & Equipment) also have subsidiary ledgers. The raw material inventory records form the subsidiary ledger for the Raw Materials Inventory account, whereas the job cost records on completed, unsold jobs form the subsidiary ledger for the Finished Goods Inventory account.

We can summarize the flow of materials costs through the T-accounts as follows:

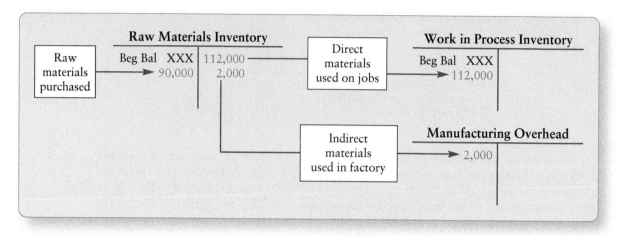

Use of Direct Labor

The labor time records of individual factory workers are used to determine exactly how much time was spent directly working on Jobs 603 and 604. The cost of this direct labor is entered on the job cost records, as shown:

Job Cost Record	
Job Number: 603 (50 Cross-trainers)	
Manufacturing Cost Information:	**Cost Summary**
Direct Materials	$40,000
Direct Labor	$10,000
Manufacturing Overhead	
Total Job Cost	

Job Cost Record	
Job Number: 604 (60 Treadmills)	
Manufacturing Cost Information:	**Cost Summary**
Direct Materials	$72,000
Direct Labor	$20,000
Manufacturing Overhead	
Total Job Cost	

Again, because the job cost records form the underlying support for Work in Process Inventory, an identical amount ($10,000 + $20,000 = $30,000) must be debited to the Work in Process Inventory account. Wages Payable is credited to show that the company has a liability to pay its factory workers:

(4)	Work in Process Inventory ($10,000 + $20,000)	30,000	
	Wages Payable		30,000
	(*to record the use of direct labor on jobs*)		

The Wages Payable liability will be removed on payday when the workers receive their pay.

Use of Indirect Labor

Recall that indirect labor consists of the salary, wages, and benefits of all factory workers who are *not* directly working on individual jobs. Examples include factory janitors, supervisors, and forklift operators. Because their time cannot be traced to particular jobs, the cost of employing these factory workers during the month (let's say $13,000) cannot be posted to individual job cost records. Thus, we record the cost of indirect labor as part of Manufacturing Overhead, *not* Work in Process Inventory:

(5)	Manufacturing Overhead	13,000	
	Wages Payable		13,000
	(to record the use of indirect labor in the factory)		

Again, the Wages Payable liability will be removed on payday when the workers receive their pay.

We can summarize the flow of manufacturing labor costs through the T-accounts as follows:

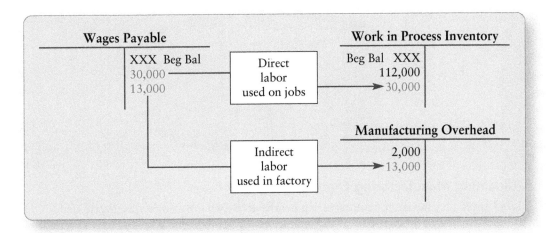

Incurring Other Manufacturing Overhead Costs

We have already recorded the indirect materials and indirect labor used in the factory during December by debiting the Manufacturing Overhead account. However, Life Fitness incurs other indirect manufacturing costs during the period, such as plant utilities ($3,000), plant and equipment depreciation ($4,000), plant insurance ($1,000), and plant property taxes ($2,000). All of these other costs of running the manufacturing plant during the month are also added to the Manufacturing Overhead account until they can be allocated to specific jobs:

(6)	Manufacturing Overhead	10,000	
	Accounts Payable *(for electric bill)*		3,000
	Accumulated Depreciation—Plant and Equipment		4,000
	Prepaid Plant Insurance *(for expiration of prepaid insurance)*		1,000
	Plant Property Taxes Payable *(for taxes to be paid)*		2,000
	(to record other indirect manufacturing costs incurred		
	during the month)		

After recording all other indirect manufacturing costs, the Manufacturing Overhead account appears as follows:

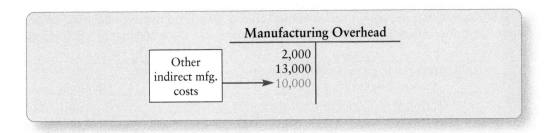

Since all MOH costs are combined, or "pooled together" into one account, the MOH account is sometimes referred to as a "cost pool." As shown in Exhibit 3-19, you might find it helpful to visualize a pool being filled with the actual MOH costs incurred during the year. In the next section, we'll see how the costs are removed from the pool and assigned to specific jobs.

EXHIBIT 3-19   Pooling Actual MOH Costs

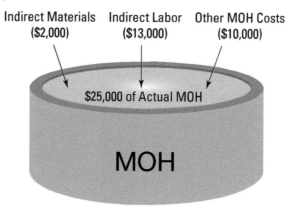

Allocating Manufacturing Overhead to Jobs

Life Fitness allocates some manufacturing overhead to each job using its predetermined MOH rate, calculated in the first half of the chapter to be $16 per direct labor hour. The total of direct labor hours used on each job is found on the labor time records and is summarized on the job cost records. Assume Job 603 used 500 DL hours and Job 604 used 1,000 DL hours. Then the amount of manufacturing overhead allocated to each job is determined as follows:

Job 603: $16 per DL hour × 500 DL hours = $8,000

Job 604: $16 per DL hour × 1,000 DL hours = $16,000

Job Cost Record

Job Number: 603 (50 Cross-trainers)

Manufacturing Cost Information:	Cost Summary
Direct Materials	$40,000
Direct Labor (500 DL hrs)	$10,000
Manufacturing Overhead	$ 8,000
Total Job Cost	

Job Cost Record

Job Number: 604 (60 Treadmills)

Manufacturing Cost Information:	Cost Summary
Direct Materials	$72,000
Direct Labor (1,000 DL hrs)	$20,000
Manufacturing Overhead	$16,000
Total Job Cost	

Again, because the job cost records form the underlying support for Work in Process Inventory, an identical amount ($8,000 + $16,000 = $24,000) must be debited to the Work in Process Inventory account. Because we accumulated all actual manufacturing overhead costs *into* an account called Manufacturing Overhead (through debiting the account), we now allocate manufacturing overhead costs *out* of the account by crediting it.

(7)	Work in Process Inventory ($8,000 + $16,000)	24,000	
	Manufacturing Overhead		24,000
	(to allocate manufacturing overhead to specific jobs)		

As shown in Exhibit 3-20, you might find it helpful to visualize the allocation process as removing, or ladling out, some of the MOH cost in the pool and allocating it to individual jobs worked on in the factory. In our example, we assumed only two jobs were worked on during the month (Jobs 603 and 604). However, if more jobs were worked on, the same allocation process would take place for each and every job. To recap, the MOH cost pool is increased through the addition of actual MOH costs as they are incurred, and decreased through the allocation of MOH to individual jobs. In the general ledger, the MOH cost pool is represented by the MOH account. Thus, the account is increased (debited) whenever an actual MOH cost is incurred, and it is credited whenever MOH costs are allocated to jobs.

EXHIBIT 3-20   Allocating MOH Costs to Individual Jobs

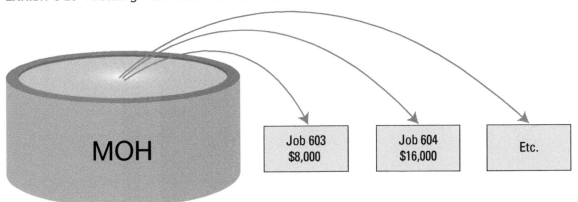

By looking at the Manufacturing Overhead T-account, you can see how actual manufacturing overhead costs are accumulated in the account through debits, and the amount of manufacturing overhead allocated to specific jobs is credited to the account:

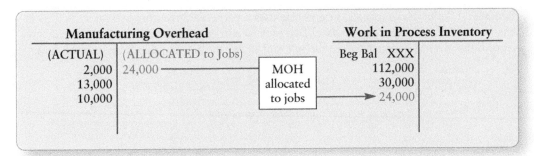

Completion of Jobs

Once the job has been completed, the three manufacturing costs shown on the job cost record are summed to find the total job cost. If the job consists of more than one unit, the total job cost is divided by the number of units to find the cost of each unit:

Job Cost Record

Job Number: 603 (50 Cross-trainers)

Manufacturing Cost Information:	Cost Summary
Direct Materials	$40,000
Direct Labor	$10,000
Manufacturing Overhead	$ 8,000
Total Job Cost	$58,000
Number of Units	÷50
Cost per Unit	$ 1,160

Job Cost Record

Job Number: 604 (60 Treadmills)

Manufacturing Cost Information:	Cost Summary
Direct Materials	$ 72,000
Direct Labor	$ 20,000
Manufacturing Overhead	$ 16,000
Total Job Cost	$108,000
Number of Units	÷60
Cost per Unit	$ 1,800

The units produced in the jobs are physically moved off of the plant floor and into the finished goods warehouse. Likewise, in the accounting records, the jobs are moved out of Work in Process Inventory (through a credit) and into Finished Goods Inventory (through a debit):

(8)	Finished Goods Inventory ($58,000 + $108,000)	166,000	
	Work in Process Inventory		166,000
	(to move the completed jobs out of the factory and into		
	Finished Goods)		

The T-accounts show the movement of completed jobs off of the factory floor:

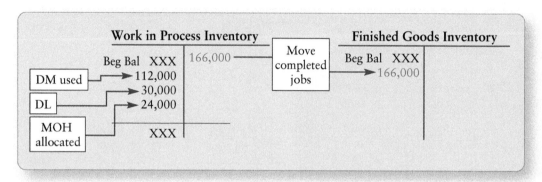

Sale of Units

For simplicity, let's assume that Life Fitness only had one sale during the month: It sold 40 cross-trainers from Job 603 and all 60 treadmills from Job 604 to the City of Westlake for its recreation centers. The sales price was $1,425 for each cross-trainer and $2,500 for each treadmill. Like most companies, Life Fitness uses a perpetual inventory system so that its inventory records are always up to date. Two journal entries are needed. The first journal entry records the revenue generated from the sale and shows the amount due from the customer:

(9)	Accounts Receivable (40 × $1,425) + (60 × $2,500)	207,000	
	Sales Revenue		207,000
	(to record the sale of 40 cross-trainers and 60 treadmills)		

The second journal entry reduces the company's Finished Goods Inventory and records the Cost of Goods Sold. From the job cost record, we know that each cross-trainer produced in Job 603 cost $1,160 to make, and each treadmill from Job 604 cost $1,800 to make. Therefore, the following entry is recorded:

(10)	Cost of Goods Sold (40 × $1,160) + (60 × $1,800)	154,400	
	Finished Goods Inventory		154,400
	(to reduce Finished Goods Inventory and record Cost of Goods Sold)		

The following T-accounts show the movement of the units out of Finished Goods Inventory and into Cost of Goods Sold:

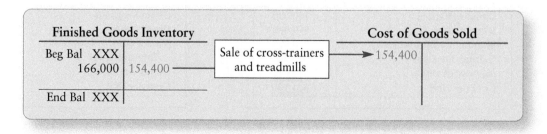

Operating Expenses

Let's assume Life Fitness also incurred $32,700 of operating expenses during the month to run its business. For example, Life Fitness incurred salaries and commissions ($20,000) for its salespeople, office administrators, research and design staff, and customer service representatives. It also needs to pay rent ($3,300) for its office headquarters. The company also received a bill from its advertising agency for marketing expenses incurred during the month ($9,400). *All costs incurred outside of the manufacturing function of the value chain* would be expensed in the current month as shown in the following journal entry:

(11)	Salaries and Commission Expense	20,000	
	Rent Expense	3,300	
	Marketing Expenses	9,400	
	Salaries and Commissions Payable		20,000
	Rent Payable		3,300
	Accounts Payable		9,400
	(*to record all non-manufacturing costs incurred during the month*)		

All non-manufacturing expenses (period costs) will be shown as "operating expenses" on the company's income statement, as shown in Exhibit 3-21 on the next page.

Closing Manufacturing Overhead

As a final step, Life Fitness must deal with the balance in the manufacturing overhead account. Because the company uses a *predetermined* manufacturing overhead rate to allocate manufacturing overhead to individual jobs, the total amount allocated to jobs will most likely differ from the amount of manufacturing overhead actually incurred.

Let's see how this plays out in the Manufacturing Overhead T-account:

1. All manufacturing overhead costs *incurred* by Life Fitness were recorded as *debits* to the Manufacturing Overhead account. These debits total $25,000 of actual manufacturing overhead incurred.

2. On the other hand, all manufacturing overhead *allocated* to specific jobs ($8,000 + $16,000) was recorded as *credits* to the Manufacturing Overhead account:

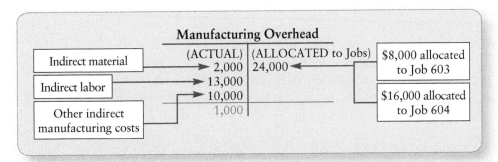

This leaves a debit balance of $1,000 in the Manufacturing Overhead account, which means that manufacturing overhead has been underallocated during the month. More manufacturing overhead costs were incurred than were allocated to jobs. Because Manufacturing Overhead is a temporary account not shown on any of the company's financial statements, it must be closed out (zeroed out) at the end of the period. Because most of the inventory produced during the period has been sold, Life Fitness will close the balance in Manufacturing Overhead to Cost of Goods Sold as follows:

(12)	Cost of Goods Sold	1,000	
	Manufacturing Overhead		1,000
	(*to close the Manufacturing Overhead account*)		

As a result of this entry, (1) the Manufacturing Overhead account now has a zero balance, and (2) the balance in Cost of Goods Sold has increased to correct for the fact that the jobs had been undercosted during the period.

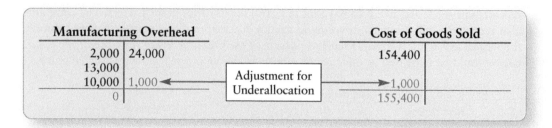

If, in some period, Life Fitness were to overallocate its overhead, the journal entry to close Manufacturing Overhead would be the opposite of that shown: Manufacturing Overhead would be debited to zero it out; Cost of Goods Sold would be credited to reduce it as a result of having overcosted jobs during the period.

Now you have seen how all of the costs flow through Life Fitness's accounts during December. Exhibit 3-21 shows the company's income statement that resulted from all of the previously shown journal entries.

EXHIBIT 3-21 Income Statement After Adjusting for Underallocated Manufacturing Overhead

	A	B	C	D
1	**Life Fitness**			
2	**Income Statement**			
3	**For the Month Ended December 31**			
4				
5	Sales Revenue	$ 207,000		
6	Less: Cost of Goods Sold	155,400		
7	Gross Profit	51,600		
8	Less: Operating Expenses	32,700		
9	Operating Income	$ 18,900		
10				

Decision Guidelines

Job Costing

The following decision guidelines describe the implications of over- or underallocating manufacturing overhead, as well as other decisions that need to be made in a job costing environment.

Decision	Guidelines
How does overallocating or underallocating MOH affect the cost of jobs manufactured during the period?	If manufacturing overhead has been *underallocated*, it means that not enough MOH was allocated to the jobs. The jobs have been undercosted as a result. On the other hand, if manufacturing overhead has been *overallocated*, it means that too much MOH was allocated to jobs. The jobs have been overcosted as a result.
What do we do about overallocated or underallocated manufacturing overhead?	Assuming most of the inventory produced during the period has been sold, manufacturers generally adjust the Cost of Goods Sold for the total amount of the under- or overallocation. If a significant portion of the inventory is still on hand, then the adjustment will be prorated between WIP Inventory, Finished Goods Inventory, and Cost of Goods Sold.
How do we know whether to increase or decrease Cost of Goods Sold (CGS)?	If manufacturing overhead has been overallocated, then Cost of Goods Sold (CGS) is too high and must be decreased through a credit to the CGS account. If manufacturing overhead has been underallocated, then Cost of Goods Sold is too low and must be increased through a debit to the CGS account.

How do we record the use of direct materials on a job?			
Work in Process Inventory		X	
Raw Materials Inventory			X

How do we record the use of direct labor on a job?			
Work in Process Inventory		X	
Wages Payable			X

How do we record actual MOH cost incurred in the factory?			
Manufacturing Overhead		X	
Raw Materials Inventory (for indirect materials)			X
Wages payable (for indirect labor)			X
Accounts payable, etc. (for other MOH)			X

How do we record the allocation of MOH costs to jobs?			
Work in Process Inventory		X	
Manufacturing Overhead			X

How do we record the completion of the job?			
Finished Goods Inventory		X	
Work in Process Inventory			X

| How does job costing work at a service firm (Appendix)? | Job costing at a service firm is very similar to job costing at a manufacturer. The main difference is that the company is allocating operating expenses, rather than manufacturing costs, to each client job. In addition, because there are no Inventory or Cost of Goods Sold accounts, no journal entries are needed to move inventory through the system. All costs are simply expensed as period costs, but separate job cost records are maintained to keep track of the costs of serving each client. |

SUMMARY PROBLEM 2

Fashion Fabrics makes custom handbags and accessories for high-end clothing boutiques. Record summary journal entries for each of the following transactions that took place during the month of January, the *first* month of the fiscal year.

Requirements

1. During January, $150,000 of raw materials was purchased on account.

2. During the month, $140,000 of raw materials was requisitioned. Of this amount, $135,000 was traced to specific jobs, while the remaining materials were for general factory use.

3. Manufacturing labor (both direct and indirect) for the month totaled $80,000. It has not yet been paid. Of this amount, $60,000 was traced to specific jobs.

4. The company recorded $9,000 of depreciation on the plant building and machinery. In addition, $3,000 of prepaid property tax expired during the month. The company also received the plant utility bill for $6,000 which will be paid at a later date.

5. Manufacturing overhead was allocated to jobs using a predetermined manufacturing overhead rate of 75% of direct labor *cost*. (*Hint:* Total direct labor cost is found in Requirement 3.)

6. Several jobs were completed during the month. According to the job cost records, these jobs cost $255,000 to manufacture.

7. Sales (all on credit) for the month totaled $340,000. According to the job cost records, the units sold cost $250,000 to manufacture. Assume the company uses a perpetual inventory system.

8. The company incurred operating expenses of $60,000 during the month. Assume that 80% of these were for marketing and administrative salaries and the other 20% were lease and utility bills related to the corporate headquarters. The expenses will be paid later.

9. In order to prepare its January financial statements, the company had to close its Manufacturing Overhead account.

10. Prepare the January income statement for Fashion Fabrics based on the transactions recorded in Requirements 1 through 9.

▪ SOLUTIONS

1. During January, $150,000 of raw materials was purchased on account.

Raw Materials Inventory	150,000	
Accounts Payable		150,000
(*to record purchases of raw materials*)		

2. During the month, $140,000 of raw materials was requisitioned. Of this amount, $135,000 was traced to specific jobs, while the remaining materials were for general factory use.

Work in Process Inventory	135,000	
Manufacturing Overhead	5,000	
Raw Materials Inventory		140,000
(*to record the use of direct materials and indirect materials*)		

3. Manufacturing labor (both direct and indirect) for the month totaled $80,000. It has not yet been paid. Of this amount, $60,000 was traced to specific jobs.

Work in Process Inventory (*for direct labor*)	60,000	
Manufacturing Overhead (*for indirect labor*)	20,000	
Wages Payable		80,000
(*to record the use of direct labor and indirect labor*)		

4. The company recorded $9,000 of depreciation on the plant building and machinery. In addition, $3,000 of prepaid property tax expired during the month. The company also received the plant utility bill for $6,000 which will be paid at a later date.

Manufacturing Overhead	18,000	
Accumulated Depreciation—Plant and Equipment		9,000
Prepaid Plant Property Tax (*for expiration of property tax*)		3,000
Accounts Payable (*for electric bill*)		6,000
(*to record other indirect manufacturing costs incurred during the month*)		

5. Manufacturing overhead was allocated to jobs using a predetermined manufacturing overhead rate of 75% of direct labor cost. (*Hint:* Total direct labor cost is found in Requirement 3.)

Work in Process Inventory (75% × $60,000 of direct labor)	45,000	
Manufacturing Overhead		45,000
(*to allocate manufacturing overhead to jobs*)		

6. Several jobs were completed during the month. According to the job cost records, these jobs cost $255,000 to manufacture.

Finished Goods Inventory	255,000	
Work in Process Inventory		255,000
(*to move the completed jobs out of the factory and into Finished Goods*)		

7. Sales (all on credit) for the month totaled $340,000. According to the job cost records, the units sold cost $250,000 to manufacture. Assume the company uses a perpetual inventory system.

Accounts Receivable	340,000	
Sales Revenue		340,000
(*to record the sales and receivables*)		

Cost of Goods Sold	250,000	
Finished Goods Inventory		250,000
(*to reduce Finished Goods Inventory and record Cost of Goods Sold*)		

8. The company incurred operating expenses of $60,000 during the month. Assume that 80% of these were for marketing and administrative salaries and the other 20% were lease and utility bills related to the corporate headquarters. The expenses will be paid later.

Salaries Expense ($60,000 × 80%)	48,000	
Lease and Utilities Expense ($60,000 × 20%)	12,000	
Salaries and Wages Payable		48,000
Accounts Payable		12,000
(to record all non-manufacturing costs incurred during the month)		

9. In order to prepare its January financial statements, the company had to close its Manufacturing Overhead account.

An analysis of the manufacturing overhead account *prior to closing* shows the following:

Manufacturing Overhead

(ACTUAL)	(ALLOCATED)
5,000	45,000
20,000	
18,000	
	2,000

Manufacturing Overhead	2,000	
Cost of Goods Sold		2,000
(to close the Manufacturing Overhead account to CGS)		

10. Prepare the January income statement for Fashion Fabrics based on the transactions recorded in Requirements 1 through 9.

	A	B	C	D
1	**Fashion Fabrics**			
2	**Income Statement**			
3	**For Month Ending January 31**			
4				
5	Sales Revenue	$ 340,000		
6	Less: Cost of Goods Sold**	248,000		
7	Gross Profit	92,000		
8	Less: Operating Expenses	60,000		
9	Operating Income	$ 32,000		
10				
11	(** $250,000 – $2,000 closing adjustment)			

Appendix 3A

How Do Service Firms Use Job Costing to Determine the Amount to Bill Clients?

So far in this chapter we have illustrated job costing in a manufacturing environment. However, job costing is also used by service firms (such as law firms, accounting firms, marketing firms, and consulting firms) and by tradespeople (such as plumbers, electricians, and auto mechanics). At these types of companies, the work performed for each individual client is considered a separate job. Service firms need to keep track of job costs so that they have a basis for billing their clients. As shown in Exhibit 3-22, the direct costs of serving the client are traced to the job, whereas the indirect costs of serving the client are allocated to the job.

7 Use job costing at a service firm as a basis for billing clients

EXHIBIT 3-22 Assigning Costs to Client Jobs

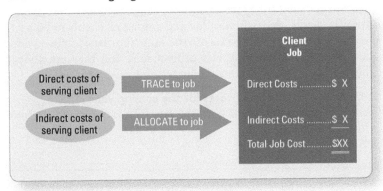

The amount billed to the client is determined by adding a profit markup to the total job cost. The main difference between job costing at a manufacturer and job costing at a service firm is that the indirect costs of serving the client are all *operating expenses* (period costs) rather than manufacturing (product) costs. In the next section, we will illustrate how job costing is used at the Bucaro & Associates law firm to determine how much to bill Client 367.

What Costs Are Considered Direct Costs of Serving a Client?

Professional labor is often the most significant direct cost at a service firm. It is considered a direct cost because professionals can use labor time records to keep track of the amount of time they spend performing work for individual clients. Because most professionals are paid an annual salary rather than an hourly wage rate, firms estimate the *hourly* professional labor cost based on the number of hours the professionals are expected to work during the year. For example, say Attorney Taylor Sweeney is paid a salary of $100,000 per year. The law firm she works for, Bucaro & Associates, expects her to spend 2,000 hours a year performing legal work for clients (50 weeks × 40 hours per week). Therefore, for job costing purposes, the law firm converts her annual salary to an hourly professional labor cost as follows:

$$\frac{\$100,000 \text{ annual salary}}{2,000 \text{ hours per year}} = \$50 \text{ per hour}$$

If the labor time record indicates that Sweeney has spent 14 hours on Client 367, then the direct professional labor cost traced to the client is calculated as follows:

14 hours × $50 per hour = $700 of direct professional labor

In addition to professional labor, any other costs that are readily identifiable with specific clients would be considered direct costs. For example, the law firm would be able to trace court filing fees to specific clients. Marketing firms would be able to trace the cost of placing print, billboard, and TV advertisements to specific clients. Plumbers, electricians, and auto mechanics would be able to trace materials (such as garbage disposals, lighting, and new tires) to specific clients. In summary, any cost that is traceable to a client would be considered a direct cost of serving the client.

What Costs Are Considered Indirect Costs of Serving a Client?

Service firms also incur general operating expenses, such as office rent, office supplies, and advertising. These costs are considered indirect because they can not be traced to individual clients. Rather, they are a joint cost of serving all clients. Since these costs cannot be traced to specific clients, they will be allocated among all clients using a *predetermined indirect cost allocation rate*. Service firms use the same four basic steps to allocate indirect costs as manufacturers use. The only real difference is that they are allocating indirect operating expenses, rather than indirect manufacturing costs (MOH).

STEP 1: Estimate the total indirect costs for the coming year.
Before the fiscal year begins, the law firm estimates the total indirect costs for the coming year:

Office rent	$190,000
Office supplies, telephone, internet access, and copier lease	10,000
Office support staff	70,000
Maintaining and updating law library for case research	25,000
Advertising	5,000
Total indirect costs	$300,000

STEP 2: Choose an allocation base and estimate the total amount that will be used during the year.
Next, the law firm chooses a cost allocation base. Service firms typically use professional labor hours as the cost allocation base. For example, Bucaro & Associates estimates that attorneys will spend a total of 10,000 professional labor hours working on client jobs throughout the coming year.

STEP 3: Compute the predetermined indirect cost allocation rate.
The predetermined indirect cost allocation rate is found as follows:

$$\text{Predetermined indirect cost allocation rate} = \frac{\text{Total estimated indirect costs}}{\text{Total estimated amount of the allocation base}}$$

$$= \frac{\$300,000 \text{ total indirect costs}}{10,000 \text{ professional labor hours}}$$

$$= \$30 \text{ per professional labor hour}$$

STEP 4: Allocate indirect costs to client jobs using the predetermined rate.
> Throughout the year, indirect costs are allocated to individual client jobs using the predetermined indirect cost allocation rate. For example, assume Taylor Sweeney spent 14 hours working on Client 367 and she was the only attorney who worked on this job. The amount of indirect cost allocated to the job is computed as follows:

> = Predetermined indirect cost allocation rate × Actual amount of allocation base used by the job
> = $30 per professional labor hour × 14 professional labor hours
> = $420

Finding the Total Cost of the Job and Adding a Profit Markup

Bucaro & Associates can now determine the total cost of serving Client 367:

Direct costs traced to Client 367 ($50 per hour × 14 hours).....................	$ 700
Indirect costs allocated to Client 367 ($30 per hour × 14 hours).............	420
Total cost of serving Client 367	$1,120

Once the total job cost is known, Bucaro & Associates can determine the amount to bill the client. Let's assume that Bucaro & Associates bills clients at 25% over its costs. Bucaro & Associates would bill Client 367 as follows:

> Job cost + Markup for profit = Amount to bill the client
> $1,120 + (25% × $1,120) = $1,400

Invoicing Clients Using a Professional Billing Rate

When service firms and tradespeople bill their clients, they don't show the actual direct costs of providing the service, the allocation of indirect costs, or the profit they earned on the job. Rather, these individual figures are hidden from the client's view. How is this done? By incorporating these costs and profit components in the labor rate, often known as the **billing rate**, charged to the customer. Consider the last time you had your vehicle repaired. A typical mechanic billing rate exceeds $48 per hour, yet the mechanic employed by the auto repair shop does not actually earn a $48-per-hour wage rate.

Let's look at the calculations a service firm performs "behind the scenes" to determine its hourly billing rates. Bucaro & Associates determines Taylor Sweeney's billing rate as follows:

> ■ **Why is this important?**
> "**Service** companies (such as **law firms**) and **tradespeople** (such as auto mechanics and plumbers) use **job costing** to determine how much to **bill** their clients."

Professional labor cost per hour...	$ 50
Plus: Indirect cost allocation rate per hour	30
Total hourly cost..	$ 80
Plus profit markup: (25% × $80 hourly cost).............................	+ 20
Hourly billing rate for Taylor Sweeney	$100

Whenever Taylor Sweeney performs legal work for a client, her time will be billed at $100 per hour. Remember, this is the *price* Bucaro & Associates charges its clients for any work performed by Taylor Sweeney. The actual invoice to Client 367 would look similar to Exhibit 3-23.

EXHIBIT 3-23 Invoice to Client

Bucaro & Associates Law Firm
Invoice: Client 367

Work performed the week of July 23: Researching and filing patent application

Attorney Taylor Sweeney: 14 hours × $100 hourly billing rate $1,400

What Journal Entries Are Needed in a Service Firm's Job Costing System?

The journal entries required for job costing at a service firm are much simpler than those used at a manufacturing company. That's because service firms typically have no inventory; hence, there is no need to record the movement of inventory through the system. Rather, all costs at a service company are treated as period costs, meaning they are immediately recorded as operating expenses in the period when they are incurred (for example, salary expense, rent expense, telephone expense, and advertising expense). The tracing of direct costs and the allocation of indirect costs is performed *only* on the client's job cost record, *not* through journal entries to the company's general ledger.

▶ Try It!

Sarah Haymeyer, CPA, pays her new staff accountant, Hannah, a salary equivalent to $25 per hour, while Sarah receives a salary equivalent to $40 per hour. The firm's predetermined indirect cost allocation rate for the year is $12 per hour. Haymeyer bills for the firm's services at 30% over cost. Assume Sarah works 5 hours and Hannah works 10 hours preparing a tax return for Michele Meckfessel.

1. What is the total cost of preparing Meckfessel's tax return?
2. How much will Sarah bill Meckfessel for the tax work?

Please see page 174 for solutions.

END OF CHAPTER

Learning Objectives

- ◼ 1 Distinguish between job costing and process costing
- ◼ 2 Understand the flow of production and how direct materials and direct labor are traced to jobs
- ◼ 3 Compute a predetermined manufacturing overhead rate and use it to allocate MOH to jobs
- ◼ 4 Determine the cost of a job and use it to make business decisions
- ◼ 5 Compute and dispose of overallocated or underallocated manufacturing overhead
- ◼ 6 Prepare journal entries for a manufacturer's job costing system
- ◼ 7 (Appendix) Use job costing at a service firm as a basis for billing clients

Accounting Vocabulary

Bill of Materials. (p. 109) A list of all of the raw materials needed to manufacture a job.

Billing Rate. (p. 145) The labor rate charged to the customer, which includes both cost and profit components.

Cost Driver. (p. 117) The primary factor that causes a cost.

Cost-Plus Pricing. (p. 120) A pricing approach in which the company adds a desired level of profit to the product's cost.

Extended Producer Responsibility (EPR). (p. 122) Laws that require product manufacturers to "take back" a large percentage of the products they manufacture at the end of the product's life in order to reduce the amount of waste ending up in landfills and the environment.

Invoice. (p. 110) Bill from a supplier.

Job Cost Record. (p. 110) A written or electronic document that lists the direct materials, direct labor, and manufacturing overhead costs assigned to each individual job.

Job Costing. (p. 106) A system for assigning costs to products or services that differ in the amount of materials, labor, and overhead required. Typically used by manufacturers that produce unique, or custom-ordered products in small batches; also used by professional service firms.

Labor Time Record. (p. 114) A written or electronic document that identifies the employee, the amount of time spent on a particular job, and the labor cost charged to a job.

Mass Customization. (p. 107) Large-scale production of customized product that allows manufacturers to meet a variety of consumer desires, while at the same time achieving the efficiencies of mass production that drive down unit costs.

Materials Requisition. (p. 113) A written or electronic document requesting that specific materials be transferred from the raw materials inventory storeroom to the production floor.

Overallocated Manufacturing Overhead. (p. 127) The amount of manufacturing overhead allocated to jobs is more than the amount of manufacturing overhead costs actually incurred; results in jobs being overcosted.

Pick. (p. 113) Storeroom workers remove items from raw materials inventory that are needed by production.

Predetermined Manufacturing Overhead Rate. (p. 117) The rate used to allocate manufacturing overhead to individual jobs; calculated before the year begins as follows: total estimated manufacturing overhead costs divided by total estimated amount of allocation base.

Process Costing. (p. 105) A system for assigning costs to a large number of identical units that typically pass through a series of uniform production steps. Costs are averaged over the units produced such that each unit bears the same unit cost.

Production Schedule. (p. 108) A written or electronic document indicating the quantity and types of inventory that will be manufactured during a specified time frame.

Purchase Order. (p. 110) A written or electronic document authorizing the purchase of specific raw materials from a specific supplier.

Raw Materials Record. (p. 109) A written or electronic document listing the number and cost of all units used and received, and the balance currently in stock; a separate record is maintained for each type of raw material kept in stock.

Receiving Report. (p. 110) A written or electronic document listing the quantity and type of raw materials received in an incoming shipment; the report is typically a duplicate of the purchase order without the quantity pre-listed on the form.

Stock Inventory. (p. 108) Products normally kept on hand in order to quickly fill customer orders.

Subsidiary Ledger. (p. 131) Supporting detail for a general ledger account.

Underallocated Manufacturing Overhead. (p. 127) The amount of manufacturing overhead allocated to jobs is less than the amount of manufacturing overhead costs actually incurred; this results in jobs being undercosted.

Quick Check

1. *(Learning Objective 1)* For which of the following would job costing *not* be appropriate?

   a. Electrician

   b. Manufacturer of mass-produced carbonated beverages

   c. Law firm

   d. Manufacturer of custom-ordered production equipment

2. *(Learning Objective 2)* Which of the following documents specifies the materials needed to produce a job?

   a. Bill of materials

   b. Raw materials records

   c. Receiving report

   d. Production schedule

3. *(Learning Objective 2)* Which of the following documents is used to accumulate all of the manufacturing costs assigned to a job?

   a. Labor time record

   b. Materials requisition

   c. Purchase order

   d. Job cost record

4. *(Learning Objective 3)* The amount of manufacturing overhead recorded on a job cost record for a particular job is found by

   a. tracing manufacturing overhead to the job.

   b. either tracing or allocating manufacturing overhead costs (management's choice).

   c. allocating manufacturing overhead to the job.

   d. None of the answers listed is correct.

5. *(Learning Objective 4)* Which of the following is *false*?

   a. Direct costing focuses on only the direct costs found on the job cost record.

   b. Job cost information is not useful for assessing the profitability of different products.

   c. A cost-plus price is determined by adding a markup to the cost.

   d. Non-manufacturing costs can be assigned to jobs only for internal decision making, never for external financial reporting.

6. *(Learning Objective 5)* Which of the following is *true*?

   a. If manufacturing overhead is underallocated, then jobs will be overcosted.

   b. If manufacturing overhead is overallocated, then jobs will be undercosted.

   c. Both of the statements are true.

   d. None of the statements is true.

7. *(Learning Objective 5)* Assuming the amount of manufacturing overhead overallocation or underallocation is not material, which account is adjusted at the end of the period?

   a. Sales Revenue

   b. Work in Process Inventory

   c. Raw Materials Inventory

   d. Cost of Goods Sold

8. *(Learning Objective 6)* Whenever direct material, direct labor, and manufacturing overhead are recorded on a job cost record, an associated journal entry is made to debit which of the following accounts?

   a. Sales Revenue

   b. Work in Process Inventory

   c. Cost of Goods Sold

   d. Finished Goods Inventory

9. *(Learning Objective 6)* When a job is completed, the total cost of manufacturing the job should be moved to which of the following general ledger accounts?

   a. Finished Goods Inventory

   b. Sales Revenue

   c. Cost of Goods Sold

   d. Work in Process Inventory

10. *(Learning Objective 7, Appendix)* Which of the following is *true* when using job costing at a service firm?

    a. Professional labor cost would be considered an indirect cost of serving the client.

    b. Office rent would be considered a direct cost of serving the client.

    c. Both direct and indirect costs are assigned to client jobs.

    d. The professional billing rate consists solely of the professionals' labor cost.

Quick Check Answers

1.b 2.a 3.d 4.c 5.b 6.d 7.d 8.b 9.a 10.c

Activity-Based Costing, Lean Operations, and the Costs of Quality

Learning Objectives

■ **1** Develop and use departmental overhead rates to allocate indirect costs

■ **2** Develop and use activity-based costing (ABC) to allocate indirect costs

■ **3** Understand the benefits and limitations of ABC/ABM systems

■ **4** Describe lean operations

■ **5** Describe and use the costs of quality framework

Andor Bujdoso/Alamy

Source: http://lifefitness.com

When Life Fitness began, it only had one product: the Lifecycle exercise bike. With time, Life Fitness expanded its product lines to include treadmills, elliptical cross-trainers, stair climbers, and strength-training equipment. As a result of increased product diversity and competition, managers often found they needed better, more accurate product cost information to help guide their business decisions. While a traditional job costing system ensures that the direct materials and direct labor traced to each job is correct, it doesn't always do an adequate job of allocating manufacturing overhead, especially when a company produces multiple product lines that use different amounts of indirect manufacturing resources. In such cases, managers benefit from using a refined cost allocation system: one that isn't based on a single, predetermined manufacturing overhead rate. Refined costing systems not only help managers more accurately determine the cost of individual jobs but also highlight the cost of wasteful activities in the production process. Armed with this knowledge, managers are able to make more profitable business decisions.

As the chapter-opening story illustrates, successful companies experience increased competition over time. In addition, companies often seek to expand their customer base by offering a more diversified line of products. Both of these factors are good for consumers, who now enjoy more product options at very competitive prices. However, these factors also present unique challenges to business managers and the accounting systems that support them. To thrive in a globally competitive market, companies must provide value to the customer by delivering a high-quality product at an attractive price, while managing costs so that the company still earns a profit. This chapter will introduce several tools that today's managers use to make their companies as competitive as possible:

- Refined costing systems
- Lean operations
- Total quality management and the costs of quality

Why and How Do Companies Refine Their Cost Allocation Systems?

The traditional overhead cost allocation system we described in Chapter 3 may not be accurate enough for some compaies. Why? Because under certain conditions, the simple system doesn't do a good job of matching the cost of overhead resources with the products that consume those resources. The following example illustrates why simple systems can lead to less-than-acceptable results.

Simple Cost Allocation Systems Can Lead to Cost Distortion

David, Matt, and Marc are three college friends who share an apartment. They agree to split the following monthly costs equally:

Rent, Internet, and utilities	$570
Cable TV	50
Covered parking fee	40
Groceries	240
Total monthly costs	**$900**

Each roommate's share is $300 (=$900/3).

Things go smoothly for the first few months. But then David calls a meeting: "Because I started having dinner at Amy's each night, I shouldn't have to chip in for the groceries." Matt then pipes in: "I'm so busy studying and using the Internet that I never have time to watch TV. I don't want to pay for the cable TV anymore. And Marc, because your friend Jennifer eats here most evenings, you should pay a double share of the grocery bill." Marc replies, "If that's the way you feel, Matt, then you should pay for the covered parking since you're the only one around here who uses it!"

What happened? The friends originally agreed to share the costs equally. But they are not participating equally in watching cable TV, using the covered parking, and eating the groceries. Splitting these costs equally is not equitable.

The roommates could use a cost allocation approach that better matches costs with the people who participate in the activities that cause those costs. This means splitting the cable TV costs between David and Marc, assigning the covered parking cost to Matt, and allocating the grocery bill one-third to Matt and two-thirds to Marc. Exhibit 4-1 compares the results of this refined cost allocation system with the original cost allocation system.

No wonder David called a meeting! The original cost allocation system charged him $300 a month, but the refined system shows that a more equitable share would be only $215. The new system allocates Marc $375 a month instead of $300. David was paying for resources he did not use (covered parking and groceries), while Marc was not paying for all of the resources (groceries) he and his guest consumed. The simple cost allocation

EXHIBIT 4-1 More Refined Versus Less Refined Cost Allocation System

A Allocation of Expenses	David	Matt	Marc	Total
More-refined cost allocation system:				
Rent, internet, and utilities	$190	$190	$190	$570
Cable TV	25	0	25	50
Covered parking	0	40	0	40
Groceries	0	80	160	240
Total cost allocated	$215	$310	$375	$900
Original cost allocation system:				
Equal allocation of expenses	$300	$300	$300	$900
Difference	($85)	$ 10	$ 75	$ 0

system the roommates initially devised had ended up distorting the cost that should be charged to each roommate: David was *overcharged* by $85 while Matt and Marc were *undercharged* by an equal, but offsetting, amount ($10 + $75 = $85). Notice that the total "pool" of monthly costs ($900) is the same under both allocation systems. The only difference is *how* the pool of costs is *allocated* among the three roommates.

Just as the simple allocation system had resulted in overcharging David, yet undercharging Matt and Marc, many companies find that the simple overhead cost allocation system described in the last chapter results in "overcosting" some of their jobs or products while "undercosting" others. <u>Cost distortion</u> occurs when some products are overcosted while other products are undercosted by the cost allocation system. As we'll see in the following sections, companies often refine their cost allocation systems to minimize the amount of cost distortion caused by the simpler cost allocation systems. By refining their costing systems, companies can more equitably assign indirect costs (such as manufacturing overhead) to their individual jobs, products, or services. As a result, less cost distortion occurs and managers have more accurate information for making vital business decisions.

In the following section, we will describe how refined cost allocation systems can be used to better allocate manufacturing overhead to specific products to reduce cost distortion. However, keep in mind that the same principles apply to allocating *any* indirect costs to *any* cost objects. Thus, even merchandising and service companies, as well as governmental agencies, can use these refined cost allocation systems to provide their managers with better cost information.

> **Why is this important?**
>
> "With better **cost information**, managers are able to make more **profitable** decisions. One company reported triple sales and a **five-fold increase** in profits after it implemented a **refined costing system**. By using better cost information for quoting jobs, **management** was able to generate a more **profitable mix** of job contracts."[1]

Review: Using a Plantwide Overhead Rate to Allocate Indirect Costs

In the last chapter, we assumed that Life Fitness allocated its manufacturing overhead (MOH) costs using one predetermined MOH rate ($16 per DL hour). This rate was based on management's estimate of the total manufacturing overhead costs for the year ($1 million) and its estimate of the total amount of the allocation base (62,500 DL hours) for the year.[2] The rate was calculated as follows:

$$\text{Predetermined MOH rate} = \frac{\$1,000,000}{62,500 \text{ DL hours}} = \$16 \text{ per direct labor hour}$$

[1]Douglas Hicks, "Yes, ABC Is for Small Business, Too," *Journal of Accountancy*, August 1999, p. 41.

[2]All references to Life Fitness in this hypothetical example were created by the authors solely for academic purposes and are not intended, in any way, to represent the actual business practices of, or costs incurred by, Life Fitness, Inc.

This rate is also known as a **plantwide overhead rate** because any job produced in the plant, whether it be treadmills, elliptical cross-trainers, or stair climbers, would be allocated manufacturing overhead using this single rate. It wouldn't matter whether the job was worked on in one department or many departments during the production process: The same rate would be used throughout the plant.

Let's see how this works for Life Fitness. Keep in mind that the company produces many different products and completes thousands of different jobs throughout the year. For simplicity of illustration, we will be following just two of those jobs:

- Job 101: One elliptical
- Job 102: One treadmill

In Chapter 3, we followed a job in which each elliptical cross-trainer required about 10 direct labor hours to make.[3] We'll continue to assume that each elliptical made by the company requires 10 direct labor hours to complete. Let's also assume that each treadmill requires 10 direct labor hours to complete. Exhibit 4-2 shows how manufacturing overhead would be allocated to a job in which one elliptical was made, and another job in which one treadmill was made, using the plantwide overhead rate.

EXHIBIT 4-2 Allocating Manufacturing Overhead Using a Plantwide Overhead Rate

	A	B	C	D	E	F	G	H	
1	Job	Plantwide Overhead Rate			Actual Use of Allocation Base			MOH Allocated to Job	
2	Job 101: One elliptical	$	16	per DL hour	×	10	DL hours	=	$ 160
3	Job 102: One treadmill	$	16	per DL hour	×	10	DL hours	=	$ 160
4									

NOTE: Arithmetic signs are only shown for illustrative teaching purposes. They are not typically displayed in spreadsheets.

The plantwide allocation system is illustrated in Exhibit 4-3.

EXHIBIT 4-3 Plantwide Allocation System

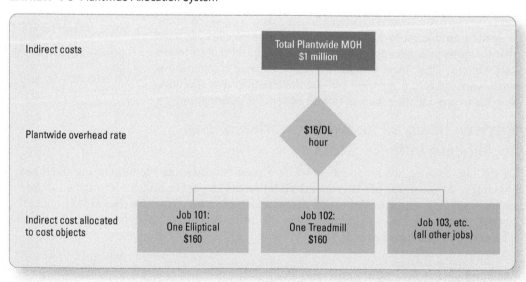

[3] Job 603, a batch of 50 elliptical cross-trainers, required 500 DL hours to complete. Thus, the average time spent on each unit was 10 DL hours.

Using Departmental Overhead Rates to Allocate Indirect Costs

The plantwide allocation system previously described works well for some companies but may end up distorting costs if the following conditions exist:

1. Different departments incur different amounts and types of manufacturing overhead.

2. Different jobs or products use the departments to a different extent.

If these circumstances exist, the company should strongly consider refining its cost allocation system. Let's see if these conditions exist at Life Fitness.

1 Develop and use departmental overhead rates to allocate indirect costs

CONDITION 1: DO DIFFERENT DEPARTMENTS HAVE DIFFERENT AMOUNTS AND TYPES OF MOH COSTS?   As shown in Exhibit 4-4, let's assume Life Fitness has two primary production departments: Machining and Assembly. The Machining Department has a lot of machinery, which drives manufacturing overhead costs such as machine depreciation, utilities, machine lubricants, and repairs and maintenance. Let's say these overhead costs are estimated to be $400,000 for the year. On the other hand, the Assembly Department does not incur as many of these types of overhead costs. Rather, the Assembly Department's manufacturing overhead costs include more indirect labor for supervision, quality inspection, and so forth. These manufacturing overhead costs are expected to total $600,000 for the year.

Exhibit 4-4 shows that the first condition is present: Each department incurs different types and amounts of MOH. Life Fitness expects to incur a total of $1 million of manufacturing overhead: $400,000 relates to the Machining Department, while $600,000 relates to the Assembly Department.

EXHIBIT 4-4 Machining and Assembly Departments' Manufacturing Overhead

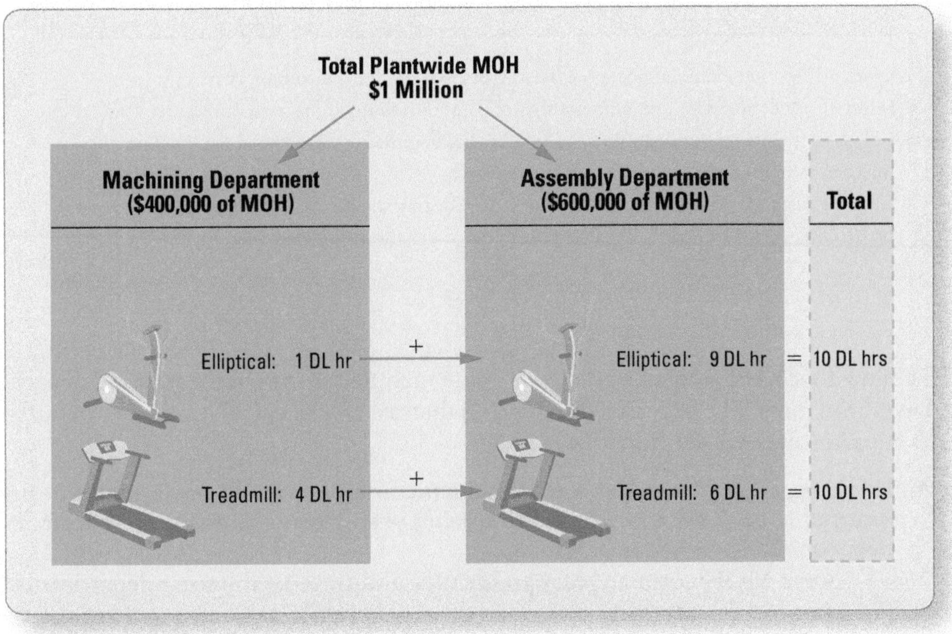

CONDITION 2: DO DIFFERENT PRODUCTS USE THE DEPARTMENTS TO A DIFFERENT EXTENT?   Although both ellipticals and treadmills take 10 direct labor hours in total to make, Exhibit 4-4 also shows that ellipticals and treadmills spend *different* amounts of time in each production department. Each elliptical only requires 1 DL hour in the Machining Department but requires 9 DL hours in the Assembly Department. Contrast that with a treadmill, which spends more time in Machining to fabricate some of its components (4 DL hours) but less time in Assembly (6 DL hours). As a result of these

differences, the second condition is also present. The company's cost allocation system would be much more accurate if it took these differences into account when determining how much manufacturing overhead to allocate to each product.

Since both conditions are present, the company should consider "fine-tuning" its cost allocation systems by establishing separate manufacturing overhead rates, known as **departmental overhead rates,** for each department. That means that Life Fitness will establish one manufacturing overhead rate for the Machining Department and another overhead rate for the Assembly Department. These rates will then be used to allocate manufacturing overhead to jobs or products based on the extent to which each product uses the different manufacturing departments.

Exhibit 4-5 shows the circumstances favoring the use of departmental overhead rates rather than a single, plantwide overhead rate.

EXHIBIT 4-5 Circumstances Favoring Use of Departmental Overhead Rates

Departmental overhead rates increase the accuracy of job costs when . . .

- Each department incurs different types and amounts of manufacturing overhead.
- Each product, or job, uses the departments to a different extent.

Four Basic Steps to Computing and Using Departmental Overhead Rates

In Chapter 3, we used four steps for allocating manufacturing overhead. These steps are summarized in Exhibit 4-6.

EXHIBIT 4-6 Four Basic Steps for Allocating Manufacturing Overhead

1. Estimate the total manufacturing overhead costs (MOH) for the coming year.
2. Select an allocation base and estimate the total amount that will be used during the year.
3. Calculate the predetermined overhead rate by dividing the total estimated MOH costs by the total estimated amount of the allocation base.
4. Allocate some MOH cost to each job worked on during the year by multiplying the predetermined MOH rate by the actual amount of the allocation base used by the job.

The same four basic steps are used to allocate manufacturing overhead using departmental overhead rates. The only real difference is that we will be calculating *separate rates* for *each* department. Let's see how this is done.

STEP 1: The company estimates the total manufacturing overhead costs that will be incurred in *each department* in the coming year. These estimates are known as departmental overhead cost pools.

Some MOH costs are easy to identify and trace to different departments. For example, management can trace the cost of lease payments and repairs to the machines used in the Machining Department. Management can also trace the cost of employing supervisors and quality control inspectors to the Assembly Department. However, other overhead costs are more difficult to identify with specific departments. For example, the depreciation, property taxes, and insurance on the entire plant would have to be split, or allocated, between the individual departments, most likely based on the square footage occupied by each department in the plant.

As shown in Exhibit 4-4, Life Fitness has determined that $400,000 of its total estimated MOH relates to its Machining Department, while the remaining $600,000 relates to its Assembly Department.

Department	Total Departmental Overhead Cost Pool
Machining Department	$ 400,000
Assembly Department	$ 600,000
TOTAL MOH	$1,000,000

STEP 2: **The company selects an allocation base for *each department* and estimates the total amount that will be used during the year.**

The allocation base selected for each department should be the cost driver of the costs in the departmental overhead pool. Often, manufacturers will use different allocation bases for the different departments. For example, machine hours might be the best allocation base for a very automated Machining Department that uses machine robotics extensively. However, direct labor hours might be the best allocation base for an Assembly Department.

Let's assume that Life Fitness's Machining Department uses a lot of human-operated machinery; therefore, the number of direct labor hours used in the department is identical to the number of hours the machines are run. While the number of machine hours is the real cost driver, direct labor hours will make an adequate surrogate. As a result, management has selected direct labor hours as the allocation base for both departments. Recall that Life Fitness estimates using a total of 62,500 direct labor hours during the year. Of this amount, management expects to use 12,500 in the Machining Department and 50,000 in the Assembly Department.

Department	Total Amount of Departmental Allocation Base
Machining Department	12,500 DL hours
Assembly Department	50,000 DL hours

STEP 3: **The company calculates departmental overhead rates using the information estimated in Steps 1 and 2:**

$$\text{Departmental overhead rate} = \frac{\text{Total estimated departmental overhead cost pool}}{\text{Total estimated amount of the departmental allocation base}}$$

Therefore, Life Fitness calculates its departmental overhead rates as follows:

$$\text{Machining Department overhead rate} = \frac{\$400,000}{12,500 \text{ DL hours}} = \$32 \text{ per DL hour}$$

$$\text{Assembly Department overhead rate} = \frac{\$600,000}{50,000 \text{ DL hours}} = \$12 \text{ per DL hour}$$

These first three steps are performed before the year begins, using estimated data for the year. Thus, departmental overhead rates are also "predetermined," just like the plant-wide predetermined manufacturing overhead rate discussed in Chapter 3. The first three steps, performed before the year begins, are summarized in Exhibit 4-7.

EXHIBIT 4-7 Steps to Calculating the Departmental Overhead Rates

	A	B	C	D	E	F	G	H
1	Department	Step 1: Total Departmental Overhead Cost Pool		Step 2: Total Amount of Departmental Allocation Base			Step 3: Departmental Overhead Rate	
2	Machining	$ 400,000	÷	12,500	DL hours	=	$ 32	per DL hour
3	Assembly	$ 600,000	÷	50,000	DL hours	=	$ 12	per DL hour
4								

NOTE: Arithmetic signs are only shown for illustrative teaching purposes. They are not typically displayed in spreadsheets.

Once these rates have been established, the company uses them throughout the year to allocate manufacturing overhead to each job as it is produced, as shown in Step 4.

STEP 4: The company allocates some manufacturing overhead from each department to the individual jobs that use those departments.

The amount of MOH allocated from each department is calculated as follows:

MOH allocated to job = Departmental overhead rate × Actual amount of departmental allocation base used by job

Exhibit 4-8 shows how these departmental overhead rates would be used to allocate manufacturing overhead to a job in which one elliptical is produced.

EXHIBIT 4-8 Allocating MOH to One Elliptical Using Departmental Overhead Rates

	A	B	C	D	E	F	G	H
1	Department	Departmental Overhead Rate (from Exhibit 4-7)			Actual Use of Departmental Allocation Base (from Exhibit 4-4)			MOH Allocated to Job 101: One Elliptical
2	Machining	$ 32	per DL hour	×	1	DL hours	=	$ 32
3	Assembly	$ 12	per DL hour	×	9	DL hours	=	$ 108
4	Total							$ 140

NOTE: Arithmetic signs are only shown for illustrative teaching purposes. They are not typically displayed in spreadsheets.

Exhibit 4-9 shows how the same rates would be used to allocate manufacturing overhead to another job in which one treadmill is produced. Because the treadmill spends more time in the Machining Department, but less time in the Assembly Department, the amount of MOH allocated to the treadmill differs from the amount allocated to the elliptical in Exhibit 4-8.

EXHIBIT 4-9 Allocating MOH to One Treadmill Using Departmental Overhead Rates

	A	B	C	D	E	F	G	H
1	Department	Departmental Overhead Rate (from Exhibit 4-7)			Actual Use of Departmental Allocation Base (from Exhibit 4-4)			MOH Allocated to Job 102: One Treadmill
2	Machining	$ 32	per DL hour	×	4	DL hours	=	$ 128
3	Assembly	$ 12	per DL hour	×	6	DL hours	=	$ 72
4	Total							$ 200
5								

NOTE: Arithmetic signs are only shown for illustrative teaching purposes. They are not typically displayed in spreadsheets.

Exhibit 4-10 illustrates the company's departmental cost allocation system.

EXHIBIT 4-10 Departmental Cost Allocation System

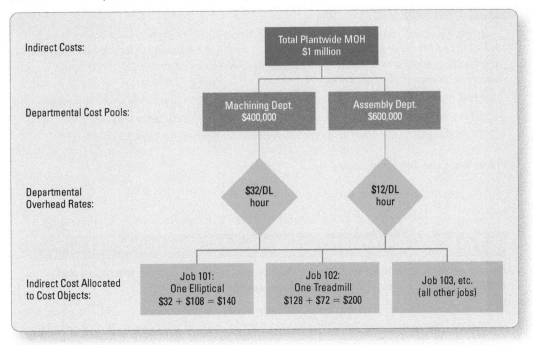

Had the Plantwide Overhead Rate Been Distorting Product Costs?

We have just seen that Life Fitness's refined cost allocation system allocates $140 of MOH to each elliptical and $200 of MOH to each treadmill (Exhibits 4-8 and 4-9). Does this differ from the amount that would have been allocated to each unit using Life Fitness's original plantwide rate? Yes. Recall from Exhibit 4-2 that if Life Fitness uses a plantwide overhead rate, $160 of manufacturing overhead would be allocated to both types of equipment, simply because both types of equipment require the *same total* number of direct labor hours (10 DL hours) to produce.

The plantwide allocation system does not pick up on the nuances of how many direct labor hours are used by the products in *each* department. Therefore, it was not able to do a very good job of matching manufacturing overhead costs to the products that use those costs. As a result, the plantwide rate would have overcosted each elliptical but undercosted each treadmill, as shown in Exhibit 4-11.

EXHIBIT 4-11 Cost Distortion Caused by Plantwide Overhead Rate

	Plantwide Overhead Rate MOH Allocation (from Exhibit 4-2)	Departmental Overhead Rates MOH Allocation (from Exhibits 4-8 and 4-9)	Amount of Cost Distortion
Job 101: One Elliptical	$160	$140	$20 *overcosted*
Job 102: One Treadmill	$160	$200	$40 *undercosted*

On the other hand, the refined cost allocation system recognizes the cost differences between departments and the usage difference between jobs. Therefore, the refined costing system does a *better job of matching* each department's overhead costs to the products that use the department's resources. This is the same thing we saw with the three roommates: The refined costing system did a better job of matching the cost of resources (cable, covered parking, groceries) to the roommates who used those resources. Because of this better matching, we believe that the departmental overhead rates *more accurately allocate* MOH costs than does a single plantwide overhead rate.

▶ Try It!

Assume a job with one stair climber requires 5 direct labor (DL) hours to produce: 3 DL hours in the Machining Department and 2 DL hours in the Assembly Department. Use the plantwide overhead rate and departmental allocation rates computed in the chapter example to answer the following:

1. How much MOH would be allocated to the job using the plantwide overhead rate?
2. How much MOH would be allocated to the job using the departmental overhead rates?
3. Does the plantwide overhead rate overcost or undercost the job? By how much?

Please see page 244 for solutions.

STOP & THINK

Do companies always have separate production departments, such as Machining and Assembly, for each step of the production process?

Answer: No. Rather than basing production departments on separate processing steps, some companies have separate production departments for each of their products. For example, Life Fitness could have one department for producing treadmills, another department for producing ellipticals, and yet another department for producing stair climbers. Each department would have all of the machinery and equipment necessary for producing its unique product. Departmental overhead rates would be formulated using the same four basic steps just discussed to determine a unique departmental overhead rate for each department. The only difference is that each product (for example, a treadmill) would travel through *only one* department (the Treadmill Department) rather than traveling through separate production departments (Machining and Assembly). Always keep in mind that the accounting system should reflect the actual production environment.

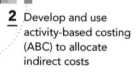

2 Develop and use activity-based costing (ABC) to allocate indirect costs

Using Activity-Based Costing to Allocate Indirect Costs

We just saw how companies can refine their cost allocation systems by using departmental overhead rates. If a company wants an even more refined system, one that reduces cost distortion to a minimum, it will use activity-based costing (ABC). **Activity-based costing (ABC)** focuses on *activities*, rather than departments, as the fundamental cost objects. ABC recognizes that activities are costly to perform, and each product manufactured may require different types and amounts of activities. Thus, activities become the building blocks for compiling the indirect costs of products, services, and customers. Companies can use ABC to more accurately estimate the cost of resources required to produce different products, to render different services, and to serve different customers.

Think about the three roommates for a moment. The most equitable and accurate cost allocation system for the roommates was one in which the roommates were charged only for the *activities* in which they participated, and the *extent* to which they participated in those activities. Likewise, activity-based costing generally causes the *least* amount of cost distortion among products because indirect costs are allocated to the products based on the (1) *types* of activities used by the product and (2) the *extent* to which the activities are used.

Four Basic Steps to Computing and Using Activity Cost Allocation Rates

ABC requires the same four basic steps listed in Exhibit 4-6. The main difference between an ABC system and a plantwide or departmental cost allocation system is that ABC systems have *separate* cost allocation rates for *each activity* identified by the company.

STEP 1: The company first identifies its primary activities and then estimates the total manufacturing overhead costs associated with *each activity*. These are known as activity cost pools.

Let's assume Life Fitness has determined that the following activities occur in its plant: First, the machines must be set up to meet the particular specifications of the production run. Next, raw materials must be moved out of the storeroom and into the Machining Department, where some of the parts for the units are fabricated. Once the parts have been fabricated, they are moved into the Assembly Department, along with additional raw materials that are needed from the storeroom. The units are then assembled by direct laborers, while production engineers supervise the process. All units are inspected after assembly. Upon passing inspection, each unit is packaged so that it is not damaged during shipment. Finally, the units are moved to the finished goods warehouse where they await shipment to customers. These activities are pictured in Exhibit 4-12.

EXHIBIT 4-12 Primary Activities Identified in the Manufacturing Plant

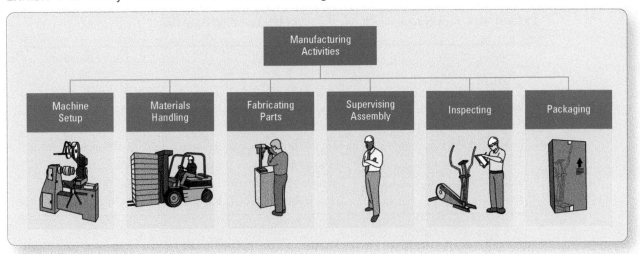

As part of this step, management must determine how much of the total estimated $1 million of MOH relates to each activity. Exhibit 4-13 shows some of the specific MOH costs that management has identified with each activity, along with the total estimated amount of each activity cost pool.

EXHIBIT 4-13 Activity Cost Pools

Activity	MOH Costs Related to the Activity	Total Activity Cost Pool
Machine Setup	Indirect labor used to set up machines	$ 80,000
Materials Handling	Forklifts, gas, operators' wages	200,000
Fabricating Parts	Machine lease payments, electricity, repairs	300,000
Supervising Assembly	Production engineers' labor	150,000
Inspecting	Testing equipment, inspection labor	170,000
Packaging	Packaging equipment	100,000
	TOTAL MOH	$1,000,000

Keep in mind that all of the costs in the activity costs pools are MOH costs; direct labor costs and direct materials costs are *not included* because they will be directly traced to specific jobs and therefore do not need to be allocated. That is why we only include supervisory labor in the overhead cost pool for the assembly activity. The machine operators and assembly-line workers are considered direct labor, so their cost will be traced to individual jobs, not allocated as part of MOH.

STEP 2: **The company selects an allocation base for each activity and estimates the total amount that will be used during the year.**

When selecting an allocation base for each activity, the company should keep the following in mind:

- The allocation base selected for each activity should be the *cost driver* of the costs in that particular activity cost pool.

- The company will need to keep track of how much of the allocation base each job or product uses. Therefore, the company must have the means to collect usage information about each allocation base. Thankfully, bar coding and other technological advances have helped make data collection easier and less costly in recent years.

Let's assume that Life Fitness has identified a cost driver for each activity and has plans for how it will collect usage data. Exhibit 4-14 shows the selected allocation bases along with the total estimated amounts for the year.

EXHIBIT 4-14 Activity Allocation Bases and Total Estimated Amount of Each

Activity	Activity Allocation Base	Total Estimated Amount of Allocation Base
Machine Setup	Number of setups	8,000 setups
Materials Handling	Number of parts moved	400,000 parts
Fabricating Parts	Machine hours	12,500 machine hours
Supervising Assembly	Direct labor hours	50,000 DL hours
Inspecting	Number of inspections	34,000 inspections
Packaging	Cubic feet packaged	400,000 cubic feet

STEP 3: **The company calculates its activity cost allocation rates using the information estimated in Steps 1 and 2.**

The formula for calculating the activity cost allocation rates is as follows:

$$\text{Activity cost allocation rate} = \frac{\text{Total estimated activity cost pool}}{\text{Total estimated activity allocation base}}$$

Exhibit 4-15 shows how this formula is used to compute a unique cost allocation rate for each of the company's production activities.

EXHIBIT 4-15 Computing Activity Cost Allocation Rates

	A	B	C	D	E	F	G	H
1	**Activity**	**Step 1: Total Activity Cost Pool (from Exhibit 4-13)**		**Step 2: Total Amount of Activity Allocation Base (from Exhibit 4-14)**			**Step 3: Activity Cost Allocation Rate**	
2	Machine Setup	$ 80,000	÷	8,000	setups	=	$ 10.00	per setup
3	Materials Handling	200,000	÷	400,000	parts	=	$ 0.50	per part
4	Fabricating Parts	300,000	÷	12,500	machine hours	=	$ 24.00	per machine hour
5	Supervising Assembly	150,000	÷	50,000	DL hours	=	$ 3.00	per DL hour
6	Inspecting	170,000	÷	34,000	inspections	=	$ 5.00	per inspection
7	Packaging	100,000	÷	400,000	cubic feet	=	$ 0.25	per cubic foot
8	Total MOH	$ 1,000,000						
9								

NOTE: Arithmetic signs are only shown for illustrative teaching purposes. They are not typically displayed in spreadsheets.

Once again, these rates are calculated based on estimated, or budgeted, costs for the year. Hence, they too are "predetermined" before the year begins. Then, during the year, the company uses them to allocate manufacturing overhead to specific jobs, as shown in Step 4.

STEP 4: **The company allocates some manufacturing overhead from each activity to the individual jobs that use the activities.**

The formula is as follows:

MOH allocated to job = Activity cost allocation rate × Actual amount of activity allocation base used by job

Exhibit 4-16 shows how these activity cost allocation rates would be used to allocate manufacturing overhead to Job 101, in which one elliptical was produced.

EXHIBIT 4-16 Allocating MOH to Job 101 (One Elliptical) Using ABC

	A	B	C	D	E	F	G	H
1	Activity	Activity Cost Allocation Rate (from Exhibit 4-15)			Actual Use of Activity Allocation Base (information collected on job cost record)			MOH Allocated to Job 101: One Elliptical
2	Machine Setup	$10.00	per setup	×	2	setups	= $	20
3	Materials Handling	$ 0.50	per part	×	20	parts	=	10
4	Fabricating Parts	$24.00	per machine hour	×	1	machine hours	=	24
5	Supervising Assembly	$ 3.00	per DL hour	×	9	DL hours	=	27
6	Inspecting	$ 5.00	per inspection	×	3	inspections	=	15
7	Packaging	$ 0.25	per cubic foot	×	52	cubic feet	=	13
8	Total						$	109
9								

NOTE: Arithmetic signs are only shown for illustrative teaching purposes. They are not typically displayed in spreadsheets.

Exhibit 4-17 shows how the same activity cost allocation rates are used to allocate MOH to Job 102, in which one treadmill was produced.

EXHIBIT 4-17 Allocating MOH to Job 102 (One Treadmill) Using ABC

	A	B	C	D	E	F	G	H
1	Activity	Activity Cost Allocation Rate (from Exhibit 4-15)			Actual Use of Activity Allocation Base (information collected on job cost record)			MOH Allocated to Job 102: One Treadmill
2	Machine Setup	$10.00	per setup	×	4	setups	= $	40
3	Materials Handling	$ 0.50	per part	×	26	parts	=	13
4	Fabricating Parts	$24.00	per machine hour	×	4	machine hours	=	96
5	Supervising Assembly	$ 3.00	per DL hour	×	6	DL hours	=	18
6	Inspecting	$ 5.00	per inspection	×	6	inspections	=	30
7	Packaging	$ 0.25	per cubic foot	×	60	cubic feet	=	15
8	Total						$	212
9								

NOTE: Arithmetic signs are only shown for illustrative teaching purposes. They are not typically displayed in spreadsheets.

Exhibit 4-18 illustrates the company's ABC system.

EXHIBIT 4-18 Illustration of the Company's ABC System

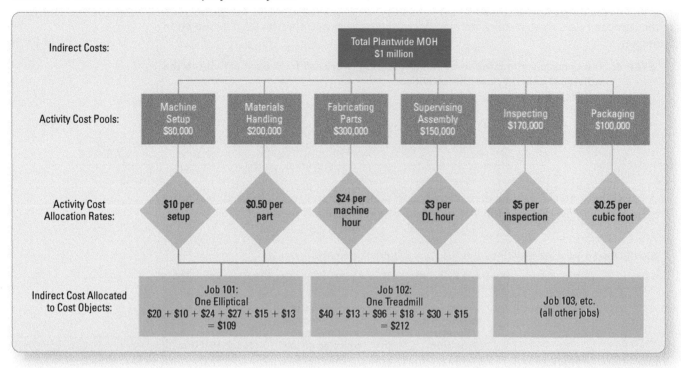

One Last Look at Cost Distortion: Comparing the Three Allocation Systems

Exhibit 4-19 compares the amount of manufacturing overhead that would have been allocated to each elliptical and each treadmill using the three cost allocation systems that we have discussed: (1) a single plantwide overhead rate, (2) departmental overhead rates, and (3) ABC.

EXHIBIT 4-19 Comparing the Three Cost Allocation Systems

	Plantwide Overhead Rate (Exhibit 4-2)	Departmental Overhead Rates (Exhibit 4-8 & 4-9)	Activity-Based Costing (Exhibit 4-16 & 4-17)
Job 101: One Elliptical	$160	$140	$109
Job 102: One Treadmill	$160	$200	$212

As you can see, each allocation system renders different answers for the amount of MOH that should be allocated to each elliptical and treadmill. Which is correct? Keep the following important rule of thumb in mind:

ABC costs are generally thought to be the most accurate because ABC takes into account (1) the *specific resources* each product uses (for example, inspecting resources) and (2) the extent to which they use these resources (for example, each elliptical required *three* inspections, while each treadmill required *six* inspections.

Exhibit 4-19 shows that the plantwide rate had been severely distorting costs: The elliptical had been overcosted by $51 ($160 − $109), and the treadmill had been undercosted by $52 ($160 − $212). Here, we have only looked at two jobs produced during the year. However, the following rule of thumb holds true:

> If we consider all of the jobs and products the company produced during the year, we will see that the *total amount* by which some products have been *overcosted* will equal the total amount by which other products have been *undercosted*.

Why? Because $1 million of MOH is being allocated: If some products are allocated too much MOH, then other products are allocated too little MOH.

Keep in mind that cost distortion is solely a result of the way indirect costs (manufacturing overhead) are allocated. The direct costs of each product (direct materials and direct labor) are known with certainty because of the precise way in which they are traced to jobs.

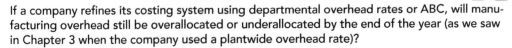

STOP & THINK

If a company refines its costing system using departmental overhead rates or ABC, will manufacturing overhead still be overallocated or underallocated by the end of the year (as we saw in Chapter 3 when the company used a plantwide overhead rate)?

Answer: Yes. The use of *any predetermined* allocation rate will result in the over- or under-allocation of manufacturing overhead. That's because *predetermined* rates are developed using *estimated* data before the actual manufacturing overhead costs and actual cost driver activity for the year are known. Refined costing systems decrease cost distortion *between* products but do not eliminate the issue of over- or underallocating total manufacturing overhead.[4] As described in Chapter 3, the Cost of Goods Sold account will need to be adjusted at year-end for the *total* amount by which manufacturing overhead has been over- or underallocated.

Sustainability and Refined Costing Systems

Refined costing systems are almost always a necessity for companies that wish to move toward environmental sustainability. Why? Because jobs and product lines do not drive environmental overhead costs equally. Even a smaller manufacturing company with only two or three product lines will often find that environmental-related overhead costs, such as:

- solid waste disposal
- water use
- energy consumption
- hazardous materials handling and training
- air emissions

are not driven equally between each product line. If a company uses a single plantwide overhead rate, environmental and nonenvironmental overhead costs will be combined within one cost pool, where they will be allocated to each of the company's product lines using the same rate.

However, refined costing systems allow companies to identify the activities driving environmental costs and separately pool and allocate these costs to the appropriate products. As a result, management will have a clearer picture of the envirommental impact of its products and can use that information to work on reducing the company's environmental footprint. This information can also be used if the company is required to report environmental impact information to its customers upstream in the supply chain (for example, Walmart and Costco assess the environmental and social impact of their suppliers).

See Exercises E4-21A and E4-32B

---

[4] In some cases, ABC may reduce the total amount of over- or underallocation of manufacturing overhead costs. How? Some activity cost pools may be overallocated, while others are underallocated, resulting in an offsetting total effect.

The Cost Hierarchy: A Useful Guide for Setting Up Activity Cost Pools

Some companies use a classification system, called the cost hierarchy, to establish activity cost pools. Companies often have hundreds of different activities. However, to keep the ABC system manageable, companies need to keep the system as simple as possible, yet refined enough to accurately determine product costs.[5] The cost hierarchy, pictured in Exhibit 4-20, helps managers understand the nature of each activity cost pool and what drives it.

EXHIBIT 4-20 The Cost Hierarchy

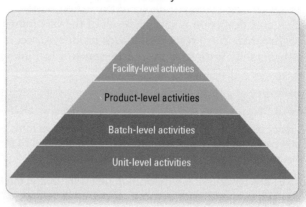

There are four categories of activity costs in this hierarchy, each determined by the underlying factor that drives its costs:

1. <u>Unit-level activities</u>—activities and costs incurred for every unit. Examples include inspecting and packaging *each* unit the company produces.

2. <u>Batch-level activities</u>—activities and costs incurred for every batch, regardless of the number of units in the batch. One example would be machine setup. Once the machines are set up for the specifications of the production run, the company could produce a batch of 1, 10, or 100 units, yet the company only incurs the machine setup cost once for the entire batch.

3. <u>Product-level activities</u>—activities and costs incurred for a particular product, regardless of the number of units or batches of the product produced. One example would be the lease payments on equipment used solely for manufacturing a particular product.

4. <u>Facility-level activities</u>—activities and costs incurred no matter how many units, batches, or products are produced in the plant. An example is facility upkeep: the cost of depreciation, insurance, property tax, and maintenance on the entire production plant.

By considering how the costs of different activities are consumed (at the unit, batch, product, or facility level), managers are often able to maintain a relatively simple, yet relatively accurate, ABC system. After initially identifying perhaps 100 different activities, managers may be able to settle on 5–15 cost pools by combining those activities that behave the same way into the same cost pools. For example, all batch-level costs might be combined into one cost pool that is allocated based on number of batches produced. Since facility-level costs do not have any particular cost driver, they are sometimes combined together in their own cost pool where they are allocated using a simple volume-based allocation base such as direct labor or machine hours, much like we saw in Chapter 3. Keep in mind that the cost hierarchy is simply a tool for helping managers think about costs and what drives them.

[5] When ABC system implementations fail, it is often due to managers' development of an overly complex system with too many cost pools and too many different cost drivers. After several redesigns of their ABC systems, Coca-Cola and Allied Signal both found that the simpler designs resulted in just as much accuracy. G. Cokins, "Learning to Love ABC," *Journal of Accountancy*, August 1999, pp. 37–39.

STOP & THINK

Do the journal entries used to record job costing differ if a manufacturer uses a refined cost allocation system (departmental overhead rates or ABC) rather than a single, plantwide overhead rate?

Answer: The journal entries used for a refined costing system are essentially the same as those described in Chapter 3 for a traditional job costing system. The only difference is that the company will typically use *several* MOH accounts (one for each department or activity cost pool) rather than *one* MOH account. By using several MOH accounts, the manufacturer obtains more detailed information on each cost pool. This information may help managers make better estimates when calculating allocation rates the next year.

How Do Managers Use the Refined Cost Information to Improve Operations?

We've just seen how companies can increase the accuracy of their product costing systems by using departmental overhead rates or ABC. Now let's consider how managers use this improved cost information to run their companies more effectively and efficiently.

3 Understand the benefits and limitations of ABC/ABM systems

Activity-Based Management (ABM)

Activity-based management (ABM) refers to using activity-based cost information to make decisions that increase profits while satisfying customers' needs. Companies can use ABC information for pricing and product mix decisions, for identifying opportunities to cut costs, and for routine planning and control decisions.

Pricing and Product Mix Decisions

Earlier in the chapter, our ABC example showed managers that ellipticals cost *less* to make and treadmills cost *more* to make than indicated by the original plantwide cost allocation system. As a result, managers may decide to change pricing on these products. For example, the company may be able to reduce its price on ellipticals to become more price-competitive. Or the company may decide to capitalize on the extra profitability of the product by leaving the price where it is but increasing demand by placing more advertisements for ellipticals. On the other hand, managers will want to reevaluate the price charged for treadmills. The price must be high enough to cover the cost of producing and selling the treadmills while still being low enough to compete with other companies and earn Life Fitness a reasonable profit.

After implementing ABC, companies often realize they are overcosting their high-volume products and undercosting their low-volume products. Plantwide overhead rates based on volume-sensitive allocation bases (such as direct labor hours) end up allocating more cost to high-volume products and less cost to low-volume products. However, ABC recognizes that not all indirect costs are driven by the number of units produced. That is to say, not all costs are unit-level costs. Rather, many costs are incurred at the batch level or product level, where they can be spread over the number of batches or product lines. As shown in Exhibit 4-21, ABC tends to increase the unit cost of low-volume products (that have fewer units over which to spread batch-level and product-level costs), and decrease the unit cost of high-volume products.

As a result of using ABC, some companies have found that they were actually losing money on some of their products while earning much more profit than they had realized on other products! By shifting the mix of products offered away from the less profitable and toward the more profitable, companies are able to generate a higher operating income.

Cutting Costs

Most companies adopt ABC to get more accurate product costs for pricing and product mix decisions, but they often reap even *greater benefits* by using ABM to pinpoint opportunities to cut costs. For example, the ABC data calculated in Exhibit 4-15 showed

EXHIBIT 4-21 Typical Result of ABC Costing

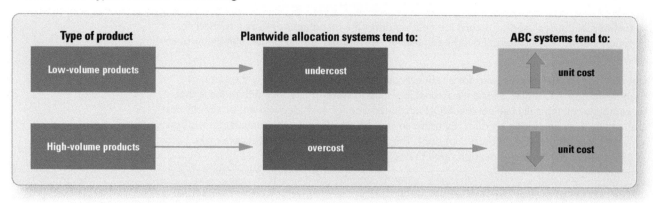

managers that each inspection costs $5, each machine setup costs $10, each part costs $0.50 to move, and so forth. This information gives production managers a starting place for cutting costs.

Once managers identify the company's activities and their related costs, managers can analyze whether all of the activities are really necessary. As the term suggests, <u>value-added activities</u> are activities for which the customer is willing to pay because these activities add value to the final product or service. In other words, these activities help satisfy the customer's expectations of the product or service. For example, fabricating component parts and assembling the units are value-added activities because they are necessary for changing raw materials into high-quality ellipticals and treadmills.

On the other hand, <u>non-value-added activities</u> (also referred to as <u>waste activities</u>), neither enhance the customer's image of the product or service nor provide a competitive advantage. These types of activities could be reduced or removed from the process with no ill effect on the end product or service. The primary goal of lean thinking, which is described in the second half of the chapter, is to make the company's processes as efficient as possible by eliminating all wasteful activities.

One way of determining whether an activity adds value is to ask if it could be eliminated or reduced by improving another part of the process. For example, could the movement of parts be eliminated or reduced by changing the factory layout? Could inventory storage be eliminated if the company only purchased the raw materials that were needed for each day's production run? Could inspection be reduced if more emphasis was placed on improving the production process, training employees, or using better-quality inputs? In the second half of the chapter we'll discuss tools that many companies have adopted to identify and eliminate these costly non-value-added activities.

Routine Planning and Control Decisions

In addition to pricing, product mix, and cost-cutting decisions, companies can use ABC in routine planning and control. Activity-based budgeting uses the costs of activities to create budgets. Managers can compare actual activity costs to budgeted activity costs to determine how well they are achieving their goals.

Using ABC Across the Value Chain and in Service and Merchandising Companies

Our chapter example revolved around using refined costing systems at a manufacturer to more accurately allocate manufacturing overhead costs. However, ABC can be used to identify the cost of *all* activities across the value chain associated with particular jobs, products, and services. For example, using ABC, a company can better determine the costs of designing or marketing new or existing products and services. It can also calculate the cost of providing customer service to different clients. The 80%/20% rule generally holds: 20% of clients often provide 80% of the company's profits once all the activities incurred on behalf of "needy" clients is taken into consideration. By more accurately allocating the cost of all activities across the value chain, businesses can focus on their most profitable products, services, and customers.

Merchandising and service companies also find ABC useful. For example, Walmart may use ABC to allocate the cost of store operating activities such as ordering, stocking, and customer service among its Housewares, Clothing, and Electronics Departments. An accounting firm may use ABC to allocate secretarial support, software costs, and travel costs between its tax, audit, and consulting clients. To implement ABC, these companies use the same four basic steps discussed earlier but apply them to indirect *operating* costs rather than indirect *manufacturing* costs (MOH). Once again, managers can use the data generated by ABC to determine which products or services to emphasize, to set prices, to cut costs, and to make other routine planning and control decisions.

STOP & THINK

Can governmental agencies use ABC/ABM to run their operations more efficiently?

Answer: Yes. ABC/ABM is not just for private-sector companies. The City of Indianapolis was able to save its taxpayers millions of dollars after using ABC to study the cost of providing city services (activities) to local citizens. Once the city determined the cost of its activities, it was able to obtain competitive bids for those same services from private businesses. As a result, the city outsourced many activities to private-sector firms for a lower cost.[6]

Passing the Cost-Benefit Test

Like all other management tools, managers must determine whether the cost of designing and implementing an ABC/ABM system is worth the benefits of having more precise information. The system should be refined enough to provide accurate product costs but simple enough for managers to understand. In our chapter example, ABC increased the number of allocation rates from the single plantwide allocation rate in the original system to six activity cost allocation rates. ABC systems are even more complex in real-world companies that have many more activities and cost drivers.

Circumstances Favoring ABC/ABM Systems

ABC and ABM pass the cost-benefit test when the benefits of adopting ABC/ABM exceed the costs.

The benefits of adopting ABC/ABM are higher for companies in competitive markets because

- accurate product cost information is essential for setting competitive sales prices that still allow the company to earn a profit.
- ABM can pinpoint opportunities for cost savings, which increase the company's profit or are passed on to customers through lower prices.

The benefits of adopting ABC/ABM are higher when the risk of cost distortion is high, for example, when

- the company produces many different products that use different types and amounts of resources. (If all products use similar types and amounts of resources, a simple plantwide allocation system works fine.)
- the company has high indirect costs. (If the company has relatively few indirect costs, it matters less how they are allocated.)
- the company produces high volumes of some products and low volumes of other products. (Plantwide allocation systems based on a volume-related driver, such as direct labor hours, tend to overcost high-volume products and undercost low-volume products.)

[6]H. Meyer, "Indianapolis Speeds Away," *The Journal of Business Strategy*, May/June 1998, pp. 41–46.

We have seen that ABC offers many benefits. However, the cost and time required to implement and maintain an ABC system are often quite high. Some companies report spending up to two to four years to design and implement their ABC systems. The larger the company, the longer it usually takes. Top management support is crucial for the success of such an expensive and time-consuming initiative. Without such support, ABC implementations might easily be abandoned for an easier, less costly accounting system. Because we know ABC systems are costly to implement, how can a company judge the costs involved with setting one up?

The costs of adopting ABC/ABM are generally lower when the company has

- accounting and information system expertise to develop the system. However, even "off-the-shelf" commercial accounting packages offer ABC modules. Small companies often find that Excel spreadsheets can be used to implement ABC, rather than integrating ABC into their general ledger software.
- information technology such as bar coding, optical scanning, Web-based data collection, or data warehouse systems to record and compile cost driver data.

Signs That the Old System May Be Distorting Costs

Broken cars or computers simply stop running. But unlike cars and computers, even broken or outdated costing systems continue to report product costs. How can you tell whether a costing system is broken and needs repair? In other words, how can you tell whether an existing costing system is distorting costs and needs to be refined by way of departmental rates or ABC?

A company's product costing system may need repair in the following situations:

Managers don't understand costs and profits:

- In bidding for jobs, managers lose bids they expected to win and win bids they expected to lose.
- Competitors with similar high-volume products price their products below the company's costs but still earn good profits.
- Employees do not believe the cost numbers reported by the accounting system.

The cost system is outdated:

- The company has diversified its product offerings since the allocation system was first developed.
- The company has reengineered its production process but has not changed its accounting system to reflect the new production environment.

Decision Guidelines

Refined Costing Systems

Several years ago, Dell decided that it needed to refine its costing system. Starting with an Excel spreadsheet, Dell developed a simple ABC system that focused on the 10 most critical activities. Here are some of the decisions Dell faced as it began refining its costing system.

Decision	Guidelines
How do we develop an ABC system?	1. Identify the activities and estimate the total MOH associated with each activity. These are known as the activity cost pools. 2. Select a cost allocation base for each activity and estimate the total amount that will be used during the year. 3. Calculate an activity cost allocation rate for each activity. 4. Allocate some MOH from each activity to the individual jobs that use the activities.
How do we compute an activity cost allocation rate?	$$\frac{\text{Total estimated activity cost pool}}{\text{Total estimated activity allocation base}}$$
How do we allocate an activity's cost to a job?	$$\text{Activity cost allocation rate} \times \text{Actual amount of activity allocation base used by job}$$
How can a refined costing system support environmental sustainability?	By creating separate cost pools for environmental related costs, managers are better able to identify those activities and products with larger environmental footprints.
What types of decisions would benefit from the use of ABC?	Managers use ABC data in ABM to make the following decisions: • Pricing and product mix • Cost cutting • Routine planning and control
What are the main benefits of ABC?	• More accurate product cost information. • More detailed information on costs of activities and associated cost drivers help managers control costs and eliminate non-value-added activities.
When is ABC most likely to pass the cost-benefit test?	• The company is in a competitive environment and needs accurate product costs. • The company makes different products that use different amounts of resources. • The company has high indirect costs. • The company produces high volumes of some products and lower volumes of other products. • The company has accounting and information technology expertise to implement the system.
How do we tell when a cost system needs to be refined?	• Managers lose bids they expected to win and win bids they expected to lose. • Competitors earn profits despite pricing high-volume products below the company's costs. • Employees do not believe cost numbers. • The company has diversified the products it manufactures. • The company has reengineered the production process but not the accounting system.

SUMMARY PROBLEM 1

Indianapolis Auto Parts (IAP) has a Seat Manufacturing Department that uses ABC. IAP's activity cost allocation rates include the following:

Activity	Allocation Base	Activity Cost Allocation Rate
Machining	Number of machine hours	$30.00 per machine hour
Assembling	Number of parts	0.50 per part
Packaging	Number of finished seats	0.90 per finished seat

Suppose Ford has asked for a bid on 50,000 built-in baby seats that would be installed as an option on some Ford SUVs. Each seat has 20 parts, and the direct materials cost per seat is $11. The job would require 10,000 direct labor hours at a labor wage rate of $25 per hour. In addition, IAP will use a total of 400 machine hours to fabricate some of the parts required for the seats.

Requirements

1. Compute the total cost of producing and packaging 50,000 baby seats. Also compute the average cost per seat.

2. For bidding, IAP adds a 30% markup to total cost. What price will the company bid for the Ford order?

3. Suppose that instead of an ABC system, IAP has a traditional product costing system that allocates manufacturing overhead at a plantwide overhead rate of $65 per direct labor hour. The baby seat order will require 10,000 direct labor hours. Compute the total cost of producing the baby seats and the average cost per seat. What price will IAP bid using this system's total cost?

4. Use your answers to Requirements 2 and 3 to explain how ABC can help IAP make a better decision about the bid price it will offer Ford.

▪ SOLUTIONS

Requirements 1 and 2

Total Cost of Order, Average Cost per Seat, and Bid Price:

	A	B	C	D	E	F	G	H
1	**Manufacturing Costs**	**Usage of Activity**			**Cost Rate**			**Total**
2	Direct Material	50,000	seats	×	$ 11.00	per seat	=	$ 550,000
3	Direct Labor	10,000	DL hours	×	$ 25.00	per DL hour	=	250,000
4	MOH:							
5	Machining	400	machine hours	×	$ 30.00	per machine hour	=	12,000
6	Assembling	1,000,000*	parts	×	$ 0.50	per part	=	500,000
7	Packaging	50,000	seats	×	$ 0.90	per seat	=	45,000
8	Total Cost							$ 1,357,000
9	Divide by: Number of units							50,000
10	Average cost per unit							$ 27.14
11								
12	**Calculation of bid price:**							
13	Total job cost							$ 1,357,000
14	Multiply by: 100% + Markup							130%
15	Bid price							$ 1,764,100
16								

*1,000,000 = 50,000 seats × 20 parts per seat.
NOTE: Arithmetic signs are only shown for illustrative teaching purposes. They are not typically displayed in spreadsheets.

Requirement 3

Bid Price (Traditional System):

	A	B	C	D	E	F	G	H
1	**Manufacturing Costs**	**Usage of Activity**			**Cost Rate**			**Total**
2	Direct Material	50,000	seats	×	$ 11.00	per seat	=	$ 550,000
3	Direct Labor	10,000	DL hours	×	$ 25.00	per DL hour	=	250,000
4	MOH:	10,000	DL hours	×	$ 65.00	per DL hour	=	650,000
5	Total Cost							$ 1,450,000
6	Divide by: Number of units							50,000
7	Average cost per unit							$ 29.00
8								
9	**Calculation of bid price:**							
10	Total job cost							$ 1,450,000
11	Multiply by: 100% + Markup							130%
12	Bid price							$ 1,885,000
13								

NOTE: Arithmetic signs are only shown for illustrative teaching purposes. They are not typically displayed in spreadsheets.

Requirement 4

IAP's bid would be $120,900 higher using the plantwide overhead rate than using ABC ($1,885,000 versus $1,764,100). Assuming that the ABC system more accurately captures the costs caused by the order, the traditional plantwide overhead system overcosts the order. This leads to a higher bid price that reduces IAP's chance of winning the bid. The ABC system shows that IAP can increase its chance of winning the bid by bidding a lower price and still make a profit.

What Is Lean Thinking?

Lean thinking is a management philosophy and strategy focused on creating value for the customer by eliminating waste. Lean is often described by the Japanese word **Kaizen**, meaning "change for the better." Lean thinking is quickly becoming the dominant business paradigm; without it, a company has little chance of long-term survival in the highly competitive global marketplace. Since management accounting systems should be designed to reflect the company's operations, it's important for you to understand the key elements of lean operations and the costs that can be reduced by eliminating waste.

One key element of creating customer value is to emphasize a short **customer response time**: the time that elapses between receipt of a customer order and delivery of the product or service. To shorten this time, companies need to reduce their own internal processing time. Although lean thinking developed in the manufacturing industry (at Toyota, in particular), the concepts and tools are being applied with great success to all types of companies. For example, service companies, such as hospitals, car repair shops, and fast-food restaurants, must also focus on eliminating the waste in their operations. No matter the industry, the bottom line is clear: By eliminating wasteful activities, companies can reduce their costs and improve their customer response time.

The Eight Wastes of Traditional Operations

Advocates of lean thinking often talk about **eight wastes** that comprise much of the waste found in traditional organizations, including service and merchandising companies. As shown in Exhibit 4-22, these wastes are easy to remember using the acronym **DOWNTIME**.[7]

EXHIBIT 4-22 The Eight Wastes

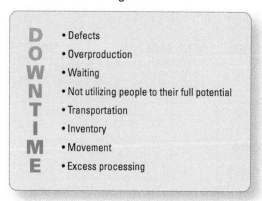

1. **Defects:** Producing defective products or services costs time and money. The product will either need to be repaired, at additional cost, or disposed of. In either case, resources are wasted. The final section of this chapter is devoted to discussing the various costs associated with poor quality of product or service.

2. **Overproduction:** Overproduction means that the company is making more product than needed or making product *sooner* than it is needed. Traditional manufacturers often make products in large batches because of long and costly machine setup times and to protect themselves against higher than expected demand for the product. Also, traditional manufacturers often make extra work in process inventory so that each department will have something to continue working on in the event production stops or slows in earlier departments. For example, in Exhibit 4-23, we see the series of production steps required to produce drill bits from bar stock. If the company keeps

[7] MAGNET (Manufacturing Advocacy and Growth Network), Cleveland, Ohio.

some work in process inventory between the grinding and smoothing operations, the smoothing operation can continue even if the shaping or grinding operations slow or come to a halt as a result of machine breakdown, absence of sick workers, or other production problems.

EXHIBIT 4-23 Sequence of Operations for Drill Bit Production

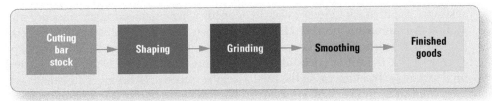

As you'll see next, overproduction can snowball into many problems, including extra wait time, extra transportation, and excess inventory build-up.

3. **Waiting:** Employees must often wait for parts, materials, information, or machine repairs before they can proceed with their tasks. In addition, because of overproduction and large batches, work in process inventory often waits in a queue for the next production process to begin. Whether it refers to people or product, wait time is wasted time. The company's customer response time could be much shorter if wait time were eliminated.

4. **Not utilizing people to their full potential:** By assuming that managers always know best, traditional companies have often underutilized their employees. In contrast, one of the key mantras of lean thinking is employee empowerment at all levels of the organization. Employees usually have excellent ideas on how their jobs could be done more efficiently and with less frustration.

5. **Transportation:** While movement of parts, inventory, and paperwork is necessary to some extent, any *excess* transportation is simply wasteful because of the equipment, manpower, energy, and time it requires. Excess transportation is often caused by poor plant layout, large centralized storage cribs, large batches, and long lead times that require product to be moved elsewhere until the next production process is ready to begin.

6. **Inventory:** Typically, traditional manufacturers buy more raw materials than they need "just in case" any of the materials are defective or the supplier is late with the next delivery. As noted earlier, they produce extra work in process inventory "just in case" something goes wrong in the production process. Also, they produce extra finished goods inventory "just in case" demand is higher than expected. In other words, large inventories are essentially a response to uncertainty. Uncertainty is a valid reason for keeping large inventories. So why are large inventories considered wasteful?

   - Inventories use cash. Companies incur interest expense from borrowing cash to finance their inventories or forgo income that could be earned from investing their cash elsewhere.

   - Large inventories hide quality problems, production bottlenecks, and obsolescence. Inventory may spoil, be broken or stolen, or become obsolete as it sits in storage and waits to be used or sold. Companies in high-tech and fashion industries are particularly susceptible to inventory obsolescence.

   - Storing and unstoring inventory is very expensive. Building space, shelving, warehouse equipment, security, computer systems, and labor are all needed to manage inventories.

7. **Movement:** In contrast to the waste of transportation, which refers to moving products and materials, the waste of movement refers to excess human motion, such as excess bending, reaching, turning, and walking. This waste is often caused by cluttered or unorganized work areas (where employees must search for the needed tools and supplies), poorly designed facilities (where employees must walk from one area of the building to another), and poorly designed workstations and work methods

(where employees must continually crouch, stretch, bend, and turn to do their tasks). Not only does excess movement take time, but also it can signal unsafe work conditions that can decrease employee morale and increase the company's exposure to workers' compensation claims.

8. **Excess processing:** This waste refers to performing additional production steps or adding features the customer doesn't care about. Often, this waste is caused when customer requirements are not clearly defined, when engineering changes are made without simultaneous process changes, or when additional steps are performed to make up for shortfalls in earlier production steps. For example, to keep its price point relatively low, IKEA flat packs all of its furniture and lets the customer perform the final assembly. By eliminating the final assembly process, IKEA gives customers what they want at a price that is affordable. Also, IKEA saves on related transportation and warehousing costs that would be incurred on bulkier, fully assembled furniture.

Characteristics of Lean Operations

One primary goal of a lean organization is to eliminate the waste of time and money that accompanies large inventories. Therefore, lean companies often adopt a **"just-in-time" (JIT)** inventory philosophy. As the name suggests, JIT inventory focuses on purchasing raw materials *just in time* for production and then completing finished goods *just in time* for delivery to customers. By doing so, companies eliminate the waste of storing and unstoring raw materials and finished goods, as pictured in Exhibit 4-24.

EXHIBIT 4-24 Traditional System Versus JIT System

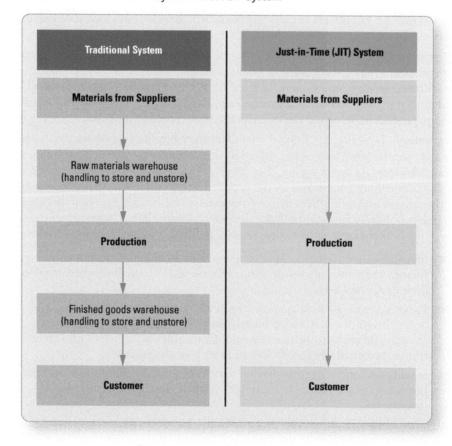

Most companies that adopt lean thinking have several common characteristics that help minimize the amount of inventory that is kept on hand, yet enable the company to quickly satisfy customer demand. These characteristics are described next.

Value Stream Mapping

Companies need to understand their current state of operations before they can attempt to remove waste and improve operations. Each family of products or services the company offers is known as a value stream. Value stream maps (VSM) are used to identify and visually illustrate the flow of materials and information for each separate value stream, all the way from order receipt to final delivery. A *current state* VSM is used to illustrate the sequence of activities, communication of information, time elapsing, and build-up of inventories that is currently occurring. After identifying waste within the current state VSM, companies prepare a *future state* VSM, with waste removed, and use it as a goal for process improvement.

Production Occurs in Self-Contained Production Cells

One of the first wastes many companies identify on the current state VSM is the waste of time, transportation, and movement that occurs as a result of poor plant or office layout. On one hand, a traditional drill bit manufacturer would group all cutting machines in one area, all shaping machines in another area, all grinding machines in a third area, and all smoothing machines in a fourth area, as illustrated in Panel A of Exhibit 4-25. On the other hand, lean companies would group the machines in self-contained production cells as shown in Panel B of Exhibit 4-25. These self-contained production cells minimize the time and cost involved with physically moving parts across the factory to other departments.

EXHIBIT 4-25 Equipment Arrangement in Traditional and Lean Production Systems

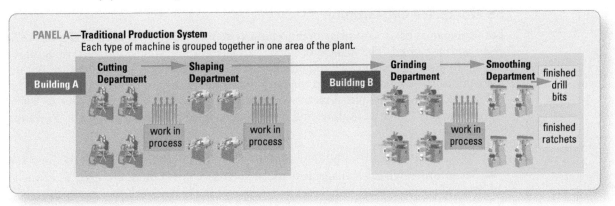

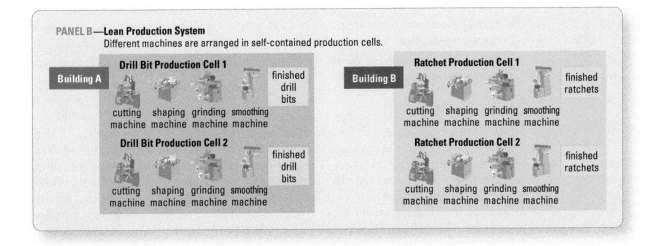

Employee Empowerment: Broad Roles and the Use of Teams

To combat the waste of not utilizing people to their full potential, lean companies focus on employee empowerment. Employees typically hold broader roles than their counterparts at traditional companies. For example, employees working in production cells do more than operate a single machine. They also conduct maintenance, perform setups, inspect their own work, and operate other machines. For example, look at Panel B of Exhibit 4-25. A worker in the Drill Bit Production Cell 1 would be cross-trained to operate all of the machines (cutting, shaping, grinding, and smoothing) in that cell. This cross-training boosts morale, lowers costs, and creates a more flexible and versatile workforce. As a result, individual workloads become much more balanced, leading to a more equitable distribution of work and a more satisfied workforce.

Lean companies also empower employees by using small teams to identify waste and develop potential solutions to the problems identified. Problem solving at lean companies involves searching for and fixing the root cause of a problem, rather than making cosmetic changes to surface issues. To find the root cause of a problem, teams are encouraged to ask "Why?" at least five times. For example, say you received a "D" grade on an exam. Your initial response might be that you didn't understand the material. However, as you dig deeper by continually asking "Why?" you might find that the root cause was not a simple failure to understand the material, but having an overloaded schedule that didn't allow you sufficient time to study and practice the material. The solution might be to lighten your semester course load or not to participate in so many extracurricular activities. Without fixing the root cause of the problem, you are apt to run into similar problems in the future.

Often, lean companies institute profit-sharing plans so that employees at all levels of the company are compensated for improving the company's overall performance. Because of employee empowerment, lean companies typically report higher job satisfaction and better employee morale.

5S Workplace Organization

Lean companies use a workplace organization system called "5S" to keep their work cells clean and organized. The mantra of 5S is, "a place for everything and everything in its place." By having a clean, well-organized, ergonomic workplace, every employee within the work cell knows where to find the tools and supplies they need to do each job in the cell as efficiently as possible. A clean workplace also leads to fewer defects (due to fewer contaminants), a safer workplace, and fewer unscheduled machine repairs. The 5S stands for the following:

- **Sort:** Infrequently used tools and supplies are removed from the workplace.
- **Set in order:** Visual management tools, such as color-coding, are used to create a logical layout of tools, supplies, and equipment in the work cell so that anyone could walk into the cell and visually understand the current situation.
- **Shine:** All machines, floors, tools, and workstations are thoroughly cleaned.
- **Standardize:** Procedures are put in place to ensure the cleanliness and organization of the workplace does not deteriorate.
- **Sustain:** Daily upkeep of the workstations is maintained, and 5S inspections are routinely performed.

Continuous Flow

Lean organizations attempt to smooth the flow of production through the plant so that the rate of production is the same as the rate of demand, thus reducing the wastes of overproduction, waiting, and inventory. The goal is to make *only* as many units as needed by the next customer, whether that be the next machine operator or the final, external customer. **Takt time,** a critical concept in lean manufacturing, is the rate of production needed to meet customer demand, yet avoid overproduction. The term comes from a German word for *rhythm* or *beat*. For example, if a product line has a takt time of five minutes, it means that one unit needs to be produced every five minutes. By carefully monitoring takt time, lean companies are able to identify bottlenecks, balance the workloads of different processes, avoid inventory build-up, and satisfy customer demand.

Pull System

In a traditional production system, batches of product are "pushed" through production according to forecasted demand. However, in a lean production system, no products are made until a customer's order has been received. The customer order triggers the start of the production process and "pulls" the batch through production. Even the necessary raw materials are usually not purchased until a customer order is received. Obviously, for this to work, companies must employ various tactics that will allow the company to quickly satisfy the customer's order. We discuss these tactics next.

Shorter Manufacturing Cycle Times

Because products are not started until a customer order is received, lean companies must focus on reducing their **manufacturing cycle time**: the time that elapses between the start of production and the product's completion. According to most experts, the majority of manufacturing cycle time is spent on non-value-added activities. Shorter manufacturing times also protect companies from foreign competitors whose cheaper products take longer to ship. Delivery speed has become a competitive weapon.

Smaller Batches

Manufacturing cycle time is highly dependent on batch size. Large batch sizes cause wasted wait time. Therefore, one of the key elements of lean production is the use of smaller batches. For example, assume that a customer has ordered 10 units and that each unit requires three unique, sequential processes: A, B, and C. Furthermore, assume that each process takes *1 minute* to complete *on each unit*. The manufacturing cycle time is illustrated in Exhibit 4-26, where each "x" stands for one unit of the product, and the capital "X" stands for the first unit in the batch. Exhibit 4-26 shows that the entire order would take 30 minutes to complete if the manufacturer uses a batch size of 10. Exhibit 4-26 also shows that 21 minutes have elapsed before the first unit in the batch is completed.

EXHIBIT 4-26 Manufacturing Cycle Time with a Batch Size of 10

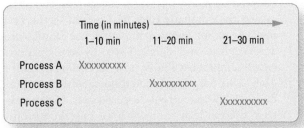

Alternatively, Exhibit 4-27 shows that the entire order could be completed in just 12 minutes if the manufacturer uses a batch size of 1. In addition, the first unit in the batch is completed after a mere 3 minutes has elapsed. Why the difference? With large batch sizes, each unit spends the bulk of the manufacturing cycle time *waiting*. Customer response time can be greatly reduced through the use of smaller batch sizes.

EXHIBIT 4-27 Manufacturing Cycle Time with a Batch Size of 1

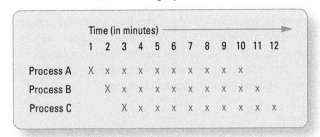

Reduced Setup Times

One key component of manufacturing cycle time is the time required to set up a machine that is used to manufacture more than one product. Employee training and technology helped Toyota cut setup times from several hours to just a few minutes. As a result, the company became more flexible in scheduling production to meet customer orders.

Point-of-Use Storage

Point-of-use storage (POUS) is a storage system used to reduce the waste of transportation and movement. In essence, tools, materials, and equipment are stored in proximity to where they will be used most frequently, rather than in a centralized storage crib. In a similar vein, those items that are used infrequently are removed from the cells and stored elsewhere.

Emphasis on Quality

Lean companies focus on producing their products right the *first* time, *every* time. Why? First, they have no backup stock to give to waiting customers if they run into production problems. Second, defects in materials and workmanship can slow or shut down production. Lean companies cannot afford the time it takes to rework faulty products. Lean companies emphasize "building in" quality rather than relying on a final inspection point to catch defects. This approach to quality, called **quality at the source**, refers to shifting the responsibility for quality adherence to the operators at each step in the value stream, rather than relying on supervisors or quality assurance personnel to catch errors. Each operator checks the incoming work, as well as his or her own outgoing work, so that defective units do not get passed on to downstream production processes.

Many lean companies also pursue the dogma of **Six Sigma**, which is the goal of producing near perfection, with less than 3.4 defects per million opportunities. The name arises from its statistical probability: a defect that is six standard deviations from the mean is highly unlikely to occur. You may hear the term *Lean/Six Sigma* together because the two approaches often go hand in hand. Six Sigma was developed by Motorola in the 1980s but has been adopted by many successful companies. GE credits Six Sigma with saving the company over $10 billion in the first five years of its use.[8] Lean/Six Sigma companies use standardization tools, such as checklists and detailed step-by-step operating procedures, to ensure employees know how to complete each process correctly. They also use visual management, root cause analysis, and other tools to "mistake-proof" each process. "Poka-yoke" is the Japanese term used in lean companies for mistake-proofing a process. Let's look at an example: at gas stations, the nozzle for diesel gasoline is larger than the nozzle for regular unleaded gas, making it virtually impossible for absent-minded customers to accidentally put diesel fuel into a car that runs on regular fuel. The process of refueling has been mistake-proofed for owners of the majority of vehicles in the United States.

> ### ◼ Why is this important?
>
> "In order to **compete** and remain **profitable**, companies must cut costs by becoming as **efficient** as possible. **Lean** thinking helps **organizations** cut costs by **eliminating waste** from the system."

Supply-Chain Management

Because there are no inventory buffers, lean production requires close coordination with suppliers. These suppliers must guarantee *on-time delivery* of *defect-free* materials. *Supply-chain management* is the exchange of information with suppliers and customers to reduce costs, improve quality, and speed delivery of goods and services from the company's suppliers, through the company itself, and on to the company's end customers. Suppliers that bear the ISO 9001 certification have proven their ability to provide high-quality products and thus tend to be suppliers for lean manufacturers.

Backflush Costing

Due to the emphasis on JIT inventory (little to no raw materials or finished goods), short manufacturing cycle times, and a "pull" system (customer is awaiting production), many lean producers use a simplified accounting system, called backflush costing, that better mirrors their production environment and eliminates wasteful bookkeeping steps. In a **backflush costing** system, the production costs are not assigned to the units until they

[8] www.sixsigmadaily.com/why-six-sigma-certification-and-training-reduces-company-costs/

are finished, or even sold, thereby saving the bookkeeping steps of moving the product through the various inventory accounts. To get an accurate measurement of the inventory accounts and Cost of Goods Sold at the end of the period, the cost of any unfinished or unsold product is "flushed" out of Cost of Goods Sold and placed back in the Work in Process Inventory and Finished Goods Inventory accounts.

Are There Any Drawbacks to a Lean Production System?

While many companies credit lean thinking with saving them millions of dollars, the system is not without problems. With no inventory buffers, lean producers are vulnerable when problems strike suppliers or distributors. For example, natural disasters, such as the tsunamis in Japan, and man-made disasters, such as terrorist attacks, have caused production shutdown at several lean manufacturers.

Lean Operations in Service and Merchandising Companies

The eight wastes and lean principles discussed previously also apply to service and merchandising firms. In fact, lean practices have become extremely popular in service companies, such as banks and hospitals, as well as merchandising companies, such as IKEA. Entire books have been written on the subject of "lean health care" and "lean offices." Through the use of lean tools, offices have been able to identify the waste caused by excessive document processing, layers of unnecessary authorization, unbalanced workloads, poor office layouts, and unclear communication channels. Through streamlining their internal operations, hospitals, such as the world-renowned Cleveland Clinic, have found that they are able to decrease patient wait time, thereby creating higher levels of customer satisfaction while at the same time decreasing their own costs.

▶ Try It!

Which of the following would you expect to see at a company that espouses lean thinking?

1. Larger inventories
2. Smaller batch sizes
3. More organized workstations
4. Longer setup times
5. Lower-level small-team problem solving
6. Centralized storage cribs
7. Pull system

Please see page 244 for solutions.

Sustainability and Lean Thinking

Sustainability and lean thinking have many similarities: both practices seek to reduce waste. However, lean operations focus on eliminating waste and empowering employees in an effort to increase economic profits. On the other hand, "lean and green" operations focus on eliminating waste and empowering employees not only to increase economic profits, but also to preserve the planet and improve the lives of *all* people touched by the company. Whereas lean practices tend to center on *internal* operational waste, green practices also consider the *external* waste that may occur as a result of the product. To become more sustainable, a lean company should be particularly cognizant of all waste that could harm the planet: packaging waste, water waste, energy waste, and emissions waste that would occur from both manufacturing the product *and* from consumers using and eventually disposing of the product.

▶ See Exercises E4-21A and E4-32B

5 Describe and use the costs of quality framework

How Do Managers Improve Quality?

Because lean companies rarely hold extra inventory to fall back on in the event of errors or defects, they use the management philosophy of <u>**total quality management (TQM)**</u> to focus on consistently generating high-quality products. The goal of TQM is to provide customers with superior products and services. Each business function in the value chain continually examines its own activities to improve quality and eliminate defects.

Costs of Quality (COQ)

As part of TQM, many companies prepare costs of quality reports. <u>**Costs of quality reports**</u> categorize and list the costs incurred by the company related to quality. Once managers know the extent of their costs of quality, they can start to identify ways for the company to improve quality while at the same time controlling costs.

Quality-related costs generally fall into four different categories: prevention costs, appraisal costs, internal failure costs, and external failure costs. These categories form the framework for a costs of quality report. We'll briefly describe each next.

Prevention Costs

<u>**Prevention costs**</u> are costs incurred to *avoid* producing poor-quality goods or services. Often, poor quality is caused by the variability of the production process or the complexity of the product design. To reduce the variability of the production process, companies often automate as much of the process as possible. Employee training can help decrease variability in nonautomated processes. In addition, reducing the complexity of the product design or manufacturing process can prevent the potential for error: The fewer parts or processes, the fewer things that can go wrong. Frequently, companies need to literally "go back to the drawing board" (the R&D and design stages of the value chain) to make a significant difference in preventing production problems.

Appraisal Costs

<u>**Appraisal costs**</u> are costs incurred to *detect* poor-quality goods or services. Intel incurs appraisal costs when it tests its products. One procedure, called burn-in, heats circuits to a high temperature. A circuit that fails the burn-in test is also likely to fail in customer use. Nissan tests 100% of the vehicles that roll off the assembly lines at its plant in Canton, Mississippi. Each vehicle is put through the paces on Nissan's all-terrain test track. Any problems are identified before the vehicle leaves the plant.

Internal Failure Costs

<u>**Internal failure costs**</u> are costs incurred on defective units *before* delivery to customers. For example, if Nissan does identify a problem, the vehicle is reworked to eliminate the defect before it is allowed to leave the plant. In the worst-case scenario, a product may be so defective that it cannot be reworked and must be completely scrapped. In this case, the entire cost of manufacturing the defective unit, plus any disposal cost, would be an internal failure cost.

External Failure Costs

<u>**External failure costs**</u> are costs incurred because the defective goods or services are not detected until *after* delivery is made to customers. News reports are filled with stories of product recalls that damage a company's reputation and can significantly harm the company's future sales. Furthermore, consumers have harnessed the power of social media and online rating sites to "spread the word" to millions of potential customers about any unsatisfying experiences they have had with products or services. As a result, a company's reputation for either good or poor quality can increase at an exponential rate. To capture the extent of a reputation for poor quality, external failure costs should include an estimate of how much profit the company is losing due to having a bad reputation.

Relationship Among Costs

Exhibit 4-28 lists some common examples of the four different costs of quality. Prevention and appraisal costs are sometimes referred to as __conformance costs__ since they are the costs incurred to make sure the product or service is not defective and therefore conforms to its intended design. On the other hand, internal and external failure costs are sometimes referred to as __nonconformance costs__. These costs are incurred when the product or service *is* defective and therefore does *not* conform to its intended design.

EXHIBIT 4-28 Four Types of Quality Costs

Prevention Costs	Appraisal Costs
Training personnel	Inspection of incoming materials
Evaluating potential suppliers	Inspection at various stages of production
Using better materials	Inspection of final products or services
Preventive maintenance	Product testing
Improved equipment	Cost of inspection equipment
Redesigning product or process	

Internal Failure Costs	External Failure Costs
Production loss caused by downtime	Lost profits from lost customers
Rework	Warranty costs
Abnormal quantities of scrap	Service costs at customer sites
Rejected product units	Sales returns and allowances due to quality problems
Disposal of rejected units	Product liability claims
Machine breakdowns	Cost of recalls

Most companies find that if they invest more in prevention costs at the front end of the value chain (R&D and design), they can generate even more savings in the back end of the value chain (production and customer service). Why? Because carefully designed products and manufacturing processes can significantly reduce the number of inspections, defects, rework, and warranty claims. Managers must make trade-offs between these costs. Companies that embrace TQM, such as Toyota, *design* and *build* quality into their products rather than having to *inspect* and *repair* later, as many traditional manufacturers do.

Costs of Quality at Service and Merchandising Companies

The costs of quality are not limited to manufacturers. Service firms and merchandising companies also incur costs of quality. For example, certified public accounting (CPA) firms spend a lot of money providing ongoing professional training to their staff. They also develop standardized audit checklists to minimize the variability of the audit procedures performed for each client. These measures help to *prevent* audit failures. Both audit managers and partners review audit work papers to *appraise* whether the audit procedures performed and evidence gathered are sufficient on each audit engagement. If audit procedures or evidence are deemed to be lacking (*internal failure*), the audit manager or partner will instruct the audit team to perform additional procedures before the firm will issue an audit opinion on the client's financial statements. This parallels the "rework" a manufacturer might perform on a product that isn't up to par. Finally, audit failures, such as those at Enron and WorldCom, illustrate just how expensive and devastating *external failure* can be to a CPA firm. The once-prestigious international CPA firm Arthur Andersen & Co. actually went out of business because of the reputation damage caused by its audit failure at Enron.

Using Costs of Quality Reports to Aid Decisions

Now that we have examined the four costs of quality, let's see how they can be presented to management in the form of a costs of quality report. Let's assume Global Fitness, another manufacturer of fitness equipment, is having difficulty competing with Life Fitness because it doesn't have the reputation for high quality that Life Fitness enjoys. To examine this issue, management has prepared the costs of quality report shown in Exhibit 4-29.

Notice how Global Fitness identifies, categorizes, and quantifies all of the costs it incurs relating to quality. Global Fitness also calculates the percentage of total costs of quality that is incurred in each cost category. This helps company managers see just how *little* they are spending on conformance costs (prevention and appraisal). Most of their costs are internal and external failure costs. The best way to reduce these nonconformance costs is to invest more in prevention and appraisal. Global Fitness managers can now begin to focus on *how* they might be able to prevent these failures from occurring.

■ Why is this important?

"Businesses **compete** with each other on the basis of price and quality. **Costs of Quality** reports help managers determine how they are **spending** money to ensure that consumers get the **best-quality** product for the price."

EXHIBIT 4-29 Global Fitness's Costs of Quality Report

	A	B	C	D
1	**Global Fitness Costs of Quality Report** **Year Ended December 31**	**Costs Incurred**	**Total Costs of Quality**	**Percentage of Total COQ**
2				
3	**Prevention Costs:**			
4	Employee training	$ 125,000		
5	Total prevention costs		$ 125,000	6.1%
6				
7	**Appraisal Costs:**			
8	Testing	$ 175,000		
9	Total appraisal costs		$ 175,000	8.5%
10				
11	**Internal Failure Costs:**			
12	Rework	$ 300,000		
13	Cost of rejected units	50,000		
14	Total internal failure costs		$ 350,000	17.0%
15				
16	**External Failure Costs:**			
17	Lost profits from lost sales due to poor reputation	$ 1,000,000		
18	Sales return processing	175,000		
19	Warranty costs	235,000		
20	Total external failure costs		$ 1,410,000	68.4%
21				
22	**Total costs of quality**		$ 2,060,000	100.0%
23				

NOTE: The percentage is calculated as the total cost of the category divided by the total costs of all categories combined.

After analyzing the costs of quality report, the CEO is considering spending the following amounts on a new quality program:

Inspect raw materials	$100,000
Reengineer the production process to improve product quality	750,000
Supplier screening and certification	25,000
Preventive maintenance on plant equipment	75,000
Total costs of implementing quality programs	$950,000

Although these measures won't completely eliminate internal and external failure costs, Global Fitness expects this quality program to *reduce* costs by the following amounts:

Reduction in lost profits from lost sales due to impaired reputation..............	$ 800,000
Fewer sales returns to be processed	150,000
Reduction in rework costs...	250,000
Reduction in warranty costs..	225,000
Total cost savings..	$1,425,000

According to these projections, Global Fitness's quality initiative will cost $950,000 but result in total savings of $1,425,000—for a net benefit of $475,000. This cost-benefit analysis can also be organized using the costs of quality framework as shown in Exhibit 4-30. By spending $850,000 more on prevention costs and $100,000 more on appraisal costs, Global Fitness will be able to save $250,000 in internal failure costs and $1,175,000 in external failure costs. In total, Global Fitness expects a net benefit of $475,000 from this quality initiative. As is usually the case, Global Fitness will be able to reduce its *overall* costs of quality by spending more on conformance costs.

EXHIBIT 4-30 Cost-Benefit Analysis of Global Fitness's Proposed Quality Program

	A	B	C	D
1	**Global Fitness Quality Initiative Cost Benefit Analysis**	**(Costs) and Cost Savings**	**Total (Costs) and Cost Savings**	
2				
3	**Prevention Costs:**			
4	Reengineer the production process	$ (750,000)		
5	Supplier screening and certification	(25,000)		
6	Preventive maintenance on equipment	(75,000)		
7	Total additional prevention costs		$ (850,000)	
8				
9	**Appraisal Costs:**			
10	Inspect raw materials	$ (100,000)		
11	Total additional appraisal costs		$ (100,000)	
12				
13	**Internal Failure Costs:**			
14	Reduction of rework costs	$ 250,000		
15	Total internal failure cost savings		$ 250,000	
16				
17	**External Failure Costs:**			
18	Reduction of lost profits from lost sales	$ 800,000		
19	Reduction of sales return	150,000		
20	Reduction of warranty costs	225,000		
21	Total external failure cost savings		$ 1,175,000	
22				
23	**Total savings (costs) from quality programs**		$ 475,000	
24				

The analysis shown in Exhibit 4-30 appears very straightforward. However, quality costs can be hard to measure. The largest external failure cost—profits lost because of the company's reputation for poor quality—does not even appear in the accounting records. This cost must be estimated based on the experiences and judgments of the Sales Department. Because these estimates may be subjective, TQM programs also emphasize nonfinancial measures such as defect rates, number of customer complaints, and number of warranty repairs that can be objectively measured.

Decision Guidelines

Lean Operations and the Costs of Quality

Toyota, the largest car manufacturer in the world, is famous for its complete commitment to both lean thinking and TQM. The following are several decisions Toyota's managers made when they helped develop and implement these two modern management techniques.

Decision	Guidelines
How will we begin to identify waste in our organization?	Most companies find that the majority of waste occurs in eight specific areas. The "eight wastes" can be remembered as DOWNTIME: • Defects • Overproduction • Waiting • Not utilizing people to their full potential • Transportation • Inventory • Movement • Excess processing
What operational features will help us become more lean?	Lean operations are typically characterized by many of the following features: • Just-in-time (JIT) inventory • Value stream mapping • Production in self-contained work cells • Employee empowerment through broader roles and use of small teams • 5S workplace organization • Point-of-use storage (POUS) • Continuous flow • Pull system • Shorter manufacturing cycle times • Reduced setup times • Smaller batches • Emphasis on quality and Six Sigma • Supply-chain management • Backflush costing
What are the four types of quality costs?	1. Prevention costs—costs incurred to avoid producing poor-quality goods and services. 2. Appraisal costs—costs incurred to detect poor-quality goods and services. 3. Internal failure costs—costs incurred on defective goods and services *before* they are delivered to the customer. 4. External failure costs—costs incurred because defective goods or services are not detected until *after* delivery is made to the customer.
How do we make trade-offs among the four types of quality costs?	Investment in prevention costs and appraisal costs reduces internal and external failure costs and usually reduces the overall costs of quality.

SUMMARY PROBLEM 2

The CEO of IAP is concerned with the quality of its products and the amount of resources currently spent on customer returns. The CEO would like to analyze the costs incurred in conjunction with the quality of the product.

The following information was collected from various departments within the company:

Warranty returns	$120,000
Training personnel	10,000
Litigation on product liability claims	175,000
Inspecting 10% of final products	5,000
Rework	10,000
Production loss due to machine breakdowns	45,000
Inspection of raw materials	5,000

Requirements

1. Prepare a costs of quality report. In addition to listing the costs by category, determine the percentage of the total costs of quality incurred in each cost category.

2. Do any additional subjective costs appear to be missing from the report?

3. What can be learned from the report?

▪ SOLUTIONS

Requirement 1

	A	B	C	D
	IAP Costs of Quality Report	Costs Incurred	Total Costs of Quality	Percentage of Total COQ
1				
2				
3	**Prevention Costs:**			
4	Personnel training	$ 10,000		
5	Total prevention costs		$ 10,000	2.7%
6				
7	**Appraisal Costs:**			
8	Inspecting raw materials	$ 5,000		
9	Inspecting 10% of final products	5,000		
10	Total appraisal costs		$ 10,000	2.7%
11				
12	**Internal Failure Costs:**			
13	Rework	$ 10,000		
14	Production loss due to machine breakdown	45,000		
15	Total internal failure costs		$ 55,000	14.9%
16				
17	**External Failure Costs:**			
18	Litigation from product liability claims	$ 175,000		
19	Warranty return costs	120,000		
20	Total external failure costs		$ 295,000	79.7%
21				
22	**Total costs of quality**		$ 370,000	100.0%
23				

Requirement 2

Because the company has warranty returns and product liability litigation, it is very possible that the company suffers from a reputation for poor-quality products. If so, it is losing profits from losing sales. Unsatisfied customers will probably avoid buying from the company in the future and may tell their friends and family not to buy from the company. Worse yet, unsatisfied customers may let their complaints be known to millions of potential customers through the use of social media and online customer satisfaction websites. As a result, this report should include an estimate of the lost profits arising from the company's reputation for poor-quality products.

Requirement 3

The costs of quality report shows that very little is being spent on prevention and appraisal, which is probably why the internal and external failure costs are so high. Management should use this information to develop quality initiatives in the areas of prevention and appraisal. Such initiatives should reduce future internal and external failure costs.

Learning Objectives

- 1 Develop and use departmental overhead rates to allocate indirect costs
- 2 Develop and use activity-based costing (ABC) to allocate indirect costs
- 3 Understand the benefits and limitations of ABC/ABM systems
- 4 Describe lean operations
- 5 Describe and use the costs of quality framework

Accounting Vocabulary

5S. (p. 202) A workplace organization system comprised of the following steps: sort, set in order, shine, standardize, and sustain.

Activity-Based Costing (ABC). (p. 184) Focusing on *activities* as the fundamental cost objects. The costs of those activities become building blocks for compiling the indirect costs of products, services, and customers.

Activity-Based Management (ABM). (p. 191) Using activity-based cost information to make decisions that increase profits while satisfying customers' needs.

Appraisal Costs. (p. 206) Costs incurred to *detect* poor-quality goods or services.

Backflush Costing. (p. 204) A simplified accounting system in which production costs are not assigned to the units until they are finished, or even sold, thereby saving the bookkeeping steps of moving the product through the various inventory accounts.

Batch-Level Activities. (p. 190) Activities and costs incurred for every batch, regardless of the number of units in the batch.

Conformance Costs. (p. 207) The combination of prevention and appraisal costs; the costs incurred to make sure a product or service is not defective and therefore conforms to its intended design.

Cost Distortion. (p. 177) Overcosting some products while undercosting other products.

Costs of Quality Report. (p. 206) A report that lists the costs incurred by the company related to quality. The costs are categorized as prevention costs, appraisal costs, internal failure costs, and external failure costs.

Customer Response Time. (p. 198) The time that elapses between receipt of a customer order and delivery of the product or service.

Departmental Overhead Rates. (p. 180) Separate manufacturing overhead rates established for each department.

DOWNTIME. (p. 198) An acronym for the eight wastes: defects, overproduction, waiting, not utilizing people to their full potential, transportation, inventory, movement, excess processing.

Eight Wastes. (p. 198) Defects, overproduction, waiting, not utilizing people to their full potential, transportation, inventory, movement, excess processing.

External Failure Costs. (p. 206) Costs incurred when the company does not detect poor-quality goods or services until *after* delivery is made to customers.

Facility-Level Activities. (p. 190) Activities and costs incurred no matter how many units, batches, or products are produced in the plant.

Internal Failure Costs. (p. 206) Costs incurred when the company detects and corrects poor-quality goods or services before making delivery to customers.

Just in Time (JIT). (p. 200) An inventory management philosophy that focuses on purchasing raw materials just in time for production and completing finished goods just in time for delivery to customers.

Kaizen. (p. 198) A Japanese word meaning "change for the better."

Lean Thinking. (p. 198) A management philosophy and strategy focused on creating value for the customer by eliminating waste.

Manufacturing Cycle Time. (p. 203) The time that elapses between the start of production and the product's completion.

Nonconformance costs. (p. 207) The combination of internal failure and external failure costs; the costs incurred when a product is defective and therefore does not conform to its intended design.

Non-Value-Added Activities. (p. 192) Activities that neither enhance the customer's image of the product or service nor provide a competitive advantage; also known as *waste activities*.

Plantwide Overhead Rate. (p. 178) When overhead is allocated to every product using the same manufacturing overhead rate.

Point of Use Storage (POUS). (p. 204) A storage system used to reduce the waste of transportation and movement in which tools, materials, and equipment are stored in proximity to where they will be used most frequently.

Prevention Costs. (p. 206) Costs incurred to *avoid* poor-quality goods or services.

Product-Level Activities. (p. 190) Activities and costs incurred for a particular product, regardless of the number of units or batches of the product produced.

Quality at the Source. (p. 204) A term that refers to shifting the responsibility for quality adherence to the operators at each step in the value stream, rather than relying on supervisors or a quality assurance department to catch errors.

Six Sigma. (p. 204) The goal of producing near perfection, with less than 3.4 defects per million opportunities.

Takt Time. (p. 202) The rate of production needed to meet customer demand, yet avoid overproduction.

Total Quality Management (TQM). (p. 206) A management philosophy of delighting customers with superior products and services by continually setting higher goals and improving the performance of every business function.

Unit-Level Activities. (p. 190) Activities and costs incurred for every unit produced.

Value-Added Activities. (p. 192) Activities for which the customer is willing to pay because these activities add value to the final product or service.

Waste Activities. (p. 192) Activities that neither enhance the customer's image of the product or service nor provide a competitive advantage; also known as non-value-added activities.

MyAccountingLab   Go to http://myaccountinglab.com/ for the following Quick Check, Short Exercises, Exercises, and Problems. They are available with immediate grading, explanations of correct and incorrect answers, and interactive media that act as your own online tutor.

Quick Check

1. *(Learning Objective 1)* Cost distortion is more likely to occur when
   a. departments incur different types of overhead and the products or jobs use the departments to a different extent.
   b. a company manufactures one type of product.
   c. all products require the same amount and type of processing activities.
   d. a company uses departmental overhead rates rather than a single plantwide overhead rate.

2. *(Learning Objective 2)* The first step in computing and using ABC is which of the following?
   a. Calculating activity cost allocation rates
   b. Identifying the company's primary activities
   c. Allocating some MOH to each job
   d. Selecting appropriate allocation bases

3. *(Learning Objective 2)* Activities incurred regardless of how many units, batches, or products are produced are called _____ activities.
   a. unit-level
   b. batch-level
   c. product-level
   d. facility-level

4. *(Learning Objective 3)* Which of the following is true?
   a. ABC is only applicable to manufacturers.
   b. Value-added activities are also referred to as waste activities.
   c. ABM refers to using activity-based cost information to make decisions.
   d. The goal of ABM is to decrease the amount of value-added activities.

5. *(Learning Objective 3)* The potential benefits of ABC/ABM are generally higher for companies that
   a. produce high volumes of some products and low volumes of other products.
   b. have low manufacturing overhead costs.
   c. are in noncompetitive markets.
   d. produce one product.

6. *(Learning Objective 4)* Lean operations are generally characterized by
   a. employee empowerment.
   b. JIT inventory systems.
   c. production in self-contained cells.
   d. all of the listed answers.

7. *(Learning Objective 4)* Which of the following is *not* one of the "eight wastes" included in the acronym DOWNTIME?
   a. Overproduction
   b. Transportation
   c. Inventory
   d. Neglect

8. *(Learning Objective 4)* Concerning lean operations, which of the following is *false*?
   a. Focus on internal and external waste
   b. Are quickly becoming the dominant business paradigm
   c. Can be found in all sectors, not just manufacturing
   d. Can leave companies vulnerable to supply-chain disruptions

9. *(Learning Objective 5)* Which of the following is *not* one of the costs of quality categories?
   a. Prevention costs
   b. Appraisal costs
   c. External failure costs
   d. Transportation costs

10. *(Learning Objective 5)* Which of the following would be considered an external failure cost?
    a. Rework costs
    b. Cost to train personnel
    c. Cost of inspecting incoming raw materials
    d. Warranty costs

Quick Check Answers

1.a 2.b 3.d 4.c 5.a 6.d 7.d 8.b 9.d 10.d

Cost Behavior

Learning Objectives

- **1** Describe key characteristics and graphs of various cost behaviors
- **2** Use cost equations to express and predict costs
- **3** Use account analysis and scatterplots to analyze cost behavior
- **4** Use the high-low method to analyze cost behavior
- **5** Use regression analysis to analyze cost behavior
- **6** Describe variable costing and prepare a contribution margin income statement

Karen W. Braun

Source: embassysuites3.hilton.com/en/about/index.html

Embassy Suites by Hilton™ differentiates itself from competing hotel brands by providing all guests with two-room suites, featuring separate bedroom and living areas, complimentary made-to-order breakfasts, and a complimentary evening reception. The evening reception provides guests with free refreshments including drinks, appetizers, and snacks. All of these amenities cost money for the hotel to provide but generate customer loyalty among travelers who have come to relish the unique and enjoyable hospitality provided by Embassy Suites.

How do hotel managers set prices high enough to cover all of these costs and earn a profit, but low enough to fill most rooms each night? They know how their costs behave. Some hotel costs, such as the complimentary morning breakfast and evening reception, rise and fall with the number of guests. But many hotel costs, such as depreciation on the building and furniture, stay the same whether the hotel is fairly vacant or 100% occupied each night. In this chapter, we'll learn more about how costs behave and how managers can use that knowledge to make better business decisions.

Up to this point, we have focused our attention on product costing. We have discussed how managers use job costing or process costing to figure out the cost of making a product or providing a service. Product costs are useful for valuing inventory and calculating cost of goods sold. Product costs are also used as a starting place for setting sales prices. However, product costs are not very helpful for planning and making many business decisions. Why? Because they contain a mixture of fixed and variable costs. Some of these costs change as volume changes, but other costs do not. To make good decisions and accurate projections, managers must understand how the company's costs will react to changes in volume.

Cost Behavior: How Do Changes in Volume Affect Costs?

1 Describe key characteristics and graphs of various cost behaviors

In order to make good decisions and accurate projections, managers must understand **cost behavior**—that is, how costs change as volume changes. Embassy Suite's managers need to understand how the hotel's costs will be affected by the number of guests staying at the hotel each night. Our chapter example will revolve around one Embassy Suites hotel, namely, the 525-room hotel overlooking Niagara Falls.

We first consider three of the most common cost behaviors, some of which were introduced in Chapter 2.

- Variable costs
- Fixed costs
- Mixed costs

Variable Costs

Variable costs are costs that are incurred for every unit of volume. As a result, total variable costs change in direct proportion to changes in volume. For example, every guest at Embassy Suites is entitled to a complimentary morning breakfast and evening refreshment hour (drinks and snacks). Guests also receive complimentary toiletries (shampoo, soap, lotion, and mouthwash) that they typically use or take with them. These costs are considered to be variable because they are incurred for every guest. In addition, the hotel's total cost for the complimentary breakfast, evening refreshments, and toiletries will increase as the number of guests increases.

Let's assume that the toiletries cost the hotel $3 per guest and that the breakfast and refreshment hour costs the hotel $10 per guest.[1] Exhibit 6-1 graphs these costs in relation to the number of guests staying at the hotel. The vertical axis (y-axis) shows total variable costs, while the horizontal axis (x-axis) shows total volume of activity (thousands of guests, in this case).

Notice a few things about these graphs:

- Graphs of variable costs always begin at the *origin*, the point that represents zero volume and zero cost. For example, if the hotel has no guests for the night, it will not incur any costs for complimentary toiletries or breakfasts.
- The *slope* of the variable cost line represents the *variable cost per unit of activity*. For example, the slope of the toiletry cost line is $3 per guest, while the slope of the breakfast and refreshment hour cost line is $10 per guest. As a result, the slope of the line representing the breakfast and refreshment hour cost is steeper than that of the toiletry cost.

> **Why is this important?**
>
> "Cost behavior is a **key** component of most **planning** and operating decisions. Without a thorough understanding of **cost behavior**, managers are apt to make less **profitable** decisions."

---

[1] All reference to Embassy Suites in this hypothetical example were created by the author solely for academic purposes and are not intended, in any way, to represent the actual costs incurred by an Embassy Suites by Hilton hotel.

EXHIBIT 6-1 Variable Costs

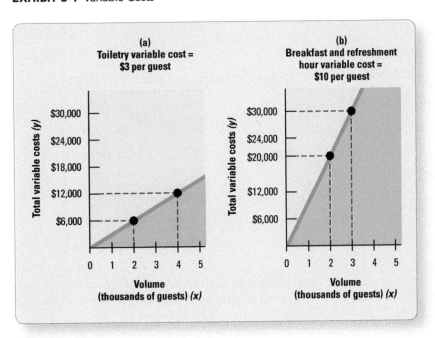

- Total variable costs change in *direct proportion* to changes in volume. In other words, if volume doubles, then total variable cost doubles. If volume triples, then total variable cost triples. For example, Exhibit 6-1(a) shows that if the hotel serves 2,000 guests, it will spend $6,000 on toiletries. However, doubling the number of guests to 4,000 likewise doubles the total variable cost to $12,000.

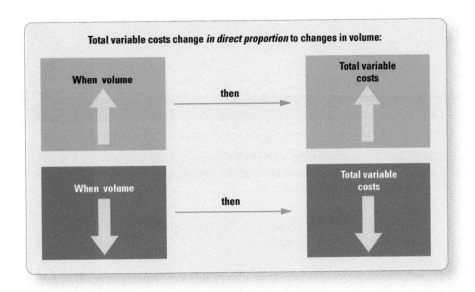

Managers do not need to rely on graphs to predict total variable costs at different volumes of activity. They can use a <u>cost equation</u>, a mathematical equation for a straight line, to express how a cost behaves. On cost graphs like the ones pictured in Exhibit 6-1, the vertical (*y*-axis) always shows total costs, while the horizontal axis (*x*-axis) shows volume of activity. Therefore, any variable cost line can be mathematically expressed as follows:

2 Use cost equations to express and predict costs

Total variable cost (y) = Variable cost per unit of activity (v) × Volume of activity (x)

Or simply:

$$y = vx$$

The hotel's total toiletry cost is as follows:

$$y = \$3x$$

where,

$$y = \text{total toiletry cost}$$
$$\$3 = \text{variable cost per guest}$$
$$x = \text{number of guests}$$

We can confirm the observations made in Exhibit 6-1(a) using the cost equation. If the hotel has no guests ($x = 0$), total toiletry costs are zero, as shown in the graph. If the hotel has 2,000 guests, total toiletry costs will be as follows:

$$y = \$3 \text{ per guest} \times 2{,}000 \text{ guests}$$
$$= \$6{,}000$$

If the hotel has 4,000 guests, managers will expect total toiletry costs to be as follows:

$$y = \$3 \text{ per guest} \times 4{,}000 \text{ guests}$$
$$= \$12{,}000$$

STOP & THINK

How much will the hotel spend on complimentary toiletries if it serves 3,467 guests?

Answer: You would have a hard time answering this question by simply looking at the graph in Exhibit 6-1(a), but cost equations can be used for any volume. We simply multiply the variable cost per guest by the expected volume:

$$y = \$3 \text{ per guest} \times 3{,}467 \text{ guests}$$
$$= \$10{,}401$$

Complimentary toiletries will cost approximately $10,401.

Now, consider Exhibit 6-1(b), the total variable costs for the complimentary breakfast and refreshment hour. The slope of the line is $10, representing the cost of providing each guest with the complimentary breakfast and refreshments. We can express the total breakfast and refreshment hour cost as follows:

$$y = \$10x$$

where,

y = total breakfast and refreshment hour cost

$10 = variable cost per guest

x = number of guests

The total cost of the breakfast and refreshment hour for 2,000 guests is as follows:

y = \$10 per guest $\times$ 2,000 guests

    = \$20,000

Both graphs in Exhibit 6-1 show how *total* variable costs vary with the number of guests. *But note that the variable cost per guest (v) remains constant in each of the graphs.* That is, Embassy Suites incurs \$3 in toiletry costs and \$10 in breakfast and refreshment hour costs for each guest no matter how many guests the hotel serves. Some key points to remember about variable costs are shown in Exhibit 6-2.

EXHIBIT 6-2 Key Characteristics of Variable Costs

- *Total* variable costs change in *direct proportion* to changes in volume
- The *variable cost per unit of activity* (v) remains constant and is the slope of the variable cost line
- Total variable cost graphs always begin at the origin (if volume is zero, total variable costs are zero)
- Total variable costs can be expressed as follows:

    $y = vx$

where,

    y = total variable cost

    v = variable cost per unit of activity

    x = volume of activity

Fixed Costs

Fixed costs are costs that do not change in total despite wide changes in volume. Many of Embassy Suites' costs are fixed because the same total cost will be incurred regardless of the number of guests that stay each month. Some of the hotel's fixed costs include the following:

- Property taxes and insurance
- Straight-line depreciation and maintenance on parking ramp, hotel, and furnishings
- Lease payments on fitness room equipment
- Cable TV and wireless Internet access for all rooms
- Salaries of hotel department managers (housekeeping, food service, special events, etc.)

Most of these costs are **committed fixed costs**, meaning that the hotel is locked in to these costs because of previous management decisions. For example, as soon as a hotel is built, management becomes locked in to a certain amount of property taxes and depreciation, simply because of the location and size of the hotel, and management's choice of furnishings and amenities (pool, fitness room, restaurant, and so forth). Management has little or no control over these committed fixed costs in the short run.

However, the hotel also incurs **discretionary fixed costs**, such as advertising expenses, that are a result of annual management decisions. Companies have more control over discretionary fixed costs.

Suppose the hotel incurs $100,000 of fixed costs each month. In Exhibit 6-3, the vertical axis (y-axis) shows total fixed costs, while the horizontal axis (x-axis) plots volume of activity (thousands of guests). The graph shows total fixed costs as a *flat line* that intersects the y-axis at $100,000 (this is known as the vertical intercept) because the hotel will incur the same $100,000 of fixed costs regardless of the number of guests that stay at the hotel during the month.

EXHIBIT 6-3 Fixed Costs

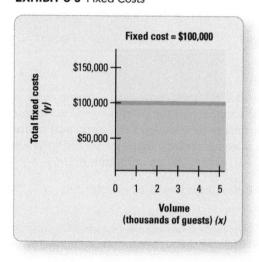

The cost equation for a fixed cost is as follows:

$$\text{Total fixed cost } (y) = \text{Fixed amount over a period of time } (f)$$

Or simply,

$$y = f$$

Embassy Suites' *monthly* fixed cost equation is as follows:

$$y = \$100,000$$

where

$$y = \text{total fixed cost per month}$$

In contrast to the *total fixed costs* shown in Exhibit 6-3, the *fixed cost per guest* depends on the number of guests that stay at the hotel during the month. If the hotel only serves 2,000 guests during the month, the fixed cost per guest is as follows:

$$\$100,000 \div 2,000 \text{ guests} = \$50/\text{guest}$$

If the number of guests *doubles* to 4,000, the fixed cost per guest is *cut in half*:

$$\$100,000 \div 4,000 \text{ guests} = \$25/\text{guest}$$

Notice that the fixed cost per guest is *inversely proportional* to the number of guests. When volume *increases*, not only does the fixed cost per guest *decrease, but it also decreases in a proportional fashion*. For example, if volume triples, then the cost per unit will be one-third of what it was at the original volume. If volume quadruples, then the cost per unit will be one quarter of what it was at the original volume. The opposite is also true: When volume *decreases*, the fixed cost per guest *increases in a proportional fashion.* In our example, cutting the number of guests in half (from 4,000 to 2,000) will double the cost per unit (from $25 per guest to $50 per guest).

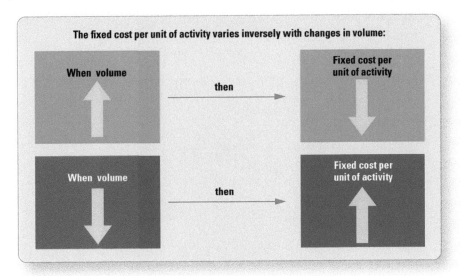

Keep the following important rule of thumb in mind:

Companies like to operate near full capacity because it drives down their fixed costs per unit. A lower cost per unit gives businesses the flexibility to decrease sales prices, which makes them more competitive.

Key points to remember about fixed costs appear in Exhibit 6-4.

EXHIBIT 6-4 Key Characteristics of Fixed Costs

- *Total* fixed costs stay *constant* over a wide range of volume
- Fixed costs *per unit of activity* vary *inversely* in proportion to changes in volume:
    - Fixed cost per unit of activity *increases* when volume *decreases*
      (*If volume is cut in half, the fixed cost per unit will double*)
    - Fixed cost per unit of activity *decreases* when volume *increases*
      (*If volume doubles, the fixed cost per unit will be cut in half*)
- Total fixed cost graphs are always flat lines with no slope that intersect the y-axis at a level equal to total fixed costs
- Total fixed costs can be expressed as $y = f$
  where,

  y = total fixed cost

  f = fixed cost over a given period of time

Try It!

Compute the (a) total fixed cost and (b) fixed cost per guest if the hotel has 16,000 guests next month. Compare the fixed cost per guest at the higher occupancy rate to the fixed cost per guest when only 2,000 guests stay during the month.

Please see page 380 for solutions.

Mixed Costs

Mixed costs contain both variable and fixed cost components. Embassy Suites' utilities are mixed costs because the hotel requires a certain amount of utilities just to operate. However, the more guests that stay at the hotel, the more water, electricity, and gas required. Exhibit 6-5 illustrates mixed costs.

EXHIBIT 6-5 Mixed Costs

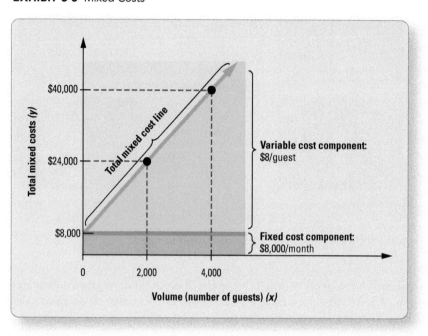

For example, let's assume that utilities for the common areas of the hotel and unoccupied rooms cost $8,000 per month. In addition, utilities increase by $8 per guest as each guest cools or heats his or her room, takes showers, turns on the TV and lights, and uses freshly laundered sheets and towels.

Notice the two components—variable and fixed—of the mixed costs in Exhibit 6-5. Similar to a variable cost, the total mixed cost line increases as the volume of activity increases. However, *the line does not begin at the origin.* Rather, it intersects the y-axis at a level equal to the fixed cost component. Even if no guests stay this month, the hotel will still incur $8,000 of utilities cost.

Managers can once again use a cost equation to express the mixed cost line so that they can predict total mixed costs at different volumes. The mixed costs equation simply *combines* the variable cost and fixed cost equations:

$$\text{Total mixed costs} = \text{Variable cost component} + \text{Fixed cost component}$$
$$y \qquad = \qquad vx \qquad + \qquad f$$

Embassy Suites' monthly utilities cost equation is as follows:

$$y = \$8x + \$8,000$$

where

$$y = \text{total utilities cost per month}$$
$$x = \text{number of guests}$$

If the hotel serves 2,000 guests this month, it expects utilities to cost:

$$y = (\$8 \text{ per guest} \times 2,000 \text{ guests}) + \$8,000$$
$$= \$24,000$$

If the hotel serves 4,000 guests this month, it expects utilities to cost:

$$y = (\$8 \text{ per guest} \times 4,000 \text{ guests}) + \$8,000$$
$$= \$40,000$$

Total mixed costs increase as volume increases, *but **not** in direct proportion to changes in volume*. The total mixed costs did *not* double when volume doubled. This is because of the fixed cost component. Additionally, consider the mixed costs *per guest*:

If the hotel serves 2,000 guests: $24,000 total cost ÷ 2,000 guests = $12.00 per guest
If the hotel serves 4,000 guests: $40,000 total cost ÷ 4,000 guests = $10.00 per guest

The mixed costs per guest did *not* decrease by half when the hotel served twice as many guests. This is because of the variable cost component. Mixed costs per unit decrease as volume increases, but ***not in direct proportion*** to changes in volume. Because mixed costs contain both fixed cost and variable cost components, they behave differently than purely variable costs and purely fixed costs. Key points to remember about mixed costs appear in Exhibit 6-6.

EXHIBIT 6-6 Key Characteristics of Mixed Costs

- *Total* mixed costs increase as volume increases because of the variable cost component
- Mixed costs *per unit* decrease as volume increases because of the fixed cost component
- Total mixed costs graphs slope upward but do *not* begin at the origin—they intersect the y-axis at the level of fixed costs
- Total mixed costs can be expressed as a *combination* of the variable and fixed cost equations:

    Total mixed costs = variable cost component + fixed cost component
    $$y = vx + f$$
    where,
    y = total mixed costs
    v = variable cost per unit of activity (slope)
    x = volume of activity
    f = fixed cost over a given period of time (vertical intercept)

Try It!

Assume the local fitness club charges a membership fee of $30 per month for unlimited use of the exercise equipment plus an additional fee of $5 for every instructor-led exercise class you attend.

1. Express the monthly cost of belonging to the fitness club as a cost equation.
2. What is your expected cost for a month in which you attend five instructor-led classes?
3. If your attendance doubles to 10 classes per month, will your total cost for the month double? Explain.

Please see page 380 for solutions.

Relevant Range

Managers always need to keep their <u>relevant range</u> in mind when predicting total costs. The relevant range is the band of volume where the following remain constant:

- *Total fixed costs*
- *Variable cost per unit*

In other words, it's the range of volume in which costs behave a certain way. A change in cost behavior means a change to a different relevant range.

Let's consider how the concept of relevant range applies to Embassy Suites. As shown in Exhibit 6-3, the hotel's current fixed costs are $100,000 per month. However, because of the hotel's popularity, the percentage of rooms occupied each night (room occupancy rate) continues to increase. To keep customer satisfaction high, management may decide to add more capacity to the common areas of the hotel, such as a new elevator bank and additional breakfast and fitness areas. This expansion, if carried out, will increase the hotel's fixed costs because of depreciation on the new fixed assets. The same sort of situation often occurs with manufacturers and merchandising companies that must expand their capacity to keep up with growing sales volume. Exhibit 6-7 illustrates different relevant ranges for the hotel's fixed costs.

EXHIBIT 6-7 Examples of Different Relevant Ranges for Fixed Costs

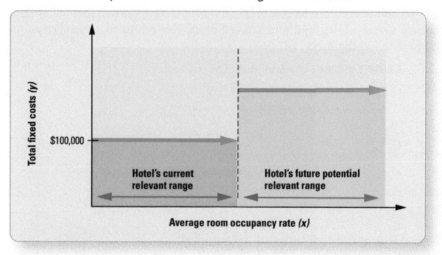

The concept of relevant range also applies to variable costs. As shown in Exhibit 6-1, the hotel's current variable cost for toiletries is $3 per guest. However, as room occupancy rates continue to grow, management hopes to negotiate greater volume discounts on the toiletries from its suppliers. These volume discounts will decrease the variable toiletries cost per guest (for example, down to $2.75 per guest). Exhibit 6-8 illustrates different relevant ranges for the hotel's variable toiletries cost.

Why is the concept of relevant range important? Managers can predict costs accurately only if they use cost information for the appropriate relevant range. For example, think about smartphone plans. Many smartphone plans offer unlimited talk and texting and a large block of data for a fixed fee each month. If the customer exceeds the allotted amount of data, the company charges an additional per-MB fee. Exhibit 6-9 shows a smartphone plan in which the first 5 GB of data each month costs $50. After 5 GB are used, the customer must pay an additional 1.5 cents per MB. This smartphone plan has two relevant ranges. The first relevant range extends from 0 to 5 GB. In this range, the $50 fee behaves strictly as a fixed cost. The customer could use 0 MB, 800 MB, or 5 GB of data and still pay a flat $50 fee that month. The second relevant range starts after 5 GB and extends indefinitely. In this relevant range, the cost is mixed: $50 plus 1.5 cents per MB of data in excess of 5 GB. To accurately predict costs, customers need to know in which relevant range they plan to operate. The same holds true for businesses.

EXHIBIT 6-8 Examples of Different Relevant Ranges for Variable Costs

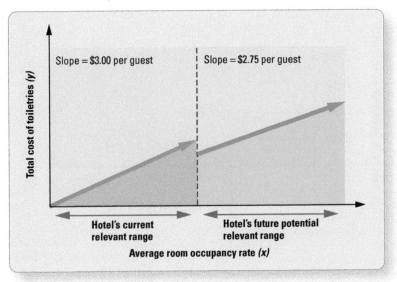

EXHIBIT 6-9 Example of Relevant Ranges

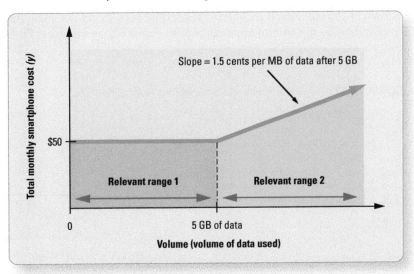

Other Cost Behaviors

While many business costs behave as variable, fixed, or mixed costs, some costs do not neatly fit these patterns. We'll briefly describe other cost behaviors you may encounter.

Step costs resemble stair steps: They are fixed over a small range of activity and then jump up to a new fixed level with moderately small changes in volume. Hotels, restaurants, hospitals, and educational institutions typically experience step costs. For example, states usually require day-care centers to limit the caregiver-to-child ratio to 1:7—that is, there must be one caregiver for every seven children. As shown in Exhibit 6-10, a day-care center that takes on an eighth child must incur the cost of employing another caregiver. The new caregiver can watch the eighth through fourteenth child enrolled at the day-care center. If the day-care center takes on a fifteenth child, management will once again hire another caregiver, costing another $20,000 in salary. The same step cost patterns occur with hotels (maid-to-room ratio), restaurants (server-to-table ratio), hospitals (nurse-to-bed ratio), and schools (teacher-to-student ratio).

EXHIBIT 6-10 Step Costs

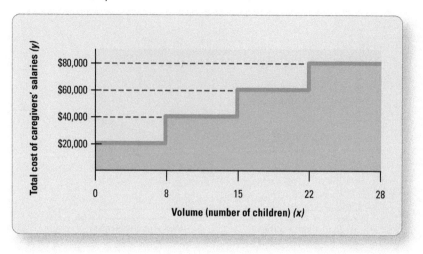

Step costs differ from fixed costs only in that they "step up" to a new relevant range with relatively small changes in volume. Fixed costs hold constant over much larger ranges of volume.

As shown by the red lines in Exhibit 6-11, **curvilinear costs** are not linear (not a straight line) and, therefore, do not fit into any neat pattern that we have discussed thus far.

EXHIBIT 6-11 Curvilinear Costs and Straight-Line Approximations

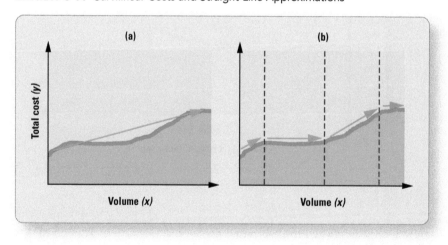

As shown by the straight green arrow in Exhibit 6-11(a), some businesses *approximate* these types of costs as mixed costs, knowing that they will have an estimation error at particular volumes. Sometimes managers also approximate step costs the same way: they simply draw a straight mixed cost line through the steps.

As shown in Exhibit 6-11(b), however, if managers need more accurate predictions, they can simply break these types of costs into smaller relevant ranges and make their predictions based on the particular relevant range. For example, the day-care center may want to predict total caregiver salaries if it enrolls 26 children. The manager knows this enrollment falls into the relevant range of 22 to 28 children, where he or she needs to employ four caregivers. The manager can then predict total caregiver salaries to be $80,000 (four caregivers × $20,000 salary per caregiver).

Sustainability and Cost Behavior

Many companies adopting sustainable business practices experience changes in the way their costs behave. For example, most banks, credit card companies, and utilities now promote the use of paperless e-banking and e-billing as a preferable alternative to sending traditional paper statements and bills through the mail. Why? Because e-banking and e-billing drives down a company's variable costs since they don't have to spend money on the paper, envelopes, printing, and postage associated with sending out paper statements. Likewise, when a customer pays electronically, rather than sending in a check, the company doesn't incur the variable cost associated with opening the mail, recording the payment to the customer's account, and processing the bank deposit. All of this is accomplished electronically by the company's software.

On the other hand, the company must incur additional fixed costs to develop and operate secure online banking and billing websites. However, we know that the variable cost savings is greater than the increase in fixed costs because many companies are either (1) offering customer incentives to switch to e-billing or (2) charging customers an additional fee for receiving paper-based bills and statements in the mail. Whether using the carrot or the stick approach, companies are shifting consumer behavior as a means to decrease total costs.

The environmental consequences of e-billing and e-banking are tremendous if you consider the entire production and delivery cycle of the bills and statements, all of the way from logging the trees in the forest to delivery of the bill at the customer's doorstep. Not only are fewer trees cut down, but also less energy is consumed in transportation of the timber, processing of the paper, distribution of the paper, delivery of the statements via the U.S. Postal Service, and final disposal of the paper at landfills or recycling centers. In addition, less waste water is generated and fewer greenhouse gas emissions are produced. The downside, from a triple-bottom-line perspective, is the loss of jobs in associated industries, such as the U.S. Postal Service.

Adoption of e-billing and e-banking services provides one means for households to embrace a greener lifestyle. For example, the average household that receives e-bills and makes electronic bill payments reduces paper consumption by 6.6 pounds and prevents 29 pounds of greenhouse gas emissions each year. Water and gasoline are also saved in the process.[2] According to the U.S. Postal Service, in 2014, 19.5 billion bills and statements (equating to approximately 900 million pounds of paper) were delivered across the country. Because of the increasing popularity of e-billing, the annual volume is actually down by over 5.5 billion pieces, or about 22%, when compared with 2008. Whereas 2010 marked the first year in history that more bills were paid electronically than by the mail, by 2014, only 34% of bills were paid by mail.[3] Thus, the huge shift toward adoption of electronic bill payment by the general public could have a significant positive impact on the environment.

▶ See Exercises 6-24A and E6-45B

We have just described the most typical cost behaviors. In the next part of the chapter, we will discuss methods managers use for determining how their costs behave.

---

[2] www.payitgreen.org/consumer/get-the-facts

[3] The Household Diary Study: Mail Use and Attributes in FY 2014 (and 2010). U.S. Postal Service.

Decision Guidelines

Cost Behavior

Suppose you manage a local fitness club. To be an effective manager, you need to know how the club's costs behave. Here are some decisions you will need to make.

Decision	Guidelines
How can you tell if a *total* cost is variable, fixed, or mixed?	• Total variable costs increase in *direct proportion* to increases in volume. • Total fixed costs stay *constant* over a wide range of volumes. • Total mixed costs increase but *not* in direct proportion to increases in volume.
How can you tell if a *per-unit* cost is variable, fixed, or mixed?	• On a per-unit basis, variable costs stay constant. • On a per-unit basis, fixed costs decrease in proportion to increases in volume (that is to say, they are inversely proportional). • On a per-unit basis, mixed costs decrease but not in direct proportion to increases in volume.
How can you tell by looking at a graph if a cost is variable, fixed, or mixed?	• Variable cost lines slope upward and begin at the origin. • Fixed cost lines are flat (no slope) and intersect the *y*-axis at a level equal to total fixed costs (this is known as the vertical intercept). • Mixed cost lines slope upward but do *not* begin at the origin. They intersect the *y*-axis at a level equal to their fixed cost component.
How can you mathematically express different cost behaviors?	• Cost equations mathematically express cost behavior using the equation for a straight line: $$y = vx + f$$ where y = total cost v = variable cost per unit of activity (slope) x = volume of activity f = fixed cost (the vertical intercept) • For a variable cost, *f* is zero, leaving the following: $$y = vx$$ • For a fixed cost, *v* is zero, leaving the following: $$y = f$$ • Because a mixed cost has both a fixed cost component and a variable cost component, its cost equation is: $$y = vx + f$$

SUMMARY PROBLEM 1

The previous manager of Fitness-for-Life started the following schedule but left before completing it. The manager wasn't sure but thought the club's fixed operating costs were $10,000 per month and the variable operating costs were $1 per member. The club's existing facilities could serve up to 750 members per month.

Requirements

1. Complete the following schedule for different levels of monthly membership, assuming the previous manager's cost behavior estimates are accurate:

	A	B	C	D
	Monthly Operating Costs	**100 Members**	**500 Members**	**750 Members**
1				
2	Total variable costs			
3	Plus: Total fixed costs			
4	Total operating costs			
5				
6	Variable cost per member			
7	Plus: Fixed cost per member			
8	Average cost per member			
9				

2. As the manager of the fitness club, why shouldn't you use the average cost per member to predict total costs at different levels of membership?

■ SOLUTIONS

Requirement 1

As volume increases, fixed costs stay constant in total but decrease on a per-unit basis. As volume increases, variable costs stay constant on a per-unit basis but increase in total in direct proportion to increases in volume:

	A	B	C	D
1	**Monthly Operating Costs**	**100 Members**	**500 Members**	**750 Members**
2	Total variable costs	$ 100	$ 500	$ 750
3	Plus: Total fixed costs	10,000	10,000	10,000
4	Total operating costs	$ 10,100	$ 10,500	$ 10,750
5				
6	Variable cost per member	$ 1.00	$ 1.00	$ 1.00
7	Plus: Fixed cost per member	100.00	20.00	13.33
8	Average cost per member	$ 101.00	$ 21.00	$ 14.33
9				

Requirement 2

The average cost per member should not be used to predict total costs at different volumes of membership because it changes as volume changes. The average cost per member decreases as volume increases due to the fixed component of the club's operating costs. Managers should base cost predictions on cost equations, not on the average cost per member.

How Do Managers Determine Cost Behavior?

Managers need to figure out how their costs behave before they can make predictions and good business decisions. In this section, we discuss the most common ways of determining cost behavior.

Account Analysis

3 Use account analysis and scatterplots to analyze cost behavior

When performing **account analysis**, managers use their judgment to classify each general ledger account as a variable, fixed, or mixed cost. For example, by looking at invoices from his or her supplier, the hotel manager knows that every guest packet of toiletries costs $3. Because guests use or take these toiletries, the total toiletries cost rises in direct proportion to the number of guests. These facts allow the manager to classify the complimentary toiletries expense account as a variable cost.

Likewise, the hotel manager uses account analysis to determine how the depreciation expense accounts behave. Because the hotel uses straight-line depreciation on the parking ramp, building, and furnishings, the manager would classify the depreciation expense accounts as fixed costs. Thus, the manager can use this knowledge of cost behavior and his or her judgment to classify many accounts as variable or fixed.

Scatterplots

The hotel manager also knows that many of the hotel's costs, such as utilities, are mixed costs. But how does the manager figure out the portion of the mixed cost that is fixed and the portion that is variable? In other words, how does the manager know from looking at the monthly utility bills that the hotel's utilities cost about $8,000 per month plus $8 more for every guest? One way of figuring this out is by collecting and analyzing historical data about costs and volume.

For example, let's assume that the hotel's manager has collected the information shown in Exhibit 6-12 about last year's guest volume and utility costs.

EXHIBIT 6-12 Historical Information on Guest Volume and Utility Costs

Month	Guest Volume (x)	Utility Costs (y)
January	13,250	$114,000
February	15,200	136,000
March	17,600	135,000
April	18,300	157,000
May	22,900	195,400
June	24,600	207,800
July	25,200	209,600
August	24,900	208,300
September	22,600	196,000
October	20,800	176,400
November	18,300	173,600
December	15,420	142,000

Once the data have been collected, the manager creates a **scatterplot** of the data.

A scatterplot, which graphs the historical cost data on the *y*-axis and volume data on the *x*-axis, helps managers visualize the relationship between the cost and volume of activity (number of guests, in our example). If there is a fairly strong relationship (correlation) between the cost and volume, the data points will fall in a linear pattern, meaning they will resemble something close to a straight line. However, if there is little or no relationship between the cost and volume, the data points will appear almost random.

Exhibit 6-13 shows a scatterplot of the data in Exhibit 6-12. Scatterplots are simple to create using Microsoft Excel (see the "Technology Makes It Simple" feature on the next page). Notice how the data points fall in a pattern that resembles something *close* to a straight line. This shows us that there is a strong relationship between the number of guests and the hotel's utility costs. In other words, the number of guests could be considered a driver of the hotel's utilities costs (recall from our discussion of ABC in Chapter 4 that cost drivers are activities that cause costs to be incurred). On the other hand, if there were a *weaker* relationship between the number of guests and the utility costs, the data points would not fall in such a tight linear pattern. They would be more loosely scattered. If there were *no* relationship between the number of guests and the utility costs, the data points would appear almost random.

> **Why is this important?**
> "Scatterplots **help managers** easily **visualize** the **relationship** between cost and volume. Scatterplots are fast and easy to prepare using Excel."

EXHIBIT 6-13 Scatterplot of Monthly Data

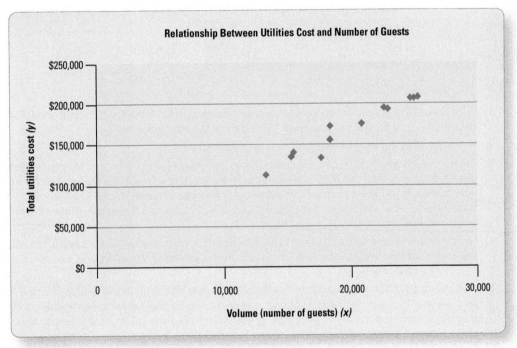

Why is this important? If the data points suggest a fairly weak relationship between the cost and the volume of the chosen activity, any cost equation based on that data will not be very useful for predicting future costs. If this is the case, the manager should consider using a different activity for modeling cost behavior. For example, many hotels use "occupancy rate" (the percentage of rooms rented) rather than number of guests as a basis for explaining and predicting variable and mixed costs.

Scatterplots are also very useful because they allow managers to identify **outliers**, or abnormal data points. Outliers are data points that do not fall in the same general pattern as the other data points. Since all data points in Exhibit 6-13 fall in the same basic pattern, no outliers appear to exist in our data. However, if a manager sees a potential outlier in the data, he or she should first determine whether the data are correct. Perhaps a clerical error was made when gathering or inputting the data. However, if the data are correct, the manager will use his or her judgment to determine whether to keep the data point in the analysis or whether to delete it.

Once the scatterplot has been prepared and examined for outliers, the next step is to determine the cost behavior that best describes the historical data points pictured in the scatterplot. Take a moment and pencil in the cost behavior line that you think best represents the data points in Exhibit 6-13. Where does your line intersect the y-axis? At the origin or above it? In other words, does the utilities cost appear to be a purely variable cost or a mixed cost? If it's a mixed cost, what portion of it is fixed?

Instead of guessing, managers can use one of the following methods to estimate the cost equation that describes the data in the scatterplot:

- High-low method
- Regression analysis

The biggest difference between these methods is that the high-low method *uses only two* of the historical data points for this estimate, whereas regression analysis uses *all* of the historical data points. Therefore, regression analysis is theoretically the better of the two methods.

We'll describe both of these methods in the next sections. Before continuing, check out the "Technology Makes It Simple" feature. It shows you just how easy it is to make a scatterplot using Microsoft Excel.

Technology Makes It Simple   Excel 2016

Creating Scatterplots

1. In an Excel 2016 spreadsheet, type in your data as pictured in Exhibit 6-12. Put the volume data in one column and the associated cost data in the next column.

2. Highlight all of the volume and cost data with your cursor.

3. Click on the "Insert" tab on the menu bar. From the chart options, choose "Scatter" as the chart type. Next, click the plain scatterplot (without any lines). You'll see the scatterplot on your screen. If you want to make the scatter graph larger, choose "Move Chart Location" from the menu bar and select "New Sheet" and "OK." Make sure the volume data is on the x-axis and the cost data is on the y-axis.

4. To add labels for the scatterplot and titles for each axis, click on the "Quick Layout" tab on the menu bar and choose the first layout pictured. Customize the chart and axis titles to reflect your data set.

5. If you want to change the way your graph looks, simply right click anywhere on the graph and use the "Format Plot Area" options. If your data consist of large numbers, the graph may not automatically start at the origin. If you want to see the origin on the graph, right-click on any of the numbers on the x- or y-axis and choose "Format Axis." Then, insert "0" (zero) as the minimum bound.

High-Low Method

4 Use the high-low method to analyze cost behavior

The **high-low method** is an easy way to estimate the variable and fixed cost components of a mixed cost. The high-low method basically fits a mixed cost line through the highest and lowest *volume* data points, as shown in Exhibit 6-14, hence the name *high-low*. The high-low method produces the cost equation describing this mixed cost line.

To use the high-low method, we must first identify the months with the highest and lowest volume of activity. Looking at Exhibit 6-12, we see that the hotel served the *most* guests in July and the *fewest* guests in January. *Therefore, we use the data from only these two months in our analysis. We ignore data from all other months.* Even if a month other than July had the highest utility cost, we would still use July. Why? Because we choose

EXHIBIT 6-14 Mixed Cost Line Using High-Low Method

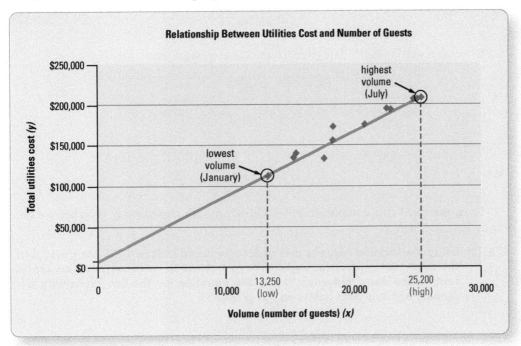

the "high" data point based on the month with the highest volume of activity (number of guests)—not the highest cost. We choose the "low" data point in a similar fashion.

STEP 1: The first step is to find *the slope of the mixed cost line* that connects the January and July data points. The slope is the variable cost per unit of activity. We can determine the slope of a line as "rise over run." The *rise* is simply the difference in cost between the high and low data points (July and January in our case), while the *run* is the difference in *volume* between the high and low data points:

$$\text{Slope} = \text{Variable cost per unit of activity } (v) = \frac{\text{Rise}}{\text{Run}} = \frac{\text{Change in cost}}{\text{Change in volume}} = \frac{y\,(\text{high}) - y\,(\text{low})}{x\,(\text{high}) - x\,(\text{low})}$$

Using the data from July (as our high) and January (as our low), we calculate the slope as follows:

$$\frac{(\$209,600 - \$114,000)}{(25,200 \text{ guests} - 13,250 \text{ guests})} = \$8 \text{ per guest}$$

The slope of the mixed cost line, or variable cost per unit of activity, is $8 per guest.

STEP 2: The second step is to find the vertical intercept—the place where the line connecting the January and July data points intersects the y-axis. This is the fixed cost component of the mixed cost. We insert the slope found in Step 1 ($8 per guest) and the volume and cost data from *either* the high or low month into a mixed costs equation:

$$\text{Total mixed costs} = \text{Variable cost component} + \text{Fixed cost component}$$
$$y = vx + f$$

For example, we can insert July's cost and volume data as follows:

$$\$209,600 = (\$8 \text{ per guest} \times 25,200 \text{ guests}) + f$$

And then solve for f:

$$f = \$8,000$$

Or we can use January's data to reach the same conclusion:

y	$=$	vx	$+ f$
$\$114,000 = (\$8 \text{ per guest} \times 13,250 \text{ guests}) + f$			

And then solve for f:

$$f = \$8,000$$

Thus, the fixed cost component is $8,000 per month regardless of whether we use July or January's data.

> **STEP 3: Using the variable cost per unit of activity found in Step 1 ($8 per guest) and the fixed cost component found in Step 2 ($8,000), write the equation representing the costs' behavior. This is the equation for the line connecting the January and July data points on our graph.**

$$y = \$8x + \$8,000$$

Where

$$y = \text{total monthly utilities cost}$$
$$x = \text{number of guests}$$

This is the equation used by the manager in the first half of the chapter to express the hotel's utility costs.

These three steps may seem familiar to you. If so, that's because you probably learned how to find the equation for a straight line ($y = mx + b$) in a high school math class. The high-low method follows the very same steps to find the equation for the straight line connecting the highest and lowest-volume data points. The only difference is in the nomenclature: cost equations use "v" to stand for the slope of the line (rather than "m") and "f" to stand for the y-intercept (rather than "b"). Otherwise, it's the exact same process you learned in your high school math class.

One major drawback of the high-low method is that it uses only two data points: January and July. Because we ignored every other month, the line might not be representative of those months. In our example, the high-low line is representative of the other data points, but in other situations, it may not be. Therefore, the better method to use is regression analysis, which is explained next.

Regression Analysis

5 Use regression analysis to analyze cost behavior

Regression analysis is a statistical procedure for determining the line and associated cost equation that best fit *all of the data points in the data set, not just the high-volume and low-volume data points*. In fact, some refer to regression analysis as "the line of best fit." Since the statistical analysis considers all of the data points when forming the line, it is usually more accurate than the high-low method. A statistic (called the R-square) generated by regression analysis also tells us *how well* the line fits the data points. Regression analysis is tedious to complete by hand but simple to do using Microsoft Excel (see the "Technology Makes It Simple" feature on page 329). Many graphing calculators also perform regression analysis.

Regression analysis using Microsoft Excel gives us the output shown in Exhibit 6-15. The output looks complicated, but for our purposes, we only need to consider the three highlighted pieces of information:

EXHIBIT 6-15 Output of Microsoft Excel Regression Analysis

	A	B	C	D	E	F	G	H	I
1	**SUMMARY OUTPUT**								
2									
3		*Regression Statistics*							
4	Multiple R		0.973273						
5	R Square		0.94726						
6	Adjusted R Square		0.941986						
7	Standard Error		8053.744						
8	Observations		12						
9									
10	**ANOVA**								
11		*df*	*SS*	*MS*	*F*	*Significance F*			
12	Regression	1	11650074512	1.17E + 10	179.6110363	1.02696E-07			
13	Residual	10	648627988.2	64862799					
14	Total	11	12298702500						
15									
16		*Coefficients*	*Standard Error*	*t Stat*	*P-value*	*Lower 95%*	*Upper 95%*	*Lower 95.0%*	*Upper 95.0%*
17	Intercept	14538.05	11898.3624	1.221853	0.249783701	-11973.15763	41049.25	-11973.16	41049.25
18	X Variable 1	7.849766	0.585720166	13.4019	1.02696E-07	6.5446997	9.154831	6.5447	9.154831

1. Intercept coefficient (this refers to the vertical intercept) = 14,538.05
2. X Variable 1 coefficient (this refers to the slope) = 7.85 (rounded)
3. The R-square value (the goodness-of-fit statistic) = 0.947 (rounded)

Let's look at each piece of information, starting with the highlighted information at the bottom of the output:

1. The Intercept coefficient is the vertical intercept of the mixed cost line. It's the fixed cost component of the mixed cost. Regression analysis tells us that the fixed component of the monthly utility bill is $14,538. Why is this different from the $8,000 fixed component we found using the high-low method? It's because regression analysis considers *every* data point, not just the high- and low-volume data points, when forming the best fitting line.

2. The "X Variable 1 coefficient" is the line's slope, or our variable cost per guest. Regression analysis tells us that the hotel spends an extra $7.85 on utilities for every guest it serves. This is slightly lower than the $8 per guest amount we found using the high-low method.

   Using the regression output, we can write the monthly utilities cost equation as follows:

   $$y = \$7.85x + \$14,538$$

   where

   y = total monthly utilities cost
   x = number of guests

> **Why is this important?**
>
> "Regression analysis is **fast** and **easy** to perform using Microsoft Excel. **Regression analysis** gives managers the most **representative** cost equations, allowing them to make the most **accurate** cost projections."

3. Now, let's look at the R-square statistic highlighted near the top of Exhibit 6-15. The R-square statistic is often referred to as a "goodness-of-fit" statistic because it tells

us how well the regression line fits the data points. The R-square can range in value from zero to one, as shown in Exhibit 6-16. If there were no relationship between the number of guests and the hotel's utility costs, the data points would be scattered randomly (rather than being in a linear pattern) and the R-square would be close to zero. If there were a *perfect* relationship between the number of guests and the hotel's utility cost, a *perfectly* straight line would run through *every* data point and the R-square would be 1.00. In our case, the R-square of 0.947 means that the regression line fits the data quite well (it's very close to 1.00). In other words, the data points *almost* fall in a straight line (as you can see in Exhibit 6-13).

EXHIBIT 6-16 Range of R-square Values

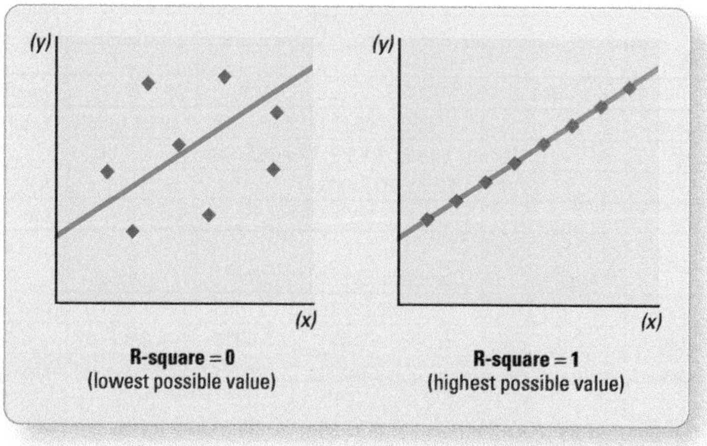

R-square = 0
(lowest possible value)

R-square = 1
(highest possible value)

The R-square provides managers with very helpful information. The higher the R-square, the stronger the relationship between cost and volume. The stronger the relationship, the more confidence the manager would have in using the cost equation to predict costs at different volumes within the same relevant range.

As a rule of thumb:

■ An R-square over 0.80 generally indicates that the cost equation is very reliable for predicting costs at other volumes within the relevant range.

■ An R-square between 0.50 and 0.80 means that the manager should use the cost equation with caution since the equation will likely result in some estimation error.

■ An R-square less than 0.50 means the equation should probably not be used. Rather, the manager should try modeling cost behavior using a different activity base (for example, room occupancy rate) because the current measure of volume is only weakly related to the costs.

Regression analysis can also help managers implement ABC. Recall from Chapter 4 that managers must choose a cost allocation base for every activity cost pool. The cost allocation base should be the primary cost driver of the costs in that pool. Management will use logic to come up with a short list of potential cost drivers for each activity cost pool. Then, management can run a regression analysis for each potential cost driver to see how strongly related it is to the activity costs in the pool. Managers compare the R-squares from each regression to see which one is highest. The regression with the highest R-square identifies the primary cost driver.

Adding a Regression Line, Regression Equation, and R-Square Value to a Scatterplot

Rather than obtaining the full regression output pictured in Exhibit 6-15 and selecting the necessary pieces of information from it, you can command Excel to add the regression equation, regression line, and R-square value directly to a scatterplot. You'll be amazed at how quickly and easily you can create a professional-quality graph using the instructions found in the "Technology Makes It Simple" feature on the next page.

Technology Makes It Simple — Excel 2016

Adding a Regression Line, Equation, and R-square to the Scatterplot

Rather than obtaining a full regression output, you can command Excel to display the regression line, the associated cost equation, and the R-square directly on the scatterplot. Just follow these simple instructions:

1. Start with the Excel scatterplot you created using the directions found on page 324.
2. Point the cursor at any data point on your scatterplot and *right* click on the mouse.
3. Choose "Add Trendline." You will see the regression line added to the chart and a "Format Trendline" dialog box will open.
4. Check the two boxes: "Display Equation on Chart" and "Display R-squared value on chart."
5. OPTIONAL: To force the regression line to stretch *back* to the y-axis fill in the "Forecast Backward" box with the *lowest* x-value (volume) in your data set. This number is easily found by hovering your cursor over the lowest volume data point on the chart.

Technology Makes It Simple — Excel 2016

Regression Analysis

1. If you created a scatterplot, you have already done this first step. In an Excel spreadsheet, type in your data as pictured in Exhibit 6-12. Put the volume data in one column and the associated cost data in the next column.
2. Click on the "Data" tab on the menu bar.
3. Next, click on "Data Analysis." If you don't see it on your toolbar, follow the directions for add-ins given below before continuing.
4. From the list of data analysis tools, select "Regression," then "OK."
5. Follow the two "Input" instructions on the screen:
    i. Highlight (or type in) the y-axis data range (this is the cost data) with your cursor.
    ii. Highlight (or type in) the x-axis data range (this is the volume data) with your cursor.
    iii. Click "OK."
6. That's all. Excel gives you the output shown in Exhibit 6-15.

DIRECTIONS FOR ADD-INs: It's easy and free to add the "Data Analysis Toolpak" if it's not already on your toolbar. You'll only need to add it once, and then it will always be on your toolbar. Simply follow these instructions:

1. Click on the "File" tab on the menu bar. Then click "Options" on the left-hand side of the screen.
2. Click "Add-Ins" on the left-hand side of the screen.
3. In the "Manage" box at the bottom of the screen, select "Excel Add-Ins" and click "GO."
4. In the "Add-Ins available" box, select the "Analysis ToolPak" check box and then click "OK." If asked, click "Yes" to install.
5. That's all. You should now see "Data Analysis" on your Excel toolbar.

Data Concerns

Cost equations are only as good as the data on which they are based. For example, if the hotel's utility bills are seasonal, management may want to develop separate cost equations for each season. For example, management might develop a winter utility bill cost equation using historical data from only the winter months and a summer utility bill using data from only the summer months. Inflation can also affect predictions. If inflation is running rampant, managers should adjust projected costs by the inflation rate. Even if the economy is experiencing low inflation rates, certain industries (such as health care and higher education) or raw material inputs (such as corn prices) may be experiencing large price changes. In our example, management would need to consider whether the rates charged by the utility companies for electricity and natural gas are expected to increase or decrease in the coming year.

Another cause for concern is outliers, or abnormal data points. Outliers can distort the results of the high-low method and regression analysis. Recall that the high-low method uses only two data points—the data points associated with the highest and lowest volumes of activity. If either of these points is an outlier, the resulting line and cost equation will be skewed. Because regression analysis uses all data points, any outlier in the data will affect the resulting line and cost equation, but to a lesser extent.

For example, let's say management's historical data set resulted in the scatterplot pictured in Exhibit 6-17. The low-volume data point looks like it might be an outlier. Notice how the high-low line is highly skewed as a result. However, the regression line remains fairly representative of the other data points, even though it is being pulled slightly toward the outlier. Remember to always investigate potential outliers to help determine whether or not to remove them from the data set before proceeding with regression or the high-low method.

EXHIBIT 6-17 Effect of Outlier on Cost Equations

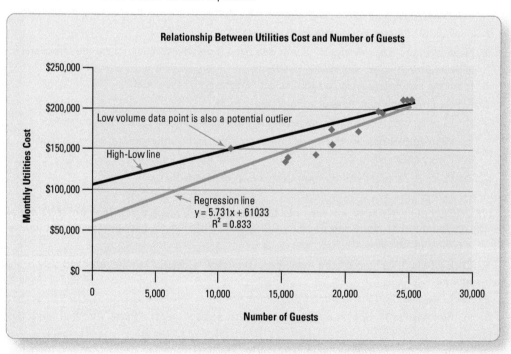

What Are the Roles of Variable Costing and the Contribution Margin Income Statement?

You have just learned about different cost behaviors. As you'll see in the coming chapters, almost all business decisions are influenced by cost behavior. In the following sections, we'll explain how the accounting system can communicate cost behavior information to managers so that they have it readily available for planning, decision-making, and performance evaluation purposes.

6 Describe variable costing and prepare a contribution margin income statement

Comparing Absorption Costing and Variable Costing

So far in this textbook, we have used a costing concept known as absorption costing. Why? Generally Accepted Accounting Principles (GAAP) requires absorption costing for external financial reporting and the Internal Revenue Service (IRS) requires it for tax preparation. Under __absorption costing__, all manufacturing-related costs, whether fixed or variable, are "absorbed" into the cost of the product. In other words, all direct materials, direct labor, and manufacturing overhead (MOH) costs are treated as product costs, as described in Chapter 2. We used absorption costing, also known as "traditional" or "full costing," when we illustrated job costing and process costing in Chapters 3, 4, and 5.

Under absorption costing, no distinction is made between manufacturing costs that rise and fall with production volume and manufacturing costs that remain fixed. As a review,

- variable manufacturing costs would include direct material, direct labor, and variable MOH costs such as the utilities used during the production process.
- fixed MOH costs would include property taxes and insurance on the plant, straight-line depreciation on the plant, lease payments on the production equipment and the portion of utilities that are not affected by changes in production volume.

Supporters of absorption costing argue that all of these costs—whether variable or fixed—are necessary for production to occur, so *all* of these costs should become part of the product cost.

Many accountants and managers do not agree, however. They argue that fixed manufacturing costs are related to the available production capacity and will be incurred *regardless* of the actual production volume that occurs during the period. Since these costs will be incurred regardless of volume, they should be treated as period costs and expensed immediately. This argument has led to the development and use of an alternative costing system known as __variable costing__ (or __direct costing__) in which only *variable* manufacturing costs are treated as product costs. Since GAAP and the IRS require absorption costing for external reporting, variable costing may only be used for internal management purposes.

One benefit of variable costing is that it often leads to better decisions. By assigning only variable manufacturing costs to each unit of product, managers can easily see how much additional manufacturing cost will be incurred every time another unit is produced. In addition, the unit cost of the product will not be affected by the number of units produced during the period, as it is when fixed manufacturing costs are absorbed into the unit cost. As we'll discuss later, another benefit of variable costing is that operating income cannot be manipulated by manufacturing more product than is needed, as absorption costing can. Therefore, variable costing can lead to better inventory management.

To summarize, keep this important rule of thumb in mind:

Managers often prefer variable costing because (1) it shows them the incremental cost of manufacturing each additional unit of product, and (2) operating income cannot be manipulated by changing inventory levels between periods.

Let's illustrate this concept using an example. Exhibit 6-18 provides the most recent annual data for ShredCo, a maker of electronic paper shredders.

EXHIBIT 6-18 ShredCo Data

Variable costs:	
Direct material cost per unit produced	$35
Direct labor cost per unit produced	$10
Variable MOH cost per unit produced	$5
Variable operating expenses per unit sold	$2
Fixed costs:	
Fixed MOH	$1,000,000
Fixed operating expenses	$300,000
Other information:	
Units produced	40,000 units
Sales price per unit	$100

Exhibit 6-19 shows the product cost of one unit under both absorption costing and variable costing. Notice that the only difference is the treatment of fixed MOH. Absorption costing includes fixed MOH ($25) in the product cost, whereas variable costing does not. The $75 product cost shown in Exhibit 6-19 will be used by the company to (1) record the value of inventory on the balance sheet and (2) record Cost of Goods Sold on the income statement when the inventory is eventually sold.

EXHIBIT 6-19 Comparing Inventoriable Product Costs

	A	B	C	
	Manufacturing Costs Per Unit	**Absorption Costing**	**Variable Costing**	
1				
2	Direct material cost per unit	$ 35	$ 35	
3	Direct labor cost per unit	10	10	
4	Variable MOH cost per unit	5	5	
5	Fixed MOH cost per unit ($1,000,000 ÷ 40,000 units)	25	0	Under variable costing, no fixed MOH is assigned to the product cost.
6	Total cost per unit	$ 75	$ 50	
7				

Why is this important?

"Variable costing **helps** manufacturers **identify** the **variable cost** of making each unit of a product. This information will be **critical** to making many business **decisions**, such as whether or not to outsource production."

Notice how variable costing shows managers exactly how much extra cost ($50) will be incurred every time a unit is made. This transparency is not the case with absorption costing, which can easily mislead managers. To illustrate, let's assume that the company decides to produce an extra 5,000 units with its existing capacity. Using variable costing, we see the additional production cost will really be $250,000 (5,000 units × $50). However, absorption costing could mislead the manager into believing that the extra cost would be $375,000 (5,000 × $75). The fallacy in this erroneous analysis stems from treating the $25 of fixed MOH in the product cost as if it were variable. In fact, the company will *not* incur an additional $25 of fixed cost with every unit produced. Rather, the company will incur $1 million of fixed cost *regardless* of the production volume, as long as the production volume stays within the company's relevant range (which in most cases is its existing production capacity). Variable costing tends be the better costing system for internal decision-making purposes because the reported unit cost is purely variable in nature.

Exhibit 6-20 illustrates period costs under both costing systems. Remember that these are often referred to as "operating expenses" in the income statement. Notice again that the only difference is the treatment of fixed MOH. Under absorption costing, *none* of the fixed MOH is expensed as a period cost. Under variable costing, *all* of the fixed MOH ($1 million) is expensed as a period cost.

EXHIBIT 6-20 Comparing Period Costs (Operating Expenses)

	A	B Absorption Costing	C Variable Costing
1	**Operating Expenses of the Period**		
2	Variable operating expenses when 40,000 units are sold (40,000 × $2)	$ 80,000	$ 80,000
3	Fixed operating expenses	300,000	300,000
4	Fixed MOH	0	1,000,000
5	Total operating expenses (period costs)	$ 380,000	$ 1,380,000
6			

> Under variable costing, fixed MOH is treated as a period cost.

Keep the following rule of thumb in mind:

The ONLY difference between absorption costing and variable costing is the treatment of fixed MOH, and the timing with which it is expensed:

- Under variable costing, fixed MOH is expensed immediately as a period cost (operating expense).
- Under absorption costing, fixed MOH becomes part of the product cost of each unit, which isn't expensed until the inventory is sold (as Cost of Goods Sold).

▶ Try It!

Sony makes DVD players and uses both absorption and variable costing. Assume Sony incurred the following manufacturing costs in producing 10,000 DVD players last month:

Manufacturing Costs	Total Cost	Per Unit Cost
Direct materials	$ 70,000	$ 7.00
Direct labor	40,000	4.00
Variable MOH	90,000	9.00
Fixed MOH	120,000	12.00
Total	$320,000	$32.00

1. What is the product cost per unit, using absorption costing?
2. How will fixed MOH be expensed if absorption costing is used?
3. What is the product cost per unit, using variable costing?
4. How will fixed MOH be expensed if variable costing is used?

Please see page 380 for solutions.

The Contribution Margin Income Statement

Now that you know the difference between absorption costing and variable costing, let's see how the information is communicated to managers using a different income statement format.

Comparing Income Statement Formats

Let's start with the situation in which the company sells *exactly* all of the units it produced during the period. In our example, this means that the company sells all 40,000 units it produced during the year. This situation occurs most frequently with lean producers who use just-in-time (JIT) inventory systems. Exhibit 6-21 shows a traditional income statement, which is based on absorption costing. Notice how Cost of Goods Sold is calculated using the $75 product cost shown in Exhibit 6-19.

EXHIBIT 6-21 Traditional Income Statement Based on Absorption Costing

	A	B	C	D
1	ShredCo			
2	Traditional Income Statement (Absorption Costing)			
3	For the Year Ended December 31			
4				
5	Sales revenue (40,000 × $100)	$ 4,000,000		
6	Less: Cost of goods sold (40,000 × $75)	3,000,000		
7	Gross profit	$ 1,000,000		
8	Less: Operating expenses [$300,000 + (40,000 × $2)]	380,000		
9	Operating income	$ 620,000		
10				

In contrast, Exhibit 6-22 shows a **contribution margin income statement**, which is an income statement organized by cost behavior. When manufacturers use variable costing, they report income internally using a contribution margin income statement format.

EXHIBIT 6-22 Contribution Margin Income Statement Using Variable Costing

	A	B	C	D
1	ShredCo			
2	Contribution Margin Income Statement (Variable Costing)			
3	For the Year Ended December 31			
4				
5	Sales revenue (40,000 × $100)	$ 4,000,000		
6	Less variable expenses:			
7	Variable cost of goods sold (40,000 × $50)	2,000,000		
8	Variable operating expenses (40,000 × $2)	80,000		
9	Contribution margin	$ 1,920,000		
10	Less fixed expenses:			
11	Fixed MOH	1,000,000		
12	Fixed operating expenses	300,000		
13	Operating income	$ 620,000		
14				

Notice the following in Exhibit 6-22:

■ The contribution margin income statement is organized by cost behavior.

■ All variable costs are expensed *above* the contribution margin line. As a result, only the *variable* product cost ($50, from Exhibit 6-19) is used when calculating Variable Cost of Goods Sold.

■ All fixed costs, including fixed MOH, are expensed *below* the contribution margin line.

■ The **contribution margin** is equal to sales revenue minus variable expenses. It shows managers how much profit has been made on sales before considering fixed costs.

■ The operating income ($620,000) is the *same* in both statements. For manufacturers, this equality will *only* occur when all of units produced during a period are also sold during that same period, resulting in no change in inventory levels.

■ For service and merchandising companies, operating income will *always* be the same regardless of the income statement format used.

The contribution margin income statement may only be used for internal management purposes, never for external reporting. Managers like the contribution margin format because it allows them to quickly see which costs will change with fluctuations in volume and which costs will remain the same. For example, if sales volume increases 10%, managers would expect sales revenue and variable costs to increase by 10%. As a result, the contribution margin should also increase 10%. On the other hand, all fixed costs shown below the contribution margin will not change as a result of changes in volume.

Why is this important?

"The **contribution margin** income statement allows **managers** to **quickly** see which costs will **change** with **volume**, and which will remain **fixed**."

Service and Merchandising Companies

Since service and merchandising companies don't manufacture products, they don't have manufacturing overhead. Therefore, variable costing and absorption costing do not apply to them because these costing concepts deal with how to treat fixed manufacturing overhead. However, many service and merchandising companies like to use the contribution margin format of the income statement for internal management purposes. Why? Because the contribution margin income statement clearly communicates cost behavior information to managers who need this information for planning and decision-making purposes. Exhibit 6-23 shows the contribution margin income statement for the service firm introduced in Chapter 2. Notice once again how all variable expenses are deducted from revenue to arrive at the company's contribution margin. Next, all fixed expenses are subtracted from the contribution margin to arrive at operating income.

EXHIBIT 6-23 Contribution Margin Income Statement of a Service Company

	A	B	C	D
1	WSC Consulting			
2	Contribution Margin Income Statement			
3	For the Year Ended December 31			
4				
5	Sales revenue	$ 160,000		
6	Less: Variable expenses	2,500		
7	Contribution margin	$ 157,500		
8	Less: Fixed expenses	127,500		
9	Operating income	$ 30,000		
10				

Note: Recall that service firms only have operating expenses and no Cost of Goods Sold.

The contribution margin income statement format is essentially the same, regardless of whether the company is a service firm, a merchandiser, or a manufacturer. The main differences are as follows:

- Service firms have no Cost of Goods Sold, so all of their costs are *operating expenses* that are simply classified as either variable or fixed. If mixed, the company first estimates the variable and fixed portions based on the methods, such as regression analysis, discussed earlier in this chapter.

- Merchandising companies have Cost of Goods Sold, but because they purchase all of their inventory, rather than manufacture it, *all of a merchandiser's Cost of Goods Sold is considered variable.* An example is pictured in Exhibit 6-24.

- For service and merchandising companies, operating income will always be the same, regardless of whether the company uses a traditional income statement or a contribution margin income statement format.

EXHIBIT 6-24 Contribution Margin Income Statement for a Merchandising Company

	A	B	C	D
1	**Wholesome Foods**			
2	**Income Statement**			
3	**For the Year Ended December 31**			
4	*(all figures shown in thousands of dollars)*			
5				
6	Sales revenue	$ 150,000		
7	Less variable expenses:			
8	Cost of goods sold	106,500		
9	Variable operating expenses	3,000		
10	Contribution margin	$ 40,500		
11	Less: Fixed operating expenses	6,000		
12	Operating income	$ 34,500		
13				

Note: For a retailer, all of Cost of Goods Sold is considered variable.

Comparing Operating Income: Variable Versus Absorption Costing

For manufacturers, operating income will not always be the same between the two costing systems. In fact, it will *only* be the same if the manufacturer sells *exactly* what it produced during the period, as was the case in Exhibits 6-21 and 6-22. This scenario is typical of a lean producer. However, traditional manufacturers in a growing economy often produce extra safety stock, *increasing* their inventory levels to ensure against unexpected demand. On the other hand, in periods of economic recession (such as in the years 2008–2009) companies often *reduce* their inventory levels to decrease costs, build cash reserves, and adjust for lower sales demand.

We will discuss how inventory levels impact operating income, for both absorption and variable costing, under three possible scenarios:

1. Inventory levels remain constant

2. Inventory levels increase

3. Inventory levels decrease

As we discuss each scenario, keep in mind that in our example, absorption costing assigned $25 of fixed MOH to each unit of product produced by ShredCo (Exhibit 6-19).

Scenario 1: Inventory Levels Remain Constant

As shown in Exhibits 6-21, 6-22, and 6-25, when inventory levels remain constant, both absorption costing and variable costing result in the *same* operating income. This scenario usually occurs at lean manufacturers since they only produce enough inventory to fill new customer orders.

EXHIBIT 6-25 Inventory Levels Remain Constant

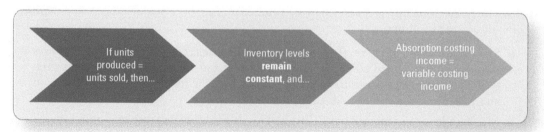

When inventory levels remain constant, *all* fixed MOH incurred during the period ($1,000,000) is expensed under both costing systems. Under variable costing, it is expensed as a period cost ($1,000,000), as shown in Exhibit 6-22. Under absorption costing, it is first absorbed into the product's cost ($25 of fixed MOH in the unit product cost) and then expensed as Cost of Goods Sold when the product is sold. As shown in Exhibit 6-21, when all product is sold in the same period as it is produced, exactly $1,000,000 (= 40,000 × $25) of fixed MOH is expensed as part of Cost of Goods Sold. As a result of expensing the same amount of fixed MOH ($1,000,000) under both costing systems, operating income will be the same regardless of which costing system is used.

Scenario 2: Inventory Levels Increase

As shown in Exhibit 6-26, when inventory levels increase, operating income will be *greater* under absorption costing than it is under variable costing. This scenario typically occurs at traditional manufacturers during times of economic growth.

EXHIBIT 6-26 Inventory Levels Increase

Recall that under variable costing, all fixed MOH incurred during the period ($1,000,000) is expensed as a period cost. However, under absorption costing when inventory levels increase, some of the fixed MOH remains "trapped" on the balance sheet as part of the cost of inventory. For example, let's say only 30,000 of the 40,000 units are sold, leaving 10,000 units still in ending inventory. As a result, $750,000 of fixed MOH is expensed as part of Cost of Goods Sold (30,000 units × $25) while $250,000 of fixed MOH (10,000 units × $25) remains in inventory. As a result, *more* fixed MOH cost is expensed under variable costing ($1,000,000) than under absorption costing ($750,000), leading to a higher operating income under absorption costing.

Thus, under absorption costing, managers can misuse their powers by continuing to build up unwarranted levels of inventory simply to increase operating income. The more inventory builds up, the more favorable operating income will be. Unfortunately, as we learned in Chapter 4, building unnecessary inventory is wasteful and should be avoided. Because of this drawback to absorption costing, many companies prefer to use variable costing to evaluate managers' performance. Since variable costing expenses all fixed MOH in the current period regardless of the amount of inventory produced, managers have no financial incentive to build unnecessary inventory.

Scenario 3: Inventory Levels Decrease

As shown in Exhibit 6-27, when inventory levels decrease, operating income will be *greater* under variable costing than it is under absorption costing. This scenario typically occurs at traditional manufacturers during times of economic recession. It also occurs when traditional manufacturers are in the process of switching to lean operations, which carry little to no inventory.

EXHIBIT 6-27 Inventory Levels Decrease

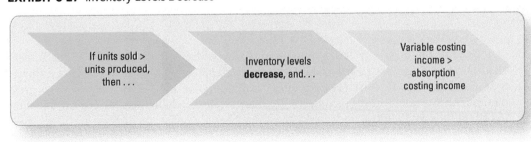

Recall that under variable costing, all fixed MOH incurred during the period ($1,000,000) is expensed as a period cost. However, under absorption costing, when inventory levels decrease all of the fixed MOH of the period is expensed as part of Cost of Goods Sold *plus* some of the fixed MOH from the previous period. For example, let's say that 45,000 units are sold, comprised of the 40,000 units produced in the current period and 5,000 units produced in the previous period. For the sake of simplicity, we'll assume the same unit costs were incurred in the previous period. As a result of selling 45,000 units this year, $1,125,000 of fixed MOH is expensed as Cost of Goods Sold (45,000 × $25). This figure consists of $1,000,000 from the current year (40,000 × $25) *plus* $125,000 from the previous year (5,000 × $25). As a result, *more* fixed MOH cost is expensed under absorption costing ($1,125,000) than under variable costing ($1,000,000), leading to a lower net income under absorption costing.

Managers who are evaluated based on absorption income have every incentive to *avoid* the situation in which inventory levels decline. However, sometimes it is in the company's best interest to decrease inventory levels. For example, companies switching over to lean production methods should experience long-run benefits from lean practices, but in the short run, inventory reductions will cause absorption-based operating income to decline. Managers switching over to lean production should be fully aware that absorption income will be temporarily affected as the company sheds itself of unnecessary inventory. The challenge for managers is to avoid thinking that lean operations are having a negative effect on the company's earnings, when, in fact, the temporary decrease in operating income is simply a result of the costing system. Again, variable costing is not affected by inventory fluctuations, making it the better costing system for evaluating performance.

Reconciling Operating Income Between the Two Costing Systems

As discussed, absorption costing is required by GAAP and the IRS, yet variable costing is preferred for internal decision-making and performance evaluation purposes. Thus, managers are often exposed to both sets of information. For manufacturers, the costing systems will yield different results for operating income when inventory levels increase or decline. Managers can easily reconcile the difference between the two income figures using the following formula:

Difference in operating income = (Change in inventory level, in units) × (Fixed MOH per unit)

We'll illustrate the use of this formula next.

Reconciling Income When Inventory Levels Increase (Scenario 2)

Let's try this formula with the example in which 40,000 units are produced, yet only 30,000 are sold. Using the formula, we predict the difference in operating income will be:

Difference in operating income = (Change in inventory level, in units) × (Fixed MOH per unit)

$250,000 = 10,000 units × $ 25

Because the inventory level has *grown*, we would expect operating income under absorption costing to be *greater* than it is under variable costing by $250,000 (see Exhibit 6-26). Exhibit 6-28, which presents comparative income statements, verifies this prediction: Absorption costing income ($390,000) is *higher* than variable costing income ($140,000) by $250,000.

EXHIBIT 6-28 Comparing Income When Inventory Levels Increase

Panel A: Absorption Costing:

	A	B	C	D
1	ShredCo			
2	Traditional Income Statement (Absorption Costing)			
3	For the Year Ended December 31			
4				
5	Sales revenue (30,000 × $100)	$ 3,000,000		
6	Less: Cost of goods sold (30,000 × $75)	2,250,000		
7	Gross profit	$ 750,000		
8	Less: Operating expenses [$300,000 + (30,000 × $2)]	360,000		
9	Operating income	$ 390,000		
10				

Panel B: Variable Costing:

	A	B	C	D
1	ShredCo			
2	Contribution Margin Income Statement (Variable Costing)			
3	For the Year Ended December 31			
4				
5	Sales revenue (30,000 × $100)	$ 3,000,000		
6	Less variable expenses:			
7	Variable cost of goods sold (30,000 × $50)	1,500,000		
8	Variable operating expenses (30,000 × $2)	60,000		
9	Contribution margin	$ 1,440,000		
10	Less fixed expenses:			
11	Fixed MOH	1,000,000		
12	Fixed operating expenses	300,000		
13	Operating income	$ 140,000		
14				

Reconciling Income When Inventory Levels Decrease (Scenario 3)

Now let's briefly consider the situation in which inventory decreases rather than increases. Let's assume that 45,000 units are sold, comprised of 40,000 that were produced in the current period plus 5,000 units that were produced in the previous period. The formula used to reconcile income suggests that operating income under absorption costing will be *lower* than it is under variable costing (see Exhibit 6-27) by $125,000:

Difference in operating income = (Change in inventory level, in units) × (Fixed MOH per unit)

$125,000 = 5,000 units × $ 25

Exhibit 6-29 verifies the truth of this prediction. Operating income under absorption costing ($735,000) is $125,000 *lower* than operating income under variable costing ($860,000).

Key Points to Remember

You have just learned about variable costing and the contribution margin income statement. Some key points to remember are summarized in Exhibit 6-30.

EXHIBIT 6-29 Comparing Income When Inventory Levels Decrease

Panel A: Absorption Costing:

	A	B	C	D
1	ShredCo			
2	Traditional Income Statement (Absorption Costing)			
3	For the Year Ended December 31			
4				
5	Sales revenue (45,000 × $100)	$ 4,500,000		
6	Less: Cost of goods sold (45,000 × $75)	3,375,000		
7	Gross profit	$ 1,125,000		
8	Less: Operating expenses [$300,000 + (45,000 × $2)]	390,000		
9	Operating income	$ 735,000		
10				

Panel B: Variable Costing:

	A	B	C	D
1	ShredCo			
2	Contribution Margin Income Statement (Variable Costing)			
3	For the Year Ended December 31			
4				
5	Sales revenue (45,000 × $100)	$ 4,500,000		
6	Less variable expenses:			
7	Variable cost of goods sold (45,000 × $50)	2,250,000		
8	Variable operating expenses (45,000 × $2)	90,000		
9	Contribution margin	$ 2,160,000		
10	Less fixed expenses:			
11	Fixed MOH	1,000,000		
12	Fixed operating expenses	300,000		
13	Operating income	$ 860,000		
14				

EXHIBIT 6-30 Key Points about Variable Costing and the Contribution Margin Income Statement

Variable Costing

- Treats all fixed MOH costs as operating expenses in the period incurred, rather than treating fixed MOH as an inventoriable product cost
- Can only be used for internal management purposes; never for external financial reporting or tax purposes
- Is often better for decision making than absorption costing because it clearly shows managers the additional cost of making one more unit of product (the variable cost per unit)
- Is often better for performance evaluation than absorption costing because it gives managers no incentive to build unnecessary inventory
- Will result in a different operating income than absorption costing for manufacturers whose inventory levels *increase* or *decrease* from the previous period

The Contribution Margin Income Statement

- Is organized by cost behavior. First, all variable expenses are deducted from sales revenue to arrive at the company's contribution margin. Next, all fixed expenses are deducted from the contribution margin to arrive at operating income
- Is often more useful than a traditional income statement for planning and decision making because it clearly distinguishes the costs that will be affected by changes in volume (the variable costs) from the costs that will be unaffected (fixed costs)
- Can only be used for internal management purposes, and never for external financial reporting
- Will show the same operating income as a traditional income statement for (1) service firms, (2) merchandising companies, and (3) manufacturers *only* if their inventory levels remain stable
- For retailers, all of Cost of Goods Sold is considered variable

Decision Guidelines

Cost Behavior

As the manager of a local fitness club, Fitness-for-Life, you'll want to plan for operating costs at various levels of membership. Before you can make forecasts, you'll need to make some of the following decisions.

Decision	Guidelines
How can I separate the fixed and the variable components of a mixed cost?	• Managers typically use the high-low method or regression analysis. • The high-low method uses only two historical data points to form the cost equation and therefore may not be very indicative of the cost's true behavior. • Regression analysis uses every data point provided to determine the cost equation that best fits the data. It is simple to do with Excel but tedious to do by hand.
I've used the high-low method to formulate a cost equation. Can I tell how well the cost equation fits the data?	The only way to determine how well the high-low cost equation fits the data is by (1) plotting the data, (2) drawing a line through the data points associated with the highest and lowest volume, and (3) visually inspecting the resulting graph to see if the line is representative of the other plotted data points.
I've used regression analysis to formulate a cost equation. Can I tell how well the cost equation fits the data?	The R-square is a "goodness-of-fit" statistic that tells how well the regression analysis cost equation fits the data. The R-square ranges from 0 to 1, with 1 being a perfect fit. When the R-square is high, the cost equation should render fairly accurate predictions.
Do I need to be concerned about anything before using the high-low method or regression analysis?	Cost equations are only as good as the data on which they are based. Managers should plot the historical data to see if a relationship between cost and volume exists (if so, the data points will fall in a linear pattern). In addition, scatterplots help managers identify outliers. Managers should consider removing outliers before further analysis. Managers should also adjust cost equations for seasonal data, inflation, and price changes.
Can I present the club's financial statements in a manner that will help with planning and decision making?	Managers often use contribution margin income statements for internal planning and decision making. Contribution margin income statements organize costs by *behavior* (fixed versus variable) rather than by *function* (product versus period).
What's the difference between absorption and variable costing?	Fixed manufacturing costs are treated as: • product costs under absorption costing. • period costs under variable costing.

Decision	Guidelines
How are product costs calculated under absorption costing and variable costing?	**Absorption Costing** Direct materials + Direct labor + Variable MOH + Fixed MOH = Product cost	**Variable Costing** Direct materials + Direct labor + Variable MOH = Product cost

Decision	Guidelines
Why is variable costing often used for internal management purposes?	• Variable costing and the contribution margin income statement help managers easily predict the cost of operating at different volumes within the relevant range. • Variable costing helps managers with decision making because it allows them to easily see the cost of making one more unit of product. • Variable costing does not give managers incentives to build up unnecessary inventory.

SUMMARY PROBLEM 2

As the new manager of a local fitness club, Fitness-for-Life, you have been studying the club's financial data. You would like to determine how the club's costs behave in order to make accurate predictions for next year. Here is information from the last six months:

Month	Club Membership (number of members)	Total Operating Costs	Average Operating Costs per Member
July	450	$ 8,900	$19.78
August	480	$ 9,800	$20.42
September	500	$10,100	$20.20
October	550	$10,150	$18.45
November	560	$10,500	$18.75
December	525	$10,200	$19.43

Requirements

1. By looking at the Total Operating Costs and the Average Operating Costs per Member, can you tell whether the club's operating costs are variable, fixed, or mixed? Explain your answer.

2. Use the high-low method to determine the club's monthly operating cost equation.

3. Using your answer from Requirement 2, predict total monthly operating costs if the club has 600 members.

4. Can you predict total monthly operating costs if the club has 3,000 members? Explain your answer.

5. Prepare the club's traditional income statement and its contribution margin income statement for the month of July. Assume that your cost equation from Requirement 2 accurately describes the club's cost behavior. The club charges members $30 per month for unlimited access to its facilities.

6. *Optional*: Perform regression analysis using Microsoft Excel. What is the monthly operating cost equation? What is the R-square? Why is the cost equation different from that in Requirement 2?

▪ SOLUTIONS

Requirement 1

By looking at Total Operating Costs, we can see that the club's operating costs are not purely fixed; otherwise, total costs would remain constant. By looking at the Average Operating Costs per Member, we can see that the operating costs are not purely variable; otherwise, the "per-member" cost would remain constant. Therefore, the club's operating costs are mixed.

Requirement 2

Use the high-low method to determine the club's operating cost equation:

Step 1: The highest volume month is November, and the lowest volume month is July. Therefore, we use **only these two months** to determine the cost equation. The first step is to find the variable cost per unit of activity, which is the slope of the line connecting the November and July data points:

$$\frac{\text{Rise}}{\text{Run}} = \frac{\text{Change in } y}{\text{Change in } x} = \frac{y \text{ (high)} - y \text{ (low)}}{x \text{ (high)} - x \text{ (low)}} = \frac{(\$10,500 - \$8,900)}{(560 - 450 \text{ members})} = \$14.55 \text{ per member (rounded)}$$

Step 2: The second step is to find the fixed cost component (vertical intercept) by plugging in the slope and either July or November data to a mixed costs equation:

$$y = vx + f$$

Using November data:

$$\$10,500 = (\$14.55/\text{member} \times 560 \text{ guests}) + f$$

Solving for *f*:

$$f = \$2,352$$

Or we can use July data to reach the same conclusion:

$$\$8,900 = (\$14.55/\text{members} \times 450 \text{ guests}) + f$$

Solving for *f*:

$$f = \$2,352 \text{ (rounded)}$$

Step 3: Write the monthly operating cost equation:

$$y = \$14.55x + \$2,352$$

where,

$$x = \text{number of members}$$
$$y = \text{total monthly operating costs}$$

Requirement 3

Predict total monthly operating costs when volume reaches 600 members:

$$y = (\$14.55 \times 600) + \$2,352$$
$$y = \$11,082$$

Requirement 4

Our current data and cost equation are based on 450 to 560 members. If membership reaches 3,000, operating costs could behave much differently. That volume falls outside our current relevant range.

Requirement 5

The club had 450 members in July and total operating costs of $8,900. Thus, its traditional income statement is as follows:

	A	B	C	D
1	FITNESS-FOR-LIFE			
2	Income Statement			
3	For the Month Ended July 31			
4				
5	Club membership revenue (450 × $30)	$ 13,500		
6	Less: Operating expenses (given)	8,900		
7	Operating income	$ 4,600		
8				

To prepare the club's contribution margin income statement, we need to know how much of the total $8,900 operating costs is fixed and how much is variable. If the cost equation from Requirement 2 accurately reflects the club's cost behavior, fixed costs will be $2,352 and variable costs will be $6,548 (= $14.55 × 450). The contribution margin income statement would look like this:

	A	B	C	D
1	FITNESS-FOR-LIFE			
2	Contribution Margin Income Statement			
3	For the Month Ended July 31			
4				
5	Club membership revenue (450 × $30)	$ 13,500		
6	Less: Variable expenses (450 × $14.55)	6,548		
7	Contribution margin	6,952		
8	Less: Fixed expenses	2,352		
9	Operating income	$ 4,600		
10				

Requirement 6

Regression analysis using Microsoft Excel results in the following cost equation and R-square:

$$y = \$11.80x + \$3,912$$

where,

$$x = \text{number of members}$$
$$y = \text{total monthly operating costs}$$

R-square = 0.8007

The cost equation is different in Requirement 6 than Requirement 2 because the regression analysis cost equation uses all of the data points, not just the data from November and July. Therefore, it better represents all of the data. The high R-square means that the regression line fits the data well and that predictions based on this cost equation should be quite accurate.

SUMMARY PROBLEM 3

Kelley Industries makes high-performance swimwear for triathletes. Kelley's manufacturing costs for the production of 100,000 swimsuits were as follows:

	Total Manufacturing Cost for 100,000 units	Absorption Costing Per unit product cost	Variable Costing Per unit product cost
Direct Materials	$1,800,000		
Direct Labor	375,000		
Variable MOH	250,000		
Fixed MOH	300,000		
Total Cost	$2,725,000		

Requirements

1. Calculate the product cost per unit using (1) absorption costing and (2) variable costing.

2. If inventory increases by 4,000 units over the preceding period, by how much would operating income differ between the two costing methods? Explain.

▪ SOLUTIONS

Requirement 1

The unit product cost is found by dividing the each manufacturing cost by the number of units produced (100,000) during the period. Under absorption costing, all manufacturing costs are "absorbed" into the product cost. However, under variable costing, only the variable manufacturing costs (DM, DL, and variable MOH) are treated as product costs. Under variable costing, the fixed MOH ($300,000) is expensed as an operating expense of the period.

	Total Manufacturing Cost for 100,000 units	Absorption Costing Per-unit product cost	Variable Costing Per-unit product cost
Direct Materials	$1,800,000	$18.00	$18.00
Direct Labor	375,000	3.75	3.75
Variable MOH	250,000	2.50	2.50
Fixed MOH	300,000	3.00	
Total Cost	$2,725,000	$27.25	$24.25

Requirement 2

When inventory levels fluctuate, operating income will differ between variable costing or absorption costing. The difference can be found as follows:

Difference in operating income = (Change in inventory level, in units) × (Fixed MOH per unit)

$12,000 = 4,000 units × $3 per unit)

When inventory levels rise, absorption costing will result in a higher operating income; in this case, by $12,000. The difference arises because under absorption costing, $3 of fixed MOH is "trapped" on the balance sheet with every unit still in inventory. However, under variable costing, all fixed MOH is expensed as a period cost. Hence, $12,000 more is expensed under variable costing than absorption costing, leading to a higher operating income under absorption costing.

END OF CHAPTER

Learning Objectives

- 1 Describe key characteristics and graphs of various cost behaviors
- 2 Use cost equations to express and predict costs
- 3 Use account analysis and scatterplots to analyze cost behavior
- 4 Use the high-low method to analyze cost behavior
- 5 Use regression analysis to analyze cost behavior
- 6 Describe variable costing and prepare a contribution margin income statement

Accounting Vocabulary

Absorption Costing. (p. 331)   The costing method where products "absorb" both fixed and variable manufacturing costs.

Account Analysis. (p. 322)   A method for determining cost behavior that is based on a manager's judgment in classifying each general ledger account as a variable, fixed, or mixed cost.

Committed Fixed Costs. (p. 311)   Fixed costs that are locked in because of previous management decisions; management has little or no control over these costs in the short run.

Contribution Margin. (p. 334)   Sales revenue minus variable expenses.

Contribution Margin Income Statement. (p. 334)   Income statement that organizes costs by *behavior* (variable costs or fixed costs) rather than by *function*.

Cost Behavior. (p. 308)   A behavior that describes how costs change as volume changes.

Cost Equation. (p. 309)   A mathematical equation for a straight line that expresses how a cost behaves.

Curvilinear Costs. (p. 318)   A cost behavior that is not linear (not a straight line).

Discretionary Fixed Costs. (p. 311)   Fixed costs that are a result of annual management decisions; fixed costs that are controllable in the short run.

Fixed Costs. (p. 311)   Costs that do not change in total despite wide changes in volume.

High-Low Method. (p. 324)   A method for determining cost behavior that is based on two historical data points: the highest and lowest volume of activity.

Mixed Cost. (p. 314)   Costs that change, but *not* in direct proportion to changes in volume. Mixed costs have both variable cost and fixed cost components.

Outliers. (p. 323)   Abnormal data points; data points that do not fall in the same general pattern as the other data points.

Regression Analysis. (p. 326)   A statistical procedure for determining the line that best fits the data by using *all of the historical data points, not just the high and low data points*.

Relevant Range. (p. 316)   The band of volume where total fixed costs remain constant at a certain level and where the variable cost *per unit* remains constant at a certain level.

Scatterplot. (p. 322)   A graph that plots historical cost and volume data.

Step Costs. (p. 317)   A cost behavior that is fixed over a small range of activity and then jumps to a different fixed level with moderate changes in volume.

Variable Costs. (p. 308)   Costs incurred for every unit of activity. As a result, total variable costs change in direct proportion to changes in volume.

Variable Costing. (p. 331)   The costing method that assigns only *variable* manufacturing costs to products. All fixed manufacturing costs (fixed MOH) are expensed as period costs. Also known as *direct costing*.

MyAccountingLab   **Go to** www.myaccountinglab.com **for the following Quick Check, Short Exercises, Exercises, and Problems. They are available with immediate grading, explanations of correct and incorrect answers, and interactive media that acts as your own online tutor.**

Quick Check

1. *(Learning Objective 1)* A graph of a variable cost starts at
   - a. any point on the *y*-axis and is horizontal.
   - b. any point on the *y*-axis and slopes upward.
   - c. the origin and slopes upward.
   - d. the origin and is horizontal.

2. *(Learning Objective 2)* Which of the following is true?
   - a. Total fixed costs increase when volume increases.
   - b. Total fixed costs decrease when volume increases.
   - c. Fixed cost per unit increases when volume increases.
   - d. Fixed cost per unit decreases when volume increases.

3. *(Learning Objective 2)* In the cost equation $y = vx + f$, the term "v" stands for
   a. total cost.
   b. variable cost per unit.
   c. fixed cost.
   d. total variable cost.

4. *(Learning Objective 2)* If $x = 35$, $v = \$100$, and $f = \$1,000$, then total costs equal
   a. $4,500.
   b. $1,100.
   c. $100.
   d. $3,500.

5. *(Learning Objective 2)* Which of the following is *false*?
   a. Step costs are fixed over small ranges of activity.
   b. Curvilinear costs can be approximated as mixed costs or broken into smaller relevant ranges for cost prediction purposes.
   c. Changes in the variable costs per unit often occur within a given relevant range.
   d. The concept of relevant range is applicable to both fixed and variable costs.

6. *(Learning Objective 3)* Which of the following is *false*?
   a. When performing account analysis, managers use their judgment to classify cost behavior.
   b. Scatterplots should be prepared to help identify outliers.
   c. When creating a scatterplot, volume should be plotted on the x-axis while cost should be plotted on the y-axis.
   d. Data points falling in a linear pattern suggest a weak relationship between cost and volume.

7. *(Learning Objective 4)* Which of the following is *false* about the high-low method?

   a. It yields an equation for a straight line connecting the high and low data points.
   b. Selection of the high and low data points should be based on cost, not volume.
   c. The slope found from the method represents the variable cost per unit.
   d. It is based on only two data points.

8. *(Learning Objective 5)* Which of the following is true about regression analysis?
   a. The resulting S-squared statistic shows how well the line fits the data points.
   b. It is based on two data points.
   c. It is sometimes referred to as the line of best fit.
   d. It is theoretically less sound than the high-low method.

9. *(Learning Objective 6)* Which of the following is true regarding variable costing?
   a. It treats variable MOH costs as period costs, rather than as product costs.
   b. It is allowed by GAAP for external reporting purposes.
   c. It treats fixed MOH costs as period costs, rather than as product costs.
   d. It is allowed by the IRS for tax preparation.

10. *(Learning Objective 6)* Which of the following is *false*?
    a. The operating income of manufacturers will always be the same, regardless of whether variable or absorption costing is used.
    b. The contribution margin is equal to sales revenue minus variable expenses.
    c. A contribution margin income statement is organized by cost behavior.
    d. Under absorption costing, the fluctuation of inventory levels will impact operating income, regardless of sales revenue.

Quick Check Answers

1. c 2. d 3. b 4. a 5. c 6. d 7. b 8. c 9. c 10. a

clivewa/Shutterstock

Source: http://corporate.art.com/aboutus/default.asp

Cost-Volume-Profit Analysis

Learning Objectives

■ **1** Calculate the unit contribution margin and the contribution margin ratio

■ **2** Use CVP analysis to find breakeven points and target profit volumes

■ **3** Use CVP analysis to measure the impact of changing business conditions

■ **4** Find breakeven and target profit volumes for multiproduct companies

■ **5** Determine a firm's margin of safety, operating leverage, and most profitable cost structure

Art.com, Inc., is the world's largest online retailer of posters, prints, photography, and framed art. The company offers over 2 million different images and has generated sales from over 19 million customers in 150 different countries. Art.com has 25 localized websites that utilize each country's native language and currency and offers local e-mail support. It also offers free iPhone and iPad apps that allow customers to turn personal photos into professionally framed art as well as preview art by importing it into a photo of their own living space. Innovations such as these continue to drive the company's success.

Before launching Art.com in 1998, how did the company's founders determine the volume of art they would need to sell just to break even? How did they estimate the volume they would need to sell to achieve their target profit? And as the company continues to operate and expand into new markets, how do managers respond to fluctuating business conditions, such as changing fixed and variable costs and pricing pressures from competitors? Cost-volume-profit analysis helps managers answer these questions.

In the last chapter, we discussed cost behavior patterns and the methods managers use to determine how the company's costs behave. We showed how managers use the contribution margin income statement to separately display the firm's variable and fixed costs. In this chapter, we show how managers identify the volume of sales necessary to achieve breakeven or a target profit. We also look at how changes in costs, sales price, and volume affect the firm's profit. Finally, we discuss ways to identify the firm's risk level, including ways to gauge how easily a firm's profits can turn to losses if sales volume declines.

How Does Cost-Volume-Profit Analysis Help Managers?

Cost-volume-profit analysis, or CVP, is a powerful tool that helps managers make important business decisions. <u>Cost-volume-profit analysis</u> expresses the relationships among costs, volume, and the company's profit. Entrepreneurs and managers use CVP analysis to determine the sales volume that will be needed just to break even or to cover costs. They also use CVP to determine the sales volume that will be needed to earn a target profit, such as $100,000 per month. And because business conditions are always changing, CVP can help managers prepare for and respond to economic changes, such as increases in costs from suppliers.

Let's begin our discussion by looking at the data needed for CVP analysis.

Data and Assumptions Required for CVP Analysis

CVP analysis relies on the interdependency of five components, or pieces of information, shown in Exhibit 7-1.

EXHIBIT 7-1 Components of CVP Analysis

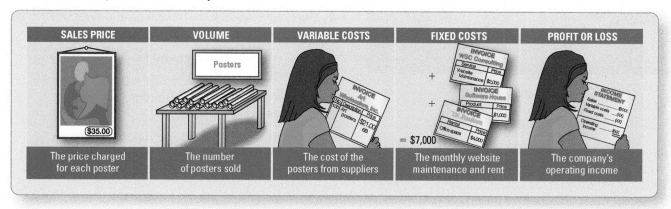

SALES PRICE	VOLUME	VARIABLE COSTS	FIXED COSTS	PROFIT OR LOSS
The price charged for each poster	The number of posters sold	The cost of the posters from suppliers	The monthly website maintenance and rent	The company's operating income

Let's examine this information in terms of a simple company example. Kay Martin, an entrepreneur, has just started a company to sell art posters through a website. Kay's software tabulates all customer orders each day and then automatically places the order to buy posters from a wholesaler. Kay buys only what she needs to fill the prior day's sales orders, so she carries no inventory. The posters cost $21 each, and Kay sells them for $35 each. Customers pay the shipping costs, so there are no other variable selling costs. Monthly fixed costs for website maintenance, software, and office rental total $7,000. Kay's relevant range extends from 0 to 2,000 posters a month. Beyond this volume, Kay will need to hire an employee and upgrade her website software to handle the increased volume. Additionally, the wholesaler will offer a volume discount if she purchases more than 2,000 posters a month.

Thus, we know the following information holds true within Kay's relevant range (0–2,000 posters per month):

- Sales price = $35 per poster
- Variable cost = $21 per poster
- Fixed costs = $7,000 per month

For CVP to be accurate, certain assumptions must be met. We'll itemize each of these assumptions, and check off whether Kay's business meets the assumptions.

1. **Sales price remains constant throughout the relevant range of volume, resulting in revenue that is linear.** In Kay's business, each poster generates $35 of sales revenue, with no volume discounts. Therefore, revenue could be graphed as a straight line beginning at the origin and sloping upward at a rate of $35 per poster sold. ✓

2. **Managers can classify each cost (or the components of mixed costs) as either variable or fixed. These costs are linear throughout the relevant range of volume.** In Kay's business, variable costs are $21 per poster, and fixed costs are $7,000 per month. These costs are expected to remain the same unless Kay's volume exceeds 2,000 posters per month. Thus, we could draw each of these costs as straight lines on a graph, just as we did in Chapter 6. ✓

3. **Inventory levels will not change.** Kay keeps no inventory. If she did, CVP analysis would still work as long as she did not allow her inventory levels to fluctuate very much from one period to the next. ✓

4. **The mix of products offered for sale remains constant. Sales mix is the combination of products that make up total sales. For example, Art.com may sell 15% posters, 25% unframed photographs, and 60% framed prints. If profits differ across products, changes in sales mix will affect CVP analysis.** Kay currently offers only one size of poster, so her sales mix is 100% posters. Later in this chapter text we will expand her product offerings to illustrate how sales mix impacts CVP analysis. ✓

Now that we know Kay's business meets these assumptions, we can proceed with confidence about the CVP results we will obtain. When assumptions are not met perfectly, managers should consider the results of CVP analysis to be approximations rather than exact figures.

The Unit Contribution Margin

The last chapter introduced the **contribution margin income statement**, which separates costs on the income statement by cost behavior rather than by function (product cost versus period cost). Many managers prefer the contribution margin income statement because it gives them the information for CVP analysis in a "ready-to-use" format. On these income statements, the contribution margin is the "dividing line"—all variable expenses go above the line, and all fixed expenses go below the line. The results of Kay's first month of operations is shown in Exhibit 7-2.

1 Calculate the unit contribution margin and the contribution margin ratio

EXHIBIT 7-2 Contribution Margin Income Statement

	A	B	C	D
1	**Kay Martin Posters**			
2	**Contribution Margin Income Statement**			
3	**Month Ended August 31**			
4				
5	Sales revenue (550 posters × $35 per poster)	$ 19,250		
6	Less: Variable expenses (550 posters × $21 per poster)	11,550		
7	Contribution margin	7,700		
8	Less: Fixed expenses	7,000		
9	Operating income	$ 700		
10				

Notice that the **contribution margin** is the excess of sales revenue over variable expenses. The contribution margin tells managers how much revenue is left—after paying variable expenses—to *contribute* toward the company's fixed expenses and operating income—hence the name contribution margin.

The contribution margin is stated as a *total* amount on the contribution margin income statement. However, managers often want to know the contribution margin on a *per unit* basis in order to get a better understanding of how profitable each unit is to the company's bottom line. A product's **contribution margin per unit**—or **unit contribution margin**—is the excess of the selling price per unit over the variable cost per unit. Kay's only variable cost is the price she pays for each poster ($21). However, some businesses pay a sales commission on each unit sold or have other variable costs, such as shipping costs, associated with each unit sold. *All variable costs, whether product costs or period costs, must be included when calculating the contribution margin per unit.* Kay's variable cost per unit is simply the price she pays for each poster. Therefore, her unit contribution margin is calculated as follows:

> ## Why is this important?
>
> "The **unit** contribution margin tells **managers** how much **profit** they make on **each unit** before considering **fixed** costs."

Sales price per poster.....................................	$ 35
Less: Variable cost per poster........................	21
Contribution margin per poster....................	$ 14

The unit contribution margin is a very powerful piece of information for owners and managers to know. Kay now knows that every time she sells a poster, she will make $14 that can be used to pay for fixed expenses and generate a profit. In other words, her operating income will *improve* by $14 every time she sells another unit. For example, let's say Kay sells 551 posters rather than 550, as pictured in Exhibit 7-2. Her operating income would be $14 higher than before ($714 instead of $700). We can prove this as shown in Exhibit 7-3:

EXHIBIT 7-3 Operating Income Comparison When One More Poster Is Sold

	A	B	C	D
1	**Kay Martin Posters**			
2	**Contribution Margin Income Statement**			
3	**Month in which 551 posters are sold**		**For comparison**	
4		**551 posters**	**550 posters**	**Difference**
5	Sales revenue (551 posters × $35 per poster)	$ 19,285	$ 19,250	$ 35
6	Less: Variable expenses (551 posters × $21 per poster)	11,571	$ 11,550	$ 21
7	Contribution margin	7,714	$ 7,700	$ 14
8	Less: Fixed expenses	7,000	$ 7,000	$ -
9	Operating income	$ 714	$ 700	$ 14
10				
11	(Notice operating income is $14 higher when one more poster is sold.)			

Keep the following important rule of thumb in mind:

Every time another unit is sold, the company's operating income will improve by the amount of the unit contribution margin ($14 in our example). This holds true whether the company is operating at a profit or at a loss. When companies offer more than one type of product, each product will have a unique unit contribution margin that shows how much profit each unit adds to the company's operating income. The higher the contribution margin per unit, the more profitable each unit is.

Managers often want to predict operating income at different sales volumes. Managers do not need to produce a full income statement to make these predictions. Rather, they can use the unit contribution margin to quickly forecast operating income at any volume within their relevant range. First, they multiply the unit contribution margin by the number of units they expect to sell in order to predict the total contribution margin from the sales. Then they simply subtract fixed costs. Let's verify using 551 posters as the volume:

Contribution margin (551 posters × $14 per poster).....................	$ 7,714
Less: Fixed expenses...	7,000
Operating income...	$ 714

Notice that this is exactly what we found above when we prepared a full income statement for a volume of 551 units. The unit contribution margin offers managers a quick shortcut to predicting operating income at different volumes of sales.

The Contribution Margin Ratio

In addition to computing the unit contribution margin, managers often compute the **contribution margin ratio**, which is the ratio of contribution margin to sales revenue. Kay can compute her contribution margin ratio at the unit level as follows:

$$\text{Contribution margin ratio} = \frac{\text{Contribution margin per unit}}{\text{Sales price per unit}} = \frac{\$14}{\$35} = 40\%$$

Kay can also compute the contribution margin ratio using any volume of sales. Let's use her current sales volume, pictured in Exhibit 7-2:

$$\text{Contribution margin ratio} = \frac{\text{Contribution margin}}{\text{Sales revenue}} = \frac{\$7,700}{\$19,250} = 40\%$$

The contribution margin ratio is the percentage of each sales dollar that is available for covering fixed expenses and generating a profit. As shown in Exhibit 7-4, each *$1.00* of sales revenue contributes $0.40 toward fixed expenses and profit, while the remaining $0.60 of each sales dollar is used to pay for variable costs.

EXHIBIT 7-4 Breakdown of $1 of Sales Revenue

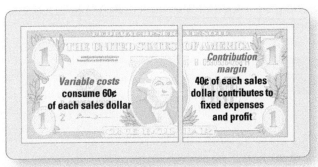

Managers can also use the contribution margin ratio to quickly forecast operating income within their relevant range. For example, let's say Kay wants to know what her operating income would be if she generates $70,000 of sales revenue one month. To find the answer, Kay simply multiplies her forecasted sales revenue ($70,000) by the contribution margin ratio (40%) to arrive at the total contribution margin. Then she subtracts fixed expenses to arrive at her predicted operating income:

Contribution margin ($70,000 sales × 40%)...................	$28,000
Less: Fixed expenses..	7,000
Operating income..	$21,000

The reason this works goes back to the definition of the contribution ratio shown above. When we multiply the contribution margin ratio by expected sales revenue, the sales revenue terms cancel out, leaving the total contribution margin. Let's verify. If Kay has $70,000 of sales revenue, she has sold 2,000 posters ($70,000 ÷ $35 per poster). Her complete contribution margin income statement would be calculated as shown in Exhibit 7-5.

EXHIBIT 7-5 Operating Income for $70,000 of Sales Revenue

	A	B	C	D
1	**Kay Martin Posters**			
2	**Contribution Margin Income Statement**			
3	**For a month with $70,000 of Sales Revenue**			
4				
5	Sales revenue (2,000 posters × $35 per poster)	$ 70,000		
6	Less: Variable expenses (2,000 posters × $21 per poster)	42,000		
7	Contribution margin (2,000 posters × $14 per poster)	28,000		
8	Less: Fixed expenses	7,000		
9	Operating income	$ 21,000		
10				

The contribution margin per unit and the contribution margin ratio help managers quickly and easily predict income at different sales volumes. However, when predicting profits, managers must keep in mind the relevant range. Recall that Kay's relevant range extends to only 2,000 posters per month. At a higher volume of sales, her variable cost per unit may be lower than $21 (due to volume discounts from her suppliers), and her monthly fixed expenses may be higher than $7,000 (due to upgrading her system and hiring an employee to handle the extra sales volume). Thus, she won't be able to predict operating income at volumes greater than 2,000 posters per month without finding out more about how her costs will change.

We've seen how managers use the contribution margin to predict income; but managers use the contribution margin for other purposes too, such as motivating the sales force. Salespeople who know the contribution margin of each product can generate more profit for the company by emphasizing high-margin products. This is why many companies base sales commissions on the contribution margins produced by sales rather than on sales revenue alone.

In the next section, we'll see how managers use CVP analysis to determine the company's breakeven point.

▶ Try It!

Rachel runs her own hot dog stand on the U of A campus. The monthly cost of the cart rental and business permit is $300. Rachel spends $0.50 on each hot dog sold, including bun and condiments. She sells each hot dog for $2.00.

1. What is the contribution margin per unit?

2. What is the contribution margin ratio?

3. Predict operating income for a month in which Rachel sells 1,000 hot dogs.

Please see page 441 for solutions.

2 Use CVP analysis to find breakeven points and target profit volumes

How Do Managers Find the Breakeven Point?

A company's **breakeven point** is the sales level at which *operating income is zero*. In other words, at the breakeven point, total revenues equal total expenses. Sales below the breakeven point result in a loss; sales above the breakeven point provide a profit. Before Kay started her business, she wanted to figure out how many posters she would have to sell just to break even.

There are three ways to calculate the breakeven point. All three approaches are based on the income statement, so they all reach the same conclusion. The first two methods find breakeven in terms of sales *units*, whereas the last approach finds breakeven in terms of sales revenue (sales dollars).

1. The income statement approach
2. The shortcut approach using the *unit* contribution margin
3. The shortcut approach using the contribution margin *ratio*

Let's examine these three approaches in detail.

> ■**Why is this important?**
>
> "Businesses **don't** want to operate at a **loss**. CVP analysis helps **managers** determine how many units they need to sell *just* to **break even**."

The Income Statement Approach

The income statement approach starts with the contribution margin income statement and then breaks it down into smaller components:

$$\text{SALES REVENUE} - \text{VARIABLE EXPENSES} - \text{FIXED EXPENSES} = \text{OPERATING INCOME}$$

$$\left(\frac{\text{Sales price}}{\text{per unit}} \times \text{Units sold}\right) - \left(\frac{\text{Variable cost}}{\text{per unit}} \times \text{Units sold}\right) - \text{Fixed expenses} = \text{Operating income}$$

Let's use this approach to find Kay's breakeven point. Recall that Kay sells her posters for $35 each and that her variable cost is $21 per poster. Kay's fixed expenses total $7,000. At the breakeven point, operating income is zero. We use this information to solve the income statement equation for the number of posters Kay must sell to break even.

$$\text{SALES REVENUE} - \text{VARIABLE EXPENSES} - \text{FIXED EXPENSES} = \text{OPERATING INCOME}$$

$$\left(\frac{\text{Sales price}}{\text{per unit}} \times \text{Units sold}\right) - \left(\frac{\text{Variable cost}}{\text{per unit}} \times \text{Units sold}\right) - \text{Fixed expenses} = \text{Operating income}$$

($35 × Units sold) −	($21 × Units sold) −	$7,000	=	$ 0
($35 −	$21) × Units sold −	$7,000	=	$ 0
	$14 × Units sold		=	$7,000
	Units sold		=	$7,000/$14
	Sales in units		=	500 posters

Kay must sell 500 posters to break even. Her breakeven point in sales revenue is $17,500 (500 posters × $35).

You can check this answer by creating a contribution margin income statement using a sales volume of 500 posters, as shown in Exhibit 7-6:

EXHIBIT 7-6 Contribution Margin Income Statement at Breakeven

◢	A	B	C	D
1	**Kay Martin Posters**			
2	**Contribution Margin Income Statement**			
3	**For a month in which 500 posters are sold**			
4				
5	Sales revenue (500 posters × $35 per poster)	$ 17,500		
6	Less: Variable expenses (500 posters × $21 per poster)	10,500		
7	Contribution margin (500 posters × $14 per poster)	7,000		
8	Less: Fixed expenses	7,000		
9	Operating income	$ 0		
10				

Notice that at breakeven a firm's fixed expenses ($7,000) equal its contribution margin ($7,000). In other words, the firm has generated *just* enough contribution margin to cover its fixed expenses but *not* enough to generate a profit.

The Shortcut Approach Using the Unit Contribution Margin

Many managers prefer to use a shortcut formula rather than the income statement approach. To develop the formula, we start with the contribution margin income statement and then rearrange some of its terms:

$$\underbrace{\text{SALES REVENUE} - \text{VARIABLE EXPENSES}}_{\text{Contribution margin}} - \text{FIXED EXPENSES} = \text{OPERATING INCOME}$$

Contribution margin − Fixed expenses = Operating income

Contribution margin = Fixed expenses + Operating income

(Contribution margin per unit × Units sold) = Fixed expenses + Operating income

As a final step, we divide both sides of the equation by the contribution margin per unit. Now we have the shortcut formula:

$$\text{Sales in units} = \frac{\text{Fixed expenses} + \text{Operating income}}{\text{Contribution margin per unit}}$$

Kay can use this shortcut approach to find her breakeven point in units. Kay's fixed expenses total $7,000, and her unit contribution margin is $14. At the breakeven point, operating income is zero. Thus, Kay's breakeven point in units is as follows:

$$\text{Sales in units} = \frac{\$7,000 + \$0}{\$14}$$
$$= 500 \text{ posters}$$

Why does this shortcut approach work? Recall that each poster provides $14 of contribution margin. To break even, Kay must generate enough contribution margin to cover $7,000 of fixed expenses. At the rate of $14 per poster, Kay must sell 500 posters ($7,000/$14) to cover her $7,000 of fixed expenses. Because the shortcut formula simply rearranges the income statement equation, the breakeven point is the same under both methods (500 posters). Keep the following important rule of thumb in mind:

Since the breakeven point occurs when operating income is equal to zero, always use "zero" as the operating income in the formula to find the company's breakeven point.

The Shortcut Approach Using the Contribution Margin Ratio

It is easy to compute the breakeven point in *units* for a simple business like Kay's which has only one product. But what about companies that have thousands of products such as Art.com, The Home Depot, and Amazon.com? It doesn't make sense for these companies to determine the number of each product they need to sell to break even. Can you imagine a Home Depot manager describing breakeven as 100,000 wood screws, two million nails, 3,000 lawn mowers, 10,000 gallons of paint, and so forth? It simply doesn't make sense. Therefore, multiproduct companies usually compute breakeven in terms of *sales revenue* (dollars).

The formula to find the sales revenue needed to break even is derived in much the same way as the earlier formula. The only difference is that to find the answer in terms of sales revenue (*dollars*) we must divide the numerator by the contribution margin *ratio* rather than the contribution margin *per unit*:

$$\text{Sales in dollars} = \frac{\text{Fixed expenses + Operating income}}{\text{Contribution margin ratio}}$$

Recall that Kay's contribution margin ratio is 40%. At the breakeven point, operating income is $0, so Kay's breakeven point in sales revenue is as follows:

$$\text{Sales in dollars} = \frac{\$7,000 + \$0}{40\%}$$
$$= \$17,500$$

This is the same breakeven sales revenue we calculated in Exhibit 7-6 (500 posters × $35 sales price = $17,500).

Why does the contribution margin ratio formula work? Recall from Exhibit 7-4 that each dollar of Kay's sales contributes $0.40 to fixed expenses and profit. To break even, she must generate enough contribution margin at the rate of $0.40 per sales dollar to cover the $7,000 fixed expenses ($7,000 ÷ 0.40 = $17,500).

When determining which formula to use, keep the following rules of thumb in mind:

- To find breakeven in terms of *units*, divide fixed expenses by the contribution margin *per unit*.
- To find breakeven in terms of sales revenue (*dollars*), divide fixed expenses by the contribution margin ratio.

Try It!

Rachel runs her own hot dog stand on the U of A campus. The monthly cost of the cart rental and business permit is $300. Rachel's contribution margin per unit is $1.50 and her contribution margin ratio is 75%.

1. How many hot dogs does Rachel need to sell each month to break even?
2. How much sales revenue does Rachel need to generate each month to break even?

Please see page 441 for solutions.

How Do Managers Find the Volume Needed to Earn a Target Profit?

Entrepreneurs and managers don't want their businesses to just break even; they want to earn a profit, and they usually have specific profit goals in mind. For example, Kay doesn't want to just break even—she wants her business to be her sole source of income. She would like the business to earn $4,900 of profit each month. How many posters must Kay sell each month to reach her target profit?

How Much Must We Sell to Earn a Target Profit?

To find the number of units a company must sell to earn a target profit, we can use the same three approaches as we used earlier in the chapter for finding breakeven. The only difference from our prior analysis is that instead of determining the sales level needed for *zero profit* (breakeven), Kay now wants to know how many posters she must sell to earn a $4,900 profit. To find

Why is this important?

"**Companies** want to make a profit. **CVP** analysis helps **managers** determine **how many** units they need to sell to earn a **target** amount of **profit**."

the answer, Kay uses the shortcut formula and simply inserts $4,900 as the target operating income:

$$\text{Sales in } \textit{units} = \frac{\text{Fixed expenses} + \text{Operating income}}{\text{Contribution margin } \textit{per unit}}$$

$$= \frac{\$7,000 + \$4,900}{\$14}$$

$$= \frac{\$11,900}{\$14}$$

$$= 850 \text{ posters}$$

This analysis shows that Kay must sell 850 posters each month to earn an operating income of $4,900 a month. Notice that this level of sales falls within Kay's current relevant range (0–2,000 posters per month), so the conclusion that she would earn $4,900 of income at this sales volume is valid. If the calculation resulted in a sales volume outside the current relevant range (greater than 2,000 units), we would need to reassess our cost assumptions.

Assume that Kay also wants to know how much sales revenue she'll need to generate each month to earn $4,900 of monthly profit. Because she already knows the number of units needed (850), she can easily translate this volume into sales revenue:

$$850 \text{ posters} \times \$35 \text{ sales price/poster} = \$29,750 \text{ sales revenue}$$

Kay could have also found the answer directly by using the shortcut formula based on the contribution margin *ratio*:

$$\text{Sales in } \textit{dollars} = \frac{\text{Fixed expenses} + \text{Operating income}}{\text{Contribution margin } \textit{ratio}}$$

$$= \frac{\$7,000 + \$4,900}{40\%}$$

$$= \frac{\$11,900}{40\%}$$

$$= \$29,750$$

Finally, Kay could have used the income statement approach to find the same answer:

SALES REVENUE	−	VARIABLE EXPENSES	−	FIXED EXPENSES	=	OPERATING INCOME
($35 × Units sold)	−	($21 × Units sold)	−	$7,000	=	$ 4,900
($35	−	$21) × Units sold	−	$7,000	=	$ 4,900
		$14 × Units sold			=	$11,900
				Units sold	=	$11,900/$14
				Units sold	=	850 posters

We can prove that our answers from any of the three approaches are correct by preparing Kay's income statement for a sales volume of 850 units, as shown in Exhibit 7-7:

EXHIBIT 7-7 Operating Income for a Volume of 850 Posters

	A	B	C	D
1	**Kay Martin Posters**			
2	**Contribution Margin Income Statement**			
3	**For a month in which 850 posters are sold**			
4				
5	Sales revenue (850 posters × $35 per poster)	$ 29,750		
6	Less: Variable expenses (850 posters × $21 per poster)	17,850		
7	Contribution margin (850 posters × $14 per poster)	11,900		
8	Less: Fixed expenses	7,000		
9	Operating income	$ 4,900		
10				

Keep the following important rule of thumb in mind:

> When finding the volume needed to earn a target profit, use the target profit as the operating income in the formulas.

▶ Try It!

Rachel runs her own hot dog stand on the U of A campus. The monthly cost of the cart rental and business permit is $300. Rachel's contribution margin per unit is $1.50, and her contribution margin ratio is 75%.

1. How many hot dogs does Rachel need to sell each month to earn a target profit of $900 a month?

2. How much sales revenue does Rachel need to generate each month to earn a target profit of $900 per month?

Please see page 441 for solutions.

Graphing CVP Relationships

By graphing the CVP relationships for her business, Kay can see at a glance how changes in the levels of sales will affect profits. As in the last chapter, the volume of units (posters) is placed on the horizontal *x*-axis, while dollars is placed on the vertical *y*-axis. Then, she follows five steps to graph the CVP relations for her business, as illustrated in Exhibit 7-8. This graph also shows the linear nature of Kay's costs and revenues. Recall that CVP analysis assumes costs and revenues will be linear throughout the relevant range.

STEP 1: Choose a sales volume, such as 1,000 posters. Plot the point for total sales revenue at that volume: 1,000 posters × $35 per poster = sales of $35,000. Draw the *sales*

EXHIBIT 7-8 Cost-Volume-Profit Graph

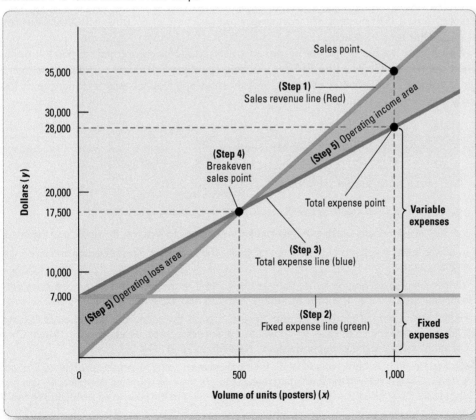

revenue line from the origin (0) through the $35,000 point. Why does the sales revenue line start at the origin? If Kay does not sell any posters, there is no sales revenue.

STEP 2: Draw the *fixed expense line*, a horizontal line that intersects the y-axis at $7,000. Recall that the fixed expense line is flat because fixed expenses are the same ($7,000) no matter how many posters Kay sells within her relevant range (up to 2,000 posters per month).

STEP 3: Draw the *total expense line*. Total expense is the sum of variable expense plus fixed expense. Thus, total expense is a *mixed* cost. So, the total expense line follows the form of the mixed cost line. Begin by computing variable expense at the chosen sales volume: 1,000 posters × $21 per poster = variable expense of $21,000. Add variable expense to fixed expense: $21,000 + $7,000 = $28,000. Plot the total expense point ($28,000) for 1,000 units. Then, draw a line through this point from the $7,000 fixed expense intercept on the dollars axis. This is the *total expense line*. Why does the total expense line start at the fixed expense line? If Kay sells no posters, she still incurs the $7,000 fixed cost for the website maintenance, software, and office rental, but she incurs no variable costs.

STEP 4: Identify the *breakeven point*. The breakeven point is the point where the sales revenue line intersects the total expense line. This is the point where sales revenue equals total expenses. Our previous analyses told us that Kay's breakeven point is 500 posters, or $17,500 in sales. The graph shows this information visually.

STEP 5: Mark the *operating income* and the *operating loss* areas on the graph. To the left of the breakeven point, the total expense line lies above the sales revenue line. Expenses exceed sales revenue, leading to an operating loss. If Kay sells only 300 posters, she incurs an operating loss. The amount of the loss is the vertical distance between the total expense line and the sales revenue line:

Sales revenue − Variable expenses − Fixed expenses = Operating income (Loss)

(300 × $35) − (300 × $21)   − $7,000   = $(2,800)

To the right of the breakeven point, the business earns a profit. The vertical distance between the sales revenue line and the total expense line equals income. Exhibit 7-8 shows that if Kay sells 1,000 posters, she earns operating income of $7,000 ($35,000 sales revenue − $28,000 total expenses).

Why bother with a graph? Why not just use the income statement approach or the shortcut approach? Graphs like Exhibit 7-8 help managers visualize profit or loss over a range of volume. The income statement and shortcut approaches estimate income or loss for only a single sales volume.

Technology Makes It Simple   Excel 2016

CVP graphs are simple to create with Microsoft Excel using these simple steps:

1. In Row 1 of a new Excel worksheet, set up column headings for Volume, Revenue, and Expenses.
2. In Row 2, enter a volume of zero. Then calculate the corresponding revenues and expenses at that volume.
3. In Row 3, enter a higher volume, such as the volume at the high end of the company's relevant range. Calculate the corresponding revenues and expenses at that volume.
4. Highlight the data. Then click on the "Insert" tab on the menu bar and choose "Scatter With a Line" as the chart type. If you want to make your graph larger, choose "Move Chart Location" from the menu bar and select "New Sheet" and "OK."
5. Click on "Insert" "Textbox" to add labels for the breakeven point, revenue line, expense line, and so forth. Play around with the formatting features to get the look you want (for example, you may want to tilt the angle of the labels or add an arrow pointing to the breakeven point, and so forth).
6. Add a title to the graph, as well as labels for the axes.

Decision Guidelines

CVP Analysis

Your friend wants to open her own ice cream parlor after college. She needs help making the following decisions:

Decision	Guidelines
How much will I earn on every ice cream cone I sell?	The unit contribution margin shows managers how much is earned on each unit sold after paying for variable *costs but before considering fixed expenses*. The unit contribution margin is the amount each unit earns that contributes toward fixed expenses and generating a profit. Each time a unit is sold, the company's operating income will improve by the amount of the unit contribution margin. It is computed as follows:

Sales price per unit

Less: Variable cost per unit

Contribution margin per unit

The contribution margin ratio shows managers how much contribution margin is earned on every $1 of sales. It is computed as follows:

$$\text{Contribution margin ratio} = \frac{\text{Contribution margin}}{\text{Sales revenue}}$$

Decision	Guidelines
Can I quickly forecast my income without creating a full income statement?	The contribution margin concept allows managers to forecast income quickly at different sales volumes. First, find the total contribution margin (by multiplying the forecasted number of units by the unit contribution margin *or* by multiplying the forecasted sales revenue by the contribution margin ratio) and then subtract all fixed expenses.
How can I compute the *number of ice cream cones* I'll have to sell to break even or earn a target profit?	**Income Statement Approach:**

$$\text{SALES REVENUE} - \text{VARIABLE EXPENSES} - \frac{\text{FIXED}}{\text{EXPENSE}} = \frac{\text{OPERATING}}{\text{INCOME}}$$

$$\left(\begin{array}{c}\text{Sales price per unit}\\ \times \text{ Units sold}\end{array}\right) - \left(\begin{array}{c}\text{Variable cost per unit}\\ \times \text{ Units sold}\end{array}\right) - \begin{array}{c}\text{Fixed}\\ \text{expenses}\end{array} = \begin{array}{c}\text{Operating}\\ \text{income}\end{array}$$

Shortcut Unit Contribution Margin Approach:

$$\text{Sales in } \textit{units} = \frac{\text{Fixed expenses} + \text{Operating income}}{\text{Contribution margin } \textit{per unit}}$$

Decision	Guidelines
How can I compute the *amount of sales revenue* (in dollars) I'll have to generate to break even or earn a target profit?	**Shortcut Contribution Margin Ratio Approach:**

$$\text{Sales in } \textit{dollars} = \frac{\text{Fixed expenses} + \text{Operating income}}{\text{Contribution margin } \textit{ratio}}$$

Decision	Guidelines
What will my profits look like over a range of volumes?	CVP graphs show managers, at a glance, how different sales volumes will affect profits.

SUMMARY PROBLEM 1

Fleet Foot buys hiking socks for $6 a pair and sells them for $10. Management budgets monthly fixed expenses of $10,000 for sales volumes between 0 and 12,000 pairs.

Requirements

1. Use the income statement approach and the shortcut unit contribution margin approach to compute monthly breakeven sales in units.

2. Use the shortcut contribution margin ratio approach to compute the breakeven point in sales revenue (sales dollars).

3. Compute the monthly sales level (in units) required to earn a target operating income of $14,000. Use either the income statement approach or the shortcut contribution margin approach.

4. Prepare a graph of Fleet Foot's CVP relationships, similar to Exhibit 7-8. Draw the sales revenue line, the fixed expense line, and the total expense line. Label the axes, the breakeven point, the operating income area, and the operating loss area.

▪ SOLUTIONS

Requirement 1
Income Statement Approach:

SALES REVENUE	−	VARIABLE EXPENSES	− FIXED EXPENSES	= OPERATING INCOME
$\left(\begin{matrix}\text{Sales price}\\\text{per unit}\end{matrix} \times \text{Units sold}\right)$	−	$\left(\begin{matrix}\text{Variable cost}\\\text{per unit}\end{matrix} \times \text{Units sold}\right)$ −	Fixed expenses	= Operating income
($10 × Units sold) −		($6 × Units sold) −	$10,000	= $ 0
($10	−	$6) × Units sold		= $10,000
		$4 × Units sold		= $10,000
		Units sold		= $10,000 ÷ $4
		Breakeven sales in units		= 2,500 units

Shortcut Unit Contribution Margin Approach:

$$\text{Sales in units} = \frac{\text{Fixed expenses} + \text{Operating income}}{\text{Contribution margin per unit}}$$

$$= \frac{\$10,000 + \$0}{(\$10 - \$6)}$$

$$= \frac{\$10,000}{\$4}$$

$$= 2,500 \text{ units}$$

Requirement 2

$$\text{Sales in dollars} = \frac{\text{Fixed expenses} + \text{Operating income}}{\text{Contribution margin ratio}}$$

$$= \frac{\$10,000 + \$0}{0.40^*}$$

$$= \$25,000$$

$$*\text{Contribution margin ratio} = \frac{\text{Contribution margin per unit}}{\text{Sales price per unit}} = \frac{\$4}{\$10} = 0.40$$

Requirement 3
Income Statement Equation Approach:

SALES REVENUE	−	VARIABLE EXPENSES	− FIXED EXPENSES	= OPERATING INCOME
$\left(\begin{array}{c}\text{Sales price} \\ \text{per unit}\end{array} \times \text{Units sold}\right)$	−	$\left(\begin{array}{c}\text{Variable cost} \\ \text{per unit}\end{array} \times \text{Units sold}\right)$ −	Fixed expenses	= Operating income
($10 × Units sold)−		($6 × Units sold) −	$10,000	= $14,000
($10	−	$6) × Units sold		= $10,000 + $14,000
		$4 × Units sold		= $24,000
		Units sold		= $24,000 ÷ $4
		Units sold		= 6,000 units

Shortcut Unit Contribution Margin Approach:

$$\text{Sales in units} = \frac{\text{Fixed expenses} + \text{Operating income}}{\text{Contribution margin per unit}}$$

$$= \frac{\$10,000 + \$14,000}{(\$10 - \$6)}$$

$$= \frac{\$24,000}{\$4}$$

$$= 6,000 \text{ units}$$

Requirement 4

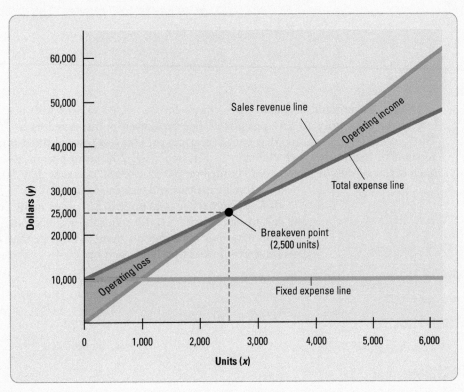

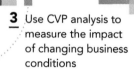

How Do Managers Use CVP to Make Decisions When Business Conditions Change?

3 Use CVP analysis to measure the impact of changing business conditions

In today's fast-changing business world, managers need to be prepared for increasing costs, pricing pressure from competitors, and other changing business conditions.

Managers use CVP analysis to conduct **sensitivity analysis**. Sensitivity analysis is a "what-if" technique that asks what results will be if actual prices or costs change or if an underlying assumption such as sales mix changes. For example, increased competition may force Kay to consider lowering her sales price. In addition, her suppliers may increase the cost of posters. How will these changes affect Kay's operating income, her breakeven point, and the volume needed to earn her target profit? How can CVP analysis help Kay respond to these changing business conditions? We'll tackle these issues next.

Changing the Sales Price and Volume

Let's assume that Kay has now been in business for several months and is typically selling 950 posters a month. Because of new competition, Kay is considering cutting her sales price from $35 to $31 per poster. If her variable expenses remain $21 per poster and her fixed expenses remain at $7,000, how many posters will she need to sell to break even? To answer this question, Kay calculates a new unit contribution margin using the new sales price:

New sales price per poster......................................	$ 31
Less: Variable cost per poster.............................	21
New contribution margin per poster..................	$ 10

She then uses the new unit contribution margin to compute breakeven sales in units:

$$\text{Sales in units} = \frac{\text{Fixed expenses} + \text{Operating income}}{\text{Contribution margin per unit}}$$

$$= \frac{\$7,000 + \$0}{\$10}$$

$$= 700 \text{ posters}$$

With the original $35 sale price, Kay's breakeven point was 500 posters. If Kay lowers the sales price to $31 per poster, her breakeven point increases to 700 posters. The lower sales price means that each poster contributes *less* toward fixed expenses ($10 versus $14 before the price change), so Kay must sell 200 *more* posters to break even. Each dollar of sales revenue would contribute $0.32 ($10/$31) rather than $0.40 toward covering fixed expenses and generating a profit.

If Kay reduces her sales price to $31, how many posters must she sell to achieve her $4,900 monthly target profit? Kay again uses the new unit contribution margin to determine how many posters she will need to sell to reach her profit goals:

$$\text{Sales in units} = \frac{\$7,000 + \$4,900}{\$10}$$

$$= 1,190 \text{ posters}$$

> **Why is this important?**
>
> "**CVP analysis** helps managers prepare for and respond to **economic** changes, such as increasing costs and **pressure** to drop sales prices, so companies can remain **competitive** and **profitable**."

With the original sales price, Kay needed to sell only 850 posters per month to achieve her target operating income. If Kay cuts her sales price (and, therefore, her contribution margin), she must sell more posters to achieve her financial goals. Exhibit 7-9 shows the effect of changes in sales price on breakeven and target profit volumes.

EXHIBIT 7-9 The Effect of Changes in Sales Price on Breakeven and Target Profit Volumes

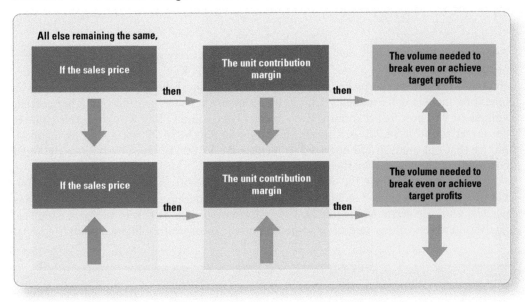

Let's also consider what will happen to Kay's operating income if she reduces the sales price from $35 per poster to $31 per poster. Exhibit 7-10 shows a "before and after" analysis of her operating income. Recall from our earlier discussion that Kay has now been in business several months and typically sells 950 posters a month. If Kay has to reduce her sales price to $31 per poster to retain her current volume of 950 posters per month, her operating income will go down by $3,800 a month from where it currently stands and she will no longer reach her target profit of $4,900 per month.

EXHIBIT 7-10 Before and After Analysis of Change in Sales Price

	A		B	C	D	F
1	**Kay Martin Posters**					
2	**Contribution Margin Income Statement**					
3	**For a month in which 950 posters are sold**	**Before Changing Price**		**After Changing Price**		**Difference**
4		**Per Unit**	**Total**	**Per Unit**	**Total**	
5	Sales revenue	$ 35	$ 33,250	$ 31	$ 29,450	$ (3,800)
6	Less: Variable expenses	21	19,950	21	19,950	0
7	Contribution margin	$ 14	$ 13,300	$ 10	$ 9,500	$ (3,800)
8	Less: Fixed expenses		7,000		7,000	0
9	Operating income		$ 6,300		$ 2,500	$ (3,800)
10						
11						

But what if Kay doesn't decrease her sales price? Let's say Kay has a loyal following of customers, and so she believes that sales volume will only decline by 10% if she leaves her sales price at $35 per poster rather than decreasing it to $31. How much will her operating income decline? Kay could create a full "before and after" income statement at the new volume, as we did in Exhibit 7-10, to find the answer. However, there is a quicker way. Kay can simply compute the *change* in operating income that would result from the decreased volume:

Contribution margin per unit given current sales price of $35..............	$ 14
Multiplied by expected decline in volume (10% × 950 posters)............	×95
Expected decline in operating income if price is not reduced............	$ 1,330

Assuming volume will only decline by 10%, we find that Kay would be better off to keep her sales price at $35 per poster than to reduce it to $31. Kay's operating income will decline by $1,330 if she keeps her sales price where it is, but Exhibit 7-10 shows that Kay's operating income will decline by $3,800 if she lowers her sales price to retain her current volume of 950 posters per month. Even at the lower volume, Kay would be able to meet her target profit of $4,900 per month ($6,300 − $1,330 = $4,970 of operating income). Notice that our analysis did not need to include the $7,000 of fixed costs since the fixed costs will not be affected by the change.

This example shows the importance of the trade-off between the unit contribution margin and volume. The higher the contribution margin per unit, the less volume is needed, and vice versa. Managers can use information such as this to perform extensive analysis between volume and price to determine the most profitable price point.

STOP & THINK

Kay believes she could dominate the e-commerce art poster business if she cut the sales price to $20. Is this a good idea?

Answer: No. The variable cost per poster is $21. If Kay sells posters for $20 each, she loses $1 on each poster. Kay will incur a loss if the sales price is less than the variable cost.

Changing Variable Costs

Let's assume that Kay does *not* lower her sales price. However, Kay's supplier raises the price for each poster to $24 (instead of the original $21). To remain competitive, Kay cannot pass this increase on to her customers, so she holds her sales price at the original $35 per poster. Her fixed costs remain $7,000. How many posters must she sell to break even after her supplier raises the price? Kay's new contribution margin per unit drops to $11 ($35 sales price per poster −$24 variable cost per poster). So, her new breakeven point is as follows:

$$\text{Sales in units} = \frac{\text{Fixed expenses + Operating income}}{\text{Contribution margin per unit}}$$

$$= \frac{\$7,000 + \$0}{\$11.00}$$

$$= 637 \text{ posters}$$

Kay will have to sell *more* units (637 versus 500 originally) just to break even. Keep the following rule of thumb in mind:

Higher variable costs have the same effect as lower selling prices—they both reduce the product's unit contribution margin. As a result, more units need to be sold to break even or achieve target profits.

As shown in Exhibit 7-11, a *decrease* in variable costs would have just the opposite effect. Lower variable costs increase the contribution margin that each poster provides and, therefore, lowers the breakeven point.

EXHIBIT 7-11 The Effect of Changes in Variable Costs on Breakeven and Target Profit Volumes

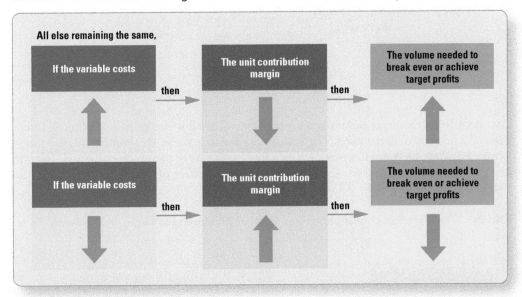

Let's also consider what will happen to Kay's operating income because of the increase in variable costs coupled with the 10% decline in volume from keeping her sales price at $35 per poster. Exhibit 7-12 shows a "before and after" analysis of Kay's operating income, starting with her original monthly income, then considering the decrease in sales volume due to competition, and finally considering the increase in variable costs from her suppliers.

EXHIBIT 7-12 Comparison of Operating Income as Volume Declines and Variable Costs Increase

	A	B		C	D		E	F	
1	**Kay Martin Posters**								
2	**Contribution Margin Income Statement**	**Originally**		**10% lower volume:**			**10% lower volume**		
3	**Per month, under various scenarios**	**950 posters**		**855 posters**			**and higher variable costs**		
4		**Per Unit**	**Total**	**Per Unit**	**Total**		**Per Unit**	**Total**	
5	Sales revenue	$ 35	$ 33,250	$ 35	$ 29,925		$ 35	$ 29,925	
6	Less: Variable expenses	21	19,950	21	17,955		24	20,520	
7	Contribution margin	$ 14	$ 13,300	$ 14	$ 11,970		$ 11	$ 9,405	
8	Less: Fixed expenses		7,000		7,000			7,000	
9	Operating income		$ 6,300		$ 4,970			$ 2,405	
10									
11									

Exhibit 7-12 shows that competition, coupled with increased costs from her suppliers, would take a drastic toll on Kay's original operating income. Thus, Kay will need to consider new business tactics to offset these detrimental factors. Perhaps she could lower her fixed costs or generate more volume by selling additional types of products. We'll consider these options next.

Changing Fixed Costs

Having considered possible changes in sales price, volume, and variable costs, Kay has now turned her attention to fixed costs. Kay has decided she really doesn't need a storefront office at a retail strip mall because she doesn't have many walk-in customers. She could drastically decrease her monthly fixed costs from $7,000 to $3,190 by moving her office out of prime retail space to an industrial park.

How will this decrease in fixed costs affect Kay's breakeven point? *Changes in fixed costs do not affect the contribution margin.* Therefore, Kay's unit contribution margin is still $11 per poster given the increased cost from her supplier ($35 sales price − $24 variable cost). However, her breakeven point changes because her fixed costs change:

$$\text{Sales in units} = \frac{\text{Fixed expenses} + \text{Operating income}}{\text{Contribution margin per unit}}$$

$$= \frac{\$3,190 + \$0}{\$11.00}$$

$$= 290 \text{ posters}$$

Because of the decrease in fixed costs, Kay will need to sell only 290 posters, rather than 637 posters, to break even. The volume needed to achieve her monthly $4,900 target profit will also decline. However, if Kay's fixed costs were to *increase*, she will have to sell *more* units to break even. Exhibit 7-13 shows the effect of changes in fixed costs on breakeven and target profit volumes.

EXHIBIT 7-13 The Effect of Changes in Fixed Costs on Breakeven and Target Profit Volumes

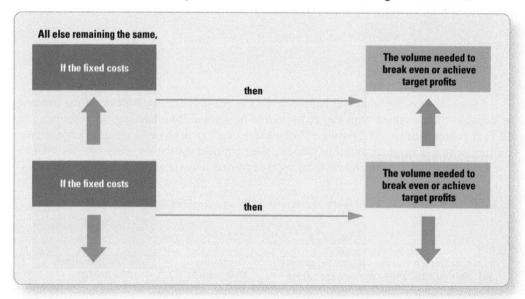

Finally, let's consider how the decreased fixed costs will affect Kay's operating income. Exhibit 7-14 shows that with the substantial decrease in fixed costs, Kay's operating income will almost be back to where it was before competition drove down her volume and suppliers increased their costs. Kay has successfully used CVP analysis to make decisions that will keep her business operating above her target operating income of $4,900 per month.

EXHIBIT 7-14 Before and After changes in Volume, Variable Costs, and Fixed Costs

	A	B		C	D
1	**Kay Martin Posters**			**10% lower volume (855)**	
2	**Contribution Margin Income Statement**	**Originally**		**higher variable costs**	
3	**Per month, under various scenarios**	**950 posters**		**and lower fixed costs**	
4		**Per Unit**	**Total**	**Per Unit**	**Total**
5	Sales revenue	$ 35	$ 33,250	$ 35	$ 29,925
6	Less: Variable expenses	21	19,950	24	20,520
7	Contribution margin	$ 14	$ 13,300	$ 11	$ 9,405
8	Less: Fixed expenses		7,000		3,190
9	Operating income		$ 6,300		$ 6,215
10					
11					

STOP & THINK

Kay has been considering advertising as a means to increase her sales volume. Kay could spend an extra $2,200 per month on website banner ads. How many *extra* posters would Kay have to sell *just to pay for the advertising?* (Use Kay's new contribution margin of $11 per poster.)

Answer: CVP is very useful for isolating and addressing individual business decisions. Instead of using *all* of Kay's fixed costs, we can isolate *just* the fixed costs relating to advertising ($2,200). This will allow us to figure out how many *extra* posters Kay would have to sell each month to break even on (or pay for) the advertising cost. Advertising is a fixed cost, so Kay's contribution margin remains $11 per poster.

$$\text{Sales in units} = \frac{\text{Fixed expenses} + \text{Operating income}}{\text{Contribution margin per unit}}$$

$$= \frac{\$2,200 + \$0}{\$11.00}$$

$$= 200 \text{ posters}$$

Kay must sell 200 *extra* posters each month just to pay for the cost of advertising. If she sells fewer than 200 extra posters, she'll increase her volume but lose money on the advertising. If she sells more than 200 extra posters, her plan will have worked—she'll increase her volume and her profit.

We have seen that changes in sales prices, variable costs, and fixed costs can have dramatic effects on the volume of product that companies must sell to achieve breakeven and target profits. Companies often turn to automation and overseas production to decrease variable labor costs, but this approach, in turn, increases their fixed costs and variable shipping costs. In recent years, many food producers have systematically reduced the size of their products to decrease the variable cost of direct materials. For example, ice cream, which in the past was primarily sold in half gallons, is now sold in smaller containers. Why make this change? Customers are less responsive, in terms of buying fewer units, to slightly smaller packages than they are to increases in prices. Thus, CVP analysis has shown that it is more profitable to decrease variable materials costs than to increase prices.

In the next section, we'll look at another tactic companies use to increase operating income: changing their sales mix to offer more products with higher contribution margins.

Sustainability and CVP

Sustainability initiatives can have a significant bearing on the cost information used in CVP analysis. For example, Coca-Cola, a recognized leader in corporate sustainability, has been working steadily to reduce the amount of packaging used for its products. The reduced use of plastic, aluminum, and cardboard translates into lower variable costs of production and distribution. Let's take a closer look at plastic beverage containers in particular.

According to the American Chemistry Council and the Association of Post-consumer Plastic Recyclers, most single-serving plastic beverage containers are made of PET (polyethylene teraphthalate), whereas larger beverage containers such as milk jugs are made from high-density polyethylene (HDPE). Both are petroleum-based products requiring the use of nonrenewable fossil fuels. Together, these two types of plastics comprise 96% of beverage containers sold in the United States. You can easily recognize these types of containers because they will be marked with either #1 (PET) or #2 (HDPE) inside of a recycling symbol. While the recycling rate for these plastics has continued to rise annually, only 31.8% of all plastic beverage containers are currently recycled. This means that nearly 6.5 billion pounds of plastic beverage containers are sent to landfills each year![1] As part of its sustainability initiatives, Coca-Cola is making strides to reduce its use of PET. First, the company is "lightweighting" its packaging; that is, it is making the bottles thinner and lighter. Its goal is to reduce all packaging by 25% by 2020. Second, the company is increasing the amount of recycled PET and renewable materials used in its beverage containers. The company's current goal is to obtain 40% of its PET from recycled PET (rPET) or renewable materials by 2020.[2] The need for increased consumer recycling plays a key role in these plans. But even more impressive, in 2015 the company released its first PET bottle made from 100% plant-based materials, such as plant waste from sugar cane operations. Why is this important? Traditionally, PET has been produced from petroleum. By reducing the need for fossil fuels, the company has reduced its carbon footprint and helped to create more sustainable packaging solutions for the long term.[3] What does this have to do with accounting? As a result of using less plastic and higher recycled content, the variable cost of packaging each unit and shipping the lighter weight containers has decreased. One might therefore assume that Coca-Cola needs to sell fewer units of product to achieve its target profit. However, keep in mind that the company had to incur many fixed costs to research, develop, and design these new bottles. As the Coca-Cola example shows, sustainability initiatives often result in both cost savings *and* additional costs. These costs and cost savings may be fixed or variable. Managers use CVP analysis to determine how these initiatives will impact the volume needed to achieve the company's operating income goals.

See Exercises E7-27A and E7-48B

Changing the Mix of Products Offered for Sale

4 Find breakeven and target profit volumes for multiproduct companies

So far, we have assumed that Kay sold only one-size posters. What would happen if she offered different types of products? Companies that sell more than one product must consider their <u>sales mix</u> when performing CVP analysis. The sales mix is the combination of products that make up total sales. Think of the sales mix as the "basket of products" sold by the company. For example, a movie theater may sell 20 popcorns, 25 sodas, and 15 boxes of candy for every 75 movie tickets sold. The combination of all of these different product sales, including the movie tickets, makes up the theater's total "sales basket." All else being equal, a company earns more operating income by selling high-contribution margin products than by selling an equal number of low-contribution margin products.

The same CVP formulas that are used to perform CVP analysis for a company with a single product can be used for any company that sells more than one product. However, the formulas use the *weighted-average contribution margin* of all products rather than the contribution margin of a sole product. Each product's contribution margin is *weighted* by the relative number of units sold. As before, the company can find the breakeven or the target profit volume in terms of units or in terms of sales revenue. We'll consider each in turn.

Multiproduct Company: Finding Breakeven in Terms of Sales Units

Suppose Kay plans to sell two types of posters. In addition to her regular-size posters, Kay plans to sell large posters. *Let's assume that none of Kay's original costs have changed.* Exhibit 7-15 shows that each regular poster will continue to generate $14 of contribution margin, while each large poster will generate $30 of contribution margin. Kay is adding the large-poster line because it carries a higher unit contribution margin.

---

[1] https://plastics.americanchemistry.com/Education-Resources/Publications/2014-National-Post-Consumer-Plastics-Bottle-Recycling-Report.pdf

[2] http://www.cokecce.com/system/file_resources/278/03_Our_sustainability_plan.pdf

[3] http://www.environmentalleader.com/2015/06/04/coca-cola-produces-worlds-first-100-plant-based-pet-bottle/

EXHIBIT 7-15 Calculating the Weighted-Average Contribution Margin per Unit

	A	B	C	D
		Regular Posters	Large Posters	Total in "basket"
1	**Calculating Weighted-Average Contribution Margin per Unit**			
2	Sales price per unit	$ 35	$ 70	
3	Less: Variable cost per unit	21	40	
4	Contribution margin per unit	$ 14	$ 30	
5	Multiply by: Sales mix (number of units in "basket")	5	3	8
6	Contribution margin	$ 70	$ 90	$ 160
7				
8	Weighted-average contibution margin per unit ($160/8 units)			$ 20
9				

For every five regular posters sold, Kay expects to sell three large posters. In other words, she expects 5/8 of the sales in her "sales basket" to be regular posters and 3/8 to be large posters. This is a 5:3 sales mix. Exhibit 7-15 shows how Kay finds the total contribution margin and total number of units in the "sales basket" and then divides the two to find the weighted-average contribution margin per unit in the basket.

Notice that none of Kay's products actually generates $20 of contribution margin. However, if the sales mix is five regular posters to every three large posters, as expected, it is *as if* the contribution margin is $20 per unit. Once Kay has computed the weighted-average contribution margin per unit, she uses it in the shortcut formula to determine the total number of posters that would need to be sold to break even:

$$\text{Sales in total units} = \frac{\text{Fixed expenses} + \text{Operating income}}{\text{Weighted-average contribution margin per unit}}$$

$$= \frac{\$7,000 + \$0}{\$20}$$

$$= 350 \text{ posters}$$

In total, Kay must sell 350 posters to break even. However, this is the case only if 5/8 of the sales basket is regular posters and 3/8 of the sales basket is large posters. As a final step, we need to separate the entire sales basket needed to break even back into the two types of products in the basket: regular posters and large posters. We do this by multiplying the total number of units needed to break even (350) by the proportion of each product in the sales basket.

Breakeven sales of regular posters (350 × 5/8)..................... <u>218.75</u> regular posters
Breakeven sales of large posters (350 × 3/8) .... <u>131.25</u> large posters

We can prove this breakeven point as follows:

Contribution margin:
    Regular posters (218.75 × $14).................. $ 3,063
    Large posters (131.25 × $30) .... <u>3,937</u>
Contribution margin .... $ 7,000
Less: Fixed expenses... <u>7,000</u>
Operating income... $ 0

As is often the case in real situations, these computations don't yield round numbers. Because Kay cannot sell partial posters, she must sell 219 regular posters and 132 large posters to avoid a loss.

We just found Kay's *breakeven* point, but Kay can also use the same steps to calculate the number of units she must sell to achieve a target profit. The only difference, as before, is that she would use *target profit*, rather than *zero*, as the operating income in the shortcut formula.

Try It!

Rachel runs her own hot dog stand on the U of A campus. The monthly cost of the cart rental and business permit is $300. Rachel's contribution margin is $1.50 per hot dog sold. She has recently added individual servings of potato chips to her product offering. Each bag of potato chips has a contribution margin of $0.75 per bag. Rachel sells 5 bags of potato chips for every 10 hot dogs.

1. What is Rachel's weighted-average contribution margin per unit?
2. How many total units must Rachel sell in a month to earn a target monthly profit of $900?
3. Of the total units needed to earn $900 of profit, how many are hot dogs and how many are bags of potato chips?

Please see page 442 for solutions.

Multiproduct Company: Finding Breakeven in Terms of Sales Revenue

Companies that offer hundreds or thousands of products (such as Walmart and Amazon .com) will not want to find the breakeven point in terms of units. Rather, they'll want to know breakeven (or target profit volumes) in terms of sales revenue. To find this sales volume, the company needs to know, or estimate, its weighted-average contribution margin ratio so that managers can use the shortcut formula introduced in the first half of the chapter. If a company prepares a contribution margin income statement that includes all of its products, the weighted-average contribution margin ratio is easily calculated as the total contribution margin divided by total sales. The contribution margin is *already* weighted by the company's *actual* sales mix! The following "Stop and Think" illustrates how Walmart would use this approach to calculate breakeven.

STOP & THINK

How would Walmart calculate its weighted-average contribution margin ratio? How much sales revenue must Walmart earn just to break even?

Answer: First, Walmart calculates its weighted-average contribution margin ratio based on its contribution margin income statement, as shown below:[4]

	A	B	C	D
1	**Walmart** **Contribution Margin Income Statement (estimated)** **For the fiscal year ended January 31, 2016**	*(in millions)*		
2	Sales revenue	$ 482,130		
3	Less: Variable expenses	370,000		
4	Contribution margin	112,130		
5	Less: Fixed expenses	88,025		
6	Operating income	$ 24,105		
7				
8	Weighted-Average Contribution Margin Ratio ($112,130/$482,130)	23.26%		
9				

Next, Walmart uses the weighted-average contribution margin ratio in the shortcut formula to predict the breakeven point:

$$\text{Sales in dollars} = \frac{\text{Fixed expenses} + \text{Operating income}}{\text{Weighted-average contribution margin ratio}}$$

$$= \frac{\$88,025 \text{ million} + \$0}{23.26\%}$$

$$= \$378,440 \text{ million (rounded)}$$

Walmart must achieve sales revenue of nearly $380,000 million just to break even.

---

[4]Estimated for teaching purposes only, based on Walmart's 2015 annual report.

Unlike Walmart, Kay's business to this point has been limited to a sole product (regular posters), which had a 40% contribution margin ratio. Since Kay is only thinking about selling large posters and doesn't yet sell them, she doesn't currently have a contribution margin income statement that includes both sizes of posters. However, she can easily estimate the weighted-average contribution margin ratio based on the expected sales mix. Exhibit 7-16 shows how Kay would first calculate the total contribution margin and total sales revenue in the sales basket based on sales mix assumptions. Next, she would divide the total contribution margin in the basket by the total sales in the basket to estimate the weighted-average contribution margin ratio.

EXHIBIT 7-16 Estimating the Weighted-Average Contribution Margin Ratio

	A	B	C	D
1	**Calculating Weighted-Average Contribution Margin Ratio**	**Regular Posters**	**Large Posters**	**Total in "basket"**
2	Contribution margin per unit	$ 14	$ 30	
3	Multiply by: Sales mix (number of units in "basket")	5	3	
4	Contribution margin	$ 70	$ 90	$ 160
5				
6	Sales price per unit	$ 35	$ 70	
7	Multiply by: Sales mix (number of units in "basket")	5	3	
8	Sales revenue	$ 175	$ 210	$ 385
9				
10	Weighted-average contribution margin ratio ($160/$385)			41.56%
11				

Notice how Kay's weighted-average contribution margin ratio (41.56%) will be higher than it was when she sold only regular posters (40%). That's because she expects to sell some large posters that have a 42.9% contribution margin ratio ($30/$70) in addition to the regular-sized posters. Because her sales mix would be changing, she would have a different contribution margin ratio.

Once Kay has calculated her weighted-average contribution margin ratio, she can use the shortcut formula to estimate breakeven in terms of sales revenue:

$$\text{Sales in dollars} = \frac{\text{Fixed expenses} + \text{Operating income}}{\text{Weighted-average contribution margin ratio}}$$

$$= \frac{\$7,000 + \$0}{41.56\%}$$

$$= \$16,844 \text{ (rounded)}$$

Kay could also use the formula to find the total sales revenue she would need to meet her target monthly operating income of $4,900.

If Kay's actual sales mix is not five regular posters to three large posters, her actual operating income will differ from the predicted amount. The sales mix greatly influences the breakeven point. When companies offer more than one product, they do not have a unique breakeven point. Every sales mix assumption leads to a different breakeven point.

STOP & THINK

Suppose Kay plans to sell a total of 800 posters in the 5:3 sales mix (500 regular posters and 300 large posters). She actually does sell 800 posters—375 regular and 425 large. The sale prices per poster, variable costs per poster, and fixed expenses are exactly as predicted. Without doing any computations, is Kay's actual operating income greater than, less than, or equal to her expected income?

Answer: Kay's actual sales mix did not turn out to be the 5:3 mix she expected. She actually sold more of the higher-margin large posters than the lower-margin regular posters. This favorable change in the sales mix causes her to earn a higher operating income than she expected.

What Are Some Common Indicators of Risk?

A company's level of risk depends on many factors, including the general health of the economy and the specific industry in which the company operates. In addition, a firm's risk depends on its current volume of sales and the relative amount of fixed and variable costs that make up its total costs. Next, we discuss how a firm can gauge its level of risk, to some extent, by its margin of safety and its operating leverage.

Margin of Safety

5 Determine a firm's margin of safety, operating leverage, and most profitable cost structure

The **margin of safety** is the excess of actual or expected sales over the sales needed to break even. This is the "cushion," or drop in sales, the company can absorb without incurring a loss. The higher the margin of safety, the greater the cushion against loss and the less risky the business plan. Managers use the margin of safety to evaluate the risk of current operations as well as the risk of new plans.

Let's continue to assume that Kay has been in business for several months and that she generally sells 950 posters a month. Let's go back to Kay's original data (selling one-size posters with a sales price of $35 per poster, variable cost of $21 per poster, and fixed costs of $7,000 per month). Kay's breakeven point in our original data is 500 posters. Kay can express her margin of safety in units, as follows:

$$
\begin{aligned}
\textbf{Margin of safety in units} &= \textbf{Expected (or actual) sales in units} - \textbf{Breakeven sales in units} \\
&= \quad\quad 950 \text{ posters} \quad\quad\quad - \quad\quad 500 \text{ posters} \\
&= \quad\quad 450 \text{ posters}
\end{aligned}
$$

Kay can also express her margin of safety in sales revenue (sales dollars):

$$
\begin{aligned}
\textbf{Margin of safety in dollars} &= \textbf{Expected (or actual) sales in dollars} - \textbf{Breakeven sales in dollars} \\
&= \quad (950 \text{ posters} \times \$35) \quad - \quad (500 \text{ posters} \times \$35) \\
&= \quad\quad \$33,250 \quad\quad\quad - \quad\quad \$17,500 \\
&= \quad\quad \$15,750
\end{aligned}
$$

Sales would have to drop by more than 450 posters, or $15,750 a month, before Kay incurs a loss. This is a fairly comfortable margin.

Managers can also compute the margin of safety as a percentage of sales. Simply divide the margin of safety by sales. We obtain the same percentage whether we use units or dollars.

In units:

$$
\begin{aligned}
\text{Margin of safety as a percentage} &= \frac{\text{Margin of safety in units}}{\text{Expected (or actual) sales in units}} \\
&= \frac{450 \text{ posters}}{950 \text{ posters}} \\
&= 47.4\% \text{ (rounded)}
\end{aligned}
$$

In dollars:

$$
\begin{aligned}
\text{Margin of safety as a percentage} &= \frac{\text{Margin of safety in dollars}}{\text{Expected (or actual) sales in dollars}} \\
&= \frac{\$15,750}{\$33,250} \\
&= 47.4\% \text{ (rounded)}
\end{aligned}
$$

The margin of safety percentage tells Kay that sales would have to drop by more than 47.4% before she would incur a loss. If sales fall by less than 47.4%, she would still earn a profit. If sales fall exactly 47.4%, she would break even. This ratio tells Kay that her business plan is not unduly risky.

Operating Leverage

A company's **operating leverage** refers to the relative amount of fixed and variable costs that make up its total costs. Most companies have both fixed and variable costs. However, companies with *high* operating leverage have *relatively more fixed costs* and relatively fewer variable costs. Companies with high operating leverage include golf courses, airlines, and hotels. Because they have fewer variable costs, their contribution margin ratio is relatively high. Recall from the last chapter that Embassy Suites' variable cost of servicing each guest is low, which means that the hotel has a high contribution margin ratio and high operating leverage.

> ### Why is this important?
>
> "The margin of safety and **operating leverage** help managers understand their **risk** if **volume** decreases due to a recession, **competition**, or other **changes** in the **marketplace**."

What does high operating leverage have to do with risk? If sales volume decreases, the total contribution margin will drop significantly because each sales dollar contains a high percentage of contribution margin. Yet, the high fixed costs of running the company remain. Therefore, the operating income of these companies can easily turn from profit to loss if sales volume declines. For example, airlines were financially devastated after September 11, 2001, because the number of people flying suddenly dropped, creating large reductions in contribution margin. Yet, the airlines had to continue paying their high fixed costs. High operating leverage companies are at *more* risk because their income declines drastically when sales volume declines.

What if the economy is growing and sales volume *increases*? High operating leverage companies will reap high rewards. Because high operating leverage companies have high contribution margin ratios, each additional dollar of sales will contribute more to the firm's operating income. Exhibit 7-17 summarizes these characteristics.

EXHIBIT 7-17 Characteristics of High Operating Leverage Firms

> • High operating leverage companies have the following:
>   —*Higher* fixed costs and *lower* variable costs
>   —*Higher* contribution margin ratios
> • For high operating leverage companies, changes in volume significantly affect operating income, so they face the following:
>   —*Higher* risk
>   —*Higher* potential for reward
> Examples include golf courses, hotels, rental car agencies, theme parks, airlines, cruise lines, etc.

In contrast, companies with low operating leverage have relatively *fewer* fixed costs and relatively *more* variable costs. As a result, they have much lower contribution margin ratios. For example, retailers incur significant levels of fixed costs, but more of every sales dollar is used to pay for the merchandise (a variable cost), so less ends up as contribution margin. If sales volume declines, these companies have relatively fewer fixed costs to cover, so they are at *less* risk of incurring a loss. If sales volume increases, their relatively small contribution margins ratios add to the bottom line, but in smaller increments. Therefore, they reap less reward than high operating leverage companies experiencing the same volume increases. *In other words, at low operating leverage companies, changes in sales volume do not have as much impact on operating income as they do at high operating leverage companies.* Exhibit 7-18 summarizes these characteristics.

EXHIBIT 7-18 Characteristics of Low Operating Leverage Firms

- Low operating leverage companies have the following:
    - —*Higher* variable costs and *lower* fixed costs
    - —*Lower* contribution margin ratios
- For low operating leverage companies, changes in volume do NOT have as significant an effect on operating income, so they face the following:
    - —*Lower* risk
    - —*Lower* potential for reward

Examples include merchandising companies and fast-food restaurants.

A company's <u>**operating leverage factor**</u> tells managers how responsive a company's operating income is to changes in volume. The greater the operating leverage factor, the greater the impact a change in sales volume has on operating income.

The operating leverage factor, *at a given level of sales*, is calculated as follows:

$$\text{Operating leverage factor} = \frac{\text{Contribution margin}}{\text{Operating income}}$$

Why do we say, "at a given level of sales"? A company's operating leverage factor will depend, to some extent, on the sales level used to calculate the contribution margin and operating income. Most companies compute the operating leverage factor at their current or expected volume of sales, which is what we'll do in our examples.

What does the operating leverage factor tell us? Keep the following rule of thumb in mind:

The operating leverage factor, at a given level of sales, indicates the percentage change in operating income that will occur from a 1% change in sales volume. In other words, it tells us how responsive a company's operating income is to changes in sales volume.

The *lowest* possible value for this factor is 1, which occurs only if the company has *no* fixed costs (an *extremely low* operating leverage company). *For a minute, let's assume that Kay has no fixed costs.* Given this scenario, her unit contribution margin ($14 per poster) contributes directly to profit because she has no fixed costs to cover. In addition, she has *no* risk. The worst she can do is break even, and that will occur only if she doesn't sell any posters. Let's continue to assume that she generally sells 950 posters a month, so this will be the level of sales at which we need to know the contribution margin and operating income:

Contribution margin (950 posters × $14 per poster)	$ 13,300
Less: Fixed expenses	0
Operating income	$ 13,300

Given this information, Kay's operating leverage factor is as follows:

$$\text{Operating leverage factor} = \frac{\$13,300}{\$13,300}$$
$$= 1$$

What does this tell us? A factor is a multiplier; therefore:

■ If Kay's volume changes by 1%, her operating income will change by 1% (= 1% × a factor of 1).

■ If Kay's volume changes by 15%, her operating income will change by 15% (= 15% × a factor of 1).

Let's now see what happens to income and operating leverage if we assume, as usual, that Kay's fixed expenses are $7,000.

Contribution margin (950 posters × $14 per poster)	$13,300
Less: Fixed expenses..	7,000
Operating income...	$ 6,300

Now that we have once again assumed that Kay's fixed expenses are $7,000, her operating leverage factor is as follows:

$$\text{Operating leverage factor} = \frac{\$13,300}{\$6,300}$$

$$= 2.11 \text{ (rounded)}$$

Notice that her operating leverage factor is *higher* (2.11 versus 1) when she has *more* fixed costs ($7,000 versus $0). Kay's operating leverage factor of 2.11 tells us how responsive her income is to changes in volume. Again, a factor is a multiplier; therefore:

■ If Kay's volume changes by 1%, her operating income will change by 2.11% (= 1% × a factor of 2.11).

■ If Kay's volume changes by 15%, her operating income will change by 31.65% (= 15% × a factor of 2.11).

Managers use the firm's operating leverage factor to determine how vulnerable their operating income is to changes in sales volume—both positive and negative.

Keep the following rule of thumb in mind:

> The larger the operating leverage factor is, the greater the impact a change in sales volume has on operating income. This is true for both increases and decreases in volume.

Therefore, companies with higher operating leverage factors are particularly vulnerable to changes in volume. In other words, they have *both* higher risk of incurring losses if volume declines *and* higher potential reward if volume increases. Hoping to capitalize on the reward side, many companies have intentionally increased their operating leverage by lowering their variable costs while at the same time increasing their fixed costs. This strategy works well during periods of economic growth but can be detrimental when sales volume declines.

Choosing a Cost Structure

Managers often have some control over how the company's costs are structured—as fixed, variable, or a combination of the two. For example, let's assume that in addition to selling posters online, Kay has decided to lease a small retail kiosk at the local mall. To keep things simple, let's assume Kay will only be selling her regular-size posters, which sell for $35 each. Let's also assume the mall leasing agent has given Kay the following two options for leasing the space:

- Option 1: Pay $300 per month plus 10% of the sales revenue generated at the kiosk.
- Option 2: Pay $1,000 per month.

Which option should Kay choose? The answer depends on how many posters Kay thinks she will sell from the kiosk each month. As we see above, Option 1 has fewer fixed costs and more variable costs than Option 2. Thus, Kay's operating leverage would be lower under Option 1 than under Option 2. As a result, Option 1 carries less financial risk if sales volume is low, but less financial reward if sales volume is high. But how high must sales volume be to make Option 2 the better choice?

To answer this question, Kay will need to figure out her **indifference point**, the point at which she would be indifferent between the two options because they both would result in the same total cost. Once Kay knows the indifference point, she can better judge which option is preferable. Let's see how this is done.

First, Kay calculates the variable and fixed costs associated with each option, as shown in Exhibit 7-19. Notice that Kay does not need to consider any of her other business expenses (such as the cost of the posters themselves or the website maintenance costs) because they will not differ between the two kiosk leasing options. In deciding which lease option to take, Kay only needs to consider those costs that are associated with the lease decision.

EXHIBIT 7-19 Costs Associated with Each Leasing Option

	Option 1	Option 2
Variable cost: 10% of sales revenue (= 10% × $35 per poster)..............	$ 3.50 per poster	0
Fixed cost:	$ 300	$ 1,000

Next, Kay develops an equation in which she sets the cost of each leasing option equal to the other. She then fills in the appropriate information and solves for number of units:

Costs under Option 1 = Costs under Option 2

Variable Costs + Fixed Costs = Variable Costs   + Fixed Costs
(# Units × Variable cost per unit) + Fixed Costs = (# Units × Variable cost per unit) + Fixed Costs

(# Units × $3.50) + $300   = (# Units × $0)   + $1,000
(# Units × $3.50) = $700
Units = 200

Based on this analysis, Kay will be *indifferent* between the two leasing options if she sells *exactly* 200 posters per month at the kiosk. At a volume of 200 units, she would pay $1,000 for the lease under Option 1 [(200 × $3.50) + $300 = $1,000] and $1,000 for the lease under Option 2. Both options would result in the same cost.

But what if sales volume is lower or higher than 200 posters per month? As shown in Exhibit 7-20, Kay will prefer the lower operating leverage alternative (Option 1) if she sells *fewer* than 200 posters a month at the kiosk. However, she will prefer the higher operating leverage alternative (Option 2) if she sells *more* than 200 posters a month at the kiosk. Her decision will be based on whether she expects sales volume at the kiosk to be lower, or higher, than the indifference point.

EXHIBIT 7-20 Using an Indifference Point to Choose the Most Profitable Cost Structure

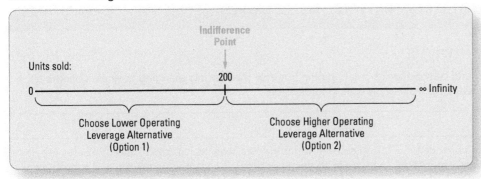

We can verify the conclusion presented in Exhibit 7-20 by calculating the lease costs at *any* volume of sales. First, let's assume that Kay expects to sell 100 posters a month at the kiosk. The lease cost under each option is calculated as follows:

Lease cost under Option 1: $300 + [10% × (100 units × $35 sales price)] = **$650**

Lease cost under Option 2: **$1,000**

As expected, when the sales volume is *lower* than the indifference point, the lease cost is lower under Option 1 than under Option 2.

Next, let's assume Kay expects to sell 500 posters a month at the mall kiosk. The lease cost is calculated as follows:

Lease cost under Option 1: $300 + [10% × (500 units × $35 sales price)] = **$2,050**

Lease cost under Option 2: **$1,000**

As expected, when the sales volume is *higher* than the indifference point, the lease cost is lower under Option 2 than under Option 1.

The following rule of thumb summarizes the conclusions presented in Exhibit 7-20:

When faced with a choice between cost structures, choose the lower operating leverage option when sales volume is expected to be lower than the indifference point. Choose the higher operating leverage option when sales volume is expected to be higher than the indifference point.

Managers can use this rule of thumb whenever they are faced with choices about how to structure their costs.

▶ Try It!

Rachel runs her own hot dog stand on the U of A campus. The monthly cost of the cart rental and business permit is currently $300, but she has been given the option of changing the arrangements to $100 plus $0.25 for every unit of product sold from her stand.

1. At what point in sales volume will Rachel be indifferent between the two options?
2. If Rachel typically sells 700 units a month, which option will she prefer?

Please see page 442 for solutions.

In this chapter, we have discussed how managers use the contribution margin and CVP analysis to predict profits, determine the volume needed to achieve breakeven or a target profit, and assess how changes in the business environment affect their profits. In the next chapter, we look at several types of short-term decisions managers must make. Cost behavior and the contribution margin will continue to play an important role in these decisions.

Decision Guidelines

CVP Analysis

Your friend opened an ice cream parlor. But now she's facing changing business conditions. She needs help making the following decisions:

Decision	Guidelines
The cost of ice cream is rising, yet my competitors have lowered their prices. How will these factors affect the sales volume I'll need to break even or achieve my target profit?	Increases in variable costs (such as ice cream) and decreases in sales prices both decrease the unit contribution margin and contribution margin ratio. You will have to sell more units in order to achieve breakeven or a target profit. You can use sensitivity analysis to better pinpoint the actual volume you'll need to sell.
Would it help if I could renegotiate my lease with the landlord?	Decreases in fixed costs do not affect the firm's contribution margin. However, a decrease in fixed costs means that the company will have to sell fewer units to achieve breakeven or a target profit. Increases in fixed costs have the opposite effect.
I've been thinking about selling other products in addition to ice cream. Will this affect the sales volume I'll need to earn my target profit?	Your contribution margin ratio will change as a result of changing your sales mix. A company earns more income by selling higher-margin products than by selling an equal number of lower-margin products. If you can shift sales toward higher contribution margin products, you will have to sell fewer units to reach your target profit.
If the economy takes a downturn, how much risk do I face of incurring a loss?	The margin of safety indicates how far sales volume can decline before you would incur a loss. It can be calculated in terms of units or sales dollars using the following formula. $$\text{Margin of safety} = \text{Expected (or actual) sales} - \text{Breakeven sales}$$ The margin of safety can also be calculated as a percentage, as follows: $$\text{Margin of safety as a percentage} = \frac{\text{Margin of safety}}{\text{Expected (or actual) sales}}$$
How can I tell whether a change in sales volume will have much of an impact on my operating income?	The operating leverage factor indicates the percentage change in operating income that will occur from a 1% change in volume. It tells you how sensitive your company's operating income is to changes in volume. At a given level of sales, the operating leverage factor is as follows: $$\text{Operating leverage factor} = \frac{\text{Contribution margin}}{\text{Operating income}}$$
What is the indifference point and how do I find it?	The indifference point is the volume of sales at which total costs under one cost structure would be the same as total costs under an alternative cost structure. The indifference point is found by setting the total costs of one option equal to the total costs of another option, and then solving for the volume that equates the two options.
If given a choice between alternative cost structures, how do I choose the most profitable one?	Choose the *lower* operating leverage option when sales volume is expected to be *lower* than the indifference point. Choose the *higher* operating leverage option when sales volume is expected to be *higher* than the indifference point.

SUMMARY PROBLEM 2

Recall from Summary Problem 1 that Fleet Foot buys hiking socks for $6 a pair and sells them for $10. Monthly fixed costs are $10,000 (for sales volumes between 0 and 12,000 pairs), resulting in a breakeven point of 2,500 units. Assume that Fleet Foot has been selling 8,000 pairs of socks per month.

Requirements

1. What is Fleet Foot's current margin of safety in units, in sales dollars, and as a percentage? Explain the results.

2. At this level of sales, what is Fleet Foot's operating leverage factor? If volume declines by 25% due to increasing competition, by what percentage will the company's operating income decline?

3. Competition has forced Fleet Foot to lower its sales price to $9 a pair. How will this affect Fleet's breakeven point?

4. To compensate for the lower sales price, Fleet Foot wants to expand its product line to include men's dress socks. Each pair will sell for $7.00 and cost $2.75 from the supplier. Fixed costs will not change. Fleet expects to sell four pairs of dress socks for every one pair of hiking socks (at its new $9 sales price). What is Fleet's weighted-average contribution margin per unit? Given the 4:1 sales mix, how many of each type of sock will it need to sell to break even?

▪ SOLUTIONS

Requirement 1

$$\text{Margin of safety in units} = \text{Expected sales in units} - \text{Breakeven sales in units}$$

$$= \quad 8{,}000 \quad - \quad 2{,}500$$

$$= \quad 5{,}500 \text{ units}$$

$$\text{Margin of safety in dollars} = \text{Expected sales in dollars} - \text{Breakeven sales in dollars}$$

$$= \quad (8{,}000 \times \$10) \quad - \quad (2{,}500 \times \$10)$$

$$= \quad \$55{,}000$$

$$\text{Margin of safety as a percentage} = \frac{\text{Margin of safety in units}}{\text{Expected sales in units}}$$

$$= \frac{5{,}500 \text{ pairs}}{8{,}000 \text{ pairs}}$$

$$= \quad 68.75\%$$

Fleet Foot's margin of safety is quite high. Sales have to fall by more than 5,500 units (or $55,000) before Fleet incurs a loss. Fleet will continue to earn a profit unless sales drop by more than 68.75%.

Requirement 2

At its current level of volume, Fleet's operating income is as follows:

Contribution margin (8,000 pairs × $4 per pair)...............	$ 32,000
Less: Fixed expenses...	10,000
Operating income..	$ 22,000

Fleet's operating leverage factor at this level of sales is computed as follows:

$$\text{Operating leverage factor} = \frac{\text{Contribution margin}}{\text{Operating income}}$$

$$= \frac{\$32,000}{\$22,000}$$

$$= 1.45 \text{ (rounded)}$$

If sales volume declines by 25%, operating income will decline by 36.25% (Fleet's operating leverage factor of 1.45 multiplied by 25%).

Requirement 3

If Fleet drops its sales price to $9 per pair, its contribution margin per pair declines to $3 (sales price of $9 − variable cost of $6). Each sale contributes less toward covering fixed costs. Fleet's new breakeven point *increases* to 3,334 pairs of socks ($10,000 fixed costs ÷ $3 unit contribution margin).

Requirement 4

	A	B	C	D
		Hiking Socks	**Dress Socks**	**Total in "basket"**
1	**Calculating Weighted-Average Contribution Margin per Unit**			
2	Sales price per unit	$ 9.00	$ 7.00	
3	Less: Variable cost per unit	6.00	2.75	
4	Contribution margin per unit	$ 3.00	$ 4.25	
5	Multiply by: Sales mix (number of units in "basket")	1	4	5
6	Contribution margin	$ 3.00	$ 17.00	$ 20.00
7				
8	Weighted-average contribution margin per unit ($20/5 units)			$ 4.00
9				

$$\text{Sales in total units} = \frac{\text{Fixed expenses} + \text{Operating income}}{\text{Weighted-average contribution margin per unit}}$$

$$= \frac{\$10,000 + \$0}{\$4}$$

$$= 2,500 \text{ pairs of socks}$$

Breakeven sales of dress socks (2,500 × 4/5)......................	2,000 pairs dress socks
Breakeven sales of hiking socks (2,500 × 1/5).....................	500 pairs hiking socks

By expanding its product line to include higher-margin dress socks, Fleet is able to decrease its breakeven point back to its original level (2,500 pairs). However, to achieve this breakeven point, Fleet must sell the planned ratio of four pairs of dress socks to every one pair of hiking socks.

Learning Objectives

■ 1 Calculate the unit contribution margin and the contribution margin ratio

■ 2 Use CVP analysis to find breakeven points and target profit volumes

■ 3 Use CVP analysis to measure the impact of changing business conditions

■ 4 Find breakeven and target profit volumes for multiproduct companies

■ 5 Determine a firm's margin of safety, operating leverage, and most profitable cost structure

Accounting Vocabulary

Breakeven Point. (p. 386) The sales level at which operating income is zero: Total revenues = Total expenses.

Contribution Margin. (p. 383) Sales revenue minus variable expenses.

Contribution Margin Income Statement. (p. 383) An income statement that groups costs by behavior rather than function; it can be used only by internal management.

Contribution Margin Per Unit. (p. 384) The excess of the unit sales price over the variable cost per unit; also called unit contribution margin.

Contribution Margin Ratio. (p. 385) Ratio of contribution margin to sales revenue.

Cost-Volume-Profit (CVP) Analysis. (p. 382) Expresses the relationships among costs, volume, and profit or loss.

Indifference Point. (p. 410) The volume of sales at which a company would be indifferent between alternative cost structures because they would result in the same total cost.

Margin of Safety. (p. 406) Excess of expected sales over breakeven sales; the drop in sales a company can absorb without incurring an operating loss.

Operating Leverage. (p. 407) The relative amount of fixed and variable costs that make up a firm's total costs.

Operating Leverage Factor. (p. 408) At a given level of sales, the contribution margin divided by operating income; the operating leverage factor indicates the percentage change in operating income that will occur from a 1% change in sales volume.

Sales Mix. (p. 402) The combination of products that make up total sales.

Sensitivity Analysis. (p. 396) A "what-if" technique that asks what results will be if actual prices or costs change or if an underlying assumption changes.

Unit Contribution Margin. (p. 384) The excess of the unit sales price over the variable cost per unit: also called contribution margin per unit.

MyAccountingLab | Go to http://myaccountinglab.com/ **for the following Quick Check, Short Exercises, Exercises, and Problems. They are available with immediate grading, explanations of correct and incorrect answers, and interactive media that acts as your own online tutor.**

Quick Check

1. *(Learning Objective 1)* The contribution margin is
   a. sales revenue minus fixed expenses.
   b. sales revenue minus cost of goods sold.
   c. sales revenue minus variable expenses.
   d. sales revenue minus operating expenses.

2. *(Learning Objective 1)* The contribution margin ratio is
   a. contribution margin divided by variable expenses.
   b. sales revenue divided by contribution margin.
   c. contribution margin divided by sales revenue.
   d. fixed expenses divided by variable expenses.

3. *(Learning Objective 2)* The formula to find the breakeven point or a target profit volume in terms of number of units that need to be sold is
   a. (Fixed expenses + Variable expenses) ÷ Sales revenue.
   b. (Fixed expenses + Operating income) ÷ Sales revenue.
   c. (Fixed expenses + Variable expenses) ÷ Contribution margin per unit.
   d. (Fixed expenses + Operating income) ÷ Contribution margin per unit.

4. *(Learning Objective 2)* On a CVP graph, the breakeven point is
   a. the intersection of the total revenue line and the fixed expense line.
   b. the intersection of the total revenue line and the total expense line.
   c. the area between the variable expense line and the fixed expense line.
   d. the area between the total revenue line and the total expense line.

5. *(Learning Objective 3)* All else being equal, if a company's variable expenses increase,
   a. its breakeven point will decrease.
   b. there will be no effect on the breakeven point.
   c. its contribution margin ratio will increase.
   d. its contribution margin ratio will decrease.

6. *(Learning Objective 3)* All else being equal, a decrease in a company's fixed expenses will:
   a. increase the sales needed to break even.
   b. increase the contribution margin.
   c. decrease the sales needed to break even.
   d. decrease the contribution margin.

7. *(Learning Objective 4)* Which of the following is true regarding a company that offers more than one product?
   a. Breakeven should be found using a simple average contribution margin.
   b. Breakeven should be found for each product individually.
   c. It has one unique breakeven point.
   d. The breakeven point is dependent on sales mix assumptions.

8. *(Learning Objective 5)* A company with a low operating leverage
   a. has relatively more risk than a company with high operating leverage.
   b. has relatively more variable costs than fixed costs.
   c. has relatively more fixed costs than variable costs.
   d. has an equal proportion of fixed and variable costs.

9. *(Learning Objective 5)* For a given level of sales, a company's operating leverage is defined as
   a. contribution margin ÷ operating income.
   b. sales revenue ÷ contribution margin.
   c. contribution margin ÷ sales.
   d. operating income ÷ contribution margin.

10. *(Learning Objective 5)* Which of the following is false regarding choosing between two cost structures:
    a. The indifference point is the point where total revenues equal total expenses.
    b. The indifference point is the point at which costs under two options are the same.
    c. Choose the higher operating leverage option when sales volume is expected to be higher than the indifference point.
    d. Choose the lower operating leverage option when sales volume is expected to be lower than the indifference point.

Quick Check Answers

1. c 2. c 3. d 4. b 5. d 6. c 7. d 8. b 9. a 10. a

Relevant Costs for Short-Term Decisions

Learning Objectives

- **1** Describe and identify information relevant to short-term business decisions
- **2** Describe and apply different approaches to pricing
- **3** Decide whether to accept a special order
- **4** Decide whether to discontinue a product, department, or store
- **5** Factor resource constraints into product mix decisions
- **6** Analyze outsourcing (make-or-buy) decisions
- **7** Decide whether to sell a product "as is" or process it further

PA Images/Alamy

Sources: Nike, Inc. 2015 10-K; www.Forbes.com/powerful-brands/#/tab:rank_page:2

NIKE, Inc., is the largest seller of athletic footwear and apparel in the world. Nike is also synonymous with outsourcing: it doesn't manufacture any of its own products. Rather, Nike leaves the actual production of its branded products to independent contractors who operate over 600 factories, most of which are overseas. By outsourcing production to others, Nike can concentrate on its core competencies—the things it is really good at—including designing, developing, marketing, and selling athletic footwear, apparel, and equipment. But outsourcing is not without risks: Nike must rely on others to follow its standards for quality and fulfill production orders on a timely basis. In addition, sourcing the product overseas opens the company to exchange rate fluctuations, trade tariffs, port strikes, and other global risks. The upside? Nike's business model has allowed the company to develop one of the most iconic and valuable brands in the world.

n Chapter 7, we saw how managers use cost behavior to determine the company's break-even point and to estimate the sales volume needed to achieve target profits. In this chapter, we'll see how managers use their knowledge of cost behavior to make six different business decisions, such as whether to outsource production to other companies. The decisions we'll discuss in this chapter usually pertain to shorter periods of time, so managers do not need to worry about the time value of money. In other words, they do not need to compute the present value of the revenues and expenses relating to the decision. In Chapter 12, we will discuss longer-term decisions (such as buying equipment and undertaking plant expansions) in which the time value of money becomes important. Before we look at the six business decisions in detail, let's consider managers' decision-making process and the information managers need to evaluate their options.

How Do Managers Make Decisions?

Exhibit 8-1 illustrates how managers decide among alternative courses of action. Management accountants participate in most aspects of the decision cycle, ranging from identifying possible courses of action to collecting and analyzing relevant information that helps guide managers' ultimate decision. Once the decision has been implemented, managerial accountants follow up on the decision, comparing actual results to expectations. If the company's goals are not being achieved as well as anticipated, the cycle will begin again with new, corrective action

EXHIBIT 8-1 How Managers Make Decisions

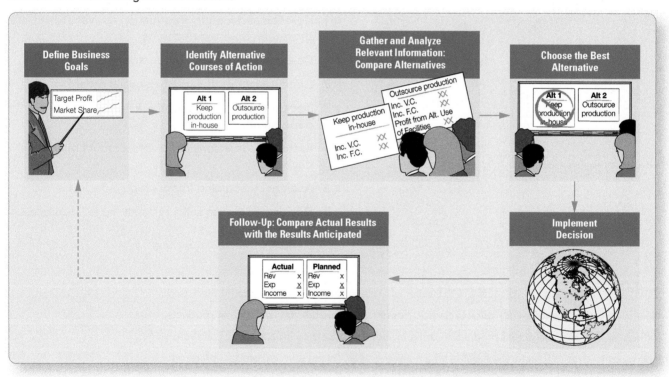

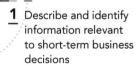

1 Describe and identify information relevant to short-term business decisions

Relevant Information

When managers make decisions, they focus only on information that is *relevant* to the decisions. Exhibit 8-2 shows that **relevant information** has two characteristics:

1. It pertains to the *future*.
2. It *differs* among alternatives.

EXHIBIT 8-2 Relevant Information

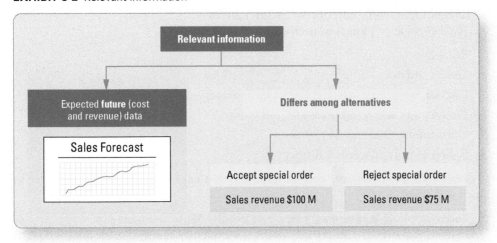

Think of a recent decision you have made, such as your decision as to which college or university to attend. What influenced your decision? Some of the relevant financial information may have included the cost of tuition, the cost of room and board, and the financial aid package you were offered, including scholarships, work study, and loans. Some of the relevant nonfinancial information may have included the size of the school, the geographic location of the school, specific extracurricular activities of interest to you, or just the feeling you got from meeting people on campus.

Think about these factors for a moment and how they influenced your decision. When you compared colleges, you probably made a mental or written list about the things you liked better about one institution over another. In other words, you concentrated on those aspects that *differed* between institutions. For example, you may have thrown out some schools because the net cost was too high and you or your parents didn't want to pay that much for tuition in the *future*. Some schools may have been more prestigious than others, causing you to believe you would get better or higher-paying job offers in the *future*. And as for the nonfinancial factors, you probably envisioned what it would be like to attend the college in the *future*. In other words, you concentrated on information that *differed* between alternatives and that would affect your *future*. The same holds true for business decisions: managers focus on financial and nonfinancial information that *differs* among alternatives and that pertains to the *future*.

With the existence of big data and ERP systems, managers can easily become overwhelmed by the sheer magnitude of data that is available. Managers must use critical thinking skills (as outlined on page 18 in Chapter 1) to zero in on the larger business issue, the specific question that needs to be addressed, and the data that are *relevant* to answering the question. Managers need to clearly identify the assumptions being made, the "gray areas" that involve judgment, and the possible implications of the decision. Throughout this chapter, you'll see that we begin each decision with a set of assumptions, but then change one or more of the assumptions to see what impact it has on the resulting decision. Since no one has a crystal ball with which to see the future, the more assumptions that have been questioned and considered, the better prepared managers will be.

> ■ **Why is this important?**
>
> "The accounting information used to make **business decisions** in this chapter focuses on one factor: **profitability**. However, in real life, managers should take a triple-bottom-line approach to decision making by considering the decision's impact on people and the environment."

Keys to Making Short-Term Special Decisions

Our approach to making short-term special decisions is called the *incremental analysis approach*. Instead of looking at the company's *entire* income statement under each decision alternative, we'll just look at how operating income would *change or differ* under each alternative. Using this approach, we'll leave out irrelevant information—the costs and revenues that won't differ between alternatives.

We'll consider six kinds of decisions in this chapter:

1. Pricing
2. Special orders
3. Discontinuing products, departments, or stores
4. Product mix when resources are constrained
5. Outsourcing (make or buy)
6. Selling as is or processing further

As you study these decisions, keep in mind the two keys to analyzing business decisions shown in Exhibit 8-3:

1. **Focus on relevant revenues, costs, and profits.** Most decisions boil down to a cost-benefit analysis. The important point is to identify and focus on only the *relevant* costs and benefits: those that will *differ* between alternatives and affect the *future*. Irrelevant information only clouds the picture and creates information overload.

2. **Use a contribution margin approach that separates variable costs from fixed costs.** Because fixed costs and variable costs behave differently, they must be analyzed separately. Traditional income statements based on absorption costing can mislead managers because they blend fixed and variable costs together. Contribution margin income statements, which isolate costs by behavior (variable or fixed), are much better suited for decision making.

Keep in mind that every business decision is unique. Just because a piece of information is relevant in one decision doesn't mean it will be relevant in the next. Each decision will need to be assessed individually to determine the relevant pieces of information. Also keep in mind that different costs are used for different purposes. For example, absorption-based costing is required by GAAP for external financial reporting purposes, yet variable costing is usually much better for decision-making purposes.

EXHIBIT 8-3 Two Keys to Making Short-Term Special Decisions

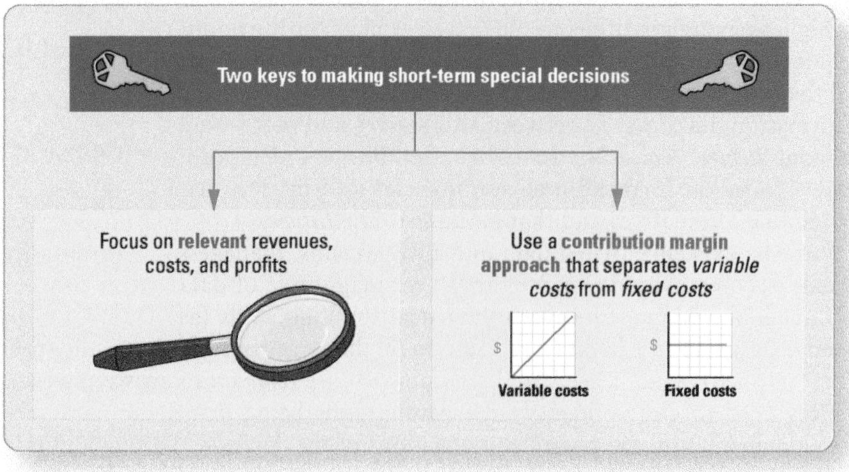

Decision Pitfalls to Avoid

Finally, there are a few common mistakes that managers sometimes make. We point out the pitfalls here so that you can train yourself to avoid them.

1. **Avoid including sunk costs in your analysis.** <u>Sunk costs</u> are costs that have been incurred in the past and cannot be changed regardless of which future action is taken. For example, a manager may have invested thousands of dollars in a computer

system that appeared to be a good investment at the time. However, with the passage of time and the speed of technological advances, using the old system may no longer be in the best interest of the organization, even if it is only one to two years old. Hindsight may even make the past decision appear foolish. When deciding whether or not to replace the system, the amount originally paid for the system is a sunk cost that should not be considered. Rather, only the *future* costs and benefits associated with continuing to use the old system versus investing in a new system should be considered.

2. **Avoid using unit costs unless they are purely variable in nature.** Recall from Chapter 6 that absorption costing includes both variable *and* fixed manufacturing costs. Variable production costs include direct material, direct labor, and variable overhead costs that will be incurred on every unit produced. On the other hand, fixed overhead cost will *not* be incurred on every unit produced but rather, will stay constant in total. Variable costing is usually better for decision-making purposes because it does not blend together the variable and fixed production costs. If you use unit costs in your analysis, make sure you first separate the fixed and variable components of the costs and then analyze the fixed cost in *total*, not on a per-unit basis.

Sustainability and Short-Term Business Decisions

For companies that embrace sustainability and the triple bottom line, almost every decision will be viewed through the lens of its impact on people and the planet, as well as profitability. For companies such as Nike that outsource key business functions, creating and maintaining sustainable practices throughout the company's supply chain can be challenging. While Nike's suppliers are contractually obligated to adhere to Nike's "Code of Conduct," which sets forth standards for equitable labor practices and environmentally sound manufacturing practices, the company's reputation could be harmed if the suppliers fail to comply. Here are just a few of the strides Nike has been making toward becoming more environmentally and socially sustainable:

- Nike is working with its contractors to create more environmentally sustainable production practices. The company's goal is to double its business, yet half its environmental impact. Since 2008, contract manufacturers have cut energy used per unit by 50%. The company aims to use 100% renewable energy by 2025. It is focused on using innovative materials and manufacturing techniques to decrease the amount of water used and carbon emitted from the manufacture of its products.

- Nike's goal by 2020 is to have zero waste from contractor factories sent to landfills. Product designers are working hard to create a cradle-to-cradle, closed-loop system where old shoes and manufacturing scraps are ground and reused in the production of new products, as well as courts, tracks, and other play surfaces. The ground recycled materials, aptly named "Nike Grind," are already incorporated into 71% of Nike's products.

- Since 2010, over 3 billion plastic bottles have been converted into recycled fibers for use in Nike's products, and approximately 30 million pairs of shoes have been recycled through the company's "reuse-a-shoe" program.

- Nike's contractors employ over one million factory workers. To make sure health, safety, and labor practices are carried out in accordance with Nike's Code of Conduct, the company employs over 150 people whose sole job is to monitor factories. Nike also works with third parties, such as the Fair Labor Association, to conduct independent monitoring. Each factory is scored on labor practices, in addition to traditional metrics such as cost, quality, and on-time delivery. Reports of noncompliance are investigated immediately, so that corrective action can be taken.

- The company is working toward forming a more diverse and inclusive workforce. Over 50% of company employees (noncontracted) are nonwhite and 41% of managers are women.

- Nike's goal is to invest at least 1.5% of annual pretax income in community impact initiatives. In 2015, Nike invested 1.9% of pretax income (approximately $80 million) in these initiatives. The company also promotes employee volunteerism and matches employee donations to nonprofits up to $10,000 per employee per year.

These are just a few of the ways Nike is embedding sustainability within the organization. You can find more information in Nike's FY14/15 Sustainable Business Report.

See Exercises E8-17A and E8-33B

Sources: Nike, Inc. 2015 10-K; Nike, Inc, FY14/15 Sustainable Business Report.

How Do Managers Make Pricing and Special Order Decisions?

2 Describe and apply different approaches to pricing

We'll start our discussion by looking at pricing decisions, which can be one of the most challenging decisions managers need to make. After that, we'll move on to special order decisions.

Regular Pricing Decisions

There is no way around it: pricing is a messy business. In your economics course, you learned that the price of a product is the point at which the supply curve and the demand curve intersect. But, in practice, what does this mean? Generally speaking, the higher the price, the lower the demand, while the lower the price, the higher the demand. To maximize its profits, a company needs to consider the *profit* that will be made at the various price points, not just the sales price alone. And as you know from earlier chapters, the profit made on a product is determined not only by its sales price, but also by its cost. In other words, cost is an important factor in determining profitability and pricing.

Exhibit 8-4 shows that managers start with three basic questions when setting regular prices for their products or services.

EXHIBIT 8-4 Regular Pricing Considerations

- What is our target profit?
- How much are customers willing to pay?
- Are we a price-taker or a price-setter for this product?

The answers to these questions are often complex and ever-changing. Let's consider each in turn.

First, managers must consider their target profit. Stockholders expect the company to achieve certain profits. Economic conditions, historical company earnings, industry risk, competition, and new business developments all affect the level of profit that stockholders expect. Stockholders usually tie their profit expectations to the amount of assets invested in the company. For example, stockholders may expect a 10% annual return on their investment. A company's stock price tends to decline if the company does not meet target profits, so managers must keep costs low while generating enough revenue to meet those targets.

Second, managers need to consider the price customers are willing to pay. The amount customers will pay depends on the competition, the product's uniqueness, whether the product is branded, the effectiveness of marketing campaigns, general economic conditions, and so forth. Focus groups and test markets are often used to help determine the price customers are willing to pay.

Third, managers must consider whether they are price-takers or price-setters. To address the third pricing question, imagine a continuum with price-takers at one end and price-setters at the other end. A company's products and services fall somewhere along this continuum, shown in Exhibit 8-5. Companies are price-takers when they have little or no control over the prices of their products or services. This occurs when their products and services are *not* unique, not branded, or when competition is heavy. Examples include food commodities (milk and corn), natural resources (oil and lumber), and generic consumer products and services (paper towels, dry cleaning, and banking).

EXHIBIT 8-5 Price-Takers Versus Price-Setters

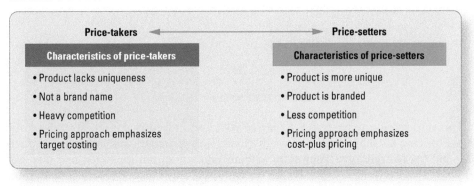

Companies are price-setters when they have more control over pricing—in other words, they can "set" prices to some extent. Companies are price-setters when their products are unique, such as original art and jewelry, specially manufactured machinery, and custom-made furniture. Companies are also price-setters when there is little competition. For example, a gas station out in the middle of nowhere can charge any price it wants because there are no other gas stations around. Finally, companies also are price-setters if they have successfully branded their products, as Nike has.

Obviously, managers would rather be price-setters than price-takers. To gain more control over pricing, companies try to differentiate their products. They want to make their products unique in terms of features, service, or quality—or at least make you *think* their product is unique or somehow better even if it isn't. How do they do this? Primarily through advertising and branding. Consider Nike's tennis shoes, Starbucks's coffee, Apple's tablets, Kleenex's tissues, Tylenol's acetaminophen, Capital One's credit cards, Shell's gas—the list goes on and on. Are these products really better than or significantly different from their lower-priced competitors? If these companies can make you think so, they've gained more control over their pricing because you are willing to pay *more* for their products or services. The downside? These companies must charge higher prices or sell more units just to cover their marketing costs.

A company's approach to pricing depends on whether its product or service is on the price-taking or price-setting side of the spectrum. Price-setters emphasize a cost-plus pricing approach; price-takers emphasize a target costing approach. Keep in mind that many products fall somewhere along the continuum. Therefore, managers tend to use both approaches to some extent.

Why is this important?

"Both **branding** and product **differentiation** give managers more control over pricing. Without such features, a **company** must often settle for selling its **product** at the same price as its competitors."

Our pricing decision rule is as follows:

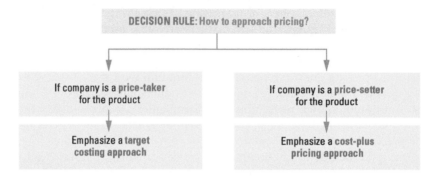

Cost-Plus Pricing

When a company is more of a price setter, such as Nike or Apple, it emphasizes a cost-plus approach to pricing. **Cost-plus pricing** starts with the product's total costs and *adds* a desired profit to determine a cost-plus price.

> Total cost
>
> Plus: Desired profit
>
> Cost-plus price

This information may seem familiar to you, and indeed it should. We talked about cost-plus pricing in Chapter 3 when we discussed how managers use job costing information to bid for custom jobs: They start with an estimate of the job's cost and then add a markup to arrive at the bid price. What we will do in this chapter is very similar, though we are going to consider an entire company rather than just one particular custom job.

For our example, let's consider Garnier Fructis, maker of branded shampoo.[1] Exhibit 8-6 contains information about the company:

EXHIBIT 8-6 Garnier's Data for the Year

Variable costs:		
Variable manufacturing costs (DM, DL, Variable MOH) per unit ....$1.20 per unit ⎫		$ 1.50 per unit
Variable operating expenses (sales commission and freight out) per unit ....$0.30 per unit ⎬		
Fixed costs:		
Fixed manufacturing overhead ....$2,000,000 ⎫		$ 3,250,000
Fixed operating expenses ....$1,250,000 ⎬		
Other information:		
Units needed		2,500,000
Plant capacity (units that could be produced with the existing capacity)		2,600,000
Total assets		$ 10,000,000
Desired return on assets		10%
Absorption cost per unit [= $1.20 variable mfg + ($2,000,000 fixed MOH ÷ 2,500,000)]		$ 2.00

Since Garnier is a branded product, the company will emphasize a cost-plus approach to pricing. In pricing decisions, *all costs are relevant* because the company must

---

[1] All references to Garnier Fructis in this hypothetical example were created by the author solely for academic purposes and are not intended, in any way, to represent the actual business practices of, or costs incurred by, Garnier.

cover all costs along the value chain before it can generate a profit. In other words, the price needs to be high enough to cover operating expenses (R&D, design, marketing, distribution, and customer service) as well as manufacturing costs. As stated in our keys to decision making, we'll separate the variable costs and fixed costs in our analysis. Exhibit 8-7 shows how Garnier would calculate its cost-plus price:

EXHIBIT 8-7 Cost-Plus Pricing Analysis

	A	B
	Cost -Plus Pricing Analysis	**Total**
2	Variable manufacturing costs ($1.20 × 2,500,000 units)	$ 3,000,000
3	Variable operating expenses ($ 0.30 × 2,500,000 units)	750,000
4	Fixed manufacturing costs	2,000,000
5	Fixed operating expenses	1,250,000
6	Total costs across the value chain	$ 7,000,000
7	Plus: Desired profit (10% × $10 million of assets)	1,000,000
8	Sales revenue desired for 2,500,000 units	$ 8,000,000
9	Divided by: Number of units	2,500,000
10	Cost-plus price per unit	$ 3.20
11		

Notice how we first found the total costs for the needed volume and then added the desired profit, just as the "cost-plus" name implies. By doing so, we arrived at the total desired amount of sales revenue. Finally, we divided by the number of units needed to arrive at the cost-plus price per unit ($3.20).

Will the company stop there? No. The next thing it will do is figure out if customers are willing to pay that much for the product. The company will use focus groups and test marketing to find out whether the cost-plus price is too high, or even possibly too low, and then it will adjust accordingly. Notice also how volume played a big role in this decision. If Garnier can produce and sell a higher volume of product, the cost-plus price will be lower. Why? Because the fixed costs will be spread over more units. Thus, management may want to test out a range of volume assumptions in its analyses.

STOP & THINK

Based on the information in Exhibit 8-7, the product cost used for inventory valuation and Cost of Goods Sold is $2.00 per unit. Why can't management simply add the 10% desired return on assets to this figure to arrive at the cost-plus price?

Answer: The absorption cost per unit only includes production costs, not operating expenses. In pricing decisions, companies must consider *all* of their costs. In addition, the absorption cost per unit includes fixed manufacturing overhead. If volume were projected to be different than 2.5 million units, the absorption cost per unit would be different than $2.00.

Target Costing

When a company is a price-taker, it has no control over the price. It must simply use the same price as its competitors or people won't buy the product. In other words, price is a "given." The only thing the company can do to ensure an adequate amount of profit is control its own costs. Companies that have little control over pricing emphasize a target costing approach. As shown below, **target costing** starts with the market price of the product (the price customers are willing to pay) and subtracts the company's desired profit to determine the product's target total cost—the *total* cost to develop, design, produce, market, deliver, and service the product:

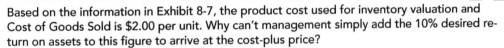

Revenue at market price

Less: Desired profit

Target total cost

As you can see, target costing is the *opposite* of cost-plus pricing. If the company's actual total costs are higher than the target total cost, managers must find ways to reduce costs so that they can meet profit goals. Managers often use activity-based costing (ABC) and lean thinking (as discussed in Chapter 4) to find ways to eliminate waste and reduce costs.

Let's look at an example of target costing. Assume that Garnier's shampoo is a *non-branded commodity* and that the current market price for similar shampoo is $3.00 per unit. Exhibit 8-8 calculates the target total cost and then compares it to the current total costs for the 2,500,000 units the company needs each year:

EXHIBIT 8-8 Target Costing Analysis

	A	B
1	**Target Costing Analysis**	**Total**
2	Revenue at market price (2,500,000 units × $3.00 sales price)	$ 7,500,000
3	Less: Desired profit (10% × $10 million of assets)	1,000,000
4	Target total cost	$ 6,500,000
5		
6	Versus: Current total costs (from Exhibit 8–7)	$ 7,000,000
7	Total cost reduction needed to achieve target profit	$ (500,000)
8		

As shown in Exhibit 8-8, Garnier's total costs are $500,000 higher than the target total cost. Therefore, the company needs to find ways to reduce total costs by $500,000 if it is to meet its profit goal. So, what are Garnier's options?

- Reduce fixed costs.
- Reduce the variable costs per unit.
- Try other strategies, such as branding, product differentiation, or adding more products to the company's product mix.
- Accept a lower profit.

Let's look at some of these options. Garnier may first try to reduce fixed manufacturing costs and fixed operating expenses. As we discussed in Chapter 6, committed fixed costs are virtually impossible to change in the short run. Therefore, the company would start by considering whether any discretionary fixed costs could be reduced or eliminated. While R&D and marketing are discretionary, cutting them may be detrimental to the company in the long run, so the managers need to carefully consider the long-term impact of cutting fixed costs.

Let's assume that Garnier has identified $100,000 of fixed cost savings. Since the company needs to reduce costs by a total of $500,000 in order to reach its profit goal, managers must now consider how to reduce the variable costs associated with each unit made and sold. Exhibit 8-9 shows that with the $100,000 reduction in fixed costs, the most Garnier can spend on each unit is $1.34 in order to meet its profit goal. The company will need to shave $0.16 off of the cost of every unit produced and sold.

EXHIBIT 8-9 Calculating Target Unit Variable Cost

	A	B
1	**Target Variable Cost per Unit**	**Total**
2	Target total cost from Exhibit 8–8	$ 6,500,000
3	Less: Fixed costs ($3,250,000 - $100,000 savings)	3,150,000
4	Target total variable cost	$ 3,350,000
5	Divided by: Number of units	2,500,000
6	Target variable cost per unit	$ 1.34
7		
8	Versus: Current variable cost per unit from Exhibit 8–6	$ 1.50
9	Cost reduction needed per unit to achieve desired profit	$ (0.16)
10		

How can managers achieve variable cost saving? Perhaps the company could renegotiate raw materials costs with its suppliers, change the packaging materials used, or restructure the way it awards sales commissions. Notice how managers need to think about *variable operating expenses*, as well as *variable manufacturing costs*. Many companies are reducing the actual size of their products to save money on direct materials. In other words, Garnier could sell slightly smaller bottles of shampoo. Smaller products also mean that more units can be shipped in the same cargo space, thereby saving on the variable cost of distributing each unit. Companies have found that consumers are less sensitive to reductions in the size of products than they are to increases in prices. Thus, trimming the contents of a product is often one strategy used to meet target variable costs.

Finally, the company can attempt different strategies that may actually include *increasing*, rather than decreasing, costs. For example, the company may need to increase marketing costs to boost volume or brand its product. It may need to spend *more* on research and development (R&D) to differentiate its product through innovation. Cost-volume-profit (CVP) analysis, as you learned in Chapter 7, can help companies determine whether these actions will be profitable. As you can see, managers don't have an easy task when the current total cost exceeds the target total cost. Sometimes, companies just can't compete given the current market price. If that's the case, they may have no other choice than to exit the market.

Special Order Decisions

A special order occurs when a customer requests a one-time order at a *reduced* sales price. Often, these special orders are for large quantities. Before agreeing to the special order, management must consider the questions shown in Exhibit 8-10.

3 Decide whether to accept a special order

EXHIBIT 8-10 Special Order Considerations

- Do we have excess capacity available to fill this order?

- Will the reduced sales price be high enough to cover the *incremental* costs of filling the order (the variable costs of filling the order and any additional fixed costs)?

- Will the special order affect regular sales in the long run?

First, managers must consider available capacity. If the company is already making as many units as possible and selling them all at its *regular* sales price, it wouldn't make sense to fill a special order at a *reduced* sales price. Therefore, excess capacity is almost a necessity for accepting a special order. This is true for companies that provide services as well as for manufacturers and merchandisers.

Second, managers need to consider whether the special reduced sales price is high enough to cover the *incremental* costs of filling the order. The special price *must* exceed the variable costs of filling the order. In other words, the special order must provide a positive contribution margin. In addition, the company must consider fixed costs. If the company has excess capacity, the existing fixed costs probably won't be affected by producing more units or delivering more service. However, in some cases, management may need to hire a consultant, pay an attorney for drawing up a contract, or incur some other fixed cost to fill the special order. If so, management will need to consider whether the special sales price is high enough to generate a positive contribution margin *and* cover the additional fixed costs.

Finally, managers need to consider whether the special order will affect regular sales in the long run. Will regular customers find out about the special order and demand a lower price? Will the special order customer come back *again and again*, asking for the same reduced price? Will the special order price start a price war with competitors? Managers must consider these questions before making their final decision. Managers may decide that any profit from the special sales order is not worth these risks.

Special Order Example

Let's assume that Garnier has successfully branded its product and is able to sell its name brand shampoo at the cost-plus price of $3.20 per bottle, as shown in Exhibit 8-7. Assume Aldi, a merchandiser that sells only generic products, has approached Garnier with an offer to buy 20,000 bottles of shampoo for $1.60 per bottle, which is half of Garnier's normal sales price. Also assume the following facts about the special order:

- Aldi wants the shampoo packaged under its own private label. The bottles used for the private-label shampoo will be slightly smaller, allowing Garnier to save $0.15 per unit on the direct material cost.

- Aldi will pay the shipping costs.

- No sales commission will be paid on this order since Aldi approached Garnier without sales people involved.

- Garnier will have to pay $2,000 in legal fees to draw up the contract.

Let's consider the issues raised in Exhibit 8-10.

First, let's find out if Garnier has excess capacity with which to produce this special order. According to Exhibit 8-6, Garnier has capacity to produce 2,600,000 units per period, but its current production and sales are only 2,500,000 per period. Thus, the company could make 100,000 more units per period with its current production capacity that would otherwise be left unused.

Second, let's consider the incremental costs of filling the order. Let's look at variable costs first. From Exhibit 8-6 we see that the variable cost to manufacture each unit is $1.20. However, Garnier will save $0.15 per bottle on direct materials. So the variable manufacturing cost associated with the order will be $1.05 per unit ($1.20 – $0.15). The variable operating expenses of $0.30 per unit (sales commission and freight out) won't be incurred on this order, so they aren't relevant to the decision.

Now let's look at fixed costs. Since Garnier has excess capacity, its *existing* fixed costs won't be affected by producing 20,000 more units. However, the company will incur an *extra* $2,000 of fixed costs to have an attorney draw up the sales contract.

Exhibit 8-11 completes the analysis by comparing the sales revenue that would be generated by the order with the incremental costs of filling the order.

EXHIBIT 8-11 Incremental Analysis of Special Sales Order

	A	B	C
			Total Order
1	**Incremental Analysis for Special Order Decision**	**Per Unit**	**(20,000 units)**
2	Revenue from special order	$ 1.60	$ 32,000
3	Less Variable expenses associated with the order:		
4	Variable manufacturing costs (DM, DL, Variable MOH)*	1.05	21,000
5	Contribution margin	$ 0.55	$ 11,000
6	Less additional fixed expenses associated with the order		2,000
7	Increase in operating income from the special order		$ 9,000
8			

*Normal variable cost of $1.20 per bottle less $0.15 savings per bottle on direct materials.

This analysis shows that Garnier could earn an extra $9,000 of operating income by accepting this special order.

Now let's consider the final issue raised in Exhibit 8-10: Will the special order affect regular sales in the long run? Since the product will be packaged under Aldi's private label, consumers won't know it is the same as Garnier's shampoo, but they may decide they like it just as much. As a result, Garnier may cannibalize sales of its own brand-name product. However, the fact that Garnier is only selling 20,000 units under the private label versus the 2.5 million units of its own label makes this risk fairly small. Plus, loyal brand-users probably won't try shampoo sold under other labels. Thus, Garnier will most likely decide to accept this order.

Notice that our analysis follows the two keys to making short-term special business decisions discussed earlier: (1) focus on relevant data (revenues and costs that *will differ* if Garnier accepts the special order) and (2) use a contribution margin approach that separates variable costs from fixed costs.

To summarize, for special sales orders, the decision rule is as follows:

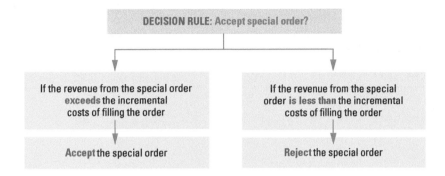

Pitfall to Avoid on Special Order Decisions

One of the most common mistakes managers make when analyzing special orders is to base their decision on the unit product cost that uses absorption costing. Recall from Chapter 6 that under absorption costing, all manufacturing costs, including fixed MOH, are "absorbed" into the unit cost of the product. Absorption costing was used as the product cost when we studied job costing and process costing in Chapters 3, 4, and 5 because it is required by Generally Accepted Accounting Principles (GAAP) for external financial reporting purposes. Using the figures found in Exhibit 8-6, we see that the product cost of each bottle of shampoo, using absorption costing, is $2.00:

Product Cost at Current Production Level	Absorption Unit Cost
Variable manufacturing costs (DM, DL, Variable MOH) per unit	$1.20
Fixed manufacturing costs (Fixed MOH of $2,000,000 ÷ 2,500,000 units)	0.80
Cost per unit using absorption costing	$2.00

The $2.00 unit cost, which GAAP mandates for inventory and cost of goods sold valuation, is *not* a good basis for making a special order decision. Why? Because it is a mixed cost, which includes both fixed and variable components. If a manager simply compared the special order sales price of $1.60 per unit to the absorption cost of $2.00 per unit, the manager would incorrectly assume that the special order would result in a loss of $0.40 per unit, or $8,000 in total (20,000 units × $0.40) before even factoring in the extra $2,000 of attorney's fees. Even considering the $0.15 per unit direct materials cost savings, absorption costing is the wrong place to start. Since there is excess capacity in the plant, the reality of the situation is that fixed MOH will remain $2,000,000 in total, regardless of whether Garnier accepts the special order. Producing 20,000 more units will *not* increase total fixed costs by $0.80 per unit. The incremental cost incurred to make each additional bottle of shampoo is the variable cost per unit, not the absorption cost per unit. Keep the following important rule of thumb in mind:

Never compare the special order sales price with the absorption cost per unit or your analysis will be flawed. Rather, use the contribution margin approach.

▶ Try It!

Assume that a Campbell's soup plant is running at 90% of its monthly capacity. Campbell's has just received a special order to produce 40,000 cases of chicken noodle soup for a national supermarket. The supermarket will sell the soup under its own private brand label. The soup will be the same in all respects, except for the label, which will cost Campbell's an extra $5,000 in total to design. The supermarket has offered to pay only $19.00 per case, which is well under Campbell's normal sales price.

Costs at the current production level (450,000 cases) are as follows:

	Total Cost	Cost per Case (450,000 cases)
Direct Materials	$4,500,000	$10.00
Direct Labor	1,350,000	3.00
Variable MOH	900,000	2.00
Fixed MOH	2,700,000	6.00
Total	$9,450,000	$21.00

1. Is there enough excess capacity to fill this order?
2. Will Campbell's operating income increase or decrease if it accepts this special order? By how much?

Please see page 506 for solutions.

Decision Guidelines

Relevant Information for Business Decisions

Nike makes pricing and special order decisions. Even though it sells mass-produced tennis shoes and sports clothing, Nike has successfully branded its products with advertising. Nike's managers consider both quantitative and qualitative factors as they make pricing decisions. Here are key guidelines that Nike's managers follow in making their decisions.

Decision	Guidelines
What information is relevant to a short-term special business decision?	Relevant information has two characteristics: 1. It pertains to the *future*. 2. It *differs* between alternatives.
What are two key guidelines in making short-term special business decisions?	1. Focus on *relevant* data. 2. Use a *contribution margin* approach that separates variable costs from fixed costs.
What are two pitfalls to avoid in making business decisions?	1. Avoid including sunk costs. 2. Avoid using the absorption cost per unit since it includes both fixed and variable components.
How does a company's commitment to sustainability affect decision making?	Companies that are committed to sustainability will judge every decision through the lens of the triple bottom line, assessing the impact of the decision not only on company profit, but also on its consequences for people and the planet.
What should Nike consider in setting its regular product prices?	Nike considers the following: 1. The profit stockholders expect 2. The price customers are willing to pay 3. Whether it is a price-setter or a price-taker
Which approach should Nike take to pricing?	Nike has differentiated its products through advertising and branding. Thus, Nike tends to be a price-setter. Nike's managers can emphasize a cost-plus approach to pricing.
Which approach should discount shoe stores such as Payless ShoeSource take to pricing?	Payless ShoeSource sells generic shoes (no-name brands) at low prices. Payless is a price-taker, so managers use a target-costing approach to pricing.
Should Nike accept a large special order from a customer at a price that is lower than the normal sales price?	If the revenue from the order exceeds the incremental variable and fixed costs of filling the order, then accepting the order will increase operating income.

SUMMARY PROBLEM 1

Linger Industries makes tennis balls. Linger's only plant can produce up to 2.5 million cans of balls per year. Current production is two million cans. Annual manufacturing, selling, and administrative fixed costs total $700,000. The variable cost of making and selling each can of balls is $1. Stockholders expect a 12% annual return on the company's $3 million of assets.

Requirements

1. What is Linger Industries' current total cost of making and selling two million cans of tennis balls? What is the total cost *per unit* of making and selling each can of balls?

2. Assume that Linger Industries is a price-taker and the current market price is $1.45 per can of balls (this is the price at which manufacturers sell to retailers). What is the *target* total cost of producing and selling two million cans of balls? Given Linger Industries' current total costs, will the company reach stockholders' profit goals?

3. Continuing with Requirement 2, if Linger Industries cannot reduce its fixed costs, what is the target variable cost per can of balls?

4. Suppose Linger Industries could spend an extra $100,000 on advertising to differentiate its product so that it could be more of a price-setter. Assuming the original volume and costs plus the $100,000 of new advertising costs, what cost-plus price will Linger Industries want to charge for a can of balls?

5. Nike has just asked Linger Industries to supply 400,000 cans of balls at a special order price of $1.20 per can. Nike wants Linger Industries to package the balls under the Nike label (Linger will imprint the Nike logo on each ball and can). As a result, Linger Industries will have to spend $10,000 to change the packaging machinery. Assuming the original volume and costs, should Linger Industries accept this special order? Assume that Linger will incur variable selling costs as well as variable manufacturing costs related to this order.

▪ SOLUTIONS

Requirement 1

The current total cost and cost per unit are calculated as follows:

Fixed costs	$ 700,000
Plus: Total variable costs (2 million cans × $1 per unit)............	2,000,000
Current total costs...	$2,700,000
Divided by number of units..	÷ 2,000,000
Total cost per can...	$ 1.35

Requirement 2

The target total cost is as follows:

Revenue at market price (2,000,000 cans × $1.45 price)	$2,900,000
Less: Desired profit (12% × $3,000,000 of assets)......................	(360,000)
Target total cost	$2,540,000

Linger Industries' *current* total costs ($2,700,000 from Requirement 1) are $160,000 higher than the *target* total costs ($2,540,000). If Linger Industries can't cut costs, it won't be able to meet stockholders' profit expectations.

Requirement 3

Assuming that Linger Industries cannot reduce its fixed costs, the target variable cost per can is as follows:

Target total cost (from Requirement 2)	$ 2,540,000
Less: Fixed costs...	(700,000)
Target total variable costs	$ 1,840,000
Divided by number of units..............................	÷ 2,000,000
Target variable cost per unit.............................	$ 0.92

Since Linger Industries cannot reduce its fixed costs, it needs to reduce variable costs by $0.08 per can ($1.00 – $0.92) to meet its profit goals. This would require an 8% cost reduction in variable costs, which may not be possible.

Requirement 4

If Linger Industries can differentiate its tennis balls, it will gain more control over pricing. The company's new cost-plus price would be as follows:

Current total costs (from Requirement 1).............	$ 2,700,000
Plus: Additional cost of advertising	100,000
Plus: Desired profit (from Requirement 2)............	360,000
Target revenue...	$ 3,160,000
Divided by number of units..................................	÷ 2,000,000
Cost-plus price per unit...	$ 1.58

Linger Industries must study the market to determine whether retailers would pay $1.58 per can of balls.

Requirement 5

First, Linger determines that it has enough extra capacity (500,000 cans) to fill this special order (400,000). Next, Linger compares the revenue from the special order with the extra costs that will be incurred to fill the order. Linger will incur $1.00 of variable costs on each can of balls, plus the additional fixed cost of $10,000 for changing the labeling machine. Notice that Linger shouldn't compare the special order price ($1.20) with the total cost of making and selling each can ($1.35) because the unit cost contains both a fixed and variable component. The correct analysis is as follows:

Revenue from special order (400,000 × $1.20 per unit)	$ 480,000
Less: Variable cost of special order (400,000 × $1.00)	(400,000)
Contribution margin from special order....................................	$ 80,000
Less: Additional fixed costs of special order.............................	(10,000)
Operating income provided by special order.............................	$ 70,000

The decision to accept the special order would increase operating income by $70,000. However, Linger Industries also needs to consider whether its regular customers will find out about the special price and demand lower prices, too. If Linger had simply compared the special order price of $1.20 to the total unit cost of making and selling each can ($1.35), it would have rejected the special order and missed out on the opportunity to make an additional $70,000 of profit.

How Do Managers Make Other Special Business Decisions?

In this part of the chapter, we'll consider four more business decisions:

- Whether to discontinue a product, department, or store
- How to factor constrained resources into product mix decisions
- Whether to make a product or outsource it (buy it)
- Whether to sell a product as is or process it further

Decisions to Discontinue Products, Departments, or Stores

Managers often must decide whether to discontinue products, departments, stores, or territories that are not as profitable as desired. For example, American Eagle and Sports Authority closed hundreds of retail locations in 2016. Kroger grocery stores eliminated obsolete movie rental departments and have replaced them with prepared meals, bulk foods, and larger produce departments. And every day, companies are deciding whether to eliminate older product lines and replace them with new product lines. How do managers make these decisions? Exhibit 8-12 shows some questions managers must consider when deciding whether to discontinue a product line, department, or retail store location.

EXHIBIT 8-12 Considerations for Discontinuing Products, Departments, or Stores

- Does the product provide a positive contribution margin?
- Are there any fixed costs that can be avoided if we discontinue the product?
- Will discontinuing the product affect sales of the company's other products?
- What could we do with the freed capacity?

In the first half of the chapter, we assumed that Garnier Fructis only made shampoo. Now, let's assume the company has other product lines, including hair styling products and skin moisturizers. Exhibit 8-13 illustrates Garnier's product line income statement in the contribution margin format. As you can see, a **product line income statement** shows the operating income of each product line, as well as the operating income for the company as a whole.

EXHIBIT 8-13 Product Line Income Statement

	A	B	C	D	E
1		Garnier Fructis			
2		Product Line Contribution Margin Income Statement			
3		For the Year Ended December 31			
4					
5		Product lines			
6		Shampoo	Styling Products	Skin Moisturizers	Company Total
7	Sales revenue	$ 8,000,000	$ 1,500,000	$ 500,000	$ 10,000,000
8	Less variable expenses:				
9	Variable manufacturing costs	3,000,000	450,000	$ 250,000	$ 3,700,000
10	Variable operating expenses	750,000	150,000	125,500	1,025,500
11	Contribution margin	$ 4,250,000	$ 900,000	$ 124,500	$ 5,274,500
12	Less fixed expenses:				
13	Fixed manufacturing costs	1,600,000	300,000	100,000	2,000,000
14	Fixed operating expenses	1,000,000	187,500	62,500	1,250,000
15	Operating income	$ 1,650,000	$ 412,500	$ (38,000)	$ 2,024,500
16					

In this exhibit, notice that the fixed costs, in total, are the same as what was shown in Exhibit 8-6. What differs is that the fixed costs have now been allocated among the various product lines. In our example, management has allocated fixed costs to each product line based on the percentage of revenue generated by the line. This is a common allocation system. It is also much like a tax: The higher the revenue, the higher the fixed cost allocation. For example, since 80% of the sales revenue is generated from shampoo sales, 80% of the fixed costs are allocated to the shampoo product line. Similarly, 15% of the fixed costs are allocated to styling products, and 5% are allocated to skin moisturizers. Keep in mind that management could have chosen another allocation system, which would have resulted in a different allocation of fixed costs.

Further, notice that the moisturizer product line appears to be unprofitable. Currently, the moisturizers have an operating loss of $38,000 per period. Without this loss, management erroneously believes the company's operating income could be $38,000 higher each period. Therefore, management is considering whether to discontinue the product line. Let's now consider how management should approach this decision.

Consider the Product's Contribution Margin and Avoidable Fixed Costs

In making this decision, management should consider the questions raised in Exhibit 8-12. The first question addresses the product line's contribution margin: is it positive or negative? Exhibit 8-13 shows that the moisturizers provide $124,500 of contribution margin. This positive contribution margin means the product line is generating enough revenue to cover its own variable costs, as well as provide another $124,500 that can be used to cover some of the company's fixed costs. Had the contribution margin been negative, management would either need to raise the price of the product or reduce variable costs. Management would rarely keep a product line with a negative contribution margin unless the product had a companion product whose sales would decline as a result. We'll discuss this possibility later.

The second question addresses fixed costs. *The important question is this: can any fixed costs be eliminated if the product line is discontinued?* Any fixed costs that can be eliminated as a result of discontinuing the product are known as **avoidable fixed costs**. These costs are relevant to the decision because they will be incurred *only* if the product line is retained. If the product line is discontinued, these costs will go away. In other words, avoidable fixed costs *differ* between alternatives.

On the other hand, **unavoidable fixed costs** are those fixed costs that will continue to be incurred even if the product line is discontinued. Unavoidable fixed costs are irrelevant to the decision because they will be incurred regardless of whether the product line is kept or discontinued. Exhibit 8-14 shows the company's fixed costs in more detail. Notice that total fixed costs ($2,000,000 of manufacturing costs and $1,250,000 of fixed operating expenses) are the same as shown in Exhibit 8-13. Managers will assess each fixed cost to determine how much, if any, is avoidable.

Exhibit 8-14 shows that management has identified $32,000 of fixed manufacturing costs and $45,000 of fixed operating expenses that can be eliminated if the moisturizers are discontinued. The avoidable fixed costs consist of a cancelable lease on equipment used to manufacture the moisturizers, advertisements for the moisturizers, and salaried employees who work solely on the moisturizer product line. Most of the fixed costs, such as property taxes, insurance, and depreciation, are unavoidable: they will continue even if the moisturizers are discontinued.

EXHIBIT 8-14 Analysis of the Company's Fixed Costs

	A	B	C
1	**Analysis of Fixed Expenses**	**Total Cost**	**Avoidable**
2	*Fixed manufacturing (Fixed MOH):*		
3	Property taxes	$ 180,000	$ -
4	Insurance	50,000	-
5	Depreciation on plant and production equipment	1,300,000	-
6	Fixed portion of utilities	70,000	-
7	Salaries of indirect labor (supervisors, janitors, etc.)	350,000	20,000
8	Equipment lease	50,000	12,000
9	Total fixed manufacturing costs	$ 2,000,000	$ 32,000
10			
11	*Fixed operating expenses (selling and administrative):*		
12	Building lease	$ 170,000	$ -
13	Telephone, internet, utilities	80,000	-
14	Depreciation on sales vehicles and office equipment	200,000	-
15	Advertisements	250,000	15,000
16	Sales and administrative salaries	550,000	30,000
17	Total fixed operating expenses	$ 1,250,000	$ 45,000
18			

With this information in hand, management can now determine whether or not to discontinue the moisturizers. Exhibit 8-15 presents management's analysis of the decision. In this analysis, managers compare the contribution margin provided by the moisturizers with the fixed costs that could be avoided if the moisturizers were discontinued.

EXHIBIT 8-15 Incremental Analysis for Discontinuing a Product Line

	A	B
1	**Incremental Analysis for Discontinuation Decision**	**Total**
2	Contribution margin lost if moisturizers are discontinued (Exhibit 8-13)	$ 124,500
3	Less fixed cost savings if moisturizers are discontinued (Exhibit 8-14):	
4	Avoidable fixed manufacturing costs	32,000
5	Avoidable fixed operating expenses	45,000
6	Operating income lost if moisturizers are discontinued	$ 47,500
7		

This analysis shows that the company's operating income would actually *decrease* by $47,500 if the moisturizers were discontinued. Therefore, the moisturizers should not be discontinued *unless* the company can use the capacity for some other product that would provide a higher profit.

Other Considerations

As noted in Exhibit 8-12, management must consider at least two other issues when making the decision to discontinue a product line, department, or store. First, will discontinuing the product line affect sales of the company's other products? As mentioned previously, some products have companion products whose sales would be hurt through discontinuing a particular product. For example, if customers always buy one bottle of shampoo every time they buy a bottle of skin moisturizer, then sales of shampoo might decline as a result of discontinuing the moisturizers. The potential loss in contribution margin on the shampoo would need to be factored into the decision. Since shampoo and styling products are not really companion products of skin moisturizers, we probably don't need to worry about the effect of discontinuing moisturizers on the sales of Garnier's other products. However, you can imagine that if the company sold shampoo and conditioner with the same fragrance, discontinuing one would affect sales of the other.

This is also true of store departments. Can you imagine a grocery store discontinuing its produce department? Sales of every other department in the store would decline as a result of shoppers' inability to purchase fruits and vegetables at the store. On the other hand, sometimes discontinuing a product, such as one particular laptop model, can increase the sales of the other company products (other laptop models). The same holds true for retail stores. For example, assume two Starbucks stores are located close to each other. If one store is closed, then sales at the other location might increase as a result.

The second question concerns freed capacity. If a product line, department, or store is discontinued, management needs to consider what it would do with the newly freed capacity. Could managers make a more profitable product or lease out the capacity to another company? For example, Kroger and other food stores used to have movie rental departments. With the advent of streaming services, such as Netflix, these departments no longer were as profitable as they were in the past. Therefore, Kroger discontinued them and replaced the retail space with larger produce departments, prepared foods, and other more profitable products. Management must consider which alternative use of the freed capacity will be most profitable. Finally, management should consider what to do with any newly freed labor capacity. To exercise corporate responsibility, management should do all it can to retrain employees for other areas of its operations rather than laying off employees.

The key to deciding whether to discontinue products, departments, or stores is to compare the lost contribution margin against the fixed costs that can be saved and to consider what could be done with the freed capacity. The decision rule is as follows:

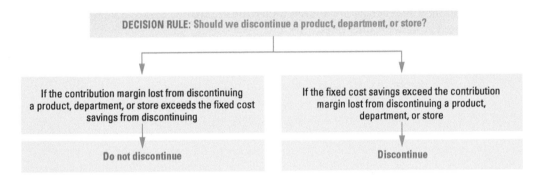

DECISION RULE: Should we discontinue a product, department, or store?

If the contribution margin lost from discontinuing a product, department, or store exceeds the fixed cost savings from discontinuing

Do not discontinue

If the fixed cost savings exceed the contribution margin lost from discontinuing a product, department, or store

Discontinue

▶ Try It!

Assume Kroger's grocery store is deciding whether to eliminate the salad bar section of its stores. The product line income statement shows the following quarterly data for the salad bar operations:

Sales revenue = $750,000

Fixed costs = $100,000

Variable costs = $600,000

1. Only $20,000 of fixed costs can be eliminated if the salad bar is eliminated. The remaining $80,000 of fixed costs are unavoidable. What will happen to Kroger's operating income if it discontinues the salad bars and does nothing with the freed capacity?

2. Management is thinking about replacing the salad bar section of the stores with a specialty olive bar, which is projected to bring in $200,000 of contribution margin each quarter while incurring no additional fixed costs. What will happen to Kroger's operating income if it replaces the salad bars with olive bars?

Please see page 506 for solutions.

Pitfall to Avoid on Discontinuation Decisions

One of the most common mistakes managers make when analyzing whether or not to discontinue a product is to base the decision on a product line income statement that contains an allocation of common fixed expenses. **Common fixed expenses** are those expenses that *cannot* be traced directly to a product line. For example, in Exhibits 8-13 and 8-14, we see that fixed MOH costs such as property taxes, insurance, and depreciation are all common production costs that have been allocated between the product lines. While appropriate for product costing purposes, the allocation of common fixed costs is not appropriate for making product discontinuation decisions. Nor is the allocation of common fixed operating expenses, such as the building lease, utilities, Internet, or depreciation of office equipment.

As shown in Exhibit 8-13, the allocation of common fixed costs suggests that the company's overall operating income would *increase* by $38,000 if the company stopped making the moisturizers. However, based on the correct analysis in Exhibit 8-15, we know the company's operating income would actually *decline* by $47,500 if the moisturizers were discontinued. Using the product line income statement with allocated common costs would have led managers to the wrong conclusion.

Since income statements with allocated common costs can potentially mislead managers, some companies prepare **segment margin income statements**, which contain *no* allocation of common fixed costs. Segment margin income statements look very similar to Exhibit 8-13, except for two differences:

1. Only direct fixed costs that can be traced to specific product lines are deducted from the product line's contribution margin. The resulting operating income or loss for each individual product line is known as a **segment margin**.

2. All common fixed costs are shown under the company "total" column but are not allocated among product lines.

We discuss and illustrate segment margin income statement in more detail in Chapter 10. Although segment margin income statements eliminate the issue surrounding the allocation of common fixed costs, they still do not completely address the question of how much operating income would be gained or lost if a product line was discontinued. Why? Because, not all direct fixed costs are avoidable. For example, Garnier may have a long-term lease on a piece of production equipment used only to make moisturizers. As a result, the lease cost is a direct cost of the moisturizer line and would be factored into the moisturizers' segment margin. However, if the lease is noncancellable, its cost cannot be avoided by discontinuing the product line. Thus, the company still needs to perform the analysis shown in Exhibit 8-15 to correctly determine the effect of discontinuing a segment on the company's operating income.

Product Mix Decisions When Resources Are Constrained

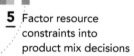

5 Factor resource constraints into product mix decisions

In Chapter 7, we learned that a product's contribution margin per unit shows the profit made on each unit *before* considering fixed costs. The higher the contribution margin per unit, the more profit is added to the company's bottom line with each sale. As a result, you might think that companies should always emphasize the products that have the highest contribution margin per unit. Sometimes this strategy is correct, but as you'll see in this section, when companies face a constraint, that strategy can actually lead to lower profit. Let's see why this is the case.

Often companies have **constraints** that restrict the amount of product they can manufacture or the amount of product they can sell. For a manufacturer, the production constraint is often the number of available machine hours. For a merchandiser, such as Walmart, the primary constraint is cubic feet of display space. To determine which products to emphasize producing or displaying, managers facing constraints should consider the questions shown in Exhibit 8-16.

EXHIBIT 8-16 Product Mix Considerations

- What constraint(s) stops us from making (or displaying) all of the units we can sell?
- Which products offer the highest contribution margin per unit of the constraint?
- Would emphasizing one product over another affect fixed costs or sales of other products?

For our example, we'll consider Union Bay, a manufacturer of shirts and jeans. As shown in Exhibit 8-17, Union Bay's shirts have a higher contribution margin per unit than the company's jeans:

EXHIBIT 8-17 Contribution Margin Data

	Per Unit	
	Shirts	**Jeans**
Sale price...	$ 30	$ 60
Less: Variable expenses	(12)	(48)
Contribution margin	$ 18	$ 12
Contribution margin ratio:		
Shirts: $18 ÷ $30..	60%	
Jeans: $12 ÷ $60		20%

Each time a shirt is sold, the company's operating income increases by $18, whereas every time a pair of jeans is sold, the company's operating income increases by $12. Therefore, managers might assume they should emphasize selling shirts rather than jeans. However, an important piece of information is missing—the time it takes to make each product.

Let's say the company uses the same machines to produce both jeans and shirts. Furthermore, the machines have only 2,000 hours of capacity per period. In this case, machine hours is a production constraint. Note that this is a short-term decision because in the long run, Union Bay could expand its production facilities. Let's also assume that Union Bay can produce either 20 pairs of jeans *or* 10 shirts per machine hour. The company will incur the same fixed costs either way, so fixed costs are irrelevant. Assuming Union Bay can sell all of the product it produces, which product should Union Bay emphasize?

To maximize profits when fixed costs are irrelevant, follow this decision rule:

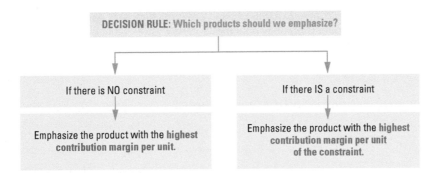

Because *machine hours* is the constraint, Union Bay needs to figure out which product has the *highest contribution margin per machine hour*. As shown in Exhibit 8-18, the company will multiply the contribution margin per unit by the number of units made per machine hour, to find the *contribution margin per machine hour*.

EXHIBIT 8-18 Calculating the Contribution Margin per Unit of Constraint

	A	B	C
1	**Product Mix Analysis When Demand Is Unlimited**	**Shirts**	**Jeans**
2	Contribution margin per unit	$ 18	$ 12
3	Multiply by: Number of units produced per machine hour	10	20
4	Contribution margin per machine hour	$ 180	$ 240
5	Multiply by: Available capacity (number of machine hours)	2,000	2,000
6	Total contribution margin at full capacity	$ 360,000	$ 480,000
7			

This analysis shows that jeans have a higher contribution margin *per machine hour* ($240) than shirts ($180). Therefore, Union Bay will earn more profit by producing jeans. Why? Because even though jeans have a lower contribution margin *per unit*, Union Bay can make twice as many jeans as shirts with the available machine hours. Exhibit 8-18 also proves that Union Bay would have a higher total profit by making and selling only jeans. Multiplying the contribution margin per machine hour by the available number of machine hours (2,000), we see that Union Bay can earn $480,000 of contribution margin by producing jeans but only $360,000 by producing shirts.

To maximize profit, Union Bay should make 40,000 jeans (2,000 machine hours × 20 jeans per hour) and zero shirts. Why zero shirts? Because for every machine hour spent making shirts, Union Bay would *give up* $60 of contribution margin ($240 per hour for jeans versus $180 per hour for shirts).

Other Considerations

We've looked at the first two questions in Exhibit 8-16, so now let's tackle the final question: Would emphasizing one product over another affect fixed costs or sales of other products?

We made a couple of assumptions about Union Bay: (1) Fixed costs wouldn't be affected by whether jeans or shirts were produced, and (2) Union Bay's sales of other products, if any, wouldn't be hurt by this decision. Let's challenge each of these assumptions.

First, let's consider fixed costs. Fixed costs become relevant if they differ between product mix alternatives. For example, what if Union Bay had a month-to-month lease on a zipper machine used only for making jeans? If Union Bay made only shirts, and no jeans, it could *avoid* the lease cost, thereby decreasing fixed costs. However, if Union Bay makes even one pair of jeans, the company will need to lease the machine. In this case, the fixed cost associated with the zipper machine becomes relevant because it differs between alternative product mixes (shirts only *versus* jeans and shirts).

STOP & THINK

If Union Bay only makes shirts and no jeans, it can cancel its monthly zipper machine lease. As a result, the company would save $20,000 of fixed costs each month. Assuming unlimited demand for its products, should Union Bay only make shirts?

Answer: Compare the profitability of the products as follows:

	A	B	C
	Product Mix Analysis When Fixed Costs Are Relevant	**Shirts**	**Jeans**
1			
2	Total contribution margin at full capacity (Exhibit 8-18)	$ 360,000	$ 480,000
3	Less: Avoidable fixed costs	0	20,000
4	Net benefit from the product at full capacity	$ 360,000	$ 460,000
5			

Even taking into consideration the cancellable zipper machine lease, we find that producing jeans is still more profitable than producing shirts.

Second, let's consider product mix on sales of other products. Could making only jeans (and not shirts) hurt sales of the company's other products? As discussed earlier in the chapter, companies must always consider companion products, that is, products that customers typically purchase together. For example, consumers who purchase spaghetti sauce will probably also purchase spaghetti noodles. In the case of Union Bay, if ties and jackets are specifically designed and produced to coordinate with Union Bay shirts, the sales of these companion products will decline as a result of no longer producing shirts.

Changing Assumptions: Product Mix When Demand Is Limited

In our Union Bay example, we assumed that the company could sell as many jeans and shirts as it could produce with the available machine capacity. Let's change that assumption. Assume that as a result of competition, demand for Union Bay's jeans is limited to 30,000 pairs per period. Because demand is no longer unlimited, Union Bay should make only as many jeans as it can sell and use the remaining machine hours to produce shirts. Let's see how this change in sales demand affects optimal production levels and profitability.

If Union Bay makes only 30,000 jeans, it will use only 1,500 machine hours (30,000 jeans ÷ 20 jeans per machine hour). That leaves 500 machine hours available for making shirts. Exhibit 8-19 shows Union Bay's contribution margin under the revised product mix:

EXHIBIT 8-19 Product Mix Under Limited Demand

	A	B	C	D
1	**Product Mix Analysis When Demand Is Limited**	**Shirts**	**Jeans**	**Total**
2	Contribution margin per machine hour (from Exhibit 8-18)	$ 180	$ 240	
3	Multiply by: Number of machine hours devoted to product	500	1,500	2,000
4	Total contribution margin at full capacity	$ 90,000	$ 360,000	$ 450,000
5				

NOTE: *30,000 jeans divided by 20 jeans per hour = 1,500 machine hours devoted to jeans. This leaves 500 available machine hours for making shirts.*

Because of the change in product mix, Union Bay's total contribution margin will fall from $480,000 (as shown in Exhibit 8-18) to $450,000, a $30,000 decline. Union Bay had to give up $60 of contribution margin per machine hour ($240 – $180) on the 500 hours it spent producing shirts rather than jeans. However, Union Bay had no choice—the company would have incurred an *actual loss* from producing jeans that it could not sell.

Pitfalls to Avoid in Constraint Decisions

When finding the contribution margin *per unit of constraint*, managers must carefully consider the mathematical operation they use. Managers always start with the contribution margin per unit, and then either *multiply* or *divide*, to arrive at the contribution margin *per unit of constraint*. In our example, an hour is the unit of constraint. The correct mathematical operation depends on whether (1) a number of units are produced per hour (such as 20 units per hour) or (2) a number of hours is needed per unit (such as 5 hours per unit). Using the correct operational sign will result in finding the contribution margin per hour:

- CM/Unit × Units/Hour = CM/Hour
- CM/Unit ÷ Hours/Unit = CM/Hour

The same logic holds true for any constraint. Always check your math to make sure you used the correct operational sign.

Outsourcing Decisions (Make or Buy)

Outsourcing decisions are sometimes called "make-or-buy" decisions because managers must decide whether to make a product or service in-house or buy it from another company. Sometimes people confuse the term *outsourcing* with the term *offshoring*.

6 Analyze outsourcing (make-or-buy) decisions

- **Outsourcing** refers to contracting an outside company to produce a product or perform a service. Outsourced work could be done domestically or overseas.
- **Offshoring** refers to having work performed overseas. Companies offshore work by either (1) operating their own manufacturing plants and call centers overseas or (2) outsourcing the overseas work to another company. Thus, offshored work is not necessarily outsourced work.

Outsourcing is not new. For years, companies have outsourced specialized services such as marketing, payroll processing, and legal work to firms that have expertise in those areas. More and more, brand-name companies are outsourcing the production of their products so that they can concentrate on their core competencies of marketing and product development. In fact, so much production is outsourced that contract manufacturing has become an entire industry. <u>Contract manufacturers</u>, such as those that Nike uses, are manufacturers that only make products for other companies, not for themselves. By using contract manufacturers, companies can avoid the risks associated with building manufacturing infrastructure. As we discussed in Chapter 7, companies with relatively more fixed costs have a riskier cost structure.

In deciding what to do, managers should consider the questions outlined in Exhibit 8-20.

EXHIBIT 8-20 Outsourcing Considerations

- How do our variable costs per unit compare to the outsourcing cost per unit?
- Are any fixed costs avoidable if we outsource?
- What could we do with the freed capacity?
- What volume do we need?

First, managers need to consider the variable cost of producing their own products (or services) with the variable costs charged by the outside company. The next two questions are similar to the questions managers consider when deciding to discontinue a product: Can any fixed costs be avoided, and what could we do with the freed capacity? Why are these questions so similar to what we considered with the discontinuation decision? Because in essence, outsourcing involves discontinuing an activity (such as production, marketing, payroll processing, and so forth) but paying another company to perform it.

Outsourcing Example

Assume that Sony is deciding whether to continue making its own earbuds or to outsource production to Shenzhen Electronics, a contract manufacturer specializing in consumer electronics. Let's assume Sony's cost to produce 2 million earbuds each period is as shown in Exhibit 8-21:[2]

EXHIBIT 8-21 Production Costs and Volume

	A	B	C	D
1	**Comparison of Variable and Absorption Costs**	**Variable Cost per Unit**	**Total Cost (2 million units)**	
2	Direct materials	$ 4.00	$ 8,000,000	
3	Direct labor	0.50	1,000,000	
4	Variable MOH	1.50	3,000,000	
5	Total variable manufacturing cost	$ 6.00	$ 12,000,000	
6	Plus: Fixed MOH		4,000,000	
7	Total manufacturing cost		$ 16,000,000	
8	Divide by: Number of units		2,000,000	
9	Total cost per unit (absorption costing)		$ 8.00	
10				

Let's further assume that Shenzhen Electronics is willing to provide earbuds to Sony for $7.00 each. Should Sony make the earbuds or should it buy them from Shenzhen? The $7.00 price is less than the full absorption cost per unit ($8.00) but greater than Sony's variable cost per unit ($6.00).

---

[2] The hypothetical cost information was created solely for academic purposes and is not intended, in any way, to represent the actual costs incurred by Sony or the price that would be charged by Shenzhen Electronics.

Let's see how the questions addressed in Exhibit 8-20 apply to our example:

- **Variable costs:** The variable cost of producing each earbud ($6.00) is less than the outsourcing cost ($7.00). Based on variable costs alone, Sony should manufacture the earbuds in-house. However, managers must still consider fixed costs.

- **Fixed costs:** Let's assume that Sony could save $500,000 of fixed costs each period by outsourcing. Most of the savings would be the result of cancellable leases on specialized machinery used for making the earbuds. However, most of the fixed manufacturing costs, such as property taxes, relate to plant capacity and will continue to exist even if the company stops making earbuds.

- **Use of freed capacity:** We'll start by assuming that Sony has no other use for the production capacity, so it will remain idle. We will change this assumption later.

Given this information, what should Sony do? Exhibit 8-22 compares the two alternatives.

> **Why is this important?**
>
> "Almost any **business activity** can be **outsourced** (for example, manufacturing, marketing, and payroll). **Companies** often choose to retain only their **core competencies**—things they are *really* good at doing—and **outsource** just about everything else to companies that can do it *better* or more cost-effectively for them."

EXHIBIT 8-22 Incremental Analysis for Outsourcing Decisions

	A	B	C	D
1	**Incremental Analysis Outsourcing Decision**	**Make Earbuds**	**Outsource Earbuds**	**Difference**
2	Variable Costs:			
3	If make: $6.00 × 2 million units If outsource: $7.00 × 2 million units	$ 12,000,000	$ 14,000,000	$ 2,000,000
4	Plus: Fixed costs	4,000,000	3,500,000	(500,000)
5	Total cost of producing 2,000,000 units	$ 16,000,000	$ 17,500,000	$ 1,500,000
6				

This analysis shows that Sony should continue to make the earbuds. Why is this the case? As shown in the last column of Exhibit 8-22, the company would spend $2,000,000 more in variable costs to outsource the earbuds but would only save $500,000 in fixed costs. The net result is a $1,500,000 increase in total costs if the company outsources production.

Rather than looking at the *total* costs under both scenarios, another way to look at this decision is to simply focus on the "Difference" column shown in Exhibit 8-22. The cost-benefit analysis in Exhibit 8-23 shows this alternative approach:

EXHIBIT 8-23 Alternative Incremental Analysis

	A	B
1	**Alternative Cost-Benefit Analysis**	
2	**Outsourcing Decision**	
3	Variable cost per unit to outsource	$ 7.00
4	Less: Variable cost per unit to manufacture	6.00
5	Incremental variable cost per unit to outsource	$ 1.00
6	Multiply by: Number of units needed	2,000,000
7	Incremental variable cost to outsource	$ 2,000,000
8	Less: Fixed costs savings from outsourcing	500,000
9	Net extra cost to outsource	$ 1,500,000
10		

Notice how the analysis in both Exhibit 8-22 and Exhibit 8-23 is affected by volume, which we've currently assumed to be 2 million earbuds per period. If Sony needs fewer than 500,000 earbuds each period, then the decision to continue making the earbuds would be reversed and Sony would outsource the production. Why is this the case? Sony will pay $1 more in variable costs per unit to outsource production but can only save $500,000 in fixed costs by outsourcing. At higher volumes, the extra variable costs outweigh the cost savings; but at lower volumes (less than 500,000 units), the fixed cost savings are greater than the extra variable costs to outsource. As this example shows, volume is a key driver in the decision of whether or not to outsource

Notice how Exhibits 8-22 and 8-23 use our two keys for decision making: (1) focus on relevant data (costs that differ between alternatives), and (2) use a contribution margin approach that separates variable costs from fixed costs. Our decision rule for outsourcing is as follows:

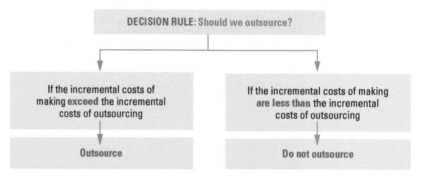

Determining an Acceptable Outsourcing Price

In Chapter 7, we used the concept of an indifference point to help managers decide how to structure costs. We can use the same concept here to determine the maximum price Sony would be willing to pay to have another manufacturer make the earbuds. By knowing up front how much it would be willing to pay, the company can proactively seek bids from multiple contract manufacturers.

Exhibit 8-24 shows how to calculate the indifference point. The exhibit begins by equating the costs of making the earbuds with the costs of outsourcing the earbuds. Next, all of the information from Exhibit 8-22 is inserted into the equations, with the exception of the variable cost per unit under the outsourcing alternative. The variable cost of outsourcing each unit is the cost we wish to solve for.

EXHIBIT 8-24 Using an Indifference Point to Find an Acceptable Outsourcing Price

Costs of making earbuds	=	Costs of outsourcing earbuds
Variable Costs + Fixed Costs	=	Variable Costs + Fixed Costs
(2,000,000 units × $6) + $4,000,000	=	(2,000,000 units × Variable cost per unit) + $3,500,000
$16,000,000	=	(2,000,000 × Variable cost per unit) + $3,500,000
$12,500,000	=	(2,000,000 × Variable cost per unit)
Variable cost per unit	=	$6.25

This analysis shows that, all else being equal, Sony would be *indifferent* between making and outsourcing 2 million earbuds if the outsourcing price was exactly $6.25 a unit. Therefore, the most Sony would be willing to pay for this volume of earbuds would be $6.25 a unit.

Notice, again, that this analysis is dependent on production volume. For example, if Sony needs 3 million units, the most it would be willing to pay would be $6.17 per unit. Why the difference? By producing more units, Sony's fixed costs are being utilized more efficiently, driving down the average cost of making each unit. As Sony's own unit cost falls, so will the price it is willing to pay some other company to make the earbuds. The opposite is also true: the fewer units Sony needs, the more it will be willing to pay another company to make the earbuds.

Alternative Use of Freed Capacity

Now let's change one of our original assumptions. Instead of assuming that the production capacity will remain idle, let's assume that Sony could lease it out to another company for $2.5 million per period. In this case, Sony must consider its **opportunity cost**, which is the benefit foregone by choosing a particular course of action. If Sony continues to make its own earbuds, it will be losing out on the opportunity to earn lease income of $2.5 million per period.

Exhibit 8-25 incorporates this information into our analysis by showing lease income as additional income that *could be made* if the company outsources production. Thus, we show the lease income in the "Outsource Earbuds" column. This income offsets some of the cost associated with outsourcing. Alternatively, we could show the $2.5 million as an *additional* cost (an opportunity cost) in the "Make Earbuds" column.

EXHIBIT 8-25 Incremental Analysis Incorporating Next Best Use of Freed Capacity

	A	B	C	D
1	Incremental Analysis Outsourcing Decision	Make Earbuds	Outsource Earbuds	Difference
2	Variable Costs:			
3	If make: $6.00 × 2 million units / If outsource: $7.00 × 2 million units	$ 12,000,000	$ 14,000,000	$ 2,000,000
4	Plus: Fixed costs	4,000,000	3,500,000	(500,000)
5	Total cost of producing 2,000,000 units	$ 16,000,000	$ 17,500,000	$ 1,500,000
6	Less: Lease income if outsource	0	2,500,000	2,500,000
7	Net cost	$ 16,000,000	$ 15,000,000	$ (1,000,000)
8				

This analysis shows that Sony will benefit by $1,000,000 each period by outsourcing production of the earbuds. This result holds regardless of whether we treat the $2.5 million lease as income in the "Outsource Earbuds" column or as an opportunity cost in the "Make Earbuds" column. Again, notice that a different production volume could potentially result in a different outcome.

Pitfall to Avoid on Outsourcing Decisions

One of the most common mistakes managers make when analyzing whether or not to outsource is to compare the absorption cost per unit ($8 in our example in Exhibit 8-21) with the outsourcing cost per unit ($7.00 in our example). Always remember that absorption costing includes fixed manufacturing costs. These costs are not *incurred* on a per-unit basis, but rather are incurred as a total, fixed amount. As we just saw in our example, some, but not all, of the fixed costs may also be avoided by outsourcing. Thus, to avoid this decision pitfall, don't ever use the absorption cost per unit; rather, compare the variable cost of producing in-house with the variable cost of outsourcing, and then factor in the relevant fixed costs.

Potential Benefits and Drawbacks of Outsourcing

Outsourcing has many benefits; otherwise so many companies wouldn't do it. As mentioned earlier, outsourcing allows companies to concentrate on their core competencies as well as take advantage of other companies' expertise and best practices. When volume is low or fluctuates greatly, outsourcing can reduce the risks associated with investing in capacity infrastructure (plant, equipment, and personnel). And, as highlighted in our analyses, outsourcing can be a lower cost alternative.

However, outsourcing is not without drawbacks. When a company outsources, it gives up control, including control over quality and production scheduling. It must rely on the supplier to provide the product or service at an agreed-upon level of quality, at agreed-upon delivery dates. Often, one or more employees are needed just to manage and oversee the relationship with the supplier. As we saw in the sustainability feature, Nike has over 150 people in house who monitor its contract manufacturers. The cost of employing any such additional personnel should also be considered when comparing the cost of outsourcing with the cost of producing in-house.

In addition, for those companies embracing the triple bottom line, outsourcing and offshoring have additional drawbacks. Why? Because, unfortunately, outsourcing often results in laying off employees. Moreover, offshored contract work is not subject to the same regulated labor practices and working conditions found in the United States. When companies offshore work, they need to make sure laborers are treated fairly and work in a safe environment. That's why Nike has a Code of Conduct for all of its contract manufacturers. While overseas labor is often cheap and readily available, the exploitation of any people, in any country, is not an acceptable business practice.

▶ Try It!

Rossignol makes downhill ski equipment. Assume that Atomic has offered to produce ski poles for Rossignol for $18 per pair. Rossignol needs 100,000 pairs of poles per period. Rossignol can only avoid $125,000 of fixed costs if it outsources; the remaining fixed costs are unavoidable. Rossignol currently has the following costs at a production level of 100,000 pairs of poles:

Manufacturing Costs	Total Cost	Cost per pair (100,000 pairs)
Direct Materials	$ 750,000	$ 7.50
Direct Labor	80,000	0.80
Variable MOH	520,000	5.20
Fixed MOH	650,000	6.50
Total	$2,000,000	$20.00

1. Should Rossignol outsource ski pole production if the next best use of the freed capacity is to leave it idle? What effect will outsourcing have on Rossignol operating income?
2. If the freed capacity could be used to produce ski boots that would provide $500,000 of operating income, should Rossignol outsource ski pole production?

Please see page 506 for solutions.

Decisions to Sell As Is or Process Further

7 Decide whether to sell a product "as is" or process it further

At what point in processing should a company sell its product? Many companies, especially those in the food processing and natural resource industries, face this business decision. Companies in these industries process a raw material (milk, corn, crude oil, lumber, and so forth) to a point before it is saleable. For example, Kraft pasteurizes raw milk before it is saleable. Kraft must then decide whether it should sell the pasteurized milk "as is" or process it further into other dairy products (reduced-fat milk, butter, sour cream, cottage cheese, yogurt, blocks of cheese, shredded cheese, and so forth). Managers consider the questions shown in Exhibit 8-26 when deciding whether to sell as is or process further.

EXHIBIT 8-26 Sell As Is or Process Further Considerations

- How much revenue will we receive if we sell the product as is?
- How much revenue will we receive if we sell the product *after* processing it further?
- How much extra will it cost to process the product further?

Let's consider Bertolli, the manufacturer of Italian food products. Suppose Bertolli spends $100,000 to process raw olives into 50,000 quarts of plain virgin olive oil. Should

Bertolli sell the olive oil as is, or should it spend more to process the olive oil into gourmet dipping oils, such as a Basil and Garlic Infused Dipping Oil? In making the decision, Bertolli's managers consider the following relevant information:[3]

- Bertolli could sell the plain olive oil for $5 per quart, for a total of $250,000 (50,000 × $5).

- Bertolli could sell the gourmet dipping oil for $7 per quart, for a total of $350,000 (50,000 × $7).

- Bertolli would have to spend $0.75 per quart, or $37,500 (50,000 × $0.75), to further process the plain olive oil into the gourmet dipping oil. This cost would include the extra direct materials required (such as basil, garlic, and the incremental cost of premium glass containers) as well as the extra conversion costs incurred (the cost of any *additional* machinery and labor that the company would need to purchase in order to complete the extra processing).

By examining the incremental analysis shown in Exhibit 8-27, Bertolli's managers can see that they can increase operating income by $62,500 by further processing the plain olive oil into the gourmet dipping oil. The extra $100,000 of revenue greatly exceeds the incremental $37,500 of cost incurred to further process the olive oil.

Notice that Bertolli's managers do *not* consider the $100,000 originally spent on processing the olives into olive oil. Why? It is a sunk cost. Recall from our previous discussion that a sunk cost is a past cost that cannot be changed regardless of which future action the company takes. Bertolli has incurred $100,000 regardless of whether it sells the olive oil as is or processes it further into gourmet dipping oils. Therefore, the cost is *not* relevant to the decision.

> ### ■ Why is this important?
>
> "Some companies are able to sell their products at **different points** of completion. For example, some furniture **manufacturers** sell flat-packed bookshelves, TV stands, and home office furniture that the consumer must **finish assembling**. A **cost-benefit analysis** helps managers choose the most **profitable point** at which to sell the company's products."

EXHIBIT 8-27 Incremental Analysis for Sell As Is or Process Further Decision

A Incremental Analysis Sell or Process Further Decision	B Sell As Is	C Process Further	D Difference
2 Revenues:			
3 If sell as is: $5.00 × 50,000 quarts If process further: $7.00 × 50,000 quarts	$ 250,000	$ 350,000	$ 100,000
4 Less: Extra cost of processing further	0	37,500	37,500
5 Net benefit to operating income	$ 250,000	$ 312,500	$ 62,500
6			

Thus, the decision rule is as follows:

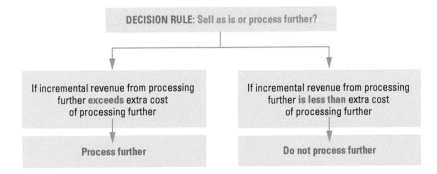

[3] All references to Bertolli in this hypothetical example were created by the author solely for academic purposes and are not intended, in any way, to represent the actual business practices of, or costs incurred by, Bertolli.

Decision Guidelines

Short-Term Special Business Decisions

Nike's managers have faced many business decisions in building one of the most recognizable brands in the world. Here are some of the guidelines they have used to make profitable decisions.

Decision	Guidelines
Should we discontinue any segment of our operations (for example, a particular product line or retail store location)?	If the segment is generating a positive contribution margin it is helping to cover the company's fixed costs. However, some costs might be avoided by discontinuing the segment. Compare the contribution margin from the segment to the fixed cost savings to determine which course of action is most profitable. In addition, consider what would be done with the freed capacity and whether the discontinuation of the segment would have any effect (positive or negative) on sales in the company's remaining segments.
What decision pitfalls should be avoided when we decide whether or not to discontinue a segment?	Avoid including any allocation of common fixed costs in the analysis. These costs will not be avoided if the segment is discontinued; therefore, they are irrelevant to the decision.
Which products should we emphasize if we have a short-term production constraint, such as limited machine hours used to produce various products?	When there is a production constraint, managers should emphasize the products that have the highest contribution margin per the constraint, rather than the products that have the highest contribution margin per unit. In addition, managers need to consider the possible effect of emphasizing one product over another on the sale of companion products (such as coordinating sportswear).
What are some of the benefits and drawbacks of outsourcing?	Potential benefits: allows companies to focus on core competencies and purchase the expertise and best practices of other companies; lower costs; decreased risk of investing in too much plant capacity; flexibility. Potential drawbacks: less control over quality, delivery timing, labor practices, and working conditions which could impact a company's reputation. In addition, offshored work may be subject to import tariffs, shipping disruptions, and exchange rate fluctuations.
What financial considerations should we make when deciding whether to outsource any aspect of our operations?	Managers should compare the in-house variable cost per unit to the outsourcing cost per unit. In addition, they should consider whether any fixed costs could be avoided by outsourcing. Finally, they should consider what they would do with the freed capacity.
How should we determine the maximum price we are willing to pay for outsourcing?	Solve for the indifference point by setting the cost to make equal to the cost to outsource. The indifference point will be the maximum price you would pay.
How should we decide whether to sell our product "as is" or process it further?	Compare the incremental revenue gained from processing further to the extra cost to process further. If the incremental revenue exceeds the incremental cost, then process further.

SUMMARY PROBLEM 2

Requirements

1. Aziz produces Standard and Deluxe sunglasses:

	Per Pair	
	Standard	**Deluxe**
Sale price..	$20	$30
Variable expenses..	16	21

The company has 15,000 machine hours available. In one machine hour, Aziz can produce 70 pairs of the Standard model or 30 pairs of the Deluxe model. Assuming machine hours is a constraint, which model should Aziz emphasize?

2. SmartSocks incurs the following costs for 20,000 pairs of its high-tech hiking socks:

Direct materials...	$ 20,000
Direct labor..	80,000
Variable manufacturing overhead	40,000
Fixed manufacturing overhead...	80,000
Total manufacturing cost	$220,000
Cost per pair ($220,000 ÷ 20,000)..	$ 11

Another manufacturer has offered to sell SmartSocks similar socks for $10 a pair, a total purchase cost of $200,000. If SmartSocks outsources *and* leaves its plant idle, it can save $50,000 of fixed overhead cost. Or the company can use the released facilities to make other products that will contribute $70,000 to profits. In this case, the company will not be able to avoid any fixed costs. Identify and analyze the alternatives. What is the best course of action?

3. A local home improvement warehouse store shows the following product line income statement for the month. All common fixed costs are allocated to departments based on percentage of sales revenue generated by the department.

	A		B		C		D		E
1			**Paint**		**Lumber**		**Lighting**		**Store Total**
2	Sales	$	500,000	$	400,000	$	100,000	$	1,000,000
3	Less: Variable Costs		300,000		160,000		50,000		510,000
4	Contribution margin		200,000		240,000		50,000		490,000
5	Less: Direct Fixed Costs		50,000		40,000		35,000		125,000
6	Less: Common Fixed Costs		100,000		80,000		20,000		200,000
7	Operating Income (Loss)	$	50,000	$	120,000		($5,000)	$	165,000
8									

Assuming $30,000 of the Lighting Department's direct fixed costs are avoidable, should the store managers discontinue the Lighting Department? The space currently occupied by the Lighting Department would be replaced with a Hardware Department that is expected to have sales of $200,000, variable costs of $80,000 and new direct fixed costs of $30,000.

▪ SOLUTIONS

Requirement 1

	A	B	C
1	**Product Mix Decision**	**Standard**	**Deluxe**
2	Sales price per unit	$ 20	$ 30
3	Less: Variable cost per unit	16	21
4	Contribution margin per unit	$ 4	$ 9
5	Multiply by: Number of units produced per machine hour	70	30
6	Contribution margin per machine hour	$ 280	$ 270
7	Multiply by: Available capacity (number of machine hours)	15,000	15,000
8	Total contribution margin at full capacity	$ 4,200,000	$ 4,050,000
9			

Decision: Emphasize the Standard model because it has the higher contribution margin per unit of the constraint—machine hours—resulting in a higher contribution margin for the company.

Requirement 2

	A	B	C	D
1	**Incremental Analysis Outsourcing Decision**	**Make Socks**	**Outsource and Leave Idle**	**Outsource and Make Other Products**
2	Variable Costs:			
3	If make: DM, DL, Variable MOH If outsource: $10 × 20,000 units	$ 140,000	$ 200,000	$ 200,000
4	Plus: Fixed costs	80,000	30,000	80,000
5	Total cost of producing 2,000,000 units	$ 220,000	$ 230,000	$ 280,000
6	Less: Profit from other products	0	0	70,000
7	Net cost	$ 220,000	$ 230,000	$ 210,000
8				

Decision: SmartSocks should outsource the socks from the outside supplier and use the released facilities to make other products.

Requirement 3

	A	B	C
1	**Incremental Analysis of Discontinuation Decision**		**Total**
2	Contribution margin lost if Lighting is discontinued		$ 50,000
3	Less: Fixed costs savings if Lighting is discontinued		30,000
4	Income lost if Lighting is discontinued		$ 20,000
5			
6	Contribution margin from Hardware Department ($200,000–$80,000)	$ 120,000	
7	Less: Direct fixed costs	30,000	
8	Segment margin provided by the Hardware Department		$ 90,000
9	Net benefit of discontinuing the Lighting Department and replacing with a Hardware Department		$ 70,000
10			

Decision: Managers should discontinue the Lighting Department and replace it with a Hardware Department.

END OF CHAPTER

Learning Objectives

- 1 Describe and identify information relevant to short-term business decisions
- 2 Describe and apply different approaches to pricing
- 3 Decide whether to accept a special order
- 4 Decide whether to discontinue a product, department, or store
- 5 Factor resource constraints into product mix decisions
- 6 Analyze outsourcing (make-or-buy) decisions
- 7 Decide whether to sell a product "as is" or process it further

Accounting Vocabulary

Avoidable Fixed Costs. (461) Fixed costs that can be eliminated as a result of taking a particular course of action.

Common Fixed Expenses. (463) Expenses that cannot be traced to a particular product line.

Constraint. (464) A factor that restricts the production or sale of a product.

Contract Manufacturers. (468) Manufacturers that make products for other companies, not for themselves.

Cost-Plus Pricing. (450) An approach to pricing used by price-setters; cost-plus pricing begins with the product's total costs and adds the company's desired profit to determine a cost-plus price.

Offshoring. (467) Having work performed overseas. Offshored work can be performed either by the company itself or by outsourcing the work to another company.

Opportunity Cost. (471) The benefit forgone by choosing a particular alternative course of action.

Outsourcing. (467) Contracting an outside company to produce a product or perform a service. Outsourced work can be done domestically or overseas.

Product Line Income Statement. (460) An income statement that shows the operating income of each product line, as well as the company as a whole.

Relevant Information. (444) Expected *future* data that *differ* among alternatives.

Segment Margin. (464) The income resulting from subtracting only the direct fixed costs of a product line from its contribution margin. The segment margin contains no allocation of common fixed costs.

Segment Margin Income Statement. (464) A product line income statement that contains no allocation of common fixed costs. Only direct fixed costs that can be traced to specific product lines are subtracted from the product line's contribution margin. All common fixed costs remain unallocated and are shown only under the company total.

Sunk Cost. (446) A past cost that cannot be changed regardless of which future action is taken.

Target Costing. (451) An approach to pricing used by price-takers; target costing begins with the revenue at market price and subtracts the company's desired profit to arrive at the target total cost.

Unavoidable Fixed Costs. (461) Fixed costs that will continue to be incurred even if a particular course of action is taken.

MyAccountingLab **Go to** http://myaccountinglab.com/ **for the following Quick Check, Short Exercises, Exercises, and Problems. They are available with immediate grading, explanations of correct and incorrect answers, and interactive media that acts as your own online tutor.**

Quick Check

1. *(Learning Objective 1)* Which of the following is *false*?
   a. Relevant information is always financial in nature.
   b. Relevant information always regards the future.
   c. Sunk costs are never relevant to a decision.
   d. Relevant information always differs among alternatives.

2. *(Learning Objective 1)* Keys to making short-term decisions include which of the following?
   a. Using a contribution margin approach that separates variable costs from fixed costs
   b. Focusing on relevant revenues, costs, and profits
   c. Both of the above
   d. None of the above

3. (*Learning Objective 2*) Which is true of price-setters?
   a. Their pricing approach emphasizes cost-plus pricing.
   b. Their pricing approach emphasizes target costing.
   c. Their products lack uniqueness.
   d. They are in highly competitive markets.

4. (*Learning Objective 3*) Which of the following should be considered for special order decisions?
   a. Whether the special order will affect regular sales in the long run
   b. Whether the special price will be high enough to cover incremental costs of filling the order
   c. Whether excess capacity exists
   d. All of the listed choices should be considered in special order decisions.

5. (*Learning Objective 2*) The formula for arriving at target cost is which of the following?
   a. Cost minus actual profit
   b. Revenue minus variable cost
   c. Revenue minus desired profit
   d. Revenue minus actual profit

6. (*Learning Objective 4*) Which of the following is *not* relevant when deciding whether or not to discontinue a product?
   a. Unavoidable fixed costs related to the product
   b. Avoidable fixed costs related to the product
   c. The product's contribution margin
   d. The effect of discontinuation on the sales of the company's other products.

7. (*Learning Objective 4*) A segment margin is the
   a. segment's contribution margin minus all fixed costs.
   b. segment's contribution margin minus allocated fixed costs.
   c. same as the segment's contribution margin.
   d. segment's contribution margin minus direct fixed costs.

8. (*Learning Objective 5*) When resources are constrained, which of the following should be used to guide product mix decisions?
   a. The products' gross margin per unit of constraint
   b. The products' contribution margin per unit of constraint
   c. The products' contribution margin
   d. The products' gross margin

9. (*Learning Objective 6*) Which of the following is *false*?
   a. Outsourcing decisions should take into consideration the intended use of freed capacity.
   b. Outsourcing refers to having work performed overseas.
   c. Outsourcing decisions are often referred to as "make-or-buy" decisions.
   d. Contract manufacturers are manufacturers that make products for other companies.

10. (*Learning Objective 7*) In making "sell as is" decisions, companies should consider all of the following EXCEPT for:
    a. Incremental costs that would be incurred by processing further.
    b. Costs incurred up to the "sell as is" decision point.
    c. Incremental revenues that would be earned by processing further.
    d. All of the above should be considered.

Quick Check Answers

1.a 2.c 3.a 4.d 5.c 6.a 7.d 8.b 9.b 10.b

Keith Homan/Alamy

Sources: Campbell Soup Company, 2015 Annual Report

The Master Budget

Learning Objectives

■ **1** Describe how and why managers use budgets

■ **2** Prepare the operating budgets

■ **3** Prepare the financial budgets

■ **4** Prepare budgets for a merchandiser

Campbell Soup Company, which has been in business for over 145 years, has had to remake itself continually as the demographic, economic, and cultural fabric of society has changed over time. The present is no different. The food industry is facing enormous demographic shifts, as consumers opt for fresher, healthier, and more organic foods and the millennial generation launches into one of the primary food-buying demographic groups. To not only cope with these changes, but also capitalize on them as business opportunities, Campbell redefined its purpose statement ("Real Food that Matters for Life Moments") and implemented new strategies. Some of these initiatives include developing new, healthier, and organic product lines, focusing more attention on digital marketing to reach the younger generation, making the company's food supply chain more transparent to consumers, increasing the company's presence in developing markets, and finally, becoming leaner and more cost-efficient. These strategies require that detailed plans be put in place. The company's managers express these plans, in financial terms, through budgets.

Budgeting is perhaps the most widely used management accounting tool employed by companies, organizations, and governments throughout the world. Even individuals, such as you and me, can benefit from creating a personal budget that shows how we plan to use our resources and to make sure our spending does not get out of control. For example, if your goal is to buy a car directly after college or a house five years after college, then you need to plan for these expenditures. Your budget should include saving enough money each year to accumulate the down payments you'll need. By carefully planning how you'll spend and save your resources, you'll have a better chance of reaching your goals.

How and Why Do Managers Use Budgets?

1 Describe how and why managers use budgets

As you'll see throughout this chapter, management uses budgeting to express its plans and to assess how well it's reaching its goals. In this section, we'll take a closer look at how budgets are used and developed, the benefits of budgeting, and the particular budgets that are prepared as part of the company's master budget.

How Are Budgets Used?

All companies and organizations use budgets for the same reasons you would in your personal life—to plan for the future and control the revenues and expenses related to those plans. Exhibit 9-1 shows how managers use budgets in fulfilling their major responsibilities of planning, directing, and controlling operations. Budgeting is an ongoing cycle: Company strategies lead to detailed plans, which in turn lead to actions. Results are then compared to the budget to provide managers with feedback. This feedback allows managers to take corrective actions and, if necessary, revise strategies, which starts the cycle over.

EXHIBIT 9-1 Managers Use Budgets to Plan and Control Business Activities

How Are Budgets Developed?

A company's budgeting process begins with its overall mission, or purpose statement, as illustrated in the chapter-opening story. Management then devises long-term strategic goals that will help the company fulfill its mission. **Strategic planning** involves setting long-term goals that may extend 5 to 10 years into the future. Long-term, loosely detailed budgets are often created to reflect expectations for these long-term goals.

Once the goals are set, management designs key strategies for attaining them. These strategies, such as Campbell's decision to launch an organic soup line and put more resources into digital marketing, are then put into place through the use of shorter-term budgets for an entire fiscal year. However, even a yearly budget is not detailed enough to guide many management decisions. For example, Campbell's soup production managers must know what month of the year they expect to receive and start using new production equipment. They must also decide how much of each raw material (organic vegetables, chicken, and so forth) to purchase each month to meet production requirements for both new and existing products. In turn, this will affect monthly cash needs. Therefore, companies usually prepare a budget for every month of the fiscal year.

Many companies set aside time during the last two quarters of the fiscal year to create their budget for the entire upcoming fiscal year. Other companies prepare rolling, or continuous budgets. A **rolling budget** is a budget that is continuously updated so that the next 12 months of operations are always budgeted. For example, as soon as January is over, the next January is added to the budget. The benefit of a rolling budget is that managers always have a budget for the next 12 months.

Who Is Involved in the Budgeting Process?

Rather than using a "top-down" approach in which top management determines the budget, most companies use some degree of participative budgeting. As the term implies, **participative budgeting** involves the participation of many levels of management. Participative budgeting is beneficial for the following reasons:

- Lower-level managers are closer to the action and should have a more detailed knowledge for creating realistic budgets.
- Managers are more likely to accept, and be motivated by, budgets they helped to create.

Participative budgeting also has disadvantages:

- The budget process can become much more complex and time consuming as more people participate in the process.
- Managers may intentionally build **slack** into the budget for their areas of operation by overbudgeting expenses or underbudgeting revenue. Why would they do this? They would do so for three possible reasons: (1) because of uncertainty about the future, (2) to make their performance look better when actual results are compared against budgeted amounts at the end of the period, and (3) to have the resources they need in the event of mandatory budget cuts.

Even with participative budgeting, someone must still have the "final say" on the budget. Often, companies use a **budget committee** to review the submitted budgets, remove unwarranted slack, and revise and approve the final budget. The budget committee frequently includes upper management, such as the CEO and CFO, as well as managers from every area of the value chain (such as research and development, marketing, and distribution). By using a cross-functional budget committee, the final budget is more likely to reflect a comprehensive view of the organization and be accepted by managers than if the budget were prepared by one person or department for the entire organization. The budget committee is often supported by full-time staff personnel devoted to updating and analyzing the budgets.

What Is the Starting Point for Developing the Budgets?

Many companies use the prior year's budgeted figures, or actual results, as the *starting point* for creating the budget for the coming year. Of course, those figures will then be modified to reflect

- new products, customers, or geographical areas;
- changes in the marketplace caused by competitors;
- changes in labor contracts, raw materials, and fuel costs;
- general inflation; and
- any new strategies.

This approach to budgeting may cause year-after-year increases that, after time, grow out of control. To prevent perpetual increases in budgeted expenses, many companies intermittently use zero-based budgeting. When a company implements <u>**zero-based budgeting**</u>, all managers begin with a budget of zero and must justify *every dollar* they put in the budget. This budgeting approach is very time consuming and labor intensive. Therefore, companies only use it from time to time in order to keep their expenses in check. For example, in 2015, as part of its quest to become leaner and more cost-efficient, Campbell's Soup Company announced plans to use zero-based budgeting to slash $200 million from its annual budget.[1]

What Are the Benefits of Budgeting?

Exhibit 9-2 summarizes three key benefits of budgeting. Budgeting forces managers to plan, promotes coordination and communication, and provides a benchmark for motivating employees and evaluating actual performance.

EXHIBIT 9-2 Benefits of Budgeting

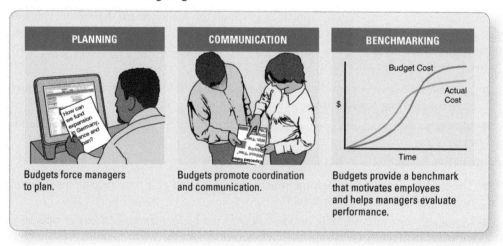

Budgets force managers to plan.

Budgets promote coordination and communication.

Budgets provide a benchmark that motivates employees and helps managers evaluate performance.

Planning

Business managers are extremely busy directing the day-to-day operations of the company. The budgeting process forces managers to spend time planning for the future, rather than only concerning themselves with daily operations. The sooner companies develop a plan and have time to act on the plan, the more likely they will achieve their goals.

Coordination and Communication

The budget coordinates a company's activities. It forces managers to consider relations among operations across the entire value chain. For example, Campbell's decision to develop new product lines will first affect the research and development (R&D) function. Once new products are developed, however, the design and production teams will need to focus on how and where the products will be mass-produced. The marketing team will need to develop attractive labeling and create a successful advertising campaign. The distribution team may need to alter its current distribution system to accommodate the new products. And customer service will need to be ready to handle any complaints or warranty issues. All areas of the value chain are ultimately affected by management's plans. The budget process helps to communicate and coordinate the effects of the plan.

Benchmarking

Budgets provide a benchmark that motivates employees and helps managers evaluate performance. The budget provides a target that most managers will try to achieve, especially if they participated in the budgeting process and the budget has been set at a realistic level. Budgets should be achievable with effort. Budgets that are too "tight" (too hard to achieve) or too "loose" (too easy to achieve) do not provide managers with much motivation.

[1] http://www.wsj.com/articles/campbell-soup-to-unveil-cost-cutting-plan-1424268625

Think about exams for a moment. Some professors have a reputation for giving "impossible" exams, while others may be known for giving "easy" exams. In either of these cases, students are rarely motivated to put much effort into learning the material because they feel they won't be rewarded for their additional efforts. However, if students feel that a professor's exam can be achieved with effort, they will be more likely to devote themselves to learning the material. In other words, the perceived "fairness" of the exam affects how well the exam motivates students to study. Likewise, if a budget is perceived to be "fair," employees are likely to be motivated by it.

Budgets also provide a benchmark for evaluating performance. At the end of the period, companies use performance reports, such as the one pictured in Exhibit 9-3, to compare "actual" revenues and expenses against "budgeted" revenues and expenses. The **variance**, or difference between actual and budgeted figures, is used to evaluate how well the manager controlled operations and to determine whether the plan needs to be revised. The use of budgets for performance evaluation will be discussed in more detail in Chapters 10 and 11. In this chapter, we focus primarily on the use of budgets for planning purposes.

EXHIBIT 9-3 Summary Performance Report

	A	B	C	D
				Variance
1	**Summary Performance Report**	**Actual**	**Budget**	**|Actual − Budget|**
2	Sales revenue	$ 478,000	$ 450,000	$ 28,000
3	Less: Variable expenses	336,000	320,000	16,000
4	Contribution margin	$ 142,000	$ 130,000	$ 12,000
5	Less: Fixed expenses	23,000	25,000	2,000
6	Operating income	$ 119,000	$ 105,000	$ 14,000
7				

What Is the Master Budget?

The **master budget** is the comprehensive planning document for the entire organization. It consists of all the supporting budgets needed to create the company's budgeted financial statements. Exhibit 9-4 shows all the components of the master budget for a manufacturer as well as the order in which they are usually prepared. The master budgets of service and merchandising firms are less complex and are discussed in the final section of the chapter.

The **operating budgets** are the budgets needed to run the daily operations of the company. The operating budgets culminate in a budgeted income statement. As Exhibit 9-4 shows, the starting point of the operating budgets is the sales budget because it affects most other components of the master budget. After estimating sales, manufacturers prepare the production budget, which determines how many units need to be produced. Once production volume is established, managers prepare individual budgets for the direct materials, direct labor, and manufacturing overhead that will be needed to meet production. Next, managers prepare the operating expenses budget. After all of these budgets are prepared, management will be able to prepare the budgeted income statement.

As you'll see throughout the chapter, cost behavior will be an important factor in developing many of the operating budgets. Total fixed costs will not change as volume changes within the relevant range. However, total variable costs will fluctuate as volume fluctuates.

The **financial budgets** include the capital expenditures budget and the cash budgets. The financial budgets culminate in a budgeted balance sheet. The capital expenditures budget shows the company's plan for purchasing property, plant, and equipment. The cash budget forecasts the cash that will be available to run the company's operations and determines whether the company will have extra funds to invest or whether the company will need to borrow cash. Finally, the budgeted balance sheet forecasts the company's position at the end of the budget period.

EXHIBIT 9-4 Master Budget for a Manufacturing Company

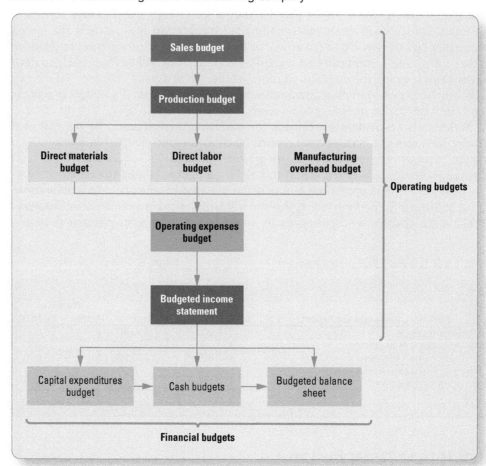

How Are the Operating Budgets Prepared?

2 Prepare the operating budgets

We will be following the budget process for Tucson Tortilla, a fairly small, independently owned manufacturer of tortilla chips. The company sells its product, by the case, to restaurants, grocery stores, and convenience stores. To keep our example simple, we will just show the budgets for the first three months of the fiscal year, rather than all 12 months. Since many companies prepare quarterly budgets (budgets that cover a three-month period), we'll also show the quarterly figures on each budget. For every budget, we'll walk through the calculations for the month of January. Then we'll show how the same pattern is used to create budgets for the months of February and March.

Sales Budget

The sales budget is the starting place for budgeting. Managers multiply the expected number of unit sales by the expected sales price per unit to arrive at the expected total sales revenue.

$$\text{Number of Unit Sales} \times \text{Sales Price per Unit} = \text{Total Sales Revenue}$$

For example, Tucson Tortilla expects to sell 30,000 cases of tortilla chips in January, at a sales price of $20 per case, so the estimated sales revenue for January is as follows:

$$30{,}000 \text{ cases} \times \$20 \text{ per case} = \$600{,}000$$

Tucson Tortilla's sales budget for the first three months of the year is shown in Exhibit 9-5. As you can see, the monthly sales volume is expected to fluctuate. January sales are expected to be higher than February sales due to the extraordinary number of chips purchased for Super Bowl parties. Also, since more tortillas chips are sold when the weather warms up, the company expects sales to begin their seasonal upward climb beginning in March.

As shown in the lower portion of Exhibit 9-5, managers may also choose to indicate the type of sale that will be made. Tucson Tortilla expects 20% of its sales to be cash (COD) sales. Companies often use **COD** ("collect on delivery"[2]) collection terms if the customer is new, has a poor credit rating, or has not paid on time in the past. Tucson Tortilla will still sell to these customers but will demand payment immediately when the inventory is delivered.

> ◼ **Why is this important?**
>
> "The **sales budget** is the **basis** for every other budget. If sales are not forecasted as **accurately** as possible, all other budgets will be **off target**."

EXHIBIT 9-5 Sales Budget

	A	B	C	D	E
1		Tucson Tortilla			
2		Sales Budget			
3		For the Quarter Ended March 31			
4		Month			
5		January	February	March	1st Quarter
6	Unit sales (cases)	30,000	20,000	25,000	75,000
7	Multiply by: Sales price per case	$ 20	$ 20	$ 20	$ 20
8	Total sales revenue	$ 600,000	$ 400,000	$ 500,000	$ 1,500,000
9					
10	**Type of sale:**				
11	Cash sales (20%)	$ 120,000	$ 80,000	$ 100,000	$ 300,000
12	Credit sales (80%)	480,000	320,000	400,000	1,200,000
13	Total sales revenue	$ 600,000	$ 400,000	$ 500,000	$ 1,500,000
14					

The remaining 80% of sales will be made on credit. Tucson Tortilla's credit terms are "net 30," meaning the customer has up to 30 days to pay for its purchases. Having this information available on the sales budget will help managers prepare the cash collections budget later.

Production Budget

Once managers have estimated how many units they expect to sell, they can figure out how many units they need to produce. Most manufacturers maintain some ending finished goods inventory, or **safety stock**, which is inventory kept on hand in case demand is higher than predicted, or the problems in the factory slow production (such as machine breakdown, employees out sick, and so forth). As a result, managers need to factor in the desired level of ending inventory when deciding how much inventory to produce. They do so as follows:

Units Needed for Sales	+	Desired Ending Inventory	=	Total Units Needed	−	Units in Beginning Inventory	=	Units to Produce

Let's walk through this calculation step by step:

- First, managers figure out how many total units they need. To do this, they add the number of units they plan to sell to the number of units they want on hand at the end

---

[2] In the past, COD meant "cash on delivery." However, as other forms of payment (such as checks, credit cards, and debit cards) have become more common, the word "cash" has been replaced with the word "collect" to incorporate these additional types of payments.

of the month. Let's assume Tucson Tortilla wants to maintain an ending inventory equal to 10% of the next month's expected sales (20,000 cases in February). Thus, the total number of cases needed in January is as follows:

30,000 cases for January sales + (10% × 20,000) = 32,000 total cases needed

- Next, managers calculate the amount of inventory they expect to have on hand at the beginning of the month. Since Tucson Tortilla desires ending inventory to be 10% of the next month's sales, managers expect to have 10% of January's sales on hand on December 31, which becomes the beginning balance on January 1:

10% × 30,000 cases = 3,000 cases in beginning inventory on January 1

- Finally, by subtracting what the company already has in stock at the beginning of the month from the total units needed, the company is able to calculate how many units to produce:

32,000 cases needed − 3,000 cases in beginning inventory = 29,000 cases to produce

Exhibit 9-6 shows Tucson Tortilla's production budget for the first three months of the year. As the red arrows show, the ending inventory from one month (January 31) always becomes the beginning inventory for the next month (February 1).

EXHIBIT 9-6 Production Budget

	A	B	C	D	E
1		Tucson Tortilla			
2		Production Budget			
3		For the Quarter Ended March 31			
4		Month			
5		January	February	March	1st Quarter
6	Unit sales (cases)	30,000	20,000	25,000	75,000
7	Plus: Desired ending inventory	2,000	2,500	3,200	3,200
8	Total needed	32,000	22,500	28,200	78,200
9	Less: Beginning inventory	3,000	2,000	2,500	3,000
10	Number of units to produce	29,000	20,500	25,700	75,200
11					

NOTE: Management wants to maintain an ending inventory equal to 10% of the next month's projected sales. Projected April sales are 32,000 units. The quarter begins January 1 and ends March 31.

Now that the company knows how many units it plans to produce every month, it can figure out the amount of direct materials, direct labor, and manufacturing overhead that will be needed. As shown in the following sections, the company will create separate budgets for each of these three manufacturing costs: direct materials, direct labor, and manufacturing overhead. Each budget will be driven by the number of units to be *produced* each month.

▶ Try It!

Assume Tucson Tortilla's sales budget shows projected sales of 32,000 cases in April and 40,000 cases in May. The company's manager would like to maintain ending safety stock equal to 10% of the next month's projected sales. How many units should be produced in April?

Please see page 582 for solutions.

Direct Materials Budget

The format of the direct materials budget is quite similar to the production budget:

Let's walk through the process using January as an example:

- First, the company figures out the quantity of direct materials (DM) needed for production. Let's assume Tucson Tortilla's only direct material is masa harina, the special corn flour used to make tortilla chips. Each case of tortilla chips requires 5 pounds of this corn flour. Therefore, the quantity of direct materials needed for January production is as follows:

    29,000 cases to be produced × 5 pounds per case = 145,000 pounds

- Next, the company adds in the desired ending inventory of direct materials. Some amount of direct materials safety stock is usually needed in case suppliers do not deliver all of the direct materials needed on time. Let's assume that Tucson Tortilla wants to maintain an ending inventory of direct materials equal to 10% of the materials needed for next month's production (102,500 required in February, as shown in Exhibit 9-7):

    145,000 pounds + (10% × 102,500) = 155,250 total pounds needed

- Next, managers determine the direct materials inventory they expect to have on hand at the beginning of the month. Tucson Tortilla expects to have 10% of the materials needed for January's production in stock on December 31, which becomes the opening balance on January 1:

    10% × 145,000 pounds = 14,500 pounds in beginning inventory

- Next, by subtracting what the company already has in stock at the beginning of the month from the total quantity needed, the company is able to calculate the quantity of direct materials it needs to purchase:

155,250 pounds needed − 14,500 pounds in beginning inventory = 140,750 pounds to purchase

- Finally, the company calculates the expected cost of purchasing those direct materials. Let's say Tucson Tortilla can buy the masa harina corn flour in bulk for $1.50 per pound.

    140,750 pounds × $1.50 = $211,125

Exhibit 9-7 shows Tucson Tortilla's direct materials budget for the first three months of the year.

EXHIBIT 9-7 Direct Materials Budget

	A	B	C	D	E
1	Tucson Tortilla				
2	Direct Materials Budget for Masa Harina Corn Flour				
3	For the Quarter Ended March 31				
4		Month			
5		January	February	March	1st Quarter
6	Units (cases) to be produced (from production budget)	29,000	20,500	25,700	75,200
7	Multiply by: Quantity (pounds) of DM needed per unit	5	5	5	5
8	Quantity (pounds) needed for production	145,000	10% 102,500	10% 128,500	376,000
9	Plus: Desired ending inventory of DM	10,250	12,850	16,150	16,150
10	Total quantity (pounds) needed	155,250	115,350	144,650	392,150
11	Less: Beginning inventory of DM	14,500	10,250	12,850	14,500
12	Quantity (pounds) to purchase	140,750	105,100	131,800	377,650
13	Multiply by: Cost per pound	$ 1.50	$ 1.50	$ 1.50	$ 1.50
14	Total cost of DM purchases	$ 211,125	$ 157,650	$ 197,700	$ 566,475
15					

NOTE: Management wants to maintain an ending inventory equal to 10% of the next month's production needs. Assume 161,500 pounds are needed for production in April.

Direct Labor Budget

The direct labor (DL) budget is determined as follows:

$$\boxed{\text{Units to Be Produced}} \times \boxed{\text{DL Hours per Unit}} = \boxed{\text{Total DL Hours Required}} \times \boxed{\text{DL Cost per Hour}} = \boxed{\text{Total Direct Labor Cost}}$$

Tucson Tortilla's factory is fairly automated, so very little direct labor is required. Let's assume that each case requires only 0.05 of an hour. Direct laborers are paid $22 per hour. Thus, the direct labor cost for January is projected to be as follows:

29,000 cases × 0.05 hours per case = 1,450 hours required × $22 per hour = $31,900

The direct labor budget for the first three months of the year is shown in Exhibit 9-8.

EXHIBIT 9-8 Direct Labor Budget

	A	B	C	D	E
1	Tucson Tortilla				
2	Direct Labor Budget				
3	For the Quarter Ended March 31				
4		Month			
5		January	February	March	1st Quarter
6	Units (cases) to be produced (from production budget)	29,000	20,500	25,700	75,200
7	Multiply by: Direct labor hours per unit	0.05	0.05	0.05	0.05
8	Total hours required	1,450	1,025	1,285	3,760
9	Multiply by: Direct labor cost per hour	$ 22	$ 22	$ 22	$ 22
10	Total direct labor cost	$ 31,900	$ 22,550	$ 28,270	$ 82,720
11					

Manufacturing Overhead Budget

The manufacturing overhead budget is highly dependent on cost behavior. Some overhead costs, such as indirect materials, are variable. For example, Tucson Tortilla considers the oil used for frying the tortilla chips to be an indirect material. Since a portion of the oil is absorbed into the chips, the amount of oil required increases as production volume increases. Thus, the cost is variable. The company also considers salt and cellophane packaging to be variable indirect materials. Tucson Tortilla expects to spend $1.25 on indirect materials for each case of tortilla chips produced, so January's budget for indirect materials is as follows:

29,000 cases × $1.25 = $36,250 of indirect materials

Costs such as utilities and indirect labor are mixed costs. Mixed costs are usually separated into their variable and fixed components using one of the cost behavior estimation methods already discussed in Chapter 6. Based on engineering and cost studies, Tucson Tortilla has determined that each case of chips requires $0.75 of variable indirect labor and $0.50 of variable utility costs as a result of running the production machinery. These variable costs are budgeted as follows for January:

29,000 cases × $0.75 = $21,750 of variable indirect labor
29,000 cases × $0.50 = $14,500 of variable factory utilities

Finally, many manufacturing overhead costs are fixed. Tucson Tortilla's fixed costs include depreciation, insurance, and property taxes on the factory. The company also incurs some fixed indirect labor (salaried production engineers who oversee the daily manufacturing operation) and a fixed amount of utilities just to keep the lights, heat, or air conditioning on in the plant, regardless of the production volume.

Exhibit 9-9 shows that the manufacturing overhead budget usually has separate sections for variable and fixed overhead costs, so that managers can easily see which costs will change as production volume changes.

EXHIBIT 9-9 Manufacturing Overhead Budget

	A	January	February	March	1st Quarter
1		Tucson Tortilla			
2		Manufacturing Overhead Budget			
3		For the Quarter Ended March 31			
4		Month			
5		January	February	March	1st Quarter
6	Cases to be produced (from production budget)	29,000	20,500	25,700	75,200
7	**Variable MOH Costs:**				
8	Indirect materials ($1.25 per case)	$ 36,250	$ 25,625	$ 32,125	$ 94,000
9	Indirect labor—variable portion ($0.75 per case)	21,750	15,375	19,275	56,400
10	Utilities—variable portion ($0.50 per case)	14,500	10,250	12,850	37,600
11	Total variable MOH	$ 72,500	$ 51,250	$ 64,250	$ 188,000
12					
13	**Fixed MOH Costs:**				
14	Depreciation on factory and production equipment	$ 10,000	$ 10,000	$ 10,000	$ 30,000
15	Insurance and property taxes on the factory	3,000	3,000	3,000	9,000
16	Indirect labor—fixed portion	15,000	15,000	15,000	45,000
17	Utilities—fixed portion	2,000	2,000	2,000	6,000
18	Total fixed MOH	$ 30,000	$ 30,000	$ 30,000	$ 90,000
19					
20	Total manufacturing overhead	$ 102,500	$ 81,250	$ 94,250	$ 278,000
21					

Now that we have completed budgets for each of the three manufacturing costs (direct materials, direct labor, and manufacturing overhead), we turn our attention to operating expenses.

Operating Expenses Budget

Recall that all costs incurred in every area of the value chain, except production, must be expensed as operating expenses in the period in which they are incurred. Thus, all research and development, design, marketing, distribution, and customer service costs will be shown on the operating expenses budget.

Some operating expenses are variable, based on how many units will be *sold* (not produced). For example, to motivate its sales force to generate sales, Tucson Tortilla pays its sales representatives a $1.50 sales commission for every case they sell.

> 30,000 sales units × $1.50 = $45,000 sales commission expense in January

The company also incurs $2.00 of shipping costs on every case sold.

> 30,000 sales units × $2.00 = $60,000 shipping expense in January

Finally, the company knows that not all of the sales made on credit will eventually be collected. Based on experience, Tucson Tortilla expects monthly bad debt expense to be 1% of its credit sales. Since January credit sales are expected to be $480,000 (from Sales Budget, Exhibit 9-5), the company's bad debt expense for January is as follows:

> $480,000 of credit sales in January × 1% = $4,800 bad debt expense for January

Other operating expenses are fixed: They will stay the same each month even though sales volume fluctuates. For example, Tucson Tortilla's fixed operating expenses include salaries of office workers, office rent, depreciation on office equipment and sales vehicles, advertising, and telephone and Internet service.

As shown in Exhibit 9-10, operating expenses are usually shown according to their cost behavior.

EXHIBIT 9-10 Operating Expenses Budget

	A	B	C	D	E
1		Tucson Tortilla			
2		Operating Expenses Budget			
3		For the Quarter Ended March 31			
4			Month		
5		January	February	March	1st Quarter
6	Number of cases to be sold (from sales budget)	30,000	20,000	25,000	75,000
7	**Variable Operating Expenses:**				
8	Sales commissions expense ($1.50 per case sold)	$ 45,000	$ 30,000	$ 37,500	$ 112,500
9	Shipping expense ($2.00 per case sold)	60,000	40,000	50,000	150,000
10	Bad debt expense (1% of credit sales)	4,800	3,200	4,000	12,000
11	Total variable operating expenses	$ 109,800	$ 73,200	$ 91,500	$ 274,500
12					
13	**Fixed Operating Expenses:**				
14	Salaries	$ 20,000	$ 20,000	$ 20,000	$ 60,000
15	Office rent	4,000	4,000	4,000	12,000
16	Depreciation	6,000	6,000	6,000	18,000
17	Advertising	2,000	2,000	2,000	6,000
18	Telephone and internet	1,000	1,000	1,000	3,000
19	Total fixed operating expenses	$ 33,000	$ 33,000	$ 33,000	$ 99,000
20					
21	Total operating expenses	$ 142,800	$ 106,200	$ 124,500	$ 373,500
22					

Budgeted Income Statement

A budgeted income statement looks just like a regular income statement, except for the fact that it uses budgeted data. A company may prepare a budget in contribution margin format for internal use or in traditional format for both internal and external use. For example, often, a company will need to supply its lending institution with budgeted financial statements. Thus, we present the traditional format here. Recall the traditional format for an income statement:

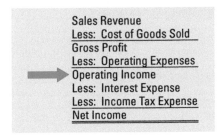

This text book has focused on a company's operating income rather than net income. However, a complete income statement would include any interest expense (and/or interest income) as well as a provision for income taxes. These additional costs are subtracted from operating income to arrive at net income.

We have already computed the budgeted sales revenue and operating expenses on separate budgets. But we still need to calculate the Cost of Goods Sold before we can prepare the income statement.

Tucson Tortilla computes its Cost of Goods Sold as follows:

This will be relatively simple for Tucson Tortilla since the company produces only one product.

The cost of manufacturing each case of tortilla chips is shown in Exhibit 9-11. Almost all of the information shown has already been presented and used to prepare the budgets for direct materials, direct labor, and manufacturing overhead. The only new piece of information is the total production volume for the year, budgeted to be 400,000 cases.

EXHIBIT 9-11 Budgeted Cost of Goods Sold per Unit

	A	B	C
1	**Budgeted Manufacturing Costs**		**Cost per Case**
2	Direct materials (5 pounds per case × $1.50 per pound)		$ 7.50
3	Direct labor (0.05 hours per case × $22 per hour)		1.10
4	Variable MOH:		
5	Indirect materials ($1.25 per case)	$ 1.25	
6	Indirect labor ($0.75 per case)	0.75	
7	Variable utilities ($.50 per case)	0.50	
8	Total variable MOH per case		2.50
9	Fixed MOH ($30,000 per month × 12 months)	$ 360,000	
10	Divided by: Budgeted production volume (cases)	400,000	
11	Total fixed MOH per case		0.90
12	Cost per case (absorption costing)		$ 12.00
13			

NOTE: Information taken from the DM, DL, and MOH budgets in Exhibits 9-7 through 9-9.

Exhibit 9-12 shows the company's budgeted income statement for January. Interest expense is budgeted to be zero since the company has no outstanding debt. The income tax expense is budgeted to be 35% of income before taxes. The company will prepare budgeted income statements for each month and quarter, as well as for the entire year.

EXHIBIT 9-12 Budgeted Income Statement

	A	B
1	**Tucson Tortilla**	
2	**Budgeted Income Statement**	
3	**For the Month Ended January 31**	
4		
5	Sales revenue (30,000 cases × $20 per case, from Exhibit 9-5)	$ 600,000
6	Less: Cost of goods sold (30,000 cases × $12.00 per case, from Exhibit 9-11)	360,000
7	Gross profit	240,000
8	Less: Operating expenses (from Exhibit 9-10)	142,800
9	Operating income	$ 97,200
10	Less: Interest expense (or add interest income)	0
11	Less: Income tax expense	34,020
12	Net income	$ 63,180
13		

NOTE: The corporate income tax rate for most companies is currently 35% of income before tax. Thus, the budgeted income tax is $34,020 (= $97,200 × 35%).

We have now completed the operating budgets for Tucson Tortilla. In the second half of the chapter, we'll prepare Tucson Tortilla's financial budgets.

Why is this important?
"The **budgeted income statement** helps managers know in advance whether their plans will result in an **acceptable** level of **income**. If not, **management** will need to consider how it can cut expenses or increase **sales revenues**."

Decision Guidelines

The Master Budget

Let's consider some of the decisions Campbell Soup Company made as it set up its budgeting process.

Decision	Guidelines
What should be the driving force behind the budgeting process?	The company's long-term goals and strategies drive the budgeting of the company's resources.
What are budgets used for?	Managers use budgets to help them fulfill their primary responsibilities: planning, directing, and controlling operations. Managers use feedback from the budgeting process to take corrective actions and, if necessary, revise strategies.
Who should be involved in the budgeting process?	Budgets tend to be more realistic and more motivational if lower-level managers, as well as upper-level managers, are allowed to participate in the budgeting process. The budgeting process tends to encompass a more comprehensive view when managers from all areas of the value chain participate in the process and serve on the budget committee.
What period of time should the budgets cover?	Long-term, strategic planning often results in forecasts of revenues and expenses 5 to 10 years into the future. Monthly and yearly budgets provide much more detailed information to aid management's shorter-term decisions.
How tough should the budget be to achieve?	Budgets are more useful for motivating employees and evaluating performance if they can be achieved with effort. Budgets that are too tight (too hard to achieve) or too loose (too easy to achieve) are not as beneficial.
What benefits should a company expect to obtain from developing a budget?	Benefits include the following: • Planning • Coordination and communication • Benchmarking (used for both motivation and performance evaluation)
What budgets should be included in a manufacturer's master budget?	The *operating budgets* include all budgets necessary to create a budgeted income statement. For a manufacturer, this includes the following: • Sales budget • Production budget • Direct materials budget • Direct labor budget • Manufacturing overhead budget • Operating expenses budget • Budgeted income statement The *financial budgets* include the capital expenditures budget, the cash budgets, and the budgeted balance sheet.

SUMMARY PROBLEM 1

Pillows Unlimited makes decorative throw pillows for home use. The company sells the pillows to home décor retailers for $14 per pillow. Each pillow requires 1.25 yards of fabric, which the company obtains at a cost of $6 per yard. The company would like to maintain an ending stock of fabric equal to 10% of the next month's production requirements. The company would also like to maintain an ending stock of finished pillows equal to 20% of the next month's sales. Sales (in units) are projected to be as follows for the first three months of the year:

January	100,000
February	110,000
March	115,000

Requirements

Prepare the following budgets for the first three months of the year, as well as a summary budget for the quarter:

1. Prepare the sales budget, including a separate section that details the type of sales made. For this section, assume that 10% of the company's pillows are cash sales, while the remaining 90% are sold on credit terms.

2. Prepare the production budget. Assume that the company anticipates selling 120,000 units in April.

3. Prepare the direct materials budget. Assume the company needs 150,000 yards of fabric for production in April.

▪ SOLUTIONS

Requirement 1

	A	B	C	D	E
1		Pillows Unlimited			
2		Sales Budget			
3		For the Quarter Ended March 31			
4		Month			
5		January	February	March	1st Quarter
6	Unit sales	100,000	110,000	115,000	325,000
7	Multiply by: Unit selling price	$ 14	$ 14	$ 14	$ 14
8	Total sales revenue	$ 1,400,000	$ 1,540,000	$ 1,610,000	$ 4,550,000
9					
10	**Type of sale:**				
11	Cash sales (10%)	$ 140,000	$ 154,000	$ 161,000	$ 455,000
12	Credit sales (90%)	1,260,000	1,386,000	1,449,000	4,095,000
13	Total sales revenue	$ 1,400,000	$ 1,540,000	$ 1,610,000	$ 4,550,000
14					

Requirement 2

	January	February	March	1st Quarter
Pillows Unlimited				
Production Budget				
For the Quarter Ended March 31				
	Month			
	January	**February**	**March**	**1st Quarter**
Unit sales	100,000	110,000	115,000	325,000
Plus: Desired ending inventory	22,000	23,000	24,000	24,000
Total needed	122,000	133,000	139,000	349,000
Less: Beginning inventory	20,000	22,000	23,000	20,000
Number of units to produce	102,000	111,000	116,000	329,000

NOTE: January 1 inventory balance (20,000) is the same as the December 31 balance, which is calculated as 20% of the projected units sales in January (100,000). March desired ending inventory (24,000) is 20% of April's projected units sales (120,000).

Requirement 3

	January	February	March	1st Quarter
Pillows Unlimited				
Direct Materials Budget				
For the Quarter Ended March 31				
	Month			
	January	**February**	**March**	**1st Quarter**
Units to be produced (from production budget)	102,000	111,000	116,000	329,000
Multiply by: Quantity (yards) of DM needed per unit	1.25	1.25	1.25	1.25
Quantity (yards) needed for production	127,500	138,750	145,000	411,250
Plus: Desired ending inventory of DM	13,875	14,500	15,000	15,000
Total quantity (yards) needed	141,375	153,250	160,000	426,250
Less: Beginning inventory of DM	12,750	13,875	14,500	12,750
Quantity (yards) to purchase	128,625	139,375	145,500	413,500
Multiply by: Cost per yard	$ 6.00	$ 6.00	$ 6.00	$ 6.00
Total cost of DM purchases	$ 771,750	$ 836,250	$ 873,000	$2,481,000

NOTE: January 1 inventory balance (12,750) is the same as the December 31 balance, which is calculated as 10% of the quantity (yards) needed for production in January (127,500). March desired ending inventory of DM (15,000) is 10% of April's projected quantity needed for production (150,000).

3 Prepare the financial budgets

How Are the Financial Budgets Prepared?

In the first half of the chapter, we prepared Tucson Tortilla's operating budgets, culminating with the company's budgeted income statement. In this part of the chapter , we turn our attention to Tucson Tortilla's financial budgets. Managers typically prepare a capital expenditures budget as well as three separate cash budgets:

1. Cash collections (or receipts) budget
2. Cash payments (or disbursements) budget
3. Combined cash budget, complete with financing arrangements

Finally, managers prepare the budgeted balance sheet. Each of these budgets is illustrated next.

Capital Expenditures Budget

The capital expenditures budget shows the company's intentions to invest in new property, plant, or equipment (capital investments). When planned capital investments are significant, this budget must be developed early in the process because the additional investments may affect depreciation expense, interest expense (if funds are borrowed to pay for the investments), or dividend payments (if stock is issued to pay for the investments). Chapter 12 contains a detailed discussion of the capital budgeting process, including the techniques managers use in deciding whether to make additional capital investments.

Exhibit 9-13 shows Tucson Tortilla's capital expenditures budget for the first three months of the year. Tucson Tortilla expects to invest in new computers, printers, delivery vans, and production equipment in January. The depreciation expense shown in the operating expenses budget and the depreciation shown in the MOH budget reflect these anticipated investments. No other capital investments are planned in the first quarter of the year.

EXHIBIT 9-13 Capital Expenditures Budget

	A	B	C	D	E
1		Tucson Tortilla			
2		Capital Expenditures Budget			
3		For the Quarter Ended March 31			
4		Month			
5		January	February	March	1st Quarter
6	Computers and printers	$ 15,000	0	0	15,000
7	Delivery vans	35,000	0	0	35,000
8	Production equipment	75,000	0	0	75,000
9	Total new capital investments	$ 125,000	0	0	$ 125,000
10					

Cash Collections Budget

The cash collections budget is all about timing: *When* does Tucson Tortilla expect to receive cash from its sales? Of course, Tucson Tortilla will receive cash immediately on its cash (COD) sales. From the Sales Budget (Exhibit 9-5), we see that the company expects the following cash sales in January:

> Cash (COD) sales = $120,000

However, most of the company's sales are made on credit. Recall that Tucson Tortilla's credit terms are "net 30 days," meaning customers have 30 days to pay. Therefore, most customers will wait nearly 30 days (a full month) before paying. However, some companies may be experiencing cash flow difficulties and may not be able to pay Tucson Tortilla on time. As a result, Tucson Tortilla doesn't expect to receive payment on all of its credit sales the month after the sale.

Based on collection history, Tucson Tortilla expects 85% of its credit sales to be collected in the month after sale, and 14% to be collected two months after the sale. Tucson Tortilla expects that 1% of credit sales will never be collected and therefore has recognized a 1% bad debt expense in its operating expenses budget. Furthermore, assume that December credit sales were $500,000 and November credit sales were $480,000.

> Anticipated January Collections of Credit Sales:
> 85% × $500,000 (December credit sales) = $425,000
> 14% × $480,000 (November credit sales) = $ 67,200

Exhibit 9-14 shows Tucson Tortilla's expected cash collections for the first three months of the year.

EXHIBIT 9-14 Cash Collections Budget

	A	B	C	D	E
1			Tucson Tortilla		
2			Cash Collections Budget		
3			For the Quarter Ended March 31		
4			Month		
5		January	February	March	1st Quarter
6	Cash sales in current month (from sales budget)	$ 120,000	$ 80,000	$ 100,000	$ 300,000
7	Collection on credit sales:				
8	85% of credit sales made one month ago	425,000	408,000	272,000	1,105,000
9	14% of credit sales made two months ago	67,200	70,000	67,200	204,400
10	Total cash collections	$ 612,200	$ 558,000	$ 439,200	$1,609,400
11					

NOTE: Cash and credit sales are shown in Sales Budget (Exhibit 9-5)
January:
$425,000 = 85% of December credit sales ($500,000)
$67,200 = 14% of November credit sales ($480,000)
February:
$408,000 = 85% of January credit sales ($480,000)
$70,000 = 14% of December credit sales ($500,000)
March:
$272,000 = 85% of February credit sales ($320,000)
$67,200 = 14% of January credit sales ($480,000)

Try It!

Assume Georgio's has the following budgeted sales for the quarter:

	January	February	March
COD sales	$ 10,000	$ 20,000	$ 15,000
Credit sales	100,000	110,000	120,000
Total sales	$110,000	$130,000	$135,000

Determine Georgio's budget for March cash collections assuming credit sales are collected as follows: 90% is collected the month after sale, 8% is collected two months after the month of sale, and 2% is never collected.

Please see page 582 for solutions.

Cash Payments Budget

The cash payments budget is also about timing: *When* will Tucson Tortilla pay for its direct materials purchases, direct labor costs, manufacturing overhead costs, operating expenses, capital expenditures, and income taxes? Let's tackle each cost, one at a time.

DIRECT MATERIALS PURCHASES Tucson Tortilla has been given "net 30 days" payment terms from its suppliers of the corn flour used to make the tortilla chips. Therefore, Tucson

Tortilla waits a month before it pays for the direct materials purchases shown in the Direct Materials Budget (Exhibit 9-7). So, the company will pay for its December purchases (projected to be $231,845) in January, its January purchases of $211,125 (Exhibit 9-7) in February, its February purchases of $157,650 (Exhibit 9-7) in March, and so forth:

	A	B	C	D	E
1	**Calculating Cash Payments for**	**Month**			
2	**Direct Materials Purchases**	**January**	**February**	**March**	**1st Quarter**
3	Total cost of DM purchases (from Exhibit 9-7)	$ 211,125	$ 157,650	$ 197,700	$ 566,475
4					
5	Cash payments for DM purchases **(paid one month after purchase)**	231,845	$ 211,125	$ 157,650	$ 600,620
6					

NOTE: December DM purchases are expected to be $231,845.

DIRECT LABOR Tucson Tortilla's factory employees are paid twice a month for the work they perform during the month. Therefore, January's direct labor cost of $31,900 (Exhibit 9-8) will be paid in January, and likewise, for each month.

	A	B	C	D	E
1		**Month**			
2	**Calculating Cash Payments for Direct Labor**	**January**	**February**	**March**	**1st Quarter**
3	Total cost of direct labor (from Exhibit 9-8)	$ 31,900	$ 22,550	$ 28,270	$ 82,720
4					
5	Cash payments for direct labor **(paid the same month)**	$ 31,900	$ 22,550	$ 28,270	$ 82,720
6					

MANUFACTURING OVERHEAD Tucson Tortilla must consider when it pays for its manufacturing overhead costs. Let's assume that the company pays for all manufacturing overhead costs except for depreciation, insurance, and property taxes in the month in which they are incurred. Depreciation is a noncash expense, so it never appears on the cash payments budget. Insurance and property taxes are typically paid on a semiannual basis. While Tucson Tortilla budgets a cost of $3,000 per month for factory insurance and property tax, it doesn't actually pay these costs on a monthly basis. Rather, Tucson Tortilla prepays its insurance and property tax twice a year, in January and July. The amount of these semiannual payments is calculated as shown:

$3,000 monthly cost × 12 months = $36,000 ÷ 2 = $18,000 payments in January and July

So, the cash payments for manufacturing overhead costs are expected to be as follows:

	A	B	C	D	E
1	**Calculating Cash Payments for**	**Month**			
2	**Manufacturing Overhead**	**January**	**February**	**March**	**1st Quarter**
3	Total manufacturing overhead (from Exhibit 9-9)	$ 102,500	$ 81,250	$ 94,250	$ 278,000
4	Less: Depreciation **(not a cash expense)**	10,000	10,000	10,000	30,000
5	Less: Property tax and insurance **(paid twice a year, not monthly)**	3,000	3,000	3,000	9,000
6	Plus: Semiannual **payments** for property taxes and insurance	18,000	0	0	18,000
7	Cash payments for manufacturing overhead	$ 107,500	$ 68,250	$ 81,250	$ 257,000
8					

OPERATING EXPENSES   Let's assume that the company pays for all operating expenses, except depreciation and bad debt expense, in the month in which they are incurred. Both depreciation and bad debt expense are noncash expenses, so they never appear on the cash payments budget. Bad debt expense simply recognizes the sales revenue that will never be collected. Therefore, these noncash expenses need to be deducted from the total operating expenses to arrive at cash payments for operating expenses:

	A	B	C	D	E
1	**Calculating Cash Payments for Operating Expenses**	**Month**			
2		**January**	**February**	**March**	**1st Quarter**
3	Total operating expenses (from Exhibit 9-10)	$ 142,800	$ 106,200	$ 124,500	$ 373,500
4	Less: Depreciation (*not a cash expense*)	6,000	6,000	6,000	18,000
5	Less: Bad debt expense (*not a cash expense*)	4,800	3,200	4,000	12,000
6	Cash Payments for operating expenses	$ 132,000	$ 97,000	$ 114,500	$ 343,500
7					

CAPITAL EXPENDITURES   The timing of these cash payments has already been scheduled on the capital expenditures budget in Exhibit 9-13. Furthermore, let's assume the capital expenditures are paid for when they are purchased.

INCOME TAXES   Corporations must make quarterly income tax payments for their estimated income tax liability. For corporations like Tucson Tortilla which have a December 31 fiscal year-end, the first income tax payment is not due until April 15. The remaining payments are due June 15, September 15, and December 15. As a result, Tucson Tortilla will not show any income tax payments in the first quarter of the year.

DIVIDENDS   Like many corporations, Tucson Tortilla pays dividends to its shareholders on a quarterly basis. Tucson Tortilla plans to pay $25,000 in cash dividends in January for the company's earnings in the fourth quarter of the previous year.

Finally, we pull all of these cash payments together onto a single budget, as shown in Exhibit 9-15.

EXHIBIT 9-15 Cash Payments Budget

	A	B	C	D	E
1	**Tucson Tortilla**				
2	**Cash Payments Budget**				
3	**For the Quarter Ended March 31**				
4		**Month**			
5		**January**	**February**	**March**	**1st Quarter**
6	Cash payments for direct materials purchases	$ 231,845	$ 211,125	$ 157,650	$ 600,620
7	Cash payments for direct labor	31,900	22,550	28,270	82,720
8	Cash payments for manufacturing overhead	107,500	68,250	81,250	257,000
9	Cash payments for operating expenses	132,000	97,000	114,500	343,500
10	Cash payments for capital investments	125,000	0	0	125,000
11	Cash payments for income taxes	0	0	0	0
12	Cash payments for dividends	25,000	0	0	25,000
13	Total cash payments	$ 653,245	$ 398,925	$ 381,670	$ 1,433,840
14					

Combined Cash Budget

The combined cash budget simply merges the budgeted cash collections and cash payments to forecast the company's ending cash position. Exhibit 9-16 shows the following:

- Budgeted cash collections for the month are added to the beginning cash balance to determine the total cash available.
- Budgeted cash payments are then subtracted to determine the ending cash balance before financing.
- Based on the ending cash balance before financing, the company knows whether it needs to borrow money or whether it has excess funds with which to repay debt or invest.

By looking at Exhibit 9-16, we see that Tucson Tortilla expects to begin the month with $36,100 of cash. However, by the end of the month, it will be short of cash. Therefore, the company's managers must plan for how they will handle this shortage. One strategy would be to delay the purchase of equipment planned for January. Another strategy would be to borrow money. Let's say Tucson Tortilla has prearranged a line of credit that carries an interest rate of prime plus 1%. A <u>line of credit</u> is a lending arrangement from a bank in which a company is allowed to borrow money as needed, up to a specified maximum amount, yet only pay interest on the portion that is actually borrowed until it is repaid.

EXHIBIT 9-16 Combined Cash Budget

	A	B	C	D	E
1		Tucson Tortilla			
2		Combined Cash Budget			
3		For the Quarter Ended March 31			
4		Month			
5		January	February	March	1st Quarter
6	Beginning cash balance	$ 36,100	$ 15,055	$ 153,980	$ 36,100
7	Plus: Cash collections (Exhibit 9-14)	612,200	558,000	439,200	1,609,400
8	Total cash available	648,300	573,055	593,180	1,645,500
9	Less: Cash payments (Exhibit 9-15)	653,245	398,925	381,670	1,433,840
10	Ending cash balance before financing	$ (4,945)	$ 174,130	$ 211,510	$ 211,660
11	Financing:				
12	Plus: New borrowings	20,000	0	0	20,000
13	Less: Debt repayments	0	20,000	0	20,000
14	Less: Interest payments	0	150	0	150
15	Ending cash balance	$ 15,055	$ 153,980	$ 211,510	$ 211,510
16					

The line of credit will enable Tucson Tortilla to borrow funds to meet its short-term cash deficiencies. Let's say that Tucson Tortilla wants to maintain an ending cash balance of at least $15,000. By borrowing $20,000 on its line of credit at the end of January, the company will have slightly more ($15,055) than its minimum desired balance.

The cash budget also shows that Tucson Tortilla will be able to repay this borrowing, along with the accrued interest, in February. Assuming Tucson Tortilla borrows the $20,000 for a full month at an interest rate of 9%, February's interest payment would be calculated as follows:

$$\$20,000 \text{ loan} \times 1/12 \text{ of the year} \times 9\% \text{ interest rate} = \$150$$

Why is this important?

"The combined **cash budget** lets managers know in **advance** when they will be short on cash and will need to **borrow** money, or when they may have **extra funds** to invest."

Exhibit 9-16 also shows that Tucson Tortilla expects to have a fairly substantial cash balance at the end of both February and March. The company's managers use the cash budgets to determine when this cash will be needed and to decide how to invest it accordingly. Since the first quarterly income tax payment is due April 15, management will want to invest most of this excess cash in a safe, short-term investment, such as a money market fund or short-term certificate of deposit. The company will also need cash in April to pay shareholders a quarterly dividend. Any cash not needed in the short run can be invested in longer-term investments. Managers exercising good cash management should have a plan in place for both cash deficiencies and cash excesses.

Budgeted Balance Sheet

Exhibit 9-17 shows Tucson Tortilla's budgeted balance sheet as of January 31. The company will prepare a budgeted balance sheet for each month of the year.

EXHIBIT 9-17 Budgeted Balance Sheet

	A	B
1	**Tucson Tortilla**	
2	**Budgeted Balance Sheet**	
3	**January 31**	
4	**Assets:**	
5	Cash, from cash budget	$ 15,055
6	Accounts receivable, net of allowance^A	549,450
7	Raw materials inventory, from DM budget (10,250 pounds × $1.50 per pound)	15,375
8	Finished goods inventory, from production budget (2,000 cases × $12.00 per case)	24,000
9	Prepaid property taxes and insurance^B	15,000
10	Total current assets	618,880
11	Property, plant, and equipment,^C net of $1,920,000 of accumulated depreciation^D	4,430,000
12	Total assets	$ 5,048,880
13		
14	**Liabilities and Stockholders' Equity:**	
15	Accounts payable^E	$ 211,125
16	Income tax liability, from Income Statement Budget	34,020
17	Other current liabilities (line of credit, from combined cash budget)	20,000
18	Total current liabilities	265,145
19	Stockholders' equity^F	4,783,735
20	Total liabilities and stockholders' equity	$ 5,048,880
21		

NOTE: Calculations for amounts itemized below.

---

^A **Accounts Receivable, Net of Allowance**

January credit sales (from sales budget, Exhibit 9-5)	$480,000
15% of December's credit sales ($500,000) yet to be collected	75,000
Accounts receivable, January 31	$555,000
Less: Allowance for uncollectible accounts (assume $750 balance prior to additional $4,800 bad debt expense, Exhibit 9-10)	(5,550)
Accounts receivable, net of allowance for uncollectible accounts	$549,450

---

^B **Prepaid Property Tax and Insurance**

Semiannual payment made in January (cash payments for MOH, p. 526)	$18,000
Less: January cost (MOH budget, Exhibit 9-9)	3,000
Prepaid property tax and insurance, January 31	$15,000

---

^C **Property, Plant, and Equipment**

December 31 balance (assumed)	$6,225,000
Plus: January's investment in new equipment (capital expenditures budget, Exhibit 9-13)	125,000
Property, plant, and equipment, January 31	$6,350,000

---

^D **Accumulated Depreciation**

December 31 balance (assumed)	$1,904,000
Plus: January's depreciation from manufacturing overhead budget, Exhibit 9-9	10,000
Plus: January's depreciation from operating expenses budget, Exhibit 9-10	6,000
Accumulated depreciation, January 31	$1,920,000

ᴱ Accounts Payable	
January's DM purchases to be paid in February (p. 526 and Exhibit 9-15).................................	211,125
Accounts payable, January 31...	$211,125

ᶠ Stockholders' Equity	
December 31 balance of common stock and retained earnings (assumed).....................................	$4,720,555
Plus: January's net income (budgeted income statement, Exhibit 9-12)......................................	63,180
Stockholders' equity, January 31..	$4,783,735

Sensitivity Analysis and Flexible Budgeting

The master budget models the company's *planned* activities. Managers try to use the best estimates possible when creating budgets. However, managers do not have a crystal ball for making predictions. Some of the key assumptions (such as sales volume) used to create the budgets may turn out to be different than originally predicted. How do managers prepare themselves for potentially different scenarios? They use sensitivity analysis and flexible budgeting.

As shown in Exhibit 9-18, **sensitivity analysis** is a *what-if* technique that asks *what* a result will be *if* a predicted amount is not achieved or *if* an underlying assumption changes. For example, *what if* shipping costs increase due to increases in gasoline prices? *What if* the cost of the corn flour increases or union workers negotiate a wage increase? *What if* sales are 15% cash and 85% credit, rather than 20% cash and 80% credit? How will any or all of these changes in key assumptions affect Tucson Tortilla's budgeted income and budgeted cash position?

EXHIBIT 9-18 Sensitivity Analysis

In addition to these "what-if" scenarios, management is particularly concerned with sales projections. Why? Because the sales budget is the driving force behind most of the other budgets. If the budgeted sales figures change, then most other budgets will also change. To address this concern, managers often prepare **flexible budgets**, which are budgets prepared for different volumes of activity. We'll discuss flexible budgets in Chapter 10, where we show how flexible budgets are often used to evaluate performance at the end of the period.

Sensitivity analysis and flexible budgeting are fairly easy to perform using Excel or special budgeting software. Managers simply change one or more of the underlying assumptions in the budgets, such as sales volume, and the software automatically computes a complete set of revised budgets based on the changes.

Armed with a better understanding of how changes in key assumptions will affect the company's bottom line and cash position, today's managers can be prepared to lead the company when business conditions change.

Technology Makes it Simple | Excel 2016

Sensitivity analysis is relatively easy to perform using spreadsheet software such as Microsoft Excel. We'll use the Direct Materials Budget pictured in Exhibit 9-7 as an example. Once the worksheet is set up, it can be used over and over for unlimited changes in assumptions. While we illustrate just one budget here, in real life, companies tie all of the individual budgets together such that if an assumption changes in one budget, the effect automatically ripples through the entire master budget. For example, a change of a key assumption in the sales budget would have an impact on almost every other budget in the master budget.

1. In a new spreadsheet, list the key factors that impact the budget (for example, units produced (Cell A19), pounds of materials needed per unit (Cell A20), cost per pound (Cell A21), desired level of ending inventory (Cell A22), and so forth).

2. Next, input the key assumptions corresponding to each of these factors (for example 29,000 units (Cell B19), 5 pounds needed per unit (Cell B20), material cost of $1.50 per pound (Cell B21), desired ending inventory equal to 10% of next month's quantity needed (Cell B22), and so forth).

3. Set up the Direct Materials Budget, as pictured in Exhibit 9-7. However, do not input any actual numbers. Rather, input cell references and formulas *for each cell*. For example:

    a. Cell B6 should reference the cell containing the number of units to be produced (=B19) and Cell B7 should reference the cell containing the assumption for pounds needed per unit (= B20).

    b. Cell B8 should have a formula multiplying units produced by pounds per unit (= B6*B7).

    c. Cell E6 should add cells B6, C6, and D6 (= B6 + C6 + D6).

4. Once you have formulated the entire budget in this manner, change one of the assumptions and notice how the effect ripples through the budget. The first time you use it, you may want to double check the figures by hand to make sure you correctly formulated the cells. Once you are sure the cell references and formulas are correct, you can use the spreadsheet for an unlimited amount of sensitivity analyses.

How Do the Budgets for Service and Merchandising Companies Differ?

Earlier in this chapter, we presented the master budget for a manufacturing company. The components of the master budget for a manufacturing company were summarized in Exhibit 9-4. The master budgets for service companies and merchandising companies are somewhat less complex and will be described next.

4 Prepare budgets for a merchandiser

Service Companies

Recall that service companies have no merchandise inventory. Therefore, their operating budgets only include the sales budget, the operating expenses budget, and the budgeted income statement, as shown in Exhibit 9-19 on the next page. Notice that the financial budgets are the same as those a manufacturer would prepare.

Merchandising Companies

Since merchandising companies purchase ready-made products, they do not need to prepare the production, direct materials, direct labor, or manufacturing overhead budgets. Replacing these budgets is a combined **cost of goods sold, inventory, and purchases budget**, as shown in Exhibit 9-20 on the next page.

EXHIBIT 9-19 Master Budget for a Service Company

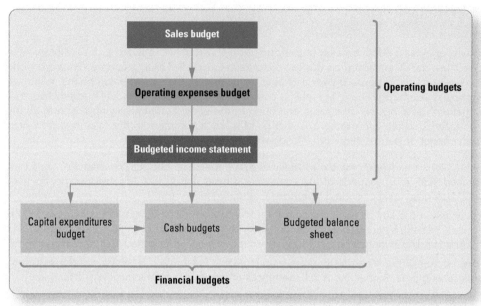

EXHIBIT 9-20 Master Budget for a Merchandising Company

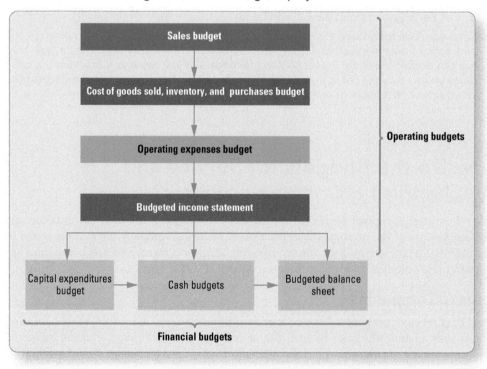

The cost of goods sold, inventory, and purchases budget follows the same general format as the manufacturer's production budget except that it is calculated at cost (in dollars) rather than in units:[3]

Cost of Goods Sold	(the inventory we plan to sell during the month, at cost)
Plus: Desired Ending Inventory	(the amount of inventory we want on hand at month's end)
Total Inventory Needed	(the total amount of inventory needed)
Less: Beginning Inventory	(the amount of inventory we have on hand)
Inventory to Purchase	(the amount of inventory we need to purchase)

[3]A merchandiser could first prepare this budget in units and then convert it to dollars. However, merchandisers usually have hundreds or thousands of products for sale, so it is often simpler to state it directly in dollars.

Notice that the format of the budget is easy to remember because it follows the name of the budget: We start with *Cost of Goods Sold*, then consider *inventory* levels, and finally arrive at the amount of inventory to *purchase*. Let's try an example:

Let's say one Circle J convenience store expects sales of $500,000 in January, $520,000 in February, $530,000 in March, and $550,000 in April. Let's also assume that management sets its prices to achieve an overall 40% gross profit. As a result, Cost of Goods Sold is 60% of the sales revenue (100% – 40%). Finally, management wishes to have ending inventory equal to 10% of the next month's Cost of Goods Sold. Exhibit 9-21 shows Circle J's cost of goods sold, inventory, and purchases budget for the first three months of the year. Keep in mind that all figures (other than Sales Revenue) are shown at cost.

EXHIBIT 9-21 Merchandiser's Cost of Goods Sold, Inventory, and Purchases Budget

	A	B	C	D	E
1		Circle J Convenience Stores			
2		Cost of Goods Sold, Inventory, and Purchases Budget			
3		For the Quarter Ended March 31			
4		Month			
5		January	February	March	1st Quarter
6	Budgeted sales revenue	$ 500,000	$ 520,000	$ 530,000	$ 1,550,000
7					
8	Cost of goods sold	$ 300,000	$ 312,000	$ 318,000	$ 930,000
9	Plus: Desired ending inventory	31,200	31,800	33,000	33,000
10	Total inventory required	331,200	343,800	351,000	963,000
11	Less: Beginning inventory	30,000	31,200	31,800	30,000
12	Amount of inventory to purchase	$ 301,200	$ 312,600	$ 319,200	$ 933,000
13					

NOTE: *Management would like to maintain an ending inventory equal to 10% of the next month's Cost of Goods Sold. The January 1 balance ($30,000) is the same as the December 31 balance, which is 10% of January's Cost of Goods Sold ($300,000). Also, assume April sales are projected to be $550,000, so April's Cost of Goods Sold is $330,000 (= 60% × $550,000).*

Figures from this budget are then used as follows:

- *Cost of Goods Sold* is used in preparing the budgeted income statement.
- *Ending Inventory* is used in preparing the budgeted balance sheet.
- *Purchases of Inventory* is used in preparing the cash payments budget.

Impact of Credit and Debit Card Sales on Budgeting

Consumers often use credit and debit cards to pay for online and in-store purchases at retailers, gas stations, and restaurants. In fact, over 26.2 billion transactions totaling roughly $4 trillion were made by credit cards in 2014.[4] What implications do these payment methods have for the merchants who accept "plastic" in place of cash or checks?

- Credit card companies (Visa, MasterCard, American Express, and Discover) and their issuing banks charge the merchant a transaction fee for each purchase made using plastic. The fee, officially known in business as "interchange," is usually a fixed amount per transaction *plus* a percentage of the amount charged. For example, the typical transaction fee for each credit card sale is between $0.05 and $0.20, *plus* 1–3% of the amount charged.[5] The actual fee will depend on the credit card brand, the merchant's industry, and whether or not the card is present (for example, online sales). Reward cards, such as those tied to frequent flyer miles, typically charge higher fees.

- In exchange for the fee, the credit card company and its issuing bank pays the merchant the entire amount of the purchase *less* the transaction fee. A deposit is made to the merchant's bank account within a few days of the sale.

[4] http://www.creditcards.com/credit-card-news/credit-card-market-share-statistics-1264.php

[5] https://www.mastercard.us/en-us/about-mastercard/what-we-do/interchange.html and https://usa.visa.com/dam/VCOM/download/merchants/Visa-USA-Interchange-Reimbursement-Fees-2015-April-18.pdf

Debit card transaction fees are usually lower than credit card transaction fees. Why?

1. Since debit card purchases require an associated personal identification number (PIN), the risk of fraud is lower than it is with a credit card. Thus, the issuing credit card company will have lower costs associated with stolen and fraudulently used cards.

2. Debit card sales are paid to the merchant using money that is in the customer's bank account, rather than money that is in essence loaned to the customer by the credit card company. Since the cash used for the deposit is not subject to credit risk, it is made with "cheaper" funds.

3. Beginning October 1, 2011, the Federal Reserve set a cap on the debit card transaction fees that banks can charge merchants. The new limit is as follows:

> Limit on *debit* card fees = $0.22 per transaction + 0.05% of the amount of the transaction

Notice that the amount charged on the value of the transaction (0.0005) is substantially less than it is for a typical credit card transaction.[6]

Although credit and debit card transaction fees are costly to merchants, the acceptance of plastic payment methods also has benefits:

■ Merchants would lose potential sales if they did not allow customers to pay with credit and debit cards. For example, Aldi, the low-cost grocery store with over 1,500 stores in the United States, only started accepting credit cards in 2016. Previously, the merchant only accepted debit cards because of the lower transaction fees. However, as part of Aldi's aggressive plan for growth in the U.S., management decided that they could attract more shoppers, and shoppers from a different socio-economic class, if they accepted credit cards in addition to debit cards.[7]

■ The acceptance of credit and debit cards decreases the costs associated with bounced checks, misappropriation of cash, and the activities associated with preparing and transporting cash deposits (sometimes via armored vehicle collection services).

■ Merchants receive the cash quickly, which may improve their cash flow.

Let's try an example:

Say a customer purchases some clothes at Urban Outfitters for $75 and uses a MasterCard to pay for the purchase. Let's also assume that MasterCard charges Urban Outfitters a transaction fee equal to $0.15 + 2% of the amount charged. The transaction fee on this sale would be:

$$\text{Transaction Fee} = \$0.15 + (2\% \times \text{Amount Charged})$$
$$\$1.65 = \$0.15 + (2\% \times \$75)$$

Within a few days, MasterCard would deposit the following amount in Urban Outfitters' bank account:

$$\text{Cash Deposited} = \text{Amount Charged on Credit Card} - \text{Transaction Fee}$$
$$\$73.35 = \$75.00 - \$1.65$$

[6] www.federalreserve.gov/newsevents/press/bcreg/20110629a.htm. Banks with less than $10 billion in assets are exempt from the new cap. In addition, if a bank does not have fraud prevention policies and procedures in place, the cap is $0.21 per transaction rather than $0.22 per transaction.

[7] http://www.cnbc.com/2016/03/02/no-frills-supermarket-aldi-to-accept-credit-cards.html

The anticipation of this credit card sale would be shown in the budgets as follows:

- The $75 sale would be shown in the sales budget, *in the month of sale.*
- The $1.65 transaction fee would be shown in the operating expenses budget, *in the month of sale.*
- The $73.35 would be shown as a cash receipt on the cash collections budget, *in the month of collection* (which is typically within one to seven days of the actual sale).

When preparing the master budget, merchants need to consider:

- The percentage of sales that will be made using debit cards and credit cards,
- The different transaction fees charged for debit and credit card transactions, and
- The length of time between the sale and the deposit.

Retail Credit Cards

Many retailers, such as Macy's and Old Navy, issue their own credit cards in addition to accepting credit cards such as Visa and MasterCard. When a customer uses a store-based credit card, no transaction fee is incurred. However, the risk of collection falls back on the merchant, rather than on a third-party credit card company. The merchant must wait for the customer to make payments on the credit card bill. The cash collection may occur over several months, several years, or never. The cash collections budget will take into account the aging of these receivables. Likewise, the operating expenses budget will need to take into consideration possible bad debts. Finally, the company will need to budget for interest income assessed on unpaid balances and any fees charged to the customer for late payments.

Exhibit 9-22 compares third-party credit cards with retail credit cards.

EXHIBIT 9-22 Comparison of Credit Cards

Third-Party Credit Cards (e.g., Visa and MasterCard)[*]
- Merchant accepts "plastic payment" in the form of a third-party credit card (e.g., Visa).
- Credit card issuer (e.g., Visa) pays merchant amount of purchase, less a transaction fee.
- Credit card issuer (e.g., Visa) assumes collection risk.
- Consumer owes credit card issuer amount of purchase, plus interest on any outstanding unpaid balance from earlier periods.

Retail Credit Cards (e.g., Macy's):
- Merchant accepts "plastic payment" in the form of the merchant's own retail card.
- No third-party transaction fee is involved.
- Merchant assumes collection risk.
- Consumer owes issuing merchant amount of purchase, plus interest on any outstanding unpaid balance from earlier periods.

[*]The actual issuers of third-party credit cards are member banks of Visa and MasterCard's network, such as JP Morgan Chase, Capital One, and Citigroup. These member banks process the payments and receive the transaction fees. They also pay additional fees to Visa and MasterCard. Thus, Exhibit 9-22 is a simplification of the actual business relationships surrounding credit cards, but serves as a useful illustration for how "plastic" payments affect merchant budgeting.

Sustainability and Budgeting

Campbell Soup Company is a recognized leader in corporate responsibility. The company has been listed on the Dow Jones Sustainability Index for the last seven consecutive years and has ranked in the Top 10 Best Corporate Citizens (large company category) by Corporate Responsibility Magazine for the fourth consecutive year.[8] How does the company do it? Managers at Campbell set long-term sustainability targets and benchmark actual yearly performance against those targets. Each of these targets requires actions that will impact the company's annual budgets. For example, the company has set long-term environmental goals for 2020 that include:[9]

- Cutting water use and greenhouse gases emissions per pound of ingredient by 20% and cutting fertilizer per pound of ingredient by 10%
- Recycling 95% of waste generated
- Reducing packaging material by 100 million pounds and delivering 100% of packaging from sustainable materials
- Reducing energy use by 35% and sourcing 40% of energy used from renewable or alternative energy sources

The adoption of these long-term goals will affect most, if not all, of the company's shorter-term budgets. For example, the reduction of water, energy, and packaging materials at the plants will affect the MOH and direct materials budget, while the recycling of waste will create some additional income. The goal of cutting greenhouse gas emissions will impact the company's capital expenditure budget, as the company invests in new technologies such as the biogas digester being used by one of the company's plants in Ohio. These plans will, in turn, affect the cash budgets.

In addition to environmental goals, the company also has social impact goals, which will be reflected in the company's budgets. These goals include:

- Increasing the nutritional value of its products
- Reducing childhood obesity and hunger
- Promoting volunteerism

These plans also play out in the company's manufacturing budgets (production of healthier products) and operating expense budgets (funding social wellness programs). While this chapter has focused on the use of budgets for planning purposes, recall that budgets also serve as benchmarks for judging performance. Each year, Campbell publishes its Corporate Social Responsibility scorecard to show how well it is achieving its environmental and social impact goals. For example, in 2014, the company had an 86% worldwide recycling rate, decreased packaging by 89 million pounds, reduced water use and greenhouse gas emissions, and gave over $70 million to charitable causes.

By using budgets for both planning and performance evaluation, Campbell is making strides in becoming the type of sustainable company envisioned by management.

See Exercises E9-17A and E9-37B

---

[8] http://www.campbellsoupcompany.com/pressrelease/campbell-named-to-the-dow-jones-sustainability-indices-for-seventh-consecutive-year/

[9] 2014 Corporate Social Responsibility Report

Decision Guidelines

The Master Budget

Let's consider some decisions managers need to make with respect to budgeting.

Decision	Guidelines
What is the key to preparing the cash collections and cash payments budgets?	The key to preparing the cash budgets is *timing*. *When* will cash be received, and *when* will cash be paid? The timing of cash collections and cash payments often differs from the period in which the related revenues and expenses are recognized on the income statement.
What can be done to prepare for possible changes in key, underlying budget assumptions?	Management uses sensitivity analysis to understand how changes in key, underlying assumptions might affect the company's financial results. This awareness helps managers cope with changing business conditions when they occur.
How does sustainability impact budgeting?	Companies that are planning on adopting any sustainable practice will want to capture those plans in their budgets. Any or all of the budgets could be impacted by plans to adopt sustainable practices.
How does the master budget of a service company differ from that of a manufacturer?	Service companies have no inventory to make or sell, thus their operating budgets are less complex. The operating budgets include the: • Sales budget • Operating expenses budget • Budgeted income statement
How does the master budget of a merchandising company differ from that of a manufacturer?	Merchandising companies buy their inventory, rather than make it. In place of the production budget, they use a "cost of goods sold, inventory, and purchases" budget. This budget follows the same basic format as the production budget. The amounts on the budget are calculated at cost, rather than in units. The operating budgets include the: • Sales budget • Cost of goods sold, inventory, and purchases budget • Operating expenses budget • Budgeted income statement
How does the acceptance of debit and credit card payments affect a merchant's budgets?	Merchants must budget for the transaction fees charged by the credit card companies and their issuing banks. The transaction fee needs to be shown on the operating expenses budget. The amount of credit and debit card sales, net of the transaction fee, will be shown on the cash collections budget.
How are credit and debit card transaction fees calculated?	The transaction fee is typically a set dollar amount per transaction, plus a percentage of the amount of sale charged on a credit or debit card. For example: Transaction Fee = \$0.25 + (2% × Amount Charged)
How does the acceptance of debit and credit cards affect the cash collection budget?	The amount of cash shown on the cash collections budget will be the net amount deposited: Cash Deposited = Amount Charged on Credit Card − Transaction Fee

SUMMARY PROBLEM 2

The following information was taken from the Pillows Unlimited sales budget, found in Summary Problem 1 on page 523:

	A	B	C	D	E
1		Pillows Unlimited			
2		Sales Budget: Type of Sale			
3		For the Quarter Ended March 31			
4		Month			
5		January	February	March	1st Quarter
6	**Type of sale:**				
7	Cash sales (10%)	$ 140,000	$ 154,000	$ 161,000	$ 455,000
8	Credit sales (90%)	1,260,000	1,386,000	1,449,000	4,095,000
9	Total sales revenue	$ 1,400,000	$ 1,540,000	$ 1,610,000	$ 4,550,000
10					

The company's collection history indicates that 75% of credit sales is collected in the month after the sale, 15% is collected two months after the sale, 8% is collected three months after the sale, and the remaining 2% is never collected.

Assume the following additional information was gathered about the types of sales made in the fourth quarter (October through December) of the previous year:

	A	B	C	D	E
1		Pillows Unlimited			
2		Sales Budget: Type of Sale			
3		For the Quarter Ended December 31			
4		Month			
5		October	November	December	4th Quarter
6	**Type of sale:**				
7	Cash sales (10%)	$ 142,800	$ 151,200	$ 137,200	$ 431,200
8	Credit sales (90%)	1,285,200	1,360,800	1,234,800	3,880,800
9	Total sales revenue	$ 1,428,000	$ 1,512,000	$ 1,372,000	$ 4,312,000
10					

The following information was taken from the Pillows Unlimited direct materials budget, found in Summary Problem 1 on page 523:

	A	B	C	D	E
1		Pillows Unlimited			
2		Excerpt from Direct Materials Budget			
3		For the Quarter Ended March 31			
4		Month			
5		January	February	March	1st Quarter
6	Total cost of DM purchases	$ 771,750	$ 836,250	$ 873,000	$ 2,481,000
7					

Assume that the total cost of direct materials purchases in December was $725,000. The company pays 40% of its direct materials purchases in the month of purchase and pays the remaining 60% in the month after purchase.

Requirements

1. Prepare the cash collections budget for January, February, and March, as well as a summary for the first quarter.

2. Prepare the cash payments budget for direct materials purchases for the months of January, February, and March, as well as a summary for the quarter.

▪ SOLUTIONS

Requirement 1

	A	B	C	D	E
1		Pillows Unlimited			
2		Cash Collections Budget			
3		For the Quarter Ended March 31			
4			Month		
5		January	February	March	1st Quarter
6	Cash sales in current month	$ 140,000	$ 154,000	$ 161,000	$ 455,000
7	Collection on credit sales:				
8	75% of credit sales made one month ago	926,100	945,000	1,039,500	2,910,600
9	15% of credit sales made two months ago	204,120	185,220	189,000	578,340
10	8% of credit sales made three months ago	102,816	108,864	98,784	310,464
11	Total cash collections	$ 1,373,036	$ 1,393,084	$ 1,488,284	$ 4,254,404
12					

NOTE: Cash and credit sales are shown on the sales budget

January:
$926,100 = 75% of December credit sales ($1,234,800)
$204,120 = 15% of November credit sales ($1,360,800)
$102,816 = 8% of October credit sales ($1,285,200)

February:
$945,000 = 75% of January credit sales ($1,260,000)
$185,220 = 15% of December credit sales ($1,234,800)
$108,864 = 8% of November credit sales ($1,360,800)

March:
$1,039,500 = 75% of February credit sales ($1,386,000)
$189,000 = 15% of January credit sales ($1,260,000)
$98,784 = 8% of December credit sales ($1,234,800)

Requirement 2

	A	B	C	D	E
1		Pillows Unlimited			
2		Cash Payments Budget			
3		For the Quarter Ended March 31			
4			Month		
5		January	February	March	1st Quarter
6	40% of current month DM purchases	$ 308,700	$ 334,500	$ 349,200	$ 992,400
7	60% of last month's DM purchases	435,000	463,050	501,750	1,399,800
8	Total cash payments	$ 743,700	$ 797,550	$ 850,950	$ 2,392,200
9					

NOTE: Payments calculated as follows:

January:
$308,700 = 40% of January DM purchases ($771,750)
$435,000 = 60% of December DM purchases ($725,000)

February:
$334,500 = 40% of February DM purchases ($836,250)
$463,050 = 60% of January DM purchases ($771,750)

March:
$349,200 = 40% of March DM purchases ($873,000)
$501,750 = 60% of February DM purchases ($836,250)

END OF CHAPTER

Learning Objectives

- 1 Describe how and why managers use budgets
- 2 Prepare the operating budgets
- 3 Prepare the financial budgets
- 4 Prepare budgets for a merchandiser

Accounting Vocabulary

Budget Committee. (p. 509) A committee comprised of upper management as well as cross-functional managers that reviews, revises, and approves the final budget.

COD. (p. 513) Collect on Delivery, or Cash on Delivery. A sales term indicating that the inventory must be paid for at the time of delivery.

Cost of Goods Sold, Inventory, and Purchases Budget. (p. 531) A merchandiser's budget that computes the cost of goods sold, the amount of desired ending inventory, and amount of merchandise to be purchased.

Financial Budgets. (p. 511) The financial budgets include the capital expenditures budget and the cash budget. It culminates in a budgeted balance sheet.

Flexible Budgets. (p. 530) Budgets prepared for different volumes of activity.

Line of Credit. (p. 528) A lending arrangement from a bank in which a company is allowed to borrow money as needed, up to a specified maximum amount, yet only pay interest on the portion that is actually borrowed until it is repaid.

Master Budget. (p. 511) The comprehensive planning document for the entire organization. The master budget includes the operating budgets and the financial budgets.

Operating Budgets. (p. 511) The budgets needed to run the daily operations of the company. The operating budgets culminate in a budgeted income statement.

Participative Budgeting. (p. 509) Budgeting that involves the participation of many levels of management.

Rolling Budget. (p. 509) A budget that is continuously updated so that the next 12 months of operations are always budgeted; also known as a *continuous budget*.

Safety Stock. (p. 513) Extra inventory kept on hand in case demand is higher than expected or problems in the factory slow production.

Sensitivity Analysis. (p. 530) A *what-if* technique that asks what a result will be if a predicted amount is not achieved or if an underlying assumption changes.

Slack. (p. 509) Intentionally overstating budgeted expenses or understating budgeted revenues in order to cope with uncertainty, make performance appear better, or make room for potential budget cuts.

Strategic Planning. (p. 508) Setting long-term goals that may extend 5 to 10 years into the future.

Variance. (p. 511) The difference between actual and budgeted figures (revenues and expenses).

Zero-Based Budgeting. (p. 510) A budgeting approach in which managers begin with a budget of zero and must justify every dollar put into the budget.

MyAccountingLab | **Go to** http://myaccountinglab.com/ **for the following Quick Check, Short Exercises, Exercises, and Problems. They are available with immediate grading, explanations of correct and incorrect answers, and interactive media that acts as your own online tutor.**

Quick Check

1. *(Learning Objective 1)* Which term describes the situation in which a manager intentionally overbudgets expenses or underbudgets revenue?
   a. Participative budgeting
   b. Budgetary slack
   c. Strategic planning
   d. Benchmarking

2. *(Learning Objective 1)* Benefits of budgeting include
   a. benchmarking.
   b. planning.
   c. coordination and communication.
   d. all of the above.

3. *(Learning Objective 1)* The comprehensive planning document for the entire organization is called the _____ budget.
   a. financial
   b. cash
   c. master
   d. operating

4. *(Learning Objective 2)* Which of the following budgets must be prepared first, as it serves as a basis for most other budgets?
   a. Production budget
   b. Operating expenses budget
   c. Cash budget
   d. Sales budget

5. *(Learning Objective 2)* The operating budgets culminate in the budgeted
   a. statement of owners' equity.
   b. balance sheet.
   c. income statement.
   d. statement of cash flows.

6. *(Learning Objective 3)* Which of the following are noncash expenses that will always result in differences between the budgeted operating expenses for a given period and the budgeted cash payments for the same period?
   a. Depreciation expense and bad debt expense
   b. Advertising expense and bad debt expense
   c. Depreciation expense and rent expense
   d. Advertising expense and rent expense

7. *(Learning Objective 3)* Which budget reflects the company's plans to invest in new property, plant, and equipment?
   a. Direct materials budget
   b. Operating expenses budget
   c. Cash collections budget
   d. Capital expenditures budget

8. *(Learning Objective 4)* Which of the following budgets is unique to merchandising companies?
   a. Direct materials budget
   b. Operating expenses budget
   c. Production budget
   d. Cost of Goods Sold, Inventory, and Purchases budget

9. *(Learning Objective 4)* Which of the following is true?
   a. Only debit card transaction fees are limited by law.
   b. Only credit card transaction fees are limited by law.
   c. Both credit card and debit card transaction fees are limited by law.
   d. Neither credit card nor debit card transaction fees are limited by law.

10. *(Learning Objective 4)* Which of the following is true for merchants who accept payments made by Visa, MasterCard, and other forms of "plastic"?
    a. Transaction fees are generally a fixed amount per month.
    b. Credit card fees are usually lower than debit card fees.
    c. Transaction fees should be budgeted for in the operating expenses budget.
    d. Retail cards (such as Target and Kohl's charge cards) have similar transaction fees to those issued by Visa and MasterCard.

Quick Check Answers

1.b 2.d 3.c 4.d 5.c 6.a 7.d 8.d 9.a 10.c

Performance Evaluation

Sources: http://www.pepsico.com/Brands/
BrandExplorer#top-global-brands

Learning Objectives

- **1** Understand decentralization and describe different types of responsibility centers
- **2** Develop performance reports
- **3** Calculate ROI, sales margin, and capital turnover
- **4** Describe strategies and mechanisms for determining a transfer price
- **5** Prepare and evaluate flexible budget performance reports
- **6** Describe the balanced scorecard and identify KPIs for each perspective

PepsiCo, which turned 50 years old in 2015, sells products in over 200 countries around the world. PepsiCo's top 22 brands each generate over $1 billion in annual sales. In addition to its well-known beverages, including Pepsi, Mountain Dew, Gatorade, and Tropicana, the company also owns all of the Frito-Lay snack brands, such as Ruffles, Doritos, and Cheetos. Pepsi also owns all of the Quaker Oat brands, such as Life and Cap'n Crunch cereals. How does such a large and diverse company coordinate, control, and evaluate such a vast array of operations? First, the company is segmented into separate operating divisions based on geographic location (for example, North America, Europe and Sub-Saharan Africa, and Latin America). In some geographic areas it is further segmented into different product types (Beverages, Quaker products, and Frito-Lay products). Second, a manager is assigned responsibility for each segment and for each operating function (production, sales, etc.) within each segment. PepsiCo's vision, *"Performance with a Purpose,"* integrates sustainability and the triple bottom line into the company's business strategy. As a result, each segment is evaluated in terms not only of its financial performance, but also its impact on society and the environment.

In Chapter 9, we saw how businesses such as Campbell Soup Company and Tucson Tortilla set strategic goals and then develop planning budgets to help reach those goals. In this chapter, we'll see how companies use budgets and other tools, such as the balanced scorecard, to evaluate performance and control operations.

How Does Decentralization Affect Performance Evaluation?

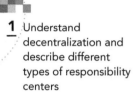

1 Understand decentralization and describe different types of responsibility centers

In a small company, such as Tucson Tortilla (discussed in Chapter 9), the owner or top manager often makes all planning and operating decisions. Small companies can use *centralized* decision making because of the smaller scope of their operations. However, when a company grows, it is impossible for a single person to manage the entire organization's operations. Therefore, most companies, like PepsiCo, decentralize as they grow.

Companies that <u>decentralize</u> split their operations into different operating segments. Top management delegates decision-making responsibility to the segment managers and determines the type of decentralization that best suits the company's strategy. For example, decentralization may be based on

- geographic area
- product line
- distribution channel (such as retail sales versus online sales)
- customer base
- business function

PepsiCo decentralizes its company by brand in North America (Frito-Lay, Quaker Foods, Pepsi Beverages) and by geographic area in other parts of the world (Latin America; Europe and Sub-Saharan Africa; Asia, Middle East, and North Africa).

Advantages and Disadvantages of Decentralization

Before we look at specific types of business segments, let's consider some of the advantages and disadvantages of decentralization.

Advantages

Most growing companies decentralize out of necessity. However, decentralization provides many potential benefits.

FREES TOP MANAGEMENT'S TIME By delegating responsibility for daily operations to segment managers, top management can concentrate on long-term strategic planning and higher-level decisions that affect the entire company.

ENCOURAGES USE OF EXPERT KNOWLEDGE Decentralization allows top management to hire the expertise each business segment needs to excel in its specific operations. Specialized knowledge often helps segment managers make better decisions than the top company managers could make.

IMPROVES CUSTOMER AND SUPPLIER RELATIONS Segment managers focus on just one segment of the company, allowing them to maintain close contact with important customers and suppliers. Thus, decentralization often leads to improved customer and supplier relations, which can result in quicker customer response times.

PROVIDES TRAINING Decentralization also provides segment managers with training and experience necessary to become effective top managers. Companies often groom their lower-level managers to move up through the company, taking on additional responsibility and gaining more knowledge of the company with each step.

IMPROVES MOTIVATION AND RETENTION   Empowering segment managers to make decisions increases managers' motivation and job satisfaction, which often improves job performance and retention.

Disadvantages

The many advantages of decentralization usually outweigh the disadvantages. However, decentralization can cause potential problems, including the following.

POTENTIAL DUPLICATION OF COSTS   Decentralization may cause a company to duplicate certain costs or assets. For example, several business segments could maintain their own payroll and human resource departments. Companies can often avoid such duplications by providing centralized services. For example, Marriott segments its hotels by property type (limited service, full-service, international), yet each hotel property shares one centralized reservations website platform.

POTENTIAL PROBLEMS ACHIEVING GOAL CONGRUENCE   <u>Goal congruence</u> occurs when the goals of the segment managers align with the goals of top management. Decentralized companies often struggle to achieve goal congruence. Segment managers may not fully understand the big picture, or the ultimate goals that upper management is trying to achieve. They may make decisions that are good for their segment but may be detrimental to another segment of the company or the company as a whole. For example, to control costs, one division may decide to offshore production to an overseas factory with poor working conditions. However, top management may embrace, promote, and market social responsibility and the use of fair labor practices. If so, the division is not acting in accordance with top management's goals.

Performance Evaluation Systems

Once a company decentralizes operations, top management is no longer involved in running the day-to-day operations of the segments. Performance evaluation systems provide upper management with the feedback it needs to maintain control over the entire organization, even though it has delegated responsibility and decision-making authority to segment managers. To be effective, performance evaluation systems should

- clearly communicate expectations,
- provide benchmarks that promote goal congruence and coordination between segments, and
- motivate segment managers (possibly through paying bonus incentives to managers who achieve performance targets).

Responsibility accounting, discussed next, is an integral part of most companies' performance evaluation systems.

What Is Responsibility Accounting?

A <u>responsibility center</u> is part of an organization whose manager is accountable for planning and controlling certain activities. Lower-level managers are often responsible for budgeting and controlling costs of a single value chain function. For example, at PepsiCo, one manager is responsible for planning and controlling the *production* of Frito-Lay products at a single plant, while another is responsible for planning and controlling the *distribution* of the product to customers. Lower-level managers report to higher-level managers, who have broader responsibilities. For example, managers in charge of production and distribution report to senior managers responsible for profits earned by an entire product line.

<u>Responsibility accounting</u> is a system for evaluating the performance of each responsibility center and its manager. Responsibility accounting performance reports compare plans (budgets) with actual results for each center. Superiors then evaluate how well each manager controlled the operations for which he or she was responsible.

Types of Responsibility Centers

Exhibit 10-1 illustrates four types of responsibility centers, as described briefly in the following paragraphs.

EXHIBIT 10-1 Four Types of Responsibility Centers

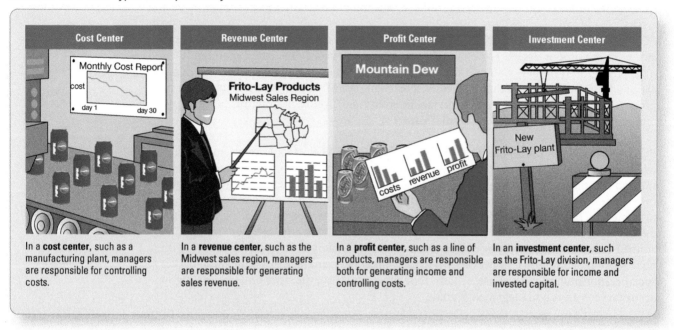

In a **cost center**, such as a manufacturing plant, managers are responsible for controlling costs.

In a **revenue center**, such as the Midwest sales region, managers are responsible for generating sales revenue.

In a **profit center**, such as a line of products, managers are responsible both for generating income and controlling costs.

In an **investment center**, such as the Frito-Lay division, managers are responsible for income and invested capital.

Cost Center

In a <u>cost center</u>, managers are accountable for costs only. Manufacturing operations, such as the Frito-Lay plant in Casa Grande, Arizona, are cost centers. The plant manager controls costs by using lean thinking to eliminate waste. The plant is near net-zero waste and uses solar energy for much of its power. The plant manager is *not* responsible for generating revenues because he or she is not involved in selling the product. The plant manager is evaluated on his or her ability to control *costs* by comparing actual costs to budgeted costs.

Revenue Center

In a <u>revenue center</u>, managers are accountable primarily for revenues. Many times, revenue centers are sales territories, such as geographic areas within the country. Revenue center performance reports compare actual revenues to budgeted revenues.

Profit Center

In a <u>profit center</u>, managers are accountable for both revenues and costs, and therefore profits. For example, at PepsiCo, a manager may be responsible for the entire line of brand products, such as Mountain Dew or Aquafina. This manager is accountable for increasing sales revenue *and* controlling costs to achieve profit goals for the entire brand or product line. Superiors evaluate the manager's performance by comparing actual revenues, expenses, and profits to the budget.

Investment Center

In an <u>investment center</u>, managers are responsible for (1) generating revenues, (2) controlling costs, and (3) efficiently managing the division's assets. Investment centers are generally large divisions of a corporation. For example, PepsiCo has six divisions:

- Frito-Lay North America
- Quaker Foods North America

- North America Beverages
- Latin America
- Europe Sub-Saharan Africa
- Asia, Middle East, and North Africa

Investment centers are treated almost as if they were standalone companies. Division managers generally have broad responsibility, including deciding how to use assets. As a result, managers are held responsible for generating as much profit as they can with those assets.

Organization Chart

Exhibit 10-2 shows a partial organization chart for a company such as PepsiCo.

- At the top level, the CEO oversees each of the divisions (*investment centers*).
- The manager of each division oversees all of the product lines (*profit centers*) in that division. For example, the VP of North America Beverages is responsible for the profitable operation of Pepsi, Gatorade, Tropicana, Mountain Dew, Aquafina, and the company's other North America beverage brands.[1]
- The manager of each product line is responsible for evaluating lower-level managers of *cost centers* (such as manufacturing plants) and *revenue centers* (such as sales territories).

EXHIBIT 10-2 Partial Organization Chart

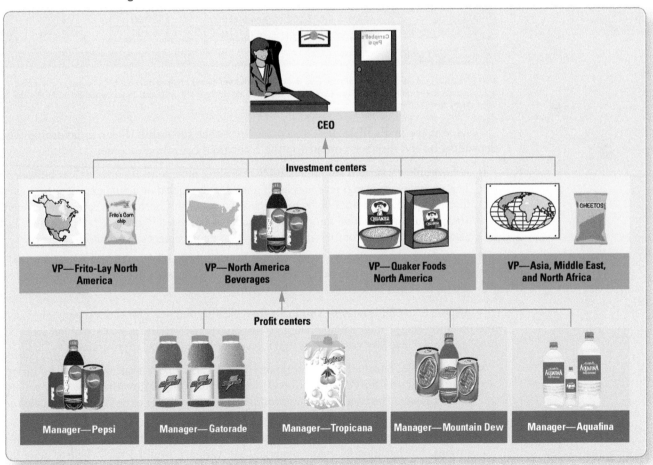

[1] For the sake of simplicity, we only illustrate four of the six divisions.

Responsibility Center Performance Reports

2 Develop performance reports

As introduced in Chapter 9, a **performance report** compares actual revenues and actual expenses against budgeted figures. The difference between actual figures and budgeted figures is known as a **variance**. The specific figures included on each performance report will depend on the type of responsibility center being evaluated. For example,

- the performance reports of cost centers will only include *costs* incurred within the center
- the performance reports of revenue centers will only include the *revenues* generated by the center

Exhibit 10-3 illustrates a partial performance report for a hypothetical revenue center—the hypothetical Midwest Sales Region of Frito-Lay products. Since the manager is only responsible for generating sales revenue, only revenues are included in the report.

EXHIBIT 10-3 Partial Performance Report for a Revenue Center

	A	B	C	D	E	F	G
1			Midwest Sales Region				
2			Monthly Performance Report				
3			For the Month Ended March 31				
4	Product	Actual Sales	Budgeted Sales	Variance		Variance Percentage	
5	Sun Chips	$ 2,367,200	$ 2,400,000	$ 32,800	U	1.37%	U
6	Doritos	15,896,000	15,000,000	896,000	F	5.97%	F
7	Lay's	9,325,500	9,000,000	325,500	F	3.62%	F
8	Tostitos	1,374,300	1,500,000	125,700	U	8.38%	U
9	Cheetos	13,500,000	13,500,000	0	F	0.00%	F
10	Fritos	4,683,100	4,500,000	183,100	F	4.07%	F
11	Total revenues	$ 47,146,100	$ 45,900,000	$ 1,246,100	F	2.71%	F
12							

NOTE: The variance percentage is calculated as the variance divided by the budgeted amount. All figures in this report are hypothetical and do not reflect PepsiCo's actual sales or budgets for these products. These hypothetical figures are used strictly for teaching purposes.

As you see in Exhibit 10-3, variances are either favorable (F) or unfavorable (U), depending on the variance's impact on the company's operating income.

- A **favorable variance** is one that causes operating income to be higher than budgeted. This occurs when actual revenues are higher than budgeted or actual expenses are lower than budgeted. A variance of "zero," such as we see with Cheetos sales revenue in Exhibit 10-3, occurs when actual figures are the same as budgeted figures. A "zero variance" is also interpreted as favorable since it means that management's expectations were met.

- An **unfavorable variance** is one that causes operating income to be lower than budgeted. This occurs when actual revenues are lower than budgeted or actual expenses are higher than budgeted.

Although favorable *revenue* variances are typically good news for the company, the same interpretation can be misleading when it comes to expense variances. Be careful *not* to interpret "favorable" expense variances as "good" and unfavorable expense variances as "bad."

- For example, on one hand, a company could spend more than originally budgeted on research and development (R&D) in order to bring innovative new products to market faster. The resulting *unfavorable* variance for R&D expenses may actually be *good* news for the company.

- On the other hand, a manager may purchase lower-quality materials to generate cost savings. The resulting *favorable* materials cost variance would actually be *bad* news for the company, since it would most likely result in reducing the quality of the end product.

Most companies' accounting software will use positive and negative numbers to indicate whether a variance is favorable or unfavorable. The direction of the sign (positive or negative) will depend on whether the variance is calculated as budget minus actual or as actual minus budget. Practice varies in this regard, especially when it comes to expense variances. To avoid any confusion over the direction of the sign, we use the U and F notation along with the absolute value of the variance. Just remember that when you are working with real companies, you will rarely see the U or F notation on the performance reports. Rather, you will see positive and negative variances that you will need to interpret using the definitions just presented.

Managers use a technique called **management by exception** when analyzing performance reports. Management by exception means that managers will only investigate budget variances that are relatively large. Let's use a personal example to illustrate this concept. Consider your monthly cell phone bill. You probably have an expectation of how large your monthly cell phone bill will be. If the actual bill is close to your expectation, you'll just pay the bill without giving it too much additional thought. However, if the actual bill is much higher or much lower than you expected, you probably will look at the detailed charges for calls, texts, and data usage to determine why the bill was so much different than what you expected.

Managers do the same thing. If the actual costs or revenues are close to budget, they assume operations are in control. However, if the variance between budget and actual is relatively large, they'll investigate the cause of the variance. Managers often have a decision rule for variance investigation that is expressed as a percentage, dollar amount, or a combination of the two. For example, the manager of the Midwest Sales Region may decide to investigate only those variances that are greater than 5% *and* $150,000. Exhibit 10-3 shows that the variance for both Doritos and Tostitos exceeds 5%. However, of the two, only the Doritos variance exceeds $150,000. Therefore, the manager would only investigate the Doritos variance.

> ### Why is this important?
>
> "Variances are always **favorable** or **unfavorable**, depending on whether they increase or decrease operating income. **Computer** software usually indicates the **directional** impact of the variance using **positive** and **negative numbers**, rather than a U or F notation."

Segment Margin

The performance reports of profit and investment centers include both revenues and expenses. Performance reports are often presented in the contribution margin format rather than the traditional income statement format. These reports often include a line called "segment margin." A **segment margin** is the operating income generated by a profit or investment center *before* subtracting common fixed costs that have been allocated to the center. Exhibit 10-4 illustrates a hypothetical performance report for Tropicana products.

EXHIBIT 10-4 Performance Report Highlighting the Profit Center's Segment Margin

	A	B	C	D	E	F	G
1		Tropicana Products					
2		Segment Margin Performance Report for the Fiscal Year Ended December 31					
3		(all figures in millions of dollars)					
4		Actual	Budgeted	Variance		Variance %	
5	Sales revenue	$ 4,314	$ 4,300	$ 14	F	0.3%	F
6	Less variable expenses:						
7	Variable cost of goods sold	1,728	1,720	8	U	0.5%	U
8	Variable operating expenses	508	515	7	F	1.4%	F
9	Contribution Margin	2,078	2,065	13	F	0.6%	F
10	Less direct fixed expenses:						
11	Fixed manufacturing overhead	1,228	1,215	13	U	1.1%	U
12	Fixed operating expenses	405	415	10	F	2.4%	F
13	Segment Margin	445	435	10	F	2.3%	F
14	Less: Common fixed expenses allocated to the profit center	36	35	1	U	2.9%	U
15	Operating income	$ 409	$ 400	$ 9	F	2.3%	F
16							

NOTE: All figures in this report are hypothetical and do not reflect the actual or budgeted sales and expense data for Tropicana products. These hypothetical figures are used strictly for teaching purposes.

As you look at Exhibit 10-4, notice that fixed expenses are separated into two categories:

- **Direct fixed expenses**, which include those fixed expenses that can be traced to the profit center. An example might include advertisements for Tropicana orange juice.

- **Common fixed expenses**, which include those fixed expenses that *cannot* be traced to the profit center. Rather, these are fixed expenses incurred by the overarching investment center (North America Beverages) that have been allocated among the different profit centers in the division. For example, these allocated costs may include the division's cost of providing a common computer information system, human resources department, payroll department, and legal department. By sharing these services, the different product lines avoid duplication of the costs and assets that would otherwise need to be maintained by the individual profit centers.

Since the manager of the profit center has little to no control over the allocation of the common fixed expenses, he or she should not be held responsible for them.[2] Therefore, the manager is typically held responsible for the center's segment margin, not its operating income.

Organization-wide Performance Reports

Exhibit 10-5 illustrates how the performance reports for each level of management shown in Exhibit 10-2 flow *up* to the top of the company. Notice the following in the exhibit:

- The operating income from each profit center, such as Tropicana products (at the bottom of the exhibit), flows into the performance report for an investment center (in the middle of the exhibit).

- Likewise, the operating income from each investment center, such as North America Beverages, flows into the performance report for the entire company (at the top of the exhibit).

- Costs incurred by corporate headquarters (shown in the top of the exhibit) are treated as a cost center and are typically not allocated to any of the divisions.

- In addition to those performance reports pictured, performance reports related to the cost and revenue centers under each profit center would exist and flow up to the profit centers.

Responsibility accounting assigns managers responsibility for their segment's performance. But superiors should not misuse the system to erroneously find fault or place blame. Some variances are controllable, while others are not.

For example, managers have no control over the general economic conditions of the country that may reduce sales. Nor do they have control over droughts, floods, and frosts that increase the cost of the agricultural materials in their products. Likewise, they have little or no control over the cost of electricity and gas used to power plants and deliver products. Managers need to carefully consider the causes of large variances so that they can focus on improving those that are controllable, while developing strategies for minimizing the risk associated with uncontrollable variances.

Evaluation of Investment Centers

3 Calculate ROI, sales margin, and capital turnover

As discussed above, investment centers are typically large divisions of a company. The duties of an investment center manager are similar to those of a CEO of an entire company. Investment center managers are responsible for *both* generating profit *and* making the best use of the investment center's assets. For example, an investment center manager has the authority to decide how much inventory to hold, what types of investments to make, how aggressively to collect accounts receivable and whether to open new stores or close old ones. In this section, we'll look at the two performance measures most commonly used

---

[2] The various methods used to allocate centralized service expenses and other common fixed expenses are covered in more advanced cost accounting textbooks.

EXHIBIT 10-5 Organization-wide Performance Reports

PepsiCo
Performance Report for the Fiscal Year Ended 2015
(all figures in millions of dollars)

Division Operating Income	Actual	Budgeted	Variance		Variance %	
Frito-Lay North America	$ 4,304	$ 4,100	$ 204	F	5.0%	F
Quaker Foods North America	560	550	10	F	1.8%	F
Latin Americas Foods	(206)	50	256	U	512.0%	U
North America Beverages	2,785	2,770	15	F	0.5%	F
Europe Sub-Saharan Africa	1,081	1,100	19	U	1.7%	U
Asia, Middle East and North Africa	941	930	11	F	1.2%	F
Corporate, unallocated	(1,112)	(1,300)	188	F	14.5%	F
Total operating income	$ 8,353	$ 8,200	$ 153	F	1.9%	F

North America Beverages
Performance Report for the Fiscal Year Ended 2015
(all figures in millions of dollars)

Product Line Operating Income	Actual	Budgeted	Variance		Variance %	
Pepsi	$ 804	$ 800	$ 4	F	0.5%	F
Mountain Dew	434	440	6	U	1.4%	U
Gatorade	614	605	9	F	1.5%	F
Aquafina	331	325	6	F	1.8%	F
Tropicana	409	400	9	F	2.3%	F
Sierra Mist	62	75	13	U	17.3%	U
Other beverages	131	125	6	F	4.8%	F
Total division operating income	$ 2,785	$ 2,770	$ 15	F	0.5%	F

Tropicana
Performance Report for the Fiscal Year Ended 2015
(all figures in millions of dollars)

	Actual	Budgeted	Variance		Variance %	
Sales revenue	$ 4,314	$ 4,300	$ 14	F	0.3%	F
Less: Variable expenses	2,236	2,235	1	U	0.0%	U
Contribution margin	2,078	2,065	13	F	0.6%	F
Less: Direct fixed expenses	1,633	1,630	3	U	0.2%	U
Segment margin	445	435	10	F	2.3%	F
Less: Allocated common expenses	36	35	1	U	2.9%	U
Operating income	$ 409	$ 400	$ 9	F	2.3%	F

NOTE: All figures in this exhibit, except for the actual operating income of each division for 2015 are hypothetical and used strictly for teaching purposes.

to assess the performance of investment centers: (1) return on investment and (2) residual income. To do this, we'll first need some financial data.

Exhibit 10-6 shows actual 2015 data for two of PepsiCo's divisions.[3] Statement of Financial Accounting Standards Number 131 (SFAS 131) requires publicly traded companies to disclose this type of segment information in the footnotes to their financial statements.[4]

---

[3] PepsiCo Inc. 2015 10(K).

[4] SFAS 131, "Disclosures about Segments of an Enterprise and Related Information," June 1997, Financial Accounting Standards Board, Norwalk, CT.

EXHIBIT 10-6 Division Information for PepsiCo Inc.

2015 Division Data (All figures are in millions of dollars)	Operating Income	Assets	Sales Revenue
PepsiCo Americas Beverages ("Beverage").....	$2,785	$28,128	$20,618
Frito-Lay North America ("Snack")..............	$4,304	$5,375	$14,782

Exhibit 10-6 shows that the Frito-Lay North America division (henceforth referred to as the Snack division) is providing more profit to the company than is PepsiCo Americas Beverages division (henceforth referred to as the Beverage division). However, a simple comparison between the operating income of each division is misleading because it does not consider the size of each division. To adequately evaluate an investment center's financial performance, top managers assess each division's operating income *in relationship to its assets*. This relationship is typically evaluated by calculating the division's return on investment or residual income.

Return on Investment (ROI)

Return on investment (ROI) measures the amount of income an investment center earns relative to the size of its assets. Companies typically define ROI as follows:

$$ROI = \frac{\text{Operating income}}{\text{Total assets}}$$

Let's calculate the ROI for both the Snack division and the Beverage division, using the income and assets of each division found in Exhibit 10-6:

$$\text{Beverage Division ROI} = \frac{\$2,785}{\$28,128} = 9.9\% \text{ (rounded)}$$

$$\text{Snack Division ROI} = \frac{\$4,304}{\$5,375} = 80.1\% \text{ (rounded)}$$

The resulting ROI indicates that the Snack division is generating much more income for every dollar of its assets than is the Beverage division:

- The Beverage division earns nearly $0.10 on every $1.00 of assets.
- The Snack division earns just over $0.80 on every $1.00 of assets.

Why is this important?

"**ROI** is one of the most commonly used **performance** metrics. It allows management to view profitability in **relation** to the size of the **investment**. Just like with your own personal investments, the **higher** the return, the **better**."

If you had $1,000 to invest, would you rather invest it in the Beverage division or the Snack division? Management would much rather have a 80% return on its investment than a 10% return. When top management decides how to invest excess funds, they often consider each division's ROI. A division with a higher ROI is more likely to receive extra funds because it has a track record of providing a higher return with the investment. However, perhaps management feels that operations could be improved in a weaker division by investing in new technology, plants, and equipment. Thus, the division with a weaker ROI may also receive an infusion of capital.

In addition to comparing ROI across divisions, management also compares a division's ROI across time to determine whether the division is becoming more or less profitable. For example, Exhibit 10-7 shows the actual ROI of the two divisions over the past five years.

EXHIBIT 10-7 Actual Division ROI over Time (rounded)

ROI (rounded)	2015	2014	2013	2012	2011
Beverage	10%	8%	9%	10%	11%
Snack	80%	76%	73%	68%	67%

The ROI of the Snack division has been trending upward over the last five years, showing just how profitable this division is to PepsiCo. However, the Beverage division's ROI has been relatively constant over the past five years. As with variances, management will investigate significant changes in ROI.

In addition to benchmarking ROI over time, management often benchmarks divisional ROI with other companies in the same industry to determine how each division is performing compared to its competitors. For example, PepsiCo may benchmark its ROI against that of the Coca-Cola Company.

Sales Margin and Capital Turnover

To determine what is driving a division's ROI, management often restates the ROI equation in its expanded form:

$$\text{ROI} = \frac{\text{Operating income}}{\text{Sales}} \times \frac{\text{Sales}}{\text{Total assets}} = \frac{\text{Operating income}}{\text{Total assets}}$$

Notice that sales, or sales revenue, is incorporated in the denominator of the first term and in the numerator of the second term. When the two terms are multiplied together, sales revenue cancels out, leaving the original ROI formula.

Why do managers rewrite the ROI formula this way? Because it helps them better understand how they can improve their ROI. The first term in the expanded equation is the **sales margin**, which focuses on profitability by showing how much operating income the division earns on every $1 of sales revenue. Sales margin is defined as:

$$\text{Sales margin} = \frac{\text{Operating income}}{\text{Sales}}$$

Let's calculate each division's sales margin using the information in Exhibit 10-6:

$$\text{Beverage Division Sales Margin} = \frac{\$2,785}{\$20,618} = 13.5\% \text{ (rounded)}$$

$$\text{Snack Division Sales Margin} = \frac{\$4,304}{\$14,782} = 29.1\% \text{ (rounded)}$$

The Beverage division is earning nearly $0.14 on every $1.00 of sales revenue, whereas the Snack division is earning about $0.29 on every $1.00 of sales revenue. Overall, the products in the Snack division are twice as profitable as the products in the Beverage division. To improve this statistic, the division manager needs to focus on cutting costs so that more operating income can be earned for every dollar of sales revenue. However, they'll need to be careful in cutting costs, so as not to jeopardize the long-term success of the division.

Next, let's consider each division's **capital turnover**, which focuses on how efficiently the division uses its assets to generate sales revenue. Capital turnover is defined as:

$$\text{Capital turnover} = \frac{\text{Sales}}{\text{Total assets}}$$

Let's calculate each division's capital turnover using the information from Exhibit 10-6:

$$\text{Beverage Division Capital Turnover} = \frac{\$20,618}{\$28,128} = 0.73 \text{ (rounded)}$$

$$\text{Snack Division Capital Turnover} = \frac{\$14,782}{\$5,375} = 2.75 \text{ (rounded)}$$

The Beverage division has a capital turnover of 0.73, which means the division generates $0.73 of sales revenue with every $1 of assets. The Snack division generates $2.75 of sales revenue with every $1.00 of assets. The Snack division uses its assets more efficiently in generating sales than does the Beverage division. To improve this statistic, the Beverage division manager should try to reduce or eliminate nonproductive assets—for example, by collecting accounts receivables more aggressively or decreasing inventory levels.

As the following table shows, the Snack division's ROI is higher than that of the Beverage division because (1) the division is earning more profit on every dollar of sales *and* (2) the division is generating more sales revenue with every dollar of assets:

	Sales Margin	×	Capital Turnover	= ROI
Beverage	13.5%	×	0.73	= 9.9% (rounded)
Snack	29.1%	×	2.75	= 80.1% (rounded)

Residual Income (RI)

Rather than using ROI to evaluate the performance of their investment centers, many companies use the concept of residual income. Similar to ROI, the residual income calculation is based on both the division's operating income and its assets, thereby measuring the division's profitability with respect to the size of its assets. However, the residual income calculation incorporates one more important piece of information: management's target rate of return. The target rate of return is the minimum acceptable rate of return that top management expects a division to earn with its assets. Management's target rate of return is based on many factors. Some of these factors include:

- the risk level of the division's business
- interest rates
- investors' expectations
- return being earned by other divisions
- general economic conditions

As these factors change over time, management's target rate of return will also change.

Residual income (RI) determines whether the division has created any excess (or residual) income above and beyond management's expectations. Residual income is calculated as follows:

$$\text{RI} = \text{Operating income} - \text{Minimum acceptable income}$$

The minimum acceptable income is defined as top management's target rate of return multiplied by the division's total assets. Thus,

$$\text{RI} = \text{Operating income} - (\text{Target rate of return} \times \text{Total assets})$$

Notice in this equation that the RI compares the division's actual operating income with the minimum operating income that top management expects *given the size of the division's assets*. A positive RI means that the division's operating income exceeds top management's target rate of return. A negative RI means the division is not meeting the target rate of return.

Let's calculate the residual income for the Beverage division, assuming a 25% target rate of return.[5] Recall that all PepsiCo data were stated in millions.

$$\text{Beverage RI} = \$2,785 - (25\% \times \$28,128) = (\$4,247) \text{ million}$$

The Beverage division's RI is negative. This means that the division did not use its assets as effectively as top management expected, and it was therefore unable to achieve the minimum ROI of 25%. Recall that the Beverage division's ROI was approximately 10%.

Let's also calculate the RI for the Snack division:

$$\text{Snack division RI} = \$4,304 - (25\% \times \$5,375) = \$2,960 \text{ million}$$

The positive RI indicates that the Snack division exceeded top management's 25% target return expectations. The RI calculation also confirms what we learned about the Snack division's ROI. Recall that the Snack division's ROI was about 80%, which is higher than the targeted minimum of 25%.

Exhibit 10-8 summarizes the performance measures we have just discussed.

EXHIBIT 10-8 Summary of Investment Center Performance Measures

Performance Measure	Formula
ROI	$\text{ROI} = \dfrac{\text{Operating income}}{\text{Total assets}}$
Sales Margin	$\text{Sales margin} = \dfrac{\text{Operating income}}{\text{Sales}}$
Capital Turnover	$\text{Capital turnover} = \dfrac{\text{Sales}}{\text{Total assets}}$
Residual Income	$\text{RI} = \text{Operating income} - (\text{Target rate of return} \times \text{Total assets})$

Goal Congruence

Since the ROI calculation already shows managers whether or not the division has reached the target rate of return, why do some companies prefer using residual income rather than ROI? The answer is that residual income often leads to better goal congruence. For example, say a manager is considering investing in a new $100,000 piece of equipment that would provide $30,000 of annual income. Upper management would want the divisions to invest in this equipment because its return (30%) exceeds the target rate (25%). But what will the division managers do?

- If evaluated based on residual income, division managers will invest in the equipment because it will increase the division's residual income by $5,000 [= $30,000 − (25% × $100,000)].

- If evaluated based on ROI, the division manager's decision may depend on its current ROI. If the division's current ROI is *less than* 30%, the manager has an incentive to invest in the equipment in order to *increase* the division's overall ROI. However,

[5] Management's actual target rate of return is unknown; 25% is used simply for illustrative purposes.

if the division's current ROI is *greater than* 30%, investing in the equipment would *decrease* the division's ROI. In this case, the manager would probably *not* invest in the equipment.

Thus, residual income enhances goal congruence, whereas ROI may or may not.

> ## ▶ Try It!
>
> Quaker Foods North America is another one of PepsiCo's divisions. The division had assets of $966 million, operating income of $695 million, and sales revenue of $2,636 million.
>
> 1. Compute Quaker's ROI, sales margin, and capital turnover.
> 2. Compute Quaker's residual income, assuming the minimum acceptable rate of return is 25%.

Please see page 652 for solutions.

Measurement Issues

The ROI and RI calculations appear to be very straightforward; however, management must come to some decisions before these calculations can be made. Most of these decisions involve how to measure the assets used in the ROI and RI calculations.

- **Which balance sheet date should we use?** Because total assets will differ between the beginning of the period and the end of the period, companies must choose a particular point in time for measuring assets. In the PepsiCo example, we chose to use total assets at the *end* of the year. Some companies use the average of the beginning of the year and the end of the year.

- **Should we include all assets?** Management must also decide if it wants to include *all* assets in the total asset figure. Many companies with retail locations are continually buying land on which to build future retail outlets. Until those stores are built and opened, the land (including any construction in progress) is a nonproductive asset, which is not generating any operating income. Including nonproductive assets in the total asset figure will drive down ROI and RI. Therefore, some firms do not include nonproductive assets in these calculations.

- **Should we use the gross book value or net book value of the assets?** The <u>gross book value</u> is the historical cost of the assets. The <u>net book value</u> is the historical cost of the assets *less* accumulated depreciation. Using the net book value of assets has a definite drawback. Because of depreciation, the net book value of assets continues to decrease over time until the assets are fully depreciated. As a result, ROI and RI get *larger over time simply because of depreciation* rather than from actual improvements in operations.

  In general, calculating ROI based on the net book value of assets gives managers an incentive to continue using old, outdated equipment because the net book value of the asset keeps decreasing. However, top management may want the division to invest in new technology to create operational efficiency. The long-term effects of using outdated equipment may be devastating as competitors use new technology to produce cheaper products and sell at lower prices. Thus, to create goal congruence, some companies prefer calculating ROI based on the gross book value of assets or even based on the assets' current replacement cost, rather than the assets' net book value.

- **Should we make other adjustments to income or assets?** Some companies use a modified residual income calculation referred to as economic value added (EVA®). To arrive at EVA, managers make several adjustments to the way income and assets are measured in the residual income formula. For example, research and development expenses are often added back to income (not viewed as expenses), while total assets are usually reduced by the company's current liabilities. EVA calculations are covered in more advanced accounting and finance textbooks.

Limitations of Financial Performance Evaluation

One serious drawback of financial performance measures is their short-term focus. Companies usually prepare performance reports and calculate ROI and RI using a time frame of one year or less. Given the short time frame, division managers have an incentive to take actions that will lead to an immediate increase in these measures, even if such actions may not be in the company's long-term interest (such as cutting back on R&D or advertising).

Many potentially positive actions, however, may take longer than one year to generate income at the targeted level. Many product life cycles start slow, even incurring losses in the early stages, before generating profit. If managers are evaluated on short-term financial performance only, they may be hesitant to introduce new products that may take time to generate acceptable profits.

As a potential remedy, management can measure financial performance using a longer time horizon, such as three to five years. Extending the time frame gives segment managers the incentive to think long term rather than short term and make decisions that will positively impact the company over the next several years.

As discussed earlier in this book, many companies are incorporating the triple bottom line (people, planet, and profit) into their performance evaluation systems. The second half of this chapter describes how the inclusion of nonfinancial performance metrics, including environmental metrics, can give managers a more balanced view of the company's performance.

What Is Transfer Pricing?

In large, diversified companies, one division will often buy products or components from another division rather than from an outside supplier. For example, one division of General Electric may purchase some of the parts it needs to produce wind turbines from another division that makes those parts. The price charged for the internal sale of product between two different divisions of the same company is known as the **transfer price**.

4 Describe strategies and mechanisms for determining a transfer price

The transfer price becomes sales revenue for the selling division and a cost for the buying division. Therefore, the operating income, ROI, sales margin, and residual income of each division will be affected by the transfer price that is used. Setting a fair transfer price is often difficult since each division will want to maximize its own profits. The selling division will want the price to be as high as possible, while the buying division will want the price to be as low as possible.

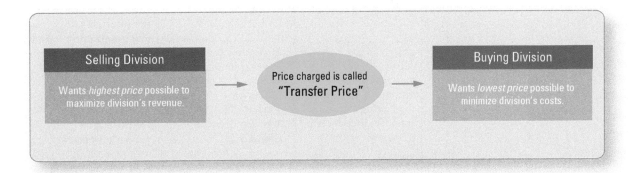

In selecting the transfer price, management's ultimate goal should be to optimize the company's *overall* profitability by encouraging a transfer to take place *only* if the company would benefit by the exchange. This benefit is usually a result of cost savings. For example, if excess capacity exists, the incremental cost of manufacturing additional product for an internal sale is the variable cost of production. Furthermore, the selling division can often avoid certain marketing or distribution costs on internal sales. **Vertical integration**, the practice of purchasing other companies within one's supply chain, is predicated on the notion that a company's profits can be maximized by owning one's supplier.

Strategies and Mechanisms for Determining a Transfer Price

The following strategies are often used to determine the transfer price.

1. **Market price:** If an outside market for the product exists, the market price is often viewed as the fairest price to use. The selling division will obtain the sales revenue it would have received on an outside sale, and the buying division will pay what it would have paid for product from an outside supplier. If the selling division can save on marketing or distribution costs, the market price could be reduced by all or a portion of the cost savings in arriving at the transfer price.

2. **Negotiated price:** Division managers negotiate until they reach agreement on a transfer price. The negotiated transfer price will usually be somewhere between the variable cost and the market price. The *lowest* acceptable price to the selling division will be the variable cost of producing and selling the product. Any lower price would result in a negative contribution margin to the selling division. The *highest* acceptable price to the buying division will be the market price. Any higher price would result in additional cost to the buying division. The disadvantage of this method is that negotiation takes time and effort, and may cause friction between company managers.

3. **Cost:** If no outside market for the product exists, then some definition of cost is often used to set the transfer price. As noted, variable cost would be the lowest fair price to use if excess capacity exists, whereas full absorption cost (including fixed manufacturing overhead) is also often viewed as a reasonable price. Additionally, a profit markup can be added to either definition of cost to arrive at a fair transfer price. The disadvantage of this method is that the selling division has no incentive to control costs since it will be reimbursed by the buying division for the costs it incurs.

These strategies are summarized in Exhibit 10-9.

> ## ■ Why is this important?
>
> "Each division's **profits** will be affected by the **transfer price** that is used. The **selling division** will want the price to be as **high** as possible, whereas the **buying division** will want it to be as **low** as possible."

EXHIBIT 10-9 Strategies for Determining Transfer Price

	Advantages	Disadvantages	Considerations
Market Price	Usually viewed as fair by both parties.	Can only be used if an outside market exists.	The market price could be reduced by any cost savings occurring from the internal sale (e.g., marketing costs).
Negotiated Price	Allows division managers to act autonomously rather than being dictated a transfer price by top management.	Takes time and effort. May lead to friction (or better understanding) between division managers.	Negotiated transfer price will generally fall in the range between: • Variable cost (low end) • Market price (high end)
Cost -or- Cost Plus a Markup	Useful if a market price is not available.	Selling division has no incentive to control costs. A "fair" markup may be difficult to determine.	Several definitions of cost could be used, ranging from variable cost to full absorption cost.

Let's try an example. Assume a division of GE produces a component used in the assembly of wind turbines. The division's manufacturing costs and variable selling expenses related to the component are as follows:

	Cost per Unit
Direct materials...	$500
Direct labor..	75
Variable manufacturing overhead	100
Fixed manufacturing overhead (at current production level)......................	150
Variable selling expenses (only incurred on sales to outside customers).....................	80

A different division of GE is just beginning to get into the turbine assembly business and is interested in purchasing the component in-house rather than buying it from an outside supplier. The production division has sufficient excess capacity with which to make the extra components. Because of competition, the market price for this component is $1,000 regardless of whether the component is produced by GE or another company.

1. **What is the highest, and possibly fairest, acceptable transfer price?** The highest acceptable transfer price is the market price of $1,000. Many would say that this is also the fairest price because the selling division would receive, and the buying division would pay, what it normally would on the open market for the component.

2. **Assuming the transfer price is negotiated between the divisions, what would be the lowest acceptable transfer price?** Because there is excess capacity, fixed costs would not increase as a result of the additional production volume; therefore, fixed costs become irrelevant. The lowest acceptable price would be the variable costs incurred by the selling division for making the component and selling it in-house. The variable manufacturing costs (direct materials, direct labor, and variable manufacturing overhead) add up to $675. In this particular case, the $80 of variable selling expense would *not* be considered because it is only incurred on sales to outside customers. Thus, the lowest acceptable transfer price would be $675. A transfer price lower than $675 would result in a negative contribution margin, which would result in a loss to the selling division. If the $80 of variable selling expense would be incurred regardless of whether the sale was made in-house or to an outside customer, then the lowest acceptable transfer price would be $755 (= $675 + $80).

3. **If GE's policy requires all in-house transfers to occur at full absorption cost plus 10%, what transfer price would be used? Assume that the increased production level needed to fill the transfer would result in fixed manufacturing overhead (MOH) decreasing by $25 per unit.** The full absorption cost includes all manufacturing costs (direct materials, direct labor, variable MOH, and fixed MOH). After ramping up production to fill this in-house order, the fixed MOH per unit would be $125 (= $150 − $25). Thus, the full absorption cost would be $800 (= $500 + $75 + $100 + $125). The transfer price would be $880, which is 10% over the full absorption cost [= $800 + (10% × $800)].

Global Considerations

In addition to these strategies for setting the transfer price, management should consider the following factors if the divisions operate in different areas of the globe:

- Do the divisions operate under different taxing authorities such that income tax rates are higher for one division than the other?

- Would the amount paid for customs and duties be impacted by the transfer price?

If either of these situations exists, then management will want to carefully craft the transfer price to avoid as much income tax, customs, and duties as legally possible.

Keep in mind that internal sales should be encouraged only if the company, overall, would profit by the exchange taking place. This additional profit is usually the result of cost savings that occur from producing the product internally rather than buying it on the open market. Any transfer price selected is simply a mechanism for dividing this additional profit between the selling and the buying divisions.

Decision Guidelines

Performance Evaluation

Let's consider some issues regarding performance evaluation.

Decision	Guidelines
How do companies decentralize?	Managers determine the type of segmentation that best suits the company's strategy. Companies often decentralize by geographic area, product line, distribution channel, customer base, or business function.
What should managers be held responsible for?	**Cost center:** Manager is responsible for costs. **Revenue center:** Manager is responsible for revenues. **Profit center:** Manager is responsible for both revenues and costs and, therefore, profits. **Investment center:** Manager is responsible for revenues, costs, and the efficient use of the assets invested in the division.
How should upper management evaluate the performance of the responsibility centers and their managers?	Actual performance should be compared with the budget. Using management by exception, any large variances should be investigated, with an emphasis on uncovering information rather than placing blame.
How are variances interpreted?	Favorable (F) variances increase income from what was budgeted, while Unfavorable (U) variances decrease income. Favorable cost variances are not necessarily "good," and unfavorable cost variances are not necessarily "bad."
What is a segment margin?	A segment margin is the operating income achieved by the segment *before* subtracting any common fixed costs that have been allocated to the segment.
What additional measures are used to evaluate investment centers?	ROI and residual income—both performance measures evaluate the division in terms of how profitable the division is relative to the size of its assets.
How is ROI calculated?	$$\text{ROI} = \frac{\text{Operating income}}{\text{Total assets}}$$ ROI can also be calculated as: $$\text{Sales margin} \times \text{Capital turnover}$$
How is sales margin calculated?	$$\text{Sales margin} = \frac{\text{Operating income}}{\text{Sales}}$$ The sales margin tells managers how much operating income is earned on every \$1 of sales revenue.
How is capital turnover calculated?	$$\text{Capital turnover} = \frac{\text{Sales}}{\text{Total assets}}$$ The capital turnover tells managers how much sales revenue is generated for every \$1 of assets invested in the division.
How is residual income calculated?	$$\text{RI} = \text{Operating income} - (\text{Target rate of return} \times \text{Total assets})$$ If residual income is positive, it means the division has earned income in excess of upper management's target rate of return. If it is negative, then the division has not met management's expectations.
What is a transfer price, and how is it determined?	A transfer price is the price charged between divisions for the internal sale of a product. The transfer price is often based on the following: • Market price of product • Negotiated price (usually between variable cost and market price) • Cost (variable or absorption) or cost plus a markup

SUMMARY PROBLEM 1

The following table contains actual segment data for two of PepsiCo's geographic divisions: (1) Europe and Sub-Saharan Africa (ESSA) and (2) Asia, Middle East, and North Africa (AMENA).

2015 Data (All figures are in millions of dollars)	Operating Income	Assets	Sales Revenue
Europe, Sub-Saharan Africa (ESSA)	$1,081	$12,225	$10,510
Asia, Middle East, North Africa (AMENA)	$941	$5,901	$6,375

Requirements

1. Compute each division's ROI.
2. Compute each division's sales margin.
3. Compute each division's capital turnover.
4. Comment on the results of the preceding calculations.
5. Compute each division's residual income, assuming upper management desires a 25% minimum rate of return.
6. How does the ROI of these two divisions compare to that of the two divisions, Beverages and Snacks, discussed in the chapter?

▪ SOLUTIONS

1. ROI

$$\text{ESSA ROI} = \frac{\$1,081}{\$12,225} = 8.8\% \text{ (rounded)}$$

$$\text{AMENA ROI} = \frac{\$941}{\$5,901} = 15.9\% \text{ (rounded)}$$

2. Sales Margin

$$\text{ESSA sales margin} = \frac{\$1,081}{\$10,510} = 10.3\% \text{ (rounded)}$$

$$\text{AMENA sales margin} = \frac{\$941}{\$6,375} = 14.8\% \text{ (rounded)}$$

3. Capital Turnover

$$\text{ESSA capital turnover} = \frac{\$10,510}{\$12,225} = 0.86 \text{ (rounded)}$$

$$\text{AMENA capital turnover} = \frac{\$6,375}{\$5,901} = 1.08 \text{ (rounded)}$$

4. ESSA has a lower ROI (8.8%) than does AMENA (15.9%). The reason for AMENA's stronger performance lies both in its ability to generate more operating income on every dollar of sales, as shown by the sales margin (14.8% versus 10.3%), and its ability to generate more sales with its assets, as shown by the capital turnover rate (1.08 versus 0.86). To increase ROI, ESSA needs to concentrate on becoming more efficient with its assets in order to increase its capital turnover. At the same time, it needs to carefully cut costs, potentially through employing lean thinking, in order to increase its sales margin.

5. Residual Income

ESSA Residual income = $1,081 − (25% × $12,225) = ($1,975) million (rounded)

AMENA Residual income = $941 − (25% × $5,901) = ($534) million (rounded)

Assuming management's minimum acceptable rate of return is 25%, the negative residual income means that neither division is generating income at an acceptable level.

6. The ROI provided by ESSA (8.8%) and the ROI provided by AMENA (15.9%) are in the same range as the ROI provided by the Beverage division (9.9%) but are significantly lower than the ROI provided by the Snack division (80.1%).

How Do Managers Use Flexible Budgets to Evaluate Performance?

In the first part of this chapter, we looked at performance reports that compared actual costs with the original planning budget. There is nothing wrong with comparing actual results against the master planning budget, as we did in Exhibits 10-3, 10-4, and 10-5; many companies do so. However, managers can often gain better insights by comparing actual results against a **flexible budget**, which is a budget prepared for a different level of volume than the one originally anticipated.

To illustrate this concept, let's return to Tucson Tortilla, the company we used in Chapter 9 to illustrate budgeting. Exhibit 10-10 shows a performance report that compares actual results against the master planning budget for the month of January. The master budget figures are drawn from the sales budget (Exhibit 9-5), operating expenses budget (Exhibit 9-10), and the budgeted cost of goods sold (Exhibits 9-11 and 9-12), while the actual results were gathered from the company's general ledger. As discussed earlier in the chapter, performance reports are often shown in contribution margin format rather than in the traditional income statement format, although either format is acceptable.

5 Prepare and evaluate flexible budget performance reports

EXHIBIT 10-10 Master Budget Performance Report

	A	B	C	D	E	F	G
1		Tucson Tortilla					
2		Master Budget Performance Report					
3		For the Month Ended January 31					
4							
5		Actual	Master Budget	Master Budget Variance		Master Budget Variance %	
6	**Sales volume (number of cases sold)**	32,370	30,000	2,370	F	7.9%	F
7							
8	Sales revenue ($20 per case)	$ 653,874	$ 600,000	$ 53,874	F	9.0%	F
9	Less variable expenses:						
10	Cost of goods sold ($12.00 per case sold)	391,540	360,000	31,540	U	8.8%	U
11	Sales commission ($1.50 per case sold)	49,860	45,000	4,860	U	10.8%	U
12	Shipping expense ($2.00 per case sold)	62,180	60,000	2,180	U	3.6%	U
13	Bad debt expense (1% of credit sales)	6,270	4,800	1,470	U	30.6%	U
14	Contribution margin	$ 144,024	$ 130,200	$ 13,824	F	10.6%	F
15	Less fixed expenses:						
16	Salaries	23,000	20,000	3,000	U	15.0%	U
17	Office rent	4,000	4,000	0	F	0.0%	F
18	Depreciation	6,000	6,000	0	F	0.0%	F
19	Advertising	3,100	2,000	1,100	U	55.0%	U
20	Telephone and internet	980	1,000	20	F	2.0%	F
21	Operating income	$ 106,944	$ 97,200	$ 9,744	F	10.0%	F
22							

NOTE: The company expects 80% of sales will be made on credit terms. Cost of Goods Sold is treated as a variable cost here for the sake of simplicity. All individual manufacturing cost variances are discussed in Chapter 11.

The difference between the actual revenues and expenses and the master planning budget is known as a **master budget variance**. This variance is really the result of an "apples-to-oranges" comparison. Why is this the case? Notice how the comparison is made between actual results for the *actual volume* of cases sold (32,370 cases) and the budgeted revenues and costs for the *planning volume* (30,000). Of course, we would expect the actual revenues and variable expenses to be higher than budgeted simply because sales volume was 7.9% higher than budgeted. However, we wouldn't expect fixed costs to change as long as the actual volume was still within the company's current relevant range. But notice that actual fixed expenses were 0% to 55% higher than expected. Management will want to understand why these variances occurred.

To provide more of an "apples-to-apples" comparison, many companies compare actual results to a flexible budget prepared *for the actual sales volume achieved* (32,370 cases).

This flexible budget will be used strictly for evaluating performance. Notice the distinction between the purposes of the two budgets:

■ The original master budget for 30,000 cases was used for *planning purposes at the beginning of the period.*

■ The new flexible budget for 32,370 cases will be used for *performance evaluation purposes at the end of the period.*

In essence, the flexible budget is the budget managers *would have* prepared at the beginning of the period if they had a crystal ball telling them the correct volume (32,370 cases rather than 30,000 cases). The flexible budget allows managers to compare actual revenues and expenses with what they would have expected given the actual sales volume. By creating a flexible budget, managers will be able to determine the portion of the master budget variance that is due to unanticipated changes in *volume* and the portion of the master budget variance that is due to factors *other than volume.*

Creating a Flexible Budget Performance Report

To create a flexible budget like the one shown in Exhibit 10-11, managers simply use the actual sales volume (32,370 cases) and the original budget assumptions (shown in parentheses on each line). For example, the flexible budget shown in bold font in Exhibit 10-11 includes the following calculations:

■ Sales Revenue: 32,370 cases × $20 per case = $647,400

■ Cost of Goods Sold: 32,370 cases × $12 per case = $388,440

■ Sales Commission: 32,370 cases × $1.50 per case = $48,555

■ Shipping Expense: 32,370 cases × $2.00 per case = $64,740

■ Bad Debt Expense: $647,400 of flexible budget sales revenue × 80% credit sales × 1% = $5,179

■ Fixed Operating Expense: the same as originally budgeted, assuming the actual volume falls within the company's current relevant range for fixed costs.

> ■ **Why is this important?**
>
> "A **flexible** budget performance report allows management to make an **"apples-to-apples"** comparison between what **actually** happened and what would have been **budgeted** if management would have known, in advance, the **actual** sales **volume** for the period."

EXHIBIT 10-11 Flexible Budget Performance Report

	A	B	C	D	E	F	G	H
1			Tucson Tortilla					
2			Flexible Budget Performance Report					
3			For the Month Ended January 31					
4								
5		Actual	Flexible Budget Variance		Flexible Budget	Volume Variance		Master Budget
6	Sales volume (number of cases sold)	32,370			32,370			30,000
7								
8	Sales revenue ($20 per case)	$ 653,874			$ 647,400			$ 600,000
9	Less variable expenses:							
10	Cost of goods sold ($12.00 per case sold)	391,540			388,440			360,000
11	Sales commission ($1.50 per case sold)	49,860			48,555			45,000
12	Shipping expense ($2.00 per case sold)	62,180			64,740			60,000
13	Bad debt expense (1% of credit sales)	6,270			5,179			4,800
14	Contribution margin	$ 144,024			$ 140,486			$ 130,200
15	Less fixed expenses:							
16	Salaries	23,000			20,000			20,000
17	Office rent	4,000			4,000			4,000
18	Depreciation	6,000			6,000			6,000
19	Advertising	3,100			2,000			2,000
20	Telephone and internet	980			1,000			1,000
21	Operating income	$ 106,944			$ 107,486			$ 97,200
22								

NOTE: The company expects 80% of sales will be made on credit terms. Cost of Goods Sold is treated as a variable cost here for the sake of simplicity. All individual manufacturing cost variances are discussed in Chapter 11.

Notice how this performance report includes the same actual costs (on the left) and master budget figures (on the right) shown in Exhibit 10-10. The flexible budget is placed in the middle column of the performance report. Two columns flank the middle column: Flexible Budget Variance and Volume Variance.

Keep the following important rule of thumb in mind:

> The flexible budget shows what revenues and expenses should have been, given the actual sales volume. It is created using the original budget assumptions for variable costs per unit and fixed costs, but calculated using the *actual sales volume* rather than the planning sales volume.

Try It!

Sam operates his own summer lawn-mowing business using a truck and equipment used solely for business purposes. Sam budgets $10 per job for variable expenses (gas for his truck and equipment) and $500 per month for fixed expenses (insurance and lease payments). Sam expected to have 100 mowing jobs during the month of June but actually had 125.

How much should be reflected in the flexible budget for (1) variable expenses, (2) fixed expenses, and (3) total operating expenses?

Please see page 652 for solutions.

Volume Variance

The **volume variance** is the difference between the master budget and the flexible budget. Recall that the only difference between these two budgets is the *volume* of units on which they are based. They both use the *same* budget assumptions but a different volume. The master planning budget is based on 30,000 cases. The flexible budget is based on 32,370 cases. The volume variance arises *only* because the volume of cases actually sold differs from the volume originally anticipated in the master budget, hence the name *volume variance*. The volume variances are shown in blue ink in Exhibit 10-12.

EXHIBIT 10-12 Volume Variances

	A	Actual	Flexible Budget Variance	Flexible Budget	Volume Variance		Master Budget
1	Tucson Tortilla						
2	Flexible Budget Performance Report						
3	For the Month Ended January 31						
6	Sales volume (number of cases sold)	32,370		32,370	2,370	F	30,000
8	Sales revenue ($20 per case)	$ 653,874		$ 647,400	47,400	F $	600,000
9	Less variable expenses:						
10	Cost of goods sold ($12.00 per case sold)	391,540		388,440	28,440	U	360,000
11	Sales commission ($1.50 per case sold)	49,860		48,555	3,555	U	45,000
12	Shipping expense ($2.00 per case sold)	62,180		64,740	4,740	U	60,000
13	Bad debt expense (1% of credit sales)	6,270		5,179	379	U	4,800
14	Contribution margin	$ 144,024		$ 140,486	$ 10,286	F $	130,200
15	Less fixed expenses:						
16	Salaries	23,000		20,000	0	F	20,000
17	Office rent	4,000		4,000	0	F	4,000
18	Depreciation	6,000		6,000	0	F	6,000
19	Advertising	3,100		2,000	0	F	2,000
20	Telephone and internet	980		1,000	0	F	1,000
21	Operating income	$ 106,944		$ 107,486	$ 10,286	F $	97,200

NOTE: For determining whether the volume variance is favorable or unfavorable, keep in mind that the master budget was the original goal. Therefore, the flexible budget is evaluated against the master budget goal.

The volume variance represents the portion of the master budget variance in Exhibit 10-10 that management would expect considering that 2,370 more cases were sold than originally anticipated. For example, because of the increase in sales volume, the volume variance shows that

- sales revenue *should have been* $47,400 higher than originally budgeted, Cost of Goods Sold *should have been* $28,440 higher than originally budgeted (and so forth with the other variable expenses),
- Fixed expenses *should have had zero variance*, and
- operating income *should have been* $10,286 higher than originally budgeted.

However, the master budget variance in Exhibit 10-10 revealed that

- sales revenue was *actually* $53,874 higher than budgeted, rather than $47,400 higher,
- Cost of Goods Sold was *actually* $31,540 higher than budgeted, rather than $28,440 higher (and so forth with the other variable expenses),
- some of the fixed costs were *actually* higher than budgeted, and
- operating income was *actually* $9,744 higher than budgeted rather than $10, 286 higher.

So, why were actual revenues and expenses still higher than they should have been, even considering the increase in number of cases sold? The answers can be found in the flexible budget variance.

Flexible Budget Variance

The **flexible budget variance** is the difference between the flexible budget and actual results. The flexible budget variances are shown in dark orange ink in Exhibit 10-13.

EXHIBIT 10-13 Flexible Budget Variances and Volume Variances

	A	Actual	Flexible Budget Variance		Flexible Budget	Volume Variance		Master Budget
1			Tucson Tortilla					
2			Flexible Budget Performance Report					
3			For the Month Ended January 31					
4								
5								
6	**Sales volume (number of cases sold)**	32,370			32,370	2,370	F	30,000
7								
8	Sales revenue ($20 per case)	$ 653,874	$ 6,474	F	$ 647,400	47,400	F	$ 600,000
9	Less variable expenses:							
10	Cost of goods sold ($12.00 per case sold)	391,540	3,100	U	388,440	28,440	U	360,000
11	Sales commission ($1.50 per case sold)	49,860	1,305	U	48,555	3,555	U	45,000
12	Shipping expense ($2.00 per case sold)	62,180	2,560	F	64,740	4,740	U	60,000
13	Bad debt expense (1% of credit sales)	6,270	1,091	U	5,179	379	U	4,800
14	Contribution margin	$ 144,024	$ 3,538	F	$ 140,486	10,286	F	$ 130,200
15	Less fixed expenses:							
16	Salaries	23,000	3,000	U	20,000	0	F	20,000
17	Office rent	4,000	0	F	4,000	0	F	4,000
18	Depreciation	6,000	0	F	6,000	0	F	6,000
19	Advertising	3,100	1,100	U	2,000	0	F	2,000
20	Telephone and internet	980	20	F	1,000	0	F	1,000
21	Operating income	$ 106,944	$ 542	U	$ 107,486	10,286	F	$ 97,200
22								

Because all variances related to volume have already been accounted for through the volume variance, the flexible budget variance highlights *causes other than volume*. For example:

- The $6,474 F variance for sales revenue means that the cases were sold at an average price *higher* than $20 per case.
- The $3,100 U variance for Cost of Goods Sold means that the cases cost more to make than $12.00 per case (we'll delve into this deeper in Chapter 11).

- The $1,305 U variance for commission expense means that the commissions were paid at a rate *higher* than $1.50 per case.

- The $2,560 F variance for shipping expense means that the shipping costs were *lower* than $2.00 per case.

- The $1,091 U variance for bad debt expense means that either more than 80% of sales were made on credit or bad debts were expensed at a rate greater than 1%.

- The fixed costs variances mean that factors other than volume caused some fixed costs to be different from what was originally planned.

Underlying Causes of the Variances

Now that we have prepared a flexible budget performance report, it's easy to see how the master budget variance in Exhibit 10-10 can be viewed as a combination of two separate variances, (1) the volume variance and (2) the flexible budget variance. For example we can see how the $9,744 F master budget variance for operating income shown in Exhibit 10-10 was the result not only of higher volume, but also of other factors. In fact, Exhibit 10-13 shows that the higher volume should have resulted in $10,286 of additional operating income, but other factors increased a number of Tucson Tortilla's costs, preventing the company from realizing the full effect of the increased volume.

Exhibit 10-14 shows that the master budget variance can be a combination of *favorable* variances (as in Panel A), a combination of *unfavorable* variances (as in Panel B), or a combination of one favorable variance *and* one unfavorable variance (as in Panel C).

EXHIBIT 10-14 Master Budget Variance

Panel A: Sales Revenue Variances (two *favorable* variances)

Flexible Budget Variance (Exhibit 10-13) $6,474 F	Volume Variance (Exhibit 10-13) $47,400 F
Master Budget Variance (Exhibit 10-10) $53,874 F	

Panel B: Sales Commission Variances (two *unfavorable* variances)

Flexible Budget Variance (Exhibit 10-13) $1,305 U	Volume Variance (Exhibit 10-13) $3,555 U
Master Budget Variance (Exhibit 10-10) $4,860 U	

Panel C: Shipping Expense Variances (one *favorable* and one *unfavorable* variance)

Flexible Budget Variance (Exhibit 10-13) $2,560 F	Volume Variance (Exhibit 10-13) $4,740 U
Master Budget Variance (Exhibit 10-10) $2,180 U	

For example, in Panel C we see that the variances for Shipping Expenses consist of a *favorable* flexible budget variance ($2,560 F) and an *unfavorable* volume variance ($4,740 U). Together, these two variances *net* to an unfavorable master budget variance of $2,180 U. This example illustrates why it's important to separate the overall master budget variance into its two components. Only by separating the variances would a manager know that the shipping expenses were actually lower per case than anticipated but higher overall due to the volume of cases shipped.

Investigating Causes for the Variances

As discussed in the first half of the chapter, managers will use *management by exception* to determine which variances to investigate. Upper management will rely on the managers of each responsibility center to provide answers to their inquiries. At other times, upper management knows the reasons for the variances, yet needs the performance report to understand how their operational decisions affected the company's finances.

For example, let's assume that upper management decided to modify its sales strategy from the original plan found in the master budget. In an attempt to increase sales, upper management decided to

- spend more on advertising,
- increase the salaries of the sales staff,
- pay a higher sales commission per case, and
- ease credit terms so that more customers qualified for credit, rather than COD terms.

The unfavorable *flexible budget variances* for advertising, salaries, commissions, and bad debt expense shown in Exhibit 10-13 reflect these operational changes. However, the variances for sales revenue shown in Exhibit 10-13 also show the positive effect of these changes: the additional sales revenue was more than enough to offset the increased costs. Not only was extra sales volume generated, but sales were also made at a higher price per case than budgeted (as shown by the favorable flexible budget variance for sales revenue). Finally, as a result of the increased volume, management was able to negotiate a lower shipping cost per case, resulting in a favorable flexible budget variance for shipping. All in all, operating income was higher than originally planned, so management's strategy paid off.

Manufacturing Cost Variances

Manufacturing cost variances receive a great deal of attention from management. The flexible budget variance is often separated into more detailed variances to better illuminate why the variance occurred. For example, was the flexible budget variance for Cost of Goods Sold due to the direct materials, direct labor, or manufacturing overhead that went into making these products? Perhaps it was due to a combination of all three. Furthermore, did the variance result from using more of these manufacturing inputs than originally anticipated (for example, more direct labor hours) or because the price of the inputs changed (for example, a higher average wage rate for factory employees)? Chapter 11 is devoted to explaining how managers dig deeply into the manufacturing cost variances to better understand why they occur.

▶ Try It!

Sam operates his own summer lawn-mowing company using a truck and equipment dedicated solely to business operations. Complete the flexible budget performance report below to answer the following questions:

1. What is the volume variance for total operating expenses? Favorable or unfavorable?
2. What is the flexible budget variance for total operating expenses? Favorable or unfavorable?
3. What is the master budget variance for total operating expenses? Favorable or unfavorable?

	A	B	C	D	E	F	G	H
1	**Sam's Mowing Business** **Flexible Budget Performance Report for June**	**Actual**	**Flexible Budget Variance**		**Flexible Budget**	**Volume Variance**		**Master Budget**
2	Sales volume (number of mowing jobs)	125			125			100
3								
4	Operating expenses:							
5	Variable operating expenses ($10 per job)	$ 1,370			$ 1,250			$ 1,000
6	Fixed operating expenses ($500 per month)	475			500			500
7	Total operating expenses	$ 1,845			$ 1,750			$ 1,500
8								

Please see page 652 for solutions.

How Do Companies Incorporate Nonfinancial Performance Measurement?

In the past, performance evaluation systems revolved almost entirely around *financial* performance. On the one hand, this focus makes sense because one of the primary goals of any company, even those companies that adhere to the notion of a triple bottom line (profit, people, and planet), is to generate profit for its owners. On the other hand, *current* financial performance tends to reveal the results of *past* decisions and actions rather than indicate *future* performance of the company. As a result, financial performance measures are known as <u>lag indicators</u>. Management also needs <u>lead indicators</u>, which are performance measures that predict future performance.

6 Describe the balanced scorecard and identify KPIs for each perspective

> ### Why is this important?
>
> "Rather than **focusing** strictly on financial performance, the **balanced scorecard** includes **operational** performance measures that give managers a **holistic** view of the company's **performance.**"

The Balanced Scorecard

In the early 1990s, Robert Kaplan and David Norton introduced the <u>balanced scorecard</u>.[6] The balanced scorecard recognizes that management must consider *both* financial performance measures *and* operational performance measures when judging the performance of a company and its segments. These measures should be linked with the company's goals and its strategy for achieving those goals. The balanced scorecard represents a major shift in corporate performance measurement: Financial indicators are no longer the sole measure of performance; they are now only *one* measure among a broader set of performance measures. Keeping score of operational performance measures *and* traditional financial performance measures gives management a "balanced," comprehensive view of the organization.

The Four Perspectives of the Balanced Scorecard

The balanced scorecard views the company from four different perspectives, each of which evaluates a specific aspect of organizational performance:

1. Financial perspective
2. Customer perspective
3. Internal business perspective
4. Learning and growth perspective

Exhibit 10-15 on the next page illustrates how the company's strategy affects, and, in turn, is affected by all four perspectives. In addition, it shows the cause-and-effect relationship linking the four perspectives. Take a moment to look at it now.

Companies that adopt the balanced scorecard develop specific objectives they want to achieve within each of the four perspectives. These objectives are critical to the company's overall success. As shown in Exhibit 10-16, companies use <u>key performance indicators (KPIs)</u>, which are summary performance metrics, to assess how well they are achieving their goals. For example, the company could use "*average customer satisfaction rating*" as a KPI to measure the company's ability to please customers. "*Number of warranty claims*" could be used to measure the company's ability to produce quality products.

KPIs are continually measured and are reported on a <u>performance scorecard</u> or performance dashboard, a report that allows managers to visually monitor and focus on managing the company's key activities and strategies as well as business risks. Performance dashboards are often updated in real time, using data from the company's ERP

---

[6] Robert Kaplan and David Norton, "The Balanced Scorecard—Measures That Drive Performance," *Harvard Business Review on Measuring Corporate Performance*, Boston, 1991, pp. 123–145; and Robert Kaplan and David Norton, *Translating Strategy into Action: The Balanced Scorecard*, Boston, Harvard Business School Press, 1996.

EXHIBIT 10-15 The Four Perspectives of the Balanced Scorecard

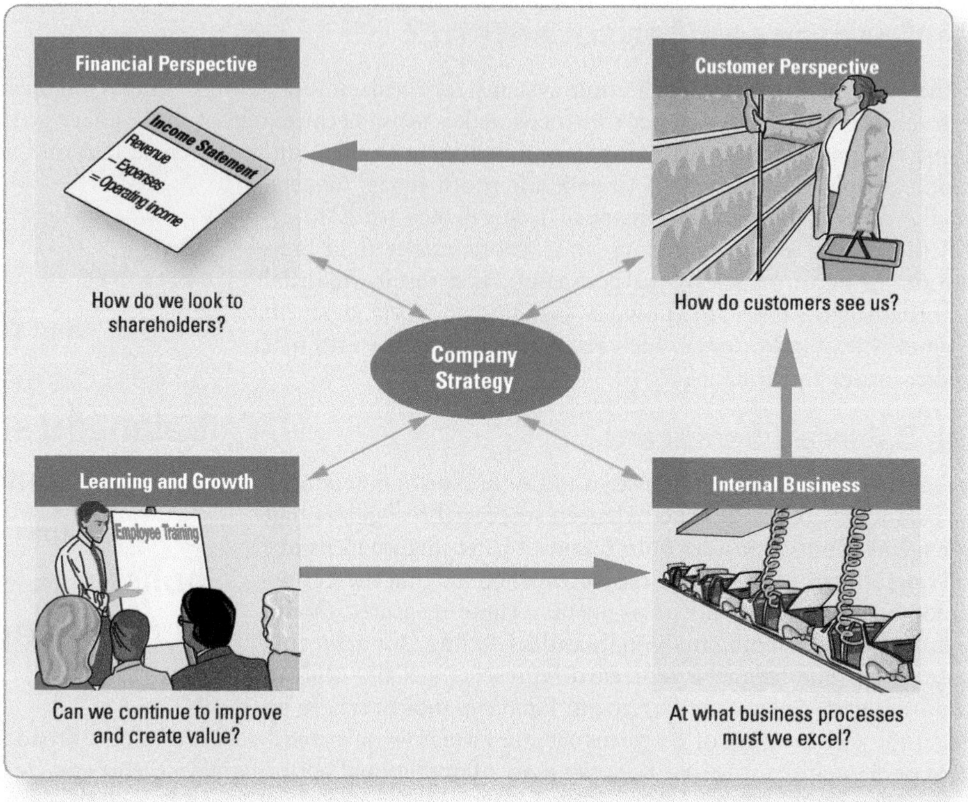

EXHIBIT 10-16 Linking Company Goals to Key Performance Indicators

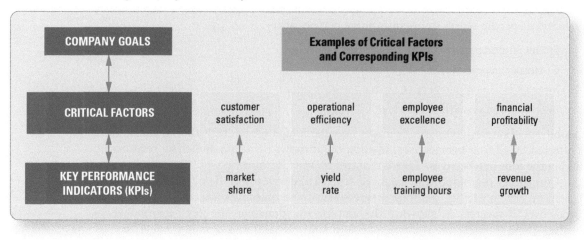

system.[7] Short-term and long-term targets for each KPI should also be displayed on the dashboard or scorecard so that managers can determine whether the company is improving and moving toward each objective, or whether new strategies need to be developed. To focus attention on the most critical elements to success and to prevent information overload, management should use only a few KPIs for each balanced scorecard perspective.

Let's now consider each of the perspectives and how they are linked together. We'll also present some of the more commonly used KPIs.

---

[7] http://www.forbes.com/sites/davelavinsky/2013/09/06/executive-dashboards-what-they-are-why-every-business-needs-one/#658ffc657568

Financial Perspective

The financial perspective helps managers answer the question, *"How do we look to share-holders?"* Shareholders are primarily concerned with the company's profitability. As shown in Exhibit 10-17, managers must continually attempt to increase profits through the following:

1. **increasing revenue:** introducing new products, gaining new customers, expanding into new markets
2. **controlling costs:** seeking to minimize costs without jeopardizing quality or long-run success, eliminating costs associated with wasteful activities
3. **increasing productivity:** using existing assets as efficiently as possible

Common KPIs: *sales revenue growth, sales margin, gross margin percentage, capital turnover, ROI, residual income, earnings per share*

EXHIBIT 10-17 Financial Perspective

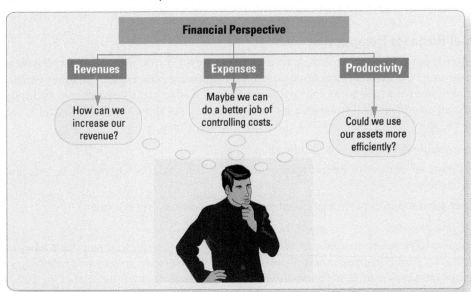

Customer Perspective

The customer perspective helps managers evaluate the question, *"How do customers see us?"* Customer satisfaction is a top priority for long-term success. If customers aren't happy, they won't come back. Therefore, customer satisfaction is critical for the company to achieve its financial goals.

As shown in Exhibit 10-18, customers are typically concerned with four product or service attributes:

1. **price:** the lower, the better
2. **quality:** the higher, the better
3. **sales service:** the importance of knowledgeable and helpful salespeople
4. **delivery time:** the shorter, the better

Common KPIs: *average customer satisfaction rating, percentage of market share, increase in the number of customers, number of repeat customers, rate of on-time deliveries.*

EXHIBIT 10-18 Customer Perspective

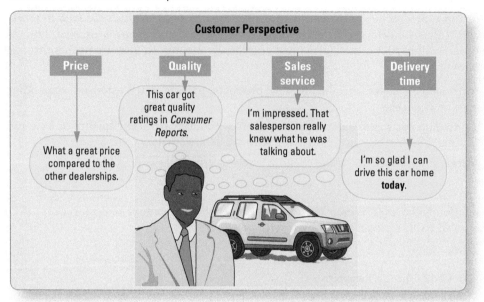

Internal Business Perspective

The internal business perspective helps managers address the question, *"At what business processes must we excel to satisfy customer and financial objectives?"* In other words, a company needs to tend to its internal operations if it is to please customers. And only by pleasing customers will it achieve its financial goals. As shown in Exhibit 10-19, the answer to that question incorporates the following three factors:

1. **innovation:** developing new products
2. **operations:** using lean operating techniques, as discussed in Chapter 4, to increase efficiency
3. **post-sales support:** providing excellent customer service after the sale

> **Common KPIs:** *number of new products developed, new product development time, defect rate, manufacturing lead time, yield rate, number of warranty claims received, average customer wait time for customer service, average repair time*

EXHIBIT 10-19 Internal Business Perspective

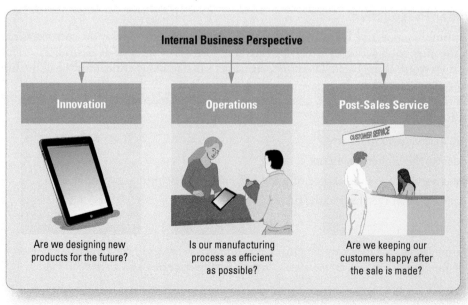

Learning and Growth Perspective

The learning and growth perspective helps managers assess the question, *"Can we continue to improve and create value?"* Much of a company's success boils down to its people. A company cannot be successful in the other perspectives (financial, customer, internal operations) if it does not have the right people in the right positions, a solid and ethical leadership team, and the information systems that employees need. Therefore, the learning and growth perspective lays the foundation needed for success in the other perspectives. As shown in Exhibit 10-20, the learning and growth perspective focuses on the following three factors:

1. **employee capabilities:** critical and creative thinkers, skilled, knowledgeable, and motivated

2. **information system capabilities:** a system that provides timely and accurate data

3. **the company's "climate for action":** the corporate culture supports communication, teamwork, change, and employee growth

Common KPIs: *hours of employee training, employee satisfaction, employee turnover, percentage of processes with real-time feedback, percentage of employees with access to real-time data, number of employee suggestions implemented, percentage of employees involved in problem solving teams, employee rating of communication and corporate culture*

EXHIBIT 10-20 Learning and Growth Perspective

Learning and Growth Perspective

Employee capabilities	Information system capabilities	Climate for action
Have we attracted and retained skilled employees?	Do we need to update our information system?	Employee morale is good, but we still could improve.

In summary, the balanced scorecard focuses on measuring those aspects of a company's operations that are critical to its success. By focusing on more than just financial metrics, it gives management a broader and more holistic view of the company's performance.

Sustainability and Performance Evaluation

Companies that embrace sustainability, like PepsiCo, incorporate sustainability-related KPIs in their performance evaluation system. Some companies will integrate sustainability-related KPIs into the four traditional balanced scorecard perspectives while others will include separate sustainability, community, or corporate responsibility sections.

For example, KPIs that fit into the four traditional perspectives might include the following:

- Financial perspective: *water cost, recycling revenues, waste-disposal costs*
- Customer perspective: *number of green products, percentage of products reclaimed after use*
- Internal Business perspective: *energy consumption, water consumption, greenhouse gas emissions*
- Learning and Growth perspective: *number of functions with environmental responsibilities, management attention to environmental issues*

Alternatively, companies may choose to add a "Sustainability" or "Community" perspective to their balanced scorecards. For example a community perspective might include the following KPIs:

- Community perspective: *percentage of profit donated to local schools and organizations, percentage of materials sourced locally, product safety ratings, number of hours devoted to local volunteering*

KPIs relating to sustainability and social responsibility should be objective and measurable, with both short-term and long-term targets specified. Baseline measurements should also be taken at the time the targets are adopted, so that managers can determine whether improvements are being made.

For example, PepsiCo's most recent corporate social responsibility report and the PepsiCo corporate website laid out a balanced scorecard approach to performance evaluation that focuses on all three aspects of the triple bottom line: people, planet, and profit. The performance perspectives used by PepsiCo, as well as some of their goals, include the following:

1. **Human Sustainability (people in society):** reduce the amount of saturated fat, sugar, and sodium in PepsiCo products; increase the amount of whole grains, nuts, seeds, and fruit in PepsiCo products; limit advertising directed at children to nutritional products; increase R&D of more affordable and nutritional products for lower-income markets

2. **Talent Sustainability (people in the company):** increase gender and racial diversity in workforce and management; reduce injury rate; increase workplace wellness programs; increase training and leadership development programs; support volunteerism and match employee charitable giving

3. **Environmental Sustainability:** improve water-use efficiency; reduce fuel and electricity use intensity, incorporate recycled PET (plastic) in containers; reduce the amount of material in packaging; reduce waste to landfill; reduce supply-chain greenhouse gas emissions; promote beverage container recycling programs; increase use of sustainable agricultural practices

4. **Financial Performance:** grow international revenues; increase operating profit; improve brand equity scores; increase market share; deliver high shareholder returns

5. **Responsible and Sustainable Sourcing:** increase use of minority- and women-owned vendors; increase use of suppliers that participate in the carbon disclosure project program

6. **Community and Philanthropy:** increase the gross dollar amount and percentage of operating income contributed through the Pepsi Foundation.

PepsiCo reports the KPIs used to evaluate these goals on its corporate website.

See Exercises E10-29A and E10-42B

Decision Guidelines

Performance Evaluation and the Balanced Scorecard

Decision	Guidelines
How can flexible budgets aid in performance evaluation?	There is nothing wrong with comparing actual results against the master planning budget. However, managers usually gain additional insights by comparing actual results against a flexible budget, which is a budget prepared for the actual volume achieved, rather than the volume originally used for planning purposes.
What is the master budget variance?	The master budget variance is the difference between the actual results and the master planning budget. This variance can be decomposed into two separate variances: (1) a volume variance and (2) a flexible budget variance, by first creating a flexible budget.
How is a flexible budget prepared?	A flexible budget is prepared by multiplying the budgeted revenue per unit and the budgeted variable cost per unit by the actual volume achieved. Since total fixed costs are not affected by changes in volume, they are the same on the flexible budget as they were on the original master budget. The flexible budget presents the revenues and expenses that management would have expected, given the actual volume achieved.
What is the volume variance?	The volume variance is the difference between the master planning budget and the flexible budget. It represents the portion of the master budget variance that was caused by actual volume being different than originally budgeted.
What is the flexible budget variance?	The flexible budget variance is the difference between actual costs and the flexible budget. It represents the portion of the master budget variance that was caused by factors *other than* volume differences.
Should the performance evaluation system include lag or lead measures?	Better performance evaluation systems include *both* lag and lead measures. Lag measures reveal the results of past actions, while lead measures predict future performance.
What are the four balanced scorecard perspectives?	1. Financial perspective 2. Customer perspective 3. Internal business perspective 4. Learning and growth perspective
How do companies include sustainability-related KPIs in their balanced scorecards?	Companies either include sustainability-related KPIs within each of the four perspectives, or they add separate perspectives for sustainability and/or corporate responsibility.

SUMMARY PROBLEM 2

Requirements

1. Each of the following describes a key performance indicator. Determine which of the balanced scorecard perspectives is being addressed (financial, customer, internal business, or learning and growth).
    a. Employee turnover
    b. Earnings per share
    c. Percentage of on-time deliveries
    d. Revenue growth rate
    e. Percentage of defects discovered during manufacturing
    f. Number of warranties claimed
    g. New product development time
    h. Number of repeat customers
    i. Number of employee suggestions implemented

2. Read the following company initiatives and determine which of the balanced scorecard perspectives is being addressed (financial, customer, internal business, or learning and growth).
    a. Purchasing efficient production equipment
    b. Providing employee training
    c. Updating retail store lighting to improve customer experience
    d. Paying quarterly dividends
    e. Updating the company's information system

▪ SOLUTIONS

Requirement 1
a. Learning and growth
b. Financial
c. Customer
d. Financial
e. Internal business
f. Internal business
g. Internal business
h. Customer
i. Learning and growth

Requirement 2
a. Internal business
b. Learning and growth
c. Customer
d. Financial
e. Learning and growth

END OF CHAPTER

Learning Objectives

- 1 Understand decentralization and describe different types of responsibility centers
- 2 Develop performance reports
- 3 Calculate ROI, sales margin, and capital turnover
- 4 Describe strategies and mechanisms for determining a transfer price
- 5 Prepare and evaluate flexible budget performance reports
- 6 Describe the balanced scorecard and identify KPIs for each perspective

Accounting Vocabulary

Balanced Scorecard. (p. 609) A performance evaluation system that integrates financial and operational performance measures along four perspectives: financial, customer, internal business, and learning and growth.

Capital Turnover. (p. 593) Sales revenue divided by total assets. The capital turnover shows how much sales revenue is generated with every $1.00 of assets.

Common Fixed Expenses. (p. 590) Fixed expenses that *cannot* be traced to the segment.

Cost Center. (p. 586) A responsibility center in which managers are responsible for controlling costs.

Decentralize. (p. 584) A process where companies split their operations into different operating segments.

Direct Fixed Expenses. (p. 590) Fixed expenses that can be traced to the segment.

Favorable Variance. (p. 588) A variance that causes operating income to be higher than budgeted.

Flexible Budget. (p. 603) A summarized budget prepared for different levels of volume.

Flexible Budget Variance. (p. 606) The difference between the flexible budget and actual results. The flexible budget variances are due to *something other than volume*.

Goal Congruence. (p. 585) When the goals of the segment managers align with the goals of top management.

Gross Book Value. (p. 596) Historical cost of assets.

Investment Center. (p. 586) A responsibility center in which managers are responsible for generating revenues, controlling costs, and efficiently managing the division's assets.

Key Performance Indicators (KPIs). (p. 609) Summary performance metrics used to assess how well a company is achieving its goals.

Lag Indicators. (p. 609) Performance indicators that reveal the results of past actions and decisions.

Lead Indicators. (p. 609) Performance measures that predict future performance.

Management by Exception. (p. 589) A management technique in which managers only investigate budget variances that are relatively large.

Master Budget Variance. (p. 603) The difference between actual results and the master budget.

Net Book Value. (p. 596) Historical cost of assets less accumulated depreciation.

Performance Reports. (p. 588) Reports that compare actual results against budgeted figures.

Performance Scorecard or Performance Dashboard. (p. 609) A report displaying the measurement of KPIs, as well as their short-term and long-term targets.

Profit Center. (p. 586) A responsibility center in which managers are responsible for both revenues and costs, and therefore profits.

Residual Income. (p. 594) Operating income minus the minimum acceptable operating income given the size of the division's assets.

Responsibility Accounting. (p. 585) A system for evaluating the performance of each responsibility center and its manager.

Responsibility Center. (p. 585) A part of an organization whose manager is accountable for planning and controlling certain activities.

Return on Investment (ROI). (p. 592) Operating income divided by total assets. The ROI measures the profitability of a division relative to the size of its assets.

Revenue Center. (p. 586) A responsibility center in which managers are responsible for generating revenue.

Sales Margin. (p. 593) Operating income divided by sales revenue. The sales margin shows how much income is generated for every $1.00 of sales.

Segment Margin. (p. 589) The operating income generated by a profit or investment center *before* subtracting the common fixed costs that have been allocated to the center.

Transfer Price. (p. 597) The price charged for the internal sale of product between two different divisions of the same company.

Unfavorable Variance. (p. 588) A variance that causes operating income to be lower than budgeted.

Variance. (p. 588) The difference between actual figures and budgeted figures.

Vertical Integration. (p. 597) The acquisition of companies within one's supply chain.

Volume Variance. (p. 605) The difference between the master budget and the flexible budget. The volume variance arises *only* because the actual sales volume differs from the volume originally anticipated in the master budget.

Quick Check

1. *(Learning Objective 1)* Companies often decentralize their operations by
   a. product line.
   b. customer base.
   c. geographic area.
   d. all of the above.

2. *(Learning Objective 1)* Which of the following is *not* an advantage of decentralization?
   a. Improved customer relations
   b. Use of expert knowledge
   c. Frees top management's time
   d. Achieving goal congruence

3. *(Learning Objective 1)* In terms of responsibility centers, a large corporate division would be considered a(n)
   a. cost center.
   b. revenue center.
   c. profit center.
   d. investment center.

4. *(Learning Objective 2)* Which of the following is true?
   a. Favorable variances should always be interpreted as "good news" for the company.
   b. Management by exception means that managers investigate all unfavorable variances but not all favorable variances.
   c. Favorable variances are variances that cause operating income to be higher than budgeted.
   d. Unfavorable variances should always be interpreted as "bad news" for the company.

5. *(Learning Objective 2)* A segment margin is the operating income generated by subtracting
   a. only direct fixed expenses from a segment's contribution margin.
   b. only common fixed expenses from a segment's contribution margin.
   c. all expenses from a segment's sales revenue.
   d. all fixed expenses from a segment's contribution margin.

6. *(Learning Objective 3)* Return on investment (ROI) can be restated as which of the following?
   a. Sales margin ÷ capital turnover
   b. Sales margin × capital turnover
   c. Residual income ÷ sales margin
   d. Residual income × sales margin

7. *(Learning Objective 4)* Which of the following is *not* a valid strategy for determining a transfer price?
   a. Using a negotiated price
   b. Using some definition of cost
   c. Using the price set by GAAP
   d. Using the market price

8. *(Learning Objective 5)* Which of the following is *false*?
   a. The volume variance is due to causes other than volume.
   b. The difference between actual results and the master budget is called the master budget variance.
   c. The master budget variance can be split into two components: a volume variance and a flexible budget variance.
   d. The flexible budget is prepared using the actual volume achieved during the period.

9. *(Learning Objective 6)* "Number of new products developed" would be a key performance indicator (KPI) for which of the four balanced scorecard perspectives?
   a. Customer
   b. Internal business
   c. Financial
   d. Learning and growth

10. *(Learning Objective 6)* "Hours of employee training" would be a key performance indicator (KPI) for which of the four balanced scorecard perspectives?
    a. Customer
    b. Internal business
    c. Financial
    d. Learning and growth

Quick Check Answers

1.d 2.d 3.d 4.c 5.a 6.b 7.c 8.a 9.b 10.d

Standard Costs and Variances

Learning Objectives

- **1** Explain how and why standard costs are developed
- **2** Compute and evaluate direct materials variances
- **3** Compute and evaluate direct labor variances
- **4** Explain the advantages and disadvantages of using standard costs and variances
- **5** Compute and evaluate variable overhead variances
- **6** Compute and evaluate fixed overhead variances
- **7** (Appendix) Record standard costing journal entries

PG Pictures/Alamy

Sources: Apple 2015 10-K
http://www.zdnet.com/article/apple-watch-costs-under-85-to-make/

Apple Inc. is well known for its innovative products such as the iPhone, iPad, and Apple Watch. But how much does it cost Apple to manufacture these products? Although Apple never releases its actual unit costs for each product, a market intelligence company by the name of IHS Technology has performed "tear-down" research to determine the cost of the direct materials in each product. For example, IHS estimates that the cost of direct materials in a 38 mm Apple Watch Sport includes $20.50 for the LG Display, $10.20 for the processor, $7.20 for the memory, $0.80 for the battery, $9.00 for the charger and spare wristband, and so forth. The total estimated cost of direct materials for an Apple Watch Sport is $83.70, purportedly giving the Apple Watch the lowest direct material cost compared to retail price ($300–$350) of any Apple product. What IHS Technology did was very similar to what many manufacturers do: They estimate how much it should cost, in terms of direct materials, direct labor, and manufacturing overhead, to produce their products. These estimates, known as standard costs, are used as performance benchmarks. They are also used by companies to prepare budgets, such as Apple's direct materials budget for the 169 million iPhones, 68 million iPads, and undisclosed number of Apple Watches sold during fiscal 2015.

In Chapter 9 we described how managers of Tucson Tortilla planned for the coming year by preparing a master budget. In Chapter 10, we saw how its managers could evaluate performance by comparing actual to budgeted revenues and costs. To gain a better understanding of the master budget variance, managers created a flexible budget to separate the master budget variance into two components: (1) a volume variance and (2) a flexible budget variance. In this chapter, we'll see how Tucson Tortilla's managers can deepen their analysis by further separating the flexible budget variance into two additional variances. To do this, we'll first need to discuss standard costs.

What Are Standard Costs?

1 Explain how and why standard costs are developed

Think of a **standard cost** as the budgeted cost for a single unit of product. For Tucson Tortilla, a single unit of product is one case of tortilla chips. A company that produces many different products will develop a standard cost for each different product. For example, Colgate-Palmolive will develop a standard cost for each type of toothpaste, soap, and laundry detergent it produces. Even service companies develop standard costs. For example, many hospitals develop standard costs for routine procedures, such as tonsillectomies. The standard cost becomes the benchmark for evaluating actual costs.

For example, let's say the standard cost of producing one case of tortilla chips is $12.00, yet the company actually incurred $12.10 to produce each case during July. The company's managers will want to know why the difference, or variance, of $0.10 per case occurred. Although $0.10 per case may not seem like much, it really is a lot when you consider that the company produces thousands of cases per month. High-volume companies like Coca-Cola, which sells 1.9 billion servings of product *each day*,[1] are eager to control every penny of cost associated with each unit of product. In highly competitive markets, the company will not be able to pass along cost increases to consumers in the form of price increases. That means that the company's profit margin will shrink with every additional penny of cost incurred. Managers' ability to understand the reasons behind cost variances is a critical factor in controlling future costs.

In our example, why did Tucson Tortilla spend more than anticipated? Perhaps the price of flour increased. Or perhaps more labor was needed than originally expected. Or extraordinarily hot weather could have driven up the cost of air conditioning used in manufacturing facility. As you can see, the variance in cost could have been due to direct materials, direct labor, manufacturing overhead, or any combination of the three. Managers will be able to understand the reasons for this unfavorable variance only by investigating further.

Types of Standards

When managers develop standard costs (often simply referred to as **standards**), they must first determine what type of standard they want to create. **Ideal standards** are standards based on perfect or ideal conditions. These types of standards, which are also known as **perfection standards**, do not allow for any poor-quality raw materials, waste in the production process, machine breakdown, or other inefficiencies. This type of standard is best suited for companies that strive for perfection, such as those that implement lean production systems described in Chapter 4.[2]

Rather than using ideal standards, many companies use **practical (or attainable) standards** that are based on currently attainable conditions. Practical standards include allowances for *normal* amounts of waste and inefficiency. Many managers believe that practical standards make the best cost benchmarks and provide the most employee motivation since they can be attained with a reasonable amount of effort.

---

[1] The Coca-Cola Company 2015 10-K.

[2] In fact, many lean producers do not advocate the use of standards at all. Since one of the primary goals of lean production is continuous improvement, advocates argue that no standard is ideal enough. Improvements can always be made.

■ Why is this important?

"Managers use **standard costs** as a **benchmark** against which to **evaluate** actual costs. If actual costs are **substantially different** than standard costs, **managers** will want to know why so that they have a basis for **improving operations**."

Information Used to Develop and Update Standards

Managers draw on many sources of information when setting standards. They consider the amount of material and labor used on each unit produced in the *past*. They also consider the *current* cost of inputs, such as negotiated labor rates and raw materials prices. Finally, they estimate how *future* changes in the economy or in the manufacturing process might affect the standards being developed. Engineering studies help determine the amount of time and quantity of material that *should be* needed to produce each unit.

In order to serve as realistic benchmarks, standards, once developed, need to be kept up to date. Standards should be reviewed at least once a year, and they should be adjusted whenever a long-term change in costs or inputs is anticipated. For example, standards should be adjusted when:

- a new labor contract is negotiated with union workers,
- a non-temporary change in raw material costs occurs, or
- a part of the production process is reengineered.

Using outdated standards defeats the entire purpose of using standards in the first place.

Computing Standard Costs

Manufacturers typically prepare standard costs for the direct material, direct labor, and manufacturing overhead required for each unit of product. With respect to manufacturing overhead (MOH), some manufacturers only set standards for the variable MOH per unit since the fixed MOH per unit will fluctuate with changes in volume. Many companies also prepare standards for operating expenses. For simplicity, we'll limit our discussion to the three manufacturing costs. We will also assume that Tucson Tortilla has decided to develop practical, rather than ideal, standards.

Standard Cost of Direct Materials

In Chapter 9, we learned that Tucson Tortilla's only direct material (DM) is *masa harina* corn flour. Engineering studies show that each case of chips requires five pounds of flour, including allowances for normal amounts of spoilage and waste. The company can purchase the flour, including freight-in and purchase discounts, for $1.50 per pound. Therefore, the standard DM cost per case of tortilla chips is calculated as follows:

Standard Quantity of DM	×	Standard Price of DM	=	Standard Cost of DM per Case
5 lbs	×	$1.50/pound	=	$7.50

This calculation reveals that Tucson Tortilla expects to spend $7.50 on the direct materials for each case of tortilla chips produced.

Standard Cost of Direct Labor

Companies compute the standard cost of direct labor (DL) in a similar fashion. In Chapter 9, we learned that each case of tortilla chips requires only 0.05 hours of direct labor. This time requirement includes allowances for cleanup, breaks, and so forth since employees are paid for that time as well as actual work time. Furthermore, direct laborers are paid $22 per hour, including payroll taxes and employee benefits. Therefore, the standard DL cost per case of tortilla chips is:

Standard Quantity of DL	×	Standard Price of DL	=	Standard Cost of DL per Case
0.05 DL hours	×	$22.00/DL hour	=	$1.10

Since the production process is fairly automated, the company only anticipates spending $1.10 of direct labor on each case.

Standard Cost of Manufacturing Overhead

Since most of Tucson Tortilla's production process is automated, the company allocates its manufacturing overhead (MOH) using machine hours (MH) as its allocation base. Engineering studies indicate that each case of chips requires 0.10 machine hours to produce. In Chapter 9, we learned that the company expects to produce 400,000 cases of chips during the year. Therefore, the total allocation base is 40,000 machine hours.

Rather than using one predetermined overhead rate as discussed in Chapter 3, some manufacturers split their manufacturing overhead into two rates: a fixed MOH rate and a variable MOH rate. Let's see how this is done.

At a volume of 400,000 cases, Tucson Tortilla expects total variable overhead to be $1,000,000. Using this information, Tucson Tortilla calculates its predetermined *variable* MOH rate as follows:

Total estimated variable MOH	÷	Total estimated amount of the allocation base	=	Variable MOH rate
$1,000,000	÷	40,000 machine hours	=	$25/machine hour

Using the variable MOH rate, Tucson Tortilla can compute the standard cost of variable manufacturing overhead per case as follows:

Standard Quantity of MH	×	Variable MOH rate	=	Standard Variable MOH per Case
0.10 machine hours	×	$25/machine hour	=	$2.50

In Chapter 9, we learned that the company expects to incur $30,000 of fixed overhead each month, resulting in a total of $360,000 for the year. Therefore, the fixed MOH rate can be calculated as follows:

Total estimated fixed MOH	÷	Total estimated amount of the allocation base	=	Fixed MOH rate
$360,000	÷	40,000 machine hours	=	$9/machine hour

The standard cost of *fixed* manufacturing overhead *per case* is calculated as follows:

Standard Quantity of MH	×	Fixed MOH rate	=	Standard Fixed MOH per Case
0.10 machine hours	×	$9/machine hour	=	$0.90

Standard Cost of One Unit

Exhibit 11-1 shows how Tucson Tortilla adds together the standard cost of direct materials, direct labor, and manufacturing overhead to determine the standard cost of producing one case of tortilla chips.

EXHIBIT 11-1 Standard Cost of Producing One Unit of Product

	A	B	C	D	E	F	G	H
1	Manufacturing Cost	Standard Quantity (SQ)			Standard Price (SP)			Standard Cost per Case
2	Direct Materials	5.00	pounds	×	$ 1.50	per pound	=	$ 7.50
3	Direct Labor	0.05	DL hours	×	$ 22.00	per DL hour	=	1.10
4	Variable MOH	0.10	machine hours	×	$ 25.00	per machine hour	=	2.50
5	Fixed MOH	0.10	machine hours	×	$ 9.00	per machine hour	=	0.90
6	Total							$ 12.00
7								

The $12-per-case figure shown in Exhibit 11-1 may look familiar to you. Indeed, it is the same budgeted unit cost that we used in Chapter 9 when we calculated Cost of Goods Sold for the budgeted Income Statement (Exhibit 9-12) used for planning purposes. We also used the $12-per-case standard cost when we calculated Cost of Goods Sold for the flexible budget used for performance evaluation purposes (Exhibit 10-10). Although we presented the budgeting chapter prior to this chapter, most companies develop standard costs *first* and *then* use that information to help develop their budgets. Standard costs ease the budgeting process by providing a basis for calculating many figures in the master budget.

Sustainability and Standards

Many companies are reengineering their products, packaging, and production processes to save environmental resources and money. For example, Apple's packaging on the iPhone 6s is 20% lighter and takes up 34% less volume than its predecessor. It also consists of 60% recycled fiber. The company also found that by focusing on the aluminum used in its iPhone enclosure, it could significantly reduce greenhouse gases. So the iPhone was reengineered to reintegrate more scrap aluminum from the production process. Whereas toxic materials, such as mercury, lead, and arsenic were once commonplace in consumer electronics and their manufacturing processes, these substances have been removed from all Apple products over the course of the last 10 years and substituted with other materials. Sustainability initiatives such as these require managers to rethink their direct materials quantity and price standards, as fewer materials and different types of materials are used.

Reengineering the production process may also result in changes to manufacturing overhead standards. For example, Apple just conducted 13 energy audits in its supplier plants in China, Taiwan, and Japan that resulted in identifying over $32 million in annual cost savings. The company is in the process of building solar arrays and investing in other clean energy projects in Asia that will reduce carbon emissions at manufacturing plants by the equivalent of taking 6 million cars off the road each year. Initiatives such as these will require management to amend existing manufacturing overhead standards.

Operating cost standards, such as the standard cost of distributing each product, will also change as the lighter products and smaller containers reduce trucking costs. The standard cost of selling each unit may also be affected by sustainability initiatives. For example 97% of all Apple retail stores and 100% of Apple data centers are now powered by 100% renewable energy. Companies may also find themselves creating standards for the amount of waste that leaves the production process in the form of air pollution, waste-to-landfill refuse, and waste water. Apple has the goal of zero-waste-to-landfill at all iPhone and Apple Watch final assembly plants by 2017, as well as all of its retail stores. It also measures corporate water use per employee and has been able to reduce that figure by 25% since 2013.

Finally, companies can create standards for operational measures that focus on the entire life cycle of the product, all the way from cradle to grave. Apple measures the environmental impact of consumer use and disposal of its products. As a result, Apple has reduced the amount of energy required to power its products by 64% from what it was less than 10 years ago, and through its "take-back" program, Apple collects and diverts products that consumers no long want. In 2015 alone, Apple recovered over 90 million pounds of e-waste. To recycle e-waste more efficiently, the company has developed a line of robots that can disassemble and sort the parts for an iPhone in only 11 seconds! The parts are sold as valuable commodities that decrease the need for mining and extraction of precious natural resources.

See Exercises E11-25A and E11-41B

Source: Apple Environmental Responsibility Report, 2016 Progress Report, covering fiscal 2015.

▶ **Try It!**

Hannah owns a fruit smoothie shop at the local mall. Each smoothie requires ¼ pound of mixed berries, which are expected to cost $4 per pound during the summer months. Shop employees are paid $10 per hour. Variable overhead consists of utilities and supplies. The variable overhead rate is $0.05 per minute of DL time. Each smoothie should require 3 minutes of DL time.

1. What is the standard cost of direct materials for each smoothie?
2. What is the standard cost of direct labor for each smoothie?
3. What is the standard cost of variable overhead for each smoothie?

Please see page 709 for solutions.

How Do Managers Use Standard Costs to Compute DM and DL Variances?

We just showed how managers develop standard costs. Managers use standards at the beginning of the period to help with the budgeting planning process. Managers also use standards at the end of the period to evaluate performance and help control future costs. Let's see how this is done.

Using Standard Costs to Develop the Flexible Budget

As we saw in the last chapter, managers often compare actual costs against a flexible budget, rather than directly against the planning budget. Recall that the flexible budget reflects the total cost that *should have been incurred, given the actual volume achieved*. In the last chapter, we created and evaluated the flexible budget performance report for the actual volume *sold* during the month of January. In this chapter, we are going to drill down farther into the company's operations, by evaluating the costs incurred to *produce* Tucson Tortilla's product.

For example, let's assume that Tucson Tortilla actually produced 31,000 cases of chips during the month of January, even though the company originally planned to produce 29,000 cases (Exhibit 9-6). Exhibit 11-2 shows the flexible budget for variable production costs. To generate the flexible budget, managers multiplied the standard costs per unit by the *actual number of units produced*. Notice the mixture of favorable and unfavorable flexible budget variances. We'll refer back to this exhibit quite often as we explore the reasons for these variances in the next sections.

EXHIBIT 11-2 Comparing Variable Production Costs with the Flexible Budget

	A	B	C	D	E	F
1	**Flexible Budget Performance Report for Variable Production Costs**	**Standard Cost per Case**	**Actual Cost for 31,000 cases**	**Flexible Budget for 31,000 Cases**	**Flexible Budget Variance**	
2	Direct materials	$ 7.50	$ 224,000	$ 232,500	$ 8,500	F
3	Direct labor	$ 1.10	$ 34,875	$ 34,100	$ 775	U
4	Variable MOH	$ 2.50	$ 85,200	$ 77,500	$ 7,700	U
5						

Direct Materials Variances

2 Compute and evaluate direct materials variances

From Exhibit 11-2 we know that Tucson Tortilla spent $8,500 less on direct materials (DM) than standards indicated would be spent to make 31,000 cases. Was this because the company *paid* less for the material than expected, *used* less material than expected, or a combination of the two?

When the amount of materials purchased is the same as the amount used (our example here), we can split the flexible budget variance for direct materials into two separate variances: a price variance and a quantity variance, as shown in Exhibit 11-3.

EXHIBIT 11-3 Splitting the Direct Material Flexible Budget Variance into Two Components

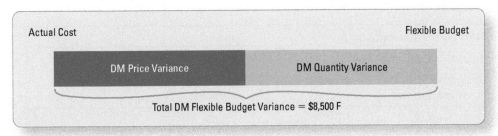

The way we do this is illustrated in Exhibit 11-4. In this model, notice that the company's actual costs are on the top-left side and are stated as Actual Quantity (AQ) × Actual Price (AP). The company's flexible budget is shown on the top-right side and is stated as the standard cost allowed *for the actual volume of output*. It is computed as the Standard Quantity Allowed (SQA) for the actual output × Standard Price (SP). As shown in the bottom box of the exhibit, the difference between the two outside terms is the total direct materials flexible budget variance, which we have shortened to "Total DM Variance" for the sake of simplicity.

EXHIBIT 11-4 Direct Materials Variances if DM Purchased Equals DM Used

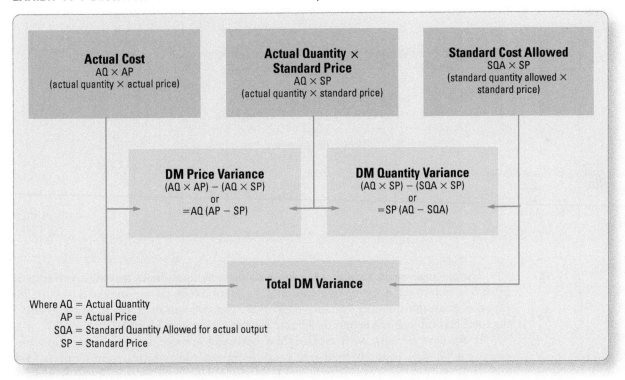

Next, we insert a middle term in the top row of the exhibit. The middle term is a mixture of the two outside terms and is defined as Actual Quantity (AQ) × Standard Price (SP). This middle term will help us separate the total flexible budget variance into two components: a price variance and a quantity variance.

The **direct materials price variance** tells managers how much of the total variance is due to paying a higher or lower price than expected for the direct materials it purchased. The **direct materials quantity variance** tells managers how much of the total variance is due to using a larger or smaller quantity of direct materials than expected. The formulas for these variances are shown in the middle row of Exhibit 11-4.

Let's see how this works for Tucson Tortilla. First, we'll need the following information:

Actual data for January:	
Number of cases produced....................	31,000 cases
Direct materials purchased....................	160,000 pounds at $1.40 per pound
Direct materials used............................	160,000 pounds

Next, we'll insert our company-specific data into the basic model, as shown in Exhibit 11-5. Notice how the "Actual Cost" of $224,000 is the same as what we showed in Exhibit 11-2. Also, the "Standard Cost Allowed" of $232,500 and the total favorable direct materials variance of $8,500 are the same as the figures shown in Exhibit 11-2.

EXHIBIT 11-5 Tucson Tortilla's Direct Materials Variances

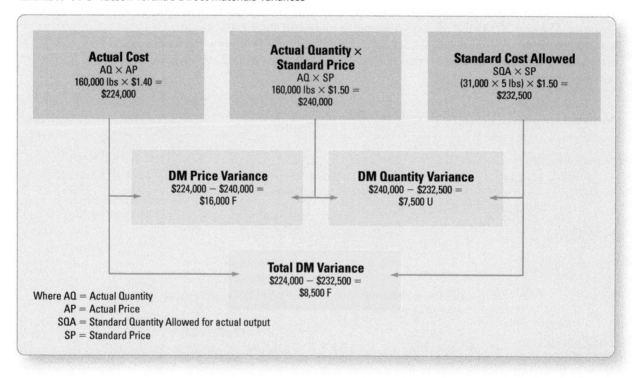

The calculations in Exhibit 11-5 show us that the total direct materials variance of $8,500 is in fact the result of two causes: (1) a favorable price variance of $16,000 and (2) an unfavorable quantity variance of $7,500. The two variances net together to equal the total favorable direct materials flexible budget variance of $8,500.

In the next sections, we'll explain these variances in more detail and show how formulas can be used as an alternative to creating the diagrams illustrated in Exhibits 11-4 and 11-5.

Direct Materials Price Variance

The direct materials price variance tells managers how much of the overall variance is due to paying a higher or lower price than expected for the quantity of materials it *purchased*. As you can see in Exhibit 11-4, the price variance is computed by comparing the company's actual costs on the left side of the model with the middle term in the model. The lavender boxes in the middle row show that we can simplify the calculations by factoring out the actual quantity (AQ) purchased from both terms in the model as follows:

$$\text{DM price variance} = (\text{AQ} \times \text{AP}) - (\text{AQ} \times \text{SP})$$
$$= \text{AQ} (\text{AP} - \text{SP})$$

The simplified equation should make sense: it simply calculates the price differential between what was paid for the direct material input (pounds of corn flour, in our case) and the price anticipated by the standards. The price differential is then multiplied by the quantity of direct materials *purchased*.

Since the amount of materials purchased may be different from the amount of materials used, we will henceforth use the notation AQP to denote the "Actual Quantity Purchased" and AQU to denote the "Actual Quantity Used." In our current example, Tucson Tortilla both purchased and used the same amount of direct materials during January. However, this more specific notation will help us later when we encounter a situation in which the amount of material *purchased* differs from the amount of material *used*.

Let's use the simplified equation to calculate Tucson Tortilla's DM price variance:

$$\begin{aligned}
\text{DM price variance} &= \text{Actual Quantity Purchased} \times (\text{Actual Price} - \text{Standard Price}) \\
&= \text{AQP} \times (\text{AP} - \text{SP}) \\
&= 160,000 \text{ lbs} \times (\$1.40 - \$1.50) \\
&= 160,000 \text{ lbs} \times (\$0.10) \\
&= \$16,000 \text{ F}
\end{aligned}$$

From this analysis we see that Tucson Tortilla spent $0.10 *less* than anticipated per pound. Since the company purchased 160,000 pounds of flour, it ended up spending $16,000 less than standards anticipated. This is a favorable variance because the cost per pound is *less* than expected.

Direct Materials Quantity Variance

Unlike the price variance, which is based on the amount of materials *purchased*, the direct materials quantity variance is based on the amount of materials *used* during the period. It tells managers how much of the total direct materials variance is due to *using* more or less materials than anticipated by the standards. As you can see in Exhibit 11-4, the quantity variance is computed by comparing the company's standard cost allowed for the actual volume of output with the middle term in the model. Again, we can algebraically simplify these calculations into the equation shown next.

$$\begin{aligned}
\text{DM quantity variance} &= \text{Standard Price} \times (\text{Actual Quantity Used} - \text{Standard Quantity Allowed}) \\
&= \text{SP} \times (\text{AQU} - \text{SQA}) \\
&= \$1.50 \times [160,000 \text{ lbs} - (31,000 \text{ cases} \times 5 \text{ lbs/case})] \\
&= \$1.50 \times (160,000 \text{ lbs} - 155,000 \text{ lbs}) \\
&= \$1.50 \times 5,000 \text{ lbs} \\
&= \$7,500 \text{ U}
\end{aligned}$$

Note the following:

1. Since this variance addresses the efficiency with which materials were used, the calculation involves the quantity of direct materials *used* during the period (AQU), *not* the quantity purchased (AQP).

2. To calculate the standard quantity of materials allowed (SQA), we start with the number of units actually produced (31,000 cases) and then multiply it by the standard quantity of material allowed per unit (5 lb per case). The result (155,000 lb) tells us how much direct material the company expected to use given the actual volume of output.

From this analysis, we see that the company used 5,000 more pounds of corn flour during the period than standards indicated should be used. At a standard price of $1.50 per pound, the excess use of flour cost the company an unanticipated $7,500. This variance is unfavorable because the company used more direct materials than it should have.

Evaluating Direct Materials Variances

Exhibit 11-6 shows us that the favorable total direct materials flexible budget variance of $8,500 resulted from

1. purchasing the corn flour at a better-than-expected price, resulting in a savings of $16,000, and

2. using more corn flour than expected, resulting in an additional cost of $7,500.

EXHIBIT 11-6 Summary of Direct Materials Variances

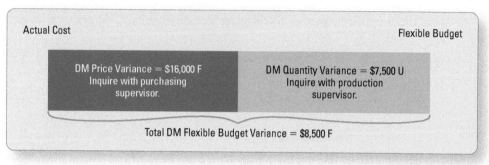

Management will want to know why both of these variances occurred. The best source of information about the price variance is the purchasing supervisor. The supervisor should know why the company was able to purchase the materials at a better-than-expected price. Perhaps alternative suppliers entered the market. Or a bumper crop of corn pushed down corn flour prices at all suppliers. On the other hand, perhaps the company was able to make use of faster payment terms and as a result was able to obtain the flour at a greater discount. Maybe the purchasing agent bought lower-grade corn flour. Many possibilities exist.

Note that while the variance is referred to as "favorable," the result may not necessarily be a "good" thing. For example, if the company bought lower-grade corn flour, did it have a detrimental impact on the taste of the tortilla chips? Or did it cause additional waste or spoilage that might account for the unfavorable quantity variance?

Management will learn more about the quantity variance by talking with the production supervisor. The production supervisor is in the best position to know why extra corn flour was used. Was something wrong with the corn flour when it arrived (torn bags, inadequate moisture content, and so forth)? Did an accident occur in transporting the corn flour from the raw material storage area to the production area? Was a batch of chips ruined by adding too much salt? Again, many possibilities exist.

Management will want to uncover the root cause of each variance to determine whether or not the extra cost was controllable. For example, if the corn flour was in poor condition when it arrived, Tucson Tortilla may be able to receive a credit from its supplier or the transportation company that trucked in the flour. Additionally, Tucson Tortilla may want to search for a new supplier. If the cause was a human error in the factory, precautionary measures might be developed that would prevent such errors in the future.

Computing DM Variances when the Quantity of DM Purchased Differs from the Quantity of DM Used

In the example just illustrated, we assumed that the quantity of direct materials purchased was the same as the quantity of direct materials used. This is often the case with lean producers since they buy inventory "just in time" to use it in production. However, traditional manufacturers often buy extra safety stock to ensure they have enough raw materials on hand to meet production if sales demand exceeds the forecast. Recall that we took safety stock into consideration in Chapter 9 when we budgeted the amount of direct materials to purchase (see Exhibit 9-7). As a result, manufacturers often buy slightly more than they immediately need. If raw materials inventory has grown too large, however, companies will intentionally buy less than the amount required for production in order to shrink their inventory. In either case, the quantity of direct materials purchased may differ from the quantity of direct materials used.

When this occurs, managers still compute the price and quantity variances but keep the following important points in mind:

1. The DM price variance will be based on the quantity of DM *purchased* (AQP).

2. The DM quantity variance will be based on the quantity of DM *used* (AQU).

3. The DM price and quantity variances will no longer sum (or net) to the total flexible budget variance.

Let's try an example. Assume that the following activity took place in February:

Actual data for February:	
Number of cases produced......................................	20,000 cases
Direct materials purchased....................................	105,000 pounds at $1.45 per pound
Direct materials used...	98,000 pounds

We can compute the DM price and quantity variances using the same formulas developed in the preceding section.

The price variance is based on the actual quantity *purchased* (AQP):

$$
\begin{aligned}
\text{DM price variance} &= \text{AQP} \times (\text{AP} - \text{SP}) \\
&= 105{,}000 \text{ lbs} \times (\$1.45 - \$1.50) \\
&= 105{,}000 \text{ lbs} \times (\$0.05) \\
&= \$5{,}250 \text{ F}
\end{aligned}
$$

By purchasing 105,000 pounds of corn flour at a price that was $0.05 less than standard, the company saved $5,250.

The quantity variance is based on the actual quantity of materials *used* (AQU):

$$
\begin{aligned}
\text{DM quantity variance} &= \text{SP} \times (\text{AQU} - \text{SQA}) \\
&= \$1.50 \times [98{,}000 \text{ lbs} - (20{,}000 \text{ cases} \times 5 \text{ lbs/case})] \\
&= \$1.50 \times (98{,}000 \text{ lbs} - 100{,}000 \text{ lbs}) \\
&= \$1.50 \times (2{,}000 \text{ lbs}) \\
&= \$3{,}000 \text{ F}
\end{aligned}
$$

This analysis reveals that the company used 2,000 fewer pounds of corn flour than standards projected, resulting in a cost savings of $3,000.

▶ Try It!

Hannah owns a fruit smoothie shop at the local mall. Each smoothie requires ¼ pound of mixed berries, which are expected to cost $4 per pound during the summer months. During the month of June, Hannah purchased and used 1,300 pounds of mixed berries at a cost of $3.75 per pound. Hannah's shop sold 5,000 smoothies during the month.

1. Calculate the DM price variance. Is the variance favorable or unfavorable?

2. Calculate the DM quantity variance (also known as a DM efficiency variance). Is the variance favorable or unfavorable?

3. Calculate the total DM variance. Is the variance favorable or unfavorable?

Please see page 709 for solutions.

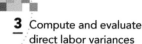

3 Compute and evaluate direct labor variances

Direct Labor Variances

From Exhibit 11-2 we know that Tucson Tortilla only spent $775 more than anticipated on direct labor. Because this is such a small variance, some managers might not consider investigating it. However, it's possible that the total variance is made up of large but off-setting individual variances, similar to what we saw with the direct materials variances. By splitting the total direct labor variance into two separate variances, a rate variance and an efficiency variance, we can find out whether the company *paid a higher wage rate* to the factory workers than expected, *used* more time in making the chips than expected, or some combination of these two factors.

Let's assume the following information about Tucson Tortilla's January operations:

Actual data for January:

Number of cases produced.............. 31,000 cases

Direct labor hours........................... 1,500 hours

Direct labor cost............................. $34,875 (resulting in an average wage rate of $23.25/hr*)

---

* $34,875/1,500 hours = $23.25/hr

Exhibit 11-7 shows that the general model for direct labor (DL) variances is almost identical to the model used for direct materials variances. The only real difference is in the names of the variances. For example, instead of a DM *price* variance, we have a DL *rate* variance. The <u>direct labor rate variance</u> tells managers how much of the total direct labor variance is due to paying a higher or lower hourly wage rate than anticipated.

Likewise, instead of the DM *quantity* variance, we have a DL *efficiency* variance. The quantity of time used in production tells management how efficiently employees were working. Therefore, the <u>direct labor efficiency variance</u> tells managers how much of the total labor variance is due to using a greater or lesser amount of time than anticipated.

While the terminology for DL variances is slightly different than it was for DM variances, the calculations are essentially the same.

EXHIBIT 11-7 Calculation of Tucson Tortilla's Direct Labor Variances

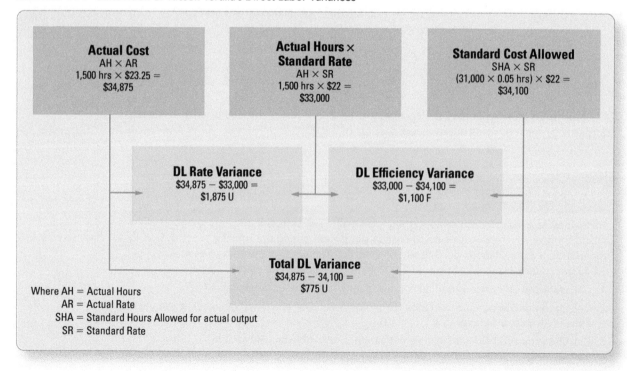

Although the total direct labor variance is small ($775), Exhibit 11-7 shows us the importance of digging down deeper: the total variance is made up of (1) an unfavorable rate variance of $1,875 and (2) an offsetting favorable efficiency variance of $1,100. In the next sections, we'll go over these variances in more detail.

Direct Labor Rate Variance

As shown in Exhibit 11-7, the direct labor rate variance is computed on the left side of the model by comparing the company's actual costs with the middle term in the model. Alternatively, we can algebraically simplify the equation, just like we did for the direct materials variances. The resulting simplified equation is as follows:

$$
\begin{aligned}
\text{DL rate variance} &= \text{Actual Hours} \times (\text{Actual Rate} - \text{Standard Rate}) \\
&= \text{AH} \times (\text{AR} - \text{SR}) \\
&= 1{,}500 \text{ hrs} \times (\$23.25 - \$22.00) \\
&= 1{,}500 \text{ hrs} \times \$1.25 \\
&= \$1{,}875 \text{ U}
\end{aligned}
$$

This analysis shows management the overall dollar impact of paying an average wage rate that was higher than anticipated. The human resources supervisor and the production supervisor should be able to explain why this happened. Several possibilities exist. For example, perhaps some lower paid employees were sick or on vacation, and higher paid employees filled in during their absence. Perhaps a wage premium was offered to workers during January to keep morale up during this peak production month. Even though the variance was "unfavorable," neither of these possible explanations suggests poor management. Rather, they simply explain why the average wage rate paid was higher than expected, resulting in an unanticipated additional cost of $1,875.

Direct Labor Efficiency Variance

As you can see in Exhibit 11-7, the efficiency variance is computed on the right side of the model by comparing the company's standard cost allowed with the middle term in the model. Again, we can algebraically simplify these calculations as follows:

$$
\begin{aligned}
\text{DL efficiency variance} &= \text{Standard Rate} \times (\text{Actual Hours} - \text{Standard Hours Allowed}) \\
&= \text{SR} \times (\text{AH} - \text{SHA}) \\
&= \$22.00 \times [1{,}500 \text{ hrs} - (31{,}000 \text{ cases} \times 0.05 \text{ hrs/case})] \\
&= \$22.00 \times (1{,}500 \text{ hrs} - 1{,}550 \text{ hrs}) \\
&= \$22.00 \times (50 \text{ hrs}) \\
&= \$1{,}100 \text{ F}
\end{aligned}
$$

Notice that to calculate the standard hours of time allowed (SHA), we start with the actual number of units produced (31,000 cases) and multiply it by the standard amount of time allowed per unit (0.05 hours per case). The result (1,550 hours) tells us how many hours of direct labor the company expected to use given the actual volume of output.

From this analysis, we see that the company used 50 fewer hours of direct labor than standards indicated would be used. At a standard labor rate of $22.00 per hour, the efficient use of time saved the company an unanticipated $1,100. This variance is favorable, because workers used *less* time than anticipated.

Although this variance is fairly small, management may still want to investigate. The production supervisor would be in the best position to explain the favorable variance. Perhaps by using higher-skilled, higher-paid individuals, the work was performed at a faster speed. By searching out the root cause, management may gain a better understanding of how the efficiency occurred and whether similar efficiencies might be replicated in the future or in other areas of operations. Exhibit 11-8 summarizes Tucson Tortilla's direct labor variances for January.

EXHIBIT 11-8 Summary of Direct Labor Variances

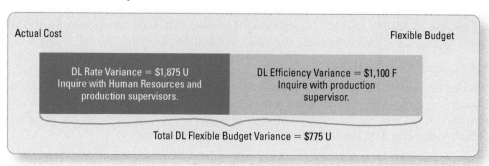

Summary of Direct Materials and Direct Labor Variances

Exhibit 11-9 summarizes the formulas for the direct materials and direct labor variances, as well as the party responsible for best explaining why the variance occurred.

EXHIBIT 11-9 Summary of DM and DL Variance Formulas

Variance	Formula	Inquire with...
Direct Materials Price Variance	= Actual Quantity Purchased × (Actual Price − Standard Price) = AQP × (AP − SP)	Purchasing Supervisor
Direct Materials Quantity Variance	= Standard Price × (Actual Quantity Used − Standard Quantity Allowed) = SP × (AQU − SQA)	Production Supervisor
Direct Labor Rate Variance	= Actual Hours × (Actual Rate − Standard Rate) = AH × (AR − SR)	Human Resources and Production Supervisors
Direct Labor Efficiency Variance	= Standard Rate × (Actual Hours − Standard Hours Allowed) = SR × (AH − SHA)	Production Supervisor

Advantages and Disadvantages of Using Standard Costs and Variances

4 Explain the advantages and disadvantages of using standard costs and variances

The practice of using standard costs and variances was developed in the early twentieth century, during the advent and growth of mass manufacturing. Although many manufacturers continue to use standard costs and variances, others do not. Management must weigh the costs against the benefits to decide whether they want to use standard costs and perform detailed variance analysis. Even if management uncovers variances, they will want to use management by exception to determine which variances are significant enough to warrant investigation.

Advantages

- **Cost benchmarks:** One of the greatest advantages of using standard costs is having a benchmark by which to judge actual costs. However, this benchmark is valid only if the standards are kept up to date.
- **Usefulness in budgeting:** Standards are often used as the basis for many components in the master budget, such as the direct materials, direct labor, and manufacturing overhead budgets.

- **Motivation:** The use of practical, or attainable, standards should increase employee motivation because it gives employees a reasonable goal to achieve.
- **Standard costing systems simplify bookkeeping:** Many manufacturers use standards as the backbone to their standard costing system. In a standard costing system, all manufacturing costs entering Work in Process Inventory are recorded at standard cost rather than actual cost. Variances between actual costs and standard costs are immediately captured in variance accounts in the general ledger. This type of costing system is described in the appendix to this chapter.

Disadvantages

Despite the prevalence of standard costing over the past century, many contemporary manufacturers are moving away from the use of standards. Here are some of the reasons:

- **Outdated or inaccurate standards:** As mentioned previously, standard costs can quickly become outdated or inaccurate as the cost of inputs or the production process changes. Standards should be reviewed and updated at least yearly. They should also be updated whenever a change in process or input costs is considered to be nontemporary. Keeping standards up to date is costly.
- **Lack of timeliness:** In the past, variances were often computed once a month. In today's fast-paced world, such information is often too old to be useful. As a result, some companies are moving toward the daily calculation of variances.
- **Focus on operational performance measures and visual management:** Because of the need for timely data, many lean producers are placing greater emphasis on operational performance measures that are collected daily, or even hourly, and visually displayed where front-line workers can immediately see performance levels. They find such visual reminders much more effective for motivating front-line employees than relying on price and efficiency variances.
- **Lean thinking:** As discussed in Chapter 4, lean companies strive for continual improvement. That means that current standards are not "good enough." Rather than focusing on whether or not production has met current standards, lean producers focus on finding new ways to decrease waste, increase efficiency, and increase quality. They concentrate on looking forward rather than looking at the past.
- **Increase in automation and decrease in direct labor:** Most manufacturers have shifted toward automated production processes. For many manufacturers, direct labor is no longer a primary component of production or a driver of overhead costs. In addition, for companies that pay employees a salary rather than an hourly wage rate, direct labor is a fixed cost, rather than a variable cost. Finally, at lean companies, employees tend to be multiskilled and cross-trained to perform a number of duties rather than a single, repetitive task. These front-line workers are held in high esteem by management and are considered to be part of a team effort rather than a labor force to be controlled. To these companies, direct labor standards are no longer relevant or helpful.
- **Unintended behavioral consequences:** Use of traditional standards can cause unintended behavioral consequences. For example, to obtain a favorable price variance, the purchasing supervisor may buy larger quantities of raw materials than needed. Likewise, a production manager may overproduce to obtain a favorable fixed overhead volume variance (discussed in the second half of the chapter). However, as we learned in Chapter 4, holding or producing excess quantities of inventories is wasteful and costly, and should be avoided.

Decision Guidelines

Standard Costs and Variances

Let's consider some decisions management must make with regard to standard costs and variances.

Decision	Guidelines
What is a standard cost and how can it be used?	A standard cost is a budget for a single unit of product. Standards costs are used as performance benchmarks against which to evaluate actual costs. Standards costs are also used for developing the direct materials, direct labor, and manufacturing overhead budgets.
Should we use ideal (perfection) standards or practical (attainable) standards?	Since ideal standards are only achievable under flawless conditions, they are best suited for lean producers that strive for perfection. Practical standards, which are attainable with effort, are typically used by traditional manufacturers that want to use motivational, yet realistic, benchmarks.
What information is used to develop standards?	Companies use a combination of historical, current, and projected data to develop standards. Managers often use engineering time and motion studies to determine the quantity of time and materials needed to produce each unit.
How often should standard costs be updated?	Standard costs should be reviewed at least once a year and updated whenever a non-temporary change in costs, inputs, or processes occurs.
How is the direct materials price variance computed?	$= \text{Actual Quantity Purchased} \times (\text{Actual Price} - \text{Standard Price})$ $= \text{AQP} \times (\text{AP} - \text{SP})$
How is the direct materials quantity variance computed?	$= \text{Standard Price} \times (\text{Actual Quantity Used} - \text{Standard Quantity Allowed})$ $= \text{SP} \times (\text{AQU} - \text{SQA})$
How is the direct labor rate variance computed?	$= \text{Actual Hours} \times (\text{Actual Rate} - \text{Standard Rate})$ $= \text{AH} \times (\text{AR} - \text{SR})$
How is the direct labor efficiency variance computed?	$= \text{Standard Rate} \times (\text{Actual Hours} - \text{Standard Hours Allowed})$ $= \text{SR} \times (\text{AH} - \text{SHA})$
Who is usually in the best position to explain why the variances occurred?	DM price variance: Purchasing Supervisor DM quantity variance: Production Supervisor DL rate variance: Production and Human Resources Supervisors DL efficiency variance: Production Supervisor

SUMMARY PROBLEM **1**

Memoirs, Inc., produces several different styles and sizes of picture frames. The collage frame consists of 12 interconnected matted picture slots, each surrounded by a wood frame. Engineering studies indicate that each collage frame will require the following direct materials and direct labor:

Materials and Labor:	Quantity of Input	Price of Input
Wood trim for frame borders	18 feet	$ 0.35 per foot
Mattes for individual pictures	12 mattes	$ 0.05 per matte
Sheet glass top	4 square feet	$ 4.00 per square foot
Pressboard frame backing	4 square feet	$ 0.25 per square foot
Direct Labor	0.25 hours	$16 per hour

The following activity regarding direct labor and wood trim occurred during March:

Number of frames produced	25,000 frames
Wood trim purchased	450,000 feet at $0.37 per foot
Wood trim used	455,000 feet
Direct labor hours	6,500 hours
Direct labor cost	$100,750 (resulting in an average wage rate of $15.50/hr*)

* $100,750/6,500 hours = $15.50/hr

Requirements
1. Calculate the standard direct materials cost and standard direct labor cost for each collage frame.
2. Calculate the wood trim direct materials price and quantity variances for the month of March.
3. Calculate the direct labor rate and efficiency variances for the month of March.

▪ SOLUTIONS

Requirement 1
The standard cost of direct materials and direct labor is calculated by multiplying the standard quantity of input needed for each collage frame by the standard price of the input:

Materials and Labor:	Quantity of Input (a)	Price of Input (b)	Standard Cost (a × b)
Wood trim for frame borders	18 feet	$ 0.35 per foot	$ 6.30
Mattes for individual pictures	12 mattes	$ 0.05 per matte	0.60
Sheet glass top	4 square feet	$ 4.00 per square foot	16.00
Pressboard frame backing	4 square feet	$ 0.25 per square foot	1.00
Direct material cost per unit			$23.90
Direct Labor	0.25 hours	$16 per hour	$ 4.00

Requirement 2

The direct materials price variance is based on the quantity of materials (wood trim) *purchased*:

$$
\begin{aligned}
\text{DM price variance} &= \text{AQP} \times (\text{AP} - \text{SP}) \\
&= 450{,}000 \text{ ft} \times (\$0.37 - \$0.35) \\
&= 450{,}000 \text{ ft} \times \$0.02 \\
&= \$9{,}000 \text{ U}
\end{aligned}
$$

The company spent $0.02 per foot more than anticipated on the 450,000 feet of wood trim that it purchased, resulting in an unfavorable price variance of $9,000.

The direct materials quantity variance is based on the quantity of materials (wood trim) *used*:

$$
\begin{aligned}
\text{DM quantity variance} &= \text{SP} \times (\text{AQU} - \text{SQA}) \\
&= \$0.35 \times [455{,}000 \text{ ft} - (25{,}000 \text{ frames} \times 18 \text{ ft/frame})] \\
&= \$0.35 \times (455{,}000 \text{ ft} - 450{,}000 \text{ ft}) \\
&= \$0.35 \times 5{,}000 \text{ ft} \\
&= \$1{,}750 \text{ U}
\end{aligned}
$$

This analysis reveals that using 5,000 more feet of wood trim than anticipated resulted in an unanticipated additional cost of $1,750.

Requirement 3

The direct labor rate variance is computed as follows:

$$
\begin{aligned}
\text{DL rate variance} &= \text{AH} \times (\text{AR} - \text{SR}) \\
&= 6{,}500 \text{ hrs} \times (\$15.50 - \$16.00) \\
&= 6{,}500 \text{ hrs} \times (\$0.50) \\
&= \$3{,}250 \text{ F}
\end{aligned}
$$

The company spent $0.50 less per hour than anticipated, resulting in a $3,250 F variance over the 6,500 hours that were worked.

The direct labor efficiency variance is calculated as follows:

$$
\begin{aligned}
\text{DL efficiency variance} &= \text{SR} \times (\text{AH} - \text{SHA}) \\
&= \$16.00 \times [6{,}500 - (25{,}000 \text{ frames} \times 0.25 \text{ hrs/frame})] \\
&= \$16.00 \times (6{,}500 - 6{,}250 \text{ hrs}) \\
&= \$16.00 \times 250 \text{ hrs} \\
&= \$4{,}000 \text{ U}
\end{aligned}
$$

At a standard labor rate of $16.00 per hour, the extra use of direct labor hours cost the company an unanticipated $4,000.

How Do Managers Use Standard Costs to Compute MOH Variances?

In the first half of the chapter we learned how Tucson Tortilla developed standard costs and then used those standards to evaluate its direct materials and direct labor costs. In this half of the chapter, we'll look at the four manufacturing overhead (MOH) variances that are typically computed: two related to variable MOH costs and two related to fixed MOH costs.

Variable Manufacturing Overhead Variances

From Exhibit 11-2, we learned that Tucson Tortilla had an unfavorable variable overhead flexible budget variance of $7,700. But why did this unexpected additional cost occur?

5 Compute and evaluate variable overhead variances

Manufacturers usually split the total variable MOH variance into rate and efficiency variances, just as they do for direct labor. Exhibit 11-10 (on the next page) shows that the general model for calculating variable MOH rate and efficiency variances is almost identical to the model used for direct labor rate and efficiency variances. The only real difference in the calculations is the rate that is used: we use the *variable manufacturing overhead rate*, not the direct labor wage rate. And since Tucson Tortilla allocates its overhead using machine hours, the hours refer to machine hours rather than direct labor hours.[3] Here is the information from January's operations:

Data for January	
Number of cases produced......................	31,000 cases
Standard variable MOH rate..................	$ 25 per machine hour
Standard hours required per case	0.10 machine hours
Actual machine hours............................	3,000 machine hours
Actual variable MOH costs....................	$85,200 (resulting in an *actual* variable MOH rate of $28.40 per machine hour)*

* $85,200/3,000 hours = $28.40/machine hour

Variable Overhead Rate Variance

As shown in Exhibit 11-10, the **variable overhead rate variance** is the difference between the actual variable MOH costs incurred during the period ($85,200) and the amount of variable MOH costs expected ($75,000) considering the actual machine (mch) hours used. It tells managers whether more or less was spent on variable overhead than expected given the actual machine hours run. As a result, the variable overhead rate variance is also sometimes called the **variable overhead spending variance**. The variance formula can be algebraically simplified into the following formula:

$$\text{Variable MOH rate variance} = \text{Actual Hours} \times (\text{Actual Rate} - \text{Standard Rate})$$
$$= \text{AH} \times (\text{AR} - \text{SR})$$
$$= 3{,}000 \text{ mch hrs} \times (\$28.40 - \$25.00)$$
$$= 3{,}000 \text{ mch hrs} \times (\$3.40)$$
$$= \$10{,}200 \text{ U}$$

The interpretation of this variance is not quite as straightforward as the interpretation of the direct labor rate variance. First, variable MOH is made up of a number of different costs, including indirect materials, indirect labor, and other variable overhead costs

[3] Many companies allocate manufacturing overhead using direct labor hours rather than machine hours. For these companies, the hours used in calculating the manufacturing overhead variances will be *identical* to the hours used in calculating the direct labor variances.

EXHIBIT 11-10 Calculation of Variable Overhead Variances

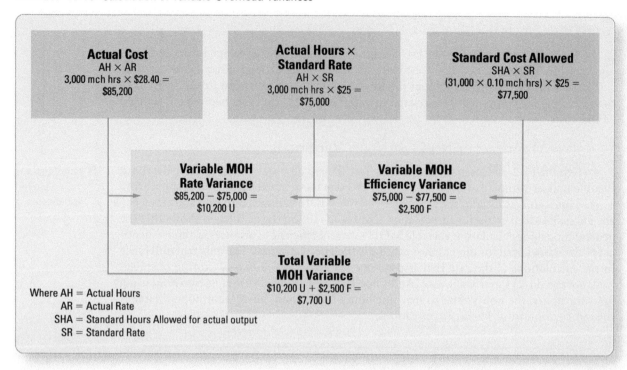

such as the variable portion of the utility bill. One particular cost (for example, indirect materials) could be higher than expected, yet another cost (for example, indirect labor) could be less than expected. As a result, the variance could be due to more than one input.

Second, we don't know if the variance is due to *using* more of the input than expected (for example, using more indirect materials than expected) or because the input *cost more* than expected from the suppliers. On average, management expected variable overhead to cost $25 per machine hour. However, we see that the actual rate ($28.40 per machine hour) turned out to be quite a bit higher. The production supervisor and purchasing manager are usually in the best position to help management understand why this variance occurred.

Variable Overhead Efficiency Variance

As shown in Exhibit 11-10, the <u>variable overhead efficiency variance</u> is the difference between the actual machine hours run and the standard machine hours allowed for the actual production volume, calculated at the standard variable MOH rate. Again, it can be algebraically simplified into the following formula:

Variable MOH efficiency variance = Standard Rate × (Actual Hours − Standard Hours Allowed)

$$= SR \times (AH - SHA)$$

$$= \$25 \times [3{,}000 \text{ mch hrs} - (31{,}000 \text{ cases} \times 0.10 \text{ mch hrs/case})]$$

$$= \$25 \times (3{,}000 \text{ mch hrs} - 3{,}100 \text{ mch hrs})$$

$$= \$25 \times (100 \text{ mch hrs})$$

$$= \$2{,}500 \text{ F}$$

The efficiency variance does not tell management anything with regard to how efficiently variable manufacturing overhead was used. Rather, it is directly tied to the efficiency with which the machine hours were used. It tells managers how much of the total variable MOH variance is due to using more or fewer machine hours than anticipated for the actual volume of output. The production supervisor would be in the best position to explain why this variance occurred.

Fixed Manufacturing Overhead Variances

The calculation and interpretation of the fixed overhead variances are much different than the variances we have discussed thus far. Why? Because all of the manufacturing costs we have analyzed thus far have been *variable* costs. However, fixed overhead is expected to remain constant, regardless of volume fluctuations.

6 Compute and evaluate fixed overhead variances

As shown in Chapter 9 (Exhibit 9-9), Tucson Tortilla expects to incur $30,000 of fixed overhead each month. Fixed overhead costs such as straight-line depreciation on the plant, property insurance, property tax, and the monthly salaries of indirect laborers should not vary month to month as production levels fluctuate to meet demand. However, let's assume that the company actually incurred $31,025 of fixed overhead.

Fixed Overhead Budget Variance

The <u>fixed overhead budget variance</u> measures the difference between the actual fixed overhead costs incurred and the budgeted fixed overhead costs. This variance is sometimes referred to as the <u>fixed overhead spending variance</u> because it specifically looks at whether the company spent more or less than anticipated on fixed overhead costs. As shown in Exhibit 11-11, the calculation of this variance is straightforward. The difference between Tucson Tortilla's actual fixed overhead costs ($31,025) and its budgeted fixed overhead costs ($30,000) results in an unfavorable fixed overhead budget variance of $1,025. The variance is unfavorable if actual fixed overhead costs are more than budgeted and favorable if actual costs are lower than budgeted.

EXHIBIT 11-11 Calculation of Fixed Overhead Variances

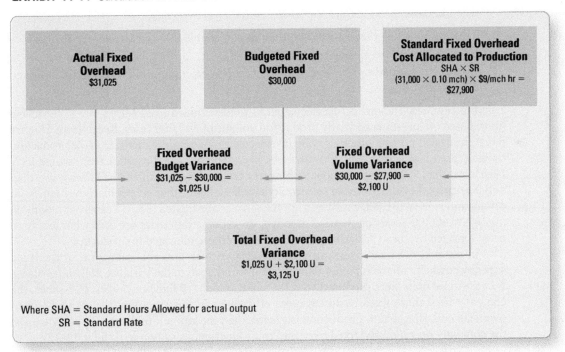

The best way to uncover the cause of the fixed overhead budget variance is to compare each fixed overhead cost component against the budgeted amount. Perhaps indirect laborers received a raise that was not foreseen when the budget was prepared. Perhaps the insurance company increased its premiums or the city increased property taxes. Although the variance is labeled "unfavorable," the reason for the variance may not be a bad thing. Nor may it be controllable. For example, let's say the unfavorable variance was caused by a raise in salary given to certain indirect laborers in the plant. The raise may result in a boost to employee morale, leading to better productivity. If the unfavorable variance was caused by an increase in city property taxes, management may have little recourse. If, however, the variance was caused by an increase in insurance premiums, management may decide to shop around for a different insurance carrier. As these potential explanations indicate, the variance could be due to a number of different factors.

Fixed Overhead Volume Variance

As shown in Exhibit 11-11, the <u>fixed overhead volume variance</u> is the difference between the budgeted fixed overhead cost and the *standard fixed overhead cost* allocated to production.[4] The standard cost is calculated the same way we calculated earlier standard costs: we start with the actual volume produced (31,000 cases) and then multiply it by the standard hours allowed per case (0.10 machine hrs) to get the standard hours allowed. Finally, we multiply the standard hours allowed by the fixed MOH rate ($9/machine hour) to get the standard fixed overhead cost allocated to production:

$$
\begin{aligned}
\text{Standard Fixed Overhead Cost Allocated to Production} &= (\text{Standard Hours Allowed} \times \text{Standard Rate}) \\
&= (31{,}000 \text{ cases} \times 0.10 \text{ mch hrs/case}) \times \$9/\text{mch hr} \\
&= 3{,}100 \text{ mch hrs} \times \$9/\text{mch hr} \\
&= \$27{,}900
\end{aligned}
$$

Now that we have calculated the standard fixed overhead allocated to production, we can compute the fixed overhead volume variance as follows:

$$
\begin{aligned}
\text{Fixed Overhead Volume Variance} &= \text{Budgeted Fixed Overhead Cost} - \text{Standard Fixed Overhead Cost} \\
&\quad\quad\quad\quad\quad\quad\quad\quad\quad\quad\quad\quad\quad\quad\quad\quad \text{Allocated to Production} \\
&= \$30{,}000 - \$27{,}900 \\
&= \$2{,}100 \text{ U}
\end{aligned}
$$

The fixed overhead volume variance results from two causes:

1. Treating fixed overhead costs *as if* they were variable in order to allocate the costs to individuals units of product; and

2. Incorrectly estimating the level of activity when calculating the predetermined fixed MOH rate.

For example, Tucson Tortilla calculated its predetermined fixed MOH rate ($9/machine hour) based on an estimated yearly production volume of 400,000 cases. Recall from Chapter 6 that fixed costs per unit of activity vary inversely with changes in volume. Had the production estimate been higher than 400,000 cases, the predetermined fixed overhead rate would have been lower than $9 per machine hour. If, however, the production estimate had been lower than 400,000 cases, the fixed overhead rate would have been higher than $9 per machine hour. Since production volume (31,000 cases) was not the same as anticipated (33,333 cases per month on average = 400,000 cases per year/12 months), we expect a difference between what was budgeted for fixed overhead and the amount of fixed overhead allocated to production.

In essence, the fixed overhead volume variance measures the utilization of the fixed capacity costs. If volume is higher than originally anticipated, the variance will be favorable because more units were produced with the same amount of fixed resources. In essence, the company used those fixed resources more efficiently. In this situation, the standard fixed overhead cost allocated to production is *greater* than the amount budgeted. In other words, the company *overallocated* fixed overhead to production, as shown in Exhibit 11-12.

EXHIBIT 11-12 Favorable Fixed Overhead Volume Variance

[4] In Chapter 3 we learned about a *normal* costing system in which manufacturing overhead is allocated to production using a predetermined MOH rate multiplied by the actual quantity of the allocation base used (such as actual machine hours used by the job). In a *standard* costing system, companies allocate manufacturing overhead to production differently: they multiply the predetermined manufacturing overhead rate by the *standard quantity of the allocation base allowed* rather than by the *actual quantity of the allocation base used*.

In contrast, if production volume is lower than anticipated, the variance is denoted as unfavorable due to the fact that fixed costs were not used to produce as many units as anticipated. Since the number of units produced (31,000 cases) was less than anticipated (33,333 on average per month), production capacity was used less efficiently than anticipated, leading to an unfavorable volume variance. In this situation, the standard fixed overhead cost allocated to production is less than the amount budgeted. In other words, the company *underallocated* fixed overhead, as shown in Exhibit 11-13.

EXHIBIT 11-13 Unfavorable Fixed Overhead Volume Variance

Keep the following rule of thumb in mind:

> When production volume is *higher* than anticipated, the fixed overhead volume variance will be *favorable*. When it is *lower* than anticipated, the fixed overhead volume variance will be *unfavorable*.

Extreme caution should be used when interpreting the volume variance. Again, favorable does not equate with "good," nor does unfavorable equate with "bad." For companies striving to create lean production environments, production levels will naturally fall as the company sheds itself of excess inventory, leading to an unfavorable volume variance. Has a "bad" decision been made? Absolutely not. The lean producer will generally be much more efficient in the long run than its traditional counterpart. The challenge during the transition phase will be for management to determine how to best use the newly freed capacity, and not be misled by the resulting temporary unfavorable volume variances that may occur.

▶ Try It!

Hannah owns a fruit smoothie shop at the local mall. The budgeted monthly fixed overhead costs consist of the store lease payment ($1,000), advertising ($250), equipment depreciation ($125), and store Wi-Fi ($80). Actual fixed overhead expenses for June were $1,600. When calculating the fixed overhead rate, Hannah anticipated selling 4,800 smoothies during each summer month. She actually sold 5,000 in June.

1. What is the fixed overhead budget variance for the month of June? Is the variance favorable or unfavorable?

2. Will Hannah's fixed overhead volume variance for the month of June be favorable or unfavorable? Explain.

Please see page 709 for solutions.

Standard Costing Systems

As we have just seen, many manufacturers calculate standard costs and perform variance analysis outside of their general ledger accounting system. However, other companies integrate standards directly into their general ledger accounting. This method of accounting, called standard costing, is discussed in the appendix to this chapter.

Decision Guidelines

Standard Costs and Variances

Let's consider some of management's decisions related to overhead variances.

Decision	Guidelines
Should we calculate and interpret all manufacturing overhead variances the same way?	Variable overhead costs are expected to change in total as production volume changes. However, fixed overhead costs should stay constant within a relevant range of production. Therefore, management will want to analyze variable and fixed MOH variances separately.
What variable overhead variances should we compute?	• The variable overhead rate (or spending) variance tells managers if they spent more or less than anticipated on variable MOH costs considering the actual hours of work used. • The variable overhead efficiency variance tells managers nothing about the efficiency with which variable overhead costs were used. Rather, it is tied directly to the efficiency with which machine hours or labor hours were used.
How is the variable overhead *rate* (or *spending*) variance computed?	$= \text{Actual Hours} \times (\text{Actual Rate} - \text{Standard Rate})$ $= \text{AH} \times (\text{AR} - \text{SR})$
How is the variable overhead *efficiency* variance computed?	$= \text{Standard Rate} \times (\text{Actual Hours} - \text{Standard Hours Allowed})$ $= \text{SR} \times (\text{AH} - \text{SHA})$
What fixed overhead variances should we compute?	• The fixed overhead budget (or spending) variance tells managers if they spent more or less than anticipated on fixed overhead costs. • The fixed overhead volume variance tells managers if too much or too little fixed overhead was allocated to production due to the actual volume of production being different than the volume used to calculate the predetermined fixed MOH rate.
How is the fixed overhead *budget* variance computed?	$= \text{Actual fixed overhead} - \text{Budgeted fixed overhead}$
How is the fixed overhead *volume* variance computed?	$= \text{Budgeted fixed overhead} - \text{Standard fixed overhead cost allocated to production}$ $= \text{Budgeted fixed overhead} - (\text{SHA} \times \text{SR})$
How should management uncover the root causes of the overhead variances?	Management will want to compare the actual cost of individual MOH components (such as indirect labor, utilities, property taxes) against the budgeted costs for those same components. The purchasing and production supervisors are usually in the best position to offer insights as to why the variances occurred.
How should the fixed overhead volume variance be interpreted?	• A favorable variance means that more units were produced than originally anticipated, leading to an overallocation of fixed MOH. • An unfavorable variance means that fewer units were produced than originally anticipated, leading to an underallocation of fixed MOH.

SUMMARY PROBLEM **2**

Memoirs, Inc., produces several different styles and sizes of picture frames. The following activity describes Memoirs' overhead costs during March:

Number of frames produced	25,000 frames
Predetermined variable MOH rate	$ 6.00 per DL hour
Predetermined fixed MOH rate	$ 12.00 per DL hour
Budgeted fixed manufacturing overhead..................	$70,000
Actual direct labor hours..	6,500 hours
Actual variable manufacturing overhead.................	$40,625, resulting in an actual rate of $6.25* per DL hour
Actual fixed manufacturing overhead......................	$68,000
Standard direct labor allowed per unit	0.25 hours per frame

*$40,625/6,500 hours

Requirements

1. Calculate the variable overhead rate and efficiency variances for the month of March.
2. Calculate the fixed overhead budget and volume variances for the month of March.
3. Calculate the total fixed overhead variance for the month of March.

▪ SOLUTIONS

Requirement 1

$$\text{Variable MOH rate variance} = \text{Actual Hours} \times (\text{Actual Rate} - \text{Standard Rate})$$
$$= \text{AH} \times (\text{AR} - \text{SR})$$
$$= 6{,}500 \text{ hrs} \times (\$6.25 - \$6.00)$$
$$= 6{,}500 \text{ hrs} \times (\$0.25)$$
$$= \$1{,}625 \text{ U}$$

$$\text{Variable MOH efficiency variance} = \text{Standard Rate} \times (\text{Actual Hours} - \text{Standard Hours Allowed})$$
$$= \text{SR} \times (\text{AH} - \text{SHA})$$
$$= \$6.00 \times [6{,}500 - (25{,}000 \text{ frames} \times 0.25 \text{ hrs/frame})]$$
$$= \$6.00 \times (6{,}500 - 6{,}250 \text{ hrs})$$
$$= \$6.00 \times 250 \text{ hrs}$$
$$= \$1{,}500 \text{ U}$$

Requirements 2 & 3

The fixed overhead variances are calculated as follows:

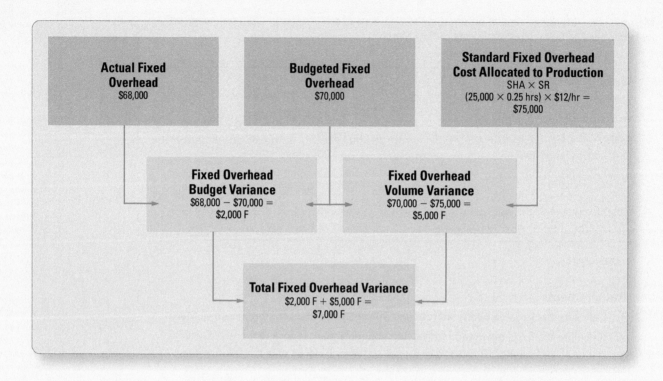

- The budget variance is favorable since less was spent on fixed overhead than budgeted.
- The volume variance is favorable since more was allocated to production than was budgeted. This means that more units were produced than budgeted.
- As a result of the two favorable variances, the total fixed overhead variance is also favorable.

Appendix 11A

Standard Costing

Many companies integrate standard costs directly into their general ledger accounting by recording inventory-related costs at standard cost rather than at actual cost. This method of accounting is called **standard costing** or **standard cost accounting**. Standard costing not only saves on bookkeeping costs but also isolates price and quantity variances as soon as they occur. The variances will be clearly displayed for management on a standard costing income statement, which we will show you in Exhibit 11-14. Before we go through the journal entries, keep the following key points in mind:

7 Record standard costing journal entries

1. Each type of variance discussed has its own general ledger account. A debit balance means that the variance is unfavorable since it decreases income (just like an expense). A credit balance means that the variance is favorable since it increases income (just like a revenue).

2. Just as in job costing, the manufacturing costs flow through the inventory accounts in the following order: raw materials → work in process → finished goods → cost of goods sold. The difference is that *standard costs* rather than actual costs are used to record the manufacturing costs entered into the inventory accounts.

3. At the end of the period, the variance accounts are closed to Cost of Goods Sold to correct for the fact that the standard costs recorded in the accounts were different from actual costs. Assuming that most inventory worked on during the period has been sold, any error from using standard costs rather than actual costs is contained in Cost of Goods Sold. Closing the variance accounts to Cost of Goods Sold corrects the Cost of Goods Sold balance and zeros out the temporary variance accounts.

Journal Entries

We use Tucson Tortilla's January transactions, just as we did in the chapter, to demonstrate standard costing.

1. **Recording Raw Materials Purchases**—Tucson Tortilla debits Raw Materials Inventory for the *actual quantity* of corn flour purchased (160,000 pounds) recorded at the *standard price* ($1.50 per pound). It credits Accounts Payable for the *actual quantity* of corn flour purchased (160,000 pounds) recorded at the *actual price* ($1.40 per pound) because this is the amount owed to Tucson Tortilla's suppliers. The difference is the direct materials *price* variance.

		Raw Materials Inventory (160,000 × $1.50)	240,000	
		Accounts Payable (160,000 × $1.40)		224,000
		DM Price Variance		16,000
		(to record purchase of raw materials)		

The favorable price variance is the same as that shown in Exhibit 11-5. Since it is favorable, it has a credit balance, which increases Tucson Tortilla's January profits.

2. **Recording Use of Direct Materials**—When Tucson Tortilla *uses* direct materials, it debits Work in Process Inventory at the *standard price* ($1.50) × *standard quantity* of direct materials that should have been used (31,000 cases × 5 lb per case = 155,000 pounds). *This maintains Work in Process Inventory at a purely standard cost.* Raw Materials Inventory is credited for the *actual quantity* of materials used in production (160,000 pounds) recorded at the *standard price* ($1.50) since this is the price at which the materials were entered into Raw Materials Inventory in the previous journal entry. The difference is the direct materials *quantity* variance. The direct

materials quantity variance is recorded when Tucson Tortilla records the *use* of direct materials:

	Work in Process Inventory (155,000 × $1.50)	232,500	
	DM Quantity Variance	7,500	
	Raw Materials Inventory (160,000 × $1.50)		240,000
	(to record use of direct materials)		

The unfavorable quantity price variance is the same as that shown in Exhibit 11-5. Since it is unfavorable, it has a debit balance, which decreases Tucson Tortilla's January profits.

3. **Recording Direct Labor Costs**—Since Work in Process Inventory is maintained at standard cost, Tucson Tortilla debits Work in Process Inventory for the *standard rate* for direct labor ($22 per hour) × *standard hours* of direct labor that should have been worked (31,000 cases × 0.05 hours per case = 1,550 hours). Tucson Tortilla credits Wages Payable for the *actual* hours worked at the *actual* wage rate since this is the amount owed to employees. At the same time, Tucson Tortilla records the direct labor rate and efficiency variances calculated in Exhibit 11-7. The *unfavorable* DL Rate Variance is recorded as a *debit*, while the *favorable DL* Efficiency Variance is recorded as a *credit*.

	Work in Process Inventory (1,550 hrs × $22)	34,100	
	DL Rate Variance (Exhibit 11-7)	1,875	
	DL Efficiency Variance (Exhibit 11-7)		1,100
	Wages Payable (1,500 hrs × $23.25)		34,875
	(to record use of direct labor)		

4. **Recording Actual Manufacturing Overhead Costs**—Tucson Tortilla records manufacturing overhead costs as usual, debiting the variable and fixed manufacturing overhead accounts and crediting various accounts. The actual costs can be found in Exhibits 11-10 and 11-11:

	Variable Manufacturing Overhead (Exhibit 11-10)	85,200	
	Fixed Manufacturing Overhead (Exhibit 11-11)	31,025	
	Various Accounts		116,225
	(to record actual overhead costs incurred)		

5. **Allocating Overhead**—In standard costing, the overhead allocated to Work in Process Inventory is computed using the standard overhead rates ($25/machine hour for variable overhead and $9/machine hour for fixed overhead) × standard quantity of the allocation base allowed for the actual output (31,000 cases × 0.10 MH per case = 3,100 MH). As usual, the Variable and Fixed Manufacturing Overhead accounts are credited when allocating overhead:

	Work in Process Inventory	105,400	
	Variable Manufacturing Overhead (3,100 MH × $25/MH)		77,500
	Fixed Manufacturing Overhead (3,100 MH × $9/MH)		27,900
	(to allocate overhead costs to Work in Process inventory)		

This journal entry corresponds with our calculations in Exhibits 11-10 and 11-11.

6. **Recording the Completion**—So far, Work in Process Inventory has been debited with $372,000 of manufacturing cost ($232,500 of direct materials + $34,100 of direct labor + $105,400 of MOH). Does this make sense? According to Exhibit 11-1, the standard cost of manufacturing one case is $12.00. If we take the $372,000 of cost and divide it by 31,000 cases, we get $12.00 per case. This is how it should be—through the standard costing journal entries, Tucson Tortilla has successfully recorded each case at its standard cost of $12. In addition, it has captured all of the variances in separate variance accounts on the general ledger. As the units are completed, the standard cost of each case is transferred out of Work in Process Inventory and into Finished Goods Inventory:

	Finished Goods Inventory (31,000 × $12.00)	372,000	
	Work in Process Inventory (31,000 × $12.00)		372,000
	(to record completion of the 31,000 cases)		

7. **Recording the Sale and Release of Inventory**—Let's assume that 32,370 cases were sold on account in January at an average price of $20.20 per case. The following journal entry would reflect the sale:

	Accounts Receivable (32,370 × $20.20)	653,874	
	Sales Revenue (32,370 × $20.20)		653,874
	(to record the sale of 32,370 cases)		

Under a perpetual inventory system, Tucson Tortilla must also release inventory for the cases it has sold. Since all cases produced during the year were recorded at standard cost ($12.00 each), they must be removed from Finished Goods Inventory and be entered into Cost of Goods Sold at the same standard cost:

	Cost of Goods Sold (32,370 × $12.00)	388,440	
	Finished Goods Inventory (32,370 × $12.00)		388,440
	(to record cost of goods sold for the 32,370 cases)		

8. **Closing Manufacturing Overhead**—Tucson Tortilla must close its temporary MOH accounts. Rather than closing them directly to Cost of Goods Sold, as we did in Chapter 3, in a standard costing system the accounts are closed to variance accounts. The company closes the Variable Manufacturing Overhead account to the variable MOH variances shown in Exhibit 11-10:

	Variable Overhead Rate Variance	10,200	
	Variable Overhead Efficiency Variance		2,500
	Variable Manufacturing Overhead		7,700
	(to close the Variable MOH account)		

Likewise, it closes the Fixed Manufacturing Overhead account to the fixed MOH variances shown in Exhibit 11-11:

		Fixed Overhead Budget Variance	1,025	
		Fixed Overhead Volume Variance	2,100	
		Fixed Manufacturing Overhead		3,125
		(to close the Fixed MOH account)		

These two journal entries zero out the two manufacturing overhead accounts.

Standard Costing Income Statement

Exhibit 11-14 shows a standard costing income statement that highlights the variances for Tucson Tortilla's management. It shows Cost of Goods Sold, first at standard cost and then at actual cost. Although the overall effect of the cost variances was minimal ($3,100 U), the report clearly shows management the size and direction of each variance. Managers will use management by exception to determine which variances, if any, they wish to investigate.

EXHIBIT 11-14 Standard Costing Income Statement

	A	B	C	D	E	F
1		Tucson Tortilla				
2		Standard Cost Income Statement				
3		For the Month Ended January 31				
4						
5	Sales revenue (32,370 × $20.20)				$	653,874
6	Less: Cost of goods sold, *at standard cost* (32,370 × $12)			$ 388,440		
7	Plus/(less) manufacturing cost variances:					
8	DM price variance	$ (16,000)	F			
9	DM quantity variance	7,500	U			
10	DL rate variance	1,875	U			
11	DL efficiency variance	(1,100)	F			
12	Variable MOH rate variance	10,200	U			
13	Variable MOH efficiency variance	(2,500)	F			
14	Fixed MOH budget variance	1,025	U			
15	Fixed MOH volume variance	2,100	U			
16	Total manufacturing cost variances			3,100	U	
17	Cost of goods sold, at actual cost					391,540
18	Gross Profit					262,334
19	Less: Operating expenses					155,390
20	Operating income				$	106,944
21						

As a final step at the end of the period, all of the cost variance accounts are closed to zero-out their balances. Why? For two reasons: (1) The financial statements prepared for *external* users never show variances (variances are only for internal management's use) and (2) the general ledger must be corrected for the fact that standard costs, rather than actual costs, were used to record manufacturing costs. Since all of the cases produced were sold, the error in costing currently exists in the Cost of Goods Sold account. Although we do not show the journal entry to close the variance accounts here, all favorable variance accounts would be debited, while all unfavorable variance accounts would be credited. The net unfavorable amount of the variances of $3,100 would be debited to Cost of Goods Sold to increase the balance in this account to its correct amount.

END OF CHAPTER

Learning Objectives

- 1 Explain how and why standard costs are developed
- 2 Compute and evaluate direct materials variances
- 3 Compute and evaluate direct labor variances
- 4 Explain the advantages and disadvantages of using standard costs and variances
- 5 Compute and evaluate variable overhead variances
- 6 Compute and evaluate fixed overhead variances
- 7 (Appendix) Record standard costing journal entries

Accounting Vocabulary

Attainable Standards. (p. 654) Standards based on currently attainable conditions that include allowances for normal amounts of waste and inefficiency. Also known as practical standards.

Direct Labor Efficiency Variance. (p. 664) This variance tells managers how much of the total labor variance is due to using a greater or lesser amount of time than anticipated. It is calculated as follows: $SR \times (AH - SHA)$.

Direct Labor Rate Variance. (p. 664) This variance tells managers how much of the total labor variance is due to paying a higher or lower hourly wage rate than anticipated. It is calculated as follows: $AH \times (AR - SR)$.

Direct Materials Price Variance. (p. 659) This variance tells managers how much of the total direct materials variance is due to paying a higher or lower price than expected for the direct materials it purchased. It is calculated as follows: $AQP \times (AP - SP)$.

Direct Materials Quantity Variance. (p. 659) This variance tells managers how much of the total direct materials variance is due to using a larger or smaller quantity of direct materials than expected. It is calculated as follows: $SP \times (AQU - SQA)$.

Fixed Overhead Budget Variance. (p. 673) This variance measures the difference between the actual fixed overhead costs incurred and the budgeted fixed overhead costs. This variance is sometimes referred to as the fixed overhead spending variance because it specifically looks at whether the company spent more or less than anticipated on fixed overhead costs.

Fixed Overhead Spending Variance. (p. 673) Another name for the Fixed Overhead Budget Variance. This variance measures the difference between the actual fixed overhead costs incurred and the budgeted fixed overhead costs.

Fixed Overhead Volume Variance. (p. 674) This variance is the difference between the budgeted fixed overhead cost and the *standard fixed overhead cost* allocated to production. In essence, the fixed overhead volume variance measures the utilization of the fixed capacity costs. If volume is higher than originally anticipated, the variance will be favorable. If volume is lower than originally anticipated, the variance will be unfavorable.

Ideal Standards. (p. 654) Standards based on perfect or ideal conditions that do not allow for any waste in the production process, machine breakdown, or other inefficiencies. Also known as perfection standards.

Perfection Standards. (p. 654) Standards based on perfect or ideal conditions that do not allow for any waste in the production process, machine breakdown, or other inefficiencies. Also known as ideal standards.

Practical Standards. (p. 654) Standards based on currently attainable conditions that include allowances for normal amounts of waste and inefficiency. Also known as attainable standards.

Standard Cost. (p. 654) The budgeted cost for a single unit of product. Also simply referred to as standards.

Standard Cost Accounting. (p. 679) Another common name for standard costing.

Standard Costing. (p. 679) Also known as standard cost accounting. A method of accounting in which product costs are entered into the general ledger inventory accounts at standard cost rather than actual cost. The variances are captured in their own general ledger accounts and displayed on a standard costing income statement prior to being closed out at the end of the period.

Standards. (p. 654) Another common name for standard costs.

Variable Overhead Efficiency Variance. (p. 672) This variance tells managers how much of the total variable MOH variance is due to using more or fewer hours of the allocation base (usually machine hours or DL hours) than anticipated for the actual volume of output. It is calculated as follows: $SR \times (AH - SHA)$.

Variable Overhead Rate Variance. (p. 671) Also called the variable overhead spending variance. This variance tells managers whether more or less was spent on variable overhead than they expected would be spent for the hours worked. It is calculated as follows: $AH \times (AR - SR)$.

Variable Overhead Spending Variance. (p. 671) Another common name for variable overhead rate variance.

> MyAccountingLab **Go to** http://myaccountinglab.com/ **for the following Quick Check, Short Exercises, Exercises, and Problems. They are available with immediate grading, explanations of correct and incorrect answers, and interactive media that acts as your own online tutor.**

Quick Check

1. (*Learning Objective 1*) Which of the following is true?
   a. Ideal standards are based on currently attainable conditions.
   b. Practical standards are based on ideal conditions.
   c. A standard cost is the budgeted cost for one unit.
   d. Standards should never be updated.

2. (*Learning Objective 2*) The direct material price variance can be defined as which of the following?
   a. Standard quantity allowed × (Actual price – Standard price)
   b. Actual quantity purchased × (Actual price – Standard price)
   c. Standard price × (Actual quantity used – Standard quantity allowed)
   d. Actual price × (Actual quantity used – Standard quantity allowed)

3. (*Learning Objective 2*) The direct material quantity variance can be defined as which of the following?
   a. Actual price × (Actual quantity used – Standard quantity allowed)
   b. Standard quantity allowed × (Actual price – Standard price)
   c. Standard price × (Actual quantity used – Standard quantity allowed)
   d. Actual quantity purchased × (Actual price – Standard price)

4. (*Learning Objective 3*) The direct labor rate variance can be defined as which of the following?
   a. Actual hours × (Actual rate – Standard rate)
   b. Actual rate × (Actual hours – Standard hours allowed)
   c. Standard hours allowed × (Actual rate – Standard rate)
   d. Standard rate × (Actual hours – Standard hours allowed)

5. (*Learning Objective 3*) The direct labor efficiency variance can be defined as which of the following?
   a. Standard hours allowed × (Actual rate – Standard rate)
   b. Standard rate × (Actual hours – Standard hours allowed)
   c. Actual hours × (Actual rate – Standard rate)
   d. Actual rate × (Actual hours – Standard hours allowed)

6. (*Learning Objective 4*) Which of the following is **not** an advantage of using standard costs?
   a. Standards can cause unintended behavioral consequences.
   b. Standards are useful for budgeting.
   c. Standards serve as cost benchmarks.
   d. Standards can simplify bookkeeping.

7. (*Learning Objective 5*) The variable overhead rate variance can be defined as which of the following?
   a. Standard hours allowed × (Actual rate – Standard rate)
   b. Standard rate × (Actual hours – Standard hours allowed)
   c. Actual rate × (Actual hours – Standard hours allowed)
   d. Actual hours × (Actual rate – Standard rate)

8. (*Learning Objective 6*) Which of the following is **not** true about the fixed overhead budget variance?
   a. It is the difference between actual fixed overhead and budgeted fixed overhead.
   b. It is the difference between the budgeted fixed overhead and the standard fixed overhead allocated to production.
   c. It can be either favorable or unfavorable.
   d. It is sometimes referred to as the fixed overhead spending variance.

9. (*Learning Objective 6*) Which of the following is **not** true about the fixed overhead volume variance?
   a. It is partially the result of treating fixed overhead costs as if they were variable for allocating the costs to individual units of production.
   b. If production volume is lower than originally anticipated, then fixed overhead cost would be underallocated.
   c. It is partially the result of incorrectly estimating the level of activity when calculating the predetermined fixed manufacturing overhead rate.
   d. If production volume is greater than originally anticipated, the variance will be unfavorable.

10. (*Learning Objective 7—Appendix*) Which of the following is **not** true about standard costing systems?
    a. A standard cost income statement shows cost of goods sold at standard, along with all of the variances needed to adjust cost of goods sold back to actual.
    b. Each type of variance has its own general ledger account.
    c. At the end of the period, the variances are closed to the Sales Revenue account.
    d. Standard costs are used to record the manufacturing costs entered into the inventory accounts.

Quick Check Answers

1. c 2. b 3. c 4. a 5. b 6. a 7. d 8. b 9. d 10. c

12

Capital Investment Decisions and the Time Value of Money

Wendy M. Tietz

Sources: Cedarpoint.com; Cedar Fair, L.P. 2015 10(K) filing, http://www.toledoblade.com/Retail/2015/09/10/Cedar-Point-plans-new-241-foot-tall-ride.html; http://coaster-nation.com/2015-golden-ticket-award-winners-announced/

Learning Objectives

- ■ **1** Describe the importance of capital investments and the capital budgeting process

- ■ **2** Use the payback and accounting rate of return methods to make capital investment decisions

- ■ **3** Use the time value of money to compute the present and future values of single lump sums and annuities

- ■ **4** Use discounted cash flow models to make capital investment decisions

- ■ **5** Compare and contrast the four capital budgeting methods

Cedar Fair Entertainment Company is a leading operator of amusement parks in the United States and Canada, entertaining over 24 million guests each year. The company's flagship park, Cedar Point, in Sandusky, Ohio, is known as the "Roller Coaster Capital of the World." The park has a world-record-breaking collection of 18 roller coasters, as well as an abundance of non-coaster rides and attractions. The newest roller coaster, "Valravn," which opened in 2016, is set to break 10 world records, including the tallest, fastest, and longest dive roller coaster in the world. Valravn cost about $25 million to build. Historical evidence has shown management that park attendance, revenues, profits, and spending per guest are driven by their ability to invest in new attractions. Thus, the company routinely spends well over $100 million a year in capital improvements at all of its amusement parks, continually adding new attractions that will draw people to the parks. The results of management's strategy are clear: Cedar Point has been voted the "Best Amusement Park in the World" for 16 consecutive years by *Amusement Today*'s international survey.

As the chapter-opening story shows, companies must continually evaluate whether they need to invest in new property, buildings, equipment, or projects in order to remain competitive or increase their revenue stream. Companies also initiate capital improvements in order to save on existing costs. For example, many companies are investing in highly efficient heating, ventilation, and air-conditioning (HVAC) systems to save millions of dollars on annual energy costs while at the same time reducing the use of fossil fuels. Management must carefully consider whether the additional revenues or cost savings will be worth the high price of these new capital investments. In this chapter, we'll see how companies such as Cedar Fair use net present value, payback period, and other capital investment analysis techniques to assess possible new investments.

What Is Capital Budgeting?

The process of making capital investment decisions is often referred to as **capital budgeting**. Companies make capital investments when they acquire *capital assets*—assets used for long periods of time. Capital investments include investments in new equipment, new plants, new vehicles, and new information technology. In addition to affecting operations for many years, capital investments usually require large sums of money. Cedar Point's decision to spend $25 million on the Valravn roller coaster will tie up resources for years to come.

Capital investment decisions affect all types of businesses as they try to become more efficient by automating production and implementing new technologies. For example, within the last 10 years, self-service checkout machines at grocery stores and self-service check-in kiosks at airports have become commonplace. These devices end up decreasing the company's labor costs by shifting the burden of labor to the end consumer. Businesses are always striving to cut costs, improve customer response time, decrease waste, and improve quality by implementing the latest technologies. These new technologies cost money up front but end up saving businesses cash in the long run. How do managers decide whether these expansions in plant, technology, and equipment will be good investments? They use capital budgeting analysis.

1 Describe the importance of capital investments and the capital budgeting process

Four Popular Methods of Capital Budgeting Analysis

In this chapter, we discuss four common methods of analyzing potential capital investments:

1. Payback period
2. Accounting rate of return (ARR)
3. Net present value (NPV)
4. Internal rate of return (IRR)

The first two methods, payback period and accounting rate of return, work well for capital investments that have a relatively short lifespan, such as computer equipment and software. They also work well as screening devices to quickly weed out less desirable investments from those that show more promise. The payback period provides management with valuable information on how fast the cash invested in the asset will be recouped. The accounting rate of return indicates the profitability of the investment with respect to its impact on operating income. Despite the insights provided by the payback period and ARR, these two methods are inadequate if the capital investments have a longer lifespan. Why? Because these methods do not consider the time value of money. The last two methods, net present value and internal rate of return, factor in the time value of money, so they are more appropriate for longer-term capital investments such as Cedar Fair's new roller coasters and rides. Management often uses a combination of methods to make final capital investment decisions.

> **Why is this important?**
> "Each of these **four methods** help managers **decide** whether it would be wise to **invest** large sums of money in **new technologies**, buildings, or equipment."

Focus on Cash Flows

Generally Accepted Accounting Principles (GAAP) is based on accrual accounting, but capital budgeting focuses on cash flows. The desirability of a capital asset depends on its ability to generate *net cash inflows*—that is, inflows in excess of outflows—over the asset's useful life. Recall that operating income based on accrual accounting contains noncash expenses such as depreciation expense and bad debt expense. The capital investment's *net cash inflows*, therefore, will differ from the operating income generated from the asset. Of the four capital budgeting methods covered in this chapter, only the accounting rate of return method uses accrual-based accounting income. The other three methods use the investment's projected *net cash inflows*.

What do the projected net cash inflows include? Cash *inflows* include future cash revenue generated from the investment, any future savings in ongoing cash operating costs resulting from the investment, and any future residual value of the asset. To determine the investment's *net* cash inflows, the inflows are *netted* against the investment's future cash *outflows*, such as the investment's ongoing cash operating costs and refurbishment, repairs, and maintenance costs. The initial investment itself is also a significant cash outflow. However, in our calculations, *we refer to the amount of the initial investment separately from all other cash flows related to the investment.*

While the capital budgeting methods discussed in this chapter seem procedurally cut and dry, remember that they are based on estimates and assumptions about cash flows in an uncertain future. These predictions must consider many unknown factors, such as changing consumer preferences, competition, resource costs, general economic conditions, and government regulations. The further into the future the decision extends, the more likely actual results will differ from predictions. In general, decisions that rely on long-term estimates are riskier than those that rely on short-term estimates. Much of capital investment analysis revolves around estimating future cash flows as accurately as possible. The "answers" given by the four methods will only be as good as the assumptions used in predicting future cash flows.

Capital Budgeting Process

As shown in Exhibit 12-1, the first step in the capital budgeting process is to identify potential capital investments—for example, new technology and equipment that may make the company more efficient, competitive, and profitable. Employees, consultants, and outside sales vendors often submit capital investment proposals to management. The second step is to estimate the investments' future net cash inflows. In other words, managers must make realistic estimates about future costs, revenues, and savings that are expected to occur as a result of making the capital investment. As discussed previously, this step can be very challenging. However, managers must make the best estimates possible given the information that is currently available.

The third step is to analyze the investments using one or more of the four methods listed earlier in the chapter. Sometimes the analysis involves a two-stage process. In the first stage, managers screen the investments using one or both of the methods that do *not* incorporate the time value of money: payback period or accounting rate of return. These simple methods quickly weed out undesirable investments. Potential investments that "pass the initial test" go on to a second stage of analysis. In the second stage, managers further analyze the potential investments using the net present value or internal rate of return method. Because these methods consider the time value of money, they provide more accurate information about the potential investment's profitability. Since each method evaluates the potential investment from a different angle, some companies use all four methods to get the most complete picture they can about the investment.

Because of limited resources, most companies cannot immediately invest in every capital project that appears promising. Therefore, the fourth step of the budgeting process, pictured in Exhibit 12-1, is to engage in **capital rationing**. Capital rationing means the company must choose among alternative investments due to limited funds. Managers often rank the order in which they will pursue investments, based on which investments are deemed most important, have the shortest payback period, or are expected to yield the highest return. The list of potential investments is constantly revisited as consumer tastes, newer technologies, competition, and general economic forces continually change.

EXHIBIT 12-1 Capital Budgeting Process

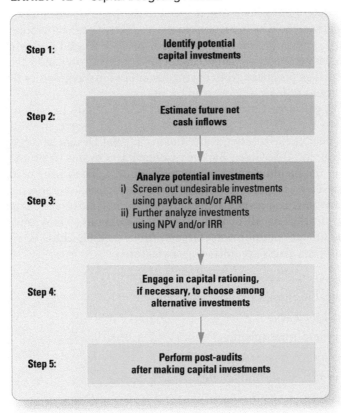

Step 1:	**Identify potential capital investments**
Step 2:	**Estimate future net cash inflows**
Step 3:	**Analyze potential investments** i) Screen out undesirable investments using payback and/or ARR ii) Further analyze investments using NPV and/or IRR
Step 4:	**Engage in capital rationing, if necessary, to choose among alternative investments**
Step 5:	**Perform post-audits after making capital investments**

As a final step in the capital budgeting process, most companies perform **post-audits** in which they compare the investment's actual net cash inflows with the net cash inflows that were originally estimated. Post-audits help companies determine whether the investments are going as planned and deserve continued support or whether new strategies need to be developed to improve the profitability of underperforming assets. Managers also use feedback from post-audits to better estimate net cash inflows for future projects. If managers expect routine post-audits, they will more likely submit realistic estimates with their capital investment proposals.

Sustainability and Capital Investments

Investments in environmentally friendly technology often require large capital outlays that are assessed using capital investment analysis. In recent years, companies have focused a great deal of attention on the amount and type of energy used in their corporate and retail buildings, manufacturing plants, and delivery fleets. Investments in renewable energy have risen dramatically in recent years, especially with respect to wind and solar energy projects, which have become much more financially attractive as a result of the decreasing cost of wind turbines and photovoltaic technology. For example, Intel, Johnson & Johnson, and Toyota use solar energy panels on their manufacturing rooftops, and Staples and UPS are investing in hybrid delivery fleets. Technological strides in energy-monitoring sensors and HVAC (heating, ventilation, and air conditioning) systems have also enabled companies to become more energy efficient.

Regulation is impacting capital investments, too. For example, beginning in 2017 all new construction in San Francisco will be required to have rooftop solar systems. At the historic 2015 Paris Climate Conference (COP 21), 195 countries agreed to take action that will limit global warming to less than 2 degrees Celsius. As a result, additional investment in clean energy is expected in future years. Companies need to be aware of grants and tax breaks that governmental agencies sometimes offer for investing in green technology. Government-sponsored incentives should be treated as reductions in the initial cost of the investment or as periodic cost savings, depending on how the incentive is structured and when it is received. When analyzing more sustainable capital investments, companies should factor in future cost savings produced from having fewer lawsuits, regulatory fines, and cleanup costs as a result of investing in green technology.

One of the largest movements toward sustainability in built environments can be traced to the LEED certification process, which began in 2000. **LEED,** which stands for Leadership in Energy and Environmental Design, is a certification system developed by the U.S. Green Building Council as a means of promoting sustainable practices in the building and construction industry. The LEED certification process is meant to serve as a guide for the design, construction, operation, and maintenance of built environments. Some companies, such as Starbucks, are committed to seeking LEED certification on all of their new retail locations. Many university campuses have made similar commitments. Organizations seeking LEED certification for their building projects assess the following six factors:

1. Location and Transportation
2. Sustainable Sites
3. Water Efficiency
4. Energy and Atmosphere
5. Materials and Resources
6. Indoor Environmental Quality

LEED projects can be certified at the basic (certified), silver, gold, or platinum level, depending on the number of points earned over all of the categories. For example, Toyota's new $1 billion North American headquarters that will open in 2017 is seeking the highest "Platinum" level of LEED certification. Over 80,000 buildings have been certified to date, and another 1 million are currently in process. Why do companies care about LEED certification? Besides being better for the planet and the people who work in the buildings, LEED-certified buildings typically have lower operating costs, which often result in higher returns on the investment. Additionally, LEED-certified buildings have a competitive advantage over noncertified buildings. As a result, LEED-certified buildings often attract more potential buyers and command higher lease prices. You can learn more about LEED certification at USGB.org.

See Exercises E12-23A and E12-42B

Sources: usgbc.org; http://newsroom.unfccc.int/unfccc-newsroom/finale-cop21; www.environmentalleader .com/2016/05/03/hybrid-electric-delivery-trucks-extend-ups-fleet-range-improve-fuel-economy/; www .environmentalleader.com/2016/06/07/toyotas-new-hq-targets-leed-platinum-houses-7-7mw-solar-system/; www.environmentalleader.com/2011/07/06/staples-coke-ge-among-newest-clean-fleets-partners/; www .starbucks.com/responsibility/environment/leed-certified-stores; www.environmentalleader.com/2016/06/08/ breeam-green-building-rating-system-arrives-in-us/

How Do Managers Calculate the Payback Period and Accounting Rate of Return?

2 Use the payback and accounting rate of return methods to make capital investment decisions

Payback Period

Payback period is the length of time it takes to recover, in net cash inflows, the cost of the capital outlay. The payback period measures how quickly managers expect to recover their investment dollars. The shorter the payback period, the more attractive the asset, *all else being equal.* Why? The quicker an investment pays itself back, the less the inherent risk that the investment will become unprofitable. The method used to compute the payback period depends on whether net cash inflows are expected to be equal each year or whether they will vary each year. To illustrate, we'll discuss three capital investments being considered by Tierra Firma, a company that makes and sells camping equipment. For the sake of simplicity, let's assume that each of the following potential investments is expected to cost $240,000:

- An updated energy-efficient HVAC system for the company's corporate offices. (*Estimated six-year useful life with no residual value; equal annual net cash energy savings of $60,000*)

- Investment in hardware and software to develop a business-to-business (B2B) portal that will allow the company to reduce the cost of purchasing components throughout its supply chain. (*Estimated three-year useful life with no residual value; equal annual net cash savings of $80,000*)

- New production equipment designed to reduce waste, time, manual labor, and energy consumption (*Estimated six-year useful life with $30,000 residual value; unequal yearly net cash savings as pictured later in Exhibit 12-3*)

> ■ **Why is this important?**
>
> "Companies want to **recover their cash** as quickly as possible. The **payback period** tells managers **how long** it will take before the investment is **recouped**."

Payback Period with Equal Annual Net Cash Inflows

When net cash inflows are equal each year, managers compute the payback period as follows:

$$\text{Payback period} = \frac{\text{Initial investment}}{\text{Expected annual net cash inflow}}$$

Since the new HVAC system will cost $240,000 and is expected to generate equal annual net cash inflows of $60,000, we compute the payback period as follows:

$$\text{Payback period for HVAC system} = \frac{\$240,000}{\$60,000} = 4 \text{ years}$$

The left side of Exhibit 12-2 verifies that Tierra Firma expects to recoup the $240,000 investment in the HVAC system by the end of Year 4, when the accumulated net cash inflows total $240,000.

EXHIBIT 12-2 Payback Period—Equal Annual Net Cash Inflows

	A	B	C	D	E	F	G
1		Payback Analysis for HVAC				Payback Analysis for B2B portal	
2		Initial Investment: $240,000				Initial Investment: $240,000	
3	Year	Annual Net Cash Inflow	Accumulated Net Cash Inflow		Year	Annual Net Cash Inflow	Accumulated Net Cash Inflow
4	1	$ 60,000	$ 60,000		1	$ 80,000	$ 80,000
5	2	$ 60,000	120,000		2	$ 80,000	160,000
6	3	$ 60,000	180,000		(3)	$ 80,000	(240,000)
7	(4)	$ 60,000	(240,000)				
8	5	$ 60,000	300,000				
9	6	$ 60,000	360,000				
10							

Likewise, Tierra Firma can compute the payback period of the B2B portal using the same formula. Recall that the B2B portal will cost $240,000 and result in equal annual cash inflows of $80,000:

$$\text{Payback period for B2B portal} = \frac{\$240,000}{\$80,000} = 3 \text{ years}$$

The right side of Exhibit 12-2 verifies that Tierra Firma will recoup the $240,000 investment for the B2B portal by the end of Year 3, when the accumulated net cash inflows total $240,000.

Payback Period with Unequal Net Cash Inflows

The payback formula only works when net cash inflows are the same each period. When periodic cash flows are expected to be unequal, managers must accumulate net cash inflows until the amount of the investment is recovered. Recall that Tierra Firma is also considering investing in new production equipment that has (1) *unequal* net cash inflows during its six-year life and (2) a $30,000 residual value at the end of its life. The production equipment is expected to generate net cash inflows of $100,000 in Year 1, $80,000 in Year 2, $50,000 each year in Years 3–5, $30,000 in Year 6, and $30,000 when it is sold at the end of its life. Exhibit 12-3 shows the payback schedule for these unequal annual net cash inflows.

EXHIBIT 12-3 Payback Period—Unequal Annual Net Cash Inflows

	A	B	C
1	**Payback Analysis for Production Equipment** *Unequal* **Net Cash Inflows**		
2	**Initial Investment: $240,000**		
3	**Year**	**Annual Net Cash Inflow**	**Accumulated Net Cash Inflow**
4	1	$ 100,000	$ 100,000
5	2	80,000	180,000
6	3	50,000	230,000
7	4	50,000	280,000
8	5	50,000	330,000
9	6	30,000	360,000
10	Residual value	30,000	390,000
11			

Payback period is between 3 and 4 years. After 3 years, there is still $10,000 to recoup before payback of $240,000 is reached.

By the end of Year 3, the company has recovered $230,000 of the $240,000 initially invested and is only $10,000 short of payback. Because the expected net cash inflow in Year 4 is $50,000, by the end of Year 4, the company will have recovered *more* than the initial investment. Therefore, the payback period is somewhere between three and four years. Assuming that the cash flow occurs evenly throughout the fourth year, the payback period is calculated as follows:

$$\text{Payback Period} = 3 \text{ years} + \frac{\$10,000 \text{ (amount needed to complete recovery in Year 4)}}{\$50,000 \text{ (projected net cash inflow in Year 4)}}$$

$$= 3.2 \text{ years}$$

Criticism of the Payback Period Method

A major criticism of the payback method is that it focuses only on time, not on profitability. The payback period considers only those cash flows that occur *during* the payback period. This method ignores any cash flows that occur *after* that period, including any residual value. For example, Exhibit 12-2 shows that the HVAC system will continue to generate net cash inflows for two years after its payback period. These additional net cash inflows amount to $120,000 ($60,000 × 2 years), yet the payback method ignores this extra cash. A similar situation occurs with the production equipment. As shown in Exhibit 12-3, the production equipment will provide an additional $150,000 of net cash inflows, including residual value, after its payback period of 3.2 years. In contrast, the B2B portal's useful life, as shown in Exhibit 12-2, is the *same* as its payback period (three years). Since no additional cash flows occur after the payback period, the B2B portal will merely cover its cost and provide no profit. Because this is the case, the company has little or no reason to invest in the B2B portal, even though its payback period is the shortest of all three investments.

Exhibit 12-4 compares the payback period of the three investments. As the exhibit illustrates, the payback method does not consider the asset's profitability. *The method only tells management how quickly it will recover its cash.* Even though the B2B portal has the shortest payback period, both the HVAC system and the production equipment are better investments because they provide profit. The key point is that the investment with the shortest payback period is best *only when all other factors are the same.* Therefore, managers usually use the payback method as a screening device to "weed out" investments that will take too long to recoup. They rarely use payback period as the sole method for deciding whether to invest in the asset.

EXHIBIT 12-4 Comparing Payback Periods Between Investments

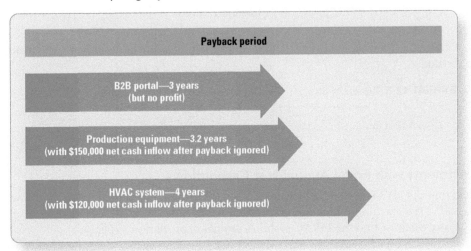

When using the payback period method, managers are guided by the following decision rule:

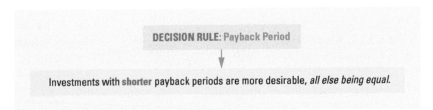

DECISION RULE: Payback Period

Investments with **shorter** payback periods are more desirable, *all else being equal.*

▶ Try It!

The Bruce Company is considering investing in a wind turbine to generate its own power. Any unused power will be sold back to the local utility company. Between cost savings and new revenues, the company expects to generate net cash inflows of $750,000 per year from the turbine. The turbine would cost $4 million and is expected to have a 20-year useful life, with no residual value. Calculate the payback period.

Please see page 777 for solutions.

Accounting Rate of Return (ARR)

Companies are in business to earn profits. One measure of profitability is the **accounting rate of return (ARR)** on an asset:[1]

$$\text{Accounting rate of return} = \frac{\text{Average annual operating income from asset}}{\text{Initial investment}}$$

[1] Some managers prefer to use the average investment, rather than the initial investment, as the denominator. For simplicity, we will use the initial amount of the investment.

The ARR focuses on the *operating income, not the net cash inflow*, that an asset generates. The ARR measures the average annual rate of return over the asset's life. Operating income is based on *accrual accounting*. Therefore, any noncash expenses such as depreciation expense must be subtracted from the asset's net cash inflows to arrive at its operating income. Assuming that depreciation expense is the only noncash expense relating to the investment, we can rewrite the ARR formula as follows:

$$\text{ARR} = \frac{\text{Average annual net cash inflow} - \text{Annual depreciation expense}}{\text{Initial investment}}$$

Exhibit 12-5 reviews how to calculate annual depreciation expense using the straight-line method.

EXHIBIT 12-5 Review of Straight-Line Depreciation Expense Calculation

$$\text{Annual straight-line depreciation expense} = \frac{\text{Initial cost of asset} - \text{Residual value}}{\text{Useful life of asset (in years)}}$$

Investments with Equal Annual Net Cash Inflows

Recall that the HVAC system, which costs $240,000, has equal annual net cash inflows of $60,000, a six-year useful life, and no residual value.

First, we must find the HVAC system's annual depreciation expense:

$$\text{Annual depreciation expense} = \frac{\$240,000 - 0}{6 \text{ years}} = \$40,000$$

Now, we can complete the ARR formula:

$$\text{ARR for HVAC system} = \frac{\$60,000 - \$40,000}{\$240,000} = \frac{\$20,000}{\$240,000} = 8.33\% \text{ (rounded)}$$

The HVAC system will provide an average annual accounting rate of return of 8.33%.

Investments with Unequal Net Cash Inflows

Now, consider the company's potential investment in new production equipment. Recall that the new production equipment would also cost $240,000 but it had unequal net cash inflows during its life (as pictured in Exhibit 12-3) and a $30,000 residual value at the end of its life. Since the yearly net cash inflows vary in size, we need to first calculate the equipment's *average* annual net cash inflows:[2]

Total net cash inflows *during* operating life of asset (does not include the residual value at the end of life)[2] from Exhibit 12-3.........................	$360,000
Divide by: Asset's operating life (in years)..	÷ 6 years
Average annual net cash inflow from asset...	$ 60,000

Now, let's calculate the asset's annual depreciation expense:

$$\text{Annual depreciation expense} = \frac{\$240,000 - \$30,000}{6 \text{ years}} = \$35,000$$

---

[2] The residual value is not included in the net cash inflows *during* the asset's operating life because we are trying to find the asset's average *annual operating* income. We assume that the asset will be sold for its expected residual value ($30,000) at the *end* of its life, resulting in no additional accounting gain or loss.

Notice how the expected residual value drives down the annual depreciation expense. Now that we have calculated the terms for the numerator, we can complete the ARR calculation as follows:

$$\text{ARR for production equipment} = \frac{\$60,000 - \$35,000}{\$240,000} = \frac{\$25,000}{\$240,000} = 10.42\% \text{ (rounded)}$$

Companies usually have a minimum required accounting rate of return for new investments. If Tierra Firma required an ARR of at least 10%, its managers would not approve the HVAC investment but would approve the production equipment investment. The decision rule is as follows:

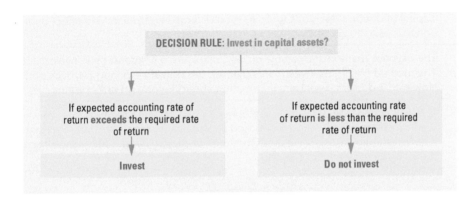

In summary, the payback period focuses on the time it takes for a company to recoup its cash investment. However, it ignores all cash flows occurring after the payback period, including any residual value. As a result, the payback period does not consider the profitability of the project.

On the other hand, the ARR measures the profitability of the asset over its entire life. The ARR is the only method that focuses on accrual-based accounting income rather than net cash inflows. Since investors tend to focus on accounting earnings, it is important for managers to understand what impact an investment will have on the company's operating income.

The payback period and ARR methods are simple and quick to compute, so managers often use them to screen out undesirable investments and to gain a more complete picture of the investment's desirability. However, both methods ignore the time value of money. In the next sections, we will review the theory behind the time value of money and then apply it to capital investments using the NPV and IRR methods.

Try It!

The Bruce Company is considering investing in a wind turbine to generate its own power. Any unused power will be sold back to the local utility company. Between cost savings and new revenues, the company expects to generate $750,000 per year in net cash inflows from the turbine. The turbine would cost $4 million and is expected to have a 20-year useful life with no residual value. Calculate the accounting rate of return (ARR).

Please see page 777 for solutions.

Decision Guidelines

Capital Budgeting

Amazon.com started as a virtual retailer. It held no inventory. Instead, it bought books and CDs only as needed to fill customer orders. As the company grew, its managers decided to invest in their own warehouse facilities. Why? Owning warehouse facilities allows Amazon.com to save money by buying in bulk. Also, shipping all items in the customer's order in one package from one location saves shipping costs. Here are some of the guidelines Amazon.com's managers used as they made the major capital budgeting decision to invest in building warehouses.

Decision	Guidelines
Why is this decision important?	Capital budgeting decisions typically require large investments and affect operations for years to come.
What method shows us how soon we will recoup our cash investment?	The payback method shows how quickly managers will recoup their investment. The method highlights investments that are too risky due to long payback periods. However, it doesn't reveal any information about the investment's profitability.
Does any method consider the impact of the investment on accrual-based accounting income?	The accounting rate of return is the only capital budgeting method that shows how the investment will affect accrual-based accounting income, which is important to financial statement users. All other methods of capital investment analysis focus on the investment's net cash inflows.
How do we compute the payback period if cash flows are *equal*?	$$\text{Payback period} = \frac{\text{Initial investment}}{\text{Expected annual net cash inflow}}$$
How do we compute the payback period if cash flows are *unequal*?	Accumulate net cash inflows until the amount invested is recovered.
How do we compute the ARR?	$$\text{Accounting rate of return} = \frac{\text{Average annual operating income from asset}}{\text{Initial investment}}$$ We can also write this formula as follows: $$\text{ARR} = \frac{\text{Average annual net cash inflow} - \text{Annual depreciation expense}}{\text{Initial investment}}$$

SUMMARY PROBLEM **1**

Sonoma is considering investing in solar paneling for the roof of its large distribution facility. The investment will cost $9 million and have a six-year useful life and no residual value. Because of rising utility costs, the company expects the yearly utility savings to increase over time, as follows:

Year 1	$1,000,000
Year 2	$1,500,000
Year 3	$2,000,000
Year 4	$2,500,000
Year 5	$3,500,000
Year 6	$4,500,000

The company uses the payback period and ARR to screen potential investments. Company policy requires a payback period of less than five years and an ARR of at least 10%. Any potential investments that do not meet these criteria will be removed from further consideration.

1. Calculate the payback period of the solar panels.
2. Calculate the ARR of the solar panels.
3. Should Sonoma turn down the solar panel investment or consider it further?

▪ SOLUTIONS

1. Since the net cash flows are uneven, Sonoma cannot use the simple payback formula. Rather, Sonoma must add up the accumulated net cash inflows until payback is reached, as follows:

	A	B	C	D	E
1	Payback Analysis for Solar Panels				
2	*Unequal* Net Cash Inflows				
3	Initial Investment: $9 million				
4					
5	Year	Annual Net Cash Inflow	Accumulated Net Cash Inflow		
6	1	$ 1,000,000	$ 1,000,000		
7	2	1,500,000	2,500,000		
8	3	2,000,000	4,500,000		
9	4	2,500,000	7,000,000		
10	5	3,500,000	10,500,000		
11	6	4,500,000	15,000,000		
12					

Payback occurs between four and five years. After four years, $2 million is left to be recouped before payback is reached. Since the company expects $3.5 million of savings in Year 5, we can further estimate the payback period as follows:

$$\text{Payback} = 4 \text{ years} + \frac{\$2 \text{ million}}{\$3.5 \text{ million}} = 4.57 \text{ years}$$

2. The ARR formula is as follows:

$$\text{ARR} = \frac{\text{Average annual net cash inflow} - \text{Annual depreciation expense}}{\text{Initial investment}}$$

To use this formula, we first need to find the *average* annual net cash inflows of the solar panels. We find the average by taking the total expected cash inflows during the six-year life of the asset ($15 million) and dividing it by six years:

Total net cash inflows during six-year life................................	$15,000,000
Divide by: Useful life..	÷ 6 years
Average annual net cash inflow...	$ 2,500,000

Next, find annual depreciation expense:

Annual depreciation = $9 million ÷ 6 years = $1,500,000

Finally, use these figures in the ARR formula:

$$\text{ARR} = \frac{\$2,500,000 - \$1,500,000}{\$9,000,000} = 11.11\%$$

3. The payback period is less than five years and the ARR is greater than 10%. Therefore, the company should further consider the solar panel proposal.

How Do Managers Compute the Time Value of Money?

A dollar received today is worth more than a dollar to be received in the future. Why? Because you can invest today's dollar and earn extra income with it. The fact that invested money earns income over time is called the **time value of money**. Because of the time value of money, cash flows received sooner in time are worth more than cash flows received later in time. In other words, the timing of the cash flows received from a capital investment is important. The NPV and IRR methods of analyzing capital investments take the time value of money into consideration. This section reviews time value of money concepts to make sure you have a firm foundation for discussing these two methods.

3 Use the time value of money to compute the present and future values of single lump sums and annuities

Factors Affecting the Time Value of Money

The time value of money depends on several key factors:

1. The principal amount (p)
2. The number of periods (n)
3. The interest rate (i)

The principal (p) refers to the amount of the investment or borrowing. Because this chapter deals with capital investments, we'll primarily discuss the principal in terms of investments. However, the same concepts apply to borrowings (which you probably discussed in your financial accounting course when you studied bonds payable). We state the principal as either a single lump sum or an annuity. For example, if you want to save money for a new car after college, you may decide to invest a single lump sum of $10,000 in a certificate of deposit (CD). However, you may not currently have $10,000 to invest. Instead, you may invest funds as an annuity, depositing $2,000 at the end of each year in a bank savings account. An **annuity** is a stream of *equal installments* made at *equal time intervals*. An *ordinary annuity* is an annuity in which the installments occur at the *end* of each period. Throughout this chapter, all references to annuities will be treated as ordinary annuities because they are best suited to capital budgeting cash flow assumptions.[3]

> ### Why is this important?
>
> "The **time value of money** is a critical factor in many management **decisions**. In addition to its use in capital investment analysis, it's also used for **personal financial planning** (such as retirement planning), **business valuation** (for purchasing businesses), and **financing decisions** (borrowing and lending)."

The number of periods (n) is the length of time from the beginning of the investment until termination. All else being equal, the shorter the investment period, the lower the total amount of interest earned. If you withdraw your savings after four years rather than five years, you will earn less interest. If you begin to save for retirement at age 22 rather than age 45, you will earn more interest before you retire. In this chapter, the number of periods is stated in years.[4]

The interest rate (i) is the annual percentage earned on the investment. **Simple interest** means that interest is calculated *only* on the principal amount. **Compound interest** means that interest is calculated on the principal *and* on all interest earned to date. *Compound interest assumes that all interest earned will remain invested at the same interest rate, not withdrawn and spent.* Exhibit 12-6 compares simple interest (6%) on a five-year, $10,000 CD with interest compounded yearly. As you can see, the amount of compound interest earned each year grows as the base on which it is calculated (principal plus cumulative interest to date) grows. Over the life of this particular investment, the total amount of compound interest is about 13% more than the total amount of simple interest. Most investments yield compound interest, so we assume compound interest rather than simple interest for the rest of this chapter.

---

[3] In contrast to an *ordinary annuity*, an *annuity due* is an annuity in which the installments occur at the *beginning* of each period.

[4] The number of periods can also be stated in days, months, or quarters. If so, the interest rate needs to be adjusted to reflect the number of time periods in the year.

EXHIBIT 12-6 Simple Versus Compound Interest for a Principal Amount of $10,000 at 6% over Five Years

	A	B	C	D	E	F	G	H	I
1		Simple Interest Calculation					Compound Interest Calculation		
2	Year	Principal	Interest rate	Interest		Year	Principal*	Interest rate	Interest
3	1	$ 10,000	6%	600		1	$ 10,000	6%	$ 600
4	2	$ 10,000	6%	600		2	$ 10,600	6%	$ 636
5	3	$ 10,000	6%	600		3	$ 11,236	6%	$ 674
6	4	$ 10,000	6%	600		4	$ 11,910	6%	$ 715
7	5	$ 10,000	6%	600		5	$ 12,625	6%	$ 758
8				$ 3,000					$ 3,383
9									
10									

*NOTE: For compound interest calculations, the principal is the original amount ($10,000) plus the cumulative interest earned to date. For example, the principal amount in Year 2 ($10,600) is the original $10,000 plus the $600 of interest earned during Year 1. The principal amount in Year 3 ($11,236) is the original principal ($10,000) plus the interest earned in Year 1 and Year 2 ($600 + $636).

Fortunately, time value calculations involving compound interest do not have to be as tedious as those shown in Exhibit 12-6. Rather, they can be easily performed using Excel financial functions, a business calculator, or formulas and tables. Using these tools simplifies the calculations. In the next sections, we will discuss how to use these tools to perform time value of money calculations.

Future Values and Present Values: Points Along the Time Continuum

Consider the time line in Exhibit 12-7. The future value or present value of an investment simply refers to the value of an investment at different points in time.

EXHIBIT 12-7 Present Value and Future Value Along the Time Continuum

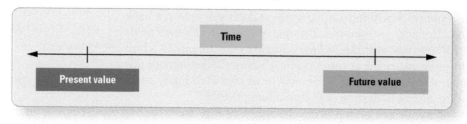

We can calculate the future value or the present value of any investment by knowing (or assuming) information about the three factors listed earlier: (1) the principal amount, (2) the number of periods, and (3) the interest rate. For example, in Exhibit 12-6, we calculated the interest that would be earned on (1) a $10,000 principal (2) invested for five years (3) at 6% interest. The future value of the investment is its worth at the end of the five-year time frame—the original principal *plus* the interest earned. In our example, the future value of the investment is as follows:

Future value = Principal + Interest earned
= $10,000 + $3,383
= $13,383

If we invest $10,000 *today*, its *present value* is simply the $10,000 principal amount. So, another way of stating the future value is as follows:

Future value = Present value + Interest earned

We can rearrange the equation as follows:

$$\begin{array}{rcl} \text{Present value} & = & \text{Future value} \; - \; \text{Interest earned} \\ \$10,000 & = & \$13,383 \quad - \quad \$3,383 \end{array}$$

The only difference between present value and future value is the amount of interest that is earned in the intervening time span.

Future Value and Present Value Factors

Calculating each period's compound interest, as we did in Exhibit 12-6, and then adding it to the present value to determine the future value (or subtracting it from the future value to determine the present value) is tedious. Fortunately, mathematical formulas simplify future value and present value calculations. Mathematical formulas have been developed that specify future values and present values for unlimited combinations of interest rates (i) and time periods (n). Separate formulas exist for single lump-sum investments and annuities.

The formulas have been calculated using various interest rates and time periods. The results are displayed in tables. The formulas and resulting tables are shown in Appendix 12A at the end of this chapter:

1. Present Value of $1 (Table A, p. 743)—*used for lump-sum amounts*
2. Present Value of Annuity of $1 (Table B, p. 744)—*used for annuities*
3. Future Value of $1 (Table C, p. 745)—*used for lump-sum amounts*
4. Future Value of Annuity of $1 (Table D, p. 746)—*used for annuities*

Take a moment to look at these tables because we are going to use them throughout the rest of the chapter. Note that the columns are interest rates (i) and the rows are periods (n).

The data in each table, known as future value factors (FV factors) and present value factors (PV factors), are for an amount of $1. To find the future value or present value of an amount other than $1, you simply multiply the factor found in the table by the actual amount of the lump sum or annuity.

Rather than using these tables, you may wish to use Microsoft Excel or a business calculator that has been programmed with time value of money functions. These technology applications make time value of money computations much easier because you do not need to find the correct PV and FV factors in the tables. Rather, you simply enter the principal amount, interest rate, and number of time periods in the electronic device and instruct the technology to solve for the present or future value for you.

Why is this important?

"The **easiest** way to find **present values** (PV) and **future values** (FV) is to use the PV and FV functions in **Excel**. The 'Technology Makes it Simple' **features** will show you how."

Throughout the remainder of this chapter, we will be displaying technology features that provide you with easy instruction on how to perform time value of money, NPV, and IRR calculations using Excel. In addition, Appendix 12B illustrates the exact Excel keystrokes to use to solve every chapter example. Appendix 12C also illustrates how to solve every chapter example using a TI-83 or TI-84 graphing calculator.

As you will see, using a programmed calculator or Excel results in slightly different answers than those presented in the text when using the tables. The differences are due to the fact that the PV and FV factors found in the tables have been rounded to three digits. Finally, all end-of-chapter homework material in MyAccountingLab has been solved using the tables, Excel, and programmed calculators so that you will have the exact solution for the method you choose to use.

Calculating Future Values of Single Sums and Annuities Using FV Factors

Let's go back to our $10,000 lump-sum investment. If we want to know the future value of the investment five years from now at an interest rate of 6%, we determine the FV factor from the table labeled Future Value of $1 (Appendix 12A, Table C). We use this table for lump-sum amounts. We look down the 6% column and across the five periods row and find that the future value factor is 1.338. We finish our calculations as follows:

$$\text{Future value} = \text{Principal amount} \times (\text{FV factor for } i = 6\%, n = 5)$$
$$= \$10,000 \times (1.338)$$
$$= \$13,380$$

This figure agrees with our earlier calculation of the investment's future value ($13,383) in Exhibit 12-6. (The difference of $3 is due to two facts: (1) the tables round the FV and PV factors to three decimal places, and (2) we rounded our earlier yearly interest calculations in Exhibit 12-6 to the nearest dollar.)

Let's also consider our alternative investment strategy: investing $2,000 at the end of each year for five years. The procedure for calculating the future value of an annuity is similar to calculating the future value of a lump-sum amount. This time, we use the Future Value of Annuity of $1 table (Appendix 12A, Table D). Assuming 6% interest, we once again look down the 6% column. Because we will be making five annual installments, we look across the row marked 5 periods. The Annuity FV factor is 5.637. We finish the calculation as follows:

$$\text{Future value} = \text{Amount of each cash installment} \times (\text{Annuity FV factor for } i = 6\%, n = 5)$$
$$= \$2,000 \times (5.637)$$
$$= \$11,274$$

This is considerably less than the future value ($13,380) of the lump sum of $10,000 even though we invested $10,000 out of pocket either way.

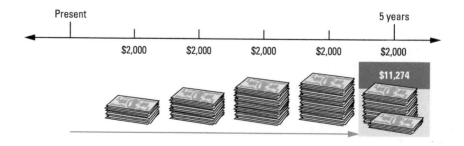

STOP & THINK

Explain why the future value of the annuity is less than the future value of the lump sum even though you are investing a total of $10,000 in both situations.

Answer: Even though you invested $10,000 out of pocket in both situations, the timing of the investment significantly affects the amount of interest earned. The $10,000 lump sum invested immediately earns interest for the full five years. However, the annuity doesn't begin earning interest until Year 2 (because the first installment isn't made until the *end* of Year 1). In addition, the amount invested begins at $2,000 and doesn't reach a full $10,000 until the end of Year 5. Therefore, the base on which the interest is earned is smaller than the lump-sum investment for the entire five-year period.

Technology Makes It Simple   Excel 2016

Future Value Computations

1. In an Excel spreadsheet click on **Formulas**.
2. Click on **Financial**.
3. Choose **FV** from the dropdown list. The following will appear as a dialog box:

   Rate

   Nper

   Pmt

   Pv

   Type

4. Fill in the interest **Rate**, in decimal format (for example, 14% would be input as .14).
5. Fill in the number of periods (for example, five years would be input as 5 in the space by **Nper**).
6. If the amount is an annuity, fill in the yearly installment as a negative number in the space by **Pmt**.
7. If the amount is a lump sum, fill in the lump sum as a negative number in the space by **Pv**.
8. Leave the space by **Type** blank.
9. The future value is shown under the dialog box.

Note: Appendix 12B illustrates each chapter example using these basic Excel instructions.

Calculating Present Values of Single Sums and Annuities Using PV Factors

The process for calculating present values—often called discounting cash flows—is similar to the process for calculating future values. The difference is the point in time at which you are assessing the investment's worth. Rather than determining its value at a future date, you are determining its value at an earlier point in time (today). For our example, let's assume that you've just won the lottery after purchasing one $5 lottery ticket. The state offers you three payout options for your after-tax prize money:

Option #1: $1,000,000 now

Option #2: $150,000 at the end of each year for the next 10 years

Option #3: $2,000,000 10 years from now

Which alternative should you take? You might be tempted to wait 10 years to "double" your winnings. You may be tempted to take the money now and spend it. However, let's assume that you plan to prudently invest all money received—no matter when you receive it—so that you have financial flexibility in the future (for example, for buying a house, retiring early, and taking vacations). How can you choose among the three payment alternatives when the *total amount* of each option varies ($1,000,000 versus $1,500,000 versus $2,000,000) and the *timing* of the cash flows varies (now versus some each year versus later)? Comparing these three options is like comparing apples to oranges—we just can't do it—unless we find some common basis for comparison. Our common basis for comparison will be the prize money's worth at a certain point in time—namely, today. In other words, if we convert each payment option to its *present value*, we can compare apples to apples.

We already know the principal amount and timing of each payment option, so the only assumption we'll have to make is the interest rate. The interest rate will vary depending on the amount of risk you are willing to take with your investment. Riskier investments (such as stock investments) command higher interest rates; safer investments (such as FDIC-insured bank deposits) yield lower interest rates. Let's assume that after investigating possible investment alternatives, you choose an investment contract with an 8% annual return.

We already know that the present value of Option #1 is $1,000,000. Let's convert the other two payment options to their present values so that we can compare them. We'll need to use the Present Value of Annuity of $1 table (Appendix 12A, Table B) to convert payment Option #2 (since it's an annuity) and the Present Value of $1 table (Appendix 12A, Table A) to convert payment Option #3 (because it's a single lump sum). To obtain the PV factors, we look down the 8% column and across the 10 period row. Then, we finish the calculations as follows:

Option #1

Present value = $1,000,000

Option #2

Present value = Amount of each cash installment $\times$ (Annuity PV factor for $i = 8\%, n = 10$)
Present value = $150,000 \times (6.710)$
Present value = $1,006,500

Option #3

Present value = Principal amount $\times$ (PV factor for $i = 8\%, n = 10$)
Present value = $2,000,000 \times (0.463)$
Present value = $926,000

Exhibit 12-8 shows that we have converted each payout option to a common basis—its worth today—so we can make a valid comparison of the options. Based on this comparison, we should choose Option #2 because its worth, in today's dollars, is the highest of the three options.

EXHIBIT 12-8 Comparing Present Values of Lottery Payout Options at *i* = 8%

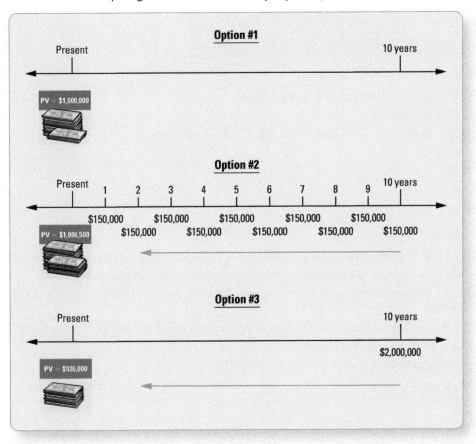

STOP & THINK

Suppose you decide to invest your lottery winnings very conservatively. You decide to invest in a risk-free investment that earns only 3%. Would you still choose payout Option #2? Explain your decision.

Answer: Using a 3% interest rate, we find that the present values of the payout options are as follows:

Payment Options	Present Value of Lottery Payout (Present value calculation, *i* = 3%, *n* = 10)
Option #1..	$1,000,000 (already stated at its present value)
Option #2..	$1,279,500 (= $150,000 × 8.530)
Option #3..	$1,488,000 (= $2,000,000 × 0.744)

When the lottery payout is invested at 3% rather than 8%, the present values change. Option #3 is now the best alternative because its present value is the highest. Present values and future values are extremely sensitive to changes in interest rate assumptions, especially when the investment period is relatively long.

Now that we have studied time value of money concepts, we will discuss the two capital budgeting methods that incorporate the time value of money: net present value (NPV) and internal rate of return (IRR).

Technology Makes It Simple — Excel 2016

Present Value Computations

1. In an Excel spreadsheet click on **Formulas**.
2. Click on **Financial**.
3. Choose **PV** from the dropdown list. The following will appear as a dialog box:

   Rate

   Nper

   Pmt

   FV

   Type

4. Fill in the interest **Rate**, in decimal format (for example, 14% would be input as .14).
5. Fill in the number of periods (for example, five years would be input as 5).
6. If the amount is an annuity, fill in the yearly installment as a negative number in the space by **Pmt**.
7. If the amount is a lump sum, fill in the lump sum as a negative number in the space by **FV**.
8. Leave the space by **Type** blank.
9. The present value is shown under the dialog box.

Note: Appendix 12B illustrates each chapter example using these basic Excel instructions.

How Do Managers Calculate the Net Present Value and Internal Rate of Return?

4 Use discounted cash flow models to make capital investment decisions

Neither the payback period nor the ARR incorporates the time value of money. *Discounted cash flow methods*—the NPV and the IRR—overcome this weakness. These methods incorporate compound interest by assuming that companies will reinvest future cash flows when they are received. Most companies use discounted cash flow methods to help make capital investment decisions.

The NPV and IRR methods rely on present value calculations to compare the cost of the initial investment with the expected net cash inflows that will result from making the investment. Recall that an investment's *net cash inflows* include all *future* cash flows related to the investment, such as future increased revenues and cost savings netted against the investment's future cash operating costs. Because the cash outflow for the investment occurs *now* but the net cash inflows from the investment occur in the *future*, companies can make valid "apple-to-apple" comparisons only when they convert the cash flows to the *same point in time*—namely, the present. Companies use the present value rather than the future value to make the comparison because the investment's initial cost is already stated at its present value.[5] As shown in Exhibit 12-9, a favorable investment is one in which the present value of the investment's net cash inflows exceeds the initial cost of the investment.

Why is this important?

"The **NPV method** lets managers make an **'apples-to-apples' comparison** between the **cash flows** they will receive in the **future** from the investment and the **price** they must **currently pay** to 'purchase' those future cash flows (the cost of the initial **investment**)."

---

[5] If the investment is to be purchased through lease payments, rather than a current cash outlay, we would still use the current cash price of the investment as its initial cost. If no current cash price is available, we would discount the future lease payments back to their present value to estimate the investment's current cash price.

EXHIBIT 12-9 Comparing the Present Value of an Investment's Net Cash Inflows Against the Cost of the Initial Investment

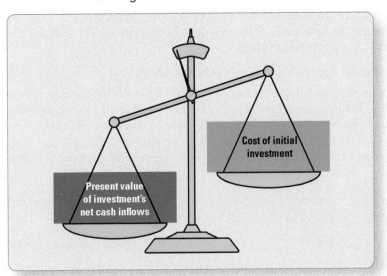

Net Present Value (NPV)

To illustrate how these discounted cash flow methods work, we'll consider two investments currently under consideration by Allegra. Allegra is a contract manufacturer that is considering producing smartphones and Bluetooth speakers for potential name-brand customers. The products require different specialized manufacturing equipment. To keep things simple, let's say that each piece of equipment costs $1 million, has a five-year expected life, and zero residual value. From now on, we'll refer to these potential investments as the Smartphone project and the Speaker project: The two potential investments have different patterns of predicted net cash inflows:

	Annual Net Cash Inflows	
Year	Smartphones	Speakers
1	$ 305,450	$ 500,000
2	305,450	350,000
3	305,450	300,000
4	305,450	250,000
5	305,450	40,000
Total	$1,527,250	$1,440,000

As you can see from the data, the Smartphone project is expected to generate more net cash inflows in total, but the Speaker project is expected to bring cash in sooner. To decide how attractive each investment is, we find its **net present value (NPV)**. The NPV is the *difference* between the present value of the investment's net cash inflows and the cost of the initial investment. We *discount* the net cash inflows to their present value—just as we did in the lottery example—using Allegra's minimum desired rate of return. This rate is called the **discount rate** because it is the interest rate used for the present value calculations. It's also called the **required rate of return** or **hurdle rate** because the investment must meet or exceed this rate to be acceptable. The discount rate depends on the riskiness of investments. The higher the risk, the higher the discount rate. Allegra's discount rate for these investments is 14%.

We compare the present value of the net cash inflows to the cost of the initial investment to decide which projects meet or exceed management's minimum desired rate of return. In other words, management is deciding whether the $1 million is worth more (because the company would have to give it up now to invest in the project) or whether the project's future net cash inflows are worth more. Managers can make a valid comparison between the two sums of money only by comparing them at the *same* point in time—namely, at their present value.

NPV with Equal Annual Net Cash Inflows (Annuity)

Allegra expects the Smartphone project to generate $305,450 of net cash inflows each year for five years. Because these cash flows are equal in amount and occur every year, they are an annuity. Therefore, we use the Present Value of Annuity of $1 table (Appendix 12A, Table B) to find the appropriate Annuity PV factor for $i = 14\%$, $n = 5$.

The present value of the net cash inflows from Allegra's Smartphone project is as follows:

$$\text{Present value} = \text{Amount of each cash inflow} \times (\text{Annuity PV factor for } i = 14\%, n = 5)$$
$$= \$305{,}450 \times (3.433)$$
$$= \$1{,}048{,}610$$

Next, we subtract the investment's initial cost ($1 million) from the present value of the net cash inflows ($1,048,610). The difference of $48,610 is the net present value (NPV), as shown in Exhibit 12-10.

EXHIBIT 12-10 NPV of Equal Net Cash Inflows—Smartphone Project

	A	B	C	D	E	F
1	**NPV Calculation for *Equal* Annual Net Cash Inflows**	**Annuity PV Factor (*i* = 14%)**		**Annual Net Cash Inflow**		**Present Value**
2	Present value of annuity, n = 5	3.433	× $	305,450	= $	1,048,610
3	Less: Initial investment					1,000,000
4	Net present value (NPV)					$ 48,610
5						

NOTE: Arithmetic signs are only shown for illustrative teaching purposes. They are not typically displayed in spreadsheets.

A *positive* NPV means that the investment earns *more* than the required rate of return. A *negative* NPV means that the investment fails to earn the required rate of return. This leads to the following decision rule:

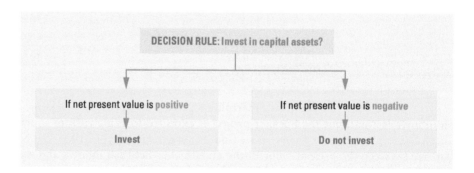

In Allegra's case, the Smartphone project is an attractive investment. The $48,610 positive NPV means that the Smartphone project earns *more than* Allegra's 14% target rate of return. In other words, management would prefer to give up $1 million today to receive the Smartphone project's future net cash inflows. Why? Because those future net cash inflows are worth more than $1 million in today's dollars (they are worth $1,048,610).

Another way managers can use present value analysis is to start the capital budgeting process by computing the total present value of the net cash inflows from the project to determine the *maximum* the company can invest in the project and still earn the target rate of return. For Allegra, the present value of the net cash inflows is $1,048,610. This means that Allegra can invest a maximum of $1,048,610 and still earn the 14% target rate of return. Because Allegra's managers believe they can undertake the project for $1 million, the project is an attractive investment.

▶ Try It!

The Bruce Company is considering investing in a wind turbine to generate its own power. Any unused power will be sold back to the local utility company. Between cost savings and new revenues, the company expects to generate $750,000 per year in net cash inflows from the turbine. The turbine would cost $4 million and is expected to have a 20-year useful life with no residual value. Calculate the NPV assuming the company uses a 12% hurdle rate.

Please see page 778 for solutions.

NPV with Unequal Annual Net Cash Inflows

In contrast to the Smartphone project, the net cash inflows of the Speaker project are unequal—$500,000 in Year 1, $350,000 in Year 2, and so forth. Because these amounts vary by year, Allegra's managers *cannot* use the annuity table to compute the present value of the Speaker project. They must compute the present value of each individual year's net cash inflows *separately, as separate lump sums received in different years*, using the Present Value of $1 table (Appendix 12A, Table A).

Exhibit 12-11 shows that the $500,000 net cash inflow received in Year 1 is discounted using a PV factor of $i = 14\%$, $n = 1$, while the $350,000 net cash inflow received in Year 2 is discounted using a PV factor of $i = 14\%$, $n = 2$, and so forth. After separately discounting each of the five years' net cash inflows, we find that the *total* present value of the Speaker project's net cash inflows is $1,078,910. Finally, we subtract the investment's cost ($1 million) to arrive at the Speaker project's NPV: $78,910.

EXHIBIT 12-11 NPV with Unequal Net Cash Inflows—Speaker Project

	A	B	C	D	E	F
1	**NPV Calculation for *Unequal* Net Cash Inflows**	**PV Factor (*i* = 14%)**		**Net Cash Inflow**		**Present Value**
2	Present value of net cash inflows:					
3	Year 1 (*n* = 1)	0.877	× $	500,000	= $	438,500
4	Year 2 (*n* = 2)	0.769	×	350,000	=	269,150
5	Year 3 (*n* = 3)	0.675	×	300,000	=	202,500
6	Year 4 (*n* = 4)	0.592	×	250,000	=	148,000
7	Year 5 (*n* = 5)	0.519	×	40,000	=	20,760
8	Total present value of net cash inflows					$ 1,078,910
9	Less: Initial investment					1,000,000
10	Net present value (NPV)					$ 78,910
11						

Because the NPV is positive, Allegra expects the Speaker project to earn more than the 14% target rate of return, making this an attractive investment.

Capital Rationing and the Profitability Index

Exhibits 12-10 and 12-11 show that both the Smartphone and Speaker projects have positive NPVs. Therefore, both are attractive investments. Because resources are limited, companies are not always able to invest in all capital assets that meet their investment criteria. For example, Allegra may not have the funds to pursue both the Speaker and Smartphone projects at this time. In this case, the Speaker project is more profitable because it yields a higher NPV. The Speaker project should earn an additional $78,910 beyond the 14% required rate of return, while the Smartphone project returns an additional $48,610.

This example illustrates an important point. The Smartphone project promises more *total* net cash inflows. But the *timing* of the Speaker cash flows—loaded near the beginning of the project—gives the Speaker investment a higher NPV. The Speaker project is more attractive because of the time value of money. Its dollars, which are received sooner, are worth more now than the more distant dollars of the Smartphone project. In addition, the payback period for the Speaker project is 2.5 years, whereas the payback period for the Smartphone project is 3.27 years. Considering both methods, the Speaker project seems like the more prudent investment.

Comparing the NPV of the Smartphone and Speaker projects is valid *only* because both projects require the same initial cost—$1 million. In contrast, Exhibit 12-12 summarizes three capital investment options that Raycor, a sporting goods manufacturer, faces. Each capital project requires a different initial investment. All three projects are attractive because each yields a positive NPV. Assuming that Raycor can invest in only one project at this time, which one should it choose? Project B yields the highest NPV, but it also requires a larger initial investment than the alternatives.

EXHIBIT 12-12 Raycor's Capital Investment Options

	A	B	C	D
1	**Comparing NPVs**	**Project A**	**Project B**	**Project C**
2	Present value of net cash inflows	$ 150,000	$ 238,000	$ 182,000
3	Less: Initial investment	125,000	200,000	150,000
4	Net present value (NPV)	$ 25,000	$ 38,000	$ 32,000
5				

To choose among the projects, Raycor computes the **profitability index** (also known as the **present value index**). The profitability index is computed as follows:

Profitability index = Present value of net cash inflows ÷ Initial investment

The profitability index computes the number of dollars returned for every dollar invested, *with all calculations performed in present value dollars*. It allows us to compare alternative investments in present value terms, like the NPV method, but it also considers differences in the investments' initial cost. Let's compute the profitability index for all three alternatives.

Present value of net cash inflows	÷	Initial investment	=	Profitability index
Project A: $150,000	÷	$125,000	=	1.20
Project B: $238,000	÷	$200,000	=	1.19
Project C: $182,000	÷	$150,000	=	1.21

The profitability index shows that Project C is the best of the three alternatives because it returns $1.21 in present value dollars for every $1.00 invested. Projects A and B return slightly less.

Let's also compute the profitability index for Allegra's Smartphone and Speaker projects:

Present value of net cash inflows	÷	Initial investment	=	Profitability index
Smartphones: $1,048,610	÷	$1,000,000	=	1.049
Speakers: $1,078,910	÷	$1,000,000	=	1.079

The profitability index confirms our prior conclusion that the Speaker project is more profitable than the Smartphone project. The Speaker project returns $1.079 (in present value dollars) for every $1.00 invested. This return is beyond the 14% return already used to discount the cash flows. We did not need the profitability index to determine that the Speaker project was preferable because both projects required the same investment ($1 million).

NPV of a Project with Residual Value

Many assets yield cash inflows at the end of their useful lives because they have residual value. Companies discount an investment's residual value to its present value when determining the *total* present value of the project's net cash inflows. The residual value is discounted as a single lump sum—not an annuity—because it will be received only once, when the asset is sold.

Suppose Allegra expects the Smartphone project equipment to be worth $100,000 at the end of its five-year life. This represents an additional *lump-sum* future cash inflow from the Smartphone project. To determine the Smartphone project's NPV, we discount the residual value ($100,000) using the Present Value of $1 table ($i = 14\%$, $n = 5$) (see Appendix 12A, Table A). We then *add* its present value ($51,900) to the present value of the Smartphone project's other net cash inflows ($1,048,610), as shown in Exhibit 12-13:

EXHIBIT 12-13 NPV of a Project with Residual Value

	A	B	C	D	E	F
1	**NPV Calculation Including Residual Value**	**PV Factor (i = 14%)**		**Net Cash Inflow**		**Present Value**
2	Present value of annuity, n = 5	3.433	× $	305,450	= $	1,048,610
3	Plus: Present value of residual value, end of Year 5	0.519	×	100,000	=	51,900
4	Total present value					$ 1,100,510
5	Less: Initial investment					1,000,000
6	Net present value (NPV)					$ 100,510
7						

Because of the expected residual value, the Smartphone project is now more attractive than the Speaker project because its NPV ($100,510) is higher than the Speaker project ($78,910) and both projects require the same investment ($1 million).

Technology Makes It Simple   Excel 2016

Net Present Value (NPV) Calculations

1. In an Excel spreadsheet, type in the future cash flows expected from the investment. Begin with the cash flow expected in Year 1. In the next cell, type in the cash flow expected in Year 2. Continue in the same fashion until all future cash flows are shown in separate cells, in the order in which they are expected to be received.

2. Click on **Formulas**.

3. Click on **Financial**.

4. Choose **NPV** from the drop down list. The following will appear as a dialog box:

    Rate

    Value 1

5. Fill in the interest **Rate**, in decimal format (for example, 14% would be input as .14).

6. Next to **Value 1**, highlight the array of cells containing the cash flow data from Step 1.

7. The **"Formula result"** will appear at the bottom of the dialog box. The result is the present value of the future cash flows.

8. Finally, subtract the initial cost of the investment to obtain the NPV.

Note: Appendix 12B illustrates each chapter example using these basic Excel instructions.

Sensitivity Analysis

Capital budgeting decisions affect cash flows far into the future. Allegra's managers might want to know whether their decision would be affected by any of their major assumptions. For example, consider the following:

- Changing the discount rate from 14% to 12% or to 16%
- Changing the net cash inflows by 10%
- Changing an expected residual value

Managers can use Excel or programmed calculators to quickly perform sensitivity analysis.

Internal Rate of Return (IRR)

The NPV method only tells management whether the investment exceeds the hurdle rate. Since both the Smartphone player and Speaker projects yield positive NPVs, we know they provide *more* than a 14% rate of return. But what exact rate of return would these investments provide? The IRR method answers that question.

The <u>**internal rate of return (IRR)**</u> is the rate of return, based on discounted cash flows, that a company can expect to earn by investing in the project. *It is the interest rate that makes the NPV of the investment equal to zero:*

$$NPV = 0$$

Let's look at this concept in another light by inserting the definition of NPV:

$$\text{Present value of the investment's net cash inflows} - \text{Initial investment} = 0$$

Or if we rearrange the equation:

$$\text{Initial investment} = \text{Present value of the investment's net cash inflows}$$

Why is this important?

"In the past, finding an investment's **IRR** was time consuming and difficult. However, using **Excel** now makes it **fast** and **easy**."

In other words, the IRR is the *interest rate* that makes the cost of the investment equal to the present value of the investment's net cash inflows. The higher the IRR, the more desirable the project. Like the profitability index, the IRR can be used in the capital rationing process.

IRR computations are very easy to perform using Excel or programmed calculators. (See the "Technology Makes It Simple" feature at the end of this section.) However, IRR computations are much more cumbersome to perform using the tables.

IRR with Equal Annual Net Cash Inflows (Annuity)

When the investment is an annuity, we can develop a formula that will tell us the Annuity PV factor associated with the investment's IRR. We start with the equation given previously and then substitute in as follows:

Initial investment = Present value of the investment's net cash inflows

Initial investment = Amount of each equal net cash inflow × Annuity PV factor ($i = ?, n =$ given)

Finally, we rearrange the equation to obtain the following formula:

$$\frac{\text{Initial investment}}{\text{Amount of each equal net cash inflow}} = \text{Annuity PV factor } (i = ?, n = \text{given})$$

Let's use this formula to find the Annuity PV factor associated with Allegra's Smartphone project. Recall that the project would cost $1 million and result in five equal yearly cash inflows of $305,450:

$$\frac{\$1,000,000}{\$305,450} = \text{Annuity PV factor } (i = ?, n = 5)$$

$$3.274 = \text{Annuity PV factor } (i = ?, n = 5)$$

Next, we find the interest rate that corresponds to this Annuity PV factor. Turn to the Present Value of Annuity of $1 table (Appendix 12A, Table B). Scan the row corresponding to the project's expected life—five years, in our example. Choose the column(s) with the number closest to the Annuity PV factor you calculated using the formula. The 3.274 annuity factor is in the 16% column.

Therefore, the IRR of the Smartphone project is 16%.

Allegra expects the project to earn an internal rate of return of 16% over its life. Exhibit 12-14 confirms this result: Using a 16% discount rate, the project's NPV is zero. In other words, 16% is the discount rate that makes the cost of the initial investment equal to the present value of the investment's net cash inflows.

EXHIBIT 12-14 IRR of the Smartphone Project

	A	B	C	D	E	F
1	**NPV Calculation for *Equal* Annual Net Cash Inflows**	**Annuity PV Factor (*i* = 16%)**		**Annual Net Cash Inflow**		**Present Value (rounded)**
2	Present value of annuity, *n* = 5	3.274	× $	305,450	= $	1,000,000
3	Less: Initial investment					1,000,000
4	Net present value (NPV)				$	0
5						

To decide whether the project is acceptable, compare the IRR with the minimum desired rate of return. The decision rule is as follows:

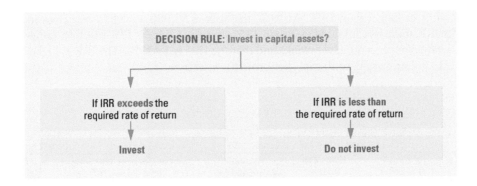

DECISION RULE: Invest in capital assets?

If IRR exceeds the required rate of return → Invest

If IRR is less than the required rate of return → Do not invest

Recall that Allegra's hurdle rate is 14%. Because the Smartphone project's IRR (16%) is higher than the hurdle rate (14%), Allegra would find the project to be an attractive investment.

In the Smartphone project, the exact Annuity PV factor (3.274) appears in the Present Value of an Annuity of $1 table (Appendix 12A, Table B). Many times, the exact factor will not appear in the table. For example, let's find the IRR of Tierra Firma's proposed HVAC system. Recall that the HVAC system would cost $240,000 and result in annual net cash inflows of $60,000 over its six-year life. We find its Annuity PV factor using the formula given previously:

$$\frac{\text{Initial investment}}{\text{Amount of each equal net cash inflow}} = \text{Annuity PV factor } (i = ?, n = \text{given})$$

$$\frac{\$240,000}{\$60,000} = \text{Annuity PV factor } (i = ?, n = 6)$$

$$4.00 = \text{Annuity PV factor } (i = ?, n = 6)$$

Now, look in the Present Value of Annuity of $1 table in the row marked 6 periods (Appendix 12A, Table B). You will not see 4.00 under any column. The closest two factors are 3.889 (at 14%) and 4.111 (at 12%).

Thus, the HVAC's IRR is somewhere between 12% and 14%.

Using Excel's IRR function, we would find the exact IRR is 12.98%. If Tierra Firma had a 14% hurdle rate, it would *not* invest in the HVAC system because its IRR is less than 14%.

▶ **Try It!**

The Bruce Company is considering investing in a wind turbine to generate its own power. Any unused power will be sold back to the local utility company. Between cost savings and new revenues, the company expects to generate $750,000 per year in net cash inflows from the turbine. The turbine would cost $4 million and is expected to have a 20-year useful life with no residual value. Calculate the internal rate of return (IRR).

Please see page 778 for solutions.

IRR with Unequal Annual Net Cash Inflows

Because the Speaker project has unequal cash inflows, Allegra cannot use the Present Value of Annuity of $1 table to find the asset's IRR. Rather, Allegra must use a trial-and-error procedure to determine the discount rate that makes the project's NPV equal to zero. Recall from Exhibit 12-11 that the Speaker's NPV using a 14% discount rate is $78,910. Since the NPV is *positive*, the IRR must be *higher* than 14%. Allegra performs the trial-and-error process using *higher* discount rates until it finds the rate that brings the net present value of the Speaker project to *zero*. Exhibit 12-15 shows that at 16%, the Speaker has an NPV of $40,390; therefore, the IRR must be higher than 16%. At 18%, the NPV is $3,980, which is very close to zero. Thus, the IRR must be slightly higher than 18%. If we use Excel's IRR function rather than the trial-and-error procedure, we would find that the IRR is 18.23%. The IRR is higher than Allegra's 14% hurdle rate, so the Speaker project is attractive.

EXHIBIT 12-15 Finding the Speaker's IRR Through Trial and Error

	A	B	C	D	E	F	G	H	I	J	K	L
1		Calculations using 16% interest rate						Calculations using 18% interest rate				
2	**NPV Calculation for *Unequal* Net Cash Inflows**	**PV Factor** (i = 16%)		**Net Cash Inflow**		**Present Value at 16%**		**PV Factor** (i = 18%)		**Net Cash Inflow**		**Present Value at 18%**
3	Present value of net cash inflows:											
4	Year 1 (n = 1)	0.862	×	$ 500,000	=	$ 431,000		0.847	×	$ 500,000	=	$ 423,500
5	Year 2 (n = 2)	0.743	×	350,000	=	260,050		0.718	×	350,000	=	251,300
6	Year 3 (n = 3)	0.641	×	300,000	=	192,300		0.609	×	300,000	=	182,700
7	Year 4 (n = 4)	0.552	×	250,000	=	138,000		0.516	×	250,000	=	129,000
8	Year 5 (n = 5)	0.476	×	40,000	=	19,040		0.437	×	40,000	=	17,480
9	Total present value of net cash inflows					$ 1,040,390						$ 1,003,980
10	Less: Initial investment					1,000,000						1,000,000
11	Net present value (NPV)					$ 40,390						$ 3,980
12												

Technology Makes It Simple   Excel 2016

Internal Rate of Return (IRR) Calculations

1. In an Excel spreadsheet, first type in the initial investment as a negative number—for example, –1000000 for a $1 million investment. In the next cell, type in the cash flow expected in Year 1. In the following cell, type in the cash flow expected in Year 2. Continue in the same fashion until all future cash flows are shown in separate cells, in the order in which they are expected to be received.

2. Click on **Formulas**.

3. Click on **Financial**.

4. Choose **IRR** from the dropdown list. The following will appear as a dialog box: **Values**

5. Next to **Values**, highlight the array of cells containing the data from Step 1.

6. The **"Formula result"** will appear at the bottom of the dialog box. The result is the Internal Rate of Return (IRR).

Note: Appendix 12B illustrates each chapter example using these basic Excel instructions.

How Do the Capital Budgeting Methods Compare?

We have discussed four capital budgeting methods commonly used by companies to make capital investment decisions—two that ignore the time value of money (payback period and ARR) and two that incorporate the time value of money (NPV and IRR). Exhibit 12-16 summarizes the similarities and differences between the two methods that ignore the time value of money.

5 Compare and contrast the four capital budgeting methods

EXHIBIT 12-16 Capital Budgeting Methods That *Ignore* the Time Value of Money

Payback Period	ARR
• Simple to compute	• The only method that focuses on the accrual-based operating income from the investment, rather than cash flows
• Focuses on the time it takes to recover the company's cash investment	• Shows the impact of the investment on operating income, which is important to financial statement users
• Ignores any cash flows occurring after the payback period, including any residual value	• Measures the average profitability of the asset over its entire life
• Highlights risks of investments with longer cash recovery periods	• Ignores the time value of money
• Ignores the time value of money	

Exhibit 12-17 considers the similarities and differences between the two methods that incorporate the time value of money.

EXHIBIT 12-17 Capital Budgeting Methods That *Incorporate* the Time Value of Money

NPV	IRR
• Incorporates the time value of money and the asset's net cash inflows over its entire life	• Incorporates the time value of money and the asset's net cash inflows over its entire life
• Indicates whether the asset will earn the company's minimum required rate of return	• Computes the project's unique rate of return
• Shows the excess or deficiency of the asset's present value of net cash inflows over the cost of the initial investment	• No additional steps needed for capital rationing decisions when assets require different initial investments
• The profitability index should be computed for capital rationing decisions when the assets require different initial investments	

Keep in mind that managers often use more than one method to gain different perspectives on the risks and returns of potential capital investments.

STOP & THINK

A pharmaceutical company is considering two research projects that require the same initial investment. Project A has an NPV of $232,000 and a 3-year payback period. Project B has an NPV of $237,000 and a payback period of 4.5 years. Which project would you choose?

Answer: Many managers would choose Project A even though it has a slightly lower NPV. Why? The NPV is only $5,000 lower, yet the payback period is significantly shorter. The uncertainty of receiving operating cash flows increases with each passing year. Managers often forgo small differences in expected cash inflows to decrease the risk of investments.

Decision Guidelines

Capital Budgeting

Here are more of the guidelines Amazon.com's managers used as they made the major capital budgeting decision to invest in building warehouses.

Decision	Guidelines
Which capital budgeting methods are best?	No one method is best. Each method provides a different perspective on the investment decision.
Why do the NPV and IRR models calculate the present value of an investment's net cash flows?	Because an investment's cash inflows occur in the future, yet the cash outlay for the investment occurs now, all of the cash flows must be converted to a common point in time. These methods use the *present* value as the common point in time.
How do we know if investing in warehouse facilities will be worthwhile?	Investment in warehouse facilities may be worthwhile if the NPV is positive or the IRR exceeds the required rate of return.
How do we compute the net present value (NPV) if the investment has equal annual cash inflows?	Compute the present value of the investment's net cash inflows using the Present Value of an Annuity of $1 table and then subtract the investment's cost. Alternatively, use the NPV function in Excel (see Appendix 12B for instructions).
How do we compute the net present value (NPV) if the investment has unequal annual cash inflows?	Compute the present value of each year's net cash inflows using the Present Value of $1 (lump sum) table, sum the present value of the inflows, and then subtract the investment's cost. Alternatively, use the NPV function in Excel (see Appendix 12B for instructions).
How do we compare potential investments that have differing initial costs?	Use the profitability index, which is computed as $$\text{Profitability index} = \text{Present value of net cash inflows} \div \text{Initial investment}$$
How do we compute the internal rate of return (IRR) if the investment has equal annual cash inflows?	Find the interest rate that yields the following Annuity PV factor: $$\text{Annuity PV factor} = \frac{\text{Initial investment}}{\text{Amount of each equal net cash inflow}}$$
How do we compute the internal rate of return (IRR) if the investment has unequal annual cash inflows?	Use trial and error. Alternatively, use the IRR function in Excel (see Appendix 12B for instructions).

SUMMARY PROBLEM 2

Sonoma is considering investing in solar paneling for the roof of its large distribution facility. The investment will cost $9 million and have a six-year useful life and no residual value. Because of rising utility costs, the company expects the yearly utility savings to increase over time, as follows:

Year 1...	$1,000,000
Year 2...	$1,500,000
Year 3...	$2,000,000
Year 4...	$2,500,000
Year 5...	$3,500,000
Year 6...	$4,500,000

The solar panels have already passed the payback period and ARR screening (see Summary Problem 1 on pages 721–722).

1. Compute the NPV of the solar panels, given the company's 12% hurdle rate.

2. Estimate the IRR of the solar panels or use Excel to find the exact IRR.

3. Should Sonoma invest in the solar paneling? Why or why not?

▪ SOLUTIONS

1. The NPV of the solar panels is found by subtracting the initial cost of the solar panels ($9 million) from the present value of the future cash flows as follows:

	A	B	C	D	E	F
1	**NPV Calculation for *Unequal* Net Cash Inflows**	**PV Factor** (*i* = 12%)		**Net Cash Inflow**		**Present Value**
2	Present value of net cash inflows:					
3	Year 1 (*n* = 1)	0.893	× $	1,000,000	= $	893,000
4	Year 2 (*n* = 2)	0.797	×	1,500,000	=	1,195,500
5	Year 3 (*n* = 3)	0.712	×	2,000,000	=	1,424,000
6	Year 4 (*n* = 4)	0.636	×	2,500,000	=	1,590,000
7	Year 5 (*n* = 5)	0.567	×	3,500,000	=	1,984,500
8	Year 6 (*n* = 6)	0.507	×	4,500,000	=	2,281,500
9	Total present value of net cash inflows				$	9,368,500
10	Less: Initial investment					9,000,000
11	Net present value (NPV)				$	368,500
12						

Alternatively, the NPV can be found using the NPV function in Excel. First, click on "Formulas," then "Financial," then "NPV." Next, input the hurdle rate (12%) and highlight the array of yearly cash flows to find their present value. Finally, subtract the $9 million initial investment. Note that the NPV will be slightly different ($366,838) from that shown above ($368,500) because the PV factors in the table are rounded to three decimal points.

2. Since the NPV is positive when a hurdle rate of 12% is used, the IRR must be higher than 12%. If we calculate the NPV using a hurdle rate of 14%, the NPV is negative, meaning the IRR is less than 14%. Thus, the IRR is somewhere between 12% and 14%. Alternatively, the IRR can be found using the IRR function in Excel. First, click on "Formulas," then "Financial," then "IRR." Next, highlight the array of numbers that first contains the initial investment as a negative cash flow (−9,000,000) and then contains the yearly cash flows shown above. The IRR is displayed as 13.126%.

3. The solar panel proposal meets all of the company's capital investment criteria. It has a payback of less than five years, an ARR greater than 10%, and an IRR of over 12%. Therefore, the solar panels appear to be a good capital investment from both a financial and environmental standpoint.

Appendix 12A

Present Value Tables and Future Value Tables

Table A Present Value of $1

							Present Value of $1						
Periods	1%	2%	3%	4%	5%	6%	8%	10%	12%	14%	16%	18%	20%
1	0.990	0.980	0.971	0.962	0.952	0.943	0.926	0.909	0.893	0.877	0.862	0.847	0.833
2	0.980	0.961	0.943	0.925	0.907	0.890	0.857	0.826	0.797	0.769	0.743	0.718	0.694
3	0.971	0.942	0.915	0.889	0.864	0.840	0.794	0.751	0.712	0.675	0.641	0.609	0.579
4	0.961	0.924	0.888	0.855	0.823	0.792	0.735	0.683	0.636	0.592	0.552	0.516	0.482
5	0.951	0.906	0.863	0.822	0.784	0.747	0.681	0.621	0.567	0.519	0.476	0.437	0.402
6	0.942	0.888	0.837	0.790	0.746	0.705	0.630	0.564	0.507	0.456	0.410	0.370	0.335
7	0.933	0.871	0.813	0.760	0.711	0.665	0.583	0.513	0.452	0.400	0.354	0.314	0.279
8	0.923	0.853	0.789	0.731	0.677	0.627	0.540	0.467	0.404	0.351	0.305	0.266	0.233
9	0.914	0.837	0.766	0.703	0.645	0.592	0.500	0.424	0.361	0.308	0.263	0.225	0.194
10	0.905	0.820	0.744	0.676	0.614	0.558	0.463	0.386	0.322	0.270	0.227	0.191	0.162
11	0.896	0.804	0.722	0.650	0.585	0.527	0.429	0.350	0.287	0.237	0.195	0.162	0.135
12	0.887	0.788	0.701	0.625	0.557	0.497	0.397	0.319	0.257	0.208	0.168	0.137	0.112
13	0.879	0.773	0.681	0.601	0.530	0.469	0.368	0.290	0.229	0.182	0.145	0.116	0.093
14	0.870	0.758	0.661	0.577	0.505	0.442	0.340	0.263	0.205	0.160	0.125	0.099	0.078
15	0.861	0.743	0.642	0.555	0.481	0.417	0.315	0.239	0.183	0.140	0.108	0.084	0.065
20	0.820	0.673	0.554	0.456	0.377	0.312	0.215	0.149	0.104	0.073	0.051	0.037	0.026
25	0.780	0.610	0.478	0.375	0.295	0.233	0.146	0.092	0.059	0.038	0.024	0.016	0.010
30	0.742	0.552	0.412	0.308	0.231	0.174	0.099	0.057	0.033	0.020	0.012	0.007	0.004
40	0.672	0.453	0.307	0.208	0.142	0.097	0.046	0.022	0.011	0.005	0.003	0.001	0.001

The factors in the table were generated using the following formula:

$$\text{Present value of } \$1 = \frac{1}{(1 + i)^n}$$

where:

i = annual interest rate
n = number of periods

Table B Present Value of Annuity of $1

Periods	1%	2%	3%	4%	5%	6%	8%	10%	12%	14%	16%	18%	20%
1	0.990	0.980	0.971	0.962	0.952	0.943	0.926	0.909	0.893	0.877	0.862	0.847	0.833
2	1.970	1.942	1.913	1.886	1.859	1.833	1.783	1.736	1.690	1.647	1.605	1.566	1.528
3	2.941	2.884	2.829	2.775	2.723	2.673	2.577	2.487	2.402	2.322	2.246	2.174	2.106
4	3.902	3.808	3.717	3.630	3.546	3.465	3.312	3.170	3.037	2.914	2.798	2.690	2.589
5	4.853	4.713	4.580	4.452	4.329	4.212	3.993	3.791	3.605	3.433	3.274	3.127	2.991
6	5.795	5.601	5.417	5.242	5.076	4.917	4.623	4.355	4.111	3.889	3.685	3.498	3.326
7	6.728	6.472	6.230	6.002	5.786	5.582	5.206	4.868	4.564	4.288	4.039	3.812	3.605
8	7.652	7.325	7.020	6.733	6.463	6.210	5.747	5.335	4.968	4.639	4.344	4.078	3.837
9	8.566	8.162	7.786	7.435	7.108	6.802	6.247	5.759	5.328	4.946	4.607	4.303	4.031
10	9.471	8.983	8.530	8.111	7.722	7.360	6.710	6.145	5.650	5.216	4.833	4.494	4.192
11	10.368	9.787	9.253	8.760	8.306	7.887	7.139	6.495	5.938	5.453	5.029	4.656	4.327
12	11.255	10.575	9.954	9.385	8.863	8.384	7.536	6.814	6.194	5.660	5.197	4.793	4.439
13	12.134	11.348	10.635	9.986	9.394	8.853	7.904	7.103	6.424	5.842	5.342	4.910	4.533
14	13.004	12.106	11.296	10.563	9.899	9.295	8.244	7.367	6.628	6.002	5.468	5.008	4.611
15	13.865	12.849	11.938	11.118	10.380	9.712	8.559	7.606	6.811	6.142	5.575	5.092	4.675
20	18.046	16.351	14.877	13.590	12.462	11.470	9.818	8.514	7.469	6.623	5.929	5.353	4.870
25	22.023	19.523	17.413	15.622	14.094	12.783	10.675	9.077	7.843	6.873	6.097	5.467	4.948
30	25.808	22.396	19.600	17.292	15.372	13.765	11.258	9.427	8.055	7.003	6.177	5.517	4.979
40	32.835	27.355	23.115	19.793	17.159	15.046	11.925	9.779	8.244	7.105	6.234	5.548	4.997

The factors in the table were generated using the following formula:

$$\text{Present value of annuity of \$1} = \frac{1}{i}\left[1 - \frac{1}{(1 + i)^n}\right]$$

where:

i = annual interest rate

n = number of periods

Table C Future Value of $1

						Future Value of $1							
Periods	1%	2%	3%	4%	5%	6%	8%	10%	12%	14%	16%	18%	20%
1	1.010	1.020	1.030	1.040	1.050	1.060	1.080	1.100	1.120	1.140	1.160	1.180	1.200
2	1.020	1.040	1.061	1.082	1.103	1.124	1.166	1.210	1.254	1.300	1.346	1.392	1.440
3	1.030	1.061	1.093	1.125	1.158	1.191	1.260	1.331	1.405	1.482	1.561	1.643	1.728
4	1.041	1.082	1.126	1.170	1.216	1.262	1.360	1.464	1.574	1.689	1.811	1.939	2.074
5	1.051	1.104	1.159	1.217	1.276	1.338	1.469	1.611	1.762	1.925	2.100	2.288	2.488
6	1.062	1.126	1.194	1.265	1.340	1.419	1.587	1.772	1.974	2.195	2.436	2.700	2.986
7	1.072	1.149	1.230	1.316	1.407	1.504	1.714	1.949	2.211	2.502	2.826	3.185	3.583
8	1.083	1.172	1.267	1.369	1.477	1.594	1.851	2.144	2.476	2.853	3.278	3.759	4.300
9	1.094	1.195	1.305	1.423	1.551	1.689	1.999	2.358	2.773	3.252	3.803	4.435	5.160
10	1.105	1.219	1.344	1.480	1.629	1.791	2.159	2.594	3.106	3.707	4.411	5.234	6.192
11	1.116	1.243	1.384	1.539	1.710	1.898	2.332	2.853	3.479	4.226	5.117	6.176	7.430
12	1.127	1.268	1.426	1.601	1.796	2.012	2.518	3.138	3.896	4.818	5.936	7.288	8.916
13	1.138	1.294	1.469	1.665	1.886	2.133	2.720	3.452	4.363	5.492	6.886	8.599	10.699
14	1.149	1.319	1.513	1.732	1.980	2.261	2.937	3.797	4.887	6.261	7.988	10.147	12.839
15	1.161	1.346	1.558	1.801	2.079	2.397	3.172	4.177	5.474	7.138	9.266	11.974	15.407
20	1.220	1.486	1.806	2.191	2.653	3.207	4.661	6.728	9.646	13.743	19.461	27.393	38.338
25	1.282	1.641	2.094	2.666	3.386	4.292	6.848	10.835	17.000	26.462	40.874	62.669	95.396
30	1.348	1.811	2.427	3.243	4.322	5.743	10.063	17.449	29.960	50.950	85.850	143.371	237.376
40	1.489	2.208	3.262	4.801	7.040	10.286	21.725	45.259	93.051	188.884	378.721	750.378	1,469.772

The factors in the table were generated using the following formula:

Future value of $1 = (1 + i)^n$

where:

i = annual interest rate

n = number of periods

Table D Future Value of Annuity of $1

Future Value of Annuity of $1

Periods	1%	2%	3%	4%	5%	6%	8%	10%	12%	14%	16%	18%	20%
1	1.000	1.000	1.000	1.000	1.000	1.000	1.000	1.000	1.000	1.000	1.000	1.000	1.000
2	2.010	2.020	2.030	2.040	2.050	2.060	2.080	2.100	2.120	2.140	2.160	2.180	2.200
3	3.030	3.060	3.091	3.122	3.153	3.184	3.246	3.310	3.374	3.440	3.506	3.572	3.640
4	4.060	4.122	4.184	4.246	4.310	4.375	4.506	4.641	4.779	4.921	5.066	5.215	5.368
5	5.101	5.204	5.309	5.416	5.526	5.637	5.867	6.105	6.353	6.610	6.877	7.154	7.442
6	6.152	6.308	6.468	6.633	6.802	6.975	7.336	7.716	8.115	8.536	8.977	9.442	9.930
7	7.214	7.434	7.662	7.898	8.142	8.394	8.923	9.487	10.089	10.730	11.414	12.142	12.916
8	8.286	8.583	8.892	9.214	9.549	9.897	10.637	11.436	12.300	13.233	14.240	15.327	16.499
9	9.369	9.755	10.159	10.583	11.027	11.491	12.488	13.579	14.776	16.085	17.519	19.086	20.799
10	10.462	10.950	11.464	12.006	12.578	13.181	14.487	15.937	17.549	19.337	21.321	23.521	25.959
11	11.567	12.169	12.808	13.486	14.207	14.972	16.645	18.531	20.655	23.045	25.733	28.755	32.150
12	12.683	13.412	14.192	15.026	15.917	16.870	18.977	21.384	24.133	27.271	30.850	34.931	39.581
13	13.809	14.680	15.618	16.627	17.713	18.882	21.495	24.523	28.029	32.089	36.786	42.219	48.497
14	14.947	15.974	17.086	18.292	19.599	21.015	24.215	27.975	32.393	37.581	43.672	50.818	59.196
15	16.097	17.293	18.599	20.024	21.579	23.276	27.152	31.772	37.280	43.842	51.660	60.965	72.035
20	22.019	24.297	26.870	29.778	33.066	36.786	45.762	57.275	72.052	91.025	115.380	146.628	186.688
25	28.243	32.030	36.459	41.646	47.727	54.865	73.106	98.347	133.334	181.871	249.214	342.603	471.981
30	34.785	40.568	47.575	56.085	66.439	79.058	113.283	164.494	241.333	356.787	530.312	790.948	1,181.882
40	48.886	60.402	75.401	95.026	120.800	154.762	259.057	442.593	767.091	1,342.025	2,360.757	4,163.213	7,343.858

The factors in the table were generated using the following formula:

$$\text{Future value of annuity of } \$1 = \frac{(1 + i)^n - 1}{i}$$

where:

i = annual interest rate
n = number of periods

Appendix 12B

Solutions to Chapter Examples Using Microsoft Excel

Technology Makes It Simple   Excel 2016

Future Value Examples from Chapter

Example 1: Future Value of a Lump Sum

Let's use our lump-sum investment example from page 726 of the text. Assume that you invest $10,000 for five years at an interest rate of 6%. Use the following procedure to find its future value five years from now:

1. In an Excel spreadsheet, click on **Formulas**.
2. Click on **Financial**.
3. Choose **FV** from the dropdown list. The following will appear as a dialog box. Fill in the variables as follows:

   Rate = **.06**

   Nper = **5**

   Pmt = (leave blank since this is used for annuities)

   PV = –**10000** (the negative sign indicates that the amount is a cash outflow, not inflow)

   Type = (leave blank)
4. The future value now appears under the dialog box as = **$13,382.26** (rounded).

Example 2: Future Value of an Annuity

Let's use the annuity investment example from page 726 of the text. Assume that you invest $2,000 at the end of each year for five years. The investment earns 6% interest. Use the following procedures to find the investment's future value five years from now.

1. In an Excel spreadsheet, click on **Formulas**.
2. Click on **Financial**.
3. Choose **FV** from the dropdown list. The following will appear as a dialog box. Fill in the variables as follows:

   Rate = **.06**

   Nper = **5**

   Pmt = –**2000** (the negative sign indicates that the amount is a cash outflow, not inflow)

   PV = (leave blank because this is used for lump-sum amounts)

   Type = (leave blank)
4. The future value now appears under the dialog box as = **$11,274.19** (rounded).

Present Value Examples from Chapter

Example 1: Present Value of an Annuity—Lottery Option #2

Let's use the lottery payout Option #2 from pages 727–728 of the text for our example. Option #2 was to receive $150,000 at the end of each year for the next 10 years. The interest rate was assumed to be 8%. Use the following procedures to find the present value of the payout option:

1. In an Excel spreadsheet, click on **Formulas**.
2. Click on **Financial**.
3. Choose **PV** from the dropdown list. The following will appear as a dialog box. Fill in the variables as follows:

   Rate = **.08**

   Nper = **10**

   Pmt = **–150000**

   Fv = (leave blank since this is used for lump sums)

   Type = (leave blank)
4. The present value answer now appears under the dialog box as = **$1,006,512.21** (rounded).

Example 2: Present Value of a Lump Sum—Lottery Option #3

Let's use the lottery payout Option #3 from pages 727–728 of the text for our example. Option #3 was to receive $2 million 10 years from now. The interest rate was assumed to be 8%. Use the following procedures to find the present value of the payout option:

1. In an Excel spreadsheet, click on **Formulas**.
2. Click on **Financial**.
3. Choose **PV** from the dropdown list. The following will appear as a dialog box. Fill in the variables as follows:

   Rate = **.08**

   Nper = **10**

   Pmt = (leave blank since this is used for annuities)

   FV = **–2000000**

   Type = (leave blank)
4. The present value answer now appears under the dialog box as = **$926,386.98** (rounded).

NPV Examples from Chapter

Example 1: NPV of Allegra's Smartphone Project—An Annuity

Recall from page 731 of the text that the Smartphone project required an investment of $1 million and was expected to generate equal net cash inflows of $305,450 each year for five years. The company's discount rate was 14%.

1. In an Excel spreadsheet, type in the future cash flows expected from the investment in the order in which they are expected to be received. Your spreadsheet should show five consecutive cells as follows: 305450, 305450, 305450, 305450, 305450.
2. Click on **Formulas**.
3. Click on **Financial**.

Capital Investment Decisions and the Time Value of Money

4. Choose **NPV** from the dropdown list. The following will appear as a dialog box. Fill in the variables as follows:

   Rate = .14

   Value 1 = (Highlight array of cells containing the cash flow data from Step 1)

5. The present value of the cash flows appears at the bottom of the dialog box as = **1,048,634.58.**

6. Finally, subtract the initial cost of the investment ($1 million) to obtain the NPV = **$48,634.58**.

Example 2: NPV of Allegra's Speaker Project—Unequal Cash Flows

Recall from page 733 of the text that the Speaker project required an investment of $1 million and was expected to generate the unequal periodic cash inflows shown in Exhibit 12-11. The company's discount rate was 14%.

1. In an Excel spreadsheet, type in the future cash flows expected from the investment in the order in which they are expected to be received. Your spreadsheet should show five consecutive cells with the following values in them: 500000, 350000, 300000, 250000, 40000.

2. Click on **Formulas**.

3. Click on **Financial.**

4. Choose **NPV** from the dropdown list. The following will appear as a dialog box. Fill in the variables as follows:

   Rate = .14

   Value 1 = (Highlight array of cells containing the cash flow data from Step 1)

5. The present value of the cash flows appears at the bottom of the dialog box as = **1,079,196.40 (rounded)**.

6. Finally, subtract the initial cost of the investment ($1 million) to obtain the NPV = **$79,196.40** (rounded).

Example 3: NPV of an Investment with a Residual Value

If an investment has a residual value, simply add the residual value as an additional cash inflow in the year in which it is to be received. For example, assume as we did in Exhibit 12-13 on page 735 that the Smartphone project equipment will be worth $100,000 at the end of its five-year life. This represents an additional expected cash inflow to the company in Year 5. The company's discount rate was 14%.

1. In an Excel spreadsheet, type in the future cash flows expected from the investment in the order in which they are expected to be received. Your spreadsheet should show five consecutive cells with the following values in them: 305450, 305450, 305450, 305450, 405450

2. Click on **Formulas**.

3. Click on **Financial**.

4. Choose **NPV** from the dropdown list. The following will appear as a dialog box. Fill in the variables as follows:

   Rate = .14

   Value 1 = (Highlight array of cells containing the cash flow data from Step 1)

5. The present value of the cash flows appears at the bottom of the dialog box as = **1,100,571.45 (rounded)**.

6. Finally, subtract the initial cost of the investment ($1 million) to obtain the NPV = **$100,571.45** (rounded).

IRR Examples from Chapter

Example 1: IRR of Allegra's Smartphone Project—An Annuity

Recall from page 737 that the Smartphone project required an investment of $1 million and was expected to generate equal net cash inflows of $305,450 each year for five years.

1. In an Excel spreadsheet, first type in the initial investment as a negative number and then type in the future cash flows expected from the investment in the order in which they are expected to be received. Your spreadsheet should show the following consecutive cells: **–1000000, 305450, 305450, 305450, 305450, 305450.**
2. Click on **Formulas.**
3. Click on **Financial.**
4. Choose **IRR** from the dropdown list. The following will appear as a dialog box. Fill in the variables as follows:

   Values = (Highlight array of cells containing the data from Step 1)
5. The IRR appears at the bottom of the dialog box as = **16.01% (rounded).**

Example 2: IRR of Allegra's Speaker Project—Unequal Cash Flows

Recall from page 733 that the Speaker project required an investment of $1 million and was expected to generate the unequal periodic cash inflows shown in Exhibit 12-11.

1. In an Excel spreadsheet, first type in the initial investment as a negative number and then type in the future cash flows expected from the investment in the order in which they are expected to be received. Your spreadsheet should show the following consecutive cells: **–1000000, 500000, 350000, 300000, 250000, 40000.**
2. Click on **Formulas.**
3. Click on **Financial.**
4. Choose **IRR** from the dropdown list. The following will appear as a dialog box. Fill in the variables as follows:

   Values = (Highlight array of cells containing the data from Step 1)
5. The IRR appears at the bottom of the dialog box as = **18.23% (rounded).**

Example 3: IRR of an Investment with a Residual Value

If an investment has a residual value, simply add the residual value as an additional cash inflow in the year in which it is to be received. For example, assume as we did in Exhibit 12-13 on page 735 that the Smartphone project equipment will be worth $100,000 at the end of its five-year life. This represents an additional expected cash inflow to the company in Year 5.

1. In an Excel spreadsheet, type in the future cash flows expected from the investment in the order in which they are expected to be received. Your spreadsheet should show six consecutive cells with the following values in them: **–1000000, 305450, 305450, 305450, 305450, 405450.**
2. Click on **Formulas.**
3. Click on **Financial.**
4. Choose **IRR** from the dropdown list. The following will appear as a dialog box. Fill in the variables as follows:

   Values = (Highlight array of cells containing the data from Step 1)
5. The IRR appears at the bottom of the dialog box as = **17.95% (rounded).**

Appendix 12C

Using a TI-83, TI-83 Plus, TI-84, or TI-84 Plus Calculator to Perform Time Value of Money Calculations

Technology Makes It Simple

Time Value of Money Calculations

Using a TI-83, TI-83 Plus, TI-84, or TI-84 Plus Calculator to Perform Time Value of Money Calculations

Steps to perform basic present value and future value calculations:

1. On the TI-83 Plus or TI-84 Plus: Press [APPS] *to show the applications menu.*

   On the TI-83 or TI-84: Press [2nd] [X⁻¹] [ENTER] *to show the applications menu.*

2. Choose **Finance** *to see the finance applications menu.*

3. Choose **TVM solver** *to obtain the list of time value of money (TVM) variables:*

   N = *number of periods (years)*

   I% = *interest rate per year* (**do not convert percentage to a decimal**)

   PV = *present value*

   PMT = *amount of each annuity installment*

   FV = *future value*

   P/Y = *number of compounding periods per year* (**leave setting at 1**)

   C/Y = *number of coupons per year* (**leave setting at 1**)

   PMT: **End** or Begin *(leave setting on End to denote an ordinary annuity)*

4. **Enter the known variables** and **set all unknown variables to zero** (except P/Y and C/Y, which need to be left set at 1).

5. To compute the unknown variable, scroll to the line for the variable you want to solve and then press [ALPHA] [ENTER].

6. The answer will now appear on the calculator.

7. Press [2nd] [QUIT] *to exit the TVM solver when you are finished.* **If you would like to do more TVM calculations, you do not need to exit. Simply repeat Steps 4 and 5 using the new data.**

Comments:

i. The order in which you input the variables does not matter.

ii. The answer will be shown as a negative number unless you input the original cash flow data as a negative number. **Use the [(-)] key to enter a negative number, not the minus key; otherwise you will get an error message.** The calculator follows a cash flow sign convention that assumes that all positive figures are cash inflows and all negative figures are cash outflows.

iii. The answers you get will vary slightly from those found using the PV and FV tables in Appendix 12A. Why? Because the PV and FV factors in the tables have been rounded to three digits.

Example 1: Future Value of a Lump Sum

Let's use our lump-sum investment example from the text. Assume that you invest $10,000 for five years at an interest rate of 6%. Use the following procedure to find its future value five years from now:

1. On the TI-83 Plus or TI-84 Plus: Press [APPS] *to show the applications menu.*

   On the TI-83 or TI-84: Press [2nd] [X⁻¹] [ENTER] *to show the applications menu.*

2. Choose **Finance** *to see the finance applications menu.*

3. Choose **TVM solver** *to obtain the list of time value of money (TVM) variables.*

4. Fill in the variables as follows:

   N = **5**

   I% = **6**

   PV = **−10000** *(Be sure to use the negative number (−) key, not the minus sign.)*

   PMT = **0**

   FV = **0**

   P/Y = 1

   C/Y = 1

   PMT: **End** or Begin

5. To compute the unknown future value, scroll down to **FV** and press [ALPHA] [ENTER].

6. The answer will now appear as **FV = 13,382.26** (rounded).

If you forgot to enter the $10,000 principal as a negative number (in Step 4), the FV will be displayed as a negative number.

Example 2: Future Value of an Annuity

Let's use the annuity investment example from the text. Assume that you invest $2,000 at the end of each year for five years. The investment earns 6% interest. Use the following procedure to find the investment's future value five years from now:

1. On the TI-83 Plus or TI-84 Plus: Press [APPS] *to show the applications menu.*

   On the TI-83 or TI-84: Press [2nd] [X⁻¹] [ENTER] *to show the applications menu.*

2. Choose **Finance** *to see the finance applications menu.*

3. Choose **TVM solver** *to obtain the list of time value of money (TVM) variables.*

4. Fill in the variables as follows:

   N = **5**

   I% = **6**

   PV = **0**

   PMT = **−2000** *(Be sure to use the negative number (−) key, not the minus sign.)*

   FV = **0**

   P/Y = 1

   C/Y = 1

   PMT: **End** or Begin

5. To compute the unknown future value, scroll down to **FV** and press [ALPHA] [ENTER].

6. The answer will now appear as **FV = 11,274.19 (rounded).**

If you forgot to enter the $2,000 annuity as a negative number (in Step 4), the FV will be displayed as a negative number.

Example 3: Present Value of an Annuity—Lottery Option #2

Let's use the lottery payout Option #2 from the text for our example. Option #2 was to receive $150,000 at the end of each year for the next 10 years. The interest rate was assumed to be 8%. Use the following procedure to find the present value of this payout option:

1. On the TI-83 Plus or TI-84 Plus: Press [APPS] *to show the applications menu.*

   On the TI-83 or TI-84: Press [2nd] [X⁻¹] [ENTER] *to show the applications menu.*

2. Choose **Finance** *to see the finance applications menu.*

3. Choose **TVM solver** *to obtain the list of time value of money (TVM) variables.*
4. Fill in the variables as follows:

N = **10**

I% = **8**

PV = **0**

PMT = **–150000** *(Be sure to use the negative number (–) key, not the minus sign.)*

FV = **0**

P/Y = 1

C/Y = 1

PMT: **End** or Begin

5. To compute the unknown present value, scroll down to **PV** and press [ALPHA] [ENTER].
6. The answer will now appear as **PV = 1,006,512.21** (rounded).

Had we not entered the annuity as a negative figure, the present value would have been shown as a negative number.

Example 4: Present Value of a Lump Sum—Lottery Option #3

Let's use the lottery payout Option #3 from the text as our example. Option #3 was to receive $2 million 10 years from now. The interest rate was assumed to be 8%. Use the following procedure to find the present value of this payout option:

1. On the TI-83 Plus or TI-84 Plus: Press [APPS] *to show the applications menu.*

   On the TI-83 or TI-84: Press [2nd] [X^{-1}] [ENTER] *to show the applications menu.*
2. Choose **Finance** *to see the finance applications menu.*
3. Choose **TVM solver** *to obtain the list of time value of money (TVM) variables.*
4. Fill in the variables as follows:

N = **10**

I% = **8**

PV = **0**

PMT = **0**

FV = **–2000000** *(Be sure to use the negative number (-) key, not the minus sign.)*

P/Y = 1

C/Y = 1

5. PMT: **End** or Begin
6. To compute the unknown present value, scroll down to **PV** and press [ALPHA] [ENTER].
7. The answer will now appear as **PV = 926,386.98** (rounded).

Had we not entered the $2 million future cash flow as a negative, the present value would have been shown as a negative number.

Technology Makes It Simple

NPV Calculations

Using a TI-83, TI-83 Plus, TI-84, or TI-84 Plus calculator to perform NPV calculations

Steps to performing NPV calculations:

If you are currently in the TVM solver mode, exit by pressing [2nd] [Quit].

1. On the TI-83 Plus or TI-84 Plus: Press [APPS] *to show the applications menu.*

   On the TI-83 or TI-84: Press [2nd] [X^{-1}] [ENTER] *to show the applications menu.*
2. Choose **Finance** *to see the finance applications menu.*

3. Choose **npv** *to obtain the NPV prompt:* **npv(**.

4. Fill in the following information, being careful to use the correct symbols: **npv (hurdle rate, initial investment*, {cash flow in Year 1, cash flow in Year 2, etc.})**

5. To compute the NPV, press [ENTER].

6. The answer will now appear on the calculator.

7. To exit the worksheet, press [CLEAR]. Alternatively, if you would like to change any of the assumptions for sensitivity analysis, you may press [2nd] [ENTER] to recall the formula, edit any of the values, and then recompute the new NPV by pressing [ENTER].

Note: If you would like to find just the present value (not the NPV) of a stream of unequal cash flows, use a zero (0) for the initial investment.

Example 1: NPV of Allegra's Smartphone Project—An Annuity

Recall that the Smartphone project required an investment of $1 million and was expected to generate equal net cash inflows of $305,450 each year for five years. The company's discount, or hurdle rate, was 14%.

1. On the TI-83 Plus or TI-84 Plus: Press [APPS] *to show the applications menu.*

   On the TI-83 or TI-84: Press [2nd] [X^{-1}] [ENTER] *to show the applications menu.*

2. Choose **Finance** *to see the finance applications menu.*

3. Choose **npv** *to obtain the NPV prompt:* **npv(**.

4. Fill in the following information, paying close attention to using the correct symbols:

   npv (14, –1000000, {305450, 305450, 305450, 305450, 305450}) *(Be sure to use the negative number (–) key, not the minus sign.)*

5. To compute the NPV, press [ENTER].

6. The answer will now appear on the calculator: **48,634.58** (rounded).

7. [CLEAR] the worksheet or recall it [2nd] [ENTER] for sensitivity analysis.

Example 2: NPV of Allegra's Speaker Project—Unequal Cash Flows

Recall that the Speaker project required an investment of $1 million and was expected to generate the unequal periodic cash inflows shown in Exhibit 12-11. The company's discount rate was 14%.

1. On the TI-83 Plus or TI-84 Plus: Press [APPS] *to show the applications menu.*

   On the TI-83 or TI-84: Press [2nd] [X^{-1}] [ENTER] *to show the applications menu.*

2. Choose **Finance** *to see the finance applications menu.*

3. Choose **npv** *to obtain the NPV prompt:* **npv(**.

4. Fill in the following information, paying close attention to using the correct symbols:

   npv (14, –1000000, {500000, 350000, 300000, 250000, 40000}) *(Be sure to use the negative number (–) key, not the minus sign.)*

5. To compute the NPV, press [ENTER].

6. The answer will now appear on the calculator: **79,196.40** (rounded).

7. [CLEAR] the worksheet or recall it [2nd] [ENTER] for sensitivity analysis.

Example 3: Investment with a Residual Value

If an investment has a residual value, simply add the residual value as an additional cash inflow in the year in which it is to be received. For example, assume as we did in Exhibit 12-13 that the Smartphone project equipment will be worth $100,000 at the end of its five-year life. This represents an additional expected cash inflow to the company in Year 5, so we'll show the cash inflow in Year 5 to be $405,450 (= $305,450 + $100,000). The company's discount rate was 14%.

1. On the TI-83 Plus or TI-84 Plus: Press [APPS] *to show the applications menu.*

   On the TI-83 or TI-84: Press [2nd] [X^{-1}] [ENTER] *to show the applications menu.*

2. Choose **Finance** *to see the finance applications menu.*

*The initial investment must be entered as a negative number.

3. Choose **npv** to obtain the NPV prompt: **npv(**.
4. Fill in the following information, paying close attention to using the correct symbols:

   npv (14, –1000000, {305450, 305450, 305450, 305450, 405450}) (Be sure to use the negative number (–) key, not the minus sign.)
5. To compute the NPV, press [ENTER].
6. The answer will now appear on the calculator: **100,571.45** (rounded).
7. [CLEAR] the worksheet or recall it [2nd] [ENTER] for sensitivity analysis.

Technology Makes It Simple

IRR Calculations

Using a TI-83, TI-83 Plus, TI-84, or TI-84 Plus calculator to perform IRR calculations

The procedure for finding the IRR is virtually identical to the procedure used to find the NPV. The only differences are that we choose IRR rather than NPV from the Finance menu and we don't insert a given hurdle rate.

Steps to performing IRR calculations:

If you are currently in the TVM solver mode, exit by pressing [2nd] [Quit].

1. On the TI-83 Plus or TI-84 Plus: Press [APPS] to show the applications menu.

   On the TI-83 or TI-84: Press [2nd] [X⁻¹] [ENTER] to show the applications menu.
2. Choose **Finance** to see the finance applications menu.
3. Choose **irr** to obtain the IRR prompt: **irr(**.
4. Fill in the following information, paying close attention to using the correct symbols: **irr (initial investment*, {cash flow in Year 1, cash flow in Year 2, etc.})**
5. To compute the IRR press [ENTER].
6. The answer will now appear on the calculator.
7. To exit the worksheet, press [CLEAR]. Alternatively, if you would like to change any of the assumptions for sensitivity analysis, you may press [2nd] [ENTER] to recall the formula, edit any of the values, and then recompute the new IRR by pressing [ENTER].

Example 1: IRR of Allegra's Smartphone Project—An Annuity

Recall that the Smartphone project required an investment of $1 million and was expected to generate equal net cash inflows of $305,450 each year for five years. Use the following procedure to find the investment's IRR:

1. On the TI-83 Plus or TI-84 Plus: Press [APPS] to show the applications menu.

   On the TI-83 or TI-84: Press [2nd] [X⁻¹] [ENTER] to show the applications menu.
2. Choose **Finance** to see the finance applications menu.
3. Choose **irr** to obtain the IRR prompt: **irr(**.
4. Fill in the following information, paying close attention to using the correct symbols:

   irr (–1000000, {305450, 305450, 305450, 305450, 305450}) (Be sure to use the negative number (–) key, not the minus sign.)
5. To compute the IRR, press [ENTER].
6. The answer will now appear on the calculator: **16.01** (rounded).
7. [CLEAR] the worksheet or recall it [2nd] [ENTER] for sensitivity analysis.

*The initial investment must be entered as a negative number.

Example 2: IRR of Allegra's Speaker Project—Unequal Cash Flows

Recall that the Speaker project required an investment of $1 million and was expected to generate the unequal periodic cash inflows shown in Exhibit 12-11. Use the following procedures to find the investment's IRR:

1. On the TI-83 Plus or TI-84 Plus: Press [APPS] *to show the applications menu.*

    On the TI-83 or TI-84: Press [2nd] [X⁻¹] [ENTER] *to show the applications menu.*
2. Choose **Finance** *to see the finance applications menu.*
3. Choose **irr** *to obtain the IRR prompt:* **irr(**.
4. Fill in the following information, paying close attention to using the correct symbols:

    irr (–1000000, {500000, 350000, 300000, 250000, 40000}) *(Be sure to use the negative number (–) key, not the minus sign.)*
5. To compute the IRR, press [ENTER].
6. The answer will now appear on the calculator: **18.23** (rounded).
7. [CLEAR] the worksheet or recall it [2nd] [ENTER] for sensitivity analysis.

Example 3: Investment with a Residual Value

If an investment has a residual value, simply add the residual value as an additional cash inflow in the year in which it is to be received. For example, assume as we did in Exhibit 12-13 that the Smartphone project equipment will be worth $100,000 at the end of its five-year life. This represents an additional expected cash inflow to the company in Year 5, so we'll show the cash inflow in Year 5 to be $405,450 (= $305,450 + $100,000).

1. On the TI-83 Plus or TI-84 Plus: Press [APPS] *to show the applications menu.*

    On the TI-83 or TI-84: Press [2nd] [X⁻¹] [ENTER] *to show the applications menu.*
2. Choose **Finance** *to see the finance applications menu.*
3. Choose **irr** *to obtain the IRR prompt:* **irr(**.
4. Fill in the following information, paying close attention to using the correct symbols:

    irr (–1000000, {305450, 305450, 305450, 305450, 405450}) *(Be sure to use the negative number (–) key, not the minus sign.)*
5. To compute the IRR, press [ENTER].
6. The answer will now appear on the calculator: **17.95** (rounded).
7. [CLEAR] the worksheet or recall it [2nd] [ENTER] for sensitivity analysis.

END OF CHAPTER

Learning Objectives

- 1 Describe the importance of capital investments and the capital budgeting process
- 2 Use the payback and accounting rate of return methods to make capital investment decisions
- 3 Use the time value of money to compute the present and future values of single lump sums and annuities
- 4 Use discounted cash flow models to make capital investment decisions
- 5 Compare and contrast the four capital budgeting methods

Accounting Vocabulary

Accounting Rate of Return (ARR). (p. 717) A measure of profitability computed by dividing the average annual operating income from an asset by the initial investment in the asset.

Annuity. (p. 723) A stream of equal installments made at equal time intervals.

Capital Budgeting. (p. 711) The process of making capital investment decisions. Companies make capital investments when they acquire *capital assets*—assets used for a long period of time.

Capital Rationing. (p. 712) Choosing among alternative capital investments due to limited funds.

Compound Interest. (p. 723) Interest computed on the principal *and* all interest earned to date.

Discount Rate. (p. 731) Management's minimum desired rate of return on an investment; also called the hurdle rate and required rate of return.

Hurdle Rate. (p. 731) Management's minimum desired rate of return on an investment; also called the discount rate and required rate of return.

Internal Rate of Return (IRR). (p. 736) The rate of return (based on discounted cash flows) that a company can expect to earn by investing in a capital asset. The interest rate that makes the NPV of the investment equal to zero.

LEED. (p. 714) LEED, which stands for Leadership in Energy and Environmental Design, is a certification system developed by the U.S. Green Building Council as a way of promoting and evaluating environmentally friendly construction projects.

Net Present Value (NPV). (p. 731) The *difference* between the present value of the investment's net cash inflows and the investment's cost.

Payback Period. (p. 714) The length of time it takes to recover, in net cash inflows, the cost of a capital outlay.

Post-Audits. (p. 713) Comparing a capital investment's actual net cash inflows to its projected net cash inflows.

Present Value Index. (p. 734) An index that computes the number of dollars returned for every dollar invested, *with all calculations performed in present value dollars*. It is computed as present value of net cash inflows divided by investment; also called profitability index.

Profitability Index. (p. 734) An index that computes the number of dollars returned for every dollar invested, *with all calculations performed in present value dollars*. Computed as present value of net cash inflows divided by investment; also called present value index.

Required Rate of Return. (p. 731) Management's minimum desired rate of return on an investment; also called the discount rate and hurdle rate.

Simple Interest. (p. 723) Interest computed *only* on the principal amount.

Time Value of Money. (p. 723) The fact that money can be invested to earn income over time.

Quick Check

1. *(Learning Objective 1)* Which of the following methods of analyzing capital investments factors in the time value of money?
   a. Payback period
   b. Accounting rate of return
   c. Internal rate of return
   d. All of the above methods factor in the time value of money.

2. *(Learning Objective 2)* After identifying potential capital investments, the next step in the capital budgeting process is which of the following?
   a. Performing post-audits of the capital investments
   b. Engaging in capital rationing
   c. Analyzing potential investments through at least one of the four methods
   d. Estimating the future net cash inflows of the investments

3. *(Learning Objective 2)* Which of the following is *false* with regard to the payback period?
   a. All else being equal, a shorter payback period is more desirable than a longer payback period.
   b. It is computed as follows, regardless of whether cash flows are equal or unequal: Initial investment ÷ Expected annual net cash inflow.
   c. The payback period is the length of time it takes to recover the initial cost of the capital investment.
   d. The payback period gives no indication of the investment's profitability.

4. *(Learning Objective 2)* Which of the following methods focuses on the operating income an asset generates rather than the net cash inflows it generates?
   a. Payback period
   b. Accounting rate of return
   c. Internal rate of return
   d. Net present value

5. *(Learning Objective 2)* In order to convert the *average annual net cash inflow* from the asset back to the *average annual operating income* from the asset, one must
   a. add annual depreciation expense.
   b. subtract annual depreciation expense.
   c. multiply by annual depreciation expense.
   d. divide by annual depreciation expense.

6. *(Learning Objective 3)* The time value of money depends on which of the following factors?
   a. Principal amount
   b. Interest rate
   c. Number of periods
   d. All of the above

7. *(Learning Objective 4)* The internal rate of return is which of the following?
   a. The internal management's minimum required rate of return
   b. The accounting rate of return minus 1%
   c. The interest rate that makes the NPV of an investment equal to zero
   d. The amount of time it takes to recoup the initial investment

8. *(Learning Objective 4)* An investment's NPV is calculated as which of the following?
   a. The present value of the net cash inflows from the investment minus the investment's initial investment
   b. The investment's initial investment minus the present value of the investment
   c. The future value of the investment minus the investment's initial investment
   d. The investment's initial investment minus the future value of the investment

9. *(Learning Objective 4)* When potential capital investments of different size are compared, management should choose the one with the
   a. highest NPV.
   b. lowest IRR.
   c. lowest NPV.
   d. highest profitability index.

10. *(Learning Objective 5)* Which of the following methods calculates the investment's unique rate of return?
    a. Internal rate of return
    b. Payback period
    c. Net present value
    d. Accounting rate of return

Quick Check Answers

1. c 2. d 3. b 4. b 5. b 6. d 7. c 8. a 9. a 10. a

15

Sustainability

Markus Mainka/Alamy

Sources: 2015 Southwest Airlines One Report; Southwest Airlines Co. 2015 10-K filing.

Learning Objectives

- **1** Describe sustainability and how it can create business value
- **2** Describe sustainability reporting and the GRI framework
- **3** Describe EMA systems and their uses and challenges

Southwest Airlines is renowned for having a positive corporate culture that embraces employees as the heart of its operations. Unlike other major airlines, after 9/11 and the economic crisis of 2008, Southwest refused to lay off employees. The result? Southwest has been listed for 22 consecutive years on Forbes's list of the "World's Most Admired Companies." It has also made Forbes's "Best Employer" list and *Corporate Responsibility* magazine's "Best Corporate Citizens" list. How does Southwest do it? The company embraces the triple bottom line: people, planet, and profit. Not only does Southwest treat its employees well, returning over $620 million to employees in 2015 as part of its profit sharing plan, but it also treats customers well by offering two free checked bags, no change fees, and frequent flyer points that can be used to book any flight at any time. From an environmental perspective, Southwest has been able to increase its jet fuel efficiency by 29% since 2005 and the company has increased recycling efforts, not only with in-flight and corporate waste, but even with its used airplane seats and billboards. As a result, Southwest earned the 2015 "Airports Going Green Award" from the Chicago Department of Aviation. How have all of these measures affected the company's profitability? Southwest has had 43 consecutive years of profit, which is unheard of in the airline industry, especially during the turbulent periods following 9/11 and the latest economic crisis.

In this chapter, we'll explore why sustainability has become such a driving force in business. We'll also look at how sustainability reporting and environmental management accounting (EMA) can help support an organization's journey toward sustainability. Finally, we'll consider some of the challenges associated with setting up and using EMA systems.

What Is Sustainability, and How Does It Create Business Value?

The dictionary definition of <u>sustainability</u> refers to the ability of a system to maintain its own viability, endure without giving way, or use resources so they are not depleted or permanently damaged.[1] In other words, it's the ability of a system, including our economic system, to operate in such a manner that it is able to continue indefinitely. With respect to business, the most widely used definition of sustainability traces its roots to a report developed by the United Nations (UN) in 1987 in which sustainable development was defined as "development that meets the needs of the present generation without compromising the ability of future generations to meet their own needs."[2] As shown in Exhibit 15-1, the report identified three factors relating to sustainability: environmental, social, and economic. The UN's 2030 Agenda for Sustainable Development, which was ratified in 2015, continues to reaffirm the importance of each of these factors on a global scale.[3]

1 Describe sustainability and how it can create business value

EXHIBIT 15-1 Three Interrelated Factors of Sustainability

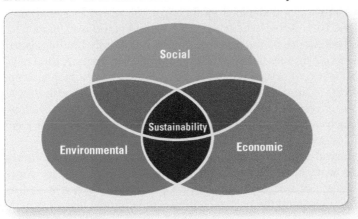

As a result of the UN report, forward-thinking businesses, such as Southwest Airlines, adhere to the notion of a triple bottom line. The <u>triple bottom line</u> is a concept that views a company's performance not only in terms of its ability to generate economic profits for its owners, as has traditionally been the case, but also in terms of its impact on people and the planet. A company will only be viable, or sustainable, in the long run if all three of these factors are considered when making business decisions. For example, a company will not be able to survive in the long run if the natural resources it relies on (e.g., air, water, soil, minerals, plants, fuel supplies, etc.) or people it relies on (e.g., suppliers, customers, employees, communities) are in jeopardy. The world is a system connected by space and time. Air pollution in North America, for example, affects air quality in Europe and the melting of polar ice caps (space connections). Choices we make about

---

[1] www.merriam-webster.com; http://dictionary.reference.com

[2] Brundtland Report, World Commission on Environment and Development (WCED), 1987, www.un-documents.net/our-common-future.pdf

[3] https://sustainabledevelopment.un.org/post2015/transformingourworld

our energy sources today will impact future generations (time connections). Because of these connections, companies that do not incorporate sustainability into their core business values put their own long-term success at risk, as well as the long-term survival of the planet's inhabitants.

Historical Overview

The Industrial Revolution, which began roughly 200 years ago, is based on what is sometimes referred to as a linear "take–make–waste" system in which companies "take" natural resources (lumber, minerals, water, fossil fuels), "make" them into products, and then sell the products to consumers or commercial enterprises that eventually dispose of the products and packaging as "waste."[4] Since the end of World War II, the U.S. economy has developed a consumer mindset that has focused on using (consuming) and throwing away products for the sake of convenience, rather than conserving resources for future generations. In essence, we have become a disposable society. However, because of the limited supply of natural resources, including potable water, tillable soil, and fossil-based fuels, we have realized that the current linear economic system is not sustainable in the long run. As a result, the last 30 years have seen an increased interest in creating more sustainable business models. This interest has escalated dramatically in the last 10 years. Whereas the business community often fought pressures to become more environmentally friendly from **non-governmental organizations (NGOs)**, such as Greenpeace and the Sierra Club, in the latter part of the last century, businesses now are finding ways to partner with these same organizations to develop better, more sustainable business practices.

December 2015 was a watershed moment for the world as 196 countries gathered and negotiated the Paris Agreement at the 2015 United Nations Climate Change Conference (COP21). The essence of the agreement, which is legally binding, is to limit global warming to less than 2 degrees Celsius above pre-industrial levels. A total of 175 countries signed the agreement on Earth Day, 2016. This agreement is a major stepping stone in international efforts to limit global warming. It sends a strong signal to businesses and the capital markets to invest in a technology and business models that have low greenhouse gas emissions (such as carbon dioxide and methane). No doubt, further environmental regulations will follow as a result of this agreement.[5]

The new, forward-thinking business model of the twenty-first century takes cues from the creative ways in which natural ecological systems create zero waste. In nature, the output and death of one organism or process become the input to life of another. Nothing becomes waste, and the system continues indefinitely. It is a *circular*, rather than *linear*, system. Likewise, businesses are now beginning to adopt operating strategies that will conserve natural resources and eliminate waste, through reducing inputs and reusing, repurposing, and recycling outputs. Business executives are now beginning to take a "systems thinking" approach. Rather than concerning themselves with only **internal costs** (those costs that are incurred and paid for by the organization and recorded in their GAAP-based accounting records), managers and accountants are now considering the **external costs** borne by society as a result of the company's operations and the products and services it sells. For example, greenhouse gas emissions caused by distribution trucks and landfill sites are external costs borne by society that impact the health and wellness of the planet and its inhabitants. To decrease harmful emissions, many distributors are now switching to hybrid and natural gas vehicles, while many landfills are capturing the methane and using it to generate power.

Both internal and external costs can be illuminated through the use of life-cycle assessment. As shown in Exhibit 15-2, **life-cycle assessment, or LCA**, involves studying the

---

[4] Paul Hawken, *The Ecology of Commerce*, 1993, New York: HarperCollins.
[5] www.un.org/sustainabledevelopment/blog/2015/12/the-paris-agreement-faqs

environmental and social impact of each product or service over the course of its *entire life*, from "cradle to grave" (all the way from sourcing to disposal). One of the ultimate goals of LCA is to replace the current cradle-to-grave system with a circular cradle-to-cradle system, such that the company's end product and packaging never go to waste, but are fully used (such as ice cream packaged in an ice cream cone) or become input to another product (such as Nike's creation of fitness apparel from recycled plastic beverage containers). LCA illuminates both internal and external costs, so that companies have a more complete set of information from which to generate cost-effective solutions to environmental and social concerns.

EXHIBIT 15-2 LCA: Assessing Product Impact from Cradle-to-Grave

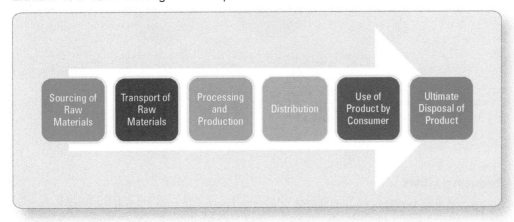

Business is now at a tipping point. The twentieth-century business model that often gravitated toward the exploitation of nature and people in pursuit of profit is changing into a life-sustaining business model. Because of their global reach and economic power, large corporations are recognizing that they are often in a better position to bring about positive world change than are many national governments and nonprofit agencies. As a result, businesses are beginning to embed sustainability into their core business functions, rather than simply tacking on isolated and temporary solutions to environmental and social issues brought to their attention by activists. Rather than taking a defensive stance as many companies did during the twentieth century, businesses are going on the offensive by making sustainability a driving force in every aspect of the value chain.

The Business Case for Sustainability

Businesses are continuing to evolve: they are now realizing they can act as positive agents of change while at the same time upholding their fiduciary responsibility to stockholders. In fact, in a recent survey, CEOs indicated that sustainability has become a more strategic and integral part of their business operations.[6] The outdated tension between profit creation and social responsibility is evaporating, as corporations recognize the business opportunity and value created through embedding sustainability throughout their core business functions. They are beginning to realize that sustainability and profitability are not at odds but often go hand in hand. In other words, sustainability simply makes good business sense. In this section, we explore some of the most compelling business reasons for adopting sustainable business practices, as illustrated in Exhibit 15-3.

---

[6] www.mckinsey.com/business-functions/sustainability-and-resource-productivity/our-insights/sustainabilitys-strategic-worth-mckinsey-global-survey-results

EXHIBIT 15-3 Business Reasons for Adopting Sustainable Practices

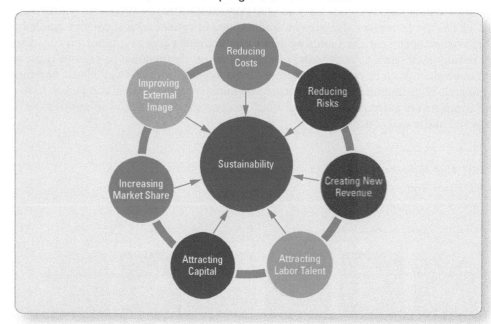

Reducing Costs

Enormous cost savings can be achieved through becoming more sustainable. What's good for the environment can also be good for the bottom line. Most of these savings come through the reduction of waste, such as the waste of materials, packaging, and energy. In fact, a relatively new term, **eco-efficiency**,[7] has been coined to signify the economic savings that can be achieved by producing goods and services with fewer ecological resources. A few examples are as follows:

- Companies are evaluating the energy intensity of their buildings. Many companies are changing out their old incandescent light bulbs to energy-efficient LED (light-emitting diode) or CFL (compact fluorescent lamp) lighting, which often results in a payback of energy cost savings in less than one year. In addition, these types of bulbs have a longer life, thus requiring lower labor cost to change them when they burn out. For example, the Clark County School District (Las Vegas) replaced the lighting in 152 of its buildings. This energy efficiency initiative alone saved the District over $2.25 million in just one year.[8] Likewise, the city of Las Vegas installed new LED streetlights that are saving the city over $2 million per year.[9] New, energy-efficient HVAC systems (heating, ventilating, and air conditioning) are likewise providing companies with enormous savings. The environmental savings are clear: less fossil fuel is used, fewer greenhouse gasses are emitted, and less material is needed to produce replacement bulbs.

- Companies with large fleets, such as UPS, Walmart, and Staples, are investing in hybrid vehicles as a means of reducing their fuel needs. They are also reassessing their route logistics to decrease the number of miles traveled per unit of product delivered. These measures not only conserve fossil fuels and prevent air pollution but also save money. For example, between 2005 and 2015, Walmart *doubled* its fleet efficiency (cases shipped per gallon of fuel), sparing the planet of 650,000 metric tons of CO_2 per year and saving the company nearly $1 *billion* in 2015 alone.[10]

---

[7] This term was coined by the World Business Council for Sustainable Development in its 1992 publication, "Changing Course."

[8] www.environmentalleader.com/2013/10/30/las-vegas-school-district-saves-12500-per-day-from-lighting-retrofit

[9] www.environmentalleader.com/2013/09/12/led-street-lights-save-las-vegas-2-million-per-year

[10] http://news.walmart.com/news-archive/2015/11/17/walmart-marks-fulfillment-of-key-global-responsibility-commitments

■ Companies are performing **waste audits,** in which they study the stream of waste coming from their operations (solid waste, water discharge, chemicals, etc.) to identify waste that can be avoided and alternative uses for the remaining waste. By reducing the amount of waste sent to landfills, companies are able to avoid the tipping fees charged by waste collection companies. For example, in 2016, Unilever announced that it has now achieved "zero waste to landfill" at all 240 of its factories worldwide, plus 400 other facilities, such as offices and distribution centers. According to Unilever, its waste diversion efforts have saved the company over $225 million.[11]

■ Companies are assessing the amount of materials and packaging used with their products. For example, by making its products thinner and lighter, Apple has been able to significantly reduce its carbon emissions while at the same time making the products more desirable to consumers. Even the smallest changes in packaging can have monumental effects. For example, one pizza producer saved over $600,000 in one year just from shaving 1/8" × 1/8" × 1/32" off of each pizza box. The savings resulted from a reduction in materials used for each pizza box (the equivalent of 3,000 trees) *and* the ability to ship 6,848 more pizzas in each truckload (saving on gasoline).[12] In another example, IKEA saved over 1.2 million euros in a single year just from figuring out a way to reduce the amount of packaging needed for one of its sofas.[13] Companies are now considering packaging, as much as manufacturing, when designing their products.

■ Companies are also assessing the waste that occurs simply from the way they've always operated their businesses. For example, hotels used to change sheets and towels every day. Now, most hotels are moving toward changing sheets and towels every two or three days, instead of once a day, unless requested otherwise by the customer. This measure saves the cost of maid time (labor) as well as the cost of laundering (water, energy, detergent) while also benefiting the environment. Since implementing its Travel with Purpose strategy, Hilton says it has reduced energy use by 14.5%, carbon output by 20.9%, waste output by 27.6%, and water use by 14.1%, compared to 2009 levels. In the process, Hilton's worldwide environmental management is credited with saving the company over $550 million.[14]

These are just a few examples of how companies are reducing their environmental impact while at the same time reducing costs. For more examples, you may wish to sign up for a free daily e-mail at Environmentalleader.com. The daily e-mail provides current news on the sustainability initiatives of well-known businesses so that you can see more examples of how businesses are reducing their environmental impact while at the same time improving their bottom line.

Generating New Revenue Streams

Sustainable product innovation can provide companies with new revenue streams. Some entrepreneurial businesses begin with a mission of providing only sustainable products. For example, Method gained market share by providing consumers with biodegradable household cleaners and soaps. Clif Bar is now a leading maker of organic energy and nutrition foods, and Terracycle makes all of its products out of recycled materials. Existing companies can also benefit from developing more sustainable products. For example, Procter & Gamble used LCA to determine that the majority of energy consumed in the life cycle of its laundry detergent was the result of consumers washing their clothes in hot water. As a result, the company developed Tide Coldwater®, which is effective as a laundering agent in cold water.

Why is this important?

"In order to **grow** the company, **managers** must listen to what their **customers**, stockholders, employees, and creditors want. Increasingly, these stakeholders want **more sustainable** operations."

---

[11] www.triplepundit.com/2015/02/unilever-zero-waste-program-saves-225-million-creating-jobs
[12] www.chainalytics.com/ikea-save-millions-packaging-optimization/
[13] www.wsj.com/articles/ikea-cant-stop-obsessing-about-its-packaging-1434533401
[14] www.environmentalleader.com/2016/01/07/hilton-cuts-carbon-output-20-9-saves-550m/

Recycling and repurposing can also provide companies with new revenue streams. After performing waste audits, companies seek alternative uses for the materials in their waste streams. By finding commercial alternatives to sending waste to landfills, companies are often able to reap significant recycling revenues. Unilever found innovative uses for the materials formerly in its waste stream. For example, the scraps left over from cutting tea bags out of fabric rolls are now sold to another company that uses the material for making pet beds. Rather than paying for these materials to be sent to landfills, as was done in the past, Unilever is now earning revenues from selling the materials.

Sustainability can also provide a competitive advantage for companies that become first movers. For example, Toyota was the first company to develop and market an affordable hybrid vehicle. As a result, the Toyota Prius still dominates the hybrid vehicle market even though most major car manufacturers are offering hybrid alternatives.

Finally, with the new Paris Agreement in place, companies will be looking for new products and services that will help them achieve their low-emission goals. Over 87% of companies of all sizes have made public commitments to decrease emissions and increase energy efficiency.[15] The demand for low-emission technology will spur product and service innovations.

Increasing Market Share

Consumers, supply-chain customers, and special interest groups are also putting pressure on companies to become more socially and environmentally sustainable. Consumers are increasingly selecting products not only on the basis of price and quality, but also on the basis of environmental and social impact. For example, many consumers now demand environmentally sensitive packaging, such as recyclable containers or packaging made from post-consumer-use materials. Companies, such as GE, Unilever, and Target, are capitalizing on this market trend. Each of these companies generates over $1 billion a year in sales from sustainable products. In 2014, over 50% of Unilever's market growth came from its Sustainable Living Brands.[16] In other words, sustainable products are driving sales and market share.

Many companies are now practicing **supply-chain assessment**, whereby purchasing decisions are influenced by how well suppliers manage the social and environmental impact of their operations. Companies can, and do, refuse to purchase materials from suppliers that do not adhere to their environmental and social justice standards. As a result, companies that don't adopt sustainable practices are likely to lose business, while those that embed sustainability through their entire organization are likely to gain market share.

Improving External Image

Community members and special interest groups can also place pressure on businesses by boycotting or picketing companies with poor environmental and social practices. A company's external image can either hurt or improve sales. For example, in 2004, Walmart started a "green" campaign, along with significant changes to its operations, because of bad publicity over its environmental impact. Because of Walmart's sheer size, even one small move by the company has enormous effects on the environment. Likewise, The Home Depot intensified its journey to sustainability after protestors headlined the company's lumber procurement practices. Even Apple has received bad press due to the labor conditions at overseas factories in the company's supply chain. Thus, companies need to carefully scrutinize not only their own internal operations, but all of the companies in their supply chain. Social responsibility is now a determining factor in shaping a company's image.

Reducing Compliance and Litigation Risks

In many cases, companies must become more sustainable to assure regulatory compliance. If they do not comply with environmental regulations, they will face substantial fines, thus compromising their profitability. In the United States, the Environmental Protection Agency (EPA), which began operations in 1970, is the regulatory agency charged with writing, implementing, and enforcing environmental laws passed by Congress. These regulations pertain to air quality, water quality, land issues, chemicals, hazardous substances, and so forth.

---

[15] www.environmentalleader.com/2016/07/07/tide-of-global-climate-agreements-produces-a-wave-of-products-and-services
[16] www.environmentalleader.com/2016/01/07/how-unilever-ge-ikea-turn-a-profit-from-sustainability

European countries, in general, have even more stringent environmental laws and regulations. For example, in the United Kingdom, the Climate Change Act (2008) commits the UK to an 80% reduction in carbon emissions by 2050. Because many U.S. companies have foreign operations, they need to be aware of the environmental regulations in each geographic location in which they operate.

Rather than simply adhering to current regulations, companies need to anticipate more stringent regulations in the future. The Paris Agreement mentioned earlier in the chapter makes future regulation all the more likely. Rather than just complying with current regulations, companies may benefit from getting ahead of the game. For example, DuPont foresaw the eventual regulation of chlorofluorocarbons (CFCs), which are potent greenhouse gases. DuPont was able to gain substantial market share by developing CFC alternatives and phasing out its CFC production far ahead of its competitors that simply struggled to meet regulatory requirements.[17]

Regulatory fines and environmental litigation can be extremely costly. For example, in 2016 Volkswagen agreed to a $15.3 billion settlement as a result of rigging the environmental tests of its diesel vehicles to hide the fact that they were emitting more pollutants than allowed under California regulations. The agreement "should send a very clear message that when you break the laws designed to protect public health in this country, there are serious consequences," stated EPA Administrator Gina McCarthy.[18] Another notable environmental fine relates to the BP *Deepwater Horizon* oil spill of 2010. In 2015, BP reached a $20.8 billion litigation settlement with the U.S. Department of Justice. In addition, BP paid out billions in operations response and cleanup costs, claims to individuals and businesses, and other proposed litigation settlements. BP estimates the total cost for the disaster at $54.6 billion.[19]

Attracting and Retaining Labor Talent

In a recent survey of CFOs, "improving employee morale and hiring" was listed as one of the top five reasons for becoming more sustainable.[20] Companies are finding that they are better able to recruit top talent and retain employees longer when the organization is more sustainable. Because hiring and training new employees is costly, organizations save money by retaining good employees longer. Currently, the average employee tenure is less than five years.[21] Thus, preventing turnover can result in cost savings.

Companies are also realizing "soft" benefits from providing more sustainable work environments. These benefits include higher productivity, less absenteeism, more employee engagement, and lower health-care costs. For example, KeyBank has redesigned the physical layout of its headquarters such that all of the cubicles are positioned near the exterior windows of the building in order to provide employees with natural light. Higher-level managers have their offices in the interior of the building but have glass walls to allow the natural light to penetrate. This is the opposite of traditional office configurations in which the higher-level executives receive outer offices that block the natural light from getting to the interior cubicles. KeyBank employees also have the option of using treadmill workstations and mobile workstations that are not pre-assigned to specific personnel. Another example comes from Intel. Intel provides employees in its Chandler, Arizona, operations with free, healthy fresh fruit all day long and access to a free onsite fitness facility. Initiatives such as these help boost employee health and wellness, as well as employee morale.

Costco, a large national retailer, provides another good example. Bucking the trend of most retailers to pay minimum wage, Costco's starting wage rate for employees is more than $3 per hour greater than minimum wage. Most employees also received health-care benefits. The company believes their policy is more profitable in the long run because it decreases turnover and maximizes employee productivity and loyalty. Costco is supporting a move in Congress to increase the national minimum wage rate.[22]

[17] Chris Laszlo, *Sustainable Value: How the World's Leading Companies Are Doing Well by Doing Good*, 2008, Stanford University Press.

[18] www.bloomberg.com/news/articles/2016-06-28/volkswagen-to-pay-14-7-billion-to-settle-u-s-emissions-claims

[19] http://money.cnn.com/2015/10/06/news/companies/deepwater-horizon-bp-settlement

[20] www.fuqua.duke.edu/news_events/news-releases/cfo-survey-2013-q2/#.UffCPYHD_IU

[21] http://bls.gov/news.release/pdf/tenure.pdf

[22] The Plain Dealer, March 7, 2013. "Costco pays more than norm, backs higher minimum wage."

Attracting Capital

Many institutional and retail investors (individual investors) are taking sustainability into account when making investment decisions. The growth of socially responsible investment indices, such as the Dow Jones Sustainability Index (DJSI), NASDAQ OMX CRD Global Sustainability Index, and FTSE4Good Index, has put increasing pressure on corporations to pay attention to sustainability.

Principles for Responsible Investment (PRI)

As of 2016, over 1,500 institutional investors with over $62 trillion of assets under management had become signatories of the UN-backed **Principles for Responsible Investment (PRI)**. In short, these six principles include a commitment of signatories to incorporate environmental, social, and governance issues into investment analysis and decision making as part of their fiduciary responsibility to act in the long-term interests of their beneficiaries.[23] Furthermore, a 2015 survey conducted by the CFA Institute revealed that 73% of investors (portfolio managers and research analysts) take ESG (Environmental, Social, and Governance) information into account when making investment decisions.[24]

In addition to investors, lenders are increasingly taking sustainability into account when making credit decisions. Companies that do not adhere to sustainable practices may be at greater risk of defaulting on future loan payments. Why? Because they may be subject to future liabilities related to their detrimental impact on society and the environment.

In this section, we have shown why adopting sustainable practices makes good business sense. In the next section, we describe how sustainability reporting is used to move companies in a more sustainable direction.

2 Describe sustainability reporting and the GRI framework

What Is Sustainability Reporting?

Sustainability reporting is best viewed as a *process* that helps companies set goals, measure performance, and manage change as they move toward an economic model that produces long-term economic profit as well as environmental care and social responsibility.[25] A **sustainability report** is the primary document used for communicating a company's performance on all three pillars of the triple bottom line: economic, environmental, and social. Sustainability reports are often referred to as *Corporate Social Responsibility (CSR) reports* or *Environmental, Social, and Governance (ESG) reports*.

Current State of Sustainability Reporting

The vast majority of large companies now issue CSR reports. Over 80% of companies on the S&P 500 issued CSR reports in 2015, whereas in 2011, only 20% did.[26] Internationally, 92% of the Global 250 companies (the largest 250 companies in the world) now issue CSR reports.[27] As a result, large corporations that do not issue CSR reports are now in the minority.

Although sustainability reporting is still a voluntary practice in the United States, some countries (such as France, Denmark, Norway, Indonesia, and South Africa) and some stock exchanges (such as those in Brazil, Malaysia, and Singapore) require certain sustainability disclosures. In the United States, the NASDAQ urges listed companies to report on issues such as greenhouse gas emissions, water use, and gender equality—or to explain why they don't.[28] In late 2015, the World Federation of Exchanges (the trade association representing 64 public stock exchanges around the globe, whose 44,000 listed companies represent 75% of the world's GDP) issued guidance and recommendations about sustainability-related key performance indicators (KPIs) that could be reported to

---

[23] http://unpri.org

[24] Environment, Social, and Governance (ESG) Survey, CFA Institute, June 2015.

[25] Global Reporting Initiative, G4 Reporting Guidelines, Reporting Principles, and Standard Disclosures, http://globalreporting.org

[26] www.ga-institute.com/nc/issue-master-system/news-details/article/flash-report-eighty-one-percent-81-of-the-sp-500-index-companies-published-corporate-sustainabi.html

[27] Currents of change: The KPMG Survey of Corporate Responsibility Reporting 2015.

[28] http://www.sustainability-reports.com/titel-1150/

investors to ensure more efficient and transparent capital markets.[29] While these guidelines are not binding, they do send a clear signal that sustainability disclosures are important to the capital markets.

The Securities and Exchange Commission (SEC) requires publicly traded companies to disclose any material information that would be necessary to prevent misleading the readers of financial statements. With respect to the environment, companies must disclose any aspects of their business operations, pending lawsuits, and risk factors that are deemed to be material. Examples include the cost of complying with environmental laws and regulations, potential monetary damages from health and environmental litigation, and risks associated with the scarcity of water and raw materials needed for operations. Additionally, any material risks specific to the company as a result of global warming must also be disclosed.

Finally, while not required, there is a growing trend for companies to include some CSR information in their annual reports, as well as issue standalone reports. Of the largest 100 companies in 45 different countries (4,500 companies in all), 56% include some CSR information in their annual reports, while 73% issue standalone sustainability reports.[30]

Reasons for Sustainability Reporting

Sustainability reporting is a costly process, so why do firms do it? They must believe the benefits exceed the cost. As outlined earlier in the chapter, economic profit often goes hand in hand with a business's journey toward sustainability. Sustainability reporting serves several business-enhancing purposes:

1. Sustainability reporting is used as an internal change management tool. A familiar phrase in business is, "You can't manage what you don't measure." A similar adage is, "What gets measured gets managed . . . and what gets managed, gets done." Thus, measurement is a key driver of organizational change. Companies need baseline measurements to assess where they currently stand on social and environmental performance before they are able to set realistic goals and develop strategies and initiatives to move toward those goals.

   At its core, management accounting seeks to measure, collect, analyze, and report data that are relevant to managers as they plan, direct, and control company operations. Viewed in this light, sustainability reporting is simply an expansion of the cost and revenue data traditionally used in the management process. Sustainability reporting simply adds a layer of quantifiable nonfinancial data to the decision-making process.

2. Companies use their CSR reports as a means of disclosing their social and environmental impact information to

   - consumers,
   - companies in their supply chain,
   - investors and creditors,
   - stock exchanges and organizations that identify and rank the most sustainable companies in a wide variety of industries, and
   - other stakeholders, such as NGOs, local communities, and employees.

Framework for Sustainability Reporting

The **Global Reporting Initiative (GRI)**, a nonprofit organization founded in 1997, has developed the leading framework used for sustainability reporting by companies worldwide. The GRI's mission is to make sustainability reporting standard practice by providing

---

[29] World Federation of Exchanges ESG Recommendation Guidance and Metrics, October 2015.
[30] Currents of change: The KPMG Survey of Corporate Responsibility Reporting 2015.

guidance and support to organizations.[31] The GRI has continued to refine and update its reporting guidelines based on the experiences and needs of CSR preparers and users. The latest guidelines, G4, were released in May 2013.

While use of the GRI framework is not mandatory for sustainability reporting, over 24,000 CSR reports have been issued that reference the GRI framework.[32]

Development of the G4 Guidelines

The G4 Guidelines are the outcome of a multi-stakeholder process that included experts, businesses, and civil labor organizations from all over the world. Public opinion was also gathered during a public comment period. The G4 Guidelines were developed so that they could be used universally by organizations of any size in any region of the world. A consortium of large businesses, such as GE, Goldman Sachs, and Alcoa, as well as all of the **Big Four** accounting firms (Deloitte, EY, KPMG, and PricewaterhouseCoopers), provided financial support for the project and expertise on its technical features. Since the root business of the Big Four firms is auditing, the consortium's inclusion of the Big Four lends credibility to the verifiability of the metrics (KPIs) included in the reporting guidelines.

Summary of the G4 Guidelines

The heart of the G4 Guidelines focuses on the concepts of materiality and the triple bottom line: Organizations should report on those environmental, social, and economic aspects of their business that are *material* to their stakeholders. **Materiality** is loosely defined as those aspects that "reflect the organization's significant economic, environmental and social impact; or substantively influence the assessments and decisions of stakeholders."[33] As a result, one of the first steps in preparing a CSR report is to identify and engage stakeholders, including stockholders, creditors, suppliers, employees, community members, and NGOs, in a meaningful ongoing conversation to identify material aspects of the organization's operations.

Organizations and their stakeholders use the framework shown in Exhibit 15-4 to identify the aspects of the triple bottom line that are material to their organization. Note the following in Exhibit 15-4:

- The G4 framework is organized around the three "categories" of the triple bottom line: economic, environmental, and social. In addition, the social category contains four subcategories: (1) labor practices and decent work, (2) human rights, (3) society, and (4) product responsibility.

- Within each category, the framework identifies several "aspects" of business that might be material to the organization.

- Each "aspect" can be measured and reported on using one or more "indicators." Metrics such as these are often referred to as KPIs (key performance indicators). The number of indicators for each aspect is listed in parentheses in Exhibit 15-4. A detailed description of each indicator can be found in the G4 Guidelines at globalreporting.org.

Let's look at an example from Exhibit 15-4. "Water" is the third aspect listed in the "Environmental" category. In applying the G4 guidelines, a company and its stakeholders would need to decide how significant water is to the company's operations. If water is considered to be material, then the company should disclose information about its use of water in its CSR report. To do this, the company would measure and report on the three indicators listed for water in the G4 Guidelines: (1) total water withdrawn by source (such as groundwater, surface water, municipal water), (2) water sources significantly affected by withdrawal (such as size of water source and its importance to indigenous peoples), and (3) percentage and total volume of water recycled and reused.

---

[31] www.globalreporting.org

[32] http://database.globalreporting.org/

[33] Global Reporting Initiative, G4 Reporting Guidelines, Reporting Principles and Standard Disclosures, http://globalreporting.org

EXHIBIT 15-4 Aspects (and Number of Indicators) Within Each G4 Category

Economic Category:

- Economic Performance (4 indicators)
- Market presence (2)
- Indirect economic impacts (2)
- Procurement practices (1)

Environmental Category:

- Materials (2 indicators)
- Energy (5)
- Water (3)
- Biodiversity (4)
- Emissions (7)
- Effluents and waste (5)
- Products and services (2)
- Compliance (1)
- Transport (1)
- Overall (1)
- Supplier environmental assessment (2)
- Environmental grievance mechanism (1)

Social Category:

Subcategory: Labor Practices and Decent Work

- Employment (3 indicators)
- Labor/management relations (1)
- Occupational health and safety (4)
- Training and education (3)
- Diversity and equal opportunity (1)
- Equal remuneration for women and men (1)
- Supplier assessment for labor practices (2)
- Labor practices grievance mechanisms (1)

Subcategory: Human Rights

- Investment (2)
- Non-discrimination (1)
- Freedom of association and collective bargaining (1)
- Child labor (1)
- Forced or compulsory labor (1)
- Security practices (1)
- Indigenous rights (1)
- Assessment (1)
- Supplier human rights assessment (2)
- Human rights grievance mechanism (1)

Subcategory: Society

- Local communities (2)
- Anti-corruption (3)
- Public policy (1)
- Anti-competitive behavior (1)
- Compliance (1)
- Supplier assessment for impacts on society (2)
- Grievance mechanisms for impacts on society (1)

Subcategory: Product Responsibility

- Customer health and safety (2)
- Product and service labeling (3)
- Marketing communications (2)
- Customer privacy (1)
- Compliance (1)

Let's apply this information to a real-life example. Intel's manufacture of semiconductors is a very water-intensive process. Intel would not be able to survive as a company without access to billions of gallons of water per year. Thus, the company would not be viable, nor could it be profitable, without access to this natural resource. Thus, water is a material aspect of Intel's business. Likewise, water is a main ingredient in Coca-Cola's beverages, so Coca-Cola also considers water to be a material aspect of its business. On the other hand, water is not material to a financial institution, such as KeyBank, that uses very little water. As a result of focusing on material aspects of individual businesses, the GRI framework is customizable to every type of organization.

Since water is a material environmental aspect of Intel's business, Intel's CSR report discloses information on several water indicators: total water withdrawn, the source and geographic location of water supplies, the amount of water lost to evaporation, the amount of water conserved, and the amount of water discharged. Because water is so critical to Intel's business, the company has performed and disclosed a complete water footprint analysis. (You may wish to look at this information on page 86 of Intel's 2015 CSR report.)

Organizations have a choice as to whether they wish to issue a <u>core report</u> or a <u>comprehensive report</u>. The reports differ as to how many indicators are included:

- Core report—*at least one* indicator related to each identified material aspect must be disclosed.

- Comprehensive report—*all indicators* related to each identified material aspect must be disclosed.

As noted, Intel has reported on all three indicators relating to water.

In addition to the specific disclosures just discussed, all CSR reports that reference the G4 Guidelines must also contain general disclosures regarding the following:

- Strategy and analysis (vision and strategy for managing triple bottom line impacts)

- Organizational profile (summary of the company's location, size, products, and brands)

- Identified material aspects and boundaries (process for determining materiality; the portion of the company included in the report, that is, the whole company or only certain segments)

- Stakeholder engagement (identification and selection of stakeholders, and frequency of engagement)

- Report profile (reporting period and content index)

- Governance (governance structure and composition)

- Ethics and integrity (mechanisms for seeking advice and reporting concerns about unethical or unlawful behavior)

This section of the text only provides a brief overview of the G4 Guidelines. A complete description of the G4 Guidelines and reporting process is available at globalreporting.org.

Assurance of Data in CSR Reports

CSR reports gain more credibility if they are verified by external parties, much like financial statements become more credible when they are audited by independent CPAs. Whereas the SEC requires that publicly traded companies have their financial statements audited annually, no such requirement exists for CSR reports. Nonetheless, two-thirds of the Global 250 companies have invested in assurance services on at least some aspects of their CSR reports.[34] **Assurance** is a term used to denote an independent party's external validation of management's assertions. The Big Four accounting firms are the leading assurance service providers for CSR reports.[35] The Big Four firms hire many experts in other fields, such as engineers, to aid accountants in their assurance service practices. If you would like to see an example of an assurance report, the Independent Accountants' Review Report can be found on page 80 of Intel's 2015 CSR report. The report lists the indicators that were assured, as well as the criteria used for assurance. You'll note that the GRI G4 guidelines are referenced in the report.

Sustainability Accounting Standards Board (SASB)

The GRI is not the only organization working on sustainability reporting. The Sustainability Accounting Standards Board (SASB) is an independent non-profit whose mission is to develop and disseminate sustainability accounting standards that help public corporations disclose material, decision-useful information to investors.[36]

---

[34] Currents of change: The KPMG Survey of Corporate Responsibility Reporting 2015.
[35] http://research.verdantix.com/index.cfm/papers/Press.Details/press_id/105/verdantix-global-survey-finds-the-big-four-accounting-firms-continue-to-dominate-the-sustainability-brands-landscape
[36] SASB.org

Whereas the GRI provides companies with complete freedom in determining the aspects of sustainability that are material to their organization, SASB is trying to standardize reporting to make it more comparable between companies within the same industry. In March 2016, the SASB released the culmination of a four-year project in which it issued *provisional* standards for all 79 SIC (Standard Industrial Classification) industries. For each industry, SASB has devised a list of sustainability topics that are material to the industry, a list of metrics to be reported for each topic, and protocols for how to collect and measure the metrics. Thus, as stated in its mission, SASB is attempting to standardize the sustainability information that would be provided by publicly traded companies in any given industry. You can go on the website (SASB.org), put in a stock ticker symbol for any publicly traded company, and find the provisional sustainability topics, metrics, and protocols applicable to that company.

For example, let's look at Southwest Airlines. SASB lists four main sustainability-related topics that should be reported for airlines:

1. Environmental footprint of fuel use
2. Labor relations
3. Competitive behavior (since only four airlines account for 75% of the market)
4. Accidents and safety management

SASB lists metrics and protocols for each of these topics. For example, fuel use has several metrics, including Scope 1 emissions (direct emissions from the company's own operations), management's short-term and long-term strategy for managing emissions, total fuel used, and percentage of renewable fuel used. Keep in mind that these provisional standards were just released in 2016 and are still under comment and review. They are not yet mandatory.

Note that the GRI Framework and SASB are not at odds but rather, are complementary. Both have the common goal of advancing sustainability reporting. Whereas the GRI attempts to provide guidance to all companies in disclosing sustainability information that is relevant to a multitude of stakeholders, SASB more specifically wishes to create mandatory, industry-specific disclosures for companies that are publicly traded on U.S. stock exchanges and targets investors as the audience for this information.[37]

You can keep up with recent developments at SASB.org.

▶ Try It!

Classify each of the following GRI aspects according to GRI category: economic, environmental, or social. If it is social, further classify it according to its subcategory. Use Exhibit 15-4 as a guide.

1. Customer health and safety
2. Child labor
3. Emissions
4. Market presence
5. Equal remuneration for women and men
6. Energy
7. Anti-corruption
8. Procurement practices

Please see page 944 for solutions.

---

[37] www.sasb.org/approach/key-relationships

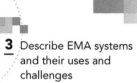

What Is Environmental Management Accounting (EMA)?

In the last section, we described sustainability reporting and CSR reports. In this section, we describe the information needed for sustainability reporting. We also describe some of the uses of this information, as well as the challenges in collecting it.

EMA Systems

<u>Environmental management accounting (EMA)</u> is a system used for the identification, collection, analysis, and use of information needed for internal decision making and external reporting. EMA collects two types of information: monetary and physical.

Monetary Information

<u>Monetary information</u> is the type of information traditionally used in accounting systems. Although presented in monetary terms, the categories of costs are quite different from what has traditionally been collected and reported by financial and management accounting systems. For example, the monetary information reported in an EMA system may include:[38]

1. **Materials costs of product outputs:** These costs include the purchase costs of natural resources that are converted into products. An example would be the purchase cost of lumber for the manufacture of picnic tables. This category is similar to direct materials, since these materials become part of the final product.

2. **Materials costs of non-product outputs:** These costs include the costs of water and energy that become nonproduct output, such as air emissions and waste. An example would be the cost of water used as a coolant in a plant's manufacturing system.

3. **Waste and emission control costs:** These costs include the costs for handling, treating, and disposing of all forms of waste and emissions, including solid waste, hazardous waste, wastewater, and air emissions. An example would be the cost associated with treatment and disposal of hazardous by-products at a chemical production facility.

4. **Prevention costs:** These costs are incurred to prevent environmental costs. An example would be the costs of monitoring water output for contaminants.

5. **Research and development (R&D) costs:** These costs include the costs of R&D projects related to environmental issues. An example would be the costs of running a laboratory aimed at developing biodegradable products.

6. **Intangible costs:** These costs include the costs of future liabilities, future regulations, productivity, company image, and stakeholder relations. An example would be the cost of a future lawsuit filed for an infringement of environmental regulations.

Physical Information

<u>Physical information</u> has not traditionally been part of managerial accounting systems, but it is a vital part of EMA systems. Examples of physical information include the following:

1. Quantity of air emissions
2. Tons of solid waste generated
3. Gallons of wastewater generated
4. Pounds of packaging recycled
5. Total amount of water consumed

By collecting and measuring physical information, such as tons of waste sent to landfills, EMA systems provide managers with a clearer view of the company's physical impact on the environment. The adage "You can't manage what you don't measure" applies. If a company doesn't measure physical impact information, management has little chance of trying to reduce it.

[38] International Federation of Accountants (IFAC), 2005, *International Guidance Document of EMA*, New York: IFAC.

Materials Flow Accounting

To track their environmental inputs and outputs, organizations can use **materials flow accounting (MFA)**. As shown in Exhibit 15-5, MFA involves tracking all of the physical inputs (materials, energy, water, and so forth) and reconciling them with the output generated (including product units, wastewater generated, air emissions, packaging, and by-products). The goal is to track where everything is going; once it is visible, steps can be taken to reduce usage or to increase efficiencies. Essentially, MFA calculates the amount of waste and emissions from a manufacturing system by tracing materials (including energy) to the finished product. Identifying the processes that lead to waste and emissions can highlight opportunities for improvement.

EXHIBIT 15-5 Materials Flow Accounting: Equating Inputs with the Company's Outputs

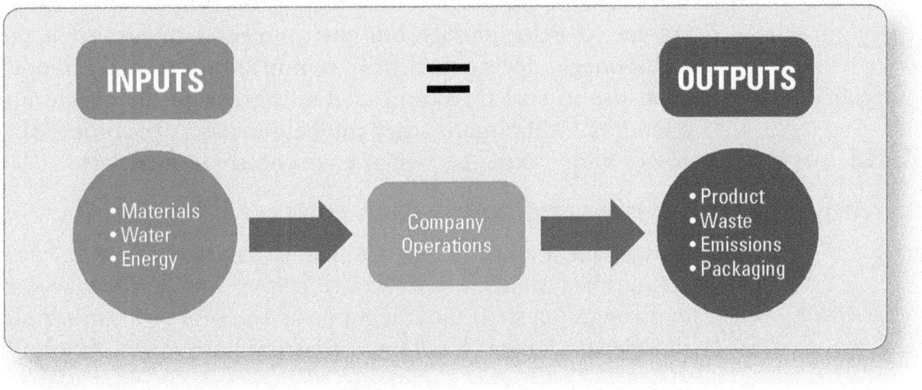

ISO 14000

How do companies gain the knowledge and expertise necessary to develop and implement EMA systems? The International Organization for Standardization (ISO) has developed the ISO 14000 series of standards, which address various aspects of EMA systems. The ISO 14000 series has more than 22 standards and guidelines pertaining to environmental sustainability. In the words of the ISO, the standards provide a "practical toolbox" that help organizations implement environmental management systems. Some of these tools include LCA, greenhouse gas accounting, materials flow accounting, eco-efficiency assessment, environmental product labeling, and others.[39]

Uses of Environmental Management Accounting Information

The information contained in and produced by an organization's EMA system is designed to help support managers' primary responsibilities: planning, directing, controlling, and decision making. Specific operational and decision-making situations where management accountants can support sustainability efforts include compliance, strategy development, systems and information flow, costing, investment appraisal, performance management, and external reporting. We'll discuss each of these areas next.

Compliance

Companies are confronted with many environmental laws and regulations that can impact their operations. An EMA system gathers the information necessary to ensure that the organization complies with these laws and regulations. Management accountants also use this information to help managers understand the potential financial implications of pending environmental legislation and of past practices that may have caused environmental damage.

---

[39] International Standards Organization, "ISO 14000—Environmental Management," 2009, www.iso.org/iso/home/standards/management-standards/iso14000.htm

For example, **Extended Producer Responsibility (EPR) laws** require manufacturers in certain industries to "take back" a large percentage of their products at the end of the products' life in order to reduce the amount of waste ending up in landfills and the environment. EPR laws are gaining traction, especially in the electronics industry due to the volume of e-waste produced each year. However, they are also beginning to surface in other industries. For example, Rhode Island recently passed an EPR law related to mattresses. The EMA system would help gather the physical information required by these laws as well as provide managers with the costs of both compliance and noncompliance. The financial ramifications should drive product engineers to develop ways of recycling, repurposing, or reusing product components.

Strategy Development

In order to succeed in the long term, organizations need to integrate sustainability into their business strategy. Management accountants can use the information from the EMA system to help identify the environmental impact of a potential strategic decision, identify opportunities to make more efficient use of resources, and take advantage of the organization's strengths. Additionally, they can help to assess the potential costs of *not* undertaking particular environmental initiatives.

Systems and Information Flow

Management accountants can help to assess the need for new information systems. They can also help to implement new systems and suggest system modifications as the organization's information needs change. New environmental laws, new products, new processes, and new technologies all create demand for new or updated information systems.

> ### ■ Why is this important?
>
> "Management **accountants** are increasingly called upon to incorporate **environmental impact** information in the **analyses** they **provide** to management."

Costing

Management accountants can help to make environmental costs more visible. Methods can be improved for allocating environmental costs (such as waste removal, water, and energy costs) to specific products, activities, or departments. Management accountants can also help to identify and estimate potential future environmental costs that should be recognized as potential liabilities in current periods.

Investment Appraisal

Management accountants can help to ensure that environmental and social costs and savings are included in capital investment analysis. Investment appraisals should include traditionally ignored factors, such as enhanced reputation, improved employee morale, and reduction of litigation and compliance risk. An analytical tool known as **Social Return on Investment (SROI)** can be used to explain social and environmental value in monetary terms. SROI works similarly to ROI calculations, but it includes estimates of the social and environmental costs and savings. Inclusion of this information can dramatically affect the results of traditional ROI calculations. LCA, described earlier, can also provide companies with the financial rationale for making new investments, such as exemplified by Procter & Gamble's investment in developing a cool-water detergent.

Performance Management

As discussed earlier, sustainability reporting is most often used as an internal change management tool, whereby performance is measured across a variety of environmental and social metrics, goals are set, and progress toward the goals is measured. Thus, performance management is at the heart of sustainability reporting.

Many companies are now beginning to disclose their carbon and water footprints. A **carbon footprint** is a measure of the total emissions of carbon dioxide and other greenhouse gases (GHGs), often expressed for simplicity as tons of equivalent carbon dioxide. It can be calculated for individual products, individual processes, or the organization as a whole. Once the carbon footprint has been measured, managers can work toward reducing it. Additionally, the **Carbon Disclosure Project**, a nonprofit organization, collects carbon footprint information from the world's largest companies each year and disseminates that information to institutional investors and other stakeholders.

Some companies, such as Timberland and Disney, are investing in reforestation projects to offset their carbon footprints in an effort to become more carbon neutral. Other companies provide customers with the opportunity to purchase carbon offsets. For example, United Airlines has partnered with Sustainable Travel International to provide a carbon offset program for its customers. At United's website, travelers have the option to calculate the carbon emissions associated with their travel and then purchase enough carbon offsets to make their travel carbon neutral. The carbon offsets are typically invested in reforestation and renewable energy projects.[40]

Similarly, a <u>water footprint</u> is the total volume of water use associated with the processes and products of a business. Some companies, such as Coca-Cola and Intel, measure their water footprint, thus enabling production engineers to consider means for reducing the footprint.

Christopher Steer/E+/Getty Images

External Reporting

As discussed earlier, EMA systems provide the information used for the sustainability reporting process. Thus, EMA systems collect the information that is necessary for companies to produce CSR reports.

Challenges to Implementing EMA Systems

There are several challenges inherent in implementing and using an EMA system within an organization. Communication issues, hidden costs, aggregated accounting information, the historical orientation of accounting, and the newness of environmental management accounting are all potentially challenging areas.

Communication Issues

For an EMA system to work effectively, many different employees within the organization need to communicate and work together. For example, members of the environmental staff possess knowledge about environmental issues impacting the organization. Technical and production engineers have experience with the flow of materials, energy, and water throughout the company operations. Management accountants have expertise in accounting, cost assignment, and regulatory reporting. In reality, all areas of the value chain will need to coordinate efforts if sustainability is to be embedded within the fabric of the organization. Communication and coordination can sometimes be challenging, yet it is necessary in order to provide the information needed to strategically manage the organization's journey toward sustainability.

Hidden Costs

In a traditional accounting system, many indirect costs are assigned to overhead because they are difficult to trace directly to a product or process. As a result, many environmental costs may get buried in the overhead account. Making environmental costs visible is a vital step in managing environmental costs.

Aggregated Accounting Information

Depending on the sophistication of the company's information system, accounting data are often aggregated into a limited number of accounts. For example, some companies still post material purchases into one "Purchases" account. Such a basic system does not allow management to identify the specific types and quantities of materials purchased (for example, hazardous and nonhazardous), the cost per unit for the material, or the product for which it was purchased. If this specific information is tracked on the production floor, it is often not connected to the general ledger accounting data. In a similar vein, labor costs are often simply recorded as payroll expense or part of manufacturing overhead, rather than specifying whether the labor was related to product output, waste management, or environmental damage prevention. For an EMA system to be effective, accounting information will need to be tagged with multiple identifiers to serve various information needs.

---

[40] http://united.com

Historical Orientation of Accounting

Financial accounting systems focus on providing the historical, transaction-based cost information needed for preparing financial statements in accordance with Generally Accepted Accounting Principles (GAAP). However, for an EMA system to be effective in helping management make good decisions, it will need to include a more open-minded and forward-looking definition of cost. For example, an EMA system might include an estimate of the cost of lost sales resulting from poor environmental performance. Or it might include an estimate of the cost of losing access to markets with environment-related product restrictions. It might also include an estimate of costs externalized to society. Both accountants and management will need to expand their view of what constitutes a "cost" as they develop EMA systems for their companies.

Undeveloped Field

Environmental management accounting is a relatively new, undeveloped field. Tools for providing environmental management accounting information are being developed and refined constantly as the field evolves. Organizations are still working to discover what information they need and how it can be reported in an accurate, timely, verifiable, and relevant manner.

> ## ■ Why is this important?
>
> "In order to provide managers with relevant **environmental information**, accountants will need to rethink their **traditional views** on what constitutes a **'cost'** and expand their costing systems to provide more **detailed information**."

Future of Environmental Management Accounting

This chapter has briefly summarized the state of environmental management accounting as it exists today. There are a number of valid business reasons for organizations to commit to sustainability reporting and producing CSR reports. Organizations can use EMA, utilizing both monetary and physical information, to support these efforts. The field of environmental management accounting is relatively new and so can be challenging to implement. However, advances are being made every day.

Sustainability is a growing concern worldwide. Management accountants have a critical responsibility and opportunity to assist their organizations in supporting sustainability through the use of environmental management accounting information that is accurate, timely, and relevant.

Decision Guidelines

Decision	Guidelines
What three performance factors should be considered if a company wishes to become more sustainable?	The three pillars of sustainability are economic, environmental, and social performance. Together, these three factors are known as the triple bottom line.
Why can't companies continue to operate under the linear "take–make–waste" economic model?	Because of the earth's limited resources, the old economic model is not viable in the long run.
Why should a company use life-cycle assessment (LCA) to evaluate its products and services?	LCA helps companies assess the social and environmental impacts of its products and services all the way from cradle to grave. Thus, it helps uncover previously hidden external costs, as well as traditionally captured internal costs. By understanding the full costs of the product, companies can work toward reducing negative impacts and increasing positive impacts.
How does sustainability increase business value?	Sustainable practices help companies: 1. Reduce costs 2. Generate new revenue streams 3. Increase market share 4. Improve external image 5. Reduce risks 6. Attract labor talent 7. Attract capital
What is sustainability reporting, and why should companies adopt it?	Sustainability reporting is a process used by companies to set goals, measure performance, and manage change as they move toward a more sustainable economic model. Sustainability reporting is used as an internal management change tool, as well as a basis for preparing CSR reports.
How prevalent are CSR reports, and who uses them?	The majority of large domestic and international companies prepare CSR reports, thus putting peer pressure on those who currently do not issue reports. CSR reports are used as a way of communicating sustainability performance to a wide variety of external stakeholders.
Is there a common framework used by all CSR reports?	The Global Reporting Initiative (GRI) has developed the most widely used framework. The G4 Guidelines are the most recent version of the framework.
How is the framework organized?	The framework is organized around the three categories of the triple bottom line: economic, environmental, and social. Companies report on those aspects of each category that are material to their operations.
What types of information should an environmental management accounting (EMA) system collect and analyze?	EMA systems focus on both monetary and physical information. Materials flow accounting (MFA) is often used to track all physical inputs and reconcile them with all of the company's outputs, including waste and emissions.
How is EMA information used?	EMA information is used to support management in planning, directing, and controlling operations. EMA information assists managers in determining how to best integrate sustainable practices throughout the organization. EMA also generates the information needed for external reporting purposes.
What challenges does management face in implementing EMA systems?	EMA systems provide much more detail than traditional accounting systems and will require effective communication throughout the organization. The existing accounting system will need to be revamped, replaced, or supplemented to provide management with the environmental information it needs. Accountants will need to rethink the traditional definitions of "cost" and expand traditional cost categories as they develop EMA systems.

END OF CHAPTER

Learning Objectives

- 1 Describe sustainability and how it can create business value
- 2 Describe sustainability reporting and the GRI framework
- 3 Describe EMA systems and their uses and challenges

Accounting Vocabulary

Assurance. (p. 906)   An independent party's external validation of management's assertions.

Big Four. (p. 904)   The largest four accounting firms in the world: Deloitte, EY, KPMG, and PriceWaterhouseCoopers.

Carbon Disclosure Project. (p. 910)   A nonprofit organization that collects and disseminates carbon footprint information.

Carbon Footprint. (p. 910)   A measure of the total emissions of carbon dioxide and other greenhouse gases (GHGs), often expressed for simplicity as tons of equivalent carbon dioxide.

Comprehensive Report. (p. 906)   A GRI-referenced report in which *all indicators* related to each identified material aspect are disclosed.

Core Report. (p. 906)   A GRI-referenced report in which *at least one* indicator related to each identified material aspect is disclosed.

Eco-Efficiency. (p. 898)   Achieving economic savings by producing goods and services with fewer ecological resources.

Environmental Management Accounting (EMA). (p. 908)   A system used for the identification, collection, analysis, and use of two types of information for internal decision making—monetary and physical information.

Extended Producer Responsibility (EPR) laws. (p. 910)   Laws that require product manufacturers to "take back" a large percentage of the products they manufacture at the end of the product's life in order to reduce the amount of waste ending up in landfills and the environment.

External Costs. (p. 896)   Costs borne by society as a result of a company's operations and the products and services it sells.

Global Reporting Initiative (GRI). (p. 903)   A nonprofit organization whose mission is to make sustainability reporting standard practice by providing guidance and support to organizations. The developer of the G4 Guidelines.

Internal Costs. (p. 896)   Costs that are incurred and paid for by the organization and recorded in GAAP-based accounting records.

Life-Cycle Assessment (LCA). (p. 896)   Studying the environmental and social impacts of a product or service over its entire life, from "cradle to grave."

Materiality. (p. 904)   An important concept in CSR reporting defined as those aspects of a business that reflect the organization's significant economic, environmental, and social impacts, or substantively influence the assessments and decisions of stakeholders.

Materials Flow Accounting (MFA). (p. 909)   An accounting system in which all physical inputs to an organization's operations are reconciled with output generated. The goal is to track where all physical inputs are going.

Monetary Information. (p. 908)   The type of information traditionally used in accounting systems.

Non-Governmental Organizations (NGOs). (p. 896)   Not-for-profit organizations that serve the public interest, such as Greenpeace and Sierra Club.

Physical Information. (p. 908)   A vital part of environmental management accounting systems. Examples include: quantity of air emissions, tons of solid waste generated, gallons of wastewater generated, pounds of packaging recycled, and total amount of water consumed.

Principles for Responsible Investment (PRI). (p. 902)   Six principles of investing, including a commitment to incorporate environmental, social, and governance issues into investment analysis and decision making.

Social Return on Investment (SROI). (p. 910)   An analytical tool that is used to explain social and environmental value in monetary terms.

Supply-Chain Assessment. (p. 900)   Making purchase decisions based partially on how well suppliers manage the social and environmental impact of their operations.

Sustainability. (p. 895)   The ability of a system to endure without giving way or to use resources so that they are not depleted or permanently damaged. In business, sustainability is also defined as the ability to meet the needs of the present without compromising the ability of future generations to meet their own needs.

Sustainability Report. (p. 902)   The primary document used for communicating a company's performance on all three pillars of the triple bottom line: economic, environmental, and social. Also known as a Corporate Social Responsibility (CSR) report.

Sustainability Reporting. (p. 902)   A process that helps companies set goals, measure performance, and manage change as they move toward an economic model that produces long-term economic profit as well as environmental care and social responsibility.

Triple Bottom Line. (p. 895)   Evaluating a company's performance not only by its ability to generate economic profits, but also by its impact on people and the planet.

Waste Audits. (p. 899)   Studying the stream of waste coming from company operations (solid waste, water discharge, chemicals, etc.) to determine waste that can be avoided and alternative uses for the remaining waste.

Water Footprint. (p. 911)   The total volume of water use associated with the processes and products of a business.

Go to http://myaccountinglab.com/ for the following Quick Check, Short Exercises, Exercises, and Problems. They are available with immediate grading, explanations of correct and incorrect answers, and interactive media that acts as your own online tutor.

MyAccountingLab

Quick Check

1. *(Learning Objective 1)* Which of the following is *not* one of the three factors related to sustainability?
   a. Ecologic
   b. Social
   c. Environment
   d. Economic

2. *(Learning Objective 1)* Which of the following items would be considered an *external* cost?
   a. Monthly trash hauling fee
   b. Annual audit by public accounting firm
   c. Impact of oil spill on aquatic life
   d. Salary cost of sustainability officer

3. *(Learning Objective 1)* LCA stands for which of the following?
   a. Life costs aggregated
   b. Lower cost always
   c. Lowest-cost audit
   d. Life-cycle assessment

4. *(Learning Objective 1)* Which of the following would *not* be a reason to adopt sustainable business practices?
   a. Improving external image
   b. Reducing costs
   c. Increasing compliance risks
   d. Producing new revenue streams

5. *(Learning Objective 2)* What is the current status of sustainability reporting in the United States?
   a. The SEC requires that publicly traded companies disclose any material information to prevent misleading the readers of financial statements.
   b. Sustainability reporting using the GRI G4 reporting guidelines is required for all companies doing business in the United States, regardless of size.
   c. All companies listed on the New York Stock Exchange (NYSE) must issue sustainability reports using the NYSE's sustainability reporting guidelines.
   d. Sustainability reporting using the GRI G4 reporting guidelines is required for all publicly traded companies.

6. *(Learning Objective 2)* Which of the following would be a reason for a company to undertake sustainability reporting?
   a. The sustainability report can communicate the company's social and environmental impact to consumers, investors, and other stakeholders.
   b. Sustainability reporting can be an internal change management tool.
   c. Neither a nor b is a reason for sustainability reporting.
   d. Both a and b are reasons for sustainability reporting.

7. *(Learning Objective 2)* Which of the following aspects would *not* be included in the environmental category of the GRI G4 reporting guidelines?
   a. Emissions
   b. Transport
   c. Training and education
   d. Energy

8. *(Learning Objective 2)* Which of the following aspects would *not* be included in the economic category of the GRI G4 reporting guidelines?
   a. Indirect economic impacts
   b. Market presence
   c. Procurement practices
   d. Equal remuneration for women and men

9. *(Learning Objective 2)* Which of the following aspects would *not* be included in the social category of the GRI G4 reporting guidelines?
   a. Child labor
   b. Environmental grievance mechanism
   c. Anti-corruption
   d. Labor/management relations

10. *(Learning Objective 3)* Which of the following is *not* a challenge to implementing and using an environmental management accounting system?
    a. Communication issues
    b. Hidden costs
    c. Historical orientation of accounting
    d. All of the above items are challenges.

Quick Check Answers

1.a 2.c 3.d 4.c 5.a 6.d 7.c 8.d 9.b 10.d

GLOSSARY/INDEX

Combined Glossary/Subject Index

Note: Page references including the letter "n" indicate content appears in a footnote on that page.

5S. A workplace organization system comprised of the following steps: sort, set in order, shine, standardize, and sustain, 202

10-K filings, 842, 849, 859

A

Absorption costing. The costing method where products "absorb" both fixed and variable manufacturing costs, 331–333, 447, 455
  income statement, 334
  reconciling operating income, 338–340
  variable costing vs, 336–338

Account analysis. A method for determining cost behavior that is based on a manager's judgment in classifying each general ledger account as a variable, fixed, or mixed cost, 322

Accounting. *See also specific types of accounting*
  within organizational structure, 9–10
  perception and reality of, 6

Accounting rate of return (ARR). A measure of profitability computed by dividing the average annual operating income from an asset by the initial investment in the asset, 711, 717–719, 739

Accounts payable. *See also* Liabilities
  budgeted balance sheet, 530
  statement of cash flows, 781, 793, 800–801

Accounts receivable. *See also* Sales
  acid-test ratio, 850
  budgeted balance sheet, 529
  cash flow, indirect method, 791
  collection of, 590, 594, 851–852
  financial statement analysis, 841, 851–852
  statement of cash flow, 781, 784, 791, 793, 800

Accounts receivable turnover. Measures a company's ability to collect cash from credit customers. To compute accounts receivable turnover, divide net credit sales by average net accounts receivable, 851, 860

Accrual basis of accounting. Revenues are recorded when they are earned (when the sale takes place) rather than when cash is received on the sale. Likewise, expenses are recorded when they are incurred rather than when they are paid, 784

Accumulated depreciation, 795

Acid-test ratio. Ratio of the sum of cash plus short-term investments plus net current receivables to total current liabilities. It tells whether the entity can pay all of its current liabilities if they come due immediately; also called the *quick ratio*, 850, 860

Activity cost pools, 185
  setting up, 190–191

Activity-based costing (ABC). Focusing on *activities* as the fundamental cost objects. The costs of those activities become building blocks for compiling the indirect costs of products, services, and customers, 184
  to allocate indirect costs, 184–189
  circumstances favoring, 193–194
  results of, 192
  target costing, 452

Activity-based management (ABM). Using activity-based cost information to make decisions that increase profits while satisfying customers' needs, 191

circumstances favoring, 193–194
cutting costs, 191–192
pricing and product mix decisions, 191
routine planning and control decisions, 192
using ABC across value chain, 192–193

Actual cost
  direct labor variances, 664–666
  direct materials variances, 660
  manufacturing overhead variances, 671–672

Actual Quantity (AQ), 660–663

Actual Quantity Purchased (AQP), 661–663

Actual Quantity Used (AQU), 661–663

Aggregated accounting information, 911

Air pollution, 910–911. *See also* Sustainability
  environmental management accounting and, 908

Allocate. To assign an indirect cost to a cost object, 56
  ABC and, 184–189

American Institute of Certified Public Accountants (AICPA). The world's largest association representing the accounting profession; together with the Chartered Institute of Management Accountants (CIMA), offers the Chartered Global Management Accountant (CGMA) designation, 11

Amortization expense. *See* Depreciation

Annuity. A stream of equal installments made at equal time intervals, 723
  future value calculations, 726
  internal rate of return, 736–739
  net present value, 732–733
  present value calculations, 727–730

Appraisal costs. Costs incurred to *detect* poor-quality goods or services, 206, 207

Assets
  cash payments and receipts, 800–802
  debt ratio, 852
  investing activities, indirect method, 794–796
  operating activities, indirect method, 788–794
  performance evaluation measures, 596
  profitability, measuring, 853–856
  return on investment, 592–597
  statement of cash flows, 781
  working capital, 849

Assign. To attach a cost to a cost object, 55, 56

Assurance. An independent party's external validation of management's assertions, 906

Attainable standards. Standards based on currently attainable conditions that include allowances for normal amounts of waste and inefficiency. Also known as practical standards, 654

Audit committee. A subcommittee of the board of directors that is responsible for overseeing both the internal audit function and the annual financial statement audit by independent CPAs, 9, 10

Average cost. The total cost divided by the number of units, 74

Average unit costs, 257–258

Avoidable fixed costs. Fixed costs that can be eliminated as a result of taking a particular course of action, 461–462

B

Backflush costing. A simplified accounting system in which production costs are not assigned to the units until they are finished, or even sold, thereby saving the bookkeeping steps of moving the product through the various inventory accounts, 204–205

Bad debt expense, 518

Balance sheet
  budgeted balance sheet, 528–530
  comparative balance sheet, 788, 789
  horizontal analysis, 841
  inventory on, 70
  performance evaluation measures, 596
  vertical analysis, 844–845

Balanced scorecard. A performance evaluation system that integrates financial and operational performance measures along four perspectives: financial, customer, internal business, and learning and growth, 609–615

Batch-level activities. Activities and costs incurred for every batch, regardless of the number of units in the batch, 190

Benchmarking. The practice of comparing a company with other companies or industry averages, 845
  budgets, benefits of, 510
  common-size statements, 845
  standard costs and, 666–667

Benefits, employee. *See also* Labor
  attracting and retaining talent, 901
  job cost record, 114–116
  labor compensation costs, 62
  Manufacturing costs, 60–61

Big data, 18–19

Big Four. The largest four accounting firms in the world: Deloitte, EY, KPMG, and PriceWaterhouseCoopers, 904, 906

Bill of materials. A list of all of the raw materials needed to manufacture a job, 109

Billing rate. The labor rate charged to the customer, which includes both cost and profit components, 145–146

Biofuels, 54

Biomimicry. A means of product design in which a company tries to mimic, or copy, the natural biological process in which dead organisms (plants and animals) become the input for another organism or process, 53–54

Board of Directors. The body elected by shareholders to oversee the company, 9

Book value, gross vs. net, 596, 789–790

Book value per share of common stock. Common stockholders' equity divided by the number of shares of common stock outstanding. It is the recorded amount for each share of common stock outstanding, 858, 861

BP Deepwater Horizon oil spill, 901

Breakeven point. The sales level at which operating income is zero: Total revenues = Total expenses, 386–389
  calculation methods, 386–389, 402–405
  contribution margin ratio, shortcut approach using, 388–389
  cost-volume-profit graphs, 391–392
  fixed cost change, 399–400
  income statement approach, 387, 390
  multiproduct companies, 402–405
  risk indicators, 406–411
  sales price changes, 396
  sales revenue, 404–405
  sales units and, 402–403
  unit contribution margin, shortcut approach using, 388
  variable cost changes, 398–399
  weighted-average contribution margin, 402–405

Prepare, Apply, and Confirm

- **Auto-Graded Excel Projects**—Using proven, field-tested technology, MyAccountingLab's new auto-graded Excel Projects allow instructors to seamlessly integrate Excel content into their course without having to manually grade spreadsheets. Students have the opportunity to practice important Accounting skills in Microsoft Excel, helping them to master key concepts and gain proficiency in Excel. Students simply download a spreadsheet, work live on an accounting problem in Excel, and then upload that file back into MyAccountingLab, where they receive reports on their work that provide personalized, detailed feedback to pinpoint where they went wrong on any step of the problem. Available with select titles.

- **Enhanced eText**—The Pearson eText gives students access to their textbook anytime, anywhere. In addition to note-taking, highlighting, and bookmarking, the Pearson eText offers interactive and sharing features. Students actively read and learn through auto-graded practice, author videos, and more. Instructors can share comments or highlights, and students can add their own, for a tight community of learners in any class.

- Keep students engaged in learning on their own time, while helping them achieve greater conceptual understanding of course material through author-created solutions videos, opportunities to Try It!, and live exhibits.

- **Dynamic Study Modules**—With a focus on key topics, these modules work by continuously assessing student performance and activity in real time and, using data and analytics, provide personalized content to reinforce concepts that target each student's particular strengths and weakness.

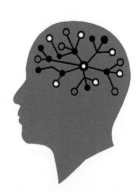

P Pearson

with MyAccountingLab®

- **Hallmark Features**—Personalized Learning Aids, like Help Me Solve This, Demo Docs, and instant feedback are available for further practice and mastery when students need the help most!

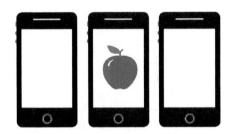

- **Learning Catalytics**—Generates classroom discussion, guides lecture, and promotes peer-to-peer learning with real-time analytics. Now, students can use any device to interact in the classroom.

- **Personalized Study Plan**—Assists students in monitoring their own progress by offering them a customized study plan based on Homework, Quiz, and Test results. Includes regenerated exercises with unlimited practice, as well as the opportunity to earn mastery points by completing quizzes on recommended learning objectives.

- **Worked Solutions**—Provide step-by-step explanations on how to solve select problems using the exact numbers and data that were presented in the problem. Instructors will have access to the Worked Out Solutions in preview and review mode.

Prepare, Apply, and Confirm with MyAccountingLab®

- **Algorithmic Test Bank**—Instructors have the ability to create multiple versions of a test or extra practice for students.

- **Reporting Dashboard**—View, analyze, and report learning outcomes clearly and easily. Available via the Gradebook and fully mobile-ready, the Reporting Dashboard presents student performance data at the class, section, and program levels in an accessible, visual manner.

- **LMS Integration**—Link from any LMS platform to access assignments, rosters, and resources, and synchronize MyLab grades with your LMS gradebook. For students, new direct, single sign-on provides access to all the personalized learning MyLab resources that make studying more efficient and effective.